THE RULE OF EMPIRES

THE RULE OF EMPIRES

Those Who Built Them,
Those Who Endured Them,
and Why They Always Fall

Timothy H. Parsons

OXFORD
UNIVERSITY PRESS

2010

UNIVERSITY PRESS

Oxford University Press, Inc., publishes works that further
Oxford University's objective of excellence
in research, scholarship, and education.

Oxford   New York
Auckland   Cape Town   Dar es Salaam   Hong Kong   Karachi
Kuala Lumpur   Madrid   Melbourne   Mexico City   Nairobi
New Delhi   Shanghai   Taipei   Toronto

With offices in
Argentina   Austria   Brazil   Chile   Czech Republic   France   Greece
Guatemala   Hungary   Italy   Japan   Poland   Portugal   Singapore
South Korea   Switzerland   Thailand   Turkey   Ukraine   Vietnam

Published by Oxford University Press, Inc.
198 Madison Avenue, New York, New York 10016

www.oup.com

Oxford is a registered trademark of Oxford University Press

Library of Congress Cataloging-in-Publication Data
Parsons, Timothy, 1962–
The rule of empires : those who built them,
those who endured them,
and why they always fall / Timothy H. Parsons.
p.   cm.
ISBN 978-0-19-530431-2
1. Colonies—History.   2. Colonization—History.
3. Imperialism—History.   I. Title.
JV61.P33 2010
325'.3—dc22   2009044192

1 3 5 7 9 8 6 4 2

Printed in the United States of America
on acid-free paper

For Annie, always

CONTENTS

ACKNOWLEDGMENTS

As a social historian of twentieth-century Africa, I incurred considerable scholarly debts in writing on so many different empires that are far outside my own area of specialization. Bruce Masters introduced me to the study of Islamic societies more than two decades ago, and Ahmet Karamustafa continued this education with his close reading of the Umayyad Spain chapter. Matthew Restall read the initial proposal for this book as an anonymous reviewer for Oxford University Press and then was immensely supportive in helping me find my way in Spain's American empire. Mark Burkholder and Rick Walter each reviewed that chapter closely and also made numerous suggestions and corrections. Similarly, Tom Metcalf generously helped me navigate the complexities of the history of British rule in South Asia, and Hillel Kieval did the same for the Nazi empire in Europe. I have drawn inspiration from Dane Kennedy's and Lori Watt's views of empire, and I am particularly grateful to my dear friend Derek Peterson for his close and critical reading of the introduction. Richard Davis was an equally important source of wise advice, and I particularly valued Keith Bennett's patience and encouragement during the writing process. Although they were not fully aware of it, my graduate students John Aerni, Muey Saeteurn, and Meghan Ference made an important intellectual contribution to the book's central arguments through their thoughtful and probing questions. Rethinking empire from the perspectives of subject peoples has been a difficult and complex process, and so of course I alone am responsible for any errors of fact or interpretation that have crept into this exercise in academic trespassing.

The logistics of researching and writing a project of this scope have been equally daunting. The Inter-Library Loan and Circulation units of Washington University's Olin Library did a remarkable job in locating and producing a diverse and unusually obscure array of historical sources. Most importantly, I never could have organized this material or written this book without the assistance and unflagging support of my friends on the faculty and staff of our African and African-American Studies Program. My colleagues Mungai Mutonya, Garrett Duncan, Rafia Zafar, Priscilla Stone, Cameron Monroe, and Amina Gautier were always encouraging, and in running the program office Raye Maheney and Adele Tuchler spoiled me by making sure that I had all the time and resources necessary to finish the book. On this score, Molly Shaikewitz and four successive years of work-study students also deserve mention: Nancy Kim, Josh Lubatkin, Karen Wang, Danielle Roth, Lily Huang, Brandon Williams, Molissa Thomas, and Michael Musgrave. Sheryl Peltz and Brendan Akos were similarly helpful in giving me extra time for research and writing.

A number of people played equally key roles in bringing this book into print. My agent, Jeff Gerecke, was smart and deft in helping me refine my abstract ideas about empire, and Peter Ginna shared my conviction that conventional imperial histories are flawed because they ignore the central role of imperial subjects. But I never would have been able to follow through on the grand promises that I made to Oxford University Press and my editor, Tim Bent, without Ann Parsons's help in reading and rereading countless draft chapters. I am also particularly grateful to Tim for his incisive guidance in shaping the final manuscript and for addressing my concerns thoughtfully and patiently. Tim's assistant, Dayne Poshusta, also merits a word of thanks on this score.

Finally, I never would have been able to write this book without the unflagging encouragement of my friends and family. Showing infinite and largely undeserved patience, they never gave into the temptation of asking, "Aren't you done yet?"

THE RULE OF EMPIRES

INTRODUCTION

The Subjects of Empire

Looking back to his youth, when Britain ruled Kenya and he served in its East African army, seventy-four-year-old Daniel Wambua Nguta's hatred for his former colonial rulers remains undiminished. "A European is no good. He rolls you like a ball at his will. And you have to live by his commands."[1] Nguta's characterization of British rule is strikingly different from the idealized and romantic notions of empire.

The conquerors of Kenya would have dismissed men like Nguta as barbarous tribesmen. The British peer Baron Cranworth claimed that he and his fellow Kenyan settlers brought progress and modernity to the "primitive" peoples of the East African highlands.

> We give peace where war was. We give justice where injustice ruled. We give law and order where the only law was the law of strength. We give Christianity, or a chance of it, where Paganism ruled. Whether the native looks on it in that light is another matter. I am afraid that possibly he doesn't as yet truly appreciate his benefits.[2]

Cranworth made his case in 1912, but the current archbishop of Canterbury, Rowan Williams, echoed his sentiments almost a century later when he criticized the United States' occupation of Iraq by lauding Britain's rule of India. "It is one thing to take over a territory and then pour energy and resources into administering it and normalising it. Rightly or wrongly that's what the British Empire did in India."[3]

Today, few westerners doubt this argument. Confident in the superiority of their technology and culture, they believe that the empires of the last century performed the necessary service of dragging backward counties into the modern world.

The twentieth-century western empires were probably the most humane imperial enterprises in history. In contrast to brutal and nakedly exploitive ancient and medieval empires, French and British administrators tried to make good on promises to improve the lives of their subjects. But such imperial humanitarianism rested on the premise that nonwestern peoples were in need of salvation. To Cranworth, Africans were only marginally human. "They lie, they steal, they poison; they conspire, they are intensely lazy, and they are callously cruel. Still, there they are, and such as they are we must make the best of them."[4]

It is hardly surprising that the rulers and the ruled had differing perspectives on empire. The myth of the liberal empire survives to this day because the voices of men like Nguta were either silenced or never recorded at all. Instead, popular history romanticizes Caesars, emirs, conquistadors, viceroys, nabobs, explorers, soldiers, and missionaries. Westerners like to think that they are the heirs of an omnipotent and enlightened imperial Rome.

Imperial nostalgia diminished as the last formal global European empires broke up after the Second World War, and the Soviet Union and Red China, imperial powers in their own right, won allies in the developing world by championing their cause. The Latin American, African, and Asian nations that dominated the United Nations General Assembly by the 1960s further redefined imperial rule as foreign domination, economic exploitation, and ultimately a violation of fundamental human rights. European liberals consequently repudiated their own imperial history or conveniently forgot that their nations had ever even ruled empires. Similarly, most Americans ignore the fate of Amerindians by viewing themselves as a uniquely anti-imperial people. Recalling the Revolutionary War as a struggle against British despotism, they viewed the United States as an egalitarian republic protecting the world from communist imperial expansion.

The terrorist attacks of 2001 gave imperial methods, if not actual empire building, a new lease on life. Puncturing the illusion of domestic security, they gave credence to those who called for a more aggressive stance in defending America's national interests. The best way to protect the United States from further attacks was to use military force, or hard power, to change regimes and restructure conquered societies. This imperial assumption was in no way masked by President George W. Bush's assertion in the run-up to the invasion of Iraq that "America has no empire to extend or utopia to establish. We wish for others only what we wish for ourselves—safety from violence, the rewards of liberty, and the hope for a better life."[5]

Fears that collapsed states would become havens for terrorists and that rogue nations might give them nuclear, chemical, or biological weapons led political commentators and analysts of all ideological stripes to accept the necessity of imposing order on an increasingly chaotic world. By overthrowing Saddam Hussein, the Bush administration and its allies calculated that they could remake Iraqi politics and society. Deployed creatively, hard power could instill new cultural values. The United States would use its unrivaled military and economic might to bolster failed states and control totalitarian regimes through benevolent imperial-style trusteeship.

The primary advocates of this strategy were those we now call neoconservatives, joined by Christian evangelicals and right-wing ideologues who welcomed the opportunity to put their faith in hard power and unilateralism into practice. Other enthusiasts were professional and amateur theorists and historians. Harvard historian Niall Ferguson, for one, publicly declared himself a "fully paid-up member of the neo-imperialist gang." Echoing Baron Cranworth's depiction of the British Empire as a civilizing force that underwrote a worldwide "liberalized economic system," Ferguson asserted that global security depended on America's readiness to become an imperial power on the British model. Championing the invasion of Iraq, he urged the United States to intervene in the domestic affairs of foreign nations to impose peace and promote his conception of liberal capitalism.[6] Economist Deepak Lal similarly lauded earlier western empire builders for laying the foundations of global capitalism. Envisioning an American empire as a benevolent Hobbesian Leviathan that would sponsor an "international moral order," Lal promised that this benign application of hard power would defuse the Islamicist threat by forcibly integrating Muslim states into a liberal worldwide capitalist economy.[7]

While other scholars and public intellectuals were less bold or dogmatic in promoting an American imperial agenda, a surprising number shared the confidence that imperial methods could restore global stability if applied in conjunction with responsible international institutions. Harold James and Strobe Talbott suggested that a renewed and updated western imperial order might mitigate the negative and destabilizing consequences of the free movement of goods, diseases, and would-be terrorists around the world by serving as a quasi-global government. The legal scholar Amy Chua similarly believed empires could be a force for global stability if they were sufficiently diverse, pluralistic, and tolerant.[8]

This reading of history ignores the essential characteristic of empire: the permanent rule and exploitation of a defeated people by a conquering power. By their very nature, empires can never be—and never were—humane, liberal, or tolerant. Would-be Caesars throughout history sought glory, land, and, most important, plunder. This true nature of empire was more obvious in premodern times when it was unnecessary to disguise such base motives. In recent centuries, however, imperial conquerors have tried to hide their naked self-interest by promising to rule for the good of their subjects. This was and always will be a cynical and hypocritical canard. Empire has never been more than naked self-interest masquerading as virtue.

Defenders (and even critics) of twenty-first-century imperial projects employ abstract, romanticized, and top-down perspectives of empire. This book will do the opposite, employing concrete examples of how empires actually ruled. In looking at the experience of empire from the bottom up, it does not claim to speak for the voiceless or to right past wrongs. Injustice is a constant in human history, and certainly no sainthood is conferred by being conquered. Nevertheless, the empires covered in this book demonstrate that imperial rule always meant denigration and exploitation. Ultimately, the fundamental reality of empires is that they are unsustainable because their subjects find them intolerable.

This book will prove this by examining the actual experience of imperial rule in seven empires: Roman Britain, Umayyad Spain, Spanish Peru, India under the British East India Company, Napoleonic Italy, Britain's Kenya colony, and Nazi-occupied France. Each example in its own way shows why empires are unbearable and eventually untenable. Rome remains the standard by which all empires are judged, yet it actually lacked the power to intervene in the daily lives of its subjects in Britain. The Umayyad Caliphate in medieval Spain demonstrates that conquered people could swallow up imperial rulers who could not maintain the distinction between *citizen* and *subject*. Taking this lesson to heart, the Spanish wrung unprecedented wealth out of the peoples of the Peruvian highlands by using religion and culture to define them as inherently different. A century later, the British East India Company carved out a private commercial empire in South Asia by stepping into the shoes of the Mughal emperors, but the company's shareholders and employees similarly enriched themselves by depicting Indians as distinctly different and exploitable. The gradual development of larger national identities blocked Napoleon from using similar tactics in Italy, and the collapse of his brief empire marked the end of viable imperial rule in Europe. While empire appeared reborn in Africa and Asia during the "new imperialism" of the late nineteenth century, the equally short-lived and often brutal British imperial state in Kenya exploded the notion that empires could ever be liberal or humanitarian. Adolf Hitler's brief but vicious tenure as the imperial ruler of France affirmed this reality by pushing the inherent logic of empire building to its brutal and inevitable limit.

Of course, these examples are neither definitive nor exhaustive. There is no shortage of empires to choose from—the Byzantine, Chinese, Persian, Ottoman, Portuguese, Russian, Japanese, and Soviet empires also would have furnished examples—but collectively these particular examples chart the evolution and demise of empires. They are linked, with each empire drawing on the ideologies and practices of its predecessors. The Romans conquered the ancestors of the British, the Umayyad Arabs occupied Spain, the Spanish seized the Andes from the Inkas, the British built an empire in Mughal India, the French turned the Italian descendants of the Romans into subjects, modern Britons added Kenya to their empire, and the Nazis ruled France as an imperial power.

Beginning with Rome is essential because imperial enthusiasts portray it as the model for future empires. In fact, we know very little about what life was like for common people under Roman rule. Ancient Britons lived at the edges of the empire, but most were typical "subjects," meaning slaves, tenants, and peasant farmers. Their rulers relied on assimilated, "romanized" local elites to actually govern. Commoners in Britain and indeed the rest of the provinces were too divided by local customs and habits to band together to resist this domination. Roman rule was therefore exploitive but long-lived in Britain precisely because its reliance on assimilated local allies made it seem less crushing.

Most modern histories of empire rarely mention medieval Muslim Spain (Al-Andalus), and the Umayyad Arabs never actually claimed to be imperial rulers. Nevertheless, Al-Andalus shared many of the same characteristics as Rome. Initially a remote and resistive province of the larger Umayyad Caliphate, Iberia became an autonomous emirate under a refugee Umayyad prince. At first glance, the imperial state he founded, which lasted from the eighth to twelfth centuries, appeared to match Rome in its stability and limitations. Like the Romans, the Umayyads shared power with assimilated local notables, but the Muslim empire builders' religious obligation to convert conquered populations undermined their status as a ruling elite. Even more than in the ancient era, the necessity of recruiting local allies allowed large numbers of urban Iberians to escape subjecthood by converting to Islam, thereby gradually changing the character of the imperial state itself. By the high point of Spanish Umayyad rule in the tenth century, intermarriage and conversion had thoroughly blurred the distinction between Arab and Iberian ruling elites. Rural and common people, however, probably did not convert to Islam in large numbers. Their overlords may have shifted from Christianity to Islam and then back again during the Reconquista, but the oppressive realities of imperial rule led most Iberians to seek protection within their local communities.

In the fifteenth century, empires gained a greater capacity to place more systematic and sustainable demands on their subjects. However, these early modern states still bore little resemblance to the empires of popular contemporary imagination. Francisco Pizarro and the Spanish conquistadors became fabulously wealthy by looting the Inkan Empire, but to actually govern common Andeans their successors fell back on the systems of imperial control pioneered by the Romans and Umayyads. Consequently, although the Spanish Crown's empire in South America lasted into the nineteenth century, it struggled to exert direct control over the hybrid local communities of Spanish settlers, Andeans, and African slaves that emerged from the wreckage of the Inkan Empire.

The apparent longevity and coherence of Britain's empire in India is equally misleading. It was the British East India Company, not the Crown, that won the right to collect taxes in Bengal in the name of the Mughal emperors. Posing as Mughal vassals, grasping company employees known as nabobs wrung enormous profits out of Bengal and the rest of India by taking over its revenue collection systems. Ordinary Bengalis probably paid little attention because one set of tribute collectors simply appeared to replace another, but in time they realized that their new overseers had an insatiable appetite for revenue. Imperial enthusiasts credit the British East India Company with integrating India into the global capitalist order, but the cost for common people was economic dislocation, cultural degradation, and in some cases famine.

Conversely, the development of the nation-state in the late eighteenth century rendered empire unsustainable in the west. Premodern empires were relatively stable because local customs and identities were strong enough to mitigate the crushing effects of foreign rule. Nationalism, which imagined that populations were culturally and ethnically homogeneous, made it more difficult to recruit these allies. It also rendered imperial rule far more onerous by alienating those who clung to local identities.[9] Napoleon Bonaparte's empire was supposedly based on the universalizing ideals of the French Revolution—liberty, equality, fraternity—but for local communities Napoleonic rule meant unyielding demands for tribute and military conscripts. This was a new and more burdensome kind of nationalistic and extractive empire building, one that employed modern bureaucratic and policing tools to intervene more extensively into the daily lives of conquered people than ever before. Yet the beginnings of nationalism also inspired many people in Italy and throughout Europe to defend their autonomy, which contributed to the rapid demise of Napoleon's short-lived empire.

Although formal imperial rule was no longer feasible in Europe, in the late nineteenth century westerners engaged in a final spasm of empire building, known as the "new imperialism," in Africa and Asia. With the exception of Russia, the nations that took part in this "scramble" were, to varying degrees, liberal democracies. Pandering to the humanitarian concerns of western voting publics, empire builders promised both to extract profits and to civilize. While the invention of advanced weapons such as the Maxim gun was hardly a great cultural achievement, the new imperial conquerors equated military weakness with racial inferiority. The result was a brutal and humiliating system of imperial domination. In practice, however, these empires were viable only as long as subject populations identified themselves in local terms. Once the common experience of imperial subjugation inspired Africans and Asians to think collectively (if not nationally), imperial rule collapsed.

The Third Reich was also a twentieth-century empire. Counting Nazi-occupied France as an imperial case study may seem controversial because it equates suffering under German rule with the experiences of Africans and Asians. Yet in many ways Hitler was the most honest empire builder of the modern era. Where the British and French used racist rhetoric to give their imperial projects a humanitarian veneer, Hitler was an unapologetic social Darwinist who conquered, plundered, and murdered in the name of the German *Volk*. This was the logical endpoint of the legitimizing pseudoscientific racial ideologies of the new imperialism. Furthermore, the French experience of Nazi imperial domination demonstrated that any defeated people, no matter how "advanced," could be transformed into subjects. Just as some Kenyans worked with the British to further personal and communal interests, a surprisingly large number of Frenchmen supported Marshal Philippe Pétain's attempt to reach an accord with the Nazi occupiers. In contrast to ancient Rome, Hitler's imperial project failed because it was too efficient. The Nazis' nakedly exploitive rule turned all of Europe against them.

Taken as a whole, these historical examples show that no one became an imperial subject voluntarily. Empires were viable only when conquerors could recruit local allies, and the common people overlooked by conventional accounts of empire had the capacity to render imperial institutions unworkable. This remains true today. Stable imperial rule is an impossibility in an era when self-determination has become a basic human right and transnational flows of wealth, people, ideas, and weapons mean that no community is truly isolated.

Yet many still look for lessons and models in empires and imperial methods. In part, this is because of the fuzziness in definitions of *citizen* and *subject*, or *citizenship* and the slightly awkward if unavoidable *subjecthood*. There is also a popular tendency to label any form of dictatorial rule *imperial*. Definitions matter; hazy meanings facilitate misunderstandings, both honest and intentional.

In its purest and most basic form, *empire* entails the formal, direct, and authoritarian rule of one group of people over another. It is born of the attempt to leverage military advantage for profit. Global dominance, economic coercion, and the unbridled use of hard power may be unjust, but they are not necessarily imperial actions. Some empires did engage in such behavior, but the now common practice of using empire as a metaphor for any unequal power relationship has blurred its meaning. Autocratic institutions may have imperial qualities, but the equation of slavery with empire or the characterization of the modern European Union as an "empire by invitation" is misleading.[10]

The word *empire* itself comes from the Latin *imperare*, "to command." An *imperium* was the territory where an *imperator* (general) could and did command. In time, Roman kings, republican consuls, military tribunes, and dictators all came to hold and exercise this power. By the first century A.D., the *imperium Romanum* meant the vast territory ruled by Rome.[11] When the western self-described heirs of Rome traveled to Asia in the early modern era, they called khans, sultans, shoguns, and other potentates "emperors," and versions of the term gradually entered into common usage in most of the world's major languages.

The Romans actually had no expression that corresponded to the modern meaning of *imperialism*, and the word came into common usage only in the mid-nineteenth century. Initially it was a pejorative expression that British commentators coined to accuse Napoleon III of despotism. During the Cold War, communist propagandists used *imperialism* to describe a new kind of exploitation linked to the global spread of capitalism.[12] These doctrinal implications of the word mean that it is better to speak of the process of conquering and ruling as *empire building* rather than *imperialism*. *Imperial methods* is an even more imprecise term, but in this book the phrase means an attempt to use hard power to reorder and transform a conquered society.

The terms *colonization* and *colonialism* create further confusion because they are often used interchangeably with *imperialism*. Like *empire*, the word *colony* had Roman origins. From the Latin *colonia*, referring to an outpost or village in a conquered territory, it came to mean a settlement of one group of people on the lands of another. In most cases, these settlers at first retained citizenship in their original societies, but in time colonies often became fully sovereign states. While empire building entailed the permanent control of one people or nation by another, colonization was the permanent settlement of the lands of a conquered people. In most cases, the original inhabitants were either wiped out or segregated and reduced to second-class status, which explains why *imperialism* and *colonialism* have become synonymous. But a conquest resulted in an empire only when the victors attempted to rule and exploit a defeated foe permanently.

There were also instances where colonies of settlement existed within empires. This was the case in Kenya, where a privileged class of British settlers exploited the labor of subject local communities in addition to seizing their land. In this instance, Kenya's status as a colony was a by-product of empire building because the British government did not explicitly sanction the conquest of East Africa to seize new land for its citizens. Imperial enthusiasts often promised to relieve population pressure in the metropole (from the Greek for "mother city") by founding settlement colonies, but in reality the primary motive was the extraction of wealth and labor from subject peoples. It is therefore more accurate to speak of this process as empire building or imperialism rather than colonialism.

Historians and theorists have also made distinctions between *formal* and *informal* empire. The former meant the direct rule of subject peoples, while the latter implied the exercise of influence and privilege over a particular state or population without direct conquest. This influence might rest on the threat of military action, but it could also take the form of example, persuasion, and assistance. As such, these informal imperial methods could be termed *soft power*. Some scholars alternatively describe this kind of influence as *hegemony*. Based on the Greek *hegemon* (preeminence, leadership), hegemony meant the exercise of power through status, affluence, and cultural preeminence.

In this sense, less powerful actors or communities might voluntarily subordinate themselves to an informal empire or hegemon to acquire status and protection. More significantly, soft power often paid greater dividends than formal imperial conquest. Britain, for example, used its economic and military dominance in the mid-nineteenth century to build a global financial and commercial network of influence without incurring the expense of formal and direct imperial rule. This was in fact the "liberal empire" that captured the imagination of the modern imperial lobby. Similarly, the United States pegged out Central America and the Caribbean as its own sphere of influence. Contemporary imperial apologists depict the hegemony of the liberal international financial and commercial order underwritten by the western capitalist powers as a force for good.[13] This is open to debate, but it is clear that these systems of persuasion and influence are not imperial in the formal sense of the term.

Direct imperial rule, by definition, produces subjects. In common western usage, a subject is a person under the domination of a sovereign, but in the imperial context a subject refers to an outsider open to exploitation. Barbarians, outlanders, tribesmen, and other categories of peoples allegedly on the lower rungs of the ladder of civilization and human development were by their very nature ineligible for citizenship in metropolitan society. Conversely, a citizen (from the Latin *civitas*) was a person possessing the rights and privileges of full membership in a city or state. Citizens were autonomous individuals, free people, and, ultimately, fully realized human beings. Imperial subjects, by comparison, lived on the periphery in territories, both geographically and ideologically removed from the "civilized" metropole. They were, by definition, primitive and exploitable. In most cases, the prospect of assimilation into the supposedly superior metropolitan society was a chimera. To be profitable and sustainable, empires by their very nature had to codify and enshrine inequality.

There is of course no universalistic or timelessly "pure" model of empire, and comparing historical experiences of imperial rule is not a quest for natural laws or universal qualities of the human condition. This is simply a history that compares the experience of imperial rule in the ancient (Rome), medieval (Muslim Spain), early modern (the Spanish Americas; British rule in India), and modern (Napoleonic Europe; British Kenya; Nazi Europe) imperial eras. What stands out in each case is the resolve of subject majorities to throw off the yoke of an alien power that treated them as perpetual strangers and exploitable primitives.

Most empires shared certain central features and characteristics resulting from their attempts to subjugate a conquered people permanently. The first is that, far from confirming some sort of hierarchical ranking of advanced and primitive human societies, empires were simply the products of a temporary advantage in military technology, wealth, and political will. They were the result of the uneven integration of diverse populations into an emerging world economy and culture. These processes of "globalization" were quite old and probably began with the development of long-distance Eurasian commercial networks in the ancient era. It was therefore relatively rare for one state to maintain an economic or technological advantage over another for a significant length of time.

Successful empires exploited these temporary imbalances. In the sixteenth century, for example, New World peoples had never been exposed to highly contagious Old World diseases, lacked horses for civil and military transport, and had no knowledge of the advanced metallurgical technologies needed to produce iron-based armor, edged weapons, and firearms. Consequently, small bands of Spaniards won cheap but decisive victories over much larger Inkan and Aztec armies.

But it took more than a short-term economic, technological, and epidemiological imbalance to create an empire. In the ancient and medieval worlds, it was rare for one society or state to be significantly more advanced than another. In such cases, personal greed and cultural aggression were the decisive factors. Ancient Rome was rarely at peace with its neighbors, and both missionary zeal and an appetite for plunder motivated the Arab Muslims who built the Umayyad Caliphate. The British East India Company also had no significant military advantage over rival Indian princes, but the endemic warfare of early modern Europe taught its employees to be ruthless in expanding the company's influence in South Asia. Even the Nazi armies that won decisive victories in 1939 and 1940 were not substantially better equipped than their European rivals. Instead, their advantage lay in their tactics and willingness to discard the conventional rules of warfare by violating the rights of neutrals and attacking civilians.

These realities meant that imperial subjecthood was initially nothing more than an indication that a particular people had lost the ability to defend themselves. Over the long term these structural imbalances evened out. The most vulnerable societies were those divided sharply along the lines of class, religion, ethnicity, or some other form of identity. These divisions led to military weakness, hindered organized resistance, and made it easier for conquering powers to recruit local allies.

Ironically, imperial states were themselves vulnerable in this regard. The Umayyads took Iberia from the Visigothic kings with relative ease, the Spanish conquistadors toppled a highly unpopular and oppressive Inkan regime, and the British East India Company had little difficulty stepping into the shoes of Mughal imperial officials. Successful conquerors exploited parochialism. In Italy Napoleon's men faced little initial opposition from insular rural communities. The British adventurers filled out armies in East Africa by exploiting local rivalries to recruit "native auxiliaries." One might have expected France to be immune to these sorts of divide-and-rule tactics. But virtual civil war between political factions in the 1930s left the country unprepared for war. The rise of the left-wing Popular Front embittered the French right to the point where Pétain was willing to seek an accommodation with the Nazi occupiers.

The poor, the angry, and the blatantly opportunistic often had reason to cooperate with a new political order. The initial anarchy of imperial rule offered at least some people an opportunity to preserve or even improve their status by making themselves useful to the new regime. In both Napoleonic Italy and Nazi-occupied France, common people settled grievances large and small by denouncing rivals and enemies to their new masters. Alternatively, British chieftains and Visigothic nobles allied with the Romans to preserve their rank. Modern nationalism rendered this kind of pragmatism indefensible. Therefore, the regimes that returned to power in Europe after the Second World War redefined cooperation as the prosecutable crime of "collaboration." In premodern times, however, when identities were primarily local and cooperation was not yet treason, it was much easier to recruit intermediaries.

Contemporary critics often link imperial ambition with capitalism. Actually, the most stable and long-lived empires belonged to the premodern era, when local communities were more isolated from imperial demands for tribute and labor after the initial phases of conquest and plunder. This also meant that they had less cause to resist because the weight of their subjecthood was comparatively lighter. One of the primary reasons that empires in modern Europe became unsustainable was that the combination of imperial avarice and racialized nationalism made them unbearable.

The new imperialism of the late nineteenth century appeared viable because it targeted peoples with precapitalist economies who had not yet begun to think collectively. Most African subjects were actually relatively self-sufficient peasants or pastoralists who proved strikingly successful in resisting efforts to force them to participate in the imperial economy. There were very few prospects for profitable capitalist enterprise in the new territories, which meant that regimes had to court investors and entrepreneurs with the promise of cheap labor. It took an array of illiberal measures, ranging from thinly disguised slavery to excessive taxation, to drive subject Africans into the labor market. The French justified the *code de l'indigénat*, which gave them the summary authority to brutalize their subjects into working on state and private projects, on the grounds that it was a form of social education.

Modern conquerors endeavored to make their empires profitable and morally defensible by identifying subject peoples as inherently exploitable. Put more bluntly, their victims had to become less than human. Rulers consequently portrayed their subjects as culturally or racially inferior. The first category left open the possibility of jumping the boundary between subject and citizen through assimilation into the dominant imperial order. Racial inferiority implied that subjecthood was permanent and inescapable. In both cases, a vocabulary for subjecthood evolved. Subjects were not fully formed individuals; their primary identities were communal and collective. If they had rights to land, property, or protection, it was as members of a clan, caste, or tribe. They were "traditional" peoples who made no progress and indeed were barely aware of the passage of time.

The distinction between subject and citizen was less important in premodern eras when rulers unapologetically exploited their own domestic populations, and as late as the eighteenth century only a small percentage of the global population could even be classified as "free." Sovereigns and nobles generated surplus wealth by exploiting tenants, peasants, serfs, and laborers. In return, these marginal peoples received some measure of protection. In sharing even the most minimal bonds of kinship with their rulers, they qualified as nominally human. The European nationalist regimes that transformed their lower orders into citizens in the eighteenth and nineteenth centuries also resorted to harsh tactics that might appear, at first glance, imperial in character. But ultimately these peasants and townsmen emerged as full and equal members of a nation-state. Real assimilation, forced or otherwise, was part of the process of nation building, not empire building. Empires needed permanently exploitable subjects, not rights-holding citizens, to remain viable. Lucrative extraction was possible on a long-term basis only so long as subject peoples remained alien and inassimilable. The question of identity, what determined who was a subject and who was a citizen, is essential to understanding the true nature of empires, and to their history.

Yet the nation was not the end of history. Indeed, the accelerated expansion of global networks of culture, commerce, investment, and migration in the second half of the twentieth century provided a powerful counterweight to the nation-state. Some scholars have gone so far as to argue that global capital now constitutes a new, more powerful form of sovereignty that has eclipsed the national variety.[14] Transnational forces have also created new forms of pan-national identity that give like-minded groups of people additional means to challenge, if not thwart, the agendas of national governments, multinational corporations, and would-be empire builders.

Although the era of formal empire is conclusively over, policy debates, particularly after the terrorist attacks of 2001, frequently revolved around imperial themes. Critics on the left indicted the United States for behaving imperially in adopting an aggressive foreign policy, while right-wing revisionists and neoconservatives sought to rehabilitate empire to demonstrate that military force was the most effective way to impose order and stability on a global scale. No one in the Bush administration seriously aspired to acquire an empire when they invaded Iraq in 2003; even the most ardent imperial apologists knew that this was simply no longer possible or politically defensible. Rather, the architects of the Iraqi occupation believed that they could use authoritarian methods to replace an enemy regime with a liberal prowestern government. Like earlier generations of conquerors, they continued to believe that hard power could be used creatively to persuade, inspire, and reeducate a defeated "inferior" people.

Critics on the American and European left were equally ignorant of the historical precedents they invoked in their attacks
on the "Bush doctrine." Even some of the harshest opponents of
the war in Iraq failed to recognize that imperial rule was no longer feasible in an era that accepts national self-determination as
a basic human right. Castigating the Bush administration for its
unrestrained use of hard power, they produced a raft of books and
editorials warning ominously that the United States risked emulating ancient Rome in shifting from an egalitarian republic to an
authoritarian empire.[15] Rather than rebutting the neoconservative
hawks with the far more effective argument that imperial methods
are no longer possible or feasible, these critics allowed themselves
to be sidetracked into a moralistic debate over whether America
had become an empire.

The left's failure to make this case effectively allowed the neoimperial lobby to win over the American public by resurrecting the
myth of the liberal progressive empire. In doing so, they conveniently
forgot how these empires came apart under the pressure of nationalism in the 1960s. What mattered was that the notion of empire still
retained a seductive hold on the popular imagination. Western civilization courses teaching that modern nation-states are the heirs of a
culturally advanced and nearly omnipotent imperial Rome promote
an inherent respect for empire. Moreover, the media's tendency to
still depict nonwesterners as tribal, traditional, and backward meant
that the civilizing propaganda that legitimized the new imperialism
continued to carry weight with the general public in the United States
and its partners in the "coalition of the willing."

Striving to legitimize the Iraqi occupation, the revisionists gave
the failed imperial enterprises of the last century credit for introducing free trade around the world, imposing the rule of law on
anarchic regions, protecting private property, installing responsible
government, safeguarding speculative capitalist investment, and
sowing the seeds of democracy in modern nonwestern nations such
as India. The neoimperial lobby's case rested on the balance sheet
approach used by 1960s imperial apologists such as L. H. Gann and
Peter Duignan to claim that the collective good of hospitals, schools,
railways, roads, and industries far outweighed the sacrifices they
required of individual subjects.[16] This is how Niall Ferguson could

argue that the evils of indentured servitude, which was a brutal but highly effective means of compelling subject peoples to work, was necessary to achieve the greater good of increasing the global output of rubber and gold.[17]

To some degree, the attempt to rehabilitate the British and French empires represented an attempt by conservative Britons and Frenchmen to put a positive spin on their nations' imperial record and legacy. The French politicians who managed to temporarily pass a law in 2005 directing schools to teach the "positive role of the French overseas presence" clearly had this agenda. In this sense modern imperial romanticism is reminiscent of nostalgia in the American South for a lost and overly idealized antebellum slaveholding society. It also explains how most Americans conveniently overlook their nation's mistreatment of subject Amerindians, Filipinos, and other marginalized peoples.

The most serious flaw of the unbalanced balance sheet defense was that it ignored, either accidentally or willfully, subject perspectives. At best, the common Africans and Asians who lived under these supposedly benevolent empires were simply missing from the equation. At worst, the apologists fell back on the dehumanizing, if not outright racist, ideologies that legitimized imperial ambitions in the first place. Conversely, looking at empire from the bottom up exposes the mendacity of imperial balance sheets. As the anthropologist Nicholas Dirks aptly charged: "When imperial history loses any sense of what empire meant to those who were colonized, it becomes complicit in the history of empire itself."[18] Without question, subject peoples must be the central focus of any true assessment of an empire or the feasibility of imperial adventures.

This is more than just an issue of morality. Defeated populations did not automatically become saintly when they became subjects, and many of the subject peoples featured in this book were once autocratic imperial powers themselves. Sad to say, history also abounds with nonimperial rulers who brutally exploited their own people. Nonetheless, the implication that imperial methods remain viable because nonwestern peoples are still backward has allowed the naive, the venal, and the corrupt to continue to promise that imperial hard power can enhance national defense, improve international security, serve humanitarian causes, and fight the "war on terror."

This top-down view of empire disguises the fundamental reality that imperial subjecthood was and remains intolerable. Even the liberal British and French empires of the last century were born of blood and conquest. Ferguson may have excused the initial violence of empire building as "imperial overkill," but there is no escaping the almost genocidal viciousness in the satisfaction the British deputy commissioner of Bechuanaland took in the slaughter of Ndebele soldiers during the conquest of Rhodesia (Zimbabwe). "I must confess that it would offer me sincere and lasting satisfaction if I could see the Matabele Matjaha cut down by our own rifles and machine guns like a cornfield by a reaping machine and I would not spare a single one if I could have my way."[19]

The establishment of more formal rule ended the overt violence of these Orwellian "pacification campaigns," but Africans continued to die for imperial masters while working in the fields and mines. As in earlier eras, the labor of common people remained the only significant source of profit in the new empires. The supposedly modernizing imperial states of the last century relied on unfree labor, privileged foreign commercial interest, and discouraged the diversification of commodity production. They were hardly free and liberal. Eloquently rebutting the imperial apologists' balance sheets, the poet Aimé Césaire declared: "They throw facts at my head, statistics, mileages of roads, canals, and railroad tracks. I am talking about thousands of men sacrificed to the Congo-Ocean [railway]. I am talking about those who…are digging the harbor of Abidjan by hand."[20] Césaire was not exaggerating the lethality of imperial labor. The Belgian, French, and British authorities expended the lives of roughly eighteen hundred coerced African workers in the construction of a single railway line from Matadi to Léopoldville in the Belgian Congo.[21] Like the schools and hospitals enumerated by Gann and Duignan, the Matadi-Léopoldville line served western empire builders. If the new imperialists left independent African nations with a rudimentary capitalist infrastructure, it was by chance, not design.

The common experience of imperial rule throughout history has been oppression. In their scorn for these supposedly "liberal" French and British empires, Césaire and the former soldier Daniel Nguta provide a powerful rejoinder to modern scholars and policy makers who invoke historical examples to extol the virtues and rewards of imperial ventures. For there were Daniel Ngutas in every empire, even ancient Rome. Imperial apologists can laud the Romans for bringing civilization to the British Isles because the names and experiences of the common Britons who became Roman subjects have been lost to history. Yet the story of how simple people have the power to thwart grand imperial projects begins in this remote and backward corner of the Roman Empire.

Roman Britain

1

ROMAN BRITAIN

The Myth of the Civilizing Empire

Unlike most imperial projects, Roman Britain began with a formal, premeditated state-sponsored invasion. Emperor Claudius's most likely pretext for sending forty thousand legionnaires and auxiliaries across the English Channel in A.D. 43 was to restore the exiled king and Roman client Verica to power. The emperor's bid to conquer a cold, remote land that the Romans knew very little about also served pragmatic personal ends. Coming to the imperial purple with the backing of the Praetorian Guard, Claudius needed a heroic victory to establish his legitimacy and to pay off his military backers. Julius Caesar had led a pair of speculative expeditions to the island in 56 and 54 B.C., and Claudius's predecessor Gaius (Caligula) had aborted an invasion in A.D. 40. Britain was thus one of the last unconquered territories in western Europe. By adding it to the Roman Empire, Claudius sought to win over the army, burnish his imperial credentials, and answer critics in the Senate by accomplishing what his more distinguished predecessors could not.

Political considerations aside, Britain's actual value was less clear. The extractive worth of the island's population remains a matter of debate. Modern historians have alternately depicted southern Britain as either a rich commercial and agricultural region with a dense population and considerable tax potential or a mist-shrouded land that Emperor Augustus deemed too undeveloped to warrant the cost of conquest. The Greek geographer Strabo recorded that Caesar's military expeditions intimidated the Britons into paying tribute and returned with slaves and plunder. Yet he also suggested that the overall value of the island was not worth the cost of permanent occupation.

This may have been why Claudius's legions initially refused to cross the channel. The Greek historian Cassius Dio recorded that Claudius's freedman Narcissus convinced them to board the ships by appealing to their pride, but the promise of extra pay and plunder was probably the real inducement. Claudius delegated command of the four-legion invasion force, drawn primarily from the German provinces, to Aulus Plautius, whom Dio considered a "senator of great renown." There was no initial opposition to the Roman landings. Most Britons probably viewed the invasion as another short-term military expedition and hoped that the Claudian army would follow Caesar's example by withdrawing with its loot. They therefore avoided direct combat, gathering for battle only when it became apparent that the Romans were not leaving. Organized by the Catuvellaunian brothers Caratacus and Togodumnus, a British confederation fought the Romans and lost on the banks of the river Medway in southeastern England. Dio recorded that eleven British kings surrendered after Togodumnus died in the fighting and Caratacus retreated northward.

With southern Britain in Roman hands, Claudius arrived to claim the fruits of victory and founded a colony near Camulodunum, the closest thing to a British capital at the time. The emperor then left for Rome with a parting order to Plautius to "subjugate the remaining [British] districts." By A.D. 82, the legions had overrun all of modern England and Wales and most of lowland Scotland.[1]

Claudius's imperial adventure helps to explain why modern debates about the nature and utility of empire invariably begin with Rome. The Roman Empire's scope, power, cultural accomplishments, and longevity made it the standard by which westerners measured all other imperial states. The Romans' spectacular art, architecture, engineering, and literature reflected the wealth and sophistication of their empire, but the passage of time obscures the reality that ruthless extraction made these achievements possible. Ancient generals sought the immediate rewards of loot and plunder, but subject populations represented the most durable and sustainable dividends of an imperial conquest. In time, most eventually developed new methods of resisting central authority, but the Romans were particularly adept at creating sustainable bureaucratic systems to draw this process out and make the most efficient use of their enormous subject population. From the top down, these institutions seem rational and relatively benign, but in reality it took intimidation, naked force, and institutionalized slavery to produce all the grand monuments and cultural achievements of the ancient world.

Popular histories of Rome ignore these realities because Roman subjects are largely missing from the historical record. Ancient historians and geographers such as Strabo, Tacitus, Cassius Dio, Suetonius, and Zosimus provide rich and colorful accounts of Roman empire building, but their descriptions of the "barbarians" who became the subjects of the empire cannot be taken at face value. Concerned primarily with domestic issues, classical authors used the empire as a backdrop for critiques of Roman politics and society. Epigraphs, legal texts, bronze copies of discharge diplomas, and census data help to contextualize and correct the classical historians. Archaeology is also particularly helpful because it shows how people actually lived rather than what others said about them. But many archaeologists are drawn to grand monuments and stately villas, and too few pay attention to the Roman conquest's violence and disruption. Consequently, simple farmsteads and urban dwellings remain largely unexamined.

There is therefore no comprehensive picture of what it meant to be a common Roman subject. A careful reading of the ancient historians in fact suggests that the Romans themselves knew very little about the peoples of the empire, regardless of how long they ruled them. Indeed, it is almost certain that Roman officials and tax collectors were no more successful in governing captive territory directly than their more modern successors were.

This fogginess surrounding the realities of the Roman past allowed succeeding generations of historians and theorists to follow Tacitus and Cassius Dio in reinterpreting the Roman Empire to speak to contemporary concerns. In the early modern Andes, Spanish conquerors used Roman imperial analogies to understand and govern the conquered Inkan Empire. Edward Gibbon's *Decline and Fall of the Roman Empire* voiced worries about the decline of the first British Empire in the late eighteenth century. A century later, late Victorian and Edwardian imperial enthusiasts imagined themselves the heirs of a grand imperial Rome that had uplifted their Iron Age ancestors.[2]

As the dominant force in the ancient world for more than five centuries, Rome exemplified imperial power and became a yardstick for westerners to measure the empires that succeeded it. The Roman Empire was therefore a blank slate. Variously, the Rome of Cicero and Virgil stood for high culture, Caesar's assassination was a triumph of republican virtues, Augustus's principate embodied imperial greatness, and the excesses of Caligula and Nero were cautionary tales about the corrupting influences of imperial power.[3] Rome thus is the starting point for today's debates over the nature and efficacy of empire building.

In contrast to the liberal western empires of the twentieth century that pretended to govern in the interests of their subjects, the Romans made no apology for expanding *imperium Romanum* by violence and conquest. They also did not initially see any incompatibility between empire building and their democratic institutions. It was actually the Roman republic that built the *imperium Romanum*. Invoking Rome's destiny for universal rule, the republican statesman Cicero declared in 56 B.C. that "it has now finally come about that the limits of our empire and of the earth are one and the same." This view continued into the imperial era. Augustus bragged that Rome controlled the world, and the poet Virgil had Jupiter sanctify the empire in the *Aeneid*: "For these [Romans] I place neither physical bounds nor temporal limits; I have given empire without end."[4]

Yet the Romans were by no means as self-assured as these boastful quotes suggest. They actually acquired most of their territory in piecemeal, almost accidental fashion. Claudius's planned invasion of Britain was an exception. Almost universally, the Romans of the post-Augustus era were more concerned with stability and control than with expansion for its own sake. Moreover, they needed allies to exercise power at the local level. In this sense, the *imperium Romanum* was actually an administrative grid imposing control on an enormously diverse range of local polities and cultures. Strength alone was not enough to consign an entire population to permanent subjecthood, and so the Romans shared power with useful local elites to govern the larger subject majority. Like all of the empires that came after it, the Roman Empire established its authority through militarism and terror, but it needed these partners and intermediaries to actually rule.

The Romans were generally more open to easing the line between citizen and subject than their successors in later empires. At a time when identities were highly fluid and flexible, Roman elites were usually willing to accept any person of status as Roman provided he or she spoke Latin and embraced Roman culture. The Senate was quite generous in granting citizenship to friends and allies during the republican era, and the emperors continued this practice to the point where Caracalla bestowed blanket citizenship on all residents of the empire in A.D. 212. Those who prefer to imagine the Roman Empire as a civilizing force cite this mass enfranchisement as evidence of its benevolence, but it is more likely that Caracalla's concession was a pragmatic acknowledgment that the boundaries of true subjecthood had blurred to the point where the Roman Empire was actually no longer an imperial institution by strict definition.

In other words, if empire is the direct and authoritarian rule of one group of people by another, then Rome ceased to be truly imperial when it turned its subjects into officially recognized Romans. The Roman state certainly exploited its lower orders, but Caracalla's action suggests that the respectable and military classes of the empire had become so romanized that the distinction between citizen and subject no longer mattered at the elite level. This universal enfranchisement must have tempered the extractive power of the state and may have contributed to the financial crisis that beset the later Roman Empire.

The Romans' assimilationist policies were possible in part because modern conceptions of race did not apply. They did not conceive of "Romanness" in terms of race or blood, but they had a strong sense of their own distinct identity and considered themselves inherently superior to everyone who did not share their culture and morality. While they inherited the Greek perception of foreigners as barbarians, they also borrowed freely from subject cultures even as they despised them. Confident of their superiority, the Romans assumed that "tribal" peoples became less virile and easier to handle once they embraced Roman culture. Assimilation was thus a coercive and administrative tool as well as an affirmation of Roman preeminence. Contrary to modern assumptions, it did not convey blanket equality or release common people from the responsibility to serve the empire with their tribute and labor.[5]

For all their self-confidence, Roman intellectuals were also profoundly anxious about the consequences of empire building. In a
speech condemning an abusive governor in Sicily, Cicero warned that
misrule would turn the world against the Rome. "Within the bounds
of Ocean there is no longer any place so distant or so out of the way
that the wanton and oppressive deeds of our countrymen have not
penetrated there in recent years. Rome can no longer hold out against
the whole world—I do not mean against its power and arms in war,
but against its groans and tears and lamentations."[6]

Like-minded statesmen worried that unchecked imperial expansion would eventually destroy the republic. The limits of travel
and communication in the ancient world raised serious concerns in
the Senate about whether Roman representative institutions could
include remote alien populations. Even the Greeks brought the threat
of degenerative decadence through their enticing learning, arts, and
material luxuries. Far from exalting in Rome's triumph over Greece,
Pliny lamented that "through conquering we have been conquered."[7]
Conversely, subjugating northern peoples brought the reverse threat
of contamination through the adulteration and debasement of the
superior Roman culture.

Indeed, promiscuity in granting citizenship to useful allies eventually transformed the very nature of the empire. The Greeks defied
assimilation, but in the west, where identities were more fluid, imperial rule produced a new hybrid ruling culture. But this process of
romanization, a modern academic concept, did not mean the meta-
morphosis of tribal barbarians into civilized Romans. Imperial rule
actually transformed the Romans themselves: as the empire absorbed
a vast array of conquered peoples and cultures, imperial institutions
and values evolved constantly as new groups of elites became citizens.
It is therefore better to think of the culture of the empire as mixed
and borrowed rather than homogenously Roman.

Romans believed that the primary basis of identity in Britain and
the rest of the western empire was the *civitas*. In the Mediterranean
world this term meant a city-state inhabited by citizens (*cives*). In
western Europe, where there were few actual cities, the *civitas* became
a tribal unit. These *civitates* (tribes) were small-scale nonliterate polities, sometimes anchored by an urban center or *oppidum*, in other
cases not. It is tempting to refer to them as "Celts" on the assumption

that they spoke variants of the same language and shared a common culture. Herodotus called the inhabitants of southern Gaul "Keltoi," but archaeologically there were significant variations in the material cultures of western Europe in the preconquest era.

Identities were overwhelmingly local in the ancient world, and a tribal label was not a mark of barbarity. Even the Romans began as a tribal people. The original inhabitants of the city of Rome divided themselves into thirty-five tribes, which made tribal membership a marker of citizenship. Noncitizens in Rome were, by definition, tribeless. Under the republic, the tribe became an electoral unit that organized citizens for military service and taxation. Romans officially inherited tribal identities from fathers and patrons, but the republic also had the authority to shift citizens from one tribe to another.

In Britain and the rest of western Europe, the Romans assumed that "barbaric" tribal peoples in the more conventional modern sense represented a less advanced stage of social development. But in fact these tribal identities probably emerged in response to Roman imperial expansion. Conventional historical narratives often excused empire building as a defensive response to hostile "tribal" peoples, but it is more likely that culturally diverse and multilingual groups on the imperial frontier coalesced into more coherent political and social units when faced with economic domination and possible conquest by a powerful expansionist state. The opportunities and risks that came with closer political and commercial ties to Rome disrupted local patronage and authority, and the resulting political centralization was thus both a defensive response and an opportunistic one. This is most likely what produced the "tribes" in southern Britain in the era between Julius Caesar's raids and the Claudian occupation. Having conquered a territory, the Romans explicitly encouraged the codification of tribal identities to make better sense of alien and fluid societies. Drawing on the eastern practice of governing through the leading citizens of Greek city-states, the Romans treated tribes as urban *civitates*.

The leaders of these new tribes became romanized as they shared in the benefits of the Roman imperial project, but it is much harder to judge the impact of romanization on conquered majorities. Co-opted tribal aristocrats contributed to the evolving imperial culture, but almost certainly most common people continued to identify more strongly with their localities than with distant Rome. Assimilation did not turn entire populations into Romans and probably did not bring much relief from demands for tribute, labor, and taxes. The empire's aristocratic classes exploited their lower classes without regard as to whether they were Roman or not. For the vast majority of people, the Roman conquest did not bring assimilation and a chance to live a better life. While it exposed subject peoples to new ideas and cultures, imperial rule primarily brought greater tribute demands and more efficient extraction.

Ironically, Rome's great imperial expansion took place under the republic, making it a de facto empire before it actually had an emperor. Rome began as a small city-state in the eighth century B.C., and its first subjects were its neighbors in the Latin League. The league, a coalition of culturally related cities, was a mutual defense alliance, but by the early fourth century B.C. it was firmly under the sway of Rome. The Romans then imposed their will on central Italy and drove the Greeks from the south. By the mid-third century B.C. they had become a dominant power in the Mediterranean by defeating Carthage in the First Punic War. In the last years of the republic, Rome acquired Greece, most of Spain, Gaul, Libya, Numidia, Egypt, Syria, and substantial stretches of Asia Minor and the Balkans. Where the early republican leaders were initially reluctant to make their annexations permanent, after the civil war of 81 B.C., ambitious senators and military men often seized territory to further personal ambitions.

At first the Romans were not conscious empire builders. Sometimes Rome acquired territory at the behest of weak states that sought its protection; in other instances Romans fought stronger, threatening powers. In Asia Minor, Rome added Pergamum to the empire when its rulers made the Roman people their legal heirs. The Romans usually claimed that they fought to defend themselves, but as their empire grew, they became increasingly confident that it was their destiny to become a great power. As Cicero declared in 56 B.C.: "It was by piety and religious scruples and our sagacious understanding of a single truth, that all things are directed and ruled by the gods' will, that we have conquered all peoples and nations."[8]

While popular history lauds the egalitarian virtues of the Roman Republic, the republic was almost constantly at war. Fighting and rapacious plunder were facts of life. Victorious generals who killed more than five thousand foreigners were entitled to a grand parade in Rome. The Romans held more than three hundred of these "triumphs" between 509 and 19 B.C., which means that the republic dispatched roughly 1.5 million of its enemies during this period.[9] These triumphs also demonstrate the naked avarice that lay behind Rome's conquests. Livy reported that Titus Quinctius Flamininus, who defeated Philip V in the Second Macedonian War, showcased a staggering amount of wealth during his three-day triumph in 194 B.C.:

> On the first day, Flamininus put armour, weaponry, and statues of bronze and marble on display.... On the second he displayed gold and silver wrought, unwrought, and coined. There were 18,270 pounds of unwrought silver.... In coined silver 84,000 "Attic" coins.... There were 3,714 pounds of gold, a shield made of solid gold and 14,514 gold Philippics. On the third day 114 golden crowns which had been gifts from the city-states were carried in the procession.... Before the triumphal chariot there were many prisoners and hostages of noble birth, including Demetrius, son of king Philip, and Armenes the Spartan, son of the tyrant Nabis.[10]

Ambitious men such as Flamininus turned over most of this wealth to imperial coffers, but they also were careful to give their common soldiers a healthy share of the plunder.

Unlike the empire builders of later eras, the Romans did not enjoy a significant technological advantage over their opponents. Most classical Mediterranean armies used similar equipment, and the Romans' victories came from the superior organization, training, and aggression of their legions. Consisting of five thousand citizens subdivided into cohorts and centuries, the republican legion was a highly trained fighting force. Roman commanders augmented the regular army with auxiliary cohorts consisting of non-Roman subjects and officered by aristocratic Romans. These auxiliaries usually earned Roman citizenship if they survived their full term of service. The need to keep the legions busy and out of politics spurred military adventures on the frontiers.

Those who resisted Roman expansion did so at their peril. The Greek historian Polybius recorded in graphic detail how Scipio Africanus made an example of New Carthage in 209 B.C. by ordering his men to slaughter the entire population of the city. "They do this,

I think, to inspire terror, so that when towns are taken by the Romans one may often see not only the corpses of human beings, but dogs cut in half, and the dismembered limbs of other animals."[11] Roman forces similarly destroyed Corinth sixty-three years later. The Romans nevertheless were inclined to treat surrendering rulers generously. The same Scipio who destroyed Carthage was magnanimous toward Heraclea in Asia Minor: "We shall endeavor, now that you have come under our protection, to take the best possible care of you.... We grant freedom, with the right to administer all your affairs your-selves, under your own laws."[12] The fate of Heraclea demonstrated that it was safer and wiser to be within the empire than outside it.

Imperial expansion eventually destroyed the republic, but in the short term the resulting plunder brought marked benefits to Rome: citizens paid no taxes. In Italy allied states were liable for taxes and military service until their revolt in the Social War of 90 B.C. forced the Romans to grant them citizenship. This set a precedent for the wider empire. In Greece, where the greatest returns were through commerce rather than crude extortion, Rome enfranchised the entire population of cooperative city-states. In the west, tribal leaders could earn citizenship, but their small numbers ensured that this generos-ity did not reduce the flow of tribute.

The actual mechanisms of Roman imperial administration, which seem so familiar as the standard template of imperial rule, evolved gradually over time. Sovereignty in republican Rome rested with the consuls, the Senate, and the citizenry, but their influence was lim-ited by the ancient world's realities of time and distance. The Senate exercised authority over remote territories by assigning consuls or magistrates who had finished their term in office to complete specific tasks in the wider empire. Proconsuls collected revenue, secured food for Rome, conducted censuses, supervised trade, and, most impor-tant, fought wars. Their *provincia*, assignments or tasks, gradually took on specific territorial dimensions. A province came to mean a magistrate's geographic scope of operations, and these administrative boundaries were largely set by the first century B.C.

Appointed by the Senate, their governors were usually ex-consuls with command of the provincial military garrison. There was no per-manent imperial bureaucracy, and these wealthy proconsuls relied on their personal resources and small private staffs to govern. Their primary responsibility was to maintain order and collect tribute. Governors sometimes had to obey senatorial orders, but for the most part they had considerable autonomy in dealing with local issues and threats. Although the Senate barred them from moving troops outside their provinces without permission, many found the temptation to enrich themselves through self-serving wars irresistible.

Before 150 B.C., the Romans ruled only Sicily, Corsica, Sardinia, and Spain directly. Although unapologetic conquerors, they were also deft practitioners of soft power. When possible, Rome preferred to exert influence through semiautonomous client kings whom the Senate euphemistically termed "friends of the Roman people." Putting aside their avowed disdain for kings, senators bestowed ivory scepters, embroidered togas, and other markers of Etruscan royalty on puppet rulers as symbols of their allegiance to Rome. More significantly, the Romans often helped cooperative monarchs remain in power with direct payments of coins and material goods. Acceptance of these royal trappings and subsidies signified that an ally deferred to imperial authority, and the Romans interpreted any defiance of their will as an overt revolt. They also intervened freely in local succession disputes to replace unsuitable clients.

In the Greek portions of the empire, many city-states were so cooperative that imperial administration was not a problem. But in most other conquered territories the governors and their tiny staffs needed local help to collect taxes and maintain order. In the west, where there were fewer useful centralized institutions of authority, the Romans encouraged their creation by rewarding cooperative allies with citizenship. The Romans also engaged in formal colonization by settling former soldiers in veterans' colonies and providing land grants to citizens and allies.

While tribute from client states and provincial taxes poured new riches into Rome, the imperial windfall had an enormous hidden cost. The common farmers, who made up the backbone of the early republican armies, faced bankruptcy because they could not compete with cheap grain from Sicily and Spain. Many gravitated to the city of Rome to take advantage of the free grain ration after wealthy and connected families bought up their lands. This urban poor became a dangerous rabble ready to support any conquering hero who promised to feed and entertain them.

Powerful proconsuls such as Pompey, Crassus, and Caesar played to the mob and turned their legions into private armies by using imperial plunder to reward soldiers with pensions and land grants. Having gained sufficient strength and fame in the provinces, they marched on Rome in a bid for absolute power. Imperial plunder thus had a corrupting and corrosive impact on the republic. Countless problems afflicted the late Roman Republic, but Caesar's rise stemmed from the inability of its representative institutions to incorporate its far-flung provinces and this was a key factor in its demise. The slow transmission of orders and messages in the ancient world gave Roman generals and governors far too much power and autonomy, and the Senate failed to find a way to balance Rome's representative institutions with the inherent tyranny of imperial rule in the provinces.

Julius Caesar's murder at the hands of the Senate in 44 B.C. appeared to reaffirm Rome's republican values, but it paved the way for the rise of his adopted son and heir, Octavian, who took the name Augustus Caesar after coming to power in 31 B.C. Four years later, Augustus made a show of giving up the dictatorial powers he had assumed during the struggle for power. The citizenry of Rome still elected consuls and other lesser magistrates, but Augustus effectively brought the republic to an end. He made himself a tribune for life, which gave him the power to veto legislation and made his person sacred. Augustus thus had absolute power over the city of Rome and its empire. He did not claim to be a god during his lifetime, but by sanctioning the Senate's deification of his adoptive father, Julius Caesar, he established his divine lineage. Adding the title *imperator*, an honorific that soldiers voted to victorious generals, Augustus finally gave Rome an emperor to go with its de facto empire (the principate). With a population of forty million people, four million of whom were citizens, the Roman Empire reached the height of its power under his despotic rule.

Facing few serious foreign threats, Augustus and the Julio-Claudian emperors who succeeded him focused on securing virtually all of the agriculturally productive regions of Europe and the Mediterranean borderlands. They pushed imperial boundaries to their natural frontiers at mountain ranges, dense forests, deserts, and impassable bodies of water. There was no formal line on a map marking the conclusive limits of Roman territory. Rather, the Romans bounded the empire with a network of roads, forts, and alliances with client kings.

Persia's Parthian Empire was the principate's only significant rival foreign power. But the "barbarians" of the west also became a serious problem. It was the ambush and annihilation of three legions (fifteen thousand men) by northern Germans in the Teutoburg Forest in A.D. 9 that cooled the aging Augustus's enthusiasm for further empire building. The massacre drove home the reality that the incorporation of unwilling frontier peoples was rarely worth the cost. Nonetheless, the republican civil wars demonstrated that successful generals were a much greater political threat.

Augustus had no direct male heir and left no formal system of succession, which meant most Julio-Claudians came to power through adoption by their predecessors and the support of powerful allies in the military. It was the Praetorian Guard who elevated Claudius to the imperial throne by assassinating Caligula. While Claudius was a reasonably moderate ruler, his adopted son and heir, Nero, was so brutal and incompetent that powerful provincial governors drove him to suicide in A.D. 68. The empire then lapsed into civil war as various military leaders competed for the imperial purple. Order returned in A.D. 69 when Vespasian, who had distinguished himself during the Claudian conquest of Britain and the Jewish revolt, came to power. The members of his Flavian dynasty and the following "five good emperors" ranged from enlightened despots to tyrants, but they presided over a century of stability and prosperity that Gibbon and later historians romanticized as Rome's golden age.

The Roman imperial administrative system came to full maturity under the Julio-Claudian and Flavian dynasties, but the actual reach of the emperors was short. Lacking the technology to issue immediate and direct orders, they relied on small personal staffs of slaves and freedmen, trustworthy aristocrats, and a relatively small clerical bureau to govern the empire. A formal bureaucracy did not develop until early in the third century A.D. The Senate retained authority over the Italian peninsula, and senatorial governors also commanded garrisons in the peaceful territories. The emperor's own men, who were often equestrians (second-rank aristocrats), controlled legions in frontier provinces. In most cases, their headquarters' staffs provided the core of the administration. The emperors made law by sending directives to provincial officials and responding to petitions from their subjects. In their capacity as magistrates, governors relied on Roman law in adjudicating cases involving Romans and followed local precedent for lesser proceedings concerning noncitizens.

At the local level the actual mechanics of government varied widely. Whenever possible, a city became the center of imperial administration because urban populations were the easiest to police and tax. The Romans ruled through long-established city-states in the Greek east, but Roman officials had to actively promote urbanization in the western provinces. Imperial rule turned Spanish village communes into formal cities with the rights of Roman citizenship (*municipia*) and encouraged Gauls and Britons to abandoned fortified strongholds for new Roman-style towns. As in the city of Rome, urban populations elected governing magistrates from among the most wealthy and influential members of the community, and these civil leaders carried the burden of funding municipal operations. The emperors also continued the republican practice of using veterans' colonies to create islands of Roman influence among conquered populations.

Governing the vast rural majority was more complicated. In the western provinces, the Romans created the semblance of *civitates* by lending money to community leaders to build capitals on the Roman model. These anchored the administration of the surrounding countryside, and over time, many of their respectable classes became leading citizens of the empire.

The army was also a powerful instrument of assimilation under the principate. Composed of long-serving professional soldiers who were mostly volunteers, its base shifted from the Italian peninsula to the provinces. Many of the principal recruits were the sons of legionnaires from army camps in Spain, North Africa, and southern Gaul, but others were auxiliaries drawn from subject communities throughout the empire. The later Roman army had almost as many auxiliary troops as it did regular Roman legionnaires, which lowered the costs of imperial rule considerably. The Romans also disciplined troublesome subjects by impressing them into ethnically based specialist units such as archers and light cavalrymen. German auxiliaries from Batavia staged a significant revolt in A.D. 69, but most subject troops earned their Roman citizenship on discharge. Imperial military officials spread thousands of these romanized veterans throughout the empire. In both cases, they constituted a substantial prop to Roman imperial rule.

The empire's subjects bore primary responsibility for supporting this 250,000-man standing army and the emperor's vast personal household. The steady flow of imperial loot and extortion meant that citizens faced little in the way of direct taxes until late in the third century A.D. In terms of currency alone, the republic minted roughly fifty tons of silver coinage per year in its final decades, the equivalent of half of the silver the Spanish imported from the Americas in the sixteenth century A.D.[13] Demands for revenue fell most heavily on subject communities living along the empire's network of roads, but over time the imperial tax system captured a greater swath of the rural population as it became more established and efficient.

Metropolitan Rome and the Italian heartland were at the center of a ring of prosperous provinces consisting of Spain, southern Gaul, North Africa, Asia Minor, Syria, and Egypt. These wealthy territories, particularly in the east, funneled tax revenues to the imperial core. Egypt and the African provinces also provided most of the free grain for the city of Rome. Plunder aside, Britain and the other outer provinces actually contributed comparatively little to the metropolitan treasury, with the bulk of their resources going to support military garrisons on the frontiers. Over time, Roman rule gradually transformed the local economies of these outlying territories as revenue demands, military purchases, and free-spending legionnaires stimulated trade and promoted the development of provincial markets.

There are no surviving records of general tax rates under the principate, which means historians disagree on whether Roman demands on their subjects were light or burdensome. At the very least, Roman subjects paid a personal tax and a land tax. Wealthier men also paid indirect levies on inheritances, houses, slaves, ships, and other forms of property and commerce. The republic delegated direct taxation in Greece and Gaul to private companies that paid for the right to collect taxes in a given region. In order to extract more revenue than they had to turn over to the state, these companies were often quite predatory. The principate ended some of the worst tax-farming abuses, but its improved efficiency in keeping track of the general population through censuses probably offset savings that taxpayers might have gained from escaping the clutches of corrupt private collectors. Romanized urban elites most likely accepted payment in agricultural produce that could be sold to generate the coinage demanded by the imperial treasury.

Aristocrats in Rome and the central provinces were the ultimate beneficiaries of this comparatively efficient extractive system. These were the senatorial and equestrian classes, which constituted less than 1 percent of the total imperial population. Senators, who numbered six hundred under the early principate, owned vast rural estates that made them the wealthiest men in the empire. Some also dabbled in moneylending, but the equestrian class, which took its name from the cavalrymen of the early republic, were the empire's most prominent financiers and businessmen. Both classes used their status to acquire substantial wealth and land holdings in the provinces.

These elites took on compliant kings and chiefs in Spain, Gaul, and Britain as clients, sponsoring their entry into imperial society. Most of these former chieftains and war leaders gradually became landed Roman gentlemen. Roman citizenship did not release them from the obligation of paying direct taxes, but it brought limited immunity from local laws and an exemption from tribute and forced labor. Non-Romans eventually accounted for a significant portion of the imperial aristocracy of the later principate. Native-born Italians constituted 90 percent of the Senate under Augustus, but by the beginning of the second century A.D. only 40 percent of all senators were from the inner provinces. There was a backlash against ennoblement of so many provincials under the Julio-Claudians, but Tacitus recorded a potent speech by Claudius defending the admission of Gallic nobles to the Senate in A.D. 48:

> What else was the downfall of Sparta and Athens, than that they held the conquered in contempt as foreigners? But our founder Romulus's wisdom made him on several occasions both fight against and naturalize a people on the same day! …If you examine the whole of our wars, none was finished in a shorter time than that against the Gauls; from then on there has been continuous and loyal peace. Now that customs, culture, and marriage ties have blended them with us, let them also bring their gold and riches instead of holding them apart.[14]

Later empire builders, who found it essential to keep their subjects at arm's length, would have found this unthinkable. Identity was far more flexible in the classical era, and Roman conquerors freely borrowed from subject cultures. They unashamedly worshipped a host of cults from Germany, Syria, Egypt, and Persia alongside their own Greco-Roman gods and the divine emperor himself. These syncretic practices allowed subject elites to embrace an imperial identity without entirely abandoning their own cultures. Emperor Caracalla's decision to make every free resident of the empire a citizen in the early third century A.D. was most likely a tacit admission that the assimilative process had gone so far that the formal distinction between citizen and subject underpinning the crudest forms of imperial exploitation had become largely meaningless.

Historians of empire often equated this romanization with the twentieth-century concepts of modernization and westernization on the assumption that it entailed the progression from barbarism to civilization. At the elite level Rome's subjects learned Latin, adopted Roman manners, copied Greco-Roman architecture, and purchased Roman products. Yet romanization did not mean the domination of one culture over another. Imperial society was never uniform at the grassroots, and the term really meant only an acceptance of Roman authority. Greeks, Jews, and Egyptians never became Romans, although to varying degrees they acknowledged Roman rule. If there was a common imperial identity at the heart of the romanization process, it emerged through cultural exchanges with the subject peoples of the empire. Romanization thus described the spread of a hybrid culture that emerged as Romans adopted local norms to govern conquered populations and conquered populations encountered Roman functionaries, celebrations, monuments, and commerce.

The scope of romanization was relatively limited in the wealthy and culturally coherent eastern provinces where Alexander the Great's empire left a Hellenic counterweight to Roman culture. It had a greater impact in the west, where less coherent tribal communities were more open to Rome's ideas and material culture. Spaniards and Gauls became senators, but romanization and token citizenship after Caracalla's decree probably meant relatively little beyond the provincial level. The evidence is scanty, but it appears that there were no British senators and few auxiliary commanders in the first century A.D.

This convenient lacuna allowed later generations to bend the Roman imperial record to suit their needs. Debates over the scope and influence of romanization predictably reflected the national, class, and methodological biases of the observer. Insisting that pre-conquest identities survived under Roman rule, nationalistic British historians and archaeologists point to the survival of popular Celtic forms in jewelry and religious shrines in arguing that romanization influenced only a thin layer of Roman British society.[15] Alternatively, just as apologists for the empires of the twentieth century adopted a balance sheet standard in counting railways, hospitals, and schools as imperial achievements, those who imagined a civilizing Rome paid the most attention to roads, aqueducts, villas, art, and literature. By their reckoning, the high material culture of the empire suggested that Roman rule was benevolent and uplifting. Depicting preconquest Britain as afflicted with Hobbesian "endemic warfare," one sympa-thetic scholar credited Roman rule with giving Britons the "freedom to live the good life."[16]

This may have been true for the *civitas* rulers who became imperial gentlemen, but the initial stages of Roman rule brought significant hardship for subject majorities. Roman conquerors plundered and disrupted local economies, seized land, and requisitioned labor. As with most imperial projects, the real wealth of the Roman Empire came from the exploitation of its subjects. Monumental construction projects and the enormous surpluses needed to sustain the impe-rial bureaucracy, military, and artistic classes most likely consumed wealth produced by huge amounts of coerced labor. Leading citizens such as Cicero occasionally urged administrators to respect the inter-ests of provincial populations, but defeated peoples were entirely at the mercy of Roman soldiers, magistrates, and politically connected metropolitan aristocrats.

Although they may appear cultured and urbane by contemporary standards, Roman empire builders enslaved conquered populations in enormous numbers. This was fairly typical behavior in the ancient world, for victorious armies had the assumed right to dispose of their captives as they wished. Republican Romans took tens of thousands, if not hundreds of thousands, of slaves from Carthage, Spain, Gaul, and captured eastern cities. Rebels continued to meet this fate under the principate, and Emperor Vespasian enslaved ninety-seven thousand residents of Jerusalem after razing the city during the Jewish Revolt. He sent most of them to hard labor in Egypt, but the healthiest and best-looking entertained the Roman mob by dying at the hands of gladiators and wild animals in arenas throughout the empire.[17]

Imperial apologists point out that educated slaves and freedmen held significant positions of authority in the emperor's household and that owners often manumitted slaves. Admittedly, enslavement did not mean permanent stigmatization in the modern sense, and Pertinax, who became emperor in the late second century A.D., was the son of a freedman. Yet these were exceptional cases, for the vast majority of Roman slaves were the meanest type of manual laborers.

Much of the empire's wealth between the second century B.C. and the second century A.D. came from slaves working on great rural estates in Italy. Slaves constituted approximately 35 percent of the population of the Italian peninsula under Augustus. An expert on Roman slavery calculated that the Romans needed to acquire up to half a million new slaves each year to maintain these levels during the late republic and early principate.[18] A great many of these slaves faced a grim fate. Their owners worked them like animals, and slaves could be tortured as a matter of procedure in criminal trials. Tellingly, massive revolts were common under the late republic. The ability of the ex-gladiator Spartacus to rally ninety thousand slaves to his rebellion in 73 B.C. testified to their hopeless and desperate condition, given that the penalty for revolt was torture and crucifixion.

The Romans treated slave revolts and provincial rebellions with such brutality because, like all empire builders, they worried that their control over their subjects was never completely secure. Defeated peoples in the Roman Empire tended to rebel in the first generation after the initial conquest, when Roman demands for labor and taxes were most severe. Organized resistance became less common late in the first century A.D. after imperial expansion came to an end. Nevertheless, the Romans still showed no mercy to those who challenged them. On learning that his generals had crushed a revolt by the Nasamones in the African province of Numidia, Emperor Domitian proudly declared to the Senate: "I have forbidden the Nasamones to exist." Similarly, Emperor Severus ordered his forces to be equally ruthless with enemies who threatened the northern frontier of Roman Britain in the third century A.D.: "Let no-one escape utter destruction at our hands; let not the infant still carried in its mother's womb, if it be male, escape from its fate."[19] Despite their military supremacy, the

Romans were ever mindful of their security, and these measures were usually sufficient to deter potential rebels.

Britons most certainly learned this lesson, but their experience of Roman imperial rule was not typical. One of the least romanized provinces in the western empire, it paid meager returns. Yet Roman Britain figures prominently in the imaginations of English-speakers, for it allows them to pretend that Great Britain is the direct heir of a grand and majestic Roman Empire. Nonetheless, the Roman era in British history was not as uplifting or influential as contemporary imperial enthusiasts might imagine.

Classical sources referred to the primary island in the British Isles as Britannia, thus the inhabitants of this island were Britons. Greek and Roman sources depict them as prototypical candidates for imperial subjugation. Casting them as giant forest-dwelling barbarians, Strabo asserted that they had "no experience in gardening or other agricultural pursuits." Caesar, who actually visited Britain, granted that the southern "tribes" were civilized through contacts with more advanced continental Gauls, but he borrowed from Strabo in describing northern Britons as ferocious tribesmen who lived solely on milk and meat, dyed themselves blue for war, and shared wives. Tacitus, who wrote well after the Claudian conquest, continued to depict northerners as wild and militaristic but added the qualification that the peace and stability of Roman rule had made them decadent.

For Roman authors and readers, Britain was an alien, exotic land that was literally beyond the known world. The English Channel was no mere maritime body. It was "Ocean," a watery boundary that marked the limits of civilization. Life in this remote, cold, inhospitable, and mist-shrouded land turned Britons into wild men. In Roman eyes they were a different order of humanity that deserved conquest.[20]

These accounts actually tell us very little about the people we now describe generically as Britons. There were strong continuities in the material culture of Iron Age southern Britain, but preconquest Britons had distinct and separate identities based on their means of subsistence, political and social organization, and perhaps even language. Regardless, classical authors invariably portrayed all barbarians— including Britons—as nomadic, cannibalistic, and sexually immoral.[21] These historians provide most of the narrative detail of the Roman conquest of Britain, but we need to read them with caution, for most used Britannia as a backdrop for debates about society and politics in metropolitan Rome. Evidence demonstrates that Britons, particularly southern Britons, were not isolated and shared a material culture with their Iron Age neighbors across Ocean in Gaul, Belgica, and Germania.

Contrary to Strabo and Caesar, late pre-Roman Iron Age communities practiced specialized agriculture; mined copper, iron, and tin; and produced wheel-thrown pottery and finished metal goods. The British Isles most likely experienced significant population growth in the first century B.C., and competition for resources probably led to friction and warfare. Britons in the more mountainous northern and western highland zones had fewer commercial and cultural contacts with continental Europe, but they produced a sufficient agricultural surplus to sustain settled communities. The agrarian lowland regions of southern Britain supported much higher population densities. In the rugged regions of Wales and southwest England, populations clustered around hill forts, while *oppida*, large semiurban settlements enclosed by extensive networks of earthen dikes, were the most common form of settlement in southeastern England.

While Iron Age Britons shared a similar material culture, they were politically fragmented. Powerful chieftains probably built hill forts between the fifth and second centuries B.C. to claim productive territories. The origins and function of the *oppida*, which first emerged in continental Gaul during the second century B.C., are less certain. Continental *oppida* were built for defense, but their British counterparts were less fortified. Archaeologists theorize that they were centers of political, social, and perhaps religious power that controlled productive river valleys and important trade routes. The *oppidum* at Camulodunum (near modern Colchester) covered twelve square miles and also may have served as a cattle enclosure. Excavations of British *oppida* yield both evidence of coin minting and wealthy warrior gravesites containing high-value imported goods including arms and armor, pottery, glass and metal work, Mediterranean wine amphorae, and Roman bronzes.

Deposits of Roman goods suggest that lowland Britons had commercial and political contacts with continental Europe and Rome well before the Caesarian invasion. They may have traded directly with

Romans or acquired Roman goods from the Gauls. Either way, south-eastern England had the most developed continental trading links in preconquest Britain, which suggests a connection between commerce and the building of *oppida*.

Both classical and modern historians speak of Britons as living in tribes under the rule of chieftains or petty kings. Certainly Britain did not have states on the Greco-Roman model, but the British tribe did not fit the stereotype of a static kin-based polity locked in a lower phase of development. It is likely that most of southern Britain was undergoing significant political and social change when Caesar invaded, suggesting that the tribes he encountered were relatively new creations. In fact, the Roman expansion into Gaul probably accelerated and intensified these changes. Although Strabo depicted Britons as aboriginal barbarians, he also admitted that they exported grain, cattle, gold, silver, iron, hides, hunting dogs, and slaves.[22] In return they received silver bullion and high-quality material goods. Passing references in the classical sources also suggest that the Romans backed cooperative British elites with subsidies and political patronage after the conquest of Gaul.

These foreign influences had a significant impact on British society. Rome's imperial shadow reordered local systems of agricultural and craft production, thereby destabilizing the political entities that drew authority from their ability to control and redistribute these resources. Inflows of wealth disrupted alliances, incited wars, and ultimately produced political centralization as the victors consolidated their power. Tribes split, reformed, and united in confederations in response to these changing circumstances. The resulting militarism and turmoil most likely contributed to the slave exports that Strabo noted.

The *oppida* may have been the centers of this new tribal power, and their extensive network of dikes and earthen berms suggests a shift from communal to private land ownership. Furthermore, much of the coinage minted at these sites carried tribal names and bore portraits of British kings in local and Roman garb. Taken as a whole, this evidence suggests an increasingly stratified social order where a warrior elite, with an appetite for Roman goods, exercised authority over peasants, artisans, and slaves through patronage and the threat of violence.

The Romans were only dimly aware of these realities when Caesar invaded Britain in 56 and 54 B.C. But the fairly extensive cross-channel trade probably brought the growing prosperity of southeast England to his attention. British support for an anti-Roman revolt in Brittany was Caesar's *casus belli*, but it is unclear whether southern Britons sympathized with the Gauls or were simply continuing long-established commercial and diplomatic ties. Moreover, Caesar received delegations from several British leaders offering hostages and submission to Rome, which suggests that the Romans were already embroiled in the island's domestic politics. Unrest in Germany and storms over the channel delayed the relatively small ten-thousand-man expeditionary force, and British resistance forced the Roman proconsul to withdraw in 55 B.C.[23]

Caesar tried again the following year with a much larger force of five legions and two thousand cavalrymen. The leader of the anti-Roman resistance, Cassivellaunus, was a Catuvelluanian noble rather than a tribal king in his own right. He seems to have been a competent general, but his war chariots were ineffective against the massed formations of heavily armored Roman legionaries. Cassivellaunus therefore came to terms with Caesar by turning over hostages, paying tribute, and acknowledging Caesar's client Mandubracius as the ruler of the Trinovantes. Distracted by the threat of a mass uprising led by the Gallic leader Vercingetorix, Caesar declared victory and withdrew. Strabo later claimed he did not need to garrison Britain because the submission of Cassivellaunus and his allied chiefs made "the whole of the island Roman property."[24]

Caesar's military adventures were a speculative attempt to add to the Roman Empire on the cheap. Protracted British resistance, more pressing continental concerns, and his political ambitions led him to realize that it was easier and less expensive to exploit Britain through informal means than to annex it directly. Augustus came to a similar conclusion when he canceled another invasion of the island in favor of continuing Caesar's policy of using diplomacy, threats, subsidies, and commerce to control the British. Cassivellaunus and the other rulers who submitted to Rome may well have become client kings. It is by no means certain that British tribes recognized kings before Caesar's invasion, but after his retreat, powerful elites began to refer to themselves as "rex" on their coins. They also appear to have acquired a taste for

Italian wine, and their graves contain impressive inventories of silver kitchenware, Mediterranean ceramics, and other high-value imports.

Frustratingly, almost none of the tribal groups and kings that Caesar mentioned appear in the historical accounts of the final Roman conquest in A.D. 43. Nevertheless, the main political developments in southeastern England during this period are relatively clear. Backed by the Romans, the Trinovantes monopolized much of the cross-channel trade and became a dominant power north of the lower Thames River. Caesar's intervention drove the Catuvellauni further inland, where they established themselves as a major force northwest of modern London. A new power emerged south of the Thames when Caesar's onetime ally Commius became king of the Atrebates. Having provoked the Romans by backing Vercingetorix's rebellion, Commius fled to Britain, where Gallic support probably helped consolidate his power among the Atrebates. Excavations at his *oppidum* at Calleva reveal quantities of imported Roman goods and coins referring to him as rex.[25]

Although these new tribal groupings grew increasingly influential by the early first century A.D., they remained under Roman sway. Many southern British leaders continued to pay tribute to the empire and dedicated religious offerings in the city of Rome. Moreover, the steady volume of slave exports to the continent suggests that the Roman appetite for captive labor may have inflamed tensions in southern Britain by inspiring the petty kings to buy their imports with captives.

Rome also continued to beckon the losers of dynastic and intertribal struggles. Refugee British princelings inspired both Augustus and Caligula to consider annexing Britain, and an appeal for help from a displaced Atrebatian king named Verica, whom the resurgent Catuvellauni had overthrown, provided Claudius with the pretext for a decisive cross-channel invasion. Under Cunobelinus, who may have been Cassivellaunus's grandson or great-grandson, and his sons Caratacus and Togodumnus, the Catuvellauni were sufficiently powerful to displace Rome's key clients and threaten the empire's interests in southern Britain.

Thus Claudius had strategic as well as personal reasons for launching his invasion. Consisting of four legions and supporting auxiliary units, Claudius's army outnumbered Caesar's first expeditionary force by four to one. Some British tribes submitted immediately after the Roman landing, but the Catuvellauni harried the Claudian forces with hit-and-run raids until their final stand on the banks of the Medway. Although the British warrior elite rode into battle on chariots, poorly trained farmers probably constituted most of their forces. Claudius's forces were far superior, and General Aulus Plautius broke the Catuvellaunian hold over the Thames River valley with relative ease by killing Togodumnus and driving Caratacus into exile in Wales.

The Dumnonii and Durotriges of southwestern England were more difficult to conquer. Vespasian, the commander of the Second Legion and a future emperor, had to subdue the region hill fort by hill fort. Suetonius recorded that the Roman general defeated two tribes/*civitates*, captured twenty *oppida*, and fought thirty battles.[26] The tenacity of the southwesterners underscored a central reality of empire building: stateless "tribal" peoples were much harder to defeat than kingdoms because they resisted individually rather than collectively. It took only a single major battle to defeat the more centralized Catuvellauni, and the Romans then easily subdued the rest of lowland England by playing various tribal factions off against each other. The conquering power rewarded cooperation and most likely kept the eleven unnamed British rulers who surrendered in power as client kings of *civitates*. By comparison, the less centralized but more defiant peoples of southwestern Britain probably faced punishing military campaigns, the loss of their lands, and enslavement.

Plautius delayed the formal end of the initial campaign to give Claudius time to arrive and take credit for the victory. With an entourage of ranking senators, Praetorian guardsmen, and elephants, the emperor annexed Britain as a province of the Roman Empire at Camulodunum, perhaps the most urbanized site in the British Isles. Before leaving for his triumph in Rome, Claudius established a veterans' colony at the site, which eventually developed into a major center of Roman influence with a theater, a triumphal arch, and a temple dedicated to the Claudian imperial cult.

It may be that Claudius and his generals intended to claim only the most agriculturally productive parts of southern England, but continued opposition by highland peoples forced them to conquer the rest of England and Wales. The surviving Catuvellaunian prince Caratacus organized stiff resistance among the Welsh Silures and Ordovices, and it took extensive military operations lasting from A.D. 47 to 84 for the Romans to subjugate all of Wales. Even then, the continued threat of unrest in the region forced them to maintain a network of Welsh forts well into the second century A.D.

Ongoing tensions on the expanding imperial frontier also drew the Romans northward. During the fighting in Wales, the Roman armies counted on Queen Cartimandua of the Brigantes, a confederation of related clans or tribes in north-central England, to protect their flanks. Cartimandua may have been one of the eleven rulers who submitted to Claudius, and it is likely that Roman support underpinned her authority over her disparate and fractious people. She repaid her sponsors by refusing to shelter Caratacus after his flight from Wales. Cartimandua's decision to turn Caratacus over to Rome split the Brigantes and forced the Romans to intervene directly to keep her in power. Interestingly, her own husband, Venutius, led the anti-Roman faction. The royal couple reconciled for a time, but Venutius forced Cartimandua from power in A.D. 69 on the grounds that she was an adulteress.

The resulting civil war destabilized northern England and compelled the Romans to take direct control of this marginally productive region. They annexed the Brigantes in A.D. 79, and under the command of Governor Julius Agricola, the historian Tacitus's father-in-law, Roman forces pushed the frontier of the empire into southern Scotland. As in England and Wales, the Roman expansion led indigenous communities to concentrate into tribes and tribal alliances for self-defense. Under the leadership of the chieftain Calgacus, the Caledonian confederacy mounted the last significant military resistance at the battle of Mons Graupius in approximately A.D. 84. Tacitus claimed Agricola's forces slaughtered ten thousand Caledonians while losing only 360 auxiliary soldiers.[27]

This seemingly decisive victory brought little long-term security to Roman Britain. Agricola therefore gave up most of his northern territory and withdrew to a fortified frontier at the edge of the modern Scottish border. Beyond this line, the Romans relied on military patrols, diplomacy, and subsidies to control the defiant Caledonians, which may well have been the most effective and economical strategy for dealing with the decentralized peoples across the frontier. It is likely that Emperor Domitian ordered the retreat because the less productive highland zones in Wales and Scotland were not worth the cost of occupation.

Even after Agricola's retreat, chronic resistance by tribal peoples in the highlands and across the northern frontier was expensive and difficult to contain. Consequently, the military garrison for Roman Britain remained at roughly forty thousand men. This force, which amounted to a significant portion of the standing Roman army, would have required eight thousand to twenty thousand metric tons of food per day.[28] Claudius's imperial triumph thus turned out to be enormously expensive, and it is not surprising that Nero seriously considered withdrawing from Britain when he came to power in A.D. 54. He did not, but the Romans were never able to reduce their British garrison significantly, and it remained a politically destabilizing drain on the empire's resources for the rest of the imperial era.

While hostile frontiersmen remained an ongoing threat to the northern imperial border, it is far from clear how the people of occupied lowland Britain reacted to becoming Roman subjects. Some scholars have argued that southern British elites were already so romanized in the immediate preconquest era that they had little real incentive to resist the invasion. Contemporary apologists maintain that many Britons recognized the civilizing benefits of Roman rule and welcomed the opportunity to join the empire.[29]

Perhaps, but there is no denying that some of Rome's closest British clients revolted during the initial decades of Roman rule. The Iceni, possibly one of the eleven kingdoms that submitted to Claudius, and the Trinovantes, whose protection provided the excuse for the Caesarian invasion, were the most serious threats. Located in the Thames region and modern East Anglia, these were two of the most romanized client states in all of Britain. The Iceni first rebelled in A.D. 47 when the Roman governor ordered them to disarm. Imperial forces crushed the revolt after storming their *oppidum*, but fourteen years later the Iceni and the Trinovantes launched one of the gravest uprisings in the early principate. Led by the Icenian queen Boudicca, the rebels sacked and burned the colony at Camulodunum, the Roman settlement at the old Catuvellaunian *oppidum* at Verulamium (St. Albans), and the commercial center of Londinium (London).

The Romans were caught entirely off guard by the scope and intensity of the revolt. The rebels destroyed part of the Ninth Legion as it attempted to defend Londinium. At Verulamium a small band of legionnaires held out in Claudius's temple for two days before the Britons massacred them. All told, Cassius Dio recorded that the rebels tortured and killed eighty thousand Romans and Roman allies: "They hung up naked the noblest and most distinguished women and then cut off their breasts and sewed them to their mouths, in order to make the victims appear to be eating them; afterwards they impaled the women on sharp skewers run lengthwise through the entire body. All this they did to the accompaniment of sacrifices, banquets, and wanton behaviour."[30] For a time it looked as though Rome might lose control of Britain, but the failure of the rebels to attract support from other *civitates* gave Governor Suetonius time to bring in reinforcements, crush the uprising, and undertake merciless reprisals.

Cassius Dio attributed the Boudiccan revolt to Roman oppression. Writing at least a century later, it is highly unlikely that he had access to firsthand accounts of the rebellion. Nevertheless, he drafted a speech for the Icenian queen, whom he depicted as terrifying and noble, that to modern ears sounds like an explicit indictment of imperial exploitation:

> What treatment is there of the most shameful or grievous sort that we have not suffered ever since these men made their appearance in Britain? Have we not been robbed entirely of most of our possessions?...Besides pasturing and tilling for them all our other possessions, do we not pay a yearly tribute for our very bodies? How much better to have been slain and to have perished than to go about with a tax on our heads![31]

Dio used Boudicca to attack the corrupting influences of empire on Roman society, but he was probably correct in linking the Icenian uprising to imperial abuses. Tacitus also charged that Roman misrule had driven the Iceni to revolt:

> Prasutagus, king of the Iceni, after a life of long and renowned prosperity, had made the emperor co-heir with his own two daughters. Prasutagus hoped by this submissiveness to preserve his kingdom and [family] from attack. [But]...kingdom and household alike were plundered like prizes of war, the one by Roman officers, the other by Roman slaves.... His widow Boudicca was flogged and their daughters raped. The Icenian chiefs were deprived of their hereditary estates as

if the Romans had been given the whole country. The king's own relatives were treated like slaves.[32]

Roman financiers, who did a good business lending money to client kings, probably provoked the crisis by unexpectedly calling in their debts. The Iceni's inability to pay apparently gave Roman officials an excuse to loot and plunder. Similarly, Tacitus charged that misbehavior by discharged legionnaires at Camulodunum provoked the Trinovantes into joining the Icenian revolt.

The rebels' destruction of temples and other symbols of Roman culture in Camulodunum and Verulamium may also have reflected popular opposition to the imperial transformation of Britain. Questions over the extent to which Britons became Romans lie at the heart of current debates over the character of Roman Britain. According to Tacitus, Agricola aimed to bind British nobles more closely to Rome by encouraging them to learn Latin, wear togas, adopt a Roman diet, and build bathhouses. Ever the critic, the Roman historian sneeringly noted that while the Britons viewed these luxuries as a mark of "civilization," in fact "they were only a feature of enslavement."[33]

In this sense, romanization went hand in hand with imperial domination, but elites could earn substantial rewards by embracing the new social order. The nobleman Togodumnus used Claudius's patronage to claim a portion of the old Atrebatian kingdom after Verica either died or was deposed by feckless Roman officials. Apparently, they conveniently forgot that returning him to power was a central excuse for the Claudian invasion. Taking the Latin name Tiberius Claudius Cogidubnus, which indicated that Claudius made him a Roman citizen, he was a key ally during the Icenian revolt. Tacitus may have considered him a dupe or slave, but his sumptuous Italian-style palace at Fishbourne, near modern Chichester, testifies to the gilded nature of his chains.[34]

Cogidubnus and his peers used Roman ties to ensure that they retained their status during the social turmoil that was an inevitable by-product of imperial conquest. This was a dangerous time when Claudius's triumph allowed senators, imperial administrators, wealthy merchants, and discharged soldiers to acquire farms and estates in Britain. The Roman colonists allowed cooperative *civitas* leaders to retain the rural bases of their authority, and the relatively limited rewards of romanization eventually did produce a hybrid but fairly narrow Romano-British cultural elite. For the most part, however, there were relatively few opportunities for Britons to play a role in Roman governance and commerce. In contrast to other territories such as Gaul and Spain, Britain produced no senators or emperors during the early empire.

Commoners in particular did not have much of a chance or incentive to embrace the new imperial culture. Most were simple farmers, and archaeological evidence suggests considerable continuity in rural settlement and landholding practices during the first century of Roman rule. Popular metalworking and pottery styles also survived into the imperial era. It is unclear if these preconquest cultural institutions persisted because rural Britons refused to be romanized or because the empire's extractive reach lessened significantly in the countryside.

The Romans may not have been able to exploit their subjects systematically, but tenacious resistance in Wales, northern England, and Scotland, the Icenian rebellion, and accusations of corruption by Tacitus and Cassius Dio suggest that romanization and the resulting reordering of British society were not particularly civilizing or benign. Almost certainly, the imperial conquest resulted in mass enslavement. Coerced British workers had to have built the grand buildings and roads that so impressed later Romanophiles. The emperors were probably the largest landowners in Britain, and farmers in the drained fenlands of East Anglia were most likely their tenants. Similarly, Roman military and civilian entrepreneurs used local labor when they developed the island's gold, silver, lead, iron, and copper deposits. Britons were also liable for conscription for military service throughout the empire, and it is unlikely that any of the men in the fourteen auxiliary units raised in the province by the end of the first century A.D. returned home. Finally, the Boudiccan uprising suggests that Roman merchants and moneylenders had an unfair commercial advantage over common Britons.

The imperial restructuring of local British institutions must have been equally traumatic. The Romans were generally tolerant of exotic religions, but Claudius made it a capital offense for Druids to practice their religion. It is not exactly certain what Druidism entailed, but it clearly became a focus of resistance, and Roman forces destroyed a Druidic center on the island of Anglesey during the conquest of Wales.

Female Britons probably also suffered in the immediate aftermath of the occupation. Excepting powerful queens such as Boudicca and Cartimandua, they are largely missing from the historical and archaeological record. But it does not take much imagination to envision that forty thousand legionnaires, who were forbidden to marry under military law, might prey on subject women.[35] It is equally impossible to know how the soldiers viewed the general population. Military records on tablets recovered near Hadrian's Wall offer a hint in their references to neighboring communities as "Brittunculi," or "wretched little Britons."[36]

Comparatively speaking, the elites of most preconquest British societies, particularly in the south, would have also looked down on the rural population. It is therefore hard to determine if the Roman empire builders treated common Britons better or worse than had the kings and chieftains they overthrew. If the foreign administrators and soldiers did in fact view the entire subject population as inferior, then Roman rule was most likely a much greater burden in the first decades of the occupation. Nonetheless, the bloody Icenian revolt must have reminded succeeding Roman governors that there was a significant risk in pushing their subjects too far.

Roman Britain did in fact become more stable by the mid-first century A.D., but this was because the city-bound postconquest administration did not exert direct authority in the countryside on a day-to-day basis. Under the early empire, the island was a single imperial province run by a governor based in London. His small staff was essentially an informal circle of friends and advisors. An equally undersized provincial bureaucracy consisting primarily of detached army officers backed by a military guard was the formal imperial administration in the province. An autonomous procurator answering directly to the emperor oversaw tax collection.

Roman rule was heavier in Wales and northern Britain, where security considerations kept these restive frontier regions under direct military control. Most Roman officials served short terms of less than three years, which further limited the influence of the comparatively minuscule civil administration. Emperor Septimus Severus was probably mindful of these realities when he introduced a greater measure of bureaucratic control in A.D. 197 by dividing the island into two separate provinces (Britannia Superior and Britannia Inferior).

Given their limited reach, Roman administrators needed local elites if they were to govern effectively. Following the template developed under the republic, they sought to tribalize preconquest polities and communities by transforming them into *civitates*. The new administrative units had fixed boundaries, urban capitals, and ruling magistrates that fitted neatly into the larger provincial bureaucracy. Although it is now lost, the Egyptian geographer Ptolemy's tribal map of Britain apparently documented the spatial dimensions of these new imperial identities. Based on the fragmentary data that survive, the preconquest Atrebatian and Catuvellaunian confederacies appear to have become the *civitates* Atrebatum, Belgarium, and Regni (or Regini) under Roman rule. These new units could have reflected existing clan or lineage divisions, but in the less centralized regions of southwest England and Wales they seem to have been pure invention.

As noted earlier, the establishment of new towns, which many scholars refer to as tribal capitals, was central to the *civitates* process. Most of the preconquest fortified settlements fell into disuse under the Romans, and only the Atrebatian and Catuvellaunian *oppida* at Calleva and Verulamium appear to have survived. The new urban sites were close to the imperial road network, and there is considerable debate over whether *civitas* leaders voluntarily built them from scratch or did so under Roman pressure. Regardless, most followed a similar metropolitan Roman template that included streets on a grid pattern, public squares, town halls, court buildings, theaters, public baths, and piped water.

Contemporary Roman apologists emphasize how these institutions "encouraged the development of a more civilised way of life," but they also gave the imperial regime greater control over local politics, commerce, and social life.[37] The provincial administration turned preconquest chiefs and kings who abandoned their arms and armor into *decurions* (councilmen) and tutored them in the art of municipal government. Roman rule thus gave British tribal identities new spatial, geographical, and urban form, and the *civitates* most likely became standardized administrative units by the second century A.D.

Although the conquerors and romanized Britons built comfortable villas in the countryside, the Roman heart of the province lay in its towns and cities, where the line between citizen and subject was the most blurred. Urban populations originally consisted primarily of imperial administrators, military men, merchants, and settlers, but a prosperous Romano-British municipal gentry emerged by the end of the first century A.D. Evidence is scanty, but it seems likely that this was due at least in part to Roman relations with local women. Londinium, neither a *civitas* town nor a veterans' colony, was the seat of government and commerce. The *colonia* of Camulodunum, Lindum (Lincoln), Glevum (Gloucester), and Eburacum (York) and select privileged British settlements such as Verulamium held charters as *municipia*, which meant that their respectable classes enjoyed Roman citizenship. The *civitas* towns generally came next in terms of influence, followed by small towns that grew up alongside commercially important roads.

These urban sites anchored the extractive machinery of imperial rule and drew in agricultural surpluses from their hinterlands. Legionary fortresses and smaller garrisons also created markets for local crafts and produce, and military wages helped introduce a cash-based economy to Britain. While this was not by design, the monetization of the rural economy made it easier to tap the wealth of the countryside through taxation. The increasingly common usage of coins, which were primarily for hoarding wealth in Iron Age Briton, must have had a profound impact on rural economies. While a regularized currency stimulated craft production and encouraged agricultural specialization by creating new markets for surpluses, the cash economy also enabled outsiders to acquire land at the expense of local communities by giving rise to a commercial land market.

The cultural impact of romanization on the subject British majority was decidedly mixed. To be sure, Latin was the language of government, law, commerce, military service, and elite urban society. The comfortable, often luxurious villas clustered in southeastern England further indicate that a measure of the aristocratic imperial culture extended into the countryside. Nevertheless, the discovery of less romanized prosperous farmsteads with rectangular stone buildings and tiled roofs suggests the continued influence of a preconquest nonimperial rural elite.

Indeed, if elements of preconquest culture survived under the Roman occupation, they did so in the countryside. Indigenous religious cults remained popular with rural peoples, who sometimes combined them with imported Roman forms. The giant chalk figure of a white horse on the Berkshire downs, already roughly a thousand years old at the time of the occupation, was maintained regularly during the imperial era. Rural archaeological sites also suggest that country folk drank domestically produced beer instead of imported wine, ate sheep and goats instead of cattle and seafood, and used relatively few foreign implements. Latin graffiti is relatively common in urban and villa sites, but there are few examples of it in the villages. Common Britons may or may not have spoken a form of vulgar Latin, but few were literate. Taken together, the evidence suggests that rural localities were insulated from the full force of Roman imperial rule.

However, most Britons eventually had to come to terms with the imperial regime. Rome never withdrew its military garrison, but the absence of walls and fortifications around most urban centers before the late second century A.D. suggests that Roman rule became relatively secure once the spectacular violence of the Icenian revolt had passed. Prosperity stemming from increased long-distance imperial trade, improved agricultural technology, and urbanization most likely enriched the respectable classes of the later generations of Britons, who did not have to endure the violence and trauma of the initial imperial conquest. As a result, southern England was largely stable until the third century A.D.

There is considerable debate as to whether the peoples of northern Britain and Scotland constituted a threat to Roman Britain. Caches of Roman coins found in lowland Scotland suggest that the Romans bought their cooperation with subsidies and cross-border trade. On the other hand, Emperor Hadrian invested enormous resources in a monumental eighty-mile-long stone wall along the frontier from the North Sea to the Irish Sea. Begun in A.D. 122, the wall was approximately fifteen feet high and was dotted with small forts garrisoned by auxiliary units. Twenty years later, Emperor Antonius Pius pushed the imperial frontier further north with a less impressive timber and earthen barricade that ran from the Firth of Forth to the Firth of Clyde at the narrowest point in the Scottish lowlands. This fortification apparently had marginal value, for the Romans abandoned it and reestablished the imperial frontier at Hadrian's Wall sometime after A.D. 160.

At first glance, these extensive fortifications indicate the presence of a formidable military presence in Scotland, a threat that may have spread behind the wall to include the peoples of northern England. Some scholars think that Scottish pressure and a rebellion by the Brigante federation forced the Romans to abandon the Antonine Wall, but alternatively the construction and maintenance of both walls could have been make-work exercises to keep the British garrison busy and out of metropolitan Roman politics.

It is impossible to know for certain because the great classical historians of Rome made very little mention of Roman Britain once the conquest phase was over. This historical silence creates an impression that the island was an outpost of stability and prosperity during the third century A.D., when the wider empire suffered from foreign attack and internal instability. Material fragments of Roman culture that appear in archaeological excavations suggest that the urban classes flourished under the empire, but this perspective ignores the rural majority that produced most of wealth consumed by the Romano-British elite. The dearth of information on the common experience invites imperial nostalgists to view the Roman Empire as benign and civilizing.

To be sure, Britain's outsized garrison kept the settled areas of the province relatively secure in an era when the rest of the empire was under threat. Resurgent Persian power in the east from the Sassanid Empire and pressure by Germanic peoples on the Rhine and Danube frontiers placed heavy demands on the Roman military, while ambitious governors and generals again looked inward with an eye to seizing the imperial throne. Echoing the turmoil of the late republic, the empire had twenty-one rulers between A.D. 235 and 284, most of whom came to power with military backing. Mutinies, coup plots, and poor leadership sapped the strength of the army, and the empire experienced its first major barbarian invasions in the middle of the fourth century A.D.

This was also at a time when civil wars and the end of plunder from imperial conquests created a severe economic crisis in the Roman Empire. Scholars tend to attribute these problems to dynastic infighting or structural weaknesses, but it may have been that accelerated assimilation and mass enfranchisement contributed to the revenue shortfall by making the empire's lower orders less exploitable. Faced with rising military costs and reduced tribute and tax flows, the emperors resorted to currency debasement. Coins that were 97 percent silver in the first century A.D. were only 40 percent silver in A.D. 250 and just 4 percent in A.D. 270.[38] The resulting hyperinflation disrupted the cash economy and forced imperial tax collectors to demand payment in goods.

Emperor Diocletian tried to arrest this inflationary spiral in A.D. 301 with an unenforceable decree fixing wages and basic commodity prices. Faced with significant shortfalls in the western half of the empire, tax collectors concentrated on the cities and towns, where magistrates faced fines and confiscations if they failed to produce sufficient revenues. Not surprisingly, the wealthy and privileged fled to the countryside, where the reach of imperial authority was inherently shorter. Many invested in feudalistic large estates worked by tenant farmers who became bound to the land by law and heredity. Lacking the means to tap into this rural wealth, the imperial government came to rely on the wealthier eastern provinces for two-thirds of its revenue.

These disparities ultimately led Diocletian to split the empire in A.D. 286. Acknowledging the economic and cultural divide between the Greek- and Latin-speaking provinces, he shifted his base of power to the east and appointed an ally, Maximian, coemperor in the west. As "Augusti," Diocletian and Maximian both adopted junior partners as heirs and deputy emperors or "Caesars," thereby creating a theoretical tetrarchy (rule by four). Further reforms reorganized the entire empire into prefectures and dioceses to improve revenue collection and security. Roman Britain, which consisted of four separate provinces in the fourth century, was part of the prefecture of Gaul.

These pragmatic steps acknowledged the reality that the empire had grown too large and complex for a single central government. More radically, they also suggest that the early principate's conventional institutions of imperial extraction were less viable in an era when most of the subject population were now technically citizens. They were of course still servile, but enfranchisement probably made them less exploitable. Either way, the tetrarchy was supposed to bring stability by ensuring an orderly political succession, but it soon broke down when the oversized British military garrison raised Constantine, the son of one of the original junior emperors, to the throne in A.D. 306. Attributing his victory to divine Christian intervention, Constantine made Christianity the imperial state religion. He also continued the eastern power shift by founding Constantinople as an alternative and rival imperial capital to Rome in A.D. 324.

These administrative realignments failed to arrest the Roman decline. Dynastic infighting continued, and the military, which Constantine reorganized into mobile field armies, was hard pressed to defend the imperial frontiers. Shrinking revenues, urban flight, and the transformation of citizens into servile tenants forced commanders to absorb large numbers of foreign Germans into the imperial forces to compensate for the shrinking recruiting base. To some extent, this was imperial conquest in reverse. Unlike the auxiliary units of the early principate, Rome's barbarian troops fought under their own kings and chieftains. Many of these leaders assumed senior positions in the Roman army, and later emperors allowed entire friendly Germanic tribes to settle within the imperial borders. Some of these groups proved to be reliable allies, but in time the most ambitious German leaders realized that they held enough power to capture the Roman Empire from within.

It is not exactly clear how the Roman imperial decline affected Britain, and the province may have actually benefited from its relative isolation. The military garrison's reduction to thirty-four thousand soldiers in the third century and the deployment of second-line troops on Hadrian's Wall suggests Britain was relatively secure. Improved farming techniques and the adoption of a heavy iron plough raised agricultural production and in all likelihood made the province more self-sufficient. The writer Eumenius noted Britain's value to the empire in A.D. 297: "Without doubt Britain was a land that the state could ill afford to lose, so plentiful are its harvests, so numerous are the pasturelands which it rejoices, so many are the metals of which seams run through it, so much wealth comes from its taxes."[39] To some degree, this was propaganda lauding Emperor Constantine, who owed his rise to the throne to the Roman garrison at York. On the other hand, it is possible that improved crop yields, the extensive road network, a strong indigenous pottery industry, and sustained silver production actually did make Britain better off than the rest of the later empire. It is not at all clear, however, how much of this prosperity trickled down to common Britons.

Regardless, the problems of the wider empire eventually reached Britain by the end of the fourth century. The expanded fortification of most towns and the construction of a series of forts on the southern English coast suggest that the British provinces were threatened by invasions from northern highlanders and seaborne Saxon raiders. Modern excavations of many urban sites dating to this period reveal a blanketing thick stratum of brackish, loamy soil, known as dark earth, that was probably decomposed animals, plants, and charcoal. This evidence of decay suggests that urban construction came to an abrupt halt in the mid-third century as public buildings in towns and cities fell into disrepair due neglect or looting. The central theater at Verulamium appears to have become a dump for broken pottery and rotted vegetables from a nearby market, and archaeological evidence suggests that the golden age of villa construction in the southern countryside was quite brief.

The historian Ammianus Marcellinus recorded that Picts from Scotland, Attacotti from the Hebrides, Scotti from Ireland, and Saxon and Frankish pirates from the continent simultaneously invaded Britain in 367. British prosperity may have attracted these opportunistic raiders, or imperial political and economic meddling might have provoked the frontier peoples. *Picti*, or "painted people" in Latin, was not a specific tribal identity, and the Picts may have simply been a larger confederation of Caledonians and Maeatae. They split into small, disorganized bands to loot and pillage on crossing into Britain, but the Romans suspected that the attacks were a part of a grand "barbarian conspiracy." According to Ammianus, Theodosius, a senior commander and father of the emperor Theodosius the Great, restored order with part of the western field army.[40] Alternatively, Ammianus may have invented a conspiracy and overstated the scope of the unrest in order to celebrate the exploits of an emperor's father. Given that archaeological evidence of widespread destruction during this period is scanty, it is again likely that classical historical accounts of the Roman Britain experience are not reliable.

The Roman Empire of the late fourth century A.D. was a mere shadow of the robust economic and military power that had annexed Britain almost four centuries earlier. Dynastic infighting, divisive religious controversies, urban decay, depopulation, recession, rampant inflation, military decline, and barbarian invasions sapped its strength and weakened its hold on the outer provinces. Romanized landowning elites, who had accepted Roman rule in return for legitimacy, opportunity, and security, began to slip the bonds of imperial control. Seeking a measure of protection in troubled times, many transferred their allegiance to invading warlords.

Still, the overextended imperial military did a reasonably good job of protecting the frontiers until the Huns moved east. Migrating from central Asia, these powerful nomads drove the peoples of eastern and central Europe to seek the comparative safety of the empire. In A.D. 378 a band of Goths who had received imperial permission to settle in Moesia turned on their Roman patrons and wiped out two-thirds of the eastern field army at the battle of Adrianople. The eastern empire recovered under Theodosius the Great, but in the west the Rhine and Danube garrisons could not hold the entire frontier.

In 405, the Ostrogothic king Radagaisus invaded northern Italy. The following year bands of Vandals, Alans, and Suevi pushed across the Rhine into Gaul and Spain, and in 408 a band of Huns invaded Dacia. Roman forces eventually reined in all three of these incursions with the assistance of friendly Germanic kings, but the politically divided and impotent western empire was doomed. The Visigothic king Alaric, a onetime Roman ally, sacked the city of Rome in 410. The eastern Roman Empire survived in various forms for another millennium, but Roman rule in the west ended when the German king Odoacer deposed the last figurehead western Roman emperor in A.D. 476.

In Britain, the turmoil of the Germanic invasions opened the way for the last of the military pretenders to bid for power. According to the historian Zosimus, the garrison followed Constantine III to the continent in 407 to deal with the trans-Rhine invasion and lay claim to the western empire. Constantine's troops never returned. This left the province without a significant imperial presence for the first time in four centuries. Historians conventionally date the end of Roman Britain to A.D. 409–10, when Romano-Britons expelled the imperial administration. Zosimus suggests that this was in response to Emperor Honorius's refusal to come to their aid during another barbarian invasion: "Accordingly the Britons took up arms and, with no consideration of the danger to themselves, freed their cities from barbarian threat.... They freed themselves, ejected the Roman magistrates, and set up home rule at their own discretion."[41] Finally liberated from direct Roman occupation, the British population took their chances as anarchy engulfed continental Europe.

Having lost its imperial protection, Britain's autonomy was ephemeral, and it appears to have lapsed into chaos under the weight of renewed invasions by Picts and Saxons. Long-distance imperial trade dried up due to the turmoil on the continent, and the Roman military retreat ended the inflow of imperial coinage for provisions and wages. The disintegration of the cash-based economy doomed manufacturing industries, ended commercial mining, and made it impossible for farmers to disposes of their surpluses. Stripped of its economic underpinnings, Romano-British society collapsed. The threat of rape and pillage appears to have given the populace little alternative but to place themselves in the hands of invading Saxon warlords or local strongmen and militia leaders. The British provinces thus split into a mix of Germanic and indigenous petty kingdoms within decades of the Roman retreat.

Archaeological evidence indicates an abrupt disappearance of Romano-British culture by the mid-fifth century. The layer of ash in many urban sites dating from this period suggests widespread destruction and flight. The remaining townsmen dismantled neglected Roman-era monuments and buildings for raw materials and built new wooden structures over older Roman stone foundations and streets. Tellingly, peasant settlements and simple farmsteads seem to have been less affected.

While imperial Roman culture survived the demise of the western empire to varying degrees in Italy, Gaul, and Spain—excepting Arthurian legends of Roman holdouts in Wales and Cornwall— Roman Britain seems almost to have disappeared overnight. Roman apologists often point out that there was no evidence that preconquest tribal identities reemerged, but it is unrealistic and ahistorical to assume that any identity or culture would have remained static for four centuries. Ultimately, the Christian church was the only significant imperial institution that remained.

German invaders on the continent became partially romanized by taking over provincial bureaucratic and economic systems, but the Saxons apparently had much less to work with in Britain, which again suggests that Roman influence on the island was relatively transitory. Conventional accounts suggest that the bulk of the British population became "Germanized" instead of taming the invaders through the lure of romanization. More likely, the rural communities that had preserved much of their autonomy during the Roman era continued to evolve by selectively incorporating elements of their new rulers' culture.

The achievements of imperial Rome were a touchstone for succeeding western empire builders. From their perspective, the Roman Empire's longevity, influence, and scientific and cultural achievements made it the measure of all empires. It was highly proficient in using the extracted wealth of conquered peoples to create a complex bureaucracy, nurture the arts, build grand stone monuments, and become a quintessentially unipolar continental power. Later imperial rulers therefore adopted its nomenclature and copied systems of administration and indirect rule.

Yet at best Rome's rise and fall was a cautionary tale about the risks of allowing military power to build up in the periphery and the inherent incompatibility of empire building and representative government. There have been no "new Romes." Born of the ancient world, the Roman Empire was a unique product of its times that offered no real precedents for later eras. It is nonsensical to assume that it was possible, much less desirable, to replicate ancient institutions in advanced industrial societies.

Furthermore, imperial enthusiasts overlook the reality that the Roman Empire's seeming durability actually stemmed from its capacity to enlist subjugated elites in extractive imperial enterprises. This was possible only in an age when subjects lacked the means and perspective to resist collectively because their identities were primarily local and fluid. Slave uprisings were relatively common under the early principate, but apart from the Jewish Revolt, there were no significant organized rebellions, much less nationalistic ones. Most of the empire's main challengers were local and "tribal," and at first glance, systemic internal weaknesses rather than popular uprisings appeared to have brought down the empire. In reality, the Roman Empire did not so much fall as evolve to reflect the new identities resulting from four centuries of imperial rule. Its weak boundaries between citizen and subject allowed conquered elites to join, if not eventually dominate, the imperial aristocracy.

The surprisingly conclusive demise of Roman Britain draws these realities into sharper focus. Ancient states relied on widespread slavery, tribute collection, and the exploitation of agricultural labor to extract the surplus needed to support an advanced bureaucracy, elite culture, and, by extension, grand art and literature. Ruling classes disdained their own lower orders and had no qualms about treating them as an exploitable resource. Initially, Roman rule in Britain was lucrative because the strange and alien population was precariously vulnerable to enslavement and unrestrained exploitation. In time, elite assimilation and Caracalla's enfranchisement turned Britons into citizens, but the bulk of the population still remained marginal and subordinate because they were common. Moreover, most free rural people in the later imperial heartland became bound to the land as impoverished tenants or outright serfs. Local partisanship and the bureaucratic limit of ancient empire allowed some protection from excessive Roman demands for treasure and labor.

While the Augustan state ruled and exploited an enormous subject population, by the fourth century Rome was no longer an empire in the conventional sense of the term. Instead, it was a dominant but decaying continental oligarchy whose downfall was due at least in part to its inability to maintain the high tribute levels of the imperial era. In this sense the stability associated with the Pax Romana is deceiving, for the decline in subject revolts and slave uprisings in the later principate may well have been a mark of weakness that reflected the Romans' diminished ability to place demands on rural populations.

Rome's grandeur understandably captured imaginations for centuries to come, and the dearth of reliable information about daily life in the provinces allowed imperial enthusiasts to ignore these realities. In their idealized top-down view, the Roman Empire was long-lived, coherent, cultured, and transformative. Rome's common subjects were largely missing apart from passing references to barbarians, tribes, revolting slaves, and the urban mob in Rome. Grittier popular perspectives on lower-class life have appeared in contemporary narratives such as Steven Saylor's Roma Sub Rosa books and Michael Apted's *Rome* series for cable television, but for the most part it was more romantic and entertaining to identify with a cultured Roman gentleman. Consequently, scholars, military strategists, and public intellectuals have found the temptation to invoke idealized stereotypes of Roman imperial greatness in contemporary policy debates irresistible. In point of fact, the Roman Empire was by definition an antiquarian product of its times, and as such it was by no means as omnipotent, durable, or uplifting as they imagine.

The Umayyad Caliphate, which succeeded Roman rule in much of the Mediterranean world, suffered from the same limitations in the medieval era. While its religiously inspired Arab founders denied that secular ambition drove their conquests, they produced a Muslim transcontinental state that was clearly an empire. Forced by necessity to adopt Roman governing practices, they inevitably also had to recruit local allies to rule and extract treasure. This was particularly true in Spain, where a branch line of the Umayyad dynasty solidified its hold on power by allowing Visigothic nobles to convert to Islam. While modern historians nostalgically recall the resulting imperial state of Al-Andalus as a paragon of learning, culture, and religious toleration during the darkest medieval centuries, it too rested on the exploitation of common subjects.

As in Rome, a conquering power built a viable imperial state by allowing a local elite to share in the spoils of empire. Although Islam provided a powerful moral justification for imperial expansion, it also complicated imperial rule by requiring pious Muslim sovereigns to convert the conquered populations. Even more than the Romans, the Andalusi Umayyads struggled to maintain a sufficiently clear boundary between citizen and subject, a failure that would allow Muslim converts from the once romanized Iberian aristocracy to eventually take over their empire.

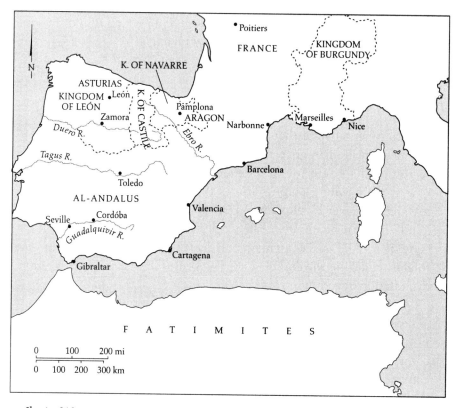

Iberia, 910

2

MUSLIM SPAIN

Blurring Subjecthood in Imperial Al-Andalus

According to myth, a looming tower built by Hercules lay on the outskirts of the Spanish capital of Toledo. It contained a powerful secret that kept the kingdom safe from invasion, and upon taking power each succeeding ruler added a lock to its gate. Twenty-six monarchs kept the tower secure until curiosity got the better of Roderic, the last Christian Visigothic ruler of Spain. Ignoring the pleas and warnings of his ministers, the king broke into the tower to find a bejeweled table belonging to Solomon sitting in a room decorated with paintings of Arab horsemen armed with swords and bows. A parchment on the table read: "Whenever this asylum is violated and the spell...broken, the people shown in the picture shall invade the land and overturn the throne of its kings. The rule of the Goths shall end and the whole country fall into the hands of...strangers." Symbolically, the violation of the tower thus led to the invasion of Spain by a mighty Arab army that later Christian sources described as "more cruel and hurtful than the wolf that comes at night to the flock of sheep."[1]

Roderic was in fact the final Visigothic Spanish king, but the tower's millenarian prophecy was an invention that helped succeeding generations of Christians explain the sudden trauma of imperial conquest. Indeed, the rapid annexation of the Iberian Peninsula by the Umayyad Caliphate must have seemed like the end of the world. Conversely, the story of Roderic's rash actions gave the victorious Muslims, who had their own version of the myth, an excuse for empire building. The parchment on Solomon's table suggested divine sanction for the conquest of Spain and the creation of Al-Andalus.

The name Iberia came from ancient Greek sources, and the Romans referred to the peninsula as Hispania. Muslim sources interpreted this as Isbania, while medieval Christians used Espania. The name Al-Andalus was an Arabic allusion to the Vandals and referred to the regions of the peninsula under Muslim rule. Contemporary Spain arose from the union of the medieval Christian kingdoms of Aragón and Castile. Although modern Portugal is a separate sovereign nation, for the purposes of this chapter the name Iberia refers to the entire peninsula south of the Pyrenees mountain range.

The first Muslim expedition to Iberia was a relatively small, speculative, and haphazard enterprise. Moreover, it was not really even Arab. Consisting primarily of approximately twelve thousand Muslim Berbers and sub-Saharan Africans under the command of Tariq ibn Ziyad, the Berber governor of Umayyad Tangier, the invading army most likely sought plunder rather than empire. Tariq had probably noticed the impotent Visigothic response to earlier, smaller raids on the Spanish coast and was almost certainly acting on his own initiative. Although devout Muslims had an obligation to work for the political and cultural supremacy of Islam, the Berber governor also knew that expanding the Umayyad imperial frontiers paid direct dividends in treasure and prestige.

Interestingly, the ramshackle Visigothic state was much more vulnerable than the decentralized "tribal" Britons. Roderic had ruled Spain for only a single year at the time of invasion. He came to power by elbowing aside a more legitimate rival named Witiza, and it is possible that, like Verica's appeal to Claudius, Witiza's partisans may have asked Tariq for aid in reclaiming the Spanish throne. Landing on a rocky promontory that is now called Jabal Tariq (the Mountain of Tariq, or Gibraltar) in A.D. 711, Tariq found little opposition and pushed easily into the heart of the Iberian Peninsula. His forces defeated Roderic in a small but decisive battle in the Guadalquivir River valley that wiped out the knights of the royal household and court. Muslim accounts credit the victory in part to the defection of Witiza's sons, who changed sides to reclaim their father's estates. Roderic apparently died in the fighting, and the swift capture of Toledo prevented the Visigoths from selecting a replacement king.

Tariq was too successful for his own good. His lightning conquest of southern Iberia attracted the attention of his superior Musa ibn

Nusayr, the Umayyad viceroy of western North Africa. Suspicious of his subordinate's achievements and coveting a share of the spoils, he directed Tariq to wait in Toledo until he arrived to take command of the operations. The Berber general nonetheless continued his northern advance. When Musa landed with a rival Arab army the following year, the invasion degenerated into a race between the Berbers and Arabs to sack wealthy Iberian cities. Urban populations that surrendered were treated relatively well, but those who resisted faced massacre and wholesale enslavement.

By the end of 712, Muslim forces had overrun the most productive and fertile areas of lowland Iberia. Musa and Tariq became wealthy and powerful, but they had little chance to enjoy the fruits of their victory. Successful imperial generals can easily become Caesars, and Caliph al-Walid I prudently recalled his adventurous vassals to Damascus two years later. The anonymous Christian author of the *Chronicle of 754* recorded that they returned with "some [Visigothic] noblemen who escaped the sword; gold and silver, assayed with zeal by the bankers; a large quantity of valuable ornaments, precious stones, and pearls; ointments to kindle a woman's desire." Yet these treasures did not appease the Umayyads, and Sulayman, who succeeded his brother as caliph in 715, convicted Musa of embezzling the state's share of the spoils and "paraded [him] with a rope around his neck."[2] Musa and Tariq apparently died in disgrace and poverty, but Visigothic Spain became the westernmost possession of the Umayyad Caliphate.

Like Roman Britain, Iberia was not a typical Umayyad possession and cannot be taken as a representative example of early Islamic imperial rule. Nevertheless, the Muslim conquerors' attempts to make sense of its diverse Roman and Visigothic heritage reflected the larger problem of defining subjecthood in the caliphate. Moreover, like the Romans in Britain, the Umayyads gave the ancestors of the Spanish people, who became a global imperial power in the early modern era, a profound lesson in what it meant to be an imperial subject.

As with the republican Romans, the Umayyads never set out to build an empire, nor did they admit to being a secular imperial power. The title *caliph* comes from *khalifah*, the Arabic word for successor. The Umayyad caliphs were a ruling dynasty that claimed to be the legitimate successors of the Prophet Muhammad. But they were temporal sovereigns rather than theocrats. They governed the caliphate, a vast Muslim state stretching from Iberia to India, as the secular protectors of the faith.

Yet there is no denying that the caliphate had all the essential qualities of an empire. Beginning as a community of believers in the Arabian entrepôt of Mecca, it grew into a diverse multiethnic imperial state through conquest. In theory, all believers were equal under Islamic law, but non-Arabs who embraced Islam under the Umayyads faced discrimination and exploitation. Those who did not convert were, by definition, subordinate, imperial subjects. The caliphate thus continued the traditions of the ancient empires of the Middle East and Mediterranean. Lacking experience governing large settled populations, the Arab Muslims used Byzantine and Persian imperial systems to manage their conquered territories. Additionally, their conquest of the settled Middle East also had a strong colonial element. Drawn by the spoils of empire building, entire communities followed the victorious Muslim armies and settled in new cities that grew around their fortified camps. Almost overnight, these pastoral nomads and merchants became a privileged imperial elite.

Despite this, the Arabs were ambivalent empire builders. Initially, Muhammad's followers fought to protect the infant Muslim community from the hostile pagan elite of Mecca; they did not set out to create the caliphate. Whereas the Roman Empire grew steadily, almost organically, over centuries of warfare, the imperial Arab caliphate exploded in a few short decades. The religious obligation to protect Islam and struggle against unbelief legitimized its conquests. The faith required Muslims to push the frontiers of Islam into the unbelieving lands of the "house of war" (*dar al-harb*) until the "house of Islam" (*dar al-Islam*) encompassed the known world. The divine obligation to create a pious universal political realm provided a moral excuse for imperial expansion, but the customs of the Muslim armies, which took time to develop into a formal doctrine of jihad, also allowed victorious soldiers to take plunder and tribute from conquered populations. Many of the early Islamic soldiers were motivated by piety, but their campaign's divine authorization provided an ideal legitimizing ideology for the blatant self-interest of secular empire building.

Islam therefore came to underpin an imperial order that extracted labor and tribute from non-Muslims. As in the Roman Empire, the true wealth of the caliphate lay in these subjects, but the Muslims found it harder than the Romans to define subjecthood conclusively. As "peoples of the book" (*dhimmi*) sharing Islam's sacred texts and traditions, Christians and Jews were entitled to comparatively fair treatment under Muslim rule. *Dhimmi* retained the right to practice their faith, but they paid a special tax and suffered institutionalized social and political discrimination. Pagans were not entitled to any protection and theoretically could be enslaved by Muslim conquerors. Consequently, there were powerful incentives for non-Muslims to embrace Islam, and in the medieval era the act of conversion was simple and straightforward. Those wishing to become Muslims simply had to make a profession of faith by declaring, "There is no God but God and Muhammad is his prophet."[3] Islamic law obligated Muslim rulers to welcome these converts into the community of believers. Conversion therefore blurred the essential line between citizen and subject that was central to empire.

Divinely sanctioned imperial expansion thus had built-in contradictions. Proselytizing religion provided a moral excuse for empire building, but it also blunted the extractive power of imperial rule. More seriously, the subject majority threatened to hijack the imperial enterprise as they became Muslims in ever larger numbers. The Roman aristocrats who opposed Claudius's plans to admit romanized Gauls to the Senate had similar concerns, but in the short term, at least, there were only a handful of Gallic senators. Early Islam aimed to encompass the entire world and was too egalitarian to define the boundaries of subjecthood and legitimize permanent imperial privilege. Later Christian missionaries did a better job of making evangelism compatible with imperial rule by reducing converts to junior believers, but the early Arab empire builders were not so nuanced. They therefore struggled to keep mass conversions from overwhelming and absorbing them.

The Arabs' sudden acquisition of an enormous multiethnic empire further complicated their conception of themselves as Arabs. The peoples of the Arabian Peninsula in the caliphate era shared a common language and culture, and they identified themselves as members of distinctive entities, which they called "tribes," subdivided into smaller clans. These were akin to the tribes of the Old Testament, and collectively the Arabs claimed descent from the prophet Abraham through his son Ishmael. The tribes of northern Arabia claimed descent directly from Ishmael, while southerners reckoned their lineage through Noah. Arab tribal identities theoretically sprang from a strongly shared belief in a common paternal ancestor, but in fact they were almost never fixed or rigid. As in preconquest Britain, tribes in pre-Islamic Arabia split and re-formed. Arab commanders further reordered clans and subclans to create largely artificial tribal regiments (*ajnad*) during the expansionist wars of the early Islamic era.[4]

These tribal identities formed the basis of citizenship under the caliphate, but they were porous and malleable. Cultural assimilation and rewritten tribal genealogies allowed the subject peoples of the caliphate to become Arabs in good standing. Upon conversion most became junior clients (*mawali*) of Arab tribal patrons, but over time the new converts aspired to redefine what it meant to be an Arab and a Muslim as they took on the tribal identities of their sponsors. In doing so they challenged the Arab elite's claim to preeminence in the caliphate. Imperial exploitation required rigid social boundaries, and, contrary to the tenets of Islam, the Arab empire builders hypocritically had to treat the *mawali* as subjects to rule them effectively.[5]

While the imperialization of the caliphate facilitated extraction, it threatened Muhammad's idealized vision of a just and egalitarian society of believers. Just as Pliny regretted the cultural adulteration resulting from Rome's conquest of Greece, many of the original Muslims worried that their victories undermined the virtuous and representative character of the original Islamic state. Yet empire was seductive, and apart from a single caliph, they never seriously considered giving up territory or recalling the conquering Muslim armies. Enticed by the prodigious spoils of imperial rule, victorious Arab caliphs and generals turned the caliphate into a grand Islamic empire.

The Umayyad Caliphate sprang from this expansion of Islam as a faith and as a political institution. Although pastoral nomadic "tribes" were the center of Arab society and politics in the pre-Islamic era, it is a mistake to classify Islam as a desert religion. It originated in the commercial cities of Mecca and Medina, which lay astride long-distance trade routes running through Arabia and the Red Sea. Muhammad ibn Abdullah belonged to a prominent merchant clan that was part of the ruling Quraysh tribe of Mecca, an entrepôt whose religious shrines made it a destination for pagan pilgrims. Mecca's status as a pre-Islamic religious sanctuary encouraged trade, which meant that the city's elites were not receptive to Muhammad's vision that the archangel Gabriel had told him he was to serve as God's messenger in preaching the central message of monotheism.

Receiving this first revelation in A.D. 610, Muhammad became the last of a line of prophets stretching back to Adam. Islam thereby continued and expanded the Judeo-Christian traditions of the Bible. As with the prophets who came before him, Muhammad felt a divine compulsion to teach that there was only a single God. In attacking pagan idol worship he provoked the Meccan establishment, who forced him to flee to the neighboring city of Medina with a small band of converts in 622. Two years later, Muhammad was strong enough to force the Quraysh and the rest of the Meccan aristocracy to embrace the new faith. Islam's Arabian origins gave it a distinctly Arab character, but Muhammad's deemphasis of tribal identities made it a powerful universalistic force that encouraged non-Arabs to join the Muslim community of believers (*umma*).

Unlike Jesus Christ, whom Muslims recognize as a prophet, Muhammad combined religious and political authority. After convincing the Meccans to submit and winning over most pastoral Arabs, he turned his attention to the settled Middle East. The Byzantine and Sassanid empires, which were distracted by protracted warfare, internal religious controversy, and natural disasters, were clearly vulnerable. The Muslim leader was in the process of laying the groundwork for a larger Muslim polity when he died in 632.

Muhammad's death created a crisis among the *umma* because he had said very little about long-term political authority and made no mention of a caliphate, much less an empire. Muslims revered him as the last of the prophets, and his successors never replicated his authority or influence. Nevertheless, the first four caliphs, who were among his original followers, had a strong measure of legitimacy. They are known in Islamic history as the *rashidun*, "rightly guided ones."

Abu Bakr, Muhammad's friend and first convert, succeeded him as the political leader of the *umma*. Ruling for only two years until his death in 634, he came to power on the acclamation of the Muslim community. As the first caliph, he stopped rebellious Arab tribes from putting forth their own prophets after Muhammad's death. The following three *rashidun* caliphs undertook the conquest of the Middle

East over the next two decades. Their forces captured Damascus in 635, defeated the Sassanid Empire in 637, and took Egypt from the Byzantines by 656. Further east, they added Khurasan (a prosperous region covering contemporary eastern Iran and western Afghanistan) to the caliphate. The evolving Islamic legal code (the *shari'a*) reserved one-fifth of the conquering armies' plunder of these settled regions for God and charity, with the commanders dividing the rest among themselves and their troops.

These successful campaigns kept the Arab soldiers occupied and provided a lucrative incentive for them to respect caliphal authority. Led by Qurayshi generals who had once opposed Muhammad, the conquering Arab armies were relatively small tribally organized forces that often were trailed by families and flocks. After their victories they essentially became colonists living apart from their new subjects. As with their Roman predecessors, the victorious Arabs did not enjoy a technological military advantage over their enemies. Instead, mobility and moral certainty allowed them to defeat much larger but less motivated Byzantine and Sassanid professional armies. The Muslims gained few converts during the initial conquest, but the Byzantines' and Sassanids' peasant subjects gave them little trouble, for they had few ties to their former imperial masters.

Truly impressive in its scope, the Umayyad Caliphate eventually stretched from Spain to China and encompassed more territory than the Roman or Chinese empires. Yet this vast empire never rivaled Rome in the imaginations of western empire builders. Where Roman expansion brought civilization and culture, later European observers saw Muslim imperialism as intrinsically hostile to the grand Greco-Roman and Christian heritage of the Mediterranean. The British historian Edward Gibbon credited the Franks with saving western Christendom by stopping the Muslim advance at Poitiers in A.D. 732.

> [An] Arabian fleet might have sailed without a naval combat into the mouth of the Thames. Perhaps the interpretation of the Koran would now be taught in the schools of Oxford, and her pulpits might demonstrate to a circumcised people the sanctity and truth of the revelation of Mahomet.[6]

These chauvinistic biases regained their potency after the terrorist attacks of September 2001, and some neoconservatives argued that modern Islamicists take the expansionist Umayyad Caliphate as an inspirational model for an "Islamic imperial dream of world domination."[7] This is anachronistic, for the Umayyads never thought in such terms. While al-Qaeda and Usama bin Laden have spoken of reclaiming Al-Andalus, they have no more chance of reviving the Umayyad Caliphate than Mussolini's Fascist Italy did of re-creating the Roman Empire.

Moreover, the original Muslims were entirely unprepared for the complexities of imperial rule. They were fortunate that earlier powers had already done much of the work of imperial subjugation for them. Initially, Arab generals simply kept Byzantine and Sassanid systems of taxation, land tenure, and governance in place. They also went to great lengths to maintain a sharp boundary between their soldier settlers and their new subjects. Worried that contact with more sophisticated urban populations would be corrupting, the second *rashidun* caliph, Umar, banned Muslim colonists from living in conquered cities. Instead the Arabs established fortified military camps (*misr*) to keep watch on major urban centers. These colonial settlements eventually grew into major cities such as Basra and Kufa in Iraq, Fustat in Egypt, and Qayrawan in Tunisia.

While appropriating preexisting imperial systems to administer newly conquered lands was easy enough, the rapid expansion of the *dar al-Islam* in territory, converts, and wealth strained the early caliphate. The Quran, which collected the original Muslims' written recollections of Muhammad's revelations, made no specific mention of a caliph. Lacking clear guidance from Islamic law, the early community of believers struggled to adapt their simple and egalitarian political system to imperial rule. Muslims believed that the *umma* had to remain united, but compromises that brought Abu Bakr and Umar to power gave way to factional disputes in 656 between Meccan elites, who were latecomers to Islam, and Muhammad's original circle of friends and converts.

The resulting civil war, which led to the deaths of the third and fourth caliphs, brought Mu'awiya, the provincial governor of Syria and founder of the Umayyad dynasty, to power in 661. A kinsman and appointee of the third caliph, Uthman, Mu'awiya was the son of a Meccan aristocrat who had led the opposition to Muhammad before becoming a convert. Ending the practice of choosing caliphs by acclamation, he turned the caliphate into a hereditary empire. Although some sources praised him for his self-control and patronage of humble clients, there was a strong anti-Umayyad bias in Islamic historiography that painted him as a usurper. The followers of the fourth caliph, Ali, who was Muhammad's kinsman and son-in-law, blamed Mu'awiya for displacing the Prophet's family. In their eyes, the Umayyads were secular kings rather than righteously guided successors to the Prophet. Their sins included moving the political seat of Islam from Mecca to Damascus and aspiring to become emperors.[8]

Ruling from 661 to 750, the Umayyads indeed played the central role in transforming the caliphate into an empire. Just as the Roman emperor Claudius sought legitimacy through empire building, Caliph Abd al-Malik launched a new phase of imperial expansion that added Sind, Transoxiana, North Africa, and Spain to the caliphate. Lacking extensive administrative experience, the Umayyads relied on local bureaucrats who had served the Byzantine and Sassanid empires to manage their conquered territories. Their central bureaucracy in Damascus was initially quite rudimentary. Originating as the keepers of the payroll (*diwan*) that shared out plunder to the Arab soldiery, the first caliphal officials expanded this military record-keeping system into simple departments for correspondence and tax collection. *Dhimmi* and clients writing in Greek and Persian staffed the original bureaus, but Arabic-speakers took over in the 690s under Caliph Abd al-Malik. His successors in the eighth century further expanded the imperial bureaucracy to include more formal departments for security, taxation, military pay, and the caliphal household.

In terms of sovereignty, the Umayyad Caliphate was theoretically a unified imperial state under the absolute authority of the caliph. Yet the limits of medieval travel and communication meant that the Umayyad caliphs' direct authority rarely reached beyond Syria. Initially, there was no standardized system of provinces on the Roman model, and the Arabs drew their territorial boundaries around their original *amsar*, or garrison cities. This created de facto viceroyalties encompassing Syria, Jazira (the territory between the Tigris and Euphrates rivers in northern Iraq), Kufa and Basra in southern Iraq, Khurasan, and Egypt and North Africa. The caliphs usually ruled Syria and Jazira directly and appointed governors to control the rest of the empire. Each viceroyalty consisted of provinces (*wilayat*) divided into districts and subdistricts.

The viceroyal capital cities were also recruiting bases for the Arab regiments (*ajnad*; sing. *jund*) who settled within their borders. The tribal organization of the original Arab armies thus shaped settlement and governance. When necessary, governor-commanders divided each *jund* into "quarters" and "fifths" to create new administrative units.

This tribally based system of civil and military administration evolved as the caliphate expanded into North Africa and Central Asia. By the time of Abd al-Malik, the Umayyad military consisted of the viceroyal field armies of Syria, Jazira, southern Iraq (Kufa and Basra), Khurasan, and Egypt. The southern Iraqi army carried out the caliphate's early eastern conquests, but disputes over the division of plunder led the caliphs to demobilize it in the late seventh century. The Jazira force almost exclusively fought the Byzantines, while the relatively small Egyptian army operated in North Africa. But the real seat of Umayyad political and military power was in Syria. Divided into five separate military districts, the province fielded a force of approximately 175,000 men who underpinned Umayyad rule and fought as expeditionary forces throughout the caliphate.

The Umayyad soldiery's regular wages came from provincial taxation, but pay rates were not uniform. The privileged Syrians earned three times more than troops in the discredited Iraqi field army, and non-Arab *mawali* clients earned even less. But inclusion on the rolls of a victorious Umayyad army was much more important than wages, for participation in a successful campaign entitled even the lowest-ranking soldier to a share of the plunder. When Muhammad ibn al-Qasim conquered Sind in 712 he duly turned over one-fifth of the loot to the caliphate. This amounted to 120 million dirhams, the equivalent of the entire land tax of Iraq. Simple calculation reveals that the general's entire haul in Sind was six hundred million dirhams. Further raids into India by his successors produced another four hundred million dirhams. These warrior-administrators became fabulously wealthy, but lower-ranking officers and common soldiers also received a generous share that far surpassed their regular wages.

Predictably, conflicts over the division of imperial spoils became a central point of tension in the caliphate. Maneuvering to monopolize the wealth of empire, the Umayyad military split into coalitions claiming descent from the tribes of northern (Qays/Mudar) and southern (Yaman) Arabia. The Yamani colonists who settled in southern Syria got the lion's share because they made up the core of the Umayyad armies. Although these supratribal factions acquired real political meaning, they were essentially genealogical inventions that emerged as commanders modified or fabricated tribal identities to reorganize their armies. Persian units that defected en masse from the Sassanid Empire became a fictive Qays subtribe, and succeeding groups of converts similarly formed subordinate components of the larger tribal regiments. In this way, the Qays and Yaman factions became the primary medium through which Arab soldiers and their clients staked their claims to wealth, prestige, and political power.

From a military standpoint, it clearly paid to become a Muslim. As with Roman tribal auxiliaries, military service offered a path to citizenship and a chance to share in the imperial spoils. This explains why Berber converts to Islam were a significant portion of the Umayyad forces that conquered North Africa. Abandoning their initial resistance, they joined the Umayyads in despoiling the Byzantine settled regions. After that, the Berber general Tariq's conquest of Iberia was the next logical step.

It was relatively easy to turn conquered peoples into expendable shock troops, but mass popular conversions were problematic. Seeking to shore up the boundaries of subjecthood, the Umayyads manipulated the tenets of early Islam to fudge the distinction between citizen and subject. Islam was the caliphate's de facto state religion, but it took more than a century for it to develop into a text-based faith with an explicitly proselytizing obligation. The Umayyads claimed to be God's secular deputies, but they did not initially push their subjects to convert. Religious men were still debating what exactly it meant to be a Muslim during the first century of Islam, and a clerical class (the *ulama*) and a fully codified religious law (the *shari'a*) did not emerge until around the turn of the eighth century. Still, empire building forced scholars and intellectuals to define Islam more precisely in a futile attempt to ensure that the much larger and more culturally sophisticated non-Muslim subject majority did not absorb and assimilate Arab soldiers and colonists. This codification of Islam facilitated imperial domination and extraction, and after the reign of

Abd al-Malik the Umayyad caliphs began to style themselves more explicitly as Islamic rulers. They also became less willing to tolerate public expressions of non-Islamic religions and cultures.

Yet the Umayyads still shied away from undertaking a systematic effort to convert non-Muslims. Uncertainty over how to incorporate outsiders into the *umma* and the desire to exploit imperial subjects were powerful counterweights to Muhammad's injunction to spread the faith. As a result, the rates of conversion under the Umayyads were generally low. Muslims were less than 10 percent of the Persian population when the Abbasids seized the caliphate in 750, and most Egyptians remained Coptic Christians until well into the ninth century.

Nevertheless, caliphal imperial rule created real incentives for certain groups to embrace Islam. Excepting Byzantine and Sassanid prisoners of war, most early converts in Iraq and Iran were peasants and tenant farmers, for, at least in theory, conversion brought a significant tax reduction. Islamic law required all Muslims to pay the *zakat,* a religious tax assessed at differing rates based on property and wealth. Non-Muslims, in contrast, paid a land tax (*kharaj*) and a head tax (*jizya*). Taken together, these obligations were considerably heavier than the *zakat* and became a major source of funding for the caliphal state. Seeking relief from tax collectors and obligations to local landlords, the Umayyads' subjects had an incentive to convert to Islam.

Anxious to protect an important imperial revenue stream, Umayyad administrators often refused to recognize the conversion of their taxpaying non-Muslim subjects. Iraqi officials sent would-be peasant converts back to the countryside, and the governor of Khurasan used circumcision, a practice required under Islam, to determine if new Muslims were sincere. Taxation became more equitable as Muslims became liable for the *kharaj* when they acquired land owned by *dhimmi* and pagans, but the Umayyads' need to tax their subjects at higher rates perverted their obligation to treat converts as equals. Ultimately, military service was the only sure way for common men to become Muslims in good standing, thereby going from taxpayers to tax recipients.

Converts usually became clients (*mawali*) of powerful Arab patrons. Under the Umayyads only Arabs were "true" Muslims, and *mawali* adopted the tribal identities of their sponsors. Even so, it was difficult to escape the stigma of their non-Arab origins, and most still paid the non-Muslim poll tax. Initially, most new Muslims were slaves, peasants, tenants, and foot soldiers. In the west, commanders converted entire communities of Berbers by promising them equal status within the Arab armies, but they used them as shock troops and denied them full shares of the spoils. The *mawali* responded to this institutionalized discrimination by inventing fictional Arab genealogies and insisting that a sincere profession of faith was all that it took to be a true Muslim. Although Islam legitimized Arab empire building, its inherent inclusiveness complicated the business of imperial rule. Given a choice, caliphal officials probably would have preferred not to convert their subjects, for they were much easier to govern and exploit while they remained non-Muslims.

Consequently, the Umayyads did not meddle too deeply in the daily lives of the subject populations. Like the Roman emperors, they lacked the means to rule directly at the local level, which meant that their demands on their non-Muslim subjects were no greater than those of the Byzantines or Sassanids. Although Islamic law obligated Muslim conquerors to either convert pagan "idolaters" or put them to death, the Umayyads generally left these communities alone if they acknowledged Muslim sovereignty and paid their taxes. Furthermore, Islamic law explicitly protected Jews and Christians from forced conversion because they shared a spiritual heritage with Islam as "peoples of the book."

Although these rules seem reasonably tolerant, there is no disguising the imperial nature of the caliphal rule. Jews and Christians could not testify against Muslims in court, nor could they marry Muslim women. The Umayyads' increased reliance on Islam for their legitimacy in the early eighth century made the status of *dhimmi* even more precarious. In 717, the famously pious Caliph Umar II issued decrees banning Christians from dressing like Muslims and limiting their right to maintain churches and display religious symbols. Conversion offered the tempting promise of social advancement, but even the *mawali* could not fully escape subjecthood.

The Umayyad Caliphate was also as dependent on slave labor as any other ancient or medieval empire. Arab armies took captives by the tens, if not hundreds of thousands, and victorious generals treated these prisoners as booty to be shared out among their troops. The conquest of Sind netted almost seven hundred thousand saleable captives, and commanders in North Africa often paid their Berber auxiliaries in slaves rather than treasure. Islamic law generally granted slaves greater legal protection and social status than Roman slaves, and Muhammad praised owners who manumitted captives as an act of piety. But plenty of Muslim masters still treated slaves as an exploitable and disposable resource. Indeed, the ninth-century rebellion of desperate African slaves (the *zanj*) in the marshes of Basra continued the long tradition of mass slave uprisings against uncaring imperial masters. Conversion to Islam did offer captives more rights and the hope of manumission, but only the most pious owners made this a viable option.

Still, the Umayyads were no more exploitive than their imperial predecessors or contemporaries, and their demise came at the hands of fellow Muslims rather than rebellious non-Muslim subjects. Ruling for less than a century, they were comparatively poor empire builders. The early caliphate was not set up to manage a sprawling intercontinental empire, nor were the Umayyads equipped to divide the enormous spoils of empire or govern large numbers of alien subjects. In this sense, the Umayyad imperial state simply grew too large and too fast to be stable.

Most of the Umayyad caliphs failed to grasp the inherent risks of empire and gave their generals and governors a free hand to acquire new territories. Umar II was one of the few rulers to understand the implications of subjugating so many non-Muslims and had grave doubts about the sustainability of the Umayyad expansion. Ruling from only 718 to 720, he concluded that the caliphate was too reliant on plunder. The enormous sums that his predecessors spent on public works, mosques, palaces, and military operations were not sustainable without constant flows of loot. The conquest of Sind may have netted the caliphate 120 million dirhams, but it took at least 60 million dirhams per year to pay the stipends of the three hundred thousand soldiers in the Umayyad armies.[9] Moreover, looting was not a sustainable revenue source; a conquered community could only be plundered so many times. The *jizya* (poll tax on non-Muslims) provided some relief, but this obligation theoretically ended with conversion. Fiscal necessity worked against this, and perceptive caliphal officials warned that the continued imposition of the *jizya* on *mawali* converts undermined the regime's legitimacy.

Umar therefore tried to keep the caliphate solvent by taking a break from empire building. Cognizant of the underlying costs of imperial expansion, he demobilized surplus military units and seriously considered withdrawing from recently conquered territories in Sind, Transoxiana, and Spain. He also reduced princely allowances and imposed the *kharaj* (land tax) on Muslims who purchased land from non-Muslims. Umar recognized that discrimination against the *mawali* was dangerous and moved to exempt them from the *jizya*. Seeking to offset the resulting loss of revenue, he tried to introduce more regular and efficient taxation policies.

Although Umar's reforms made considerable sense, he did not live to see them through. Caliph Hisham, who ruled from 724 to 743, did not share his predecessor's concerns about the costs of empire. He broke an implicit truce with the Byzantines and launched new expansionist campaigns in Central Asia, North Africa, and France. Although his forces initially won a few victories, internal revolts and stiffening resistance on the frontiers soon led to disaster. The Umayyad military fortunes turned in the late 720s when Turkish invaders wiped out entire armies in Khurasan, while widespread popular resistance forced them to retreat from India. In the west, Frankish forces under Charles Martel turned back an invading Muslim army at Poitiers in 732.

The cost of Hisham's futile campaigning alienated the soldiery and fanned popular dissatisfaction with Umayyad rule. This was particularly true in Khurasan, where Umayyad governors reimposed the *jizya* on converts, but there was also significant unrest among the Berbers in North Africa. Angered by the *jizya* and abusive Arab governors who seized conscripts and slaves as tribute, Muslim Berbers launched a massive revolt in 739 that forced Hisham to send an army of one hundred thousand men to Tunisia. When the Berbers won a decisive victory by exploiting tensions between local Arabs and Syrian units in the expeditionary force, the caliph had to rush even more troops to North Africa. The overextended Umayyad generals finally defeated the Berbers in 742, but the toll of almost ten years of continuous campaigning meant that Hisham's imperial adventures were no longer sustainable.

Exhaustion, mounting losses, and economic retrenchment resulting from military reverses opened deep divides among the Arab military elite. The Syrian field army's significant reverses in India, Central Asia, Asia Minor, North Africa, and France meant that it could no longer prop up the Umayyad regime. More seriously, tensions between the Yaman and Qays tribal cliques became so bitter under Hisham that incoming governors routinely removed officials from rival factions and imprisoned and tortured their predecessors under the guise of recovering embezzled funds. The demise of the Syrian field army, which consisted primarily of Yamanis, through overuse and military defeat created a dangerous power vacuum in Syria. The resulting civil war in 744 cost the Umayyads the caliphate. The dispersion of the surviving Syrian units throughout the provinces opened the way for rival Umayyad princes, backed by ambitious generals, to lay claim to power.

Their fratricidal infighting distracted the Umayyads from an emerging threat in the east where a rival dynastic power organized Persian *mawali* and surviving elements of the Khurasan field army into a powerful anti-Umayyad force. Angered by hypocritical tax policies, the Central Asian converts found common cause with disgruntled Arab soldiers who had married into local families. Abu al-Abbas Abdullah ibn Muhammad, the founder of the Abbasid dynasty, assumed control of this popular revolt by virtue of his descent from Muhammad's paternal uncle and his adopted ties to Ali's son. This pedigree appealed to Muslims who still believed that the *umma* should be led by a descendant of Muhammad through Ali, but the Abbasids drew their largest following by championing a universalistic non-ethnic version of Islam that recognized non-Arab converts as Muslims in good standing. Through this, they espoused an anti-imperial ideology that promised a complete and conclusive escape from subjecthood to the *mawali* who still chafed under Umayyad discrimination. Fighting under black banners that suggested that a messiah or *mahdi* from Ali's line would return to usher in a golden age of justice, the Abbasid forces swept westward out of Khurasan and defeated the last Umayyad caliph, Marwan II, in 750. They slaughtered all the Umayyad nobles they could find and desecrated the tombs of every Umayyad caliph except for that of the pious Umar II.

Although the caliphate technically lasted until the Mongol invasion of 1258, the Abbasids transformed it substantially. They shifted its capital from Damascus to Baghdad and drew more heavily on

Persian systems of imperial rule. The caliphate thus became fundamentally less Arab as easterners assumed greater roles in the bureaucracy and court. Yet the Abbasids continued to struggle with the complexities of imperial rule. There was no further institutional discrimination against non-Arab Muslims, but the "Abbasid revolution" did not make the caliphate less imperial from the perspective of its non-Muslim subjects. Indeed, Christians in Lebanon and Egypt proved particularly restive under Abbasid rule.

Although their victory over the Umayyads was total and complete, the Abbasids failed to wipe out their rivals entirely. Fleeing the carnage in Damascus, Prince Abd al-Rahman, a grandson of Caliph Hisham and the son of a Berber concubine, sought refuge with his mother's people in North Africa before crossing into Iberia. Taking control of Al-Andalus, Abd al-Rahman laid the groundwork for an independent Muslim Iberian state that lasted for two hundred years. Raised to a caliphate by his ambitious descendant Abd al-Rahman III, this Umayyad outpost ruled a substantial Christian majority. These Iberians were particularly vulnerable because they had been subjects of the Roman and Visigothic imperial states. By necessity, the Muslim conquerors appropriated and adapted the imperial institutions of their predecessors to exploit the ancestors of the Spanish conquistadors.

The people whom Tariq ibn Ziyad and Musa ibn Nusayr conquered in 711 were not Spanish in the modern national sense. Roderic and his nobles were the heirs of the "barbarians" who brought down the Roman Empire. Chapter 1 has shown how an armed migration by the Huns in the fourth century forced loosely organized bands of Goths to seek refuge within the Roman frontiers. Although the Gothic leader Alaric sacked Rome, the ancestors of the Visigoths eventually became relatively reliable Roman allies. As *foederati*, they provided military service in return for protection and a one-third share of the revenue from large Roman estates in the region.[10]

Though technically barbarians, the Visigoths became an important prop of the later Roman Empire. Emperor Honorius, who had allowed Roman Britain to slip away, granted them the right to settle in Aquitania in recognition of their assistance during further barbarian invasions. Pressure from the Franks early in the sixth century forced them into Iberia, where they challenged an earlier group of Germanic invaders known as the Sueves. The Visigothic kings made Toledo the royal capital, but they pragmatically kept Roman officials at their posts. They did not consolidate their hold on the peninsula until the mid-sixth century, when King Leovigild defeated the Sueves and drove the Byzantines from the southern regions of the peninsula.

Like many Roman successor states, Visigothic Iberia was unstable. Political succession was a problem because the Visigothic monarchs were, at least in theory, elected warrior kings. Most aspired to become hereditary rulers, and their dynastic ambitions led to constant friction with the nobility. As a conquering elite that probably numbered no more than two hundred thousand people, the Visigoths claimed sovereignty over an indigenous population approximately eight million strong.[11] As foreigners and outsiders, they were an imperial power, and their limited numbers forced them to rely on Hispano-Roman landowners to rule the Iberian majority. Living apart and lacking the means and sophistication to impose their own customs, the Visigoths relied on administrative institutions inherited from the Romans. In this sense, the Roman Empire did not fall in Iberia so much as it was simply taken over by the Visigoths. Keeping the Hispano-Roman imperial machinery running as well as it could, the Visigothic state did not govern or collect taxes directly until the late seventh century.

The Visigoths were far less successful in preserving the economic foundations of Roman Spain. The fragmentation of the empire into smaller political units, coupled with widespread banditry and outright anarchy, destroyed the networks of commerce and finance that made Roman Iberia so rich. Plagues and warfare appear to have reduced the peninsula's population from six million to four million people by the end of the seventh century.[12] The Visigoths could not keep the roads open and safe or prevent warlords from building strong points to prey on villages and travelers. Consequently, farming communities in the Guadalquivir Valley, the economic heartland of southern Roman Spain, fled their lands for the comparative protection of the hills.

As in Britain, many Roman cities fell into decline, and those that survived often consisted of decrepit Visigothic structures built on Roman ruins. The breakdown of long-distance trade and the demise of the Roman military garrison meant that coinage no longer circulated, disrupting the peninsula's market economy severely. The Iberian grain and olive oil that once were important cash crops lost their most lucrative markets in Italy, Gaul, and Britain, thereby forcing many producers to fall back on subsistence agriculture. As a result, Iberian import markets also dried up. These developments coincided with the Byzantine retreat and suggest that the peninsula became relatively isolated from the commerce of the wider Mediterranean world under the Visigoths.

This overall insecurity probably promoted localism and accelerated Spain's shift to a feudal economy, a process that was already under way in the late Roman imperial era. Faced with the anarchy of the Roman collapse, large numbers of peasant farmers most likely turned their lands over to powerful elites in exchange for protection. In doing so they joined the slave laborers who worked the vast Hispano-Roman estates, or *latifundia*, in serfdom. Tied to the soil, they surrendered a share of their crops as rent in addition to paying the Roman poll tax to the Visigothic state. These feudal systems of production generated only a fraction of the revenues of the late Roman era, and the Visigothic nobility made matters worse by confiscating former Roman imperial estates and shrinking the kingdom's tax base.

As in Britain, the impact of romanization in the Iberian countryside is difficult to measure, and it is unclear as to what extent commoners retained local identities or became Hispano-Romans. The Basques and other peoples of the northern highlands, who had withstood Roman assimilationist pressure, certainly maintained identities that were distinct from the more settled south. The medieval chroniclers who provide most of the information on Visigothic Spain were concerned primarily with the doings of nobles and high churchmen and paid almost no attention to common Iberians. It seems likely that villagers, peasants, herdsmen, hill folk, and slaves probably distrusted their Roman and Visigothic rulers equally, and the common thread that runs through the Roman, Visigothic, and Umayyad eras was the domination and exploitation of local peoples by succeeding ancient and medieval imperial powers.

At the elite level, a common aristocratic culture in Iberia was taking shape at the time of the Umayyad invasion as the Hispano-Roman aristocracy made their peace with Visigothic rule. But it is not clear how the majority of Iberians identified themselves during this period. As in the wider medieval world, Christianity was a common reference point, but the Visigoths' embrace of Arianism divided them from their Catholic subjects until the Council of Toledo created a single Iberian church in 587. Nevertheless, the role that Catholicism played in the everyday lives of common Iberians is uncertain. Christianity was synonymous with romanization under the late empire, but, as in Britain, it is difficult to determine its influence beyond the Hispano-Roman aristocracy. The veneration of St. Eulalia of Merida, popular throughout the peninsula, probably drew on a pre-Roman fertility cult. Although this suggests indigenous local beliefs shaped Spanish Christianity, it is not necessarily evidence that the church had a large popular following. Iberian values may have influenced its beliefs, but the Catholic Church was also one of the largest slave owners in the seventh century, and its close ties to the Visigothic elite probably circumscribed its popular influence.

The Visigoths' embrace of Catholicism was certainly a disaster for Iberian Jews. The Arian kings had denied them a range of rights, but the Visigoths' conversion subjected the Jews of Iberia to the full weight of the horrendous anti-Semitic laws that had become the norm in the rest of Catholic Europe. Although there is no evidence that it went into force, a 694 law actually enslaved the entire Jewish population of the peninsula. This systematic oppression led to unfounded suggestions that the Jews actively abetted the Umayyad invasion. Nonetheless, institutionalized anti-Semitism was certainly a small part of the wider oppressive and extractive policies that alienated common Iberians from the Visigothic state.

It therefore comes as little surprise that the Visigoths received scant help from the general population when Tariq invaded in 711. Roderic's problems were both personal and systemic. Coming to power after winning one of the bitter succession disputes that plagued the Visigothic monarchy, he was hard pressed to mobilize his fellow nobles against the invaders. Furthermore, falling agricultural yields and declining tax revenues undermined the Visigoths' military capacity. By 711, their manpower shortages were so serious that Roderic resorted to arming slaves.

This is why it took the Umayyads only four years to overrun most of the peninsula. By some reports, southern cities such as Córdoba and Zaragoza resisted, but the Hispano-Roman elite seems to have remained relatively neutral by retreating to their rural estates. Some of the surviving Visigothic nobles apparently buried their treasure and withdrew to the north on the assumption that the invasion was just another short-term raid. Overall, the invaders appear to have faced relatively little popular resistance, which suggests that common Iberians did not consider the Muslim conquest particularly catastrophic despite the story of Hercules's Tower.

Nonetheless, the Umayyad victory was impressive. By comparison, it took the Romans nearly two centuries to conquer Iberia. The Muslims had the advantage of being able to exploit many of the infrastructure and administrative systems that Rome bequeathed the Visigoths. Just as Leovigild kept the Roman administrative machinery running, the Umayyads now stepped into the Visigoths' shoes as Rome's imperial heirs.

At the ground level, Musa's son Abd al-Aziz, the first Umayyad governor of Al-Andalus, had no choice but to continue his predecessors' imperial strategy of ruling indirectly. The conquest of Iberia cost the Umayyads approximately three thousand men, and Abd al-Aziz did not fully trust his father's Berber auxiliaries. Lacking administrative manpower and expertise, he and his successors co-opted Romano-Visigothic governing systems and reached an accord with prominent local Iberians. Following the Umayyad practice of guaranteeing the rights and property of enemies who acceded peacefully to Muslim rule, Abd al-Aziz initially did little more than impose the *jizya* (poll tax) on cooperative Christians and Jews.

Many Visigothic nobles considered this an attractive arrangement. In 713, Theodemir (Tudmir), whom the chroniclers described as a count and governor, won Umayyad recognition of his reign over seven cities near Seville by agreeing to pay the annual *jizya* of one dinar plus measures of grain, vinegar, honey, fruit juice, and olive oil for each of his subjects. In return, Abd al-Aziz made a promise:

> We will not set special conditions on him or for any among his men, nor harass him, nor remove him from power. His followers will not be killed or taken prisoner, nor will they be separated from their women and children. They will not be coerced in matters of religion, their

churches will not be burned...[so long as] Tudmir remains sincere and faithful.[13]

Initially at least, elites such as Theodemir were thus able to keep their property and position. The Umayyad governors found land for their men by seizing the holdings of resisters and nobles who fled north. They also took the royal Visigothic estates that probably had once belonged to the Roman emperors. Per Umayyad practice, the new Arab masters of these lands were obliged to surrender one-fifth of their revenues to the caliphate.

Abd al-Aziz further cemented his ties to the Visigothic aristocracy by marrying Roderic's widow, Egilo, which most likely set a precedent for Arab soldiers with little chance of finding Muslim brides. Similarly, Witiza's granddaughter Sara the Goth traveled to Damascus to convince Caliph Hisham to reward her family's assistance during the conquest by restoring their estates. Hisham agreed and married her to an Umayyad nobleman, who returned with her to Spain. Sara converted to Islam, but, interestingly, her brothers became high-ranking Catholic clerics, thereby demonstrating that the Iberian church did not immediately suffer under Muslim rule.

The realities of empire eventually derailed these initial compromises. Estimates of the size of the initial Arab/Berber invasion force range from a conventional army of thirty thousand men to a full-scale armed migration consisting of two hundred thousand soldiers, families, clients, and slaves.[14] The first estimate is more likely, but in either case, the victorious Muslim troops settled as colonists and expected privilege, plunder, and land. The more influential Arabs took the cities and the fertile Guadalquivir and Ebro river valleys and left the arid mountainous regions to the Berbers. The actual impact of these settlements on local Iberian communities depended on the size of the invasion force. If the lower estimates are accurate, then it is likely that the seventh-century demographic collapse under the Visigoths would have left plenty of land for Muslim colonial settlement, but accommodating more than two hundred thousand migrants would have placed a considerable burden on their unwilling Iberian hosts. Either way, even the most cooperative Visigothic elites found it difficult to hold on to their estates as Muslim settlement increased over the course of the eighth century.

Struggles over the spoils of empire also strained the early Andalusi administration. Suspicions that Musa had embezzled the caliphate's fifth of the Iberian plunder led al-Walid to recall him to Damascus, and caliphal agents may have been behind the assassination of his son Abd al-Aziz in 715. Popular accounts held that Abd al-Aziz's Christian wife had convinced him to make a Caesar-style grab for power by donning a Visigothic crown, but it is more likely that the Andalusi governor was the first victim of the vicious infighting that was endemic during the first four chaotic decades of Umayyad rule in Iberia. All told, Al-Andalus had twenty governors between 716 and 756, of which only three served for more than five years and more than a few died in combat or at the hands of fellow Arabs.

Ensconced safely in the remote westernmost corner of the caliphate, the original Andalusi Arab colonists, who became known as the *baladiyyun*, guarded their autonomy jealously. Having won the peninsula by force of arms, they conspired to keep its wealth for themselves. In this sense they were no different from later conquistadors and imperial "men on the spot" who reaped the immediate rewards of empire. The *baladiyyun* paid no tribute on their new estates even though the caliphate insisted that formerly Christian lands remained subject to taxation. Their intransigence was probably a factor in Caliph Umar II's plans to withdraw from Spain. He did not, and his successor Hisham strove to impose more stringent taxation, a centralizing move that undermined *baladi* loyalty to Damascus.

Hoping that new sources of plunder would defuse these tensions, several Andalusi governors resumed the invasion of western Christendom. Muslim forces consisting primarily of Berbers under Arab leadership overran most of southern France until the Frankish ruler Charles Martel stopped them at Poitiers in 732. The Andalusis lingered in Provence until the expansion of Frankish power under Charlemagne later in the century drove them out. Their retreat to Iberia dried up the *baladiyyun*'s access to loot. Although they acknowledged the Umayyad caliphs in their Friday prayers, these Andalusi Arabs asserted their independence from Damascus in substantive matters such as land settlement and tribute.

The Umayyads' hold on Al-Andalus became even more precarious after the mass Berber revolt in 739. Angered by Arab discrimination in the division of land and wealth, the Andalusi Berbers joined their North African kinsmen in open rebellion and laid siege to the main cities of southern Iberia. While the Berber uprising appeared to threaten the Arabs' hold on power, the insurrection was also an opportunity. It allowed the *baladiyyun* to ignore Damascus until the Syrian expeditionary force in North Africa, which was largely cut to pieces by the Berbers, took refuge in Spain. The result was an Arab civil war between the *baladiyyun* and the more recent Syrian arrivals. After three years of strife and broken truces, the Syrian military commander al-Sumayl ibn Hatim massacred most of the *baladi* leaders and ran Al-Andalus as an independent state until the refugee Umayyad princeling Abd al-Rahman arrived on the peninsula in 755.

Backed by wealthy Umayyad *mawali* clients among the Syrians, Abd al-Rahman deposed al-Sumayl's pet governor within the year and forced all of the Arab factions to recognize him as the ruler of Al-Andalus. To consolidate his power he divided al-Sumayl's base by exploiting the divisions between the Yaman and Qays cliques that had so weakened the Umayyads in Syria. Abd al-Rahman then had the Syrian leader arrested and strangled in prison. He kept the *baladiyyun*, who resisted his demands for the one-fifth caliphal share of their revenues, in check by raising a new force of Umayyad loyalists, Berbers, and slave soldiers. The Umayyad prince then consolidated his power by subduing and fortifying the main Iberian cities.

Iberian Christians were initially bystanders to this second Umayyad occupation, but the land-hungry Syrians encroached on their estates, abrogating the earlier arrangements that the *baladiyyun* had made with elites such as Theodemir. Lacking sufficient land reserves to give the Syrians their own colonial holdings, the Andalusi governors revived the *foederati* system by settling the various Syrian *ajnad* on Christian estates and allotting them one-third of their revenues. Abd al-Rahman retained this arrangement, thereby placing the burden of supporting the Syrians on subject Iberians.

Abd al-Rahman thus established himself as an imperial ruler. Seeking a base from which to restore the fortunes of his family, he transformed Al-Andalus from a caliphal province into a hereditary Umayyad emirate. Initially, the term *emir* referred to an Arab provincial governor or general, but over time it became a title for an independent Muslim ruler. To common Iberians, who had endured imperial rule since Roman times, it must have seemed as though the Umayyad emirate was the same empire under new management. Following precedent, Abd al-Rahman and the succeeding Umayyad emirs retained many of the imperial institutions inherited from their predecessors. They relied on Visigothic law and legal officials in the rural areas, and employed non-Muslim magistrates, who most likely were holdovers from Roman times, to adjudicate urban cases that did not fall under Islamic law. Little, as far as the common Iberians were concerned, had changed.

The emirate's direct reach never extended very far into the countryside, but Abd al-Rahman ended the chaos of the "governors' era" by creating a more centralized administration. Shifting his capital to Córdoba, he established specialized departments for finance, justice, foreign relations, frontier defense, and the supervision of *dhimmi*. Viziers from loyal Umayyad client families ran these bureaus, but the Umayyads also employed Jews and Christians in specialized administrative and technical positions. As in most all premodern empires, their power base was largely urban. Abd al-Rahman and his heirs appointed provincial governors, but ultimately Al-Andalus was a feudal state. As such, the emirate needed powerful local elites to wage war, collect revenue, and extend its authority into the countryside. These vassals were a heterogeneous group that included *baladiyyun*, Syrians, Umayyad *mawali*, Berbers, and *muwallad* (Iberian converts). Abd al-Rahman I commanded their loyalty, but his weaker heirs often lost control.

It took the emir roughly two decades to establish his authority over the most productive southern regions of the peninsula. For a time, he fantasized about using Al-Andalus as a base to recapture the caliphate, but he eventually settled for dropping the Abbasid caliph's name from Friday prayers. The Abbasids, in turn, similarly schemed to retake their wayward province and, most likely hoping for a general uprising, sent a representative to reclaim the Iberian governorship. Abd al-Rahman returned this underling's head as a warning. Al-Andalus was thus permanently shorn from the caliphate. Like Roman Britain, it was originally one of the most remote territories of a wider empire. Yet none of the Umayyad governors or emirs were able to replicate Constantine's feat in using a power base on the periphery to claim, or in Abd al-Rahman's case recapture, the imperial metropole.

Instead, the slow pace of medieval travel and communication allowed the Andalusi emirs to set themselves up as independent rulers, a feat that eluded the Roman provincial governors.

Although Abd al-Rahman and his heirs never stopped hating the Abbasids, the emerging Christian kingdoms of northern Spain were a much more tangible threat. Neither the Romans nor the Visigoths had been able to control the people of the peninsula's northern mountainous regions fully. Christian chroniclers recorded that a minor Visigothic noble named Pelayo exploited this tradition of resistance by escaping north to found the Kingdom of Asturias. Pelayo is something of a mythical figure, but his successor and reputed son-in-law, Alfonso I, made himself known to the Umayyad emirs by raiding south into Muslim territory. Alfonso's heirs intermarried with the royal house of Pamplona/Navarre, thereby sowing the seeds of the Kingdom of Castile, which would reconquer the peninsula for Christianity in the fifteenth century.

From the hindsight of romantic nationalism and modern anti-Islamic phobia, the early northern kingdoms might appear as Christian bastions that valiantly held out against the Muslim invaders. In reality, Asturias and the other small northern kingdoms served a useful purpose by providing an opportunity to raid, loot, and establish jihadist credentials. The emirs rarely tried to seize Christian territory. Instead, they established a fortified frontier stretching from the Ebro River valley in the northeast to what is today northern Portugal in the west. Popularly known as the Thughr, or "front teeth," these borderlands consisted of small semi-independent fiefdoms ruled mostly by Berbers and *muwallad* converts. Interestingly, the Banu Qasi clan that controlled the Ebro Valley claimed descent from a Visigothic noble, Count Cassius. Musa ibn Forton, a member of this family who ruled from the city of Zaragoza in the late eighth century, married into the Pamplona royal family while remaining a vassal of the Umayyad emirs. Romantic nationalism aside, the lines between Christian and Muslim Iberia blurred markedly in the early medieval era.

This trend became more pronounced as direct Umayyad influence over Iberia declined after Abd al-Rahman I's death in 788. Struggles between his sons over succession brought a return to factionalism, and the emirate's military might waned as landed Arabs, the backbone of the Umayyad armed forces, gained the right to buy their way out of their obligation for military service. Moreover, the political unreliability of Syrian and Berber troops led the emirs to use slave soldiers as bodyguards and household troops. These foreign but more dependable forces were too expensive to be used in large numbers. The emirs therefore lost control over much of Al-Andalus to their own vassals. At its lowest point in the late ninth century the emirate had direct control over only Córdoba and its immediate suburbs, and Emir Abd Allah had to acknowledge Muslim warlords throughout the peninsula as local kings. The extended occupation of fortified hilltop settlements in the south suggests widespread rural unrest and implies that the emirate's extractive reach was also slipping.

Financial problems born of the relatively loose boundaries of subjecthood were at the root of this instability. Conversion to Islam by common Iberians reduced the emirate's revenues from the *jizya* (poll tax) and the *kharaj* (land tax). Muslims paid only the *zakat*, and perhaps the *kharaj* if they had acquired land from Christians. Although Al-Andalus recovered from the Mediterranean-wide recession following the collapse of the Roman Empire, the emirs did not have the power to tap the peninsula's commercial and agrarian wealth directly. Relying on irregular land taxes, military exemption payments, and licensing fees on frivolities such as falconry, they lost the resources to mint coins by the late ninth century.

The empty treasury forced the Umayyads to demand more taxes from all Iberians regardless of their religious status. Not surprisingly, a broad cross section of Andalusi society including Berbers, frontier warlords, Arab immigrants, *muwallad* converts, and, most likely, common Christians bitterly resisted this push for economic and administrative centralization. Iberian converts were an even bigger problem. Even though the *muwalladun* had embraced Islam, the Andalusis regarded them as second-class Muslims, a subordinate distinction that did not exist in the wider Islamic world. The taint of the *muwalladun*'s non-Islamic origins lingered, as "pure" Arabs openly derided them as inferior. Finding it easier to defend the boundaries of ethnicity than religion, the Andalusi elite made a science of genealogy to emphasize the pedigree of their Arab lineage, thereby suggesting that *muwalladun* were untrustworthy. Unlike the *mawali* of the larger caliphate, the Spanish *muwalladun* lacked patrons or sponsors to ease their absorption into the community of Muslims.

These tensions came to a head in the ninth century when systematic discrimination and the weakness of Umayyad regime inspired *muwallad* feudal elites to rebel. The *muwalladun* of Toledo, who were most likely descended from the old Visigothic aristocracy, staged a general uprising in 807 that Emir al-Hakam I crushed ruthlessly. Rural *muwallad* warlords proved much harder to deal with. Living on the rent and tribute of the rural peasantry, they were neither folk heroes nor popular anti-imperial nationalists. Rather, they were local power brokers from Iberian families that had converted to Islam to preserve their influence. Recognizing the waning power of Córdoba, they now calculated that they could safely defy the emirate.

Umar ibn Hafsun, who claimed descent from a Visigothic count, mounted the most serious challenge to Umayyad sovereignty. Operating from his fortified base at Bobastro in the Málaga Mountains, the *muwallad* warlord held sway over most of southern Iberia from 878 until his death from natural causes in 917. His forces failed to capture Córdoba, but the Umayyad military was equally incapable of dislodging him from his mountain stronghold. Putting military methods aside, Abd al-Rahman III finally captured Umar's fortress by exploiting divisions among his sons. His propagandists then sought to discredit the *muwallad* leader by claiming to have discovered that he had been buried as a Christian when they dug up his body to crucify him posthumously. There is no denying that the Hafsunid family had Christian support, but in actuality the great *fitna* (rebellion) by Umar and his fellow warlords was an attempt by rural elites to regain the autonomy they lost at the time of the Muslim conquest.

It fell to Abd al-Rahman III to revive the fortunes of the Umayyad line. The grandson of a princess of Navarre and the son of a Christian slave concubine, Abd al-Rahman was technically 75 percent Iberian. He reportedly had blue eyes, light skin, and reddish hair that he dyed black to appear more Arab. His grandfather, Emir Abdullah, chose him as his heir over a host of uncles and nephews with equally valid claims to power. Concerned with political challenges from his own offspring, the emir apparently concluded that he could trust the young man to wait to come into his political inheritance by natural means.

Taking power in 912 at the age of twenty-one, Abd al-Rahman III reorganized the emirate in a bid to reassert his authority over all of Al-Andalus. He expanded and reorganized its central bureaucracy and provincial administration, which enabled him to collect five and a half million silver dirhams per year. This was roughly eighteen times the annual income of his forebearer Abd al-Rahman I, and it provided the resources for an Umayyad military revival.[15] Warlords and petty kings who submitted retained a measure of authority, but those who resisted faced retribution at the hands of a new force consisting of Arab allies, Berbers, northern Christian mercenaries, and slave soldiers from North Africa, Europe, and sub-Saharan Africa.

Abd al-Rahman III explicitly used jihadist language to legitimize his campaigns against rebellious *muwallad* nobles, whom he accused of abandoning Islam to return to Christianity. Confident in his hold on power, in 929 he declared himself caliph of the entire Muslim world, in direct opposition to the Abbasids. His forebearers never made such a claim, but his was a less audacious move in an era when the Abbasids were mere figureheads in Baghdad and a rival Shi'a Fatimid caliphate already existed in North Africa. The declaration of an Umayyad caliphate in Al-Andalus meant very little in the wider world of Muslim politics, but it bolstered Abd al-Rahman's legitimacy at home.

The Iberian Christian kingdoms also gave the new regime a useful foil. Styling himself a champion of Islam, Abd al-Rahman resumed the raids on the north for slaves and booty. These continued until 939, when the caliph almost lost his life in an ambush. Apparently shaken by his brush with death, Abd al-Rahman shifted to extracting tribute and concessions from Christian rulers. He forced León and Navarre to acknowledge his suzerainty and restored his client Sancho the Fat to the Navarese throne.

As the greatest power in Iberia since Roman times, Abd al-Rahman III's caliphate presided over an impressive economic renewal. Rejoining the Mediterranean commercial world, Al-Andalus gained access to a broad array of useful crops, including rice, hard wheat, cotton, citrus fruits, bananas, spinach, and sugar cane, that Arab agronomists introduced into the Islamic heartland from Asia. Most of these plants required extensive irrigation for commercial production. Andalusi experts solved the problem by combining imported techniques with local Iberian irrigation practices dating from Roman times. The resulting agricultural boom raised living standards, fed the royal court, and stimulated regional commerce. In addition to exotic foodstuffs, the caliphate exported books, silks, textiles, and manufactures. Andalusis also reexported slaves and furs from western Europe in return for a variety of luxury goods ranging from Chinese porcelains to sub-Saharan gold. This rising prosperity helped the Iberian population grow from four million to ten million between the end of Visigothic rule in the early eighth century and Abd al-Rahman III's reign three hundred years later.[16]

The affluence of tenth-century Al-Andalus fueled a cultural renaissance that drew merchants and visitors from around the Mediterranean. Building on cross-cultural exchanges, Andalusis blended Hispano-Roman, Visigothic, Berber, and Arabic forms with the cultures of the wider Muslim world, which stretched to China, to create dynamic works of art, architecture, and literature. The Arab chronicler and geographer Muhammad Abu al-Qasim ibn Hawqal admiringly noted that Al-Andalus had no equal "in the whole of the Maghreb, or even in Upper Mesopotamia, Syria or Egypt, for the number of its inhabitants, its extent, the vast area taken up by markets, its cleanliness, the architecture of the mosques or the great number of baths and caravanserais."[17]

Iberian Christians could not help but be impressed by these achievements, and the northern kingdoms drew increasingly into Al-Andalus's economic and intellectual orbit. Overawed by the strength of Abd al-Rahman III's armies, many borrowed and adapted the material culture of the caliphate. More significant, subject Christians in Al-Andalus adapted to life under the Umayyads by learning Arabic and embracing Arab customs. Muslims referred to this sort of arabized Christian as a *musta'rab*, or "one who claims to be an Arab without being so." These Mozarabs played a central role in introducing Andalusi culture into the northern kingdoms. Additionally, Christian monks from the south used Cordoban geometric miniatures to decorate their manuscripts, which were often translations of Arab texts.

The achievements of tenth-century Al-Andalus were the culmination of three centuries of imperial Umayyad rule. Nevertheless, an empire's prosperity and longevity depends on its ability to extract wealth from its subjects, and the brilliance of the Andalusi caliphate ultimately rested on the exploitation of common Iberians. Like all premodern imperial regimes, the Umayyads relied heavily on coerced labor, and Musa and the succeeding governors almost certainly took slaves after their victory over the Visigoths. At the same time, most Umayyad subjects remained free Christians during the first two centuries of Muslim rule, which conveniently made them subject to higher revenue demands.

At the elite level, however, conversion did offer an escape from subjecthood. Just as romanization gave elite Britons a stake in the Roman imperial enterprise, embracing Islam allowed Hispano-Roman and Visigothic aristocrats to maintain their status under the caliphate. In effect, both romanization and islamization facilitated an alliance between imperial conquerors and local notables built on a shared project to extract rural wealth and exploit subject labor.

The Umayyads could not match the achievements of the Spanish conquistadors and later generations of imperial rulers because they had considerable difficulty maintaining the social boundaries of empire in Al-Andalus. The moral certainty of monotheistic religions such as Islam and Christianity legitimized the conquest and subjugation of nonbelievers, but the evangelical obligation of these proselytizing faiths created opportunities for conversion that blurred the line between citizen and subject. Although they portrayed themselves as devout Muslim rulers, the Andalusi Umayyads had strong economic incentives not to convert the common Iberians.

This implies that they were tyrannical imperial masters, but the actual fate of Iberian Christians under Muslim rule is far from certain. Nationalistic Spanish historians depict them as an oppressed majority that suffered for centuries until the northern Christian kingdoms liberated them. The historian Richard Bulliet offers a much different picture. Using genealogies in medieval Islamic biographical dictionaries, he estimated that the percentage of the Spanish population that was Muslim increased from 8 to 70 percent between the ninth and eleventh centuries.[18] This suggests that the bulk of the indigenous population either converted or emigrated to the Christian north.

Bulliet's precise figures are questionable because his genealogical data came primarily from elite families, and it is difficult to distinguish Iberian Muslims from Christians with Arab and Berber names. Nevertheless, it seems certain that the Muslim population of Iberia grew substantially under the caliphate. Cultural arabization facilitated conversion, but this was most likely a gradual process rather than a sharp jump from one identity to another. Indeed, the distinction between Christian and Muslim in al-Andalus was often imprecise. Conversion was most likely an urban phenomenon that had less of an impact on the much larger rural population. In the countryside, local elites probably blurred the boundaries between Christianity and Islam to protect their authority. In a society where Jews and Christians lived as cultural Arabs, it must have been difficult to determine precisely who was a Muslim.

This explains why the status of the subject majority under Umayyad rule remains one of the great unanswered questions in Spanish history. Nationalists depicted the Islamic period as a mere interruption in the organic development of modern Spain and insist that the Umayyads were an alien ruling class that had little influence on the wider population. According to this narrative, Al-Andalus's cultural achievements were due to domestic Spanish influences, and the Christian reconquest of Iberia, culminating in the fifteenth century, saved Europe from Islamic tyranny. The *muwalladun* were therefore never really Muslims or Arabs; they were simply forced converts who regained their Spanish identity when freed from the yoke of Muslim rule.[19]

Less chauvinistic and more romantic depictions of Spain's Muslim era portrayed it as a golden age of toleration when Jews, Christians, and Muslims cooperated in building a culturally and technologically advanced society. Central to this version of Andalusi history was the concept of *convivencia*, the cross-cultural borrowing that came from "living together" in harmony. The nineteenth-century American writer Washington Irving celebrated the romantic grandeur produced by *convivencia* in his *Tales of the Alhambra*. Later scholars seeking an antidote to contemporary xenophobic depictions of Islam emphasized that *convivencia* reintroduced the west to lost classical Greco-Roman writings that survived in caliphal libraries after the collapse of the Roman Empire.[20]

There is simply not enough historical evidence to reconcile these competing narratives. Most Arab accounts of the invasion in 711 dated from two to three centuries after the fact. These and later histories consisted primarily of institutionalized myths, family histories, and accounts of wars with the Christian north. They made almost no reference to the status or fate of the greater Iberian population. Spanish Christian sources were equally opaque. There are virtually no existing works by Andalusi Christian writers in Latin after the tenth century, and the earlier texts that have survived relate primarily to the arabized urban elite. Chronicles from the northern Christian kingdoms are propagandistic, contradictory, and incomplete.[21] Archaeology has the potential to fill some of these gaps, but most Iberian archaeologists focus on the Roman era.

Therefore, like Roman Britain, Muslim Spain was a relatively blank canvas for later historians to sketch out a past reflecting contemporary interests and biases. In reality, it is extremely difficult to determine the exact nature of Al-Andalus's subject majority. Visigothic and Roman nobles were a privileged elite at the time of the conquest, but it is virtually impossible to know how their rural subjects identified themselves. What is certain is that they were no more Spanish than the peoples of preconquest Roman Britain were Englishmen.

It is clear, however, that the Umayyads were most comfortable with Iberians who did not convert. Islamic law provided a clear blueprint for governing and exploiting *dhimmi*, in contrast to its relative vagueness on the thorny question of assimilating new Muslims. Thus, administrative expediency led the early emirate to assume that all Iberians were Christian. This allowed Andalusi officials to govern indirectly by transforming bishops and higher clergymen into Umayyad functionaries responsible for law and revenue collection in Christian communities. Hostigesis, the bishop of Málaga, actively assisted the late emirate in registering Christian peasants for taxation. By the tenth century, the Iberian Catholic Church had become so intertwined with the caliphate that Abd al-Rahman III had the authority to appoint bishops. Recemund, a Christian official in the royal court, earned the bishopric of Elvira as a reward for serving as the caliphal ambassador to a German prince. The Iberian church survived under Muslim rule by cooperating with the Umayyad regime, but the gradual disappearance of all but seven of its preconquest bishoprics by the eleventh century suggests that its primary constituency was shrinking.[22]

The church's steady eclipse does not appear to have been a particular hardship for non-Muslim Iberians. *Dhimmi* played important roles in the royal court throughout the Umayyad era. Christian bureaucrats served in virtually every ministry of the early emirate, and the emirs employed Christian doctors as their personal physicians. A Christian functionary named Rabi became so powerful (and unpopular) collecting taxes and overseeing al-Hakam I's palace guard that vindictive Cordobans murdered him upon the emir's death. Iberian Jews do not appear to have played as prominent a role in Al-Andalus until Abd al-Rahman III established the caliphate in the tenth century. Free to practice their religion more openly after the Visigothic demise, Jewish scholars such as Hasdai ibn Shaprut served the caliphs as doctors and diplomats.

These intimate ties with the centers of Andalusi authority gave Jews and Christians an incentive to adopt the trappings of Arab culture even if they resisted the temptation to convert to Islam. In this sense arabization rather than islamization was a key element in bringing elite non-Muslim Iberians into the Umayyad imperial system. The resulting Arab acculturation was most obvious in Córdoba and other urban centers where *dhimmi* lived in segregated neighborhoods but interacted regularly and closely with Muslims in the bureaucracy, markets, and public squares. Intermarriage with Muslims also grew increasingly common. By the ninth century, Umayyad Christian functionaries began to adopt Muslim styles of clothing, follow Islamic dietary laws, and translate Christian texts into Arabic. The popular use of high Latin and vernacular versions of the early Romance languages that would eventually evolve into Spanish waned in the south. This cultural backsliding caused the Cordoban scholar Paulus Alvarus to lament: "Alas, the Christians do not know their own law, and the Latins pay no attention to their own tongue, so that in the whole community of Christ there cannot be found one man in a thousand who can send letters of greeting properly expressed to his fellow."[23] These arabized Christians had no political ties to the northern kingdoms, which they tended to disdain as primitive and uncultured.

Yet their status as *dhimmi* limited their advance, and it is easy to see why many elite Christians eventually gave up their religion to seek greater social status. Qumis ibn Antonian, a high-ranking Cordoban civil servant under Muhammad I, converted because the emir would allow only a Muslim to serve as his chief minister. Qumis won the post after embracing Islam over the protests of Arab elites who claimed that the Abbasids would use his Iberian origins to humiliate the emirate. Conversions such as these were largely an urban phenomenon. Cities were centers of commerce, crafts, and administration and offered new Muslims the best chance of blending into the

Arab elite. Indeed, for a time many urban Andalusis may have been public Muslims and private Christians.

The blurred nature of imperial identities in the heterogeneous urban population of Al-Andalus alarmed both Muslim and Christian leaders. Mirroring concerns about the implications of conversion in the wider ninth-century Muslim world, religious scholars worried that Iberian converts influenced their fellow Muslims to adopt Christian cultural and dietary practices. Jurists of the Maliki legal school, which became the dominant form of Islamic jurisprudence in Al-Andalus, devoted themselves to rooting out these sinful innovations and equated heresy with political subversion. At all costs, they strove mightily to maintain the imperial boundaries that separated devout Muslims from their unbelieving subjects.

Christian leaders, who felt they were watching their community disappear before their eyes, were even more dismayed by these blurred identities. Drawing inspiration from the heroic martyrs of the late Roman era, a handful of scholars and Christian zealots in Córdoba began to publicly disparage Islam in the 850s. It is telling that they knew just what to say to enrage the Muslim clerical establishment. Seeking to force the Andalusi authorities to put him to death, Isaac de Tábanos, a civil servant and the son of a prominent Christian family, provoked a Muslim judge by publicly slandering those who followed Muhammad: "Such a man is full of the devil, is promoting devilish delusions, is handing out a cup of deadly poison, and will suffer the pains of eternal damnation."[24] The Muslim cleric attempted to defuse the situation by suggesting that only a drunkard or madman would be so self-destructively rash, but Isaac openly declared that he was sane and challenged the authorities to put him to death.

The Umayyads grudgingly obliged him, but the subversion continued when a prominent cleric named Eulogius publicized Isaac's defiance and sacrifice to inspire more martyrs. Between 850 and 857, the emirate executed forty-eight Cordobans for blasphemy or apostasy. Some were Christian zealots like Isaac, but others were the products of mixed marriages who were technically Muslims. Flora, who was raised a secret Christian by her mother after her Muslim father died, tried to run away to a monastery, but willingly accepted torture and death when her Muslim brother denounced her to the authorities.

The Cordoban martyrs were not anti-imperial revolutionaries. Rather, they sought to preserve their faith and identity by making Muslim rule less tolerable for Iberian Christians. They died horribly, but they succeeded in disrupting the elite alliances and compromises that held Andalusi society together. Faced with their inexcusable blasphemy, Abd al-Rahman II and his successor Muhammad I had to crack down by executing Eulogius, destroying new churches, dismissing Christian bureaucrats, and increasing taxes on non-Muslims.

The emirs also pressed the Andalusi bishops, who were equally horrified by the martyrdoms, to exercise greater discipline over their flock. The bishop of Córdoba went into hiding because he could not control the city's Christian community to the emirate's satisfaction, but in 854 a council of Christian nobles and clergymen had no choice but to denounce Isaac and his followers publicly as heretics. As Umayyad functionaries, they had little sympathy for this small group of fanatics who threatened their leadership of Christian Al-Andalus. The execution of Eulogius, who eventually became a Catholic saint, helped put an end to the organized martyrdoms in Córdoba. Even so, individuals continued to make fatal public expressions of their faith well into the tenth century despite the relatively easy option of emigrating to the Christian north.

Taken together, the ninth-century *muwallad* revolts and Christian martyrdoms demonstrate the precariousness of the imperial social boundaries defining citizen and subject in imperial Al-Andalus. While religion would appear to sharply define identity, the distinction between Christian and Muslim and between Iberian and invader blurred considerably under the Umayyads. Conversion and arabization were two of the most obvious forms of interaction, but conjugal relations and intermarriage between Muslim Arab men and Christian Iberian women introduced gender as a problematical marker of imperial identity. The Romans almost certainly established relationships with female Britons, but there is little direct historical or archaeological information about how these contacts fit into the larger processes of Roman imperialism. In contrast, documentary evidence makes it easier to tease out the implications of cross-cultural sex and marriage in Al-Andalus.

As in most empires, the conquerors of Iberia considered subject women a legitimate form of plunder. The initial phase of imperial domination under the early Arab caliphate produced clear guidelines on how Muslims could enslave or marry non-Muslim women. As *dhimmi*, Jewish and Christian females did not have an obligation to convert to Islam if they became the wives or concubines of Muslim men, but Islamic law dictated that their children had to be raised as free Muslims. The case of the Cordoban martyr Flora, however, suggests that the daughters of these unions were sometimes, perhaps often, secretly brought up as Christians. This implies that over time religion and imperial citizenship became gendered within the narrow confines of elite Andalusi families as sons identified themselves as Arabs and Muslims and daughters as Iberian and Christian.

Arab and Berber men may have subjugated Iberia politically and made Islam the dominant imperial ideology, but they were themselves assimilated into Iberian culture over succeeding generations through intimate relations with their female subjects. Iberian women introduced sons and daughters to their culture and taught them to speak local dialects. The most significant and influential of these children were the Umayyad rulers themselves. Although they proudly traced their lineage to Damascus, most members of the royal family were the sons of Christian mothers ranging in status from slave concubines to northern princesses. According to the Andalusi theologian and historian Ibn Hazm, all but one of the Andalusi caliphs had blond hair and blue eyes. By the ninth century, Muslim clerics worried openly about the contaminating influences of Christian wives. At the very least, they were free to eat pork and drink wine before they had sex with their Muslim husbands or nursed their Muslim children. More significant, they blurred the imperial social boundaries that enabled the Andalusi regime to extract wealth from its Iberian subjects.

Fortunately for the Umayyads, these cross-cultural social contacts were largely limited to city dwellers and nobles. Common rural Iberians, who interacted rarely with the Arab settlers, had far less incentive to follow the lead of their learned or urban counterparts in embracing Islam or adopting Arab cultural practices. The exploitive realities of medieval rule meant that, despite the Islamic legal protections for converts, those who did convert remained subject to tribute payments in the form of *jizya* and *kharaj* if they lived within reach of Umayyad tax collectors. By the ninth century, the Umayyads pretended that they ruled an entirely Muslim state, but it appears that relatively isolated agrarian and pastoral majorities continued to practice their version of Christianity quietly. This probably explains why Ibn Hawqal found the Iberian countryside to be still largely Christian in the mid-tenth century.

These realities did not prevent Abd al-Rahman III from making the Andalusi caliphate into a major political and economic influence in the western Mediterranean, but as was the case with his forebearer Abd al-Rahman I, his successors struggled to maintain his legacy. Following the death of his son al-Hakam II in 976, real power in the caliphate fell into the hands of a hereditary line of chamberlains who ruled through Abd al-Rahman's relatively impotent heirs. The most influential of these ministers was Muhammad ibn Abi Amir, who took the title al-Mansur, "the victorious," in celebration of his military accomplishments in the north. He copied the Quran by hand and expanded the grand mosque in Córdoba to establish his legitimacy, but his piety did not deter him from marrying a daughter of the king of Navarre. Their son Abd al-Rahman, who had the Christian nickname Sanchuelo, ended the power of the chamberlains in 1009 by rashly trying to depose the puppet Umayyad caliph. The resulting civil war, in which six different Umayyad princes tried to seize power, fatally weakened the caliphate and fragmented Al-Andalus.

This fratricidal struggle brought a final and decisive end to three centuries of Umayyad rule and produced more than sixty petty kingdoms run by *muwalladun*, Berbers, Arab elites, descendants of the chamberlains, and former slave soldiers. Lasting from 1031 to 1084, the *taifa* (faction/party) era saw the reemergence of local authority on the Iberian Peninsula. Ironically, it also marked the high point of Andalusi cultural achievement, as the various regional potentates became patrons of the arts and letters to burnish their royal credentials. The fragmentation of the caliphate into petty kingdoms also created opportunities for northern Christians. Fernando I united the kingdoms of León and Castile under a single crown, and his heirs recaptured the old Visigothic capital of Toledo. Flexing their military might, they exploited the conflicts between the *taifa* rulers and extracted tribute from Muslim clients. These payments became a significant revenue stream for the Christian kingdoms and a source of shame for the proud Islamic rulers of Al-Andalus.

The pendulum swung back in favor of the Muslims in the early eleventh century when Sinhaji Berbers invaded the peninsula. Known in Spanish history as the Almoravids, they followed charismatic Muslim clerics who preached a return to the purer form of Islam of the original *rashidun* caliphs. The Almoravids conquered Morocco in 1083 and crossed into Spain eight years later in response to a plea from a *taifa* ruler for help against the Christians. Their leader, Yusuf ibn Tashufin, reunited southern Al-Andalus but could not recapture Toledo. The Almoravids condemned the Andalusis for their decadence and weakness, but Yusuf's heir Ali himself became enamored with the rich court of life of medieval Iberia. Weakened by constant warfare with the north and revolts by Andalusi regional elites, the Almoravid regime collapsed with Ali's death in 1143. Once again, Al-Andalus broke into petty *taifa* states until a new and even more puritanical Berber movement known as the Almohads intervened four years later. For the next half century they governed southern Iberia as a province of their larger North African empire.

It is difficult to determine exactly how these developments affected non-Muslim Iberians. Interestingly, urban Christianity appears to have largely disappeared from what remained of Al-Andalus after the *taifa* era, and eleventh-century Arab historians made no further mention of Andalusi Christians. The Latin-based vernacular language, known to linguists as Romance, seems to have fallen out of use in the southern Iberian cities, and the *taifa* rulers relied largely on interpreters to communicate with non-Muslims. When King Alfonso VI of León conquered Toledo in 1085 his forces found that the population spoke only Arabic. Technically, practicing Christians required an established clergy to administer the baptismal rites to sustain a Christian identity over succeeding generations, but the church had largely disappeared from much of Al-Andalus by this period.[25]

The majority of Iberians still might have considered themselves believers, but it would have been difficult for them to remain formal Christians without the ministrations of the clergy. Moreover, archaeological evidence indicating the widespread use of North African cooking vessels and dinnerware suggests that much of the population followed the dietary and social practices of the wider Islamic world in the tenth century.[26] This does not necessarily mean that a majority of rural Iberians became Muslims. Local particularism was still more than strong enough in the medieval era that they may well have lived alongside Berber and Arab migrant communities while continuing to speak regional dialects of Romance among themselves and observe the Christian faith in their own way. Seeking to escape the tribute demands of the later caliphate, the *taifa* states, and the Berber invaders, rural communities may have disappeared from the historical record as they tried to ride out these difficult times by withdrawing deeper into their own local worlds. Consequently, they would have had little reason to revolt against "foreign" Muslim rulers.

It is likely that the majority of urban and aristocratic Mozarabs either converted to Islam, emigrated north, or retreated to the relative isolation of the countryside by the end of the *taifa* era. The Cordoban martyrdoms show that conversion had already begun to shrink the urban Christian community by the ninth century. This suggests that, as in the Roman Empire, there was a point where a sufficient percentage of the subject urban and aristocratic population merged into the dominant imperial elite that the original Arab conquerors lost control of their imperial state. Nonetheless, the prominent role of Jews and Christians as advisors, diplomats, merchants, artists, and men of letters during the caliphate demonstrates that some *dhimmi* remained in Al-Andalus until the Almoravid and Almohad purges. Indeed, they continued to play these roles for the *taifa* rulers.

Convivencia came to a conclusive end under Berber rule as the growing power of the northern kingdoms, coupled with the western European Crusades, introduced greater levels of mistrust and intolerance into Iberia. The rulers of the Christian north had never reconciled themselves to a Muslim presence on the peninsula, but this did not prevent them from intermarrying with the Umayyad royal family during the heyday of Al-Andalus. By the thirteenth century, however, northern chroniclers began to write about Muslims in increasingly uncompromising terms. The Almoravids, who were equally intolerant, responded to repeated northern attacks by declaring that the remaining Andalusi Christians were no longer entitled to protection as *dhimmi*. In the urban centers, this resulted in massacres, forced conversions, and mass flight to the north. The northern kings also contributed to the demise of Christian Al-Andalus by forcing the arabized Christian Mozarabs from "liberated" *taifa* states to emigrate to underpopulated regions in their own realms, thereby further demonstrating that people were the most valuable and exploitable imperial resource.

Technically, Al-Andalus lasted from 711 to 1492, but real Muslim power in Iberia ended with the demise of the Almohads in 1212. Weakened by new rivals in North Africa and Iberian revolts, the Almohads fell to a Vatican-brokered alliance of the kingdoms of León, Castile, Navarre, and Aragón. Their retreat to North Africa allowed the Christians to overrun all of Iberia except for a small Andalusi rump state known as the Emirate of Granada. Founded by Muhammad ibn Yusuf ibn Nasr, Granada was a weak federation of regional warlords that paid tribute to the Kingdom of Castile. In essence, Muhammad was a Castilian vassal who controlled only one-tenth of the original Al-Andalus. The emirate survived on Christian sufferance and because its mountainous borders were heavily fortified with watchtowers and castles.

The complete Christian "reconquest" of Iberia was a much longer and bloodier process than the lightning Arab-Berber invasion of 711. For a time, rulers such as Alfonso VI of León treated vanquished Muslim populations with relative tolerance. Upon capturing Toledo in 1085, he promised the city's Muslims that he would protect their property and religion. Crusading French monks and knights fighting alongside the Iberians sabotaged the accord by turning the main Toledan mosque into a church. Thereafter, massacres and mass enslavements by victorious Christian armies became the norm.

Like the Mozarabs, Iberian Muslims now faced the choice of oppression, conversion, or emigration. Most elites fled to North Africa after failed rebellions in the thirteenth century, and those who stayed behind were mostly urban artisans and peasant farmers. These Mudejars, whose name came from the Arabic *mudajjan*, "those who remain," were quite similar to the Mozarabs. Like their Christian counterparts, most spoke the language of their rulers rather than Arabic. But unlike the *dhimmi* under the caliphate, they had no legal standing or protection. They lived in segregated neighborhoods and faced torture and death for proselytizing or having sexual relations with Christian women. There was no Christian version of *convivencia*.

The increasingly precarious position of the Mudejars in the fourteenth century reflected the importance of Christianity as a legitimizing ideology for the conquest of the Iberian Peninsula. Queen Isabella of Castile and King Ferdinand of Aragón, whose marriage brought political unity to the northern kingdoms, were self-declared Catholic monarchs. Their final invasion of Granada in 1492 was a papally sanctioned Crusade that provided a moral basis for their creation of a single Spanish crown. Those Jews and Muslims who remained after the completion of the Reconquista had to convert, emigrate, or practice their faith in secret to escape the persecution of the Inquisition. The resurgent Spanish church was far more jealous and mistrustful of rivals than its Visigothic forebearer, which had learned to coexist with Umayyad rule.

Nationalist Spanish historiography tends to downplay the brutality of these times in celebrating the reemergence of the "true" Roman and Christian Spain after centuries of oppressive Muslim rule. It seems much more likely that the Reconquista was the culmination of another cultural realignment by Iberian elites who once again adapted to the changing realities of imperial rule by gradually shifting their identity. This time, however, the aggressive and intolerant strain of Christianity that legitimized the Reconquista made it virtually impossible for the remaining Muslim elites to follow the example of the Roman and Visigothic aristocracies in coming to terms with the new conquering power. Although they were not yet national, European identities were becoming much more rigid at the dawn of the early modern era.

At first glance, the original Arab caliphate and the Umayyad emirate/caliphate in Spain might not seem to fit conventional definitions of empire. Yet there is no denying the fundamental imperial character of both versions of the caliphate. They arose through military victories that transformed alien peoples into subjects who in the immediate postconquest era suffered enslavement, discrimination, and exploitation as a consequence of their inferior status. The Arabs ruled these subject majorities indirectly, a tactic they learned from their imperial Roman, Byzantine, and Sassanid predecessors. Although these conquests brought them tremendous power, Muslims also worried that the wealth and cross-cultural intimacies of imperial rule would bring corruption and social contamination. These anxieties beset all empire builders.

The Arab caliphate was relatively unstable and short-lived compared to other ancient and medieval empires. Initially, it held an advantage over Rome in having Islam as a powerful legitimizing engine of empire. While the Romans were self-confident, the first Muslim armies were absolutely certain that God sanctioned and facilitated their victories over nonbelievers. Yet Islam's clear and powerful obligation on all Muslims to proselytize complicated, and ultimately undermined, the rigid social boundaries required for sustained imperial extraction. Although the *mawali* converts suffered institutionalized discrimination by the original Muslim Arabs, they became equal partners in the imperial project within a few centuries. Conversion thus became a means of escaping subjecthood. The Abbasid revolution had complex origins and consequences, but the *mawali*'s central role in overthrowing the Umayyad regime meant that once-subject peoples had captured the empire. Although historians do not generally write of the later Roman Empire in this fashion, it seems likely that Roman empire builders suffered a similar fate. Conversely, the realities of indirect imperial rule led the Arabs to adopt and assimilate the cultural values of their subjects much more extensively than their Roman predecessors. This was romanization in reverse.

The Umayyad regime in Iberia embodied the same strengths and weaknesses as the original imperial caliphate. As a peripheral offshoot of a sprawling transcontinental empire, Al-Andalus was a far more manageable imperial unit. The Romans had already done the heavy lifting of setting up the extractive systems of empire, and the Visigoths had begun the process of adapting these institutions to the medieval era. It was therefore a relatively simple matter for the Umayyads to take up where the earlier empire builders had left off. But the caliphal imperial systems that initially proved effective in colonizing and reordering imperial Al-Andalus also floundered over the thorny question of subjecthood. Islamic evangelicalism helped win over Iberian notables by allowing them to retain their status and wealth through conversion, but the *muwallad* revolts of the ninth century represented, at least in part, an attempt by these elites to recapture their political power within an Islamic context. More significant, the cross-cultural exchanges that were at the heart of *convivencia* were profoundly incompatible with imperial rule.

In blurring the political, religious, social, and gendered boundaries between citizen and subject, *convivencia* essentially turned the Umayyads into Iberians. Abd al-Rahman I, the founder of the dynasty, was the son of a Berber woman, and his heirs had no qualms about having sex with Iberians to father their successors. Abd al-Rahman III's caliphate dominated the peninsula, but it was very much a hybrid Iberian institution that probably would have seemed quite alien and upsetting to the original *baladiyyun* Arab settlers. Just as romanization allowed subject communities to create new conceptions of Romanness, islamization in Al-Andalus gave Iberians the opportunity to redefine what it meant to be a Muslim and an Arab. The Andalusi Umayyads' inability to maintain sufficient distance from their subjects ultimately cost them their privileged imperial identity. They may have built an empire, but they failed as colonists. Cut off from the Arab heartland, they eventually became Iberians.

Later generations of Spaniards told the story of Roderic and Hercules's Tower to explain how their ancestors had suffered the indignity of becoming imperial subjects. Yet the majority of rural Iberians did not need to become Muslims. Their overlords may have shifted from Christianity to Islam and then back again, but the rural population escaped the full weight of imperial oppression because medieval empires were relatively weak.

Centuries later, the peoples of the Andean highlands invented a fable strikingly similar to the myth of the tower to explain how they had fallen victim to a much more invasive and pernicious form of imperial rule. They told the story of how the Inka emperor Wayna Qhapaq had called the conquistador descendants of the Visigoths down on them by rashly opening a box brought to him by a mysterious messenger in a black cloak. Like Roderic, he could not contain his curiosity, and opened the box to find that it contained butterflies and moths that scattered throughout the land. Clearly inspired by the Greek story of Pandora that came to the Andes with the Spaniards, the insects were "the pestilence of measles, and within two days...many [Inka] captains died, all their faces covered with scabs."[27] Faced with devastating epidemics, the collapse of Inkan power, and merciless invaders, the Andeans used this millenarian story to explain how imperial conquest had turned their world upside down.

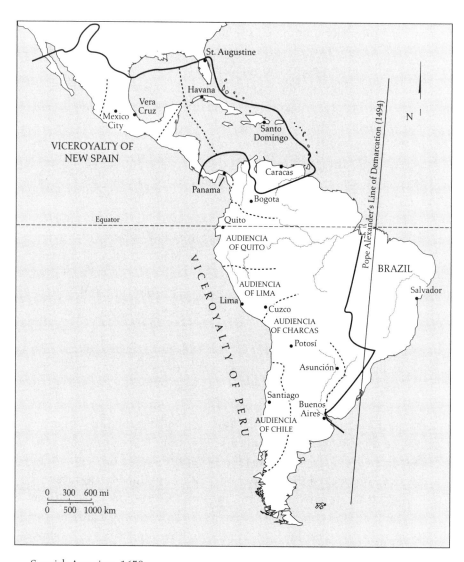

Spanish Americas, 1650

3

SPANISH PERU

Empire by Franchise

It is tempting to imagine what the Inka ruler Atawallpa was thinking as the Spanish friar Vicente de Valverde approached him, Bible in hand, on November 16, 1532. Seated high on a litter borne by his most senior nobles in the plaza of the Andean city of Cajamarca, the Sapa Inka (emperor) looked down on a delegation of foreigners. Through his interpreter Felipillo, Valverde was to speak for a small band of conquistadors who had landed on the coast two years earlier.

Atawallpa probably considered the Spaniards to be impertinent, exotic, and potentially dangerous; his spies had kept him fully aware of their activities as they made their way into the central Andes. As the Sapa Inka, Atawallpa ruled an empire encompassing almost one thousand square miles and approximately ten million subjects.[1] He had an army of at least one hundred thousand men, so it is unlikely that he considered the band of fewer than two hundred "barbarians" much of a risk. True, the Sapa Inka's advisors and generals were troubled by reports of new weapons and horses, but Atawallpa had far more serious concerns. Having just vanquished his half-brother Waskar in a brutal civil war, his main concern was to consolidate power and wrest the Inkan capital of Cuzco from his mutinous sibling. The strangers, who had left themselves dangerously exposed by rashly blundering into the heart of the Inkan Empire, could now be easily dealt with.

Although Atawallpa's priorities were entirely understandable, he should have taken the Spaniards more seriously. Led by Francisco Pizarro, the barely literate illegitimate son of a Spanish nobleman,

111

the conquistadors were a rapacious band of fortune seekers. Far from being professional soldiers, they were armed speculators who won royal sanction by promising to spread Christianity and carve out a New World empire for the Spanish Crown. Above all, these relatively common men sought to become rich enough to join the ranks of the lower nobility.

Initially, Pizarro and his partner, Diego de Almagro, struggled to find sufficiently lootable prizes along the Pacific coast of Central and South America. Their fortunes changed in 1528 when their ally Bartolomé Ruiz captured a raft carrying gold and silver jewelry, gems, and finely woven cloth. Drawn by the strong whiff of treasure, Ruiz continued southward until he found an Inkan outpost at Tumbez. Pizarro used Ruiz's booty to convince Charles V to grant him a *capit-ulación*, an imperial contract giving him the authority to conquer the Andean highlands as a knight, captain general, and, ultimately, royal governor of the new lands that came to be called Peru.[2] Almagro was to be the commandant of Tumbez with the promise of a governorship over the as yet undiscovered regions lying beyond Pizarro's realm. In return, the Spaniards promised the Crown that they would civilize the Andeans by turning them into Christians.

Armed with this royal sanction, Pizarro claimed the right to lead the expedition to Peru, which included his half-brothers Hernando, Juan, and Gonzalo, while Almagro raised reinforcements. His troop of approximately two hundred conquistadors and thirty horses reached Tumbez in 1531. When Ruiz first encountered the city three years earlier it had been secure and prosperous under the rule of Atawall-pa's father, Wayna Qhapaq. Since then, the Sapa Inka's death from what was most likely smallpox or measles had plunged the empire into a civil war between his sons so widespread in its devastation that the Pizarrists found Tumbez in ruins. Relying on captured transla-tors, they learned that the Inkas were precariously divided. Local people also warned that Atawallpa was brutal and ruthless, but the conquistadors' relatively easy victories over Inka vassals on the coast gave them the confidence to push inland.

It took Pizarro two years to reach the plaza at Cajamarca. As the conquistadors plundered their way into the highlands they learned that common Andeans had no love for their imperial rulers. Although the Spaniards did not know it, the Inka Empire was little more than a century old. It was still in the process of assimilating the recently conquered peripheral territories that the Pizarrists encountered on their inward march. Pizarro made alliances with these restive Inkan subjects as he grew more conversant in Andean politics. But he also covered his bets by sending a message to Atawallpa offering Spanish military support in the war with the Sapa Inka's brother Waskar. Atawallpa in turn granted Pizarro an audience, and the two leaders exchanged gifts through their intermediaries.

Not surprisingly, the Inkas and Spaniards both secretly prepared for a military confrontation. Plotting to entrap the conquistadors, Atawallpa bragged that he would sacrifice some of the Pizarrists to the sun god and turn the survivors into eunuchs to serve the women of his court. The nobles who attended him in the plaza concealed weapons and armor under their clothes, and a force of twelve thousand men stood at the ready throughout the town. If these forces somehow proved insufficient to deal with 62 Spanish horsemen and 106 foot soldiers, Atawallpa's seventy-thousand-man army was camped nearby.

Pizarro and his men realized the precariousness of their situation. They gambled that horses, armor, guns, military experience, and sheer ruthlessness would compensate for their lack of manpower if they could convince Atawallpa to meet them in the narrow confines of the plaza. On open ground, the Inkas would overwhelm them. Pizarro therefore sent a delegation of horsemen under Hernando de Soto to goad the Sapa Inka into granting them an audience in the town. De Soto and his men found Atawallpa sitting on a stool. Defiantly, they brought their horses so close that the animals' breath disturbed the fringe of gold and feathers that was his imperial crown. Confident in his power and unwilling to hesitate before the barbarians, Atawallpa barely blinked and agreed to meet the Spanish in the plaza the following day.

This is how Friar Vicente came to meet Atawallpa. Accompanied by Felipillo, one of the Pizarrists' kidnapped translators, his job was to fulfill the conquistador's obligations under the *capitulación* by offering to instruct the Sapa Inka in Christianity. Oblivious to this legal fig leaf, Atawallpa demanded that the Spanish return the treasure and captives they had looted on their way to Cajamarca, and he angrily flung the friar's Bible aside. This was the signal for the Spaniards to attack. Hidden about the square, the horsemen charged, yelling, "Santiago, Santiago!" while their gunmen opened fire on the massed

Andeans. Pizarro and his guard swiftly captured Atawallpa, hacking off the arms and hands of the aristocrats holding his litter above the fray. Panicked and demoralized, the Sapa Inka's troops broke down a plaza wall and trampled each other in a desperate bid to escape the carnage. Spanish chroniclers estimated that the Pizarrists slaughtered approximately six thousand to seven thousand of them, including key Inka nobles, generals, and administrators.[3]

Despite his victory, Pizarro knew full well that the massed Inkan army was camped nearby. Seeking to buy time until Almagro and his reinforcements arrived from the coast, he tried to consol Atawallpa: "You should consider it to be your good fortune that you have not been defeated by a cruel people, such as you are yourselves, who grant life to none. We treat our prisoners and conquered enemies with kindness, and only make war on those who attack us, and, being able to destroy them, we refrain from doing so, but rather pardon them."[4] The Sapa Inka in turn calculated that he could crush the Spaniards if he escaped their clutches. He therefore proposed to buy his freedom with a ransom of gold, silver, gems, and jewelry, enough to fill a 3,366-cubic-foot room in the palace. This was wealth beyond Pizarro's wildest dreams, and he settled down in Cajamarca for the eight months it took Atawallpa's followers to gather the treasure.

The conquistador captain spent this time learning about Inka politics and teaching Atawallpa how to play chess. Secure in the knowledge that the Sapa Inka had ordered the Andeans to cooperate, he sent out bands of men to loot cities and shrines throughout the Andes. More significantly, he exploited divisions in Inkan society by courting subject Andean communities and making overtures to Waskar, whom Atawallpa's men held prisoner in Cuzco. Waskar recognized that Cajamarca had rendered the civil war moot and offered to double his brother's ransom if the Spanish backed him instead. Atawallpa found this intolerable and ordered his men to drown his rival before he could conclude an alliance with the invaders.

Yet Atawallpa's days also became numbered as the room in Cajamarca slowly filled with plunder. By mid-1533, the ransom amounted to thirteen thousand pounds of gold and twenty-six thousand pounds of silver, much of it melted down into ingots from priceless works of decorative and ceremonial art. Shared out among the conquistadors, it came to forty-five pounds of gold and ninety pounds of silver per man. Horsemen received larger shares than foot soldiers, and one-fifth of the treasure, which equaled 262,259 pesos, went to the Spanish Crown. Pizarro ruled that Almagro and his contingent of 150 men, who arrived late on the scene, were not eligible for a full share, a decision that eventually would lead the conquistadors to turn on each other.[5]

This windfall had an immediate and corrupting impact on the Spaniards. Suddenly rich and powerful, men from humble backgrounds spent their time gambling, fighting, and preying upon Inkan noblewomen. Having paid his ransom, Atawallpa now became a liability. Pizarro knew full well that the Sapa Inka would seek retribution once free, and cynically condemned Atawallpa to death by garroting for the murder of his royal brother Waskar. The Sapa Inka accepted baptism before his execution on August 29, 1533, thereby earning a full Christian burial. Pizarro appointed a seemingly compliant prince named Manqu to be the new Sapa Inka.

Most Spanish chroniclers depicted the Pizarrists as daring heroes who single-handedly overthrew a mighty heathen tyrant, but in reality they hijacked one of the great empires of the New World by exploiting the deep rifts in the Inkan Empire. Although the conquistadors' guns, horses, and armor gave them a tactical advantage, these military innovations would have not amounted to much if they had encountered the Inkas at the height of their power. Old World epidemics of smallpox, measles, and influenza preceded the Pizarrists into the highlands and indirectly touched off the civil war by killing Atawallpa's father, Wayna Qhapaq. Many of Atawallpa's rivals in this fratricidal struggle joined Pizarro as foot soldiers after the carnage at Cajamarca decapitated the Inkan imperial government. Understandably, the Inkas' newly conquered subjects also viewed Atawallpa's downfall as potentially liberating and many threw in with the Spaniards. Where Claudius and Tariq ibn Ziyad needed thousands of seasoned soldiers to conquer Britain and Spain, in the early modern era Pizarro demonstrated that it was possible to build an empire with only a handful of followers if audacious imperial entrepreneurs could exploit divisions in a conquered society. In effect, the conquistadors enlisted New World peoples in their own subjugation.

Peru became a domain of the Spanish Crown, but in the immediate decades after Pizarro's coup at Cajamarca it was essentially a private imperial state. Rarely, if ever, had such a small group of marauders been able to lay their hands on the levers of imperial exploitation for such an extended period. The conquistadors' capture of the Inkan state led to an orgy of looting and naked exploitation that probably would have seemed extreme to even the most hardened ancient and medieval empire builders. Claudius and Tariq certainly plundered and enslaved vanquished Britons and Iberians. But they lacked the means, and perhaps even the will, to match the ruthless tactics that the Pizarrists used to wring wealth out of subject Andeans. While the *capitulación* gave the conquistadors' empire a veneer of royal and Christian legitimacy, Pizarro and his men viewed the Andeans as a disposable resource and raised imperial extraction to new heights of brutality.

The conquistadors had almost total freedom to do as they pleased in the New World because they were free from royal supervision. The marriage of Isabella and Ferdinand brought most of the Iberian Peninsula together by joining the kingdoms of Castile and Aragón. Through matrimony, inheritance, and dynastic alliance their grandson Charles became the ruler of Spain and Habsburg Austria. Elected Holy Roman Emperor in 1520, his realm was so large and powerful that contemporary European observers assumed that it would eventually encompass the entire world. Of this, the Americas were only a secondary concern for Charles. He profited from his share of the conquistadors' plunder, but the limits of transatlantic travel and communication kept his focus on Europe. Although Columbus's discoveries allowed Spanish monarchs to burnish their Catholic credentials through state-sanctioned evangelism in a hemisphere that had never encountered Islam, they initially had no more direct control over their American possessions than the Umayyad caliphs had over Al-Andalus.

Unlike their Muslim predecessors, the Spanish Habsburgs eventually exercised more direct control over their empire. But during the heyday of the conquistadors in the early sixteenth century they practiced empire by franchise. The Crown delegated the exploration, conquest, and exploitation of the New World to private imperial contractors such as Pizarro. These reckless adventurers were the heirs of the Christian warlords and military orders who had taken Iberia from the Muslims. Backed by the Castilian Crown, zealous nobles (*hidalgos*) won plunder and landed estates in Al-Andalus through their exploits on the battlefield. The New World conquistadors had much more common origins, but they also pursued noble status by winning new lands for Christendom. In this sense they were not unlike the Muslim fighters who built the original Arab caliphate.

As with Islam, Christianity also had the capacity to provide a powerful moral justification for empire. In 1493, Pope Alexander VI granted the Spanish Crown the exclusive right to all land in the New World beyond an arbitrary north-south line drawn 370 leagues west of the Cape Verde Islands. The Spanish thus had the right to wage a "just war" against resisting New World peoples who rejected the Pope's commandment. Although he probably never believed that he could convert Atawallpa to Christianity, Vicente de Valverde's seemingly nonsensical pantomime at Cajamarca served the very important purpose of giving the Pizarrists a legitimate right to use violence against the Inkas.

Upon encountering New World peoples, representatives of the Crown read out a formal statement, in Spanish, declaring that the Pope had given their lands to Spain. Drafted in 1510 by the Council of Castile, this *requerimiento* (requirement) warned resistors:

> With the help of God, we shall powerfully enter into your country, and shall make war against you...and shall subject you to the yoke and obedience of the Church and of their [Spanish] Highnesses; we shall take you and your wives and your children, and shall make slaves of them, and as such shall sell and dispose of them as their Highnesses may command; and we shall take away your goods, and shall do you all the mischief and damage that we can.

The pronouncement concluded with a breathtakingly hypocritical addendum: "We protest that the deaths and losses which shall accrue from this are your fault, and not that of their Highnesses, or ours."[6] Valverde most likely did not actually read out this statement to Atawallpa, but the Inka lord's violent rejection of his Bible gave the Pizarrists the right to act as if he had formally defied the *requerimiento*.

To the Spanish, indigenous Americans who rejected Christianity were degenerate heathens who needed to be saved from damnation by force. Stateless peoples were sinful enough, but the Inkas were depraved tyrants who preyed on their Andean subjects. In other words, they were guilty of empire building. Explicitly imagining themselves as the heirs of ancient Rome, the Spanish believed that these "barbarians" could be "civilized" through imperial domination. Charles's son

Philip II ordered Spanish officials to teach the defeated Amerindians to be western: "Have them dress and wear shoes and let them have many other good things heretofore prohibited to them.... Give them the use of bread, wine, oil, and other foodstuffs, cloth, silk, linen, horses, cattle, tools, arms and all the rest that Spain has had."[7] While these seemed generous instructions, the Spanish jurist and entrepreneur Juan de Matienzo was more frank in describing the real cost of these "good things": "We give them religious instruction, we teach them to live like men, and they give us silver, gold or things [of] worth."[8]

The Andeans paid a terrible price for Spain's imperial lessons. Ancient and medieval empire builders exploited their subjects on the grounds that they were alien barbarians, but they also gave at least some of them an opportunity to escape subjecthood through romanization, islamicization, and other forms of cultural assimilation. Atawallpa undoubtedly looked upon Pizarro as a barbarian, but the Spaniards' victory at Cajamarca demonstrated that the real measure of civilization in an imperial context was military supremacy. As imperial conquerors themselves, the Inkas were confident in their superiority over their own Andean subjects, but their loss to the Pizarrists now made them the barbarians. Times were changing, and Spanish rule in the Americas was shaped in part by a larger ideological shift taking place in Europe that deemed nonwesterners and non-Christians inherently and irrevocably inferior regardless of whether they were nobles or common subjects.

Philip's paternalistic order to uplift his Amerindian subjects obscured the reality that early modern subjecthood entailed a higher magnitude of dehumanizingly ruthless exploitation. Most of the laborers and peasants in sixteenth-century Iberia were barely free themselves, but in the Andes new subordinate imperial identities justified unprecedented levels of systematic plunder, sexual exploitation, and permanent servitude. We know little about how Britons and Iberians felt about becoming imperial subjects, but the chronicler Don Felipe Huamán Poma de Ayala, a direct descendant of Inkan nobles, complained bitterly to Philip about the hypocrisy of Spanish rule in the Andes.

> Just imagine, Your Majesty, being an Indian in your own country and being loaded up as if you were a horse, or driven along by a succession of blows from a stick. Imagine being called a dirty dog or a pig or a

goat....What would you and your Spanish compatriots do in these circumstances? My own belief is that you would eat your tormentors alive and thoroughly enjoy the experience.[9]

In the new overseas empire, Andeans such as Don Felipe were now inferior to Spaniards of all classes, regardless of their status or nobility. Later generations of nationalist historians protested that these negative depictions of Spanish rule were a "black legend" concocted by jealous French- and Englishmen, but there was no denying that the conquistadors destroyed the culture and civilization of the Andes in their unrelenting quest for treasure.

Although they were still deciding exactly what it meant to be Spanish, sixteenth-century Spaniards codified this new meaning of empire by creating the world's first truly global imperial state. Building on advances in maritime technology pioneered by the Portuguese, they explored and conquered vast territories in the Americas and Asia. For the first time, the constraints of travel and communication no longer limited empires to a single continental land mass. By the end of the sixteenth century, the Spanish Crown ruled over lands stretching from the Americas to the Philippines, in addition to most of western and central Europe. Yet this was a highly decentralized conglomerate empire built through European dynastic alliances, franchised New World conquests, and armed trade in Asia. Its global scope was impressive and unprecedented, but it was ungovernable by direct means. Near constant warfare in Europe and glacially slow transoceanic communication forced the Spanish Crown to delegate considerable authority to its representatives overseas. In the Americas, this autonomy created lucrative opportunities for privately funded empire builders such as Pizarro, while leaving New World communities at their mercy.

Spain's imperial project sprang from the Iberian experience of Muslim rule and the centuries of warfare resulting from the "reconquest" of most of the peninsula by the Kingdom of Castile. Beginning as one of the many small states on the northern periphery of Al-Andalus in the ninth century, Castile gradually became the dominant Christian power in Iberia after the fall of the Andalusi Umayyad caliphate. By the mid-fifteenth century, the Iberian Peninsula consisted of four primary states: Muslim Granada and the kingdoms of Castile, Aragón, and Portugal. In 1469, Isabella, who won the Castil-

ian throne in a civil war, married Ferdinand of Aragón, thereby creating the framework of modern Spain.

The marriage did not produce a single state. Castile consisted primarily of the less productive northern highlands and the new territories
wrested from the Muslims. Its knights drove the Reconquista because
they had few alternatives to conquest and plunder. It was no accident that Pizarro and many of his fellow conquistadors came from
Extremadura, the poor Castilian frontier region that was once western Al-Andalus. Aragón, by comparison, was a commercially focused
kingdom. Ferdinand was essentially a constitutional monarch who
deferred to representative assemblies in his various realms, while
Isabella's Castile was an emerging absolutist state. Although they
ruled together as Catholic sovereigns, they did not have a common
economy or army.

Under Isabella, Castile was a Catholic state that had no room for
non-Christians, and after Granada's fall in 1492 she looked for further crusading opportunities in North Africa and the Canary Islands.
The Reconquista thus provided the template for Spanish conquests in
the Americas. The rulers of Castile created the precedent for conquistadorism by granting Christian knights and military religious orders
extensive estates carved out of captured Andalusi territory. Warfare
logically became an avenue to gentlemanly status if not outright
ennoblement. Most of the Pizarrists had ordinary backgrounds, but
they sought hidalgo status by replicating the feats of the Reconquista
in the New World. Indeed, the conquistadors often equated Andeans
with Muslims.

Although they were the primary agents of Spanish empire building in the Americas, the conquistadors were largely peripheral to
the main Spanish imperial project, which remained firmly grounded
in Europe. Aragón's claim to the crowns of Sicily and Naples made
Ferdinand and Isabella Italian rulers, which drew them further into
European dynastic politics. Their daughter Juana married the son
of the Austrian Holy Roman Emperor, and in 1519 their grandson
Charles came into a great European empire by inheriting the crowns
of the Spanish kingdoms and Habsburg Austria. Disorder in the German lands led Charles to surrender the Austrian crown to his brother
Ferdinand, but as King Charles I of Spain and Emperor Charles V
of the Holy Roman Empire, he became the most powerful ruler in
Europe. His son Philip II, whose reign from 1556 to 1598 marked the

heyday of the Habsburg Spanish Empire, ruled over Spain, Portugal, much of Italy, and what came to be called the Spanish Netherlands.

Under the Habsburgs, Spain never achieved the unqualified military supremacy that drove the empire building of its ancient and medieval predecessors. Nor was it really an empire on the Roman or Umayyad model. In fact, Charles and Philip fought incessant wars to defend rather than expand their European holdings. Most early modern European rulers waged war in the name of religion rather than nationalism, and as committed Catholics, the Spanish Habsburgs became embroiled in enervating and seemingly endless conflicts in central Europe. Issues of sovereignty, trade, and taxation took on bitter religious dimensions as princes and rebels in Germany and the Netherlands embraced militant Protestantism to legitimize their opposition to Habsburg imperial rule. Finally, the burden of defending Christian Europe from Ottoman imperial expansion also fell on the Habsburgs.

It is therefore hardly surprising that the Spanish emperors paid relatively little attention to the overseas possessions that the conquistadors dropped in their laps. Ferdinand and Isabella never explicitly intended to acquire a global empire, but Pope Alexander's 1493 bull granting Spain primary title to the New World certainly encouraged them. Distracted by events in Europe, they continued the traditions of the Reconquista by granting speculators a franchise in the form of a *capitulación* to conquer new territories in their name. Like the Umayyad caliphs, they demanded one-fifth of the spoils in return.

The conquistadors themselves were mostly young, unmarried, marginal men with little military experience. In securing the license from the Crown that raised them to the status of captain general, the leaders of the conquistador bands and their backers assumed total responsibility for financing and organizing their speculative adventures. They were, in essence, amateurs who gambled their lives and meager savings in a desperate bid to wring enough wealth from the New World to become respectable Spanish gentlemen. Hernán Cortés, the conqueror of the Aztec Empire, famously remarked that he "came [to the New World] to get rich, not to till the soil like a peasant."[10] The conquistadors' appetite for treasure was so insatiable that the Inkas believed they ate gold, but if a region lacked precious metals or centralized states worth pillaging, the Spaniards turned to slave raiding. They usually ignored metropolitan authority despite enthusiastic declarations of loyalty to the Crown, and a leader's control over his men rested almost entirely on his ability to feed their limitless craving for plunder. Many of these desperate fortune hunters lost their lives to war or disease, while others slunk home penniless. This explains why there never were enough men to fill out the conquistador bands, and so the Spaniards often augmented their forces with mercenaries, Africans, and local auxiliaries. At the same time, Francisco Pizarro's share of Atawallpa's ransom came to 57,220 gold and 2,350 silver pesos, thereby demonstrating that the rewards of successful conquistadorism were truly prodigious.[11]

As a Genoese, Christopher Columbus was not a conquistador in the strictest sense, but Queen Isabella, who partially bankrolled his attempt to discover new sea routes to Asia, granted him a *capitulación*. As a governor, captain general, and admiral, he was entitled to a share of the commerce and plunder of the New World, but the miserable pickings on the island of Hispaniola, where he established a base after first making landfall in the Bahamas, led his men to revolt. The Arawak peoples who inhabited most of the islands in the Caribbean had an agricultural economy that produced little in the way of lootable treasure. Following the template of the Romans and Umayyads, the Spaniards soon realized that the real wealth of the West Indies lay in the Arawak themselves. Spanish settlers on Hispaniola raided them for slaves, and Columbus and succeeding governors rewarded their restless followers with rights to the labor of entire Arawak communities.

By the early sixteenth century, Hispaniola was the seat of Spanish power in the New World and a base for conquistador operations. Spreading like a virus in all directions, they conquered Puerto Rico, Jamaica, and Cuba and gained footholds in Florida and Panama within the first two decades of the century. From the Panamanian colony at Darien, Vasco Núñez de Balboa scoured the Pacific coast of Central and South America for treasure.

The conquests born of these early explorations produced relatively modest returns. The real prize lay in central Mexico. Building on centuries of imperial rule in the region by the Toltecs and other groups in the Valley of Mexico, Nahuatl-speaking invaders from the north founded the Aztec Empire in the thirteenth century. The Aztecs ruled over hundreds of smaller client states and were expanding into Guatemala and the coastal regions of the Gulf of Mexico when the

Spanish first arrived in the Caribbean. With approximately ten million to fifteen million subjects, they were enormously wealthy and seemingly impregnable in Tenochtitlán, their island capital, that would eventually become Mexico City. As imperial rulers, they were no more benevolent than the Inkas, and the dedication of their temple to the imperial god Huitzilopochtli included tens of thousands of human sacrifices.[12]

The Aztecs' breathtakingly rapid capitulation to a small band of Spaniards was due more to the willingness of their restive subjects to ally with foreign invaders and to epidemic disease than to the conquistadors' martial prowess. By themselves, they were hardly a formidable fighting force, and Spanish accounts from the period made virtually no mention of the thousands of New World auxiliaries and African slaves and freedmen who filled out their armies.[13] Moreover, Hernán Cortés, who arrived in Hispaniola as a clerk, was not a great military tactician. But his naked ambition and reckless aggressiveness earned him command of a Spanish expedition to the Yucatán Peninsula. Drawn by rumors of a wealthy empire in the interior, he landed with a force of five hundred men, sixteen horses, and several small cannons in 1519. The Cuban governor tried to recall the conquistador chieftain after realizing that he had slipped his control, but Cortés pressed inland. The conquistadors took enormous risks in charging into the heart of such a powerful empire, but their horses and artillery gave them a few quick victories that impressed the Aztecs' subjects. Hoping to escape bondage, local rulers raised thousands of auxiliary troops for the Spanish attack on the Aztec heartland. Romantic accounts of Cortés's expedition suggest that he almost single-handedly defeated a great empire, but he would not have stood a chance against the military might of the Aztecs without Mesoamerican help.

The Aztec ruler Montezuma II certainly recognized that the Spaniards were in a position to touch off a widespread anti-imperial uprising among his subjects. He therefore offered to become a vassal of Charles V if Cortés halted his march on Tenochtitlán. But the conquistadors were driven more by greed than by loyalty to the Crown. Making the same desperate gamble that Pizarro would take in Cajamarca thirteen years later, Cortés took the Aztec ruler hostage upon reaching the capital in 1519. He and a thousand of his local allies withstood a siege by the massed Aztec forces while fending off an attack by a Spanish "relief" column the Cuban governor had sent to replace him. Montezuma, whose weakness cost him the support of his own nobles, died in the fighting, and a well-timed smallpox epidemic killed his successor and much of the besieging force.

Cortés executed the last emperor in 1524, thereby setting the stage for the transformation of the former Aztec empire into the Viceroyalty of New Spain in 1535. By the 1560s, its dependencies even included the Philippine archipelago, which the Spaniards annexed in a bid to challenge the Portuguese monopoly of the Asian spice trade. Cortés personally reaped the benefits of these audacious conquests and became an inspiration for every conquistador. Although Spanish aristocrats sniffed at his common origins, they could not ignore the plundered wealth of the Aztecs. Charles made him the Marqués del Valle de Oaxaca, which allowed his children to marry into the Castilian nobility. Cortés's successors in New Spain pushed the Spanish frontier into North America searching for the next great plunderable New World empire, while other conquistador bands went south into the Yucatán to loot the city-states that were the remnants of the great Mayan empire.

The relative ease and stunning rapidity of these sweeping victories appeared to validate the conquistadors' conviction that they were morally and spiritually superior to New World peoples. Spanish chroniclers even advanced the hardly believable theory that the Aztecs deferred to Cortés because Montezuma mistook him for the god Quetzalcoatl, whose expected return coincided with the conquistador invasion. More plausible explanations for the Spanish success emphasize the superiority of their horses, armor, and guns over the stone weapons of the Mesoamericans. These significant advantages offset the Spaniards' sparse numbers and gave them a temporary measure of military superiority in the Americas that the Romans and Umayyads never achieved in their wars of imperial conquest.

However, the most potent weapons in the Spanish imperial arsenal were smallpox, measles, malaria, typhus, typhoid, influenza, and the plague. These were endemic maladies in the Old World, but they produced virulent pandemics when Europeans inadvertently introduced them into immunologically defenseless American populations. Exacerbated by warfare and abusive Spanish rule, these diseases virtually wiped out the Arawak population of Hispaniola less than half a century after Columbus's landing. The population of Mexico similarly dropped from roughly twenty-five million to eight hundred thousand people between Cortés's invasion in 1518 and the early seventeenth century.[14] The devastating shock of these virgin-soil epidemics, which occurred when populations had had no contact with a disease during the lifetime of their oldest members, made the trauma of imperial conquest even worse. It is easy to imagine how New World peoples could have believed the world was literally coming to an end when faced with such catastrophes.

Those who survived the brutality of the Spanish conquest became an exploitable imperial resource. Although the conquistadors had the means to seize all the land they wanted, it was worthless without people to work it. The Spanish authorities therefore exported an Iberian institution known as the *encomienda* to the New World. Conferred by the Crown and based on the Spanish verb *encomendar*, meaning to "give in charge or entrust," it accorded knights and warlords the right to collect tribute in newly conquered territories in return for military service.[15] In the Americas, this system evolved into a royal grant entitling the conquistadors to tribute in the form of labor from designated communities. While the Spanish made extensive use of African slaves, their reliance on Christianity to legitimize their New World conquests led the Crown to ban the enslavement of Native American peoples in the 1540s. The conquistadors adopted less obviously coercive methods to get their subjects to work. Eventually even clergymen and Hispanized American nobles acquired *encomienda* grants, but the original *encomienderos* were conquistadors who needed labor tribute to develop conquered lands. To justify this royally sanctioned exploitation they made a show of instructing their charges in Christianity.

In theory, an *encomienda* was thus both extractive and civilizing, but in practice it was simply systematic imperial domination dressed up in moral garb. Not surprisingly, the conquistadors-turned-*encomienderos* were shameless and ruthless in their demands for labor. Many were so successful that the *encomiendas* ultimately proved far more lucrative than unsustainable looting. Enterprising *encomienderos* forced their Indian tributaries to grow cash crops, mine precious metals, weave cloth, raise livestock, and provide domestic labor. Metropolitan Spanish authorities tried to cap the number of people subject to a single *encomienda* at five hundred, but Cortés personally controlled more than one hundred thousand Mesoamericans.

Seeking to establish themselves as landed New World nobility, the *encomienderos* strove to make their grants heritable by their offspring, but the Crown wisely refused. It was hard enough to exercise royal control across the vast expanse of the Atlantic without giving men such as Cortés and Pizarro more power. Moreover, even metropolitan Spanish officials, who had no reservations about oppressing Iberian Jews and Muslims, were embarrassed by the conquistadors' brutality. Taking their obligation to convert New World populations seriously, reformist Spanish clerics were the first to draw attention to the abuses of the *encomienda* system. In 1511, the Dominican friar Antonio Montesinos preached a blistering Christmas day sermon to an *encomiendero* congregation on Hispaniola:

> You are in mortal sin...by reason of the cruelty and tyranny that you practice on these innocent people. Tell me, by what right or justice do you hold these Indians in such cruel and horrible slavery?...Why do you so greatly oppress and fatigue them, not giving them enough to eat or caring for them when they fall ill from excessive labors, so that they die or rather are slain by you, so that you may extract and acquire gold every day? And what care do you take that they receive religious instruction and come to know their God and creator?...Are they not men? Do they not have rational souls?[16]

Montesinos's passionate homily was a new kind of attack on empire. Although Roman and Umayyad critics worried about its contaminating influences, they never concerned themselves with the fate of foreign subjects. Montesinos and Bartolomé de Las Casas, who held an *encomienda* on Hispaniola before joining the priesthood, were certain that indigenous Americans were inferior and alien, but they also believed that they could become fully human through conversion, honest labor, and paternal supervision by benevolent clergymen.

Documenting Spanish abuses in the Americas, the reformist clerics petitioned the Spanish Crown and the Pope to supervise the *encomienderos*. Las Casas asserted that the papal bull did not give the Spanish monarchs the authority to claim property in the Americas and maintained that political power in the New World carried a moral obligation to govern justly. Although the central role of Catholicism in early modern Spain prevented the Spanish authorities from dismissing Las Casas's impertinent arguments outright, this was a debate he could not win.

In answering their critics, Spanish imperial proponents painted the Inkans as tyrants and all Andeans as intrinsically backward. They invoked St. Augustine's criticism of pagan cultures in arguing that conquest and authoritarian rule were necessary to force Americans to give up unnatural practices such as idolatry, human sacrifices, and cannibalism (a charge that had no merit in the Andes). Depicting New World peoples as Aristotelian "natural slaves" lacking the ability to reason, they characterized Spanish labor demands as progressive and civilizing. Clerical apologists ruled conclusively that the *encomienderos* had a right to expect reasonable service from their subjects in return for teaching them discipline and saving their souls. They also ensured that the critical and indigenously Andean histories produced by Don Felipe and Garcialaso de la Vega did not see the full light of day. Reflecting the need to cover up the messy realities of empire, Spanish courtiers and imperial officials kept the most critical sections of their voluminous histories out of print.

Moral debates aside, the metropolitan authorities were reluctant to listen to Las Casas or enact serious reforms because they needed labor to develop the overseas empire. *Encomienderos* usually used Indian tributaries as agricultural workers, but in Peru they also adapted Inka tribute systems to turn Andeans into miners. Nevertheless, the *encomienda* system could not produce enough labor to meet the empire's needs, which meant that the Spaniards inevitably defied the Crown's ban on slave raiding in the Americas. Desperate for labor, they sent hundreds of thousands of Central American slaves to the Caribbean sugar islands and Mexican and Andean mines in the first half of the sixteenth century. When local resistance and the general demographic collapse of American populations dried up these reserves, Spanish entrepreneurs turned to the African slave trade to meet their labor needs.

Las Casas and the reformers eventually forced the Council of the Indies, which had ultimate authority over Spanish colonies in the Americas, to do a better job of protecting New World peoples. Spanish officials had few concerns about the plight of African slaves, but they made a show of benevolence in the Americas to maintain the moral veneer of empire. The "New Laws" of 1542 therefore renewed the prohibition on American slave raiding, decreed that tribute be paid in money rather than labor, and banned the creation of new *encomiendas*. Subject Americans still had to toil for the Spanish, but the reforms required employers to provide them with reasonable pay and working conditions. On paper, the New Laws appeared to restore morality to Spanish imperial rule. In actuality, they were unenforceable. Metropolitan authority in the overseas empire remained weak, and the extractive imperial economy simply had to have huge inputs of forced labor. In New Spain, local Spanish resistance to the New Laws convinced the viceroy not to even try to apply them; in Peru there were *encomiendero* revolts.

Spain's embarrassing inability to exercise real authority in the Americas stemmed from the administrative and communication problems confronting all early modern empire builders. It was hard for the Crown to hold its subordinates accountable when it took eight months for a message from the imperial court to reach Peru. Charles V and Philip II were two of the most powerful rulers in the sixteenth century, but they had direct control only over the Kingdom of Castile and ruled the rest of their European realms as separate kingdoms.

The Habsburg Spanish emperors theoretically had full control of the Americas as an inheritance from Isabella and the Crown of Castile. Initially, the Castilian Casa de Contratación (house of trade) had responsibility for both commerce and governance in the New World, but in 1524 the Council of Indies took over its duties. Administratively, the council divided the Spanish Americas into the viceroyalties, which they subdivided into smaller administrative units based on the jurisdiction of district courts of appeal (*audiencias*), regional magistracies (*corregimientos*), and urban municipalities (*cabildos*). At first glance, this formal chain of authority appeared to be a departure from the systems of indirect rule practiced by the Romans and Umayyads. Indeed, Spanish imperial law laid out a precise hierarchy of direct and formal bureaucratic rule in the Americas.

Predictably, however, imperial authority in the Spanish Americas was as faint and circumscribed as it was in earlier empires and caliphates. Viceroys ignored royal instructions and laws they deemed unworkable or disruptive simply by declaring *obedezco pero no cumplo,* "I obey but do not carry out." The emperors never tried to force the issue. They knew their reach was limited and generally tolerated disobedience if it was accompanied by regular tribute deliveries and affirmations of loyalty.

The Catholic Church was another power unto itself in the Americas. Although a 1508 papal bull gave the Spanish Crown the authority to appoint clergy and create dioceses in the New World, distance allowed both the regular Church and Catholic religious orders considerable freedom of action. Some clerics, such as Las Casas, were passionate defenders of Indian rights, but most churchmen collaborated actively with local imperial interests.

The most influential force in Spanish America, however, was the settlers who followed on the heels of the conquistadors. Over time, these colonists eclipsed imperial administrators and churchmen as the dominant power in the New World. Ancient and medieval empires rewarded victorious soldiers with land grants in conquered territories, but the Spanish Empire facilitated civilian colonization on a new and unprecedented scale. Most colonists came from Spain, but the wealth of the Americas also attracted migrants from almost every state in western Europe and, via the Spanish Philippines, China and South Asia. By the turn of the seventeenth century, locally born Spaniards (creoles) outnumbered recent immigrants, and by 1650 there were approximately half a million settlers in the Spanish colonies who claimed European origins.

Spanish women made this self-sustaining European New World population possible. Initially, the conquistadors had the implicit permission of the Crown to follow the Roman and Umayyad example of treating subject American women as imperial plunder. As in earlier times, the resulting relationships ranged from marriage to concubinage to outright rape. In some cases conquistador leaders used local women as translators or took Aztec and Inkan wives to stake their claims to noble status. The resulting hybrid generation of mestizos complicated the imperial project by unacceptably bridging the line between citizen and subject. Charles V addressed the problem by requiring *encomienderos* to marry and encouraging Spanish women to immigrate to the Americas, and many young women answered his call in the hope of inheriting the fortunes of elderly *encomienderos*.

The Americas proved such a powerful magnet because European origins brought privilege and autonomy in colonial societies stratified on the basis of "blood." The Inkan chronicler Don Felipe noted bitterly that even the lowest Spanish "tramps" used their exalted status to live off the Andean populace. "Their refrain is always 'Give me a servant' or 'Give me a present.'...Every day of their lives they eat about twelve pesos' worth of food and ride off without paying, but still give themselves the airs of gentlemen."[17] Not only could common

Iberian-born women marry far above their social station in the New World, but their blood also gave them authority over Andean men as breeding trumped gender as the key marker of imperial citizenship.

Yet it was difficult to establish a clear distinction between Spanish citizen and Andean subject. The conquistadors married royal Inkan women to buttress their claims to noble status, and Spanish men of all stripes used their privileged status to exploit Andean women sexually. The mestizo children produced by these encounters confused imperial social boundaries and made a mockery of Spanish attempts to define identity on the basis of inheritance and blood. The situation grew even more complicated when the Spaniards introduced African slaves into the Andes, who in turn produced children with Europeans, Andeans, and mestizos. In the seventeenth century, the imperial state tried to restore a measure of social order by codifying a confusing hierarchy of racial categories, known as *castas*, based on the percentage of a person's European, Andean, and African ancestry.

Imperial officials and creoles worried constantly about the contamination of Spanish blood, but the Crown's foremost concern was to keep the wealth of the Americas flowing into Spain. In an era when mercantile-minded rulers strove to build precious metal reserves, the Spanish Americas accounted for 80 percent of the world's silver and 70 percent of its gold. The sixteen million kilograms of silver that streamed into Spain between 1503 and 1660 was a windfall three times larger than the combined silver holdings of the rest of Europe. This bonanza helped lay the groundwork for the development of a global monetary system by allowing Europeans to purchase goods in Asia. The Crown claimed 20 percent of the New World bullion, which the Habsburgs used as collateral for the enormous loans that funded their European wars.

Mercantilism also inspired Spanish attempts to maintain a strict monopoly on commerce within the overseas empire. For most of the sixteenth century, transatlantic shippers had to work through the ports of Seville and Havana and sail in strictly organized biannual fleets. Trade with the Philippines, which was Spain's primary entrepôt for trade with China and Japan, was similarly restricted to one to two galleons that made one round trip per year between Manila and Mexico. Otherwise, Spanish authorities forbade the colonies to trade with each other and tried to bar all foreign merchants from its overseas territories.

Spain, however, lacked the military and economic means to enforce this closed commercial system. Spanish empire builders bit off more than they could chew in acquiring such vast overseas holdings. Castilian pride and nascent Spanish nationalism led them to try to keep the imperial spoils for themselves, but they needed foreign manpower and investment to run and develop their colonies. This meant that New World wealth eventually flowed to bankers, soldiers for hire, and military suppliers throughout Habsburg Europe. Similarly, the enormous importance of early modern Europe's trade with Asia meant that Chinese merchants ultimately acquired nearly half of the American silver.[18]

More importantly, New World plunder actually contributed to the bankruptcy of the Spanish Crown. The flood of wealth into the Iberian Peninsula allowed Spaniards to purchase the best products Europe had to offer, but it drove up prices and destroyed the once vital Castilian textile industry. The emperors themselves were the worst offenders. In 1574, the Castilian treasury took in the equivalent of six million ducats per year, but the expense of the imperial court and Spain's European wars required eight million. Facing insolvency, the Spanish emperors borrowed heavily from German and Italian bankers at high rates of interest. Cash flow problems often forced them to suspend debt payments and seize incoming private cargos of American bullion. In return, the Crown compensated the unlucky owners with low-paying government bonds known as *juros*. No one was exempt from these royal confiscations, and even the Pizarro family had to buy more than forty-seven thousand gold pieces' worth of *juros*.[19]

These desperate economic measures were symptomatic of the larger problems plaguing the Spanish Habsburgs. Although they dominated Europe from the mid-sixteenth to mid-seventeenth centuries, they could not translate the wealth of the Americas into sustainable power in Europe. It may seem nonsensical that the enormous wealth of the overseas empire would be of so little benefit to Spain, but hindsight clearly shows that plunder and extraction had toxic consequences in the imperial metropole. Imperial treasure was a windfall for men such as Cortés and Pizarro, but it weakened the Spanish Habsburg regime. Emboldened by the wealth of the Americas, Charles and Philip did not have to make constitutional concessions to their nobles to raise revenue. As a result, they became addicted to American precious metals and had no domestic reserves to fall back on when imports declined. Similarly, the relatively simple Iberian economy was ill equipped to handle the flood of New World precious metals. This unearned wealth pushed up the cost of living and discouraged economic diversification as cheaper imports drove local products out of metropolitan markets.

While most Spaniards had no direct stake in the Americas, conquistadors such as Cortés and Pizarro profited enormously from the new empire. Working through Pizarro's brother Hernando as their representative in Spain, the Pizarrists acquired extensive farms, pastures, and urban holdings in their home region of Trujillo. Most of them, including Francisco, died violently in Peru, but Hernando brought the family into the ranks of Spanish aristocracy. Nobles detested these common upstarts, but money trumped lineage in the new Spain.

The Pizarrists typified the special interest groups that enriched themselves through self-serving imperial adventures at the expense of the metropolitan population. Many contemporary Spaniards were openly critical of their new American empire. They did not share Las Casas's concern for the rights of indigenous Americans; rather they charged that speculators and foreigners were bleeding Spain of its rightful patrimony. In 1548, a Castilian councilman unknowingly acknowledged the exploitive and inflationary nature of Spanish rule when he complained that "Spain has become an Indies for the foreigner."[20] In other words, just as the conquistadors wrung treasure out of New World populations, the imperial interests drained this same wealth from Spain, albeit through far less brutal tactics.

In the New World, the Inkas were equally outraged over the reversal of fortune that made them imperial subjects. Far from being in a state of decay at the time of Pizarro's arrival in Peru, they were the ruling class of a dynamic empire that was solidifying its hold over newly conquered lands stretching from modern Ecuador to Chile. The Pizarrists could never have ruled the enormous population of the central Andes if the Inkans had not first transformed them into exploitable imperial subjects. The Inkas' rapid fall illustrated one of the fundamental realities of empire building: empires themselves were particularly vulnerable to conquest and subjugation. By necessity, imperial states created well-ordered bureaucratic and extractive machinery that could be taken over easily by even more powerful conquerors. Moreover, an empire's disenfranchised subjects had little incentive to risk their lives and property defending an oppressive foreign regime. This was a lesson that the Inkas learned well in the aftermath of Cajamarca.

Although the Spanish conquest made it appear fragile and short-lived, the Inka Empire was actually the product of centuries of imperial consolidation in the Andes. Prior to the Spanish conquest, the peoples of the highlands identified themselves primarily on the basis of their home region. These local ethnic polities or *ayllus* were paramount, and each had its own protecting spirits, known as *wakas*, that inhabited the rivers, lakes, forests, and mountains around the community. Despite their local particularism, Andeans also shared a common social framework that made their individual cultures mutually intelligible. In this sense, the Andean highlands resembled pre-Roman Britain with the Inkans playing the role of imperial conquerors.

The Inkans were not the first empire builders in the Andes. While the Umayyads were overrunning most of the Mediterranean world in the early seventh century, a centralized power that archaeologists have labeled the Wari Empire was expanding throughout southern and central Peru. Further south, a civilization known as Tiwanaku built stepped pyramids and agricultural terraces around Lake Titicaca in a region roughly corresponding to modern Bolivia. Able to mobilize labor on a substantial scale, these were centralized, if not imperial, states. Together they developed many of the bureaucratic and technological innovations that facilitated Inkan empire building. Unfortunately, they left no historical records, but archaeological evidence suggests that central authority in the highlands collapsed in the tenth or eleventh century, thereby allowing subject states and *ayllus* to reclaim their autonomy.

It seems that the Inkas were originally one of these small ethnic polities. Archaeological remains of warfare and fortifications reinforce Inkan oral traditions suggesting that they expanded gradually but militarily from their central city of Cuzco during the anarchy and disorder of the twelfth century. Overall, there seems to have been a trend toward political recentralization, but it is difficult to determine precisely what inspired Andean empire building in the centuries before the Spanish arrival. The endemic warfare of the period appears to have been driven by population growth, drought, and competition for productive land, but dynastic ambitions of individual rulers were probably also factors.

Andean tradition held that a legendary ruler named Manqu Qhapaq founded the Inkan state in Cuzco and that the following eleven Sapa Inkas built it into an empire during the fifteen and sixteenth centuries. But archaeological evidence suggests that Manqu Qhapaq and the next seven rulers were mythical figures and the process of state formation in Cuzco took longer than a mere ten generations. Either way, Pachakutiq Yupanki, the ninth Sapa Inka, was the first historically verifiable sovereign. Coming to power in 1438, he conquered most of the region around Cuzco and established many of the ideological institutions that underpinned Inkan empire building. His claim of direct descent from the sun god provided moral and political legitimacy for the imperial regime, as did the deification of previous Sapa Inkas, whose cults and mummies continued to play a role in court politics.

Pachakutiq's son and grandson drew on these divinely sanctioned imperial ideologies during the Inkan conquest of the Pacific coastal plain and the rest of the Andean highlands. By the time Pizarro arrived in Cajamarca in 1532, the Inkas had an empire encompassing most of the Andes and more than one hundred million subjects. They accomplished this feat without the wheel, a system of writing, or knowledge of the arch.

Like all empire builders, the Inkas assembled their enormous imperial state through conquest. Armed with stone and bronze-tipped weapons, they had no clear tactical or technological advantage over neighboring Andean states and communities. Instead, their victories appear to have come through unalloyed aggression and superior organizational and logistical strategies that allowed them to field huge armies. Lacking the wheel, the Inkas relied on slow-moving llama trains for their transport, but they exploited and expanded an impressive network of roads, bridges, causeways, and drainage canals inherited from their imperial predecessors to move troops quickly and efficiently. Strategically placed imperial warehouses (*qollqas*) stocked with food, clothing, and weapons allowed Inkan forces to travel lightly and campaign without having to live off the land.

All told, the Inkas appear to have been constantly at war for the century preceding the Spanish conquest. Their armies overran the highlands with relative ease, but the forests were more difficult. Like the Romans, they struggled to subdue less settled "barbarian" frontier peoples. The Inkas were most successful in yoking centralized states to their imperial project. Conquest and assimilation usually began with the arrival of Inkan envoys and merchants who distributed high-value trade goods to win local allies. In doing so, they unknowingly copied the commercial hegemony that the Romans used to draw Britons into their economic and cultural orbit as a prelude to the Claudian invasion. As in Roman Europe, massed armies followed the traders and gave Andeans the choice of accepting Inka rule or risking the disastrous consequences of armed resistance. The Inkas punished the Canari, a people of the northern Andes, for their defiance by scattering them throughout the empire as laborer-colonists and soldiers. They similarly dismantled the coastal Chimor Empire and exacted tribute from the remains in the form of skilled artisans and their crafts.

Cooperation, however, allowed local elites to join the Inkan nobility. As there were probably no more than one hundred thousand ethnic Inkans, their empire building depended on co-optation and conscription. As in the ancient and medieval empires of Europe, women played a central role in this process. The Inkas seized girls from conquered communities as a form of tribute and transformed them into *acllas*, "chosen women." Youth, beauty, and social status determined whether the *acllas* would serve Inkan religious cults, become wives for Inkan nobles, or labor as domestic servants, artisans, or entertainers. Conversely, the Inkas provided cooperative subject elites with Inkan wives, thereby binding them to the imperial project through kinship.

This "Inkanization" was comparable to Roman and Islamic processes of imperial assimilation. Like the Romans, the Inkas reinforced their mastery over their subjects by appropriating aspects of their culture. They took over the widely venerated Pacha Kamaq cult that most likely dated back to the Wari Empire and incorporated regional *wakas*, the protective natural spirits guarding individual communities, into the state religion.

In terms of administration, the Sapa Inka ruled Cuzco and its environs directly but relied on personal bonds with subject elites to extend his authority throughout the empire. Through this, the Inkas employed a variant of the standard imperial template of indirect rule. Calling their realm Tawantinsuyu (the fourfold domain), they divided its four major regions into eighty provinces split into approximately 160 districts. Members of the royal family were the equivalent of provincial governors, and the Sapa Inka's wives also filled senior administrative positions. Subject elites, who were bound to the Inkas through intermarriage, patronage, and cultural assimilation, represented imperial authority at the district level.

Real power in the Andes depended on the cooperation of the leaders (*kurakas*) of the *ayllus*, which remained the fundamental unit of identity and community in the highlands. The *kurakas* drew their power from their capacity to accumulate and redistribute wealth. They collected food, precious metals, textiles, and other material goods from their *ayllu* by virtue of their standing and influence and parceled them out to followers who acknowledged their authority. In return, the members of an *ayllu* built their *kuraka's* house, tilled his fields, wove his cloth, and tended his llama herds. The Spanish translated the term *kuraka* as "lord of the people," but the authority of these *ayllu* leaders was anything but absolute. As community representatives, the *kurakas* mediated disputes and upheld social norms, but they did not have the power to govern unilaterally. Moreover, although the Spanish falsely assumed that the *kuraka*-ship was an exclusively male position, Andean women occasionally played this role.

Once they became Inkan intermediaries, *kurakas* of both genders became responsible for ensuring that an *ayllu* met its tribute and labor obligations to the empire. Ultimately, though, they still derived their authority from their capacity to protect the interests of their community. All Andean states, including the Inkan Empire, were essentially based on hierarchically nested reciprocal relationships in which *kurakas* answered to their *ayllus* and to higher lords who rewarded their deference and cooperation with patronage, women, and resources. The number of aristocratic intermediaries in this system varied, but larger states might have quite a few layers of higher *kurakas* and nobles between the common Andean and a ruler such as the Sapa Inka.

The Inkas did not have the inclination or capacity to interfere in these reciprocal relationships. Instead, they balanced their tolerance of localism with a relatively small but efficient centralized imperial bureaucracy. Inkan functionaries used knotted *khipu* strings to keep track of revenue collection, labor service, military conscription, colonization, *aclla* women, and the inventories of the *qollqa* warehouses. Although this was not a formal writing system, it was accurate. The *khipu, qollqa,* and road network were innovations inherited from earlier Andean empires, but the Inkas improved and expanded them substantially. There were more than fifteen thousand miles of roads in the Andes that the Inkas, like the Romans, reserved for nobles, soldiers, and imperial messengers. The *qollqa* warehouses were both an economic asset and a strategic one in that they stored tribute and supplied Inkan armies. In Peru's Mantaro Valley alone there were 2,753 of these stone structures, with a storage capacity of over half a million square feet. The warehouses also underpinned Inkan authority by serving as collection and redistribution points for royal tribute.[21]

Although the Inkans rewarded their allies with the accumulated wealth of the *qollqas,* their commitment to reciprocity had its limits. There is no evidence that they had a formal legal code or police system, but they, like all imperial rulers, developed ruthless institutions of domination. Special officials known as *tokoyrikoq* (those who see all) were the eyes and ears of the Inka state in the provinces. If they uncovered disobedience or subversion, the penalties ranged from flogging for shirking work to capital punishment for speaking against the empire. The Inkas punished armed revolts or collective disobedience with wholesale slaughter. They seized the lands of rebellious communities, destroyed their shrines and *wakas,* and resettled the survivors as bound laborers on imperial estates. They made an example of disloyal *kurakas* by flaying them to death and making drums from their skin and cups from their skulls.

As in Roman Britain and Al-Andalus, subject Andean labor was the true imperial prize. The Inkas claimed ownership of all property by right of conquest and required communities to supply tribute in the form of labor to gain access to arable land. Under the *mit'a* system (*mit'a* means "to take a turn"), in which *ayllus* sent colonists to exploit distant resources, communities had to furnish the Inkan Empire with miners, soldiers, porters, craftsmen, and laborers. This was in addition to sending a portion of their produce and crafts to the *qollqa* warehouses. In most cases, the *kurakas* based these assessments on long-standing reciprocal obligations in the *ayllus.*

It also seems likely that the Inkas were in the process of developing new strategies of extraction at the time of the Spanish conquest. Their primary goal was to cut through the reciprocal institutions of authority and exchange to make empire building more lucrative. They had begun to make heavy use of *yanaconas,* men who had become divorced from their *ayllus*, in a variety of roles ranging from simple laborers to trusted imperial retainers. The Inkas' main goal in promoting this individuality over communalism was to restructure Andean society. Using careful censuses, they began to organize conquered communities for military and labor service by dividing them into units of ten, fifty, one hundred, five hundred, one thousand, five thousand, and ten thousand people. The Pizarrists interrupted this experiment, but it is clear that the enormous wealth and impressive monumental architecture of the Inkas reflected their well-honed ability to wring labor tribute from their subjects.

Competition to control these vast riches probably sparked the fratricidal civil war between Atawallpa and Waskar. Their father, Wayna Qhapaq, was pushing the Inkan borders northward into Ecuador in the 1520s when he died so unexpectedly. With the imperial inheritance uncertain, the Cuzco bureaucracy and the Inkan high command each backed a different son. As the military candidate, Atawallpa had the advantage over his half-brother, and his professional forces killed approximately sixty thousand of Waskar's Cuzco militiamen in a series of bloody battles as Pizarro and his men marched up from the coast.[22] Unaware of the true nature of the Spanish threat, Atawallpa was brutal even by Inka standards in his treatment of his brother's vanquished supporters. His men executed Waskar's wives and children after capturing Cuzco and took their revenge on *ayllus* and subject states that had unwisely taken his side in the conflict.

Atawallpa's faction justified their bloodshed and looting on the grounds that it was part of a cosmic cataclysm (*pachakuti*) that would usher in a new age. This had occurred four times in the Inkan past, and Pachakutiq Yupanki, the founder of the Inkan Empire, took his name from this "turning over of time and space."[23] In 1532, however, *pachakuti* set the stage for Pizarro and new kind of empire.

The Pizarrists did not really conquer Peru; rather, they hijacked the Inkan imperial state. For the most part, the war-weary Inkan military and bureaucracy were paralyzed for the six months the Spanish kept Atawallpa alive as a hostage in Cajamarca. Waskar's partisans foolishly but understandably hoped to use the invaders against Atawallpa's men, particularly after Pizarro installed Waskar's brother Manqu as the puppet Sapa Inka. On the other hand, many Inkan subjects similarly hoped that the Spaniards would free them from imperial servitude. Their assistance was invaluable to the undermanned and undersupplied conquistadors. Andeans tending the vast network of *qollqa* warehouses in the Mantaro Valley supplied and equipped the roughly thirty-five thousand auxiliaries, most of whom were Waskar's men, which rounded out the Spanish forces. The Pizarrists used this local support to root out and destroy the remnants of Atawallpa's army.

The Spanish relied on Andean military assistance to finish the work they began at Cajamarca, but Pizarro and his men lacked the ability and patience to maintain the Inkas' finely tuned systems of imperial extraction. Having risked their lives to topple a great empire, they expected immediate rewards. The conquistadors therefore embarked on a frenzied orgy of plunder when they took possession of Inkan shrines and cities. Waskar's supporters in Cuzco originally welcomed them as saviors, but they quickly grew disgusted as the Spaniards began to loot. Mocking Inkan traditions and customs, the Pizarrists pried hundreds of golden plaques from the Temple of the Sun and carried off its golden sacrificial altar. Nor did they confine themselves to confiscating moveable precious metals. Ill-disciplined conquistadors slaughtered the royal llama herds for their tongues, which they apparently considered a delicacy, and took *aclla* women as concubines. Rampaging conquistadors repeated this scene at every major Inkan settlement in the highlands.

The Pizarrists' relentless campaign of imperial plunder had a devastating impact on Andean society. Two centuries of Inkan rule had introduced Andeans to the realities of subjecthood, but the Spanish conquest appeared to bring the very world to an end. Established values and institutions lost their meaning as powerful cults such as Pacha Kamaq failed to predict the catastrophe or stop the looting. The Inkan priest of Apurimac, afflicted with the despair that seized the former imperial ruling class, jumped to his death in a deep river gorge as the Spanish pillaged his shrine. Similarly, the chronicler Pedro Cieza de León reported that royal women hung themselves with their own hair to escape the conquistadors, and an entire village committed suicide after falling to a Spanish attack. Gathering their wives and children with them as they flung themselves over a cliff, the village men declared: "It is better to die in freedom than to live in servitude of such cruel people."[24] The myth of Wayna Qhapaq's pestilential butterflies was surely born of this desperation.

The Pizarrists themselves faced the challenge of constructing a new world in the Andes after they had finished stripping the Inkan Empire of its lootable treasure. For the next two decades, Francisco Pizarro and his followers built a rudimentary conquistador state that was focused primarily on extorting tribute from defeated Andeans. The arrival of the first precious metal shipments in Spain in 1534 sparked a rush to the Andes that brought desperately needed reinforcements, but the flood of speculators and fortune hunters caused significant problems. Pizzaro had difficulty controlling the masses of would-be conquistadors whose main goal was to replicate his feat at Cajamarca by finding new Andean empires to overthrow. In 1535, he cleverly distracted his Spanish and Inkan rivals by encouraging his onetime partner Almagro to go on an ill-fated expedition to conquer Chile at the head of an army of twelve thousand Andean auxiliaries led by Paullu Inka, the brother of the new Sapa Inka, Manqu.

This diversion gave the Pizarrists time to solidify their hold on power. Their first priority was to force back under the imperial umbrella the subject Andean communities that had used the collapse of Inkan power to reassert their autonomy. Anchoring his regime in urban centers, Pizarro founded Lima as his capital and reorganized Cuzco along the lines of a European city. He turned the Temple of the Sun into a Dominican monastery, divided the Inkan palaces among his followers, and forbade them from settling more than one league from the city because their control over the Andean majority was still precarious.

The Pizarrists further staked their claim to the remnants of the Inkan Empire by seizing Inka noblewomen as their concubines. Although it might appear at first glance that they were continuing the Inkan practice of using intermarriage to build alliances with defeated elites, the Spanish rarely married the women they treated as imperial plunder. Instead, they formed informal conjugal relations with the wives and daughters of Inkan nobles and *kurakas*, many of whom Cieza described as "very lovely and beautiful," to claim the legitimacy and wealth of their families.[25]

Some of these women may have entered into these relationships willingly, but it is hard to see how Atawallpa's widow, Doña Angelina Yupanqui, would have welcomed the embrace of Francisco Pizarro, the man who had her husband garroted. Yet she bore him two children. Similarly, Pizarro had two children by one of Atawallpa's daughters,

Doña Inés Huaylas Yupanqui, before he married her off to one of his employees. This is why the Jesuit mestizo priest Blas Valera charged that the conquistadors pushed Inkan women into prostitution: "They counseled wives to leave their husbands, virgin daughters [to leave] their parents, and they gave [these women] over to public lewdness, a thing that had not been seen in the [Inka] kingdom for over two thousand years."[26] Without question, the most repulsive example of this sexual imperial exploitation was Cristobal Maldonado's attempt to force a nine-year-old Inkan heiress into marriage by raping her. Inkan aristocrats, who might well have been happy to give their daughters or sisters to the conquistadors in marriage under the old system, were humiliated by these unequal relationships. In keeping with the nihilism of the times, a nobleman in Quito went so far as to kill all of the women of his household to keep them out of Spanish hands.[27]

On a much wider scale, the Pizarrists similarly co-opted and perverted Andean institutions of reciprocity through the *encomienda* system. Not only did the conquistadors loot Inkan shrines and cities, they treated the whole population of the Andes as an imperial resource. Lacking the manpower to seize and exploit land, they needed Andean labor to make their new empire pay on a long-term basis. In his capacity as governor, Pizarro rewarded his followers with *encomienda* grants over entire *ayllus*. This brought the power to demand tribute in labor, but the land itself was relatively unimportant. For example, in 1534 Pizarro awarded Juan de Barrios authority over the subjects of a pair of *kurakas* and their *ayllus* near the coastal town of Ica. The grant gave Barrios sanction to use approximately 1,300 Indians on farms, mines, or "other enterprises." In return he was obliged to "teach and indoctrinate the Indians in the matters of our Holy Catholic Faith, giving them good treatment, and obey the ordinances that have been drawn up for their welfare."[28] Most *encomienda* grants also required their holders to maintain a horse and arms to deal with potential uprisings.

With Spanish military manpower stretched thin, the *encomienderos* obviously did not have the means to force hundreds of Andeans to work. They instead relied on the *kurakas* to mobilize their followers to mine gold and silver, weave cloth, and grow cash crops. The most successful *encomienderos* developed a working partnership with their *kurakas* and cut them in on a share of the profits, but the demands of the system put tremendous strain on *ayllu* leaders, whose authority depended on reciprocity. The Spaniards would replace them if they failed to deliver sufficient labor tribute, but they risked their positions and even their lives if they placed unreasonable demands on their followers.

More grasping *encomienderos* made the *kurakas'* situation even more precarious by abusing their grants. Those who fulfilled their dream of acquiring large estates struggled to compete with independent Andeans who could produce crops and crafts more cheaply, and so they assigned their Indians to work as domestic servants in Spanish homes or on labor gangs hired out to employers in Lima. Some male *encomienda* holders also exploited their power over Andean women, and it was not unusual for *encomienderos* to keep veritable harems on their estates. Even common Spanish men exploited this sexual perquisite of empire, and Don Felipe complained that innkeepers forced their female servants to work as prostitutes.[29]

The Inkan nobility found the Spanish behavior intolerable. Initially Manqu Inka took an oath of loyalty to the Spanish Crown in the hope that the conquistadors would help him prevent his subjects from reasserting their independence. But the Pizarrists' behavior in Cuzco demonstrated conclusively that they would never accept the Inkas as equal imperial partners. Not only did they strip the city of its moveable treasure, but Francisco's brother Gonzalo seized Manqu's own wife. In a speech to the surviving nobles of Cuzco, the Sapa Inka unknowingly echoed Boudicca's condemnation of Roman imperialism some fourteen centuries earlier:

> They preach one thing and do another, and they give so many admonitions, yet they do the opposite. They have no fear of God or shame, and treating us like dogs, they call us no other names. Their greed has been such that there is no temple or palace left that they have not looted. Furthermore, even if all the snow turned to gold and silver, it would not satiate them. They keep the daughters of my and other ladies, your sisters and kin, as concubines, behaving bestially in this.... They strive to have us so subjected and enslaved that we have no other care than to find them metals and to provide them with our women and livestock.[30]

Like the British Icenian queen, Manqu concluded that revolt was the only option. With Francisco Pizarro occupied in Lima, the

Spanish garrison in Cuzco under the command of his brothers consisted of only 196 conquistadors and five hundred Andean auxiliaries. The Inkan elites, who could still muster tens of thousands of soldiers, recognized that it was time to strike before the steady stream of Spaniards into the highlands became a flood.

In 1535, Manqu escaped Cuzco by promising to retrieve an Inka treasure buried in the hinterlands. Instead, he raised an army of one hundred thousand men that besieged the Inkan capital while his allies attacked Lima and the other urban centers in Peru. Francisco Pizarro brushed aside the assault on Lima relatively easily, but Manqu's troops wiped out the forces he sent to relieve Cuzco. The Inkans' enormous advantage in numbers gave them control of the countryside, placing the isolated *encomienderos* in the highlands in real jeopardy. Nevertheless, Manqu's army could not overwhelm the tiny Cuzco garrison. The Spaniards' horses allowed them to forage for supplies and terrorize the Sapa Inka's supporters, and intimidated common Andeans, who had no love of the Inkas, gave the conquistadors food, military intelligence, and even extra soldiers.

Most of Cuzco burned in the fighting, but Pizarrists broke the back of the Inkan assault by boldly seizing a key fortress overlooking the city. Juan Pizarro died in the attack, but as the porous siege dragged on, Manqu's forces drifted away to plant crops and tend to religious obligations. More significantly, many Andeans remained neutral in the hope that the Inkan and Spanish empire builders would destroy each other. In 1537, Almagro returned from his aborted invasion of Chile and raised the siege of Cuzco. Manqu retreated with his remaining forces to the remote fortress of Vilcabamba, where he held out until Spanish agents murdered him in 1545. Pizarro chose his more pliant half-brother Paullu to be the new puppet Sapa Inka, but Manqu's sons continued to reign in exile in Vilcabamba until the final demise of their neo-Inkan state in 1572.

The Spaniards put down the final revolt of the old regime in the Andes by exploiting tensions in the Inkan aristocracy, but in 1538 their own squabble over the division of imperial spoils finally turned violent. The conflict pitted the Pizarrist faction that claimed the bulk of Atawallpa's ransom and the choicest *encomiendas* against Almagro's disgruntled later arrivals. The privileges of early modern empire meant that virtually every would-be conquistador felt entitled to a personal fortune by sole virtue of his Spanishness, but even the vast

wealth of the Inkas was too finite to accommodate their lust for treasure. Rumors of another lootable Andean empire lured Almagro to
Chile, but when he found only aggressive Araucanian frontiersmen
he returned to demand a more equitable division of Peru. Claiming
that Cuzco actually fell within the *capitulación* that gave him authority over the lands south of Pizarro's realm, he attempted a coup d'état
by arresting Gonzalo and Hernando Pizarro and taking control of the
garrison.

Francisco Pizarro's position was initially precarious, but he prevailed because he had the authority of the Crown behind him. As
the legitimate governor of Peru, he had the means and the right to
destroy his treasonous rival. However, he had little time to savor his
victory. Three years later, his death at the hand of Almagro's aveng-
ing son restarted the civil war. Fed up with the squabbling, Charles V
took a greater role in the imperial administration. The first emissary
he sent to replace Pizzaro captured and executed the junior Almagro
but was too sympathetic to the conquistadors to actually reform the
Peruvian administration.

Vasco Núñez de la Vela, the first true viceroy of Peru, was
more respectful of royal authority, but he provoked the remaining
Pizarrists by trying to enforce the provisions of the 1542 New Laws
that reformed the *encomienda* system. Led by Gonzalo Pizarro, they
murdered Vela and declared their independence. Yet although it was
in a separate hemisphere, Peru was not as far from Spain in political
terms as Al-Andalus was from the seat of Umayyad power in Damascus. Gonzalo could not emulate Emir Abd al-Rahman I by transforming an imperial province into an autonomous state. The Spanish
Crown would never surrender the Andean silver, and Charles's next
viceroy, Pedro de la Gasca, arrived in Peru in 1547 at the head of a
royalist army that brought the Pizarrist era to an end by capturing
and killing Gonzalo one year later.

Thus, few of the Peruvian conquistador leaders lived long enough
to enjoy the fruits of empire. Hernando Pizarro consolidated his family's wealth by marrying his niece Francisca, who was the daughter of
an Inkan princess and was his brother Francisco's sole heir, and buying
land in Spain. But he spent most of his later life in a Spanish prison
for his role in the death of Almagro. The rest of his brothers all died
violently, as did most of the Almagrist faction. To an imperial critic
such as Cieza, the conquistadors had answered for their crimes: "God

has punished our men, and most of these leaders have died miserably in wretched deaths, a frightening thought to serve as a warning."[31]

Cieza may have been grimily satisfied with Pizarro's fate, but the passing of the conquistador generation meant relatively little in Peru. The populations of Britain and Iberia actually increased under the Romans and Umayyads, but the first century of Spanish rule was devastating for the people of the Andes. The realities of virgin-soil epidemics meant that there was no escaping Wayna Qhapaq's poisonous butterflies, and the Pizarrists' merciless imperial rule and the exploitive *encomienda* system made things even worse. Their pillaging of the Inkan warehouses wiped out important food reserves, and the sexual abuse of Andean women led to high rates of infant mortality. Early modern population estimates are notoriously unreliable, and some regions were more hard hit than others, but it appears that the Andean population fell from nine million to one million between the 1520s and the first Spanish census in 1569. In the seventeenth century it reached a low point of approximately six hundred thousand people, and gradually recovered thereafter.[32]

The conquistadors certainly did not intend to cause this demographic disaster; their *encomiendas* depended on the exploitation of Andean labor. Some *encomienderos* even promoted motherhood in a vain effort to stem the decline of tributary populations, but the fact remains that the Pizarrist conquest state was unsustainable because it consumed people. The demise of so many Andean societies during this imperial catastrophe opened the way for the resettlement of Peru by Spanish colonists, African slaves, and the offspring of unions between members of these groups. The approximately 250,000 settlers of European descent in Peru in the mid-seventeenth century were at the pinnacle of this new society.[33] The surviving Andeans became "Indians," a misnomer originating from European explorers' confusion of the Americas with Asia. Yet Indianism was far more than a Spanish geographical mistake; it was a new subordinate identity that transformed Andeans into perpetually backward imperial subjects with no rights as individuals under Spanish law.

The value of this Indian labor far outweighed the Crown's initial one-fifth share of the Pizarrists' plunder. Consequently, the emperors could not allow one of Spain's richest overseas domains to be run as a private enterprise. In the long term, silver production was much more important than the conquistadors' crude looting or the *encomienderos*' fumbling efforts to monetize Andean tribute. More-over, the growing Spanish colonial population of nobles, small farmers, merchants, professionals, and craftsmen demanded access to Andean labor and more representative and responsible government. Embarrassed by the conquistador civil wars and *encomienda* scandals, the metropolitan authorities sought to bring Peru under greater control.

Viceroy Pedro de la Gasca suspended the New Laws to undercut popular support for Gonzalo Pizarro's rebellion, but he also moved against the most abusive *encomienderos*. His investigators uncovered horrific stories of *encomienda* holders torturing their tributaries to produce silver and brought the most flagrant transgressors to trial. It was much harder, however, for the Council of the Indies to reform the overseas empire. Gasca's crackdown was short-lived, and many of his viceregal successors became enmeshed in embezzlement, bribery, and smuggling scandals.

It fell to Don Francisco de Toledo, Philip II's viceroy from 1569 to 1581, to stamp out the systematic corruption of the Pizarrist era. The younger son of a Spanish noble family, he had the influ-ence and authority to remake the original conquest state. Tellingly, he and his successors made sense of the Inkan Empire by com-paring it to ancient Rome and used Roman models in fashioning an orderly and coherent system of imperial rule for the Andes.[34] Toledo imposed a more regular administrative geography by divid-ing the region into eighty provinces encompassing 614 districts (*repartimientos*). The *encomienderos* lost their political influence, and Toledo used the segregated Republic of the Indians to rule the surviving Andean population. To this end, the *corregidor de indios*, who was the equivalent of a provincial governor, supervised the *kurakas*, collected tribute, organized tribute labor, and commanded the provincial militia.

Even with these reforms, the Spaniards lacked the linguistic and cultural understanding to rule the Indian republic directly. Toledo therefore sought greater control at the local level by transforming cooperative *kurakas* into a hereditary Indian nobility. Ignorant of the reciprocal nature of authority in the Andes, Spanish officials imag-ined them as *caciques* with total power over their *ayllus*. By this wishful thinking they hoped to turn the *kurakas* into minor imperial functionaries that would extend Spain's reach into local communities. As such, these imperial allies acquired full individual legal status in the Spanish courts and rights to call themselves *don,* own horses and guns, and wear Spanish clothing. In effect, they were to become the princes of the Republic of the Indians.

Similarly, Toledo hoped to remake common Andeans into more dependable and obedient laborers by concentrating the scattered *ayllu* settlements into supervised villages. Laid out on a Renaissance-style grid template, these *reducciones* included a central plaza, church, administrative buildings, and a jail. A council of appointed Andean elites was to run each village, with individual *ayllus* occupying assigned neighborhoods under the jurisdiction of their *kurakas.* The Andeans rightly viewed the *reducciones* as prisons, and *ayllu* leaders hired sympathetic Spanish lawyers to challenge Toledo's plan before the imperial court in Spain. Lacking the status of imperial citizenship, the Andeans of course stood little chance of convincing Philip to overrule his viceroy. Ultimately, their mass flight to the countryside was more effective in scuttling the resettlement scheme.

The popular rejection of the *reducciones* was symptomatic of the growing informal resistance to Spanish rule in late sixteenth-century Peru. As the brutal but haphazard *encomienda* system gave way to Toledo's far more intrusive Indian republic, surviving Andeans began to experience the full implications of early modern Spanish imperial rule. The Spaniards' emphasis on blood rather than culture as a marker of citizenship meant that Hispanicization offered no escape from subjecthood, even if Andeans converted to Christianity. While the conquistadors respected Inkan nobility, if only to appropriate it for themselves, Spanish colonists and creoles never viewed the descendants of the Inkans as anything more than mere Indians. Paullu Inka, a close Pizarrist ally and prince of the royal line, became a Christian and gave his sons a western education, but common Spaniards still beat and insulted him on the street. This stands in striking contrast to the Roman embrace of British chiefs and the Umayyads' respect for defeated Visigothic nobles.

It was too early to attribute discrimination against Inkan nobles to modern racism, but it is clear that the Spanish colonists guarded their privileged status far more jealously than their Roman or Umayyad predecessors had. They came to the New World to enrich and remake themselves, not to defer to faded and impotent barbarian nobles. As the historian James Lockhart aptly observed: "Getting Spaniards to respect an Indian lord was apparently like getting a cat to respect a canary."[35] Pizarro's victory at Cajamarca made the Spaniards the true lords of the Andes, regardless of their original social station.

While ennoblement and social advance were some of the greatest rewards of empire, they did not bring security. The Spanish settlers and their creole descendants never ceased to feel vulnerable as a favored minority living among a sea of subjects. Apart from the viceregal guard in Lima, there were no regular military units in Peru until the eighteenth century. Spanish imperial authority in the highlands rested primarily on armed *encomienderos* and the *corregidors'* militias, which were often made up of Andean conscripts. While Inkan nobles and wealthy *kurakas* sought relief from imperial abuses in the courts, common Andeans were more dangerous. They occasionally murdered *encomienderos* and lone Spanish travelers and quickly mastered the western weapons that had proved so effective during the original wars of conquest. In the 1560s, the authorities uncovered hidden arms caches, including guns and pikes to deal with Spanish horsemen. As a result, rumors flew among the Spanish community of a pending mass insurrection. The neo-Inkan refugee state in Vilcabamba was another constant source of anxiety until Toledo's forces captured the fortress and executed Tupac Amaru, the last true Sapa Inka, in 1572.

The children of the conquistadors and royal Inkan mothers posed an even greater threat. This first generation of mestizos, which came of the age in the 1540s, initially enjoyed the privileges of full imperial citizenship. Although metropolitan Spanish women eventually made their way to Peru in large numbers, the early Pizarrist state was a predominately male society. The conquistadors, who aspired above all else to become a hereditary nobility, needed Andean women to provide them with heirs. Hispanicized mestiza girls made suitable wives once they reached adulthood, and the Pizarrists founded the Convent of Santa Clara in Cuzco to ensure that they become proper Spaniards away from the contaminating influence of their Inka mothers. Some of these mestizas, including Francisco Pizarro's daughter Ines, even inherited their fathers' *encomienda* grants. Their brothers were harder to assimilate. Essentially, mestizas could become Spanish, while mestizos could not. This was the reverse of the situation in Al-Andalus. The male offspring of marriages between Muslim men and Iberian women tended to become Arab and Muslim; their sisters adopted the Christian faith of their mothers and remained Iberian.

The mestizos grew restless and rebellious waiting to inherit from their conquistador fathers as the arrival of Spanish women undermined their status as honorary Europeans. Fearing that the resulting generation of locally born European (creole) children would consign them to the Indian republic, in 1567 the Cuzco mestizos hatched a conspiracy to seize control of Peru. The Spanish authorities quickly uncovered the plot and exiled all mestizos in Cuzco over the age of twenty. This was over the wailing protests of their Inka mothers, who, according to the Inkan chronicler Garcialaso de la Vega, declared that Spain owed them a debt for betraying "their [Sapa] Inka, their caciques, and their lords" by helping their Pizarrist lovers conquer Peru.[36]

Other mestizos adopted more subtle forms of resistance. Blas Valera, the son of Pizarro's captain of crossbowmen and an Inkan noblewoman, joined the Jesuits a year after the Spaniards discovered the conspiracy in Cuzco. As one of the few religious orders willing to admit mestizos, the Jesuits hoped that the sons of Inka women would use their cultural expertise and linguistic skills to convert the wider Andean population to Christianity. At first, Valera appeared to live up to expectations. He worked through the highlands as a priest and evangelist before returning to Lima to help with the translation of the Catholic catechism into Quechua. But much to his superiors' dismay, the mestizo priest became an advocate for Andean rights. Even more serious, Valera found inherent similarities between Andean religions and Christianity and even went so far as to depict the murdered Atawallpa as a saint. The Jesuits covered up his heresy by convicting him of fornication, and they joined the other Catholic brotherhoods in banning mestizos from their order until the late eighteenth century.

In hindsight, the mestizos were too few in number to be a real danger to Toledo's new Peruvian state. Similarly, the Andean majority was too disorganized and demoralized by the imperial conquest and resulting epidemics to mount a direct challenge to Spanish rule. Lacking the means to resist militarily, many followed Valera's path in turning to their faith to oppose the new imperial order. Spanish missionaries often complained that "native witches" hindered their efforts by urging the population not to take part in Catholic rituals. Just as Toledo sought to move them into supervised *reducciones*, the Jesuits and the other Spanish churchmen worked to turn Andeans into disciplined Christians. Parish priests, who used the confessional to watch for signs of political or religious subversion, soon became alarmed at discovering that the *wakas* had more influence than the Church in most *ayllus*. Certain that the devil spoke through these protective spirits, the Church council in Lima ordered parish priests to destroy the shrines, *khipu* string records, and other manifestations of the blasphemous preconquest Andean culture.

While some Andeans plotted to revolt in the 1560s, others resisted by returning to the spiritual comfort of the *wakas*. Longing for the security and salvation of an idealized preconquest past, community religious leaders concluded that the Spanish had conquered them because they had abandoned their protectors. These *taquiongo* mediums were not part of the formal Inkan priesthood. Rather, they were respected local religious experts who gained a wide following in the central Andean highlands by promising that the *wakas* would return to drive out the Spanish if Andeans united to reject Christianity and western culture. Their movement came to be known as Taki Onqoy (dance sickness) because the *taquiongos* were taken over by the *wakas*, who formerly had inhabited only natural features such as hills and bodies of water. While possessed, they trembled and shook as they led their followers in songs and dances. It might be tempting to dismiss Taki Onqoy as primitive superstition, but it had much in common with later millenarian crusades such as the Sioux Ghost Dance, the Chinese Boxer Rebellion, and the Tanzanian Maji Maji revolt, which also sought a spiritual solution to western empire building after conventional methods failed.

Imperial conquerors ignored charismatic religious resistance at their peril, for these were potent popular movements that mobilized widespread support against foreign domination. The Spanish where shocked to discover the scope of Taki Onqoy in the *ayllus*. Toledo depicted it as the satanic product of Inkan devil worship, and the clergy attacked the movement directly by flogging the *taquiongos* and sending thousands of their followers to work under priestly supervision on Church estates. Many *kurakas* aided the crackdown because Taki Onqoy's pan-Andean appeal undercut their authority as local leaders.

The Church's fumbling efforts to eradicate Andean "idolatry" continued off and on into the seventeenth century without any real success. The campaign began again in earnest in the 1610s when an opportunistic priest named Francisco de Ávila won release from jail for a host of crimes, including embezzlement, exploiting Andean labor, and illicit sex, by sounding the alarm over Andean idolatry. Goaded by Avila's reminder that the *wakas* were still potent, Church leaders tried again to reorder Andean society. This was not the formal Inquisition, which focused on the Protestant threat from Europe. Instead, it was a program of "extirpation" that sought to force Andeans to embrace Catholicism. In 1617, teams of extirpators heard 5,694 confessions, captured 669 "ministers of idolatry," confiscated 603 "principal huacas" (*wakas*), and scourged sixty-three "witches."[37] They punished Andean religious experts with public humiliation, forced labor, and detention in a special jail in Lima. In time, the whole exercise devolved into an expensive series of witch hunts that overtaxed the resources of the parish clergy. Most *ayllus* continued to venerate their *wakas*, even after the Spanish destroyed their physical shrines. As one disciple told a frustrated Jesuit, "Father, are you tired of taking our idols from us? Take away that mountain if you can, since that is the God I worship."[38]

The extirpation campaigns failed because imperial rulers cannot tell their subjects what to think, but they can exploit them. The *encomienda* system lasted into the early eighteenth century, but the Peruvian state shifted to direct taxation to force *ayllu* members into the labor market. The Spanish justified this obligation as the price of Spain's gift of civilization to the Indians. Toledo's administrative reforms made systematic tribute collection feasible by keeping better track of common Andeans, a prerequisite for effective imperial extraction. Based on a 1569 census, all males had an obligation to pay roughly five or six pesos per year to their *kuraka*, who then passed on the funds to the *corregidors*. Only *kurakas* and Inkan royalty were exempt from this head tax. Furthermore, Andeans also owed tithes to their parish priests.

Toledo's primary aim in remaking Peruvian government and society was to generate revenue for the Crown. The true wealth of Peru was locked up in the labor of its people, but the Spanish struggled to find ways to force Andeans to work on imperial projects. Under what was known as the *repartimiento de mercancías*, Spanish officials, clergymen, and settlers tried to monetize the highland economy by forcing Andeans to buy imported goods at inflated prices. But European manufactures and the five-peso tribute obligation were not sufficient inducement to get Andeans to work for wages. Slaves offered only a partial solution to the problem because they were too expensive to be used on a grand scale, and the Christian legitimizing ideology of the Spanish Empire was sufficiently potent to protect Andeans from enslavement or blatant forced labor. Spanish officials and settlers predictably blamed their labor problems on immoral Indian laziness, but it is worth recalling Viceroy Conde Nieva's candid observation in 1560 that the Spanish in Peru would "rather die of hunger than take a hoe in their hands."[39]

Ultimately, Toledo had to use established Andean tribute systems to generate labor. The Spanish Crown's addiction to New World precious metals made increasing silver production his top priority. The mines of Potosí, source of the greatest deposits of Andean silver, produced 7.6 million pesos worth of bullion per year between 1580 and 1650.[40] Located within the borders of modern Bolivia, they were Spain's single most important source of revenue in all of South America, but secondary mines scattered throughout the Andes were also important.

The Inkas worked many of these deposits before the Spanish conquest by assigning subject *mit'a* laborers (*mitayos*) to the mines to fulfill their tribute obligations. As unskilled workers, they collected ore from surface veins under the supervision of their *kurakas* and turned it over to smelters, most of whom were *yanacona* specialists, who refined it using furnaces fueled by llama dung. These skilled workers were permanently detached from their *ayllus* and lived at the mines. The system continued during the Pizarrist era, except that *encomienderos* sent tributaries to the mines and collected refined ore from their *kuraka* supervisors. The work was not unacceptably burdensome while the surface veins remained productive, and many *mitayos* chose to stay at Potosí as *yanaconas* to avoid the *encomienderos'* increasingly heavy demands on their home *ayllus*.

The situation worsened as the accessible deposits played out and production dropped. The Spaniards compensated by using mercury to refine the low-grade ores they had previously discarded, but ultimately the necessity of digging deeper required considerably more labor. One of Toledo's greatest priorities as viceroy was to lower the cost of Peruvian silver production by ensuring that the mines had a steady supply of cheap Andean labor. Handcuffed by Andean resistance to joining the cash economy, he turned the preconquest *mit'a* system into a form of state-sanctioned labor conscription that required *ayllus* in the districts accessible to Potosí to send roughly 15 percent of their adult male population to work on the mines for four months. This revision of the Inkan system generally meant that every man would have to serve a tour in Potosí once every seven years. Toledo's scheme initially produced approximately thirteen thousand unskilled laborers per year.[41]

The Spaniards justified the revised *mit'a* system on the grounds that Andeans were too ignorant to recognize the benefits of honest labor. They were also careful to distinguish the *mit'a* from slavery by paying the *mitayos*, but Spanish mine owners still bought and sold these laborers when they arrived at Potosí. Most workers fell into debt buying extra rations in addition to the mining equipment, candles, and coca leaves (for increased endurance) they needed to do their jobs. Over time, mine owners became increasingly reliant on more skilled paid laborers (*mingas*) who came to Potosí voluntarily, but *mitayos* remained at the core of the mining economy in the Andes until the very end of Spanish rule.

The work itself was backbreaking and frequently lethal. With skilled salaried miners working the silver veins, the *mitayos'* main job was to carry the raw ore up the mining shaft wrapped in wool blankets knotted at their chests. They could be whipped or beaten for failing to meet a weekly quota of loads carried to the smelters. Moreover, the workers frequently contracted pneumonia as they climbed from the heat of the pits into the chilly mountain air of Potosí, which is more than thirteen thousand feet above sea level. Silicosis and mercury poisoning also killed large numbers of *mitayos* and other miners. European inspectors and specially appointed *kurakas* were supposed to ensure that conditions did not become too bad, but they had no capacity to address the abuses that were built into Potosí's mining economy.[42]

The silver demands of the Crown required Toledo to give mine owners first call on the *mit'a* drafts, but the system was so efficient in getting Andeans to work that he and his successors frequently assigned *mitayos* to their friends and allies as patronage. In the seventeenth century, enterprising Spaniards with access to *mit'a* labor drafts set up sweatshops producing high-quality textiles for export. As in Inkan times, the Andeans themselves remained the most valuable resource in Peru. Tributary Indians consequently became *prendas con pies* (assets with feet) that Spaniards vied to control. *Corregidors* and priests hid "their Indians" from the *mit'a* draft to ensure a steady flow of tribute, and ambitious *kurakas* poached the constituents of neighboring rivals to build up their own tributary populations.

Andeans sought to escape the imperial regime's labor demands by avoiding census takers, hiding their wealth, and hiring lawyers to appeal excessive tribute obligations. If all else failed, they simply fled the *mit'a* draft, particularly after the death toll at the mines began to rise. Many became *forasteros*, a new category of rootless people who permanently abandoned their home communities. Although it did not entail the protection of reciprocity, *forastero* status exploited a loophole in Spanish law that made only *ayllu* members liable for tax and tribute. Other Andeans disappeared into Lima, Quito, and other major urban centers, where they survived in the informal sector working as peddlers and day laborers. Consequently, people seemed to disappear from the Indian republic, and by the late seventeenth century the population of the sixteen provinces supplying most of Potosí's labor had dropped by 50 percent.

The reach of the Peruvian imperial state was relatively short in the first centuries of Spanish rule, which allowed Andeans to protect many of their preconquest institutions. But as the decades passed, the realities of subjecthood inevitably broke down some of this particularism and reshaped the identities and culture of later generations, though not always in the ways that the Spanish intended. Toledo's administrative reforms and *mit'a* labor demands steadily wore down the reciprocal communal relationships central to the Andean political economy under the Inkas. Spanish insistence on taxes in cash rather than produce and mandatory purchases under the *repartimiento* system gradually forced Andeans into the cash economy, which promoted private rather than communal conceptions of property. Urbanization and the explosive growth of the mining economy created new market opportunities for those with the resources to sell crops, crafts, and services.

As the princes of the Indian republic, the *kurakas* acquired the power to monopolize the resources of their *ayllus*. Some, particularly those in more remote regions, tried to follow the old reciprocal ways by using new forms of wealth to provide their *ayllus* with aid and material goods. Other *kurakas*, however, were more entrepreneurial and self-interested. They hired out their constituents to private employers or put them to work weaving cloth under contract for Spanish buyers. Those living within Potosí's orbit made fortunes by supplying the mines with food and wine. Bearing Hispanicized names with the noble honorific *don*, they essentially became minor imperial functionaries.

The *kurakas* often used this ability to earn cash to purchase land. Theoretically, *ayllu* land belonged to the community, but the pressure of tribute and taxation led Andeans to rent and sometimes sell land to generate currency. Spanish buyers acquired some of these tracts, but they had difficulty developing them because, under the law, the Indian republic was technically closed to Europeans. The *kurakas* therefore were best positioned to take advantage of the new land market, and several powerful Hispanicized *kuraka* families became important landholders in the highland regions near Lima and other urban centers. More remote *ayllus* proved more resilient, but over time common Andeans had to sell their labor in ever larger numbers as they lost access to land.

These profound economic changes gradually turned Andeans into tribute-paying Indians as local identities lost their economic underpinnings and broke down over the course of the seventeenth century. To a large extent these Indians were partially Hispanicized Christians, but this imperially driven cultural transformation rarely lived up to Spanish expectations. The idealistic rhetoric that legitimized Spanish rule obligated Peruvian administrators to make a good faith effort to "civilize" highland populations, which meant becoming culturally Spanish. Initially, the imperial authorities did not fully appreciate that Hispanicizing their subjects would complicate their ability to exploit them.

As in earlier empires, in the Andes elites were the most open to assimilation. The sons of Inkan royals and powerful *kurakas* attended Church-run boarding schools that aimed to create a Hispanicized Christian nobility for the Indian republic. Many of these boys grew up into loyal subjects, but Spanish officials often worried that they were too European and unreliable. Bearing Spanish names and titles, acculturated Andean aristocrats wore western clothing, owned slaves, and invested in urban property. In the highlands, Hispanicized Andeans, known as Ladinos, staffed the Indian republic's bureaucracy as clerks and village scribes, but the Spanish authorities similarly distrusted them and never ceased to view them as Indians.

Peruvian officials and clergymen encountered even greater problems when they tried to provide the Indian nobility with obedient Christian subjects. The lasting power of the *wakas* testified to the strength of localism and the ability of common Andeans to resist Spain's civilizing project. Priests and friars therefore struggled to win converts because they could not articulate the central tenants of Christianity in Andean terms. They made some headway by opening parish schools and producing Quechua and Aymara dictionaries and lexicons in the early seventeenth century, but they soon discovered that many Andeans adopted baptism, saints, hymns, prayer, and other trappings of Catholicism without actually internalizing their official meaning. To their horror, Spanish churchmen began to fear that the new converts were following the mestizo priest Valera's lead in Andeanizing Christianity instead of accepting the subordinate role that Spanish Catholicism assigned them in imperial society. The panic and vigor behind the Church's ill-fated extirpation campaigns against the *wakas* thus echoed the Andalusi authorities' desperate attempt to defend the boundaries of subjecthood by preventing the Mozarabs from blending Islam with Iberian Christianity.

As in Al-Andalus, gender further muddied the distinction between citizen and subject in the Andes. Peruvian administrators initially hoped to create a more comprehensible community of subjects by promoting Spanish conceptions of paternal masculinity. Drawing on their own gendered biases, they assumed that men had a natural right and responsibility to control women. They brushed aside preconquest norms that had accorded women a parallel but equal role in the Andean political economy, thereby ensuring that there would be no more female *kurakas* under Spanish rule. Toledo denied Andean women legal standing in the courts and required them to reside in their husbands' *ayllus*.

Yet the viceroy's tribute demands made a nonsense of his attempts at imperial social engineering. Marriage was the primary marker of adulthood for Andean males, which meant that taking a wife made them liable to pay tribute to the state. Imperial extraction therefore encouraged young men to either establish informal relationships with women or put off marriage. Similarly, the *mit'a* labor sweep led many to flee their *ayllus* entirely. The 1560 census found that almost half of the women in Peru's most populous province were unmarried.[43]

Far from reinforcing patriarchal supremacy, Spanish imperial rule actually undermined the influence of common men. Backed by the power of empire, the Spaniards used their prerogatives to monopolize Andean women, which led Don Felipe to complain that women "no longer love Indians but rather Spaniards, and they become big whores."[44] Andean chroniclers condemned Andean women for their disloyalty, but conjugal relations with the conquerors taught them Spanish and provided a more sophisticated knowledge of imperial society. Don Felipe's lament that "the Indians are disappearing because they have no women" reflected the reality that many women fled the patriarchal restrictions of life in the *ayllus* to pursue commercial opportunities in Peruvian cities.[45] Predictably, some Andean men responded aggressively to this increased female autonomy, which helps to explain why domestic violence and sexual disputes were a significant cause of homicide in eighteenth-century Peru.[46] This was hardly what the architects of Spanish imperial rule in Peru had in mind when they attempted to restructure Andean society.

The proliferation of *castas* was an even bigger problem. Resulting from the insistence of Spanish men on asserting their sexual power over female slaves and Andean subjects, these mixed identities further undermined the Peruvian state's attempt to create a bounded and stable Indian republic. Theoretically, the Republic of the Spaniards, which was the mirror of the Republic of the Indians, was exclusively European, but the growing population of mixed Andean, African, and Spanish offspring had no place in the Republic of the Indians. By default, they were interlopers in the Spanish Republic. The original mestizo children of the conquistadors often became Spaniards in good standing, but later generations with less aristocratic origins faced institutional discrimination.

This inability to maintain a clear distinction between rights-bearing citizens and exploitable subjects imperiled the Spanish empire in the Andes. Writing in the immediate decades following Pizarro's victory at Cajamarca, Cieza recorded a conversation between an Andean noble and a Spanish friar: "Father, you must know that God became tired of tolerating the great sins of the Indians of this land, and He sent the Inkas to punish them; they did not last very long either, and by the their fault God also tired of tolerating them, and you came and took their land in which you are; and God will also tire of tolerating you, and others will come who will replace you, as you deserve."[47] Cieza's informant correctly predicted the demise of the Pizarrists, but it took almost three centuries for God to tire of Spanish rule in Peru. The blurred lines of subjecthood in imperial society were at the root of the problem.

As in the Roman Empire and the Umayyad Caliphate, the Spanish Empire in the Americas was not overthrown by a revolution from below. Rather, it evolved over the course of the centuries into a transoceanic state that bore little resemblance to the early modern Habsburg Spanish Empire that had sanctioned Pizarro's conquest of the Andes. The War of the Spanish Succession in the early eighteenth century, which brought the Bourbon dynasty to the Spanish throne, stripped Spain of the last of its European empire. The decline of Spanish naval power, smuggling by European rivals, and assertive creole settlers in the Americas undermined the metropolitan government's control over what remained.

The absolutist Bourbon kings sought to revitalize their truncated empire by creating more efficient bureaucratic and military institutions and enforcing the rules that closed the colonies to foreigners. This ambitious agenda depended on the wholesale reform of Spain's antiquated imperial institutions. But the Viceroyalty of Peru, which encompassed the old Inkan Empire, was not in any condition to pay for the changes. Andean opposition to the *mit'a* labor demands and a shortage of mercury for refining meant that Peruvian silver production dropped from the equivalent of seven million pesos to two million pesos per year between 1600 and 1700.[48] Institutional corruption further undercut government revenues. *Corregidors* falsified census records and tax rolls to disguise the fact that they kept Andean labor for themselves and embezzled state funds. The latter practice became so widespread that audits uncovered million-peso revenue shortfalls. The viceroyalty therefore lacked the capital to develop alternatives to the dilapidated mining economy and had to borrow heavily to cover its basic operating costs.

The Bourbon reformers tried to address these problems by bringing Peru and the other American territories under more direct control by dispatching teams of investigators to audit territorial governments. In 1783, they replaced the bureaucracy of Toledo's outdated Indian republic with specially appointed metropolitan intendants and subdelegates who supplanted the venal *corregidors* in the highlands. On paper, the intendancy system appeared to make imperial rule more accountable, but corruption persisted because the subdelegates still took their salary as a share of collected tribute. The reformers also shied away from making changes in the *mit'a* system, even though it had become so embarrassingly oppressive that several viceroys asked for permission to abolish it.

More significantly, the absolutist Bourbon agenda floundered because it alienated the Peruvian creoles. According to the 1795 census, a bit more than 12 percent of the approximately one and a half million people in the viceroyalty were of European origin.[49] The vast majority of these were locally born creoles who distinguished themselves from recently arrived metropolitan *peninsulares*. After multiple generations in the New World, the Spanish settlers evolved into European Americans who were content to remain within the Spanish Empire as long as the Crown's administrative reach was too short to stretch across the Atlantic. Spanish policy theoretically barred them from serving in the imperial administration on the assumption that their self-interest would lead to corruption. This was unrealistic and unenforceable, and creoles steadily infiltrated the *audiencias*, viceregal bureaucracy, clergy, urban militias, and rural administration over the course of the seventeenth century. Not surprisingly, these entrenched imperial interests resented the Bourbon Crown's reassertion of metropolitan authority. Powerful creoles balked at paying higher taxes to fund the Spanish military buildup in the Americas and resented the superior airs of the *peninsulares* who arrived in Peru as intendants and senior military officers.

Although they had a pronounced inferiority complex in relation to Old World Spaniards, the creoles were the real rulers of Peru. With virtually uncontested control over the agricultural and mining sectors, they jealously defended their privileges against peninsular pressure from above and Andean challenges from below. As the premier imperial interest group in Peru and the true heirs of the Pizarrists, they insisted on total supremacy over the Indian, African, and *casta* peoples who constituted roughly 88 percent of the population in the eighteenth century.

This was a Peru that was markedly different from the realm of the Inkas. The Andean societies that the conquistadors violently dragged into the Spanish empire largely disappeared as coherent corporate institutions in the late sixteenth century under the hammer blows of pestilence, Spanish tribute demands, and blurred imperial identities. Preconquest British and Iberian societies also had faded away under the weight of imperial subjecthood, but those were centuries-long evolutionary processes. The Inkan imperial collapse was a cataclysmic disaster that occurred virtually overnight, but the Andeans did not descend into a self-destructive spiral of depression and anomie, as some historians have suggested. Instead, the survivors adapted Andean culture to the realities of Spanish imperial rule.[50]

A new heterogeneous ruling class in the highlands emerged by the early eighteenth century through the fusion of the surviving Inkan nobility, wealthy mestizos, and Spaniards still willing to marry across the imperial social frontier. Centered in Cuzco, as opposed to creole-dominated Lima, these "mixed-blood" *principales* (important people) were primarily wealthy landowners, merchants, and skilled artisans. Some were descended from prosperous *kurakas,* but the influence of these princes of the Indian republic declined along with Andean institutions of reciprocity. The *principales* eclipsed those lesser *kurakas* who had to borrow money and sell community land to meet tribute obligations as their communities disintegrated. The office of *kuraka* became so unpopular in the eighteenth century that it lost its noble status and often fell into the hands of simple Spanish tax collectors. The cash economy and privatization of wealth transformed common Andeans into "estate Indians" living on creole plantations, urban wage laborers, and "community Indians" who remained in what survived of the *ayllus.* Over time, many finally came to see themselves as Indians rather than as members of a particular community.

The development of this pan-Andean Indian identity was not a boon for Spanish imperial rulers, for it made their subjects harder to govern. Far from accepting their assigned role in Peruvian society, the peoples of the highlands, whether Andean, Indian, *casta,* or African, continued to contest their subjecthood. In fact, the Spanish never succeeded in pacifying the highlands fully. Frontier peoples defied the authority of Lima, and imperial officials still risked murder if they meddled too deeply in highland communities. The relative weakness of the creole militias left the Spaniards in constant fear of conspiracies and revolts, and in 1666 they actually uncovered a mestizo/Andean plot to burn down Lima.

The eighteenth century was even more turbulent. The weight of the Bourbon reforms fell most heavily on the highlands through oppressive demands for tribute and discriminatory tariffs that disrupted the growing inter-Andean trade. Between 1730 and 1814, there were more than one hundred organized revolts against the Peruvian government and the privileged creole minority. Generally speaking, they followed a common trajectory in which local disputes grew into revolts that sometimes merged into mass rebellions. Common features of this basic template included murdering the *corregidor*, attacking clergymen, burning churches and government buildings, and displaying Inkan symbols. This nostalgia for the Inkan Empire is particularly interesting given that many of the leaders of the revolts were mestizos or the descendants of some of the Inkas' more embittered opponents. Groups such as the Canari, who had suffered heavily under the Inkan imperial yoke, now looked back on the Inka era as an Andean golden age. Eighteenth-century Peruvians knew relatively little about the Inkan Empire, but they used nostalgia as a powerful anti-imperial ideology to provoke unrest by promising that the Sapa Inkas would return to drive out the Spaniards.

The Peruvian authorities took these romantic prophecies seriously and tried to ban Inkan clothing, flags, conch shell horns, and even Garcialaso de la Vega's *Royal Commentaries of the Inkas*. Their concerns were well founded. The three most serious revolts in the eighteenth century all invoked the Inkas to attract followers and establish their legitimacy. In the lowland jungle regions of the eastern Andes, a charismatic leader calling himself Juan Santos Atawallpa organized a coalition of Andeans, *castas*, escaped slaves, and forest peoples that held off repeated Spanish attacks between 1742 and 1746. Juan Santos's rebel state collapsed after he died and left no lasting impact on the highlands, but he gave other Andean groups an opportunity to rebel by distracting the Peruvian government and tying down its military assets.

In 1750, migrants from the province of Huarochiri organized an uprising in Lima timed to coincide with a feast day celebration. The plot called for armed bands to attack government buildings and murder prominent citizens. Although conspirators made extensive use of Inkan symbolism, they also recruited Africans and black Peruvians by promising to abolish slavery. The Lima authorities put down the rebellion with wholesale torture and executions, but the rebel leader Francisco Inka fled to his home province, where he continued the uprising by attacking the *mit'a* system and abusive *corregidors*. Declaring a revival of Inkan rule in Huarochiri, he swore allegiance to Juan Santos Atawallpa and promised his followers that military aid was on the way. In the end, however, armed Spanish miners and troops brought the insurrection to a swift and bloody conclusion.

Francisco Inka's uprising was a significant threat because Huarochiri controlled the main communication routes between Lima and the highlands, but it was only a prelude to the most serious outbreak of organized unrest. In 1780, a mestizo *kuraka* named José Gabriel Condorcanqui touched off a chain reaction of popular violence in a vast swath of the highlands stretching from Cuzco southward to Lake Titicaca. Claiming to be a prince of the Inka royal line, he drew approximately fifty thousand followers as Tupac Amaru II. This enormous army handed the Spanish their worst defeat in Peru since the conquistador era and followed Manqu Inka's example by laying siege to Cuzco.

Although he claimed the Inkan throne, Tupac was actually a wealthy but common mule train owner angered by the Peruvian government's imposition of higher sales taxes and increased tariffs. Many of his followers were poor mestizos and marginal creoles, and his primary demands were for free trade and a more representative and responsible government. Far from being an anti-imperial revolutionary, Tupac declared his loyalty to the Spanish Crown and claimed to be acting under royal orders to stamp out corruption and protect the true Christian faith in the highlands. Ultimately, he was more interested in supplanting the entrenched *principales* in the highlands than in bringing about real social change. The full-blooded Inkan aristocracy in Cuzco considered him an upstart, and he drew little support from commoners living around the city.[51]

The size of Tupac's army creates a false impression that he had a popular Andean following. In reality, his insurgency was an umbrella rebellion that swept up smaller local revolts by communities that were suffering under the burden of imperial tribute and knew little of the self-proclaimed Sapa Inka's true agenda. Indeed, the rebellion took on a life of its own after the Peruvian authorities captured Tupac and tortured him to death in 1781. For a time his cousins, who took the names Diego and Andrés Tupac Amaru, continued the revolt. In time, creole officers leading militia units of conscripted Andeans and lower-class *castas* hunted them down as well.

The issues driving the Tupac Amaru rebellion also resonated with people in the Aymara-speaking regions around Lake Titicaca, which were now part of the Viceroyalty of Río de la Plata. As in Peru, a minor *kuraka* family attracted followers by tapping into widespread anger over excessive tax and tribute demands. Their leader, Tomás Katari, followed Tupac Amaru's lead in affirming his allegiance to the Crown and appealed to the *audiencia* of Buenos Aires for redress, but Bolivian officials put him to death. His brothers continued the revolt at the head of a large army that unsuccessfully besieged La Paz. Seeking help against a common enemy, they swore allegiance to Tupac Amaru as the returned Sapa Inka even though their Aymara-speaking followers had no emotional ties to the Inkas. The alliance proved fruitless, and Spanish forces eventually defeated and executed the would-be Inkan viceroys.

Upon closer analysis, neither Tupac Amaru nor the Kataris were particularly central to the mass unrest in the southern Andes. Most of the common people who flocked to their call were actually rebelling against the *mit'a* system and, indirectly, the burden of the Bourbon extractive demands. Tupac Amaru aimed to supplant the *principales* in the highlands, but his followers interjected a far more populist element into the revolt as it spread south into Bolivia. In addition to rejecting imperial demands for tribute, they assaulted the privileged, ignored church sanctuary, and rejected the right to private property. Essentially, these were as much civil wars between the victims and beneficiaries of Spanish imperial rule in the highlands as they were revolts against Bourbon absolutism. Underlying all the uprisings was opposition to the institutions of imperial exploitation that drove the emerging capitalist economy in the Andes. This radical agenda provided a powerful incentive for *principales*, creole aristocrats, Inkan nobles, and imperial administrators to cooperate in stamping out the revolts. The Peruvian authorities dismissed the rebellions as an atavistic reversion to Indian barbarism, but it took them almost two years and more than one million lives to regain control of the highlands.

This enormous loss of life was a prime consideration in the Spanish government's decision to reform the rural administration. Peruvian officials also took steps to defuse the tensions that had brought on the unrest by relaxing *mit'a* obligations and giving Cuzco a representative municipal government. But no imperial power can afford to appear soft to its subjects, and vindictive and paranoid officials executed every fifth man in rebel Andean villages and tortured and beheaded their leaders. Sporadic outbursts of local unrest continued, but the Peruvian government's draconian tactics held popular resistance at a manageable level.

Ultimately, it was the privileged creoles, not the subject majority, that brought the Spanish Empire in the Americas to an end in the early nineteenth century. The *peninsulares* insinuated that creole conspirators provoked the Tupac Amaru revolt in a plot to follow the English colonists' lead in declaring their independence. This was nonsense, for the mass rebellion demonstrated that the Peruvian creoles still needed metropolitan help in controlling the Andean majority. They were far more royalist and conservative than their counterparts in the other viceroyalties because they worried that a revolutionary war would give the lower orders of Peruvian society another chance to revolt. In 1791, the bloody slave uprising in Haiti, resulting from the breakdown in authority during the French Revolution, deepened their insecurity.

Although Peruvian creoles disliked the Bourbon mercantilism that hindered trade with the rest of the Americas and resented the condescension of the *peninsulares*, it took events in Europe to finally force a break with Spain. In 1808, central authority in the empire collapsed after Napoleon placed his brother Joseph on the Spanish throne. Warfare and disorder in metropolitan Spain, coupled with the British blockade of continental Europe, gave New World Spaniards an opportunity to take more direct control of their economic and political affairs. The Bourbon government in exile refused to sanction these steps but was powerless to enforce its will on the imperial periphery. Creole leaders such as Simón Bolívar in Venezuela and Bernardo O'Higgins in Chile took advantage by founding provincial councils (*juntas*) that challenged royal authority.

While Peruvian creole leaders were not sure what to make of their newfound autonomy, in 1811 Bolívar and his fellow Venezuelan creoles took the radical step of declaring their independence. This touched off revolutionary wars between rebels and royalists throughout the continent. Ferdinand VII tried to reassert control over the colonies upon returning to power in 1814, but his troops, who sympathized with the opponents of Bourbon absolutism, mutinied. This gave creole armies led by Bolívar in the north and José de San Martín in the south the opportunity to roll up steady victories as they brought three centuries of Spanish imperial rule in almost all of South America to an end.

In Peru, however, the threat of popular revolt dressed up in neo-Inkan garb made the creole elite far less ready to break with the Crown than were their counterparts in the rest of the continent. The viceregal authorities continued to uncover small plots to restore self-proclaimed Sapa Inkas, and another Cuzco-based mass rebellion erupted in 1814 that once again shook the foundations of creole privilege. Viceregal troops restored order, but the Lima establishment, which retained relatively strong economic ties to Spain, was in no mood to leave the safety of the empire at such a precarious moment. Alarmed by the royalists' encouragement of slaves and Indians to rise up against Bolívar in Venezuela, they decided not to form a *junta*. Lima thus became a royalist redoubt sandwiched between the revolutionary regime in Venezuela and its southern allies in Argentina and Chile.

Spanish rule in Peru survived until San Martín's Army of the Andes captured Lima in 1821 and Bolívar defeated the royalist forces in the highlands three years later. Peru and Bolivia split into independent nations in 1839. Tellingly, the subject population of Peru was largely disinterested in the outcome of the independence struggle because, despite San Martín's promises to reform the tribute system and end slavery, they recognized that a revolutionary victory would not change their status. Conscripted Peruvians fought on both sides of the conflict, but Indians, *castas*, and slaves remained a subordinate majority under the new national constitution that based the franchise on property and occupation. Viceregal officials abolished the *mit'a* in 1812, but economic necessity forced the postcolonial Peruvian government to retain the head tax. Debt peonage replaced labor tribute, and slavery remained legal until the 1850s. The promise of constitutional liberalism also faded as powerful regional warlords known as *caudillos* used patronage and clientage to seize power. The Spanish Empire in South America was no more, but the descendants of the Andeans remained exploitable subjects.

Although it shared many common features with imperial Rome and the Umayyad Caliphate, Spain's three-hundred-year New World empire was the product of a revolutionary change in the systems of imperial rule. Advances in maritime technology gave Spanish empire builders the means to conquer and hold new lands beyond the once confining shores of continental Europe. Although there would still be great land empires, the defining empires of the early modern era were sprawling global entities.

The ability to bridge the oceanic barriers that had formerly kept the Americas isolated from the Old World Eurasian land mass gave the conquistadors a distinct advantage over the seemingly invincible Aztec and Inkan empires. While they were equipped with horses, superior weapons, and an aggressive Christian zealotry nurtured by the wars of the Reconquista, Spanish empire builders triumphed by exploiting the Americans' vulnerability to Old World diseases. It would take Europeans several more centuries to understand the biological nature of infection, but the explorers and settlers who followed in Columbus's footsteps unintentionally but inevitably touched off devastating virgin-soil epidemics simply by interacting with epidemiologically vulnerable New World peoples. The ensuing deaths of millions left the Inkans and Aztecs dangerously vulnerable before they even set eyes on the first conquistador. Were it not for these diseases, the Pizarrists most likely would have encountered Wayna Qhapaq at the height of his power when they blundered into the highlands. Instead, the conquistadors found a broken empire wracked by civil war between the Sapa Inka's fratricidal sons.

A healthy Wayna Qhapaq might have been able to hold off the conquistadors, but the Pizarrists' ability to hijack the Inkan state, which seems a remarkable accomplishment at face value, actually illustrated another reality common to all empires. Although imperial states appeared virtually omnipotent at the height of their dominance, they were in fact extremely fragile. Recently conquered Andeans had little reason to defend Inkan despots and largely stood by as the Pizarrists became the new lords of the highlands. Lacking popular legitimacy, the bureaucratic and extractive institutions that made the Inkan Empire possible and profitable were easily captured by outsiders with the military means to displace them.

In one sense, Pizarro and the conquistadors do not seem particularly different from earlier generations of imperialists. They were driven by self-interest and greed, but they depicted themselves as loyal servants of the Crown. Conveniently, the ships that brought them across the Atlantic were too slow and small to allow the Habsburg imperial state to supervise them directly. As a result, the Pizarrists were free to turn the machinery of Inkan imperial rule to their own ends. Unhindered by metropolitan oversight, they were exceptionally brutal in their search for plunder. But most empire builders would have done the same if given the opportunity, for when stripped to its essence, empire is nothing more than the political embodiment of unchecked avarice.

The conquistadors also began a new era of western empire building. While earlier imperial conquerors were self-servingly brutal, they never pretended to be concerned with the salvation of their subjects. The architects of the Arab caliphate used Islam to justify their conquests, but they did not claim that their tribute demands were uplifting or civilizing. The conquistadors, conversely, professed that godless New World peoples benefited from imperial exploitation.

Foreshadowing the emergence of nineteenth-century biological racism, Spanish ideologues linked imperial citizenship with blood. Where select Britons, Iberians, and even preconquest Andeans had the chance to escape subjecthood through assimilation and conversion, the New World Spaniards claimed that all indigenous Americans were so inherently different and inferior that they were destined to be permanent subjects as "Indians." As such, it was appropriate and legitimate to exploit Andean labor through the *encomienda* and *mit'a* systems. Although the origins of this protoracism lay in the Reconquista, Spanish notions of imperial exclusivity found fertile ground in the substantial settler colonies that were another new feature of the early modern overseas empires in the Americas. While Roman veterans' colonies and Arab military camps introduced a colonial dimension into ancient and medieval empires, these relatively small imperial settlements often merged with local subject communities. In contrast, Spaniards migrated to the New World in far greater numbers and created a self-sustaining colonial aristocracy that used early modern notions of blood and purity to justify their systematic exploitation of Andean labor.

In South Asia, the rulers of the Mughal Empire similarly discovered that this new kind of empire was a global phenomenon in the early modern era. Like the Sapa Inkas, the Mughal emperors paved the way for aggressive European imperial speculators by creating efficient and co-optable imperial state systems. While the Mughal emperor Shah Alam II never had to face a desperately ruthless warlord like Francisco Pizarro, he soon discovered that the clerks of the British East India Company could be as dangerous as any conquistador.

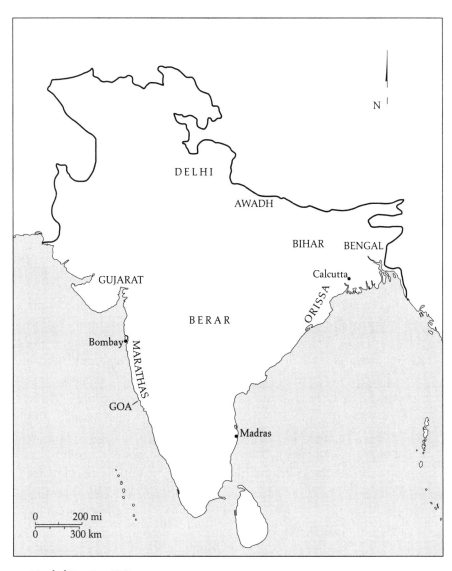

DELHI

AWADH

BIHAR

BENGAL

Calcutta

GUJARAT

BERAR

ORISSA

Bombay

MARATHAS

GOA

Madras

N

0   200 mi

0   300 km

Mughal Empire, 1960

4

COMPANY INDIA

Private Empire Building

While the conquistadors stormed into the Andes, the British Empire crept up on the *ryots* (peasant farmers) of the Mughal province of Bengal. Historians tend to mark 1757, the date of the British East India Company's victory over Nawab Siraj-ud-Daula at the battle of Plassey, as the beginning of direct British rule in eastern India.[1] But this seemingly unremarkable clash between the forces of the *nawab,* the de facto independent ruler of one of the Mughal Empire's most wealthy provinces, and a privately owned European chartered company probably did not make much of an immediate impression on the vast majority of Bengalis. Those who were aware of Siraj-ud-Daula's defeat at the hands of the barbarous but seemingly innocuous foreigners who first came to the South Asian subcontinent to buy hand-woven textiles and assorted spices well could have concluded that they had simply exchanged one set of imperial rulers for another.

Along with the territories of Bihar and Orissa, Bengal lay on the easternmost flank of the Mughal Empire in what is today northeastern India and Bangladesh. Under the British, the province of Bengal fell within the larger Bengal Presidency, which included most of the northeastern corner of the South Asian subcontinent. At the time of Plassey, Bengal was essentially an autonomous kingdom under the Mughal bureaucrats-turned-governors who exploited the declining fortunes of the empire. Murshid Quli Khan, the first of these *nawabs,* or viceroys, was a Hindu ex-slave turned bureaucrat. His successors governed through a diverse coalition of Muslim military elites and

Hindu bureaucrats who cooperated in the exploitation of the Bengali peasantry.

The *nawabs* were the last of a centuries-long succession of Hindu kings, Turkish and Afghan sultans, and Mughal imperial officials. These autocratic but remote rulers had few connections to common Bengalis, who had equally diverse origins. Some identified themselves as members of various Hindu castes, but some were converts to Islam. Most made their living by tilling the soil, but Bengal's villages also supported well-developed handicraft industries that drew foreign traders from Asia and Europe. Additionally, there were foraging and nomadic pastoral communities in the large swaths of the region that still consisted of forest and wasteland. Although religion, caste, and occupation created ties between Bengalis, the village was the primary polity, unit of economic production, and focus of social loyalty and identity.

Bengal was worth fighting over because it had a sophisticated market-based economy that linked these local economies to wider networks of South Asian trade. More important, it supported an efficient system of revenue collection developed over centuries of rule by its diverse imperial masters. Unlike ancient Britons, medieval Iberians, and early modern Andeans, the vast majority of Bengalis paid their tribute in currency rather than produce or goods. In most localities an elaborate hierarchy of elites siphoned off the rural surplus and passed it on to their superiors after reserving a share for themselves. These *zamindars* were not landed nobles in the conventional western sense; rather, they only had the hereditary right to collect wealth from a specific allotment of territory. In return, they maintained local irrigation systems and hired armed retainers to uphold law and order. The *zamindars* themselves did not actually levy tribute but instead relied on a class of petty bureaucrats to deal directly with local villages. Although the *zamindari* system was highly efficient in delivering wealth to Bengal's imperial masters, it also isolated these rulers from the greater population.

The fact that Plassey made an alien European commercial enterprise the practical master of Bengal was probably of little concern to most common Bengalis. Nevertheless, it is remarkable that the United Company of Merchants of England Trading to the East Indies, more commonly known as the East India Company (EIC), managed to seize control of such an important Mughal province. Initially, the EIC was just one of nineteen chartered companies that mobilized capital for risky foreign trading ventures in seventeenth-century England. Established in 1600, its charter from Queen Elizabeth I granted it a monopoly over all British trade with the East Indies and the implicit authority to negotiate commercial treaties, establish settlements, and, by implication, wage wars.

Although warfare seems an odd enterprise for a commercial concern, the chartered companies often used armed force to open Asian markets and defend themselves from European rivals. The EIC focused its operations on the South Asian subcontinent because the Dutch East India Company (Vereenigde Oost-indische Compagnie, or VOC) drove it out of the Indonesian Spice Islands. Drawn by India's high-quality textiles and relatively open markets, EIC representatives joined competing companies in establishing coastal trading stations throughout the subcontinent.

The Mughals were fully aware of the Europeans' militarism but were secure in their power in the seventeenth century. Rather than seeing the foreigners as a threat, they considered them useful trading partners and, after the Spanish conquest of the Americas, a lucrative source of New World silver. The Bengali governors and *nawabs* shared these views and allowed the Company to fortify its settlement on the Hugli River and purchase the right to collect revenue in the surrounding communities. In becoming a Bengali *zamindar*, the EIC also assumed judicial authority and an obligation to maintain law and order in the small enclave that grew into Calcutta under their administration.

The East India Company fortified this Bengali toehold to protect its warehouses from local unrest and French and Dutch rivals. At first glance, its decision to diversify into revenue collection was curious because it made the EIC a Mughal vassal. But it was also a good investment. The relatively small fee that it cost to buy the right to collect tribute in the regions surrounding its factory brought substantial annual returns.[2] These revenues subsidized the Company's less successful commercial operations and demonstrated that there were fortunes to be made in Bengal through administration as well as trade. The Mughals and their Bengali viceroys granted these kinds of concessions to the European companies out of self-interest rather than fear or intimidation. They clearly did not understand the dangers of giving potential empire builders intimate access to a politically unstable but wealthy society riven by class, caste, and religion.

These risks became clearer as the East India Company pushed deeper into Bengal to trade directly with weavers, spinners, and farmers. Additionally, its employees also undermined the *nawabs'* finances by using their commercial privileges to set up tax-exempt private speculative ventures. Tensions came to a head in 1756 when the Company defied Siraj-ud-Daula by fortifying its Calcutta base, abusing its trading permits, and refusing to pay him the customary presents that acknowledged his authority. In response, the *nawab* occupied Calcutta and locked more than one hundred Company employees in an overcrowded jail cell. When hysterical British reports claimed that 123 out of 146 of the prisoners smothered in this "Black Hole of Calcutta," the Company had a moral justification for deposing the *nawab*.

It fell to Robert Clive, a onetime Company clerk who had made his reputation fighting the French in southern India, to reassert British influence in Bengal. Leading a mixed force of private European troops and southern Indian soldiers, he retook Calcutta and forced the *nawab* to pay compensation for his aggression. Clive initially showed no inclination to exploit his victory by deposing the *nawab* and reaffirmed the EIC's vassal status by declaring to Siraj-ud-Daula: "I esteem your Excellency in the place of my father and mother, and myself as your son, and should think myself happy to lay down my life for the preservation of yours." The *nawab* was equally ready to make amends and rather fantastically declared that, as a Muslim, he preferred the Christian British *dhimmi* (people of the book) to his "pagan" Hindu subjects.[3]

In reality, Siraj-ud-Daula had outlived his usefulness to the Bengali elites who controlled the provincial administration and economy. The growth of Calcutta as a commercial center brought local merchants and bankers into the Company's orbit, and the *nawab*'s loss to Clive demonstrated his weakness to the military aristocrats who underwrote his authority. Sensing an opportunity, Clive and other ambitious Company employees conspired with Siraj-ud-Daula's primary local financiers to replace him with Mir Jafar, a common Arab soldier who had risen through the ranks to command the *nawab*'s army. This unimaginative Mughal general did not realize the consequences of such a Faustian bargain and promised the EIC one and a quarter million pounds in return for bringing him to power. When Clive's troops met the *nawab*'s much larger army at the village of

Plassey on June 23, 1757, Mir Jafar played his role in the conspiracy by advising the *nawab* to withdraw. With their cannons destroyed by more accurate British artillery and their cavalry mired in the mud, the Bengali troops broke and ran during the retreat. As a result, Clive found himself in possession of the battlefield.

Plassey was hardly a major military victory or a decisive imperial turning point on par with Pizarro's stroke at Cajamarca. Mir Jafar did indeed become *nawab* after his men executed Siraj-ud-Daula, but he was Clive's creature. As the EIC's governor in Bengal, Clive consolidated his hold on the province by expanding its *zamindari* rights into Calcutta's hinterlands, fending off invasions by neighboring Indian powers (including the Mughal emperor himself), and appointing and deposing *nawabs* as the Company's interests dictated. In effect, the Plassey conspiracy transformed the EIC into a princely Indian power.

Clive was thus a private speculative empire builder in the tradition of Tariq ibn Ziyad and Francisco Pizarro. But he was no crude conquistador. He was a clerk, soldier, and diplomat, but above all he was a new kind of bureaucratic conqueror. Clive's greed and personal ambition clearly matched Pizarro's, but Mughal India's advanced institutions of administration, commerce, and revenue collection made plunder unnecessary. After Plassey, he amassed a fortune of nearly a quarter million pounds by taking control of the Bengali treasury and extorting "presents" from local notables.[4]

The Company's directors in London never planned to acquire an empire, but they were powerless to prevent their opportunistic employees from parasitizing Asian imperial systems. These clerical empire builders did not need the decisive military advantage that the Pizarrists held over the Inkas; they won their victories with "foreign" Indian troops from other parts of the subcontinent. Once in control of Bengal, Clive also left the economic and political structure of the province intact because the Mughal institutions of imperial extraction were already so effective. He therefore had the luxury of playing down the consequences of Plassey by making a show of respecting Mughal sovereignty while siphoning off the province's wealth.

Clive's deference to Mughal and Bengali authority led many commoners to assume that Plassey was one of the relatively minor power shifts that occurred periodically in Bengal rather than a catastrophic stroke by imperially minded foreigners. In the short term, they were correct. Clive did not have the inclination, authority, or resources to annex the province. Instead, he lobbied his superiors for permission to supplant the *nawabs* as the primary revenue collectors in Bengal. Writing to the Company chairman in London, he declared: "It is scarcely a hyperbole to say that the whole Mogul Empire is in our hands.... We must indeed become the Nabobs ourselves in fact, if not in name, perhaps without disguise."[5] This policy had serious consequences for common Bengalis, for the EIC's shift from trade to collecting tribute drew the British ever more deeply into village life and production. Within fifteen years of Plassey, the Company's Committee of Circuit openly stated: "Revenue is beyond all question the first object of Government, that on which all the rest depends, and to which everything should be made subsidiary."[6]

From the EIC's standpoint, Clive's capture of the *nawab*-ish state and steady assumption of political authority in Bengal proved to be a trap. The enormous wealth of the province was enticing, but the costs of maintaining a government and standing army nearly bankrupted the Company. Clive's successors therefore had to squeeze the Bengali peasantry to remain solvent. By the 1770s, they were making revenue demands that earlier generations of *zamindars*, who had to negotiate tribute levels with local producers, never could have attempted.

Village *ryots* and weavers initially may have been indifferent to Siraj-ud-Daula's demise, but they suffered most under the Company's insatiable appetite for tribute and taxes. Jamiruddin Dafadar, a poet from western Bengal, wrote an epic poem recounting how their desperation led to open revolt. In it, a Muslim cleric urged local leaders to resist the British: "*Lakhs* [hundreds of thousands] of people are dying in famine, try to save their lives! The Company's agents and *picks* [armed henchmen] torture tillers and *ryots* for exorbitant revenue; and people are deserting villages." Similarly, another contemporary poem condemned the brutal methods of one of the EIC's Indian agents in Rangpur: "His only aim was to demand more and more; under severe torture a wail of agony arose."[7] Although the people of Bengal had been imperial subjects for centuries, Plassey set in motion a new bureaucratic process of rule and extraction that consigned them to a more systematically exploitive and invasive form of subjecthood.

Clive's victory in Bengal came more than a century after Pizarro and his men overthrew the Inkan Empire. Both enterprises were part of early modern Europe's global expansion, but there were considerable differences in how the relatively isolated New World societies of the Western Hemisphere and the far more integrated and complex polities of Asia responded to this threat. The Spanish conquistadors were plundering adventurers who had little interest in trade. They sought to become landed gentlemen, and their commercial activities consisted primarily of exporting the products of their *encomiendas* to Europe. Clive, on the other hand, was a salaried employee of a chartered company that focused initially on trade rather than conquest. The EIC's Dutch, French, Swedish, Danish, Spanish, and Portuguese rivals had similar agendas in Asia. But the slow pace of early modern travel and communication meant that the directors of these companies had minimal control over their employees once they were on the other side of the world. When it took half a year for a message from London to reach Bengal, self-interested opportunists such as Clive could easily turn to imperial ends the armies and navies that chartered companies had raised against European rivals.

The result was a new kind of private Asian imperial state that was very different from the early modern empires of the Western Hemisphere. Where Spanish, Portuguese, English, and French territories in the Americas quickly took on a colonial dimension by attracting significant numbers of European settlers, corporate conquerors in Asia built their empires by grafting themselves onto preexisting indigenous systems of imperial rule. The conquistadors did this to a lesser extent in Peru and Mexico, but Inkan and Aztec administrative and economic systems were less compatible with western institutions. Royal monopolies were of little value when the local population produced relatively few marketable and exportable goods and did not use convertible currencies. It was therefore more efficient and practical for the imperial powers to transform their New World conquests into settlement colonies where transplanted Europeans took on the responsibility for development and exploitation.

In the east, the chartered company empires never attracted significant numbers of migrants from Europe and could not be considered colonies in the Roman sense of the word. Europeans found the more humid and tropical Asian climates less congenial, but, more important, early modern Asian peoples and states were far better equipped to stand up to westerners. They were less vulnerable to infectious Old World diseases and had well-developed militaries that could meet the small chartered companies' private armies on equal technological terms. In short, there were no opportunities in Central and East Asia for would-be conquistadors to replicate Pizarro's Andean feat.

Men such as Clive had the freedom to dabble in speculative imperial projects because metropolitan European governments had few eastern ambitions. The English initially had little interest in an overseas empire. Empire, as conceived by Henry VIII, meant autonomy from the papacy and sovereignty over the British Isles. As in post-Reconquista Spain, it was not until the English, Scots, Welsh, and, to a much lesser extent, Irish began to envision themselves as separate and distinctive people that the "British" turned their attention overseas. The combination of the crowns of England and Scotland with the principality of Wales produced the United Kingdom in 1707. And although a vague sense of the British Isles as a coherent geographic entity dated back to Roman times, it was James I's active promotion of "Britain" as a unifying identity that encouraged his relatively diverse subjects to shift their allegiance to the Crown. Additionally, the nearly constant wars with France between 1756 and 1815, increased literacy, and the development of the Anglican Church further nurtured this broader British identity.

While it took time for common Britons to embrace the strong sense of unity and shared destiny embedded in popular nationalism, the development of a coherent sense of Britishness was an enormously powerful imperial tool at a time when most peoples of the early modern era still identified themselves primarily on the basis of locality, occupation, and religion. National sentiment paid economic and military dividends in organizing people from all walks of life to fight and fund the French wars and defend the overseas empire. The Bengal *ryots* may have been indifferent to Siraj-ud-Daula's demise at Plassey, but it did not take long for the British public to celebrate Clive's achievement as a great collective victory. Indeed, the British Empire and the wealth it generated became an inducement for the peoples of the British Isles to become "British." This is why a great many Scots played a significant role in the East India Company in the late eighteenth century.

At first, this sense of cultural superiority did not extend to Asia. Lacking the enormous advantage that they had over New World peoples, western merchant soldiers could not legitimize empire building by portraying Asians as inherently weak or backward. Instead, when

Clive and his allies built their Indian empire, they depicted rulers such as Siraj-ud-Daula as greedy and inept despots who forced them to intervene in Indian politics and society to defend legitimate commercial interests. Once in power, they found it much harder than the Pizarrists to denigrate South Asians as inferior subjects. In contrast to the American settlement colonies, company empire builders remained a small privileged minority who had to adopt local languages and customs to rule effectively and profitably.

Nevertheless, British imperial thinkers became increasingly confident that, as a free people, they had a duty to develop the world that God had given them. Divine obligation commanded them to exercise this liberty around the globe. In the decades following Plassey, the British in Bengal decided that their unique blend of liberty and commerce would rescue common Indians from the anarchy and oppression of the Mughal Empire and its successor states. Imperially minded Britons assured themselves that while they had not asked for the task of saving India, they would not shirk from it when fate and circumstance laid it at their door.

Drawing on Enlightenment ideals, evangelical Protestantism, liberalism, utilitarianism, the advances of the early industrial revolution, free trade, and English justice and good government, the imperial and reformist lobbies promised to remake India along western lines, rescue its women from sexual subjugation, and develop its resources for the greater good. Bartolomé de Las Casas and succeeding generations of Spanish imperial reformers made similar declarations, but by the nineteenth century this paternalism represented a more hypocritical kind of legitimizing imperial ideology. Answering to elected governments for their actions, empire builders tried to disguise their greed through professions of philanthropy. Clive and other Company officials became fabulously wealthy in India, the subcontinent became an important market for British manufacturers, and the metropolitan treasury depended on Company payments, but the British public was largely certain that they ruled India for its own good.

These liberalizing imperial ideologies protected Indians from the kinds of abuse that Andeans and other New World peoples suffered during the most brutal extractive phases of Spanish imperial rule. Still, the new British brand of imperial paternalism could not disguise the reality that subjecthood in Company India entailed self-serving exploitation at the hands of alien despots. British imperial rulers were therefore just as concerned with defining and defending the boundaries between citizen and subject as their Roman, Umayyad, and Spanish forerunners. Efficient and profitable extraction still depended on defining and dehumanizing conquered peoples. Opportunities for the early modern equivalent of romanization declined accordingly.

The East India Company had the freedom to develop these self-serving imperial institutions because the British Empire of the early modern era was so decentralized and incoherent. While Britons were slow to follow the Iberian lead in exploiting the opportunities of the New World, the English Crown still followed the Spanish example of relying on private speculative interests to take the lead in overseas empire building. In the Western Hemisphere, the resulting North American settlement and West Indian plantation colonies had their own particular characteristics, but they were relatively similar to their Spanish American counterparts. In Asia, however, the British East India Company was an entirely different kind of semiprivate imperial power. The Dutch East India Company, which conquered the Spice Islands and southern Africa, was its only real peer. The EIC's Indian empire differed markedly from Britain's colonies in the Americas, thereby making it difficult to speak of the larger British Empire as a single integrated institution.

The English monarchs, who had far less autonomy after the Glorious Revolution of 1688 than their Bourbon Spanish counterparts, were most concerned with forging the United Kingdom. English imperial entrepreneurs first focused primarily on founding settlement colonies in Ireland. Sixteenth-century speculators such as Sir Walter Raleigh, who later made a name for himself in the Americas, carved out "plantations" around the northern city of Ulster for English and Scottish settlers. Citing the Roman colonies in Britain as an inspiration, they claimed land in Ireland by right of conquest and depicted conquered Irish populations as uncivilized barbarians lacking the capacity to make proper use of fertile soil. Unlike the Welsh and Scots, who eventually became Britons, Irish Catholics largely remained inassimilable imperial subjects. As a result, when the Act of Union created the United Kingdom in 1707, Ireland became a de facto colony under the jurisdiction of the British Parliament.

Distracted by their Irish project and the Thirty Years' War, the cash-starved Crown left it to private commercial interests to take the lead in overseas expansion. It used the royal charter, which conferred a monopoly over all British trade in a given region, to convince entrepreneurs to accept the speculative risks of foreign ventures. Over time, these loose alliances of merchants gave way to joint stock companies that spread the risk of foreign trade and investment by raising capital collectively. Some of their shareholders were active traders, but others were passive investors seeking the greater profits of foreign commerce without leaving the safety of home. A court of directors and central office in London delegated the authority to negotiate trading rights and commercial treaties to company governors and factors who established forts and trading stations (factories) in foreign lands. Ideally, the companies exchanged European manufactures for spices, textiles, slaves, and other commodities, but in Asian markets they often had to buy the most desirable goods with precious metals. The expense of maintaining a fleet of armed merchant ships and fortified trade settlements was considerable, but the most successful firms used their monopolies to turn a profit. Technically, their charters only applied to rival British firms, but the courts of directors went to the great expense of raising private armies in an effort to force foreign rivals to respect them as well. The Crown played no role in directing their activities, but the chartered company model gave it an extremely cost-effective means of projecting imperial power overseas.

For their part, the courts of directors used their charters to raise capital for a wide variety of endeavors. Founded in 1581 as one of the first joint stock companies, the Levant Company futilely tried to develop a secure overland commercial route to Asia. In the west, the Virginia, Plymouth, and Massachusetts Bay companies purchased charters in the early seventeenth century giving them the right to establish speculative settlement colonies in North America. Later in the century, the Royal Company of Adventurers and the Royal African Company sought gold and then slaves in West Africa.

In the Americas, British charter holders and would-be empire builders had to confront the formidable but precarious Spanish Empire. Elizabeth I provided a measure of support for Francis Drake and Thomas Cavendish, but often it took force to make up for the Spanish, Portuguese, and French head start in the Western Hemisphere. Elizabeth therefore also quietly encouraged Drake and his peers to raid Spanish shipping. Taking advantage of Spain's growing impotence, British imperial entrepreneurs followed in the wake of these privateers to stake out settlement and plantation colonies in the sugar-producing islands of the West Indies and the most promising regions of coastal North America. They purchased their charters on the assumption that royally sanctioned monopolies on settlement and trade would make them great lords in the New World.

Yet the Spanish imperial model was unworkable in North America because the indigenous population was too sparse and vulnerable to disease to play the role of exploitable subjects. After an initial period of relatively peaceful coexistence, British settlers virtually wiped out most coastal Amerindian societies through warfare and enslavement. Still, the population of British North America grew from one hundred thousand to roughly two and a half million people between the mid-seventeenth and eighteenth centuries.[8] Taken as a whole, this massive overseas migration of western Europeans and unwilling African slaves produced an entrenched and expanding permanent British population in the Western Hemisphere.

In the east, the chartered company system never produced permanent settlement colonies. Most Asian societies were far too powerful and resistant to Old World diseases to suffer the fate of the Inkas. Moreover, the British East India Company was surprisingly impotent when its representatives first arrived in Asian waters. Its royal charter gave it a monopoly on all British commerce east of the Cape of Good Hope, but the EIC's 218 original stockholders were so severely undercapitalized that they had to share the costs of trading stations in the Spice Islands with Dutch partners. Further east, the Chinese refused to admit EIC ships to their ports, and in Japan Company traders ineptly tried to sell coarse English woolens to the silk-wearing Japanese. Prospects with the Company were so bad during this early period that its directors recruited many of their clerks and accountants from orphanages and charity schools.[9]

The Dutch, conversely, were the dominant western power in Asia for most of the seventeenth century. Emerging from the Thirty Years' War as an expansionist commercial power, the Dutch Republic organized Amsterdam-based companies trading with Asia into the Dutch East India Company. Chartered in 1602, the VOC had considerably more leeway than its European rivals in fighting wars and conducting diplomacy. Its fortified trading settlements in the Spice Islands and commercial contacts with Mughal India gave it the lead in capturing the lucrative long-distance trade with Europe.

The Dutch East India Company guarded its advantages jealously and was often ruthless in its pursuit of profit. For a time it tolerated the EIC's fumbling attempts to gain a portion of the pepper trade, but it lost patience with the British when they interfered with Dutch interests. Things turned ugly in 1623 when the VOC executed ten to fifteen of the EIC's employees on the island of Ambon. Unable to stand up to the Dutch militarily, the EIC turned its attention to the South Asian subcontinent, where no European company was strong enough to monopolize trade with the Mughal Empire or the independent rulers of southern India.

The Company first realized India's economic potential when it captured a Portuguese ship loaded with high-quality South Asian textiles. In 1608, it set up its first trading station at Surat, in western India, and opened another three years later at Masulipatam, on the southern coast. While these factories gave the EIC entry into the well-established Indian Ocean textile trade, it sought more direct access to the weavers in the interior to avoid the higher costs on the coast. But the Portuguese initially convinced the Mughal emperor Jahangir to deny the Company trading privileges on the grounds that it was just a minor power. It was only when the EIC's naval forces destroyed a rival Portuguese fleet, thereby demonstrating its usefulness as an ally, that the Mughals granted the British full access to Indian markets.

The Company initially purchased textiles to trade for spices in Indonesia, but it soon realized that there was a market for these fabrics in Europe. By the 1660s, its annual imports to Britain amounted to over four million square meters of cloth with a total value of nearly three-quarters of a million pounds. The East India Company sold most of this material at London auctions, but riots by English weavers in the 1690s led the Crown to impose protective tariffs on Asian textiles. In 1721, it allowed the Company to import only high-quality printed Indian calicos for reexport to Europe. These restrictions led the EIC to diversify into trading in indigo and saltpeter.

The increasing importance of the Indian trade led the Company to seek more permanent bases on the subcontinent. In the south, the EIC shifted from Masulipatam to a small fishing village that grew into Madras. Company officials also abandoned Surat for the island of Bombay, which Charles II acquired from the Portuguese as part of the dowry for his marriage to Catherine of Braganza. In Bengal, the Company established its original factory on the upper Hugli River, but Mughal pressure forced it to shift to the more strategically located coastal villages that became Calcutta. The court of directors in London appointed a council of merchants to run each of these trading stations, which came to be known as presidencies.

The Company's footprint in India was originally quite small, with each presidency rarely having more than one hundred employees. EIC traders therefore relied heavily on Indian brokers and middlemen to serve as translators and provide information on markets, weights and measures, and currency. In Bengal, the most important of these local brokers became salaried Company employees responsible for overseeing a network of rural agents who in turn contracted with weavers and farmers to supply textiles, raw silk, indigo, opium, and a range of other commodities. These lower-ranking Indian intermediaries did not work directly for the Company and made their money largely on commissions.

Similarly, the EIC's European salary levels were so low that the court of directors allowed its employees to support themselves through private trading. The most senior officials had the privilege of exporting goods on Company ships, but the royal monopoly on commerce with metropolitan Britain forced them to concentrate on Southeast Asian and Chinese markets. This tied the East India Company into larger Asian trading networks. Over the course of the seventeenth century, these official and private trading initiatives also drew the East India Company ever deeper into the affairs of the subcontinent. Seeking to cut out the middlemen who drove up prices, Company employees became more involved in Indian commerce, investment, and local politics. Many favored their private interests in undertaking ventures that did not have the approval of the court of directors in London.

The breakdown of Mughal authority in the 1730s and rising tensions with the VOC and the French Compagnie des Indes, which was a significant force in southern India, opened the way for the Company to become a territorial Indian power. Plassey was actually a side note to the Seven Years' War, a largely European conflict that took on a global dimension when France and Britain became involved. Forced to protect its commercial interests in India, the British government stiffened the EIC's small army, which consisted largely of hired Indian soldiers, with regular frontline regiments. The court of directors would have preferred to remain neutral during the conflict with the French, but this vital metropolitan backing provided the means for Clive and other ambitious employees to compete with the Bengali *nawabs* and other regional powers.

The Company's resulting Indian empire looked nothing like the British settlement colonies of the Americas. The New World territories were technically the property of the Crown, which meant that monarchs had the prerogative of intervening directly in their affairs. This was in sharp contrast to the private empire in India that answered to the EIC's two thousand proprietors (shareholders owning more than five hundred pounds' worth of stock) who elected the managing court of directors. This governing body was hardly the sort of institution equipped to run a growing overseas empire.

Its court of directors therefore worried that Clive's stroke at Plassey had saddled them with unsustainable military and administrative expenses. Most directors remained focused on commerce and maintaining the monopoly on Asian trade that finally had begun to produce impressive returns. Company stock paid annual dividends ranging from 6 to 10 percent, and between 1738 and 1742 its Asian commercial activities generated an average yearly profit of 1.1 million pounds. This made it the second-most-lucrative stock company in Britain, after the Bank of England, even before Clive emerged victorious at Plassey.[10]

The proprietors were understandably committed to protecting their charter. Facing challenges from antimercantilist critics who charged that monopolies stifled trade, they made regular loans and outright presents worth tens of thousands of pounds to the Crown. At the turn of the eighteenth century, they temporarily lost their monopoly when rival investors won permission to trade in the Indies by bribing King George I with a low-interest two-million-pound loan. Company directors responded by buying out the new company and paying the Crown 3.2 million pounds to recognize the two merged companies as the United Company of Merchants of England Trading to the East Indies.

This enormous sum amounted to the EIC's entire capital reserve. Anxious to block future challenges, the proprietors turned to politics. Company directors acquired seats in the House of Commons, where they wielded considerable influence through generous gifts and loans. Other members of Parliament also invested directly in Company stock. Over time, a network of intermarriage, kinship, and patronage developed that linked the directors with the landed elites who dominated British politics and society. Sometimes the EIC went too far and occasionally found itself caught up in insider trading and bribery scandals. Nevertheless, the Company's strong political and personal ties to the men who ran Britain safeguarded its claim to India.

Yet the real reason that the East India Company exerted such a strong hold on Bengal and the rest of South Asia was because, as in the Andes, it built on the work of imperial predecessors. Clive and his colleagues made extensive use of Mughal institutions, but the Mughals themselves were heirs to a long history of empire building on the South Asian subcontinent. Alexander the Great and a succession of ruling dynasties, petty kings, and foreign invaders did the heavy lifting of setting up stratified systems of governance, tax collection, and military recruiting. Lasting from 1526 to the end of Company rule in 1857, the Mughal Empire's imperial genius lay in its ability to adapt, expand, and systematize these indigenous institutions of exploitation. Although the EIC represented a new kind of empire, it was also a direct descendant of these earlier Indian imperial states.

The Mughals were Central Asians who invaded northern India from Afghanistan in the early sixteenth century. Muslims had been a significant presence in the region since the Umayyad general Muhammad ibn al-Qasim overran Sind in 712, and for almost a millennium Arab, Afghan, and Turkish conquerors had founded a series of imperial successor states. These Islamic empire builders ruled Hindu majorities that ranged from simple peasants to warrior castes who grudgingly accepted subject status after numerous failed rebellions. Led by Zahir-ud-din Muhammad Babur, the Mughals overthrew the Delhi Sultanate, a once-powerful Central Asian conquest state that had shattered into autonomous Afghan and Turkish fiefdoms by the sixteenth century.

Babur's grandson Jalal-ud-din Muhammad Akbar was the true architect of the Mughal Empire. Working from his base in the rich lands between the Indus and Ganges rivers, he brought most of Bengal under Mughal control by the 1580s. At its high point under Akbar's grandson Shah Jahan, the Mughal Empire ruled over approximately 1.2 million square miles and more than one hundred million subjects. This made it comparable in size and scope to Ming China, and its twenty-two provinces generated annual revenues of 220 million rupees.[11]

The Mughals extracted this fantastic wealth by imposing a rational but flexible administrative framework on the mosaic of Muslim conquest states, Hindu kingdoms, and small rural polities that made up northern and central India. Akbar and his heirs controlled the empire's nobility, which was a highly diverse mixture of Turks, Uzbeks, Indian Muslims, Shi'a Persians, and Hindu Rajputs, through a hierarchical system that rewarded loyal service with administrative posts, generous stipends, and titles. Mughal notables held a personal rank or *zat* based on the number of troops they commanded. These warrior aristocrats were Akbar's governors, generals, and ministers. This also made them *mansabdars*, a term for a Mughal official holding a specific administrative post.

Not all *mansabdars* were nobles, but only nobles were entitled to a direct share of imperial revenues in the form of a *jagir*. Based on the Turkish military fiefdom, this concession gave its holder the right to keep a portion of the collected taxes from a specific village or region. *Jagir* holders did not own the land itself and were entitled to keep only enough revenue to support themselves and their military retainers; they remitted the surplus to the imperial treasury. Nevertheless, a *jagir* was a significant perquisite that gave Mughal notables a strong personal stake in the empire, but they did not have to trouble themselves personally with the messy details of revenue gathering. Instead, this was the responsibility of lesser functionaries (known as *zamindars* in Bengal) who in turned passed the obligation on down to a ranked hierarchy of subordinate collectors ending in "village *zamindars*" or headmen.

The Mughals codified these local arrangements, but they generally remained aloof from rural affairs so long as the *zamindars* met their quotas and the *jagir* holders passed on sufficient wealth to the treasury. Provincial governors answered directly to the emperor, but their authority over common Indians was relatively circumscribed. The main political unit of the Mughal Empire was the *pargana* (sub-district), consisting of anywhere from twenty to two hundred villages where chiefs, *rajas*, clan leaders, and community elites had the greatest influence on daily life. The Mughals relied on these local authorities to extract the rural surplus.

As in all preindustrial empires, the wealth of Mughal India lay in the countryside. Land was relatively plentiful in most agricultural communities in early eighteenth-century Bengal, which meant that there was little incentive to develop a system of private ownership. Labor mobilization was as central to prosperity and social advance there as it was in the Andes. Far from being the egalitarian "rural republics" envisioned by later generations of British revenue collectors, Bengali villages were dominated by those who had the means to expand production by owning oxen or hiring salaried workers. These entrepreneurs loaned grain or money to poorer farmers in difficult times and were best equipped to invest in cash crops. Rural Bengali economies also supported a sophisticated handicraft sector that produced many of the fine textiles that drew foreign merchants to India. The *zamindars* and their subordinates tapped into this rural wealth, but the power of local authorities placed limits on what they could demand. Negotiated custom set tribute rates, and the wise collector did not meddle too deeply in village affairs. Moreover, agricultural laborers usually could move to find more favorable terms if the *zamindars'* demands became excessive.

There were enormous local variations in agricultural production throughout South Asia, but the Mughals' prosperity rested on their success in capturing local tribute systems and tying them to a dense continental web of commerce and investment. In 1585, Akbar's Hindu finance minister created the *zabt* revenue system, which aimed to survey all the *jagirs* throughout the empire, set tribute obligations, and mandated that payments be made in coin. By collecting revenues in currency the Mughals accelerated the monetization and commercialization of local economies, which gave the empire better access to rural wealth and allowed traders and speculators to move commodities and capital throughout South Asia. The *zabt* system failed in its ambitious attempt to draft an accurate and complete survey of tax collection throughout the empire, but it helped the Mughals build a sophisticated imperial economy that produced high-value export crops and fine silks and woven textiles that brought the European chartered companies to India.

These westerners played a key role in the Mughal economy by importing American and Japanese silver. This kept the economy liquid and provided the means for Indian merchants to buy Chinese goods. In the 1660s, the European chartered companies shipped thirty-four tons of silver to India each year, thereby linking the Mughal imperial economy to the Andes. In time, these commercial contacts became so well established that the Dutch and British sent unopened boxes of Peruvian silver reales directly to Indian imperial mints.[12]

The Mughals were thus indirect beneficiaries of the Spanish empire in the Americas, but it was only a matter of time before they joined the Andeans in subjecthood. Like the Inkas, they laid the groundwork for imperial conquest by setting up efficient and easily co-optable administrative and extractive systems. But the Mughal Empire was the more valuable prize. Although they lacked as much easily lootable wealth as the Inkas, the Mughals' efficient tribute collection systems and monetized economy gave British empire builders much greater access to the collective wealth of rural Indian communities. Where the Spanish had to take most of their tribute as *encomienda* labor because Andean economies were not fully commercial, the EIC captured a sophisticated integrated imperial economy that banked much of its wealth in easily accessible currency.

Clive and his allies accomplished this feat because the Mughals were as isolated and alienated from their subjects as the Inkans were from common Andeans. Akbar's heirs were Muslim emperors ruling a population that was roughly 80 percent Hindu. At the elite level, this was not as problematical as it might seem, for the Mughals co-opted Rajput Hindu kings by marrying their daughters and recognizing their authority over their own lands. The Rajput warrior elite thus accepted the Mughal emperors as legitimate sovereigns even though they were Muslims. But in doing so they set a precedent that allowed Christian Britons to step into the Mughals' shoes.

Religious toleration brought Akbar and his son Jahangir a measure of stability, but the Mughals' dependence on new sources of imperial tribute dictated a never-ending series of campaigns that fatally weakened the empire by the turn of the eighteenth century. The *zabt* revenue survey was one of the most impressive systems of imperial extraction to emerge in the early modern era, but it never captured enough rural wealth to meet the needs of the empire. The heavily stratified layers of nested revenue collection that connected local producers to the imperial court were highly inefficient and prevented the imperial authorities from fully exploiting the increasing commercialization of South Asian economies. Seeking ways to overcome local resistance, Mughal treasury officials gave revenue collectors more coercive authority by allowing them to turn their holdings into minor fiefdoms. It was only a matter of time before these well-entrenched *jagir* holders asserted their autonomy.

The decline of the *zabt* system meant that new conquests became the surest and most effective means of acquiring the new streams of wealth that the Mughals needed to sustain their expanding court and patronage system. Emperor Aurangzeb, who came to power in 1658 by overthrowing his elderly father and vanquishing rival siblings, tried to expand the empire into the southern Deccan Plateau through a series of ambitious but ultimately disastrous campaigns against the region's independent sultanates. Lasting off and on for decades, Aurangzeb's wars created a new danger to the empire by allowing the Hindu warrior elites who served the Deccan Muslim states to assert their autonomy. Known collectively as the Marathas, these independent but allied chiefdoms evolved from a nagging irritant into a significant threat as they raided northward in the first half of the eighteenth century and disrupted the commercial networks that were central to the Mughal economy.

These dire conditions spurred Aurangzeb's decision to abandon the accommodationist policies of his predecessors. Short of money to pay his troops and desperate to shore up his legitimacy, the emperor alienated his Hindu subjects by retreating to the relative security of Islamic orthodoxy. His wasteful and intolerant policies sent the empire into a downward spiral that enabled the EIC to gain its political foothold in India. His death in 1707 touched off a three-decade-long power struggle among his heirs that allowed a variety of power brokers to play the role of kingmaker in enthroning and deposing a succession of increasingly pathetic Mughal princelings. Alamgir II, the reigning emperor when Clive won his victory at Plassey, was a puppet of his chief minister, who ordered his assassination to keep him from falling into the hands of rivals. Alamgir's son Shah Alam II survived in power until his death in 1806 by attaching himself to the *nawab* of Awadh, the Marathas, invading Afghan Rohillas (who blinded him), and finally the EIC.

The Mughal Empire was a hollow shell by the mid-eighteenth century, but it did not meet the fate of its Inkan counterpart by falling to a direct western invasion. Instead, the East India Company became an Indian power by winning the scramble to fill the vacuum left by the Mughal Empire's collapse. The EIC's primary rivals were Mughal functionaries and governors who founded autonomous states in Bengal, Awadh, and Hyderabad on the Deccan Plateau. Additionally, new powers like the Marathas, Afghan Rohillas, and Sikhs also carved out states as the empire lost control of its hinterlands. In southern India, which was never under direct Mughal rule, a military adventurer in Mysore named Hyder Ali made himself a dangerous threat to the Company by allying with the French. Yet this political disorder did not do too much damage to the integrated commercial economy of South Asia. Indeed, credit was widely available, and a network of bankers funded many of the regional powers.

Bengal in particular was one of the most prosperous regions in South Asia in the decades before Plassey. Enriched by imports of American silver and the export of textiles and raw silk, sugar, pepper, opium, and other cash crops, the province had became one of the most valuable territories in the Mughal Empire at the turn of the eighteenth century. Most important, its highly commercialized cash-based economy allowed *zamindars* to collect tribute in rupees. The Mughals thus had a strong incentive to retain the province. Responding to a 1698 revolt by the local *zamindars*, Aurangzeb installed one of his grandsons as *nazim* (governor) and sent an ex-slave named Kartalab Khan to be the *diwan* (fiscal officer). Assisted by a contingent of expatriate Hindu clerks, this able bureaucrat updated the revenue rolls, removed embezzling *jagir* holders, and tortured defaulting *zamindars* into fulfilling their tribute obligations. In short order his ruthless tactics produced more than ten million rupees for the imperial treasury, which led the grateful Aurangzeb to ennoble him as Murshid Quli Khan. In time, the collapse of Mughal authority made this former slave the semi-independent *nawab* of Bengal, but he never stopped making tribute payments to the Mughal treasury in Delhi.

Murshid Quli Khan's stern but efficient rule spared Bengal much of the turmoil of the early eighteenth century, but his death in 1727 opened the way for a succession struggle among his would-be heirs. His son-in-law initially emerged victorious, but in 1740 a lesser official named Alivardi Khan seized the *nawab*ship with the backing of the Hindu bureaucracy, the powerful Jagat Seth banking family, and a personal guard of northern Indian Pathans. Alivardi Khan almost lost the province to a Maratha invasion, but he left Bengal relatively secure when died in 1756. His grandson Siraj-ud-Daula was Clive's opponent at Plassey.

It is entirely understandable that Bengali *nawabs* were not prepared to deal with the unexpectedly assertive East India Company.

The EIC's board of directors certainly was not interested the politics of the province, but at a time when it took six months to send orders from London, the Bengal Presidency made the decision to purchase *zamindari* rights in Calcutta's hinterlands entirely on its own. Becoming Mughal vassals by moving from trade into revenue collection was highly profitable, but it embroiled Company employees in the competition to succeed the Mughals in the province. The resulting private empire was thus the individual handiwork of ambitious Company employees, the most successful of whom eighteenth-century Britons nicknamed nabobs. As an English corruption of the Mughal title *nawab*, the term meant an extravagantly wealthy and powerful person who made his fortune by exploiting Indians. Far from being an honorific, it was a satirical expression of derision for grasping imperial entrepreneurs who were corrupted by greed and shameless orientalism.

Clive was the nabob personified. The son of a Shropshire squire and attorney of limited means, he arrived in India as an eighteen-year-old clerk with the unapologetic intention of acquiring a fortune. By the turn of the eighteenth century, it had become clear to ambitious social climbers that the chaos that gripped Mughal India offered opportunities to acquire wealth and status that were simply unavailable in Britain. But it also took fame and publicity to propel a junior clerk of common origins into the oligarchic ranks of landed gentlemen who dominated metropolitan politics and society. Clive's opportunity came in 1747 after he transferred to the military arm of the Company and distinguished himself by turning back a French attack on an important Indian ally of the Madras Presidency. The grateful *nawab* of Arcot awarded him the title Sabut Jang Bahadur, "firm in war," which made him a Mughal nobleman with a *zat* rank signifying the command of ten thousand soldiers and horsemen.[13] More significant, his exploits made him a minor celebrity in Britain and won him the leadership of the relief force that recaptured Calcutta from the *nawab* of Bengal.

Although Plassey was a minor battle in military terms, Clive's victory brought him the fortune and celebrity that had drawn him to India. With Mir Jafar firmly in his pocket, and assured of the support of the main Bengali merchant and banking families, he beat back a military challenge from the increasingly impotent Dutch East India Company and forced his pet *nawab* to grant the EIC *zamindari* rights over twenty-four more subdistricts (*parganas*) in eastern Bengal. Two years later, he took the enormously audacious step of secretly convincing Mir Jafar and the Mughal emperor to grant him a *jagir* over this territory, which effectively made him the Company's superior in Bengal under the terms of Mughal feudalism. Although the tribute from the Twenty-Four Parganas was substantial, the EIC was entitled to keep only 10 percent of it before turning the rest over to Clive as the recognized *jagir* holder. On average, the *jagir* netted the rising nabob a staggering annual income of twenty-seven thousand pounds.[14]

Clive's peers used similar tactics in the Madras and Bombay presidencies. In southern India, the Company became the dominant force in Madras after vanquishing the French East India Company and its local allies during the Seven Years' War. With the French threat waning and profits from conventional trade on the decline, Company employees sought fortunes in tribute collecting, loan-sharking, mercenary service to local powers, and soliciting bribes from Indian princes. Loans from Indian bankers gave them additional means to finance private trading schemes and military adventures.

In Bengal, the nabobs wrung approximately two million pounds out of the province by looting its treasury and extorting gifts from provincial elites. In 1760, Clive arrived in Britain as a conquering hero with thirty thousand pounds' worth of diamonds, Company bills of exchange totaling fifty thousand pounds, and, interestingly, two hundred and thirty thousand pounds' worth of bills issued by the rival Dutch East India Company.[15] Apparently his imperial enthusiasm did not prevent him from trafficking with the EIC's archrival.

Clive's departure left Mir Jafar and his fellow Bengali conspirators in the hands of Henry Vansittart and a cabal of senior Company officials who wasted little time in following Clive's example in exploiting their privileged position. Although *zamindari* rights in the Twenty-Four Parganas entailed only the authority to gather tribute, the EIC's dependence on revenue collection forced it to intervene more aggressively in the political and commercial life of Bengal. This gave Company employees more opportunities to seek personal fortunes, but it did not mean that they intended to carve out an empire in eastern India. They merely joined the other Mughal vassals and clients who sought to profit from the empire's collapse.

In this sense they were not very different from Mir Jafar and his Bengali backers. However, the inept old Mughal soldier was a poor custodian of the Company's interests and nearly bankrupted the province making good on his financial promises to the nabobs. The EIC therefore replaced him with his father-in-law, Mir Kasim, on the condition that the new *nawab* bestow an additional tens of thousands of pounds' worth of "presents" on Vansittart and other senior Company officials.

Once in power, Mir Kasim moved his power base beyond the Company's reach to western Bengal. Recognizing the shifting military balance in the post-Plassey era, he tried to free himself from British oversight by upgrading his army and executing fifty-six Company employees. In the ensuing war, he formed an alliance with the Mughal emperor Shah Alam II and the *nawab* of the neighboring kingdom of Awadh. The defeat of their combined forces at Buxar by Company troops in 1764 firmly established the EIC as the supreme political and military power in eastern India, which allowed Vansittart to reinstate Mir Jafar as *nawab*.

With its beachhead in Bengal secure, the East India Company forced the *nawab* of Awadh to become a client by admitting a Company supervisor into his court. This "resident" took control of his diplomatic and military affairs, which brought the kingdom squarely into the EIC's sphere of influence. Additionally, the *nawab* had to pay for the support of a Bengal army garrison. Over time, the Company's informal relationships with these sorts of Indian princes developed into the residency system, which gave it control of nominally independent rulers without adding the expense of imperial conquest and direct administration to its balance sheet.

In Bengal, however, the *nawabs* lost what remained of their authority and became simple figureheads after Mir Jafar died in 1765. The Company disbanded their armies, placed them on an allowance, and chose their heirs. Like the Inka nobility, the Bengali ruling classes suffered the disorienting loss of status that befalls vanquished imperial elites. In dismantling the *nawabs'* military and court, the Company dried up an important source of patronage, thereby threatening tens of thousands of aristocratic cavalrymen with impoverishment. Although Plassey did not produce a shock on par with Pizarro's stroke at Cajamarca, Mughal intellectuals used the Arabic and Persian term *inqilab*, a sudden "inversion of the existing order," to describe how the fall of Bengal had turned their world upside down.[16]

Company officials played down their imperial intentions by pretending to rule as Mughal vassals, but their reliance on relatively common Indian intermediaries disrupted the established social order. Becoming a successful nabob required local allies serving as interpreters, trading partners, and financiers. Far from being mere pawns, these *banians* grew wealthy on the EIC's empire building.[17] Most were new men whose influence and status humiliated the older Mughal nobility. Ghulam Hussain Khan, the son of an aristocratic court family who served both Mir Jafar and the EIC, was disgusted by the *banians'* ability to exploit the greed and ignorance of the nabobs. Writing in 1781, he complained that the young "beardless" upstarts who attached themselves to Company officials "have no view but that of their own benefit, and think of only pleasing their English masters."[18]

The nabobs owed their fortunes to these upstarts. Yet just as Hernando Pizarro discovered that no amount of looted Inka treasure could buy him respectability, Clive found that he could not escape the imperial origins of his wealth. Although he acquired a seat in Parliament, a knighthood, and a lesser Irish title as Baron Clive of Plassey in the Kingdom of Ireland, his ambitions floundered on a controversy surrounding the Bengali *jagir* that remained his primary source of income. It was understandably awkward to explain to members of Parliament that the Mughal feudal system made him the EIC's superior. Moreover, he became the personification of imperial corruption as reports of the nabobs' abuses reached London. Frustrated and facing greater scrutiny of his personal fortune, Clive accepted the directors' plan to be rid of their upstart employee by sending him back to India for a second term as the governor and commander-in-chief of Bengal.

Arriving in Calcutta in 1764, Clive consolidated and reorganized the Company's conquests. He also addressed the reports of nabob corruption that had caused a stir in London by banning private trading by Company employees and capping the gifts they could accept from Indian rulers at one thousand rupees. Conveniently forgetting the origins of his own fortune, he piously cited the need to improve the Company's reputation in India as a justification for the crackdown on nabobism: "the name of the English stink in the nostrils of a gentoo or a mussalman."[19]

Yet Clive still did not move explicitly to turn the EIC into a sovereign power. Seeking the returns of revenue collection without incurring the heavy costs of direct rule, he tried to co-opt the *nawabs'* administrative machinery. Under what became known as the dual system, roughly four hundred Europeans looked after the Company's interests and left the expensive and messy details of revenue collection, law and order, and day-to-day governance to Mughal bureaucrats and *zamindars*. A senior Bengali official named Muhammad Reza Khan supervised the operation. This was the standard imperial template of indirect rule employed by earlier generations of empire builders in the Andes, Iberia, and Britain, and it also explains why Bengali *ryots* and weavers initially failed to realize the significance of Plassey.

Although he disavowed explicit imperial pretensions, Clive remained enough of an opportunist to grasp the possibilities of the Company's victory over the Mughal emperor at Buxar. Faced with the loss of Bengali tribute and needing allies to remain in power, in 1765 Shah Alam II made the Company responsible for revenue collection in most of eastern India. Securing this *diwani* for the EIC was one of Clive's greatest coups. In return for paying the emperor less than two hundred thousand pounds per year, he promised the court of directors an annual return of two to four million pounds. The British government's share of this bounty was a guaranteed payment of four hundred thousand pounds per year, which helped keep the Crown solvent during the Seven Years' War and American Revolution. The promise of full and unfettered access to the wealth of Bengal also led to a run on the EIC's stock. Pressure from speculators pushed up dividends, and the court of directors sent detailed instructions to Clive on how to spend the expected windfall.[20]

Ultimately, the people of Bengal bore the cost of Clive's grand promises. His ambitious revenue guarantees depended on the Company's ability to bypass the hierarchal Bengali system of tribute collection to gain direct access to the wealth of local communities. This was a feat that had eluded the Mughal *jagir* holders and *zamindars* for centuries. While Akbar's *zabt* survey documented roughly half of the tribute obligations in the wider empire, more than 90 percent of Bengali villages remained unassessed at the turn of the eighteenth century. The Company could not make good on Clive's guarantees if it did not know how much wealth each village produced or how much the *zamindars* skimmed off before passing it on to their superiors. In 1769, therefore, Company officials tried in vain to conduct a thorough survey of Bengali revenues. Handcuffed by their ignorance of local circumstances, they had to base their revenue projections on estimates and speculation. Clive may have promised metropolitan Britons that the *diwani* would yield two to four million pounds a year in revenue, but in reality his men had no clear picture of Bengal's productive capacity.

At a time when most Bengali tribute came from just twelve large *zamindaris*, Company officials looked for ways to rationalize and streamline revenue collection. In the original Twenty-Four Parganas, they first tried collecting revenue directly, but when this failed to bring sufficient returns they auctioned off the task to private Bengali "revenue farmers" on three-year terms. Many of the successful bidders were so brutal in their pursuit of profit that *ryots* and laborers fled to territories outside the EIC's reach, thereby further depressing the Company's returns. Similarly, the independent local brokers responsible for channeling goods to the EIC's Indian buyers blocked the Company from taking full control of Bengal's handicraft sector.

As a result, Company officials could not make good on Clive's assurances that Bengal would yield millions of pounds in profit. Struggling under the expense of becoming a territorial and military power and the annual payments to the metropolitan treasury, they had to squeeze as much revenue as possible out of their subjects. For centuries common Bengalis had borne the weight of imperial tribute, but the EIC's escalating revenue assessments were unprecedented in their rapacity. In 1769 and 1770, the Company's demands tragically exacerbated one of the widespread famines that afflicted the region periodically. Born of flooding, crop failures, and British commercial meddling, the catastrophe killed roughly three million people. Adam Smith and other critics suggested that some Company officials shamelessly profited from the famine by manipulating rice prices, but the EIC's main culpability in the loss of so many lives lay in its unceasing revenue demands on collapsing rural economies.

The resulting degradation and depopulation of key agricultural areas further undercut the EIC's revenues and brought it to the brink of bankruptcy. In London, news of the famine burst the speculative bubble that Clive had carefully nurtured with his wild overestimates of the *diwani*'s value, but not before he made more than fifty thousand pounds speculating in Company stock. Metropolitan taxpayers also suffered in the crash, for it took a loan from the treasury of 1.4 million pounds to keep the Company solvent.[21]

Obviously things had to change, and it fell to Warren Hastings, Clive's successor as governor, to sort out the complexities of the *diwani* and imperial administration. But Hastings was just as much of a nabob as Clive. Both men arrived in India as clerks and won fame after transferring to the Company army. Where Clive was the hero of wars with the French in Arcot, Hastings made his reputation defending Bombay from a Maratha invasion. Governing Bengal from 1772 to 1885, he brought Clive's dual system to an end by replacing Mughal administrators and judges with Company employees. He also sought more direct control over the *zamindars* and other local authorities.

In effect, Hastings's reforms acknowledged that the EIC had acquired an empire, and he sought to establish the Company's legitimacy as an Indian power by codifying and systematizing indigenous administrative and legal institutions. Assuming that Bengal had fallen into decline under "foreign" Mughal despotism, Hastings and his lieutenants sought to revive its "authentic" high Hindu culture. They hired Brahmin scholars to commit "ancient" legal codes to paper, kept court records in local dialects, and became dedicated students of Sanskrit and Hindu literature and history. The reformers also became the patrons of Hindu shrines, festivals, and graves as they became increasingly enmeshed in running Bengal.

Hastings's orientalist program also recognized the value of Mughal bureaucratic institutions. The EIC adopted Persian, the Mughals' court language, as the lingua franca of day-to-day governance and reserved English for internal Company correspondence. Company courts adapted Mughal statutes to try criminal cases and used British interpretations of Hindu and Muslim law for civil matters. The new generation of young Company employee/administrators labored to learn Persian, which meant that Mughal clerks and translators remained influential. Recognizing the vital role that these intermediaries played in imperial administration, Hasting founded the Calcutta Madrassa to train Muslim elites for the civil service. Similarly, the Company continued to play its role as a dutiful Mughal vassal by sending tribute to the increasingly impotent imperial court in Delhi and minted coins bearing the emperors' portraits until well into the nineteenth century.

Despite these efforts, Company bureaucrats struggled to make sense of the enormous diversity of South Asia. Although there were broad political, religious, and cultural continuities that were common reference points at this time, most people identified themselves primarily on the basis of locality, lineage, family, occupation, and religion. Company officials, however, believed that Indians were most fundamentally defined by "caste." The actual term was in fact a European import. Based on the Latin *castus*, it had the same etymological origins as the term *castas*, which the Spanish used to describe the hybrid social categories that emerged in their New World empire. The Portuguese introduced the term to South Asia, and the Dutch and British then used it to delineate a range of Indian identities associated with Hindu religious texts and everyday life.[22]

Briefly, the notion of caste came to describe a uniquely South Asian form of ranked identity. It was based on the four *varnas* of Brahmin priests, Kshatriya warriors, Vaishya merchants, and Shudra cultivators outlined in Hindu scripture, as well as thousands of much more localized occupational categories (*jatis*) that were theoretically determined by birth. These nested identities gave Indians ways to assert authority, mobilize resources, and unite for mutual defense. Nomadic and foraging peoples were largely outside the bounds of caste, but settled Indians who converted to Islam still lived within its realities because in diverse and multiethnic village societies caste helped create order and stability.

British imperial observers believed that Indian caste, religious, and tribal identities were fixed by religion, tradition, and birth, but in fact these norms were relatively flexible and malleable, particularly in rural communities where different groups lived side by side; they were far too fluid to serve as effective instruments of imperial exploitation. Company officials needed to make better sense of Indian identity and foster sharper social boundaries to rule effectively. They therefore recruited Indian scholars and religious experts, who shared their interest in making local identities less fluid, to develop caste into a more rigid and coherent social category where communities, rather than individuals, had rights.

Nationalists and imperial critics accuse British officials of imposing caste on India as part of a larger strategy of divide and rule. In practice, no empire, least of all the East India Company, was ever even remotely powerful enough to impose new identities on an unwilling people. Instead, the EIC's empire created a new reality by introducing better communications, standardizing laws, expanding the market economy, and reducing the isolation of rural communities. This inspired Indians to reimagine personal and caste identities and codify formerly diverse and flexible religious customs and practices. Indian community leaders and legal and religious experts often cooperated with the Company's efforts to create clearly defined caste identities because it enhanced their own authority and social prestige.

Company officials never fully grasped the complexities of Bengali society, which explains why Hastings lacked the intimate knowledge of the *zamindaris* that he needed to make imperial rule in Bengal pay. In 1772 he took another stab at making the *diwani* live up to Clive's promises by fixing revenue assessments for a five-year period and by auctioning off tribute collection rights. He also tried to avoid the abuses of the 1760s by supervising the new revenue farmers more closely. A Committee of Circuit oversaw the new system, and young British officials (known as collectors) assisted by "native officers" gathered the EIC's allotted tribute from the winning bidders.

Although this Five-Year Settlement was more ordered and systematic than Clive's dismal attempts to make the *diwani* work, it also floundered on the Company's inability to exert control at the local level. The collectors were too ignorant of Bengali tribute relations to be effective, and Hastings had to replace them with their Indian deputies. Moreover, unreasonably high agricultural prices after the 1770 famine led many of the new revenue collectors to overpay for their concessions. They therefore failed to maintain the irrigation systems that sustained Bengali agriculture and continued to drive off *ryots* with their unreasonable demands for revenue.

Faced with pronounced revenue shortfalls and rising administrative and military costs, Hastings correctly recognized that real authority in Bengal required more intimate knowledge of local conditions. Investigations in some of the largest and most important *zamindaris* hinted at widespread fraud in tribute collection and suggested that large tracts of valuable land were underassessed or not assessed at all. Like earlier generations of empire builders, Company officials found, much to their frustration, that efficient imperial extraction hinged on the cooperation of local authority. The nabobs' personal fortunes, the EIC's balance sheet, and the metropolitan British government's finances all depended on their ability to make the *diwani* pay by exploiting common Bengalis.

Hastings therefore tried to circumvent the complex Bengali hier-archical system of revenue collection by gathering taxes directly from the *ryots*. This would have allowed him to dispense with the services of the petty *zamindars* and bureaucratic middlemen who took a share of the tribute in return for their services. In 1776, he appointed a special commission to conduct a new comprehensive sur-vey of Bengal with an eye to revising revenue assessments when the five-year concessions expired in 1777. The architects of Akbar's *zabt* survey had tried and failed to accomplish much the same thing sev-eral centuries earlier, and the commissioners struggled to fulfill their charge because local authorities made it difficult for them to get their hands on district revenue records. Nevertheless, they concluded that the lower-level *zamindars* and tributaries were intentionally under-reporting the value of their holdings, and they blamed the unreason-able demands of the new revenue speculators, who had replaced the Mughal *jagir* holders, for depressing production.

Both charges were largely accurate. *Zamindars* had no reason to let Company assessors know how much wealth they actually took from *ryots* and craftsmen in their concessions, and the speculative revenue farmers who had overbid for the right to collect tribute from them needed draconian tactics to meet their inflated obligations to the Company. Their desperate attempts to avoid default invariably drove some communities to revolt. This was the case in Rangpur in 1783, when an outsider named Devi Singh tried make up for a 30 percent shortfall in his collection quota by jailing noncompliant *ryots* and selling off communal land allocated to schools, mosques, and temples. Led by minor *zamindars* who also felt the weight of his demands, the tenants burned revenue records and looted storehouses. Interest-ingly, they appealed to the Company for redress and appointed their own administrators and revenue collectors. The Bengal Presidency removed Devi Singh and abolished his extra taxes, but it could not allow this expression of local autonomy to go unpunished. The forces it sent to Rangpur made quick work of *ryots* armed with sticks and farm tools, but Company troops had to remain in the district to pro-vide the law and order needed to restart revenue collection.

Garrisoning Rangpur was a considerable drain on the EIC's lim-ited resources, and the nabobs' empire would have become unwork-able if the revolt had spread. The Bengal Presidency could deal with direct and isolated challenges, but like all empire builders, Company officials were acutely aware of how little actual control they had over the countryside. Clive created special paramilitary battalions to enforce revenue collection, but Hastings disbanded them when it became clear the troops were preying on rural communities. In the 1780s, the Company stripped the *zamindars* of responsibility for local law and order and divided Bengal into twenty-square-mile police districts where British magistrates oversaw Indian inspectors and constables. These new security arrangements had little popular support and were ineffective in dealing with the banditry and burglary that spread as discharged Indian soldiers and village watchmen turned to crime to support themselves. Ultimately, violent intimidation was the most effective means of forcing common Indians to acknowledge the Company's imperial authority. After burning several villages that had rebelled against an EIC's client ruler in 1782, Major J. Gilpin candidly admitted: "Knowing from long experience no other means would prevail, I did this by way of example to [strike] a degree of terror into others, and deter them from rebellion."[23]

This was an honest acknowledgment of the inherent terror that lay below the surface of all imperial enterprises. Although the nabobs cloaked their conquests in the garb of civilization and good government, it was impossible to conceal the corruption and unalloyed self-interest that led them to turn the East India Company into an empire. Clive built his fortune through extortion, shameless stock speculation, and the "oriental despotism" of his *jagir*. He was reasonably moderate in his personal behavior, but many young Company officials were seduced by the wealth, power, and personal freedom of empire. As the growing capital of the Bengal Presidency, Calcutta acquired a reputation as a South Asian Sodom where aspiring nabobs gambled, drank, smoked opium, and fought duels.

At least the nabobs were less judgmental of their subjects than were the more staid Company bureaucrats who built on their conquests in the nineteenth century. Aspiring nabobs needed Indian help in making their fortunes and were relatively unconcerned with marking and enforcing clear boundaries between imperial citizen and subject. While they could be ruthless in demanding tribute, they also appreciated the finer qualities of high Mughal culture. Once-lowly Company clerks learned Indian languages, wore Indian clothes, and ate Indian food. Like the Pizarrists in the Andes, they often took local women as wives and mistresses because there were extremely few available European women. The opportunities for sexual exploitation in these relationships are obvious, but it was also relatively common for them to acknowledge the legitimacy of their Indian spouses and children in their wills.

The nabobs' avarice also left them open to manipulation by wealthy Indians with the means to satisfy their appetite for treasure and luxury. Nawab Muhammad Ali of Arcot even influenced metropolitan British politics by giving George Pigot, the former governor of Madras, three hundred thousand pounds to help sympathetic politicians buy seats in Parliament. Reasoning that he was secure if the nabobs had a personal stake in his rule, Muhammad Ali also bought the cooperation of Company officials with bonds backed by tribute collection. These bonds paid 20 percent interest while their holders remained in India, but the *nawab* tended to allow them to go into default when his domesticated nabobs returned to Britain. In 1775, the outraged creditors sent Pigot back to Madras to force Muhammad Ali to pay up, but the *nawab* ensured that his former client was arrested and died in jail by making two million pounds' worth of "presents" to the Madras presidential council.[24]

It was only a matter of time before these kinds of outrages provoked a backlash in Britain. The nabobs' greed and licentiousness fed fears that the contagion of empire would spread to the metropole. Assuming that all Indians were inherently corrupt, moralists charged that the embrace of their women and luxurious culture contaminated young Company men. The ability of the nabobs to buy their way into Parliament produced fears that the wealth of India was undermining the political order in Britain. Rumors that Indian princes controlled these MPs led William Pitt to warn the House of Lords: "The riches of Asia have been poured in upon us, and brought with them not only Asiatic luxury, but, I fear, Asiatic principles of government."[25] Imperial critics in Rome, Damascus, and Madrid would have understood this complaint.

Equally alarming, the nabobs' purchase of great landed estates appeared to threaten the aristocratic foundations of metropolitan society. Hastings built a grand house for himself in the English midlands that was topped with a Mughal dome and furnished with Indian art and amenities. These sorts of oriental excesses inspired Pitt to lament that "without connections, without any natural interest in the soil, the importers of foreign gold forced their way into Parliament by such a torrent of corruption, as no private hereditary fortune can resist."[26] Similarly, Edmund Burke noted that Company men used Mughal wealth to buy their way into the British elite aristocracy. Sounding an alarm, he warned his fellow gentlemen: "[The nabobs] marry into your families; they enter into your senate; they ease your estates by loans."[27]

In 1772, Samuel Foote staged a play called *The Nabob* that captured the growing public alarm over the sudden rise of men such as Clive and Hastings. In it the mayor of "Bribe'em" negotiates the sale of his borough's parliamentary seats to the nabob Sir Matthew Mite. Asked the origins of Mite's fortune, the nabob's underling Touchit explains how Company men arrived in Indian states as merchants but "cunningly encroach and fortify little by little, till at length, we grow too strong for the natives, we turn them out of their lands, and take possession of their money and jewels." Touchit reassures the mayor that the displaced Indian rulers were "little better than Tartars or Turks," to which the mayor replies, "No, no, Mr. Touchit; just the reverse; it is they have caught the Tartars in us."[28]

The nabobs' Tartarism invariably raised questions about the actual value of the Company's new Indian empire. Critics charged that metropolitan taxes paid to defend it from the French, thereby inflating the national debt. The economist Adam Smith went even further by pointing out that Clive's failure to make the *diwani* pay demonstrated that Company directors could not balance the dual role of merchant and imperial ruler. "Since they became sovereigns...they have been obliged to beg extraordinary assistance of government in order to avoid immediate bankruptcy. In their former situation, their servants in India considered themselves as the clerks of merchants: in their present situation, those servants consider themselves as the ministers of sovereigns."[29] Smith's criticism reflected widespread concerns that the Company had become uncontrollable, and rumors flew in 1784 that Hastings was planning to declare it an independent state.

It was only a matter of time before the metropolitan authorities brought the East India Company under tighter supervision. Just as the Spanish Crown prosecuted Hernando Pizarro for slipping the bonds of propriety in the Andes, the Company's enemies struck back against the nabobs. In some cases they were motivated by civic concern, but more often than not the architects of the counterstroke were Company men themselves who had been on the losing end of power struggles in India. Even Edmund Burke, who was the most eloquent metropolitan critic of the EIC, speculated in the Company's stock and suffered heavy loses during the crash of 1769.

Inevitably Clive, as the most famous nabob and the hero of Plassey, bore the brunt of the backlash. In 1773, his enemies in the House of Commons accused him of corruption and proposed to strip him of any illegally acquired wealth. In an impassioned defense Clive pointed out that his stock speculation was legal and offered a careful accounting of his finances to demonstrate that he had not accepted any private gifts during his second term as governor of Bengal. He made no mention of his conduct after Plassey. Clive justified his *jagir* as a reward for service from a grateful Mir Jafar and suggested that it spared the Company the expense of pensioning him. Wrapping himself in the newly spun garb of patriotic nationalism, he depicted himself as a loyal servant of the emerging British nation. Clive beat back the attack, but the parliamentary inquiry was humiliating. In 1774, he committed suicide at the age of forty-nine. It is not clear whether he was driven by poor health or his loss of status, but his suicide was in keeping with the ignominious demise that befell Tariq ibn Ziyad, Francisco Pizarro, and other earlier imperial conquerors.

Warren Hastings suffered similar persecution upon his return to Britain. Seeking to use the ex-governor as a lever to rein in the EIC and attack entrenched corruption in Britain, Edmund Burke brought impeachment proceedings against the nabob in the House of Commons. The trial ran intermittently from 1788 to 1795. Burke caste Hastings as an upstart oriental despot who preyed on legitimate Indian noblemen for his own selfish gain. "There is not a single prince, state, or potentate, great or small, in India, with whom they [the nabobs] have come into contact, whom they have not sold.... There is not a single treaty they have ever made, which they have not broken.... There is not a single prince or state, who ever put any trust in the company, who is not utterly ruined."[30] More specifically, Burke charged Hastings with persecuting the mother and grandmother of the *nawab* of Awadh, arranging the execution of a Bengali merchant who had charged him with taking bribes, and padding contracts to sell Company opium and provision its army.

Although he genuinely respected the nobility of Mughal aristocrats, Burke's primary aim was to ensure that the nabobs' Indian tyranny did not set a precedent for metropolitan Britain. Nicholas Dirks has also convincingly argued that Burke sought to protect the British Empire's reputation by pinning its worst abuses on the nabobs.[31] Burke was partially successful on this score, but Hastings won acquittal by drawing out the trial and presenting himself as a patriot who had saved India for Britain in the aftermath of the disastrous American Revolution and the loss of most of its New World territories. Nationalism and patriotism thus became useful camouflage for the greed and self-interest of empire building.

Nevertheless, the popular backlash against nabobery that culminated in Burke's impeachment proceedings played a central role in forcing the metropolitan government to assert more direct control over the East India Company. In effect, it had become a state unto itself, with its own revenues, army, and foreign policy. Just as the Umayyad caliphs took Iberia away from Tariq and the Spanish Crown reined in the conquistadors, the metropolitan authorities finally accepted that they had to take over the nabobs' private empire.

The attack on Clive in the House of Commons was part of a larger parliamentary inquiry into the Company's policies and accounts that began the process of bringing it under public control. The first step was the Regulating Act of 1773, which limited the ability of wealthy shareholders to dominate the court of directors and brought the Company's Indian administration under more direct metropolitan supervision. The act placed the Madras and Bombay presidencies under a governor-general in Bengal who in turn answered to a new four-man supervisory council. But this tentative move to check the Company's reckless expansionism was largely ineffective. As the first governor-general of Bengal, Hastings circumvented the council by playing the members off against each other.

Burke and the anti-Company faction in Parliament therefore proposed to bring the East India Company under more direct governmental supervision. Their draft law passed the Commons but died in the House of Lords on charges that it was a veiled attack on the private property of the EIC shareholders. More cautious politicians instead settled for a slower reformist approach to make the Company more fiscally responsible and better able to manage its own defense during an era of global war with France. The treasury secretary, John Robinson, also noted that it was preferable to keep the EIC directly accountable for the nabobs' misdeeds: "I think that the errors which must be committed in the management of such acquisitions, at so great a distance from the seat of government, had better fall upon the Directors of the Company than fall directly upon the ministers of the King."[32]

These sentiments led to the India Act of 1784, which finally stripped the East India Company of its political authority. While the court of directors retained control of the EIC's commercial operations, the act placed its political service under a new parliamentary Board of Control whose president became a de facto cabinet member. The Company's charter and monopoly came up for parliamentary review every two decades, thereby giving the metropolitan government more direct influence over its fiscal and administrative policies.

The India Act came into full force in 1786 when Lord Charles Cornwallis replaced Hastings as the governor-general. Arriving in the aftermath of his defeat at Yorktown, Cornwallis recovered from the ignominy of surrendering to the American rebels by expanding the EIC's Indian empire. This violated the intent of the parliamentary reforms, but the necessity of defending the Company's interests against Indian rivals and Napoleonic France inevitably led to further conflict and warfare. The Maratha Confederacy and the Mysore Sultanate used French aid to build well-equipped and well-trained armies. By this time most Indian rulers were fully aware of the Company's imperial agenda and belatedly tried to form a united front. In 1780, the Maratha minister of Poona wrote to the sultan of Mysore: "Divide and grab is their main principle.... They are bent upon subjugating [us] one by one, by enlisting the sympathy of one to put down the others. They know best how to destroy Indian cohesion."[33]

Yet the decaying Mughal Empire, the expansionist Muslim Mysore Sultanate, and the fractious Hindu Maratha Confederacy had competing agendas and could not create the political and social cohesion that was necessary to resist empire building. Moreover, they alienated their own subjects by imposing excessive revenue demands to fund their cripplingly expensive European-style armies. Cornwallis and his successor Richard Wellesley exploited the resulting unrest by picking off the squabbling Indian princes one by one. Britain's global struggle with France provided an excuse to annex half of Awadh and take the Mughal court and its aging emperor under its formal protection. The French revolutionary bogey gave Wellesley the excuse to finally vanquish Mysore on the grounds that Tippu Sultan had taken the title *citoyen* (citizen), planted a republican liberty tree in his capital, and was conspiring with the French governor of Mauritius. Within a few decades, the only remaining independent Indian rulers were the *nawabs* and *rajas* who remained in power by submitting to Company residents, who took control of their military, political, and diplomatic affairs.

The conquest of India was an impressive imperial achievement, but Wellesley's unauthorized wars inflated the Company's already burgeoning debt and provoked another anti-nabob backlash in Britain. His imperial adventures emboldened liberals and manufacturing interests who charged that its mercantilistic monopoly damaged the metropolitan economy by choking off trade. The court of directors' defense that the EIC needed its commercial privileges to offset the enormous expense of administering and defending its empire carried less weight at the dawn of the era of free trade and laissez faire capitalism. The Company therefore lost control over most Indian trade when its charter came up for review in 1813.

Only the monopoly on trade with China survived, and opium became the EIC's most important export. This dependency on a narcotic drug for the bulk of their commercial profits forced Company officials to take extraordinary steps to retain access to Chinese markets. Ignoring the Chinese government's ban on opium imports, they encouraged private traders to smuggle it into the country. These merchants in turn purchased tea for British markets, thereby removing the taint of drug dealing. By midcentury, opium sales accounted for 12 percent of the Company's total revenue, which made the EIC resemble a modern drug cartel.

The British government fought two wars under the banner of free trade to force China to open its markets to Indian opium, but the EIC gave up the last of its commercial functions during the next charter review in 1833. With its stock withdrawn from circulation it essentially became a department of state, albeit one whose control of revenue collection still allowed it to pay a dividend of 10.5 percent on its bonds. Moreover, as a semiprivate proxy for British rule in India, it still spared metropolitan taxpayers the full cost of maintaining an enormous Asian empire. The Company therefore still served the useful function of hiding the true economic and moral costs of empire.

This was particularly true in the case of the Company army. Its expansion from 82,000 to 214,000 mostly Indian soldiers between 1794 and 1857 turned Britain into a major imperial land power. With a professional European officer corps and a full range of artillery, cavalry, and support units, it conquered the rest of South Asia by the mid-nineteenth century. It also defrayed the costs of further conquests in the Middle East, China, Africa, and the Crimea. The burden of paying for these imperial adventures fell primarily, albeit indirectly, on Indian farmers, craftsmen, and laborers. These same Indians enlisted as *sepoys* not because they were loyal British subjects but because service in the Company army offered far greater pay, benefits, and prestige than comparable unskilled civilian positions.

The civil arm of the East India Company underwent a similar transformation when Cornwallis followed the India Act's mandate to create separate administrative, judicial, and commercial services. The immediate impact of this restructuring was that it was harder for Company officials to seek personal fortunes through private trade, *jagirs*, or buying revenue contracts through Indian proxies. Cornwallis moved to stamp out nabobery by creating a more formal political service that recruited the sons of wealthy landed and professional British families with improved pay and perquisites. Civil service academies in Calcutta and London produced a new cohort of better-trained young bureaucrats who looked on Company service as a career rather than a shortcut to easy riches.

These reforms eliminated some of the worst aspects of nabobery, but the greater metropolitan control that came with the revised charter gradually imposed a new kind of subjecthood on all South Asians. Failing to recognize that it was empire and not Indians that had corrupted so many young Britons, Cornwallis laid the foundations of a more stratified and bounded imperial state by removing Indian men from the higher ranks of Company service and discouraging Company employees from having intimate contact with local women. This was in sharp contrast to men such as Clive and Hastings, who enthusiastically embraced India's diverse cultures even as they were busily filling their pockets with its riches.

The nabobs' relatively sympathetic orientalism gradually gave way to intolerance and chauvinism as evangelical Protestants assumed a more prominent role in the Company. Hastings had characterized the empire of the nabobs as a Hindu and Muslim state governed by enlightened Christians, but he refused to promote Christianity for fear of provoking social and political unrest. This pragmatic tolerance was harder to defend after evangelicals became more politically influential in Britain and rose to leadership positions in the Company. At first, the Anglicans and Dissenters were more focused on reforming the British lower classes than in producing Indian converts, which stands in sharp contrast to the conquistadors' use of Catholicism to justify their conquests. Most of the nabobs were practicing Protestants, but they allowed the evangelicals to open schools and travel freely only so long as they did not stir up Indian anger by proselytizing. Those who refused to abide by the rules faced deportation.

This changed in the nineteenth century when the missionaries and their metropolitan supporters challenged the Company's use of Indian religious law and custom in imperial administration. Arguing that the security of British rule in India depended on mass conversions, they attacked Hindu and Muslim religious institutions as barbarous and sinful. Charles Grant, a Company director and reformed nabob, joined forces with the celebrated abolitionist William Wilberforce, who equated Hindu and Muslim influence in India with slavery. Wilberforce minced no words in dismissing these non-Christian faiths with a confident declaration: "Our religion is sublime, pure and beneficent. Theirs is mean, licentious, and cruel."[34] Making no apologies for their unalloyed bigotry, the evangelicals and abolitionists built a popular following in Britain by turning out newspapers, books, and religious tracts that featured lurid depictions of "heathen" Indian practices and titillating tales of abused women and Hindu eroticism.

The evangelical lobby used this public support to force the EIC to abolish the ban on proselytization and end its formal patronage of Indian religious institutions during the 1813 charter review. Yet the missionaries were ultimately disappointed, for these concessions failed to produce the expected rush of conversions. Becoming a Christian brought famine relief, education, and greater dignity for the poor and lower castes, but it also entailed social ostracism and the threat of physical violence. Moreover, the Company's old guard, who still believed that proselytization was disruptive, restricted religious instruction in government-funded schools and barred Christian converts from the army and civil service. Even so, the ability of Protestant leaders to influence the charter review process meant that the era of orientalist toleration was over.

In the 1820s, liberals and utilitarians sealed its demise by joining the evangelicals in calling for greater efforts to reform India. Confident that all humans could be uplifted through good government,

Christian morality, western education, and free trade, they were certain that benevolent British imperial rule would rescue Indians from heathen superstition and oriental despotism. In joining the Protestant religious lobby in proposing to save India from itself, these groups introduced a new moralizing element into the legitimizing ideology of western imperial rule. Later generations of conquerors used the belief that empire could be turned to humanitarian ends to disguise the inherent self-interest in their own imperial projects.

As central figures in the reformist lobby, James Mill and his more famous philosopher son John Stuart Mill used their senior positions in the EIC's metropolitan bureaucracy to push for utilitarianism in imperial administration. Although the Mills had little direct personal knowledge of Indian society and culture, the senior Mill was the author of a widely read and influential history of India. While James Mill was a vehement critic of nabobism, he naively believed that it was possible to use the authoritarianism of imperial rule as an instrument of moral uplift and social transformation. William Cavendish-Bentinck, the governor-general of Bengal from 1828 to 1833, tried enthusiastically to make this utilitarian agenda the basis of British rule in India.

The utilitarians hoped to use India as a laboratory to perfect rational laws and social policies that could be transplanted back to Britain to reform metropolitan political and social institutions tainted by conservatism and corruption. They joined the evangelicals in demanding that Company officials intervene more directly in Indian society to stamp out irrational and immoral practices. These alleged evil institutions included what they perceived to be infanticide, religiously sanctioned banditry (*thuggee*), and the ritual suicide of Hindu widows on their husbands' funeral pyres (*sati*).

The imperial reformers never intended to turn Indians into Britons, but they assumed that their superior civilization would have a gradual transformative impact on Indian society. The agents of this trickle-down "modernization" were to be a new class of westernized Indians who would become willing allies of the British imperial project. To this end, the charter revisions of 1813 and 1833 required the Company to set aside funds for western education. It fell to Thomas Babington Macaulay, Cavendish-Bentinck's legal advisor and the president of the General Committee of Public Instruction, to put the new system in practice. Writing in 1834, he famously declared: "We must at present do our best to form a class who may be interpreters between us and the millions whom we govern; a class of persons, Indian in colour, but English in taste, in opinions, in morals, and in intellect."[35] This state support took the form of subsidies to mission schools on the provision that they did not try to convert Hindu and Muslim students.

Macaulay and the utilitarians believed that their inherent superiority obligated them to conquer and rule India, but in practice the Company still leaned heavily on local translators, diplomats, agents, and bureaucrats to actually govern. Despite their grand philanthropic rhetoric, the reformers' main goal was still to improve the mechanisms of imperial extraction. The enormous costs of becoming a political and military power pushed the Company to the brink of bankruptcy until the metropolitan government stepped in with its 1.4-million-pound bailout. Parliament therefore insisted that the EIC support itself.

Revenue collection remained the Company bureaucracy's primary concern. Still attempting to make the *diwani* pay, Cornwallis ended the futile attempt to tap directly into the rural wealth of Bengal. Instead he agreed with Burke that the *zamindars* were the equivalent of English landed aristocrats whose legitimate rights had been usurped by decades of meddling and mistreatment by nabobs and tax-farming Indian speculators. Moreover, *zamindars* were the only people in Bengal with the intimate knowledge of local production. Cornwallis therefore concluded the Permanent Settlement with the *zamindars* in 1793, whereby they received proprietary rights as landlords over their holdings in return for an obligation to make fixed revenue payments in perpetuity. They would also have the right to claim any surplus above the set amount. In theory, this security of tenure would solve the Company's fiscal problems by giving the *zamindars* an incentive to increase production by investing in the land. The *ryots* became their tenants, but Cornwallis assumed that the *zamindars* would treat them fairly to improve yields.

Yet the fundamental problem with the Permanent Settlement was that the *zamindars* were not hereditary landlords. They were tribute collectors who had no customary rights. Cornwallis arbitrarily based the assessments on the estimated revenue returns of 1789 rather than on a systematic survey or census of Bengali wealth and production. These figures represented a nearly 20 percent increase over Mughal tribute levels. As a result, many *zamindars* defaulted and lost their holdings at auction. One-third of the land in Bengal changed hands this way between 1793 and 1822, and only one of the twelve great Bengal *zamindars* remained solvent at the turn of the nineteenth century. Cornwallis clearly did not do the *zamindars* any favors when he tried to make them the Company's primary imperial proxies in the Bengali countryside.

Officials in Madras and Bombay adopted a different strategy in trying to collect revenue directly from peasant producers, but they were no more knowledgeable about local conditions or successful than their counterparts in Bengal. Rather, they simply did not share Cornwallis's inclination to look for aristocratic allies in systematizing tribute collection. Moreover, the more peasant-centered approaches in the Madras and Bombay presidencies were not markedly more efficient in extracting rural wealth, and they ultimately forced many *ryots* into debt by demanding tribute payments in currency.

The Bengali *ryots* did not fare much better under the Permanent Settlement. Instead of becoming clients of progressive gentleman *zamindar* farmers, the defaults arising from unreasonable revenue obligations once again left them in the hands of speculators. Some of these buyers were local, but others were Calcutta merchants who had few reservations about using the coercive powers of the Permanent Settlement to meet their obligations. Tenants who fell behind on their tribute payments risked the confiscation of their entire harvest or outright eviction. This was at a time when private land titles were becoming more valuable as produce prices rose and the population of Bengal grew in the aftermath of the famines. These seismic social shifts had been under way since the beginning of the eighteenth century, but the Permanent Settlement made them more traumatic by accelerating the demise of the old *zamindar* class and the marginalization of peasant producers.

The Company's renewed effort to balance its books also placed entirely new kinds of burdens on Bengali farmers. Heavy borrowing in the 1790s inflated the EIC's debt from eighteen million pounds to thirty-two million between 1802 and 1807, which Company officials hoped to resolve by expanding cash crop exports. When the *zamindars* failed to live up to expectations, the Company resorted to draconian production quotas and enticing cash advances to push Bengali peasants into growing indigo (for dye) and poppies (for opium).

Defaulters became obligated to grow crops for European commercial firms until they or their descendants cleared their debts, which amounted to virtual debt slavery.

The failure of the Permanent Settlement and the loss of its commercial monopoly after the 1813 charter review turned the Company into a new kind of imperial power. Stripped of its mercantilist protection and privileges and subject to governmental supervision, the EIC's Indian empire now served the interests of metropolitan manufacturers and investors. British commercial firms displaced the Indian bankers who had brokered the nabobs' private trading ventures, funded the Company's wars, and financed craft production. Bengali weavers similarly suffered as the European market for Indian fabrics gradually disappeared due to rising metropolitan import duties and competition from textile factories that turned out inferior but cheaper products. After 1813, the EIC could not stop British mill owners from flooding India with these machine-woven goods. Manchester manufacturing interests used their political influence, which was at its apex at midcentury, to ensure that the Company did not adopt any of the protectionist policies that were becoming more widespread in Europe and the United States. Bengal's venerable weaving sector therefore fell into decline as South Asia shifted from one of the world's largest exporters of high-quality textiles to a raw material supplier and captive imperial market.

Although imperial apologists celebrate this transformation as a triumph of modernity and free trade, the hypocrisy of empire kept the Indian economy stunted and backward. The Company lost its monopoly, but it retained mercantilistic control over salt and opium production. Moreover, it still drew most of its revenue from tribute collection based on custom rather than formal taxes and tariffs on commercial agriculture. Each year, Company employees also transferred approximately six million pounds to Britain in the form of bullion, administrative salaries, pensions, stock dividends, and fees. In addition to these "home charges," the EIC continued to export opium to an increasingly addicted Chinese market.

From the Indian perspective, their imperial rulers ironically became more bigoted and chauvinistic as they became more respectable. Ever mindful of their precarious position as a privileged minority, British empire builders recognized that their security depended in large part on their ability to demand Indian deference and obedience. Where the nabobs had mixed freely with aristocratic Indians, their successors became obsessed with upholding their collective prestige. To this end the Company administration struggled to ensure that Indians encountered only sober, propertied, and respectable Britons.

Indeed, the life of a privileged imperial elite in India had its rewards. Cheap Indian labor allowed middle-class Britons to live like propertied metropolitan gentlemen, and phalanxes of Indian clerks, cooks, washmen, maids, gardeners, grooms, and litter bearers looked after their needs and whims. These privileges of empire trickled down to lower-class Europeans whether the East India Company liked it or not. Despite the best efforts of senior Company officials, common Britons had the power to exploit any Indian because, as members of the civilized imperial minority, they were exempt from prosecution in all but the highest presidency courts. Inevitably, a popular image of India as a country where "the black man works that the white man may be at ease" developed in Britain. As a result, the western population in India grew from approximately three thousand Europeans to eighty thousand between 1814 and 1871. This imperial elite was a tiny percentage of the overall South Asian population, but their numbers almost certainly would have been higher had not officials been so vigilant in suppressing immigration to ensure that an influx of fortune seekers did not dilute the privileges of empire.

Consequently, Company India never developed a colonial settler society on par with the Spanish Andes or British North America. Where Peruvian cities were Spanish creole bastions, Britons were ever mindful that they lived among a sea of real Indians. They became more obsessed with defending the cultural boundaries of subjecthood, and the local customs and material culture that had seemed so appealing a century earlier now threatened to conquer the conquerors through seductive assimilation. Thus, the new generation of priggish and upright Company officials and merchants replaced the nabobs' hookahs, pajamas, and curry (which was largely an Anglo-English invention) with port, formal dinner dress, and French cuisine. They lived in gated compounds where they rarely allowed Indians beyond the verandas of their bungalows, a style of segregated housing that became emblematic of British imperial society around the world.

These cultural shifts also reshaped the intimate relationships that Britons had with their Indian subjects. In the era before Plassey, it was not unusual for EIC employees to marry local women, and until the reforms of the 1780s the children of these unions, known variously as Anglo-Indians or Eurasians, grew up to enter the Company service or marry Company officials. Just as Cuzco's Convent of Santa Clara molded mestiza daughters into Spanish wives for the conquistadors, orphanages in Madras and Calcutta trained Eurasian girls to enter white society as respectable spouses for junior officials and army officers.

Although they depicted themselves as the champions and defenders of oppressed Indian women, nineteenth-century liberal and evangelical reformers introduced a new discriminatory order that closed off these opportunities. Asserting that common Indians despised "half-castes" because they shared the vices of both the western and Asian races, they barred Eurasians from the military and civil service and stigmatized conjugal relations between Europeans and local women. Sufficiently light-skinned Eurasian children could still blend into the imperial elite if they had a respectable father who acknowledged their paternity, but the children of lower-class Britons were largely doomed to join the subject majority. Over time, the entire Eurasian population, which numbered about twenty thousand in Bengal, gradually devolved into a subordinate class of imperial auxiliaries after the metropolitan government refused their repeated pleas for full British citizenship.

The arrival of greater numbers of metropolitan women in the nineteenth century further sharpened these racial boundaries. The privileges of empire meant that regardless of their social origins, these women immediately became respectable damsels and matrons upon reaching India. As such, their supposed frailty and chastity provided an excuse for new segregationist policies to protect them from allegedly lascivious "native" men. In depicting themselves as the defenders of chaste western European and degraded Indian women, British empire builders cast Indian men as both debauched and unmasculine. Macaulay was typically chauvinistic in suggesting that Plassey and the victories that followed proved that Bengal's diet, climate, and vices had turned its men soft, slothful, and effeminate. "The physical organization of the Bengali is feeble even to effeminacy.... His pursuits are sedentary, his limbs delicate, his movements languid. During many ages he has been trampled upon by men of bolder and more hard breeds."[36] Indian men were thus unfit to govern themselves.

The attempt of Macaulay and his fellow reformers to redefine Bengali masculinity was part of a larger project to impose a more precise and discriminatory kind of subjecthood on Indians. Seeking to better understand and exploit local communities, Company officials made caste and religion the central feature of governance, military service, policing, production, customary law, and, eventually, political representation. They came to believe that some Indian communities ("martial races") were natural soldiers, that a criminal sect known as *thuggee* made banditry a central feature of its devotional practices, and that certain "criminal tribes" were biological and culturally conditioned to defy central authority.

Although these caste and tribal stereotypes showed how little the British understood the workings of Indian community and identity, they allowed Indians to turn the Company's efforts to define and categorize them to their own ends. Rural Bengali elites embraced the martial label to jump to the head of the line in recruiting for the well-paying Company army. Similarly, notables in the Madras Presidency claimed superior caste status to defend land claims and demand precedence in British courts. Hindu and Muslim legal experts exploited British assumptions about the power of Indian tradition and superstition to retain a central role in advising Company jurists on the application of religious law and custom. Imposing "unclean" status on marginal groups also helped wealthy farmers and landlords lower their labor costs. Finally, common highway robbers earned higher status and even pardons by confessing to being "thugs."

Educated Hindus further countered the British reformers' attacks on their faith and culture by developing a more coherent and unified version of the eclectic religious practices that Indians had observed at the community level for centuries. The fact that British observers were the first to refer to these more standardized doctrines as "Hinduism" led some scholars to mistakenly credit them with inventing the modern version of the Hindu faith. It is far-fetched at best that a tiny imperial elite could have this kind of social impact. In reality, Hinduism was an indigenous response to the bigoted and chauvinistic assault on Indian religion and culture that legitimized the Company's empire.

Rammohun Roy, a western-educated assistant collector in the EIC's civil service, was a driving force in this movement. Drawing on centuries-old scholarly Vedic texts, he depicted Hinduism as an ancient rational monotheistic religion on par with the Judeo-Christian faiths. This enabled him to rebut the evangelists and utilitarians who cited the ritual suicide of Hindu widows, which actually was relatively rare in early nineteenth-century Bengal, as proof that Indian faith and culture were barbarous and depraved. More specifically, he argued that *sati* had no basis in Hindu scripture and collected petitions demanding that the Company ban the practice. More conservative Hindu scholars and intellectuals attacked Roy and the younger generation of western-educated Indians for tinkering with their faith to make it more compatible with western ideology, but it is striking how little contemporary British observers understood the origins and stakes of this debate. Most simply assumed that Hinduism was an ancient but degenerate pagan religion.

Like the Iberians and Andeans, Indians exploited the ignorance of their imperial rulers, but they could not escape the oppressive realities of empire. While the 1833 charter revisions explicitly declared that Indians would suffer no discrimination in applying for positions in the Company's civil service, modern conceptions of racial bigotry took on an imperial dimension. Rango Bapojee, who spent more than a decade living in Britain, echoed the bitter charges of hypocrisy that the Inkan nobleman Don Felipe Huamán Poma de Ayala had leveled against the Pizarrists nearly three centuries earlier: "The white man, or Company's servant, [is] always regarded as the embodiment of virtue and truth, incapable of wrong even in his own showing, and alone worthy of belief—the dark man, or native, [is] held up as the personification of vice and falsehood, to be accused only to be condemned, degraded, vilified, punished, imprisoned at will, tortured, beggared, and all in secret and unheard."[37]

Even Macaulay's westernized, anglicized Indian auxiliaries did not escape the taint of this imperial racism. Far from accepting them for their English "taste, opinions, morals, and intellect," Britons in India ridiculed the graduates of western schools as semieducated "baboos." *Babu* was a Persian honorific meaning "mister" or "esquire," but it evolved into a sneeringly derisive term for a partially westernized native who did not know his place. In British eyes, baboos were pretentious social climbers who used Macaulay's schooling to avoid honest work. According to the stereotype, they spoke stilted English, mixed western and Indian clothes, brazenly fed their voracious appetites for food and sex, and were inherently stupid. Such people never really existed; rather, the baboo was born of the British attempt to deny the very existence of western-educated Indians. Imperial ideologues needed reassurance that their commitment to rescuing Indians from their backwardness confirmed that they were platonic moral guardians rather than selfish tyrants.

Ironically, one of the surest ways to escape this new racially bounded subjecthood was to travel to Britain. Although Bristol street children threw stones at Rammohun Roy because they mistook him for Tippu Sultan, the Company's archenemy in Mysore, metropolitan Britons had little stake in the imperial racial hierarchy of British India. Company officials therefore went to great lengths to prevent Indians from coming to Britain. But their authority stopped at the water's edge, and Indians were free to go where they wished once they had slipped the geographical bonds of the empire. As a result, a steady parade of Indians sought redress in London. Few had any significant success, but they embarrassed the Company, particularly during the charter revisions, by publishing books and pamphlets, making speeches, and giving testimony in Parliament that drew public attention to the most abusive aspects of its Indian empire.

Moreover, not all of the Indians who traveled to Britain were aristocrats. It was not unusual for Indian wives to join their western husbands upon retirement, and their children blended into British society if they were sufficiently light-skinned. More significant, Dadabhai Naoroji, the first Indian professor at Bombay's Elphinstone Institute, entered British politics after arriving in London in 1855 as the representative of a Bombay commercial firm. As a founder of the East India Association, he accused the British Empire of draining India's wealth. Many metropolitan Britons were not offended by this carefully measured attack on the parasitism of empire, and the voters of Central Finsbury sent him to Parliament as their representative in 1892. While imperial special-interest groups built popular support for the empire as the nineteenth century progressed, Naoroji's career demonstrated that the metropolitan rule of law could trump imperial authoritarianism and racism.

These imperial exchanges also reshaped British culture. Expensive shawls from Kashmir became a mark of status for upper-class women, and the curry dishes that the new generation of empire builders dismissed as gauche in India became a central feature of metropolitan cuisine after expatriate Britons brought them home. In time, entrepreneurs brought out premixed spices (curry powder) to capitalize on popular perceptions that Indian curries were romantic, exotic, and healthy. Metropolitan cooks gradually made the dish their own by substituting apples for mangoes, lemon juice for tamarind, and flour roux in place of coconut-based thickeners, but there was no denying India's profound culinary impact on British tastes.

Similarly, words such as *calico, chintz, dungaree, seersucker, bandana, khaki, pariah*, and *pundit* entered the English language. Over time, English-speakers came to use these and other words without giving much thought to their Indian origins. This led groups like the Society for Pure English to warn of the danger of "contaminating our speech with unassimilated words, and to the disgrace, which our stupidity or laziness must bring upon us, of addressing the world in a pudding-stone and piebald language."[38]

Although its reasoning was insulting, the society was correct. Empire blurred the cultural boundaries between citizen and subject in both the imperial periphery and metropole. It was impossible to govern a people without learning and internalizing their language and culture. Macaulay and the rest of the reformist lobby may have thought they could remake Indians in their own image, but they never realized how much the Indian majority was slowly but surely remaking them. Company officials would have denied this vehemently because they understood that their ability to govern and extract wealth depended on maintaining sufficient social distance from their subjects. This explains their invention of the baboo, their denigration of everyday Indian society and culture, and the pernicious racism that steadily permeated their Indian empire in the nineteenth century.

It is therefore not surprising that Indians of every social station rejected this smothering, racially bounded subjecthood. As the educated and respectable classes attacked the inequities of British rule in print, the Company had to impose press censorship in spite of the utilitarians' commitment to the free flow of ideas. The courts also offered some relief from inequitable Company policies, which explains the baboos' reputation for litigiousness.

For common people, however, direct, often violent resistance was the only option. Landed interests sometimes thwarted the Permanent Settlement by using threats and intimidation to scare off the Calcutta merchants who considered buying up foreclosed *zamindaris*. Local communities countered Christian proselytizing by ostracizing and sometimes killing the small handful of converts won over by the missionaries. The original Baptist mission station at Semaphore needed government protection to operate, and in the 1820s the Wesleyan Missionary Society shut down its operation in Calcutta after one of its converts was murdered. There was actually very little that British authorities could do about such incidents. As in most empires, the Company's ability to exert real authority in the countryside was quite limited.

The peasant revolt also retained its potency during the final decades of the Company empire. British police officers developed a fairly extensive rural surveillance system to uncover plots in their infancy, but village headmen, Hindu and Muslim religious figures, and discharged soldiers and militiamen still tapped into widespread popular anger to organize uprisings. As a result, rebellions continued to flare up in Bengal throughout the first half of the nineteenth century. None of these incidents were large enough to threaten the imperial regime, but they demonstrated that the Company's hold on the Indian countryside remained tenuous despite its evolution from a chartered commercial concern into a more conventional territorial empire.

Indeed, the precariousness of British imperial rule became all too apparent when almost the entire Indian soldiery in Bengal rebelled en masse in 1857. *Sepoys* had revolted periodically over issues ranging from uniforms, beards, pay, and heavy campaigning since the EIC's army became a more conventional military formation in the 1770s. In this case, the Company provoked the *sepoys* by requiring them to serve overseas, cutting their pay and benefits, and lowering the status and privileges of the military profession. This came at a time when the revenue demands of the Permanent Settlement bit heavily, and soldiers from Awadh were embittered by the EIC's annexation of the rest of their province.

The revolt began in May 1857 when three regiments at Meerut executed their officers and marched on Delhi to restore the Mughal emperor. It then spread quickly to neighboring garrisons. The smaller armies of the Madras and Bombay presidencies were largely unaffected, but by the end of the year only about 8,000 troops of the 139,000-man Bengal army still obeyed British orders.[39] As a result, the EIC lost control of most of the Ganges River valley.

The mutiny of 1857 was unprecedented in its scope and threatened the very foundations of the Company empire. This breakdown of imperial law and order gave local communities an opportunity to reassert their autonomy as the unrest spread to the civilian population. Indian nationalists referred to this massive upheaval as the "First War of Indian Independence," but they were getting ahead of themselves. In reality, unconnected and largely uncoordinated popular local and regional rebellions followed the mutiny at Meerut.

To be sure, the rebels shared a deep hatred of British imperial rule. The communities that joined the revolt were in the regions that faced the heaviest revenue demands and foreclosures as a result of the Company's reforms. Many also experienced considerable economic and social instability resulting from agricultural commercialization and the spread of private land tenure. But in other cases popular Muslim religious figures stirred up revolts by calling for a jihad against Christian British rule. Finally, the Company's practice of annexing the kingdoms of rulers who did not produce a biological heir led some princes to join the uprising.

A faction of the rebels looked backward in attempting to use the elderly emperor Bahadur Shah to bring unity to the revolt, but others recognized that a century of British rule had effectively destroyed the old Mughal order. Of these, some looked to the last Maratha king, Nana Sahib, for leadership, while local leaders drew on the Company itself in imaging a new postimperial world. The village *zamindar* Shah Mal set up a "hall of justice" in the local British irrigation officer's bungalow, and the peasant leader Devi Singh created an elaborate village administrative system complete with a supreme court, a board of revenue, magistrates, and a superintendent of police.[40]

While most outbreaks of unrest during the "mutiny" had distinctly local origins, they merged into an enormous challenge to the Company empire, and it took more than a year for British forces to regain control of the Ganges heartland. The rebels exposed the inherent weakness of the Company as an imperial power, but they were too divided to win a decisive military victory. While they shared a common desire to escape their subjecthood, they could not agree on a vision for the postimperial order. Hindus distrusted Muslims, while the Muslims themselves fell out along Sunni-Shi'a lines. Sikhs had no interest in seeing a revival of the Mughal Empire, which had oppressed them for centuries, and Indian princes looked at the populist rural uprisings with alarm. Many Indians remained neutral because they calculated correctly that British power was not broken, which helps explain why *sepoys* in Bombay and Madras refused to join the mutiny. This allowed relief forces from the regular British and presidential armies to defeat the last of the rebels in 1858.

Taken as a whole, the events of 1857 stand as one of the largest popular anti-imperial uprisings in the history of empire. The mass slave insurrections of the later Roman Republic were probably larger and bloodier, but Spartacus and his men were not conventional imperial subjects. In later eras, neither the Umayyads nor the Spaniards ever had to contend with mass violent unrest on the scale of the Indian Mutiny. For good reason, the scope and ferocity of the rebellion terrified the tiny British minority in India. Bringing to life the deepest fears of all empire builders, the rebels slaughtered their imperial masters and Indian auxiliaries whenever they could find them. The Meerut *sepoys* murdered every Indian Christian in Delhi, and the followers of Nana Sahib massacred more than two hundred British men, women, and children at Kanpur after the officers of the garrison surrendered to spare their families a prolonged siege.

Newspaper reports of the rebels cutting down European women and children with clubs and bayonets enraged the British public and appeared to confirm the worst imperial stereotypes of Indian barbarism. Although later investigations revealed that the women at Kanpur had been murdered but not raped, the idea that Nana Sahib's men had violently crossed the boundaries of subjecthood by putting their hands on virtuous and vulnerable "white" women ensured an equally violent and brutal British response to the mutiny. Relief forces killed suspected rebels on sight. Armed with the legal authority to impose summary punishment without the due process of law, they cut down civilians at will and forced accused Muslim and Hindu mutineers to defile themselves by eating pork or beef before blowing them out of cannons. There are no accurate estimates for the resulting Indian loss of life, but the figures must surely run to the tens of thousands if not hundreds of thousands.

Equally troubling for a "civilized" imperial power, British commanders motivated their European and Indian troops to rush to the defense of besieged garrisons by promising them loot. But the imperial troops often did not bother to distinguish friend from foe during the chaos of the mutiny. A junior British officer candidly described what happened after the recapture of Delhi: "Sometimes [the British prize agent] finds a rich old nigger in his house, and he immediately takes him into a little room and puts a pistol to his head and tells him that he will shoot him if he doesn't tell him where the treasure is upon which the nigger takes him to some part of the house and tells him to dig, and then we sometimes find 10,000 or 100,000 Rupees hid."[41] In acknowledging that "our object is to make an example and terrify others," the governor of the Punjab admitted that more than a simple desire for revenge drove these brutal tactics. In punishing entire communities and classes for their mass defiance of imperial authority, British empire builders sought desperately to rebuild the boundaries of subjecthood that had tottered and then collapsed during the anarchy of 1857.

The vicious retribution that Britain visited upon its rebellious subjects did indeed restore its authority in India for another nine decades, but the uprising demonstrated that the East India Company had outlived its usefulness as a proxy imperial power. It took thirty-six million pounds and more than eleven thousand military casualties for the metropolitan government to regain control of Bengal. This enormous commitment of men and material resources exposed the hidden costs of empire and raised difficult questions about the overall value of India to Britain. Although it took decades for most Britons to feel remorse for the bloody conduct of their soldiers, it was clear enough in 1858 that their representatives in Indian had not behaved as benevolent and humane imperial rulers.

As tempers cooled, it was an open question whether the moral toll of empire was worth the cost. The metropolitan government, however, never considered withdrawing from South Asia as it faced increased political and economic competition from around the world. The captive Indian market became the world's largest recipient of Britain's exports by the end of the nineteenth century and was a major supplier of cotton to its textile mills. With overall British exports declining in the face of competition from newly industrialized powers, the international sale of Indian raw materials helped balance Britain's trade deficit with Europe and the United States. Furthermore, railway construction after the mutiny helped make India second only to Canada as a primary recipient of imperial investment. India also provided high salaries and generous retirement benefits for British civil servants, and Indian taxpayers funded the reconstituted Indian army, which remained an important prop of British imperial power throughout the world.

The full scope of these economic and strategic realities was not fully apparent in 1858, but the British government understood that quitting India was not an option. Instead, Prime Minister Palmerston set out once again to "reform" the Indian empire. The first step was to restore its moral veneer after the brutal realities of imperial governance and control were laid bare for all to see in the aftermath of the mutiny. Just as parliamentary investigations of Clive and Hastings helped wipe away the embarrassment of the nabobs' blatantly venial and corrupt empire building, metropolitan observers of every political stripe agreed that their nineteenth-century successors were to blame for the 1857 uprising.

Concluding that the utilitarians' modernist meddling and the evangelicals' proselytizing had provoked the fanatical and irrational Indian majority, Tory conservatives blamed the rebellion on the reformist lobby. They were particularly dismissive of Macaulay's educated auxiliaries, who failed to persuade their superstitious kinsmen to embrace British rule. Certain that Indians were not ready to live in the modern world, the conservatives cited reports that the *sepoys* rebelled in response to rumors that the cartridges for their new Lee-Enfield rifles were greased with pork and beef fat, thereby defiling Hindu and Muslims soldiers who had to rip open the paper casings with their teeth. Few stopped to consider that the Indian soldiery's supposed religious prejudices and superstition did not prevent them from using those same rifles and cartridges against the British. Liberals, on the other hand, still believed that empires could be instruments of reform, but they joined the attack on the EIC by accusing Company officials of blocking progress and inciting the mutiny by failing to properly safeguard Indian property rights under the Permanent Settlement.

Metropolitan politicians consequently agreed that the Company had to go. In 1858, Parliament passed an India Bill that finally abolished the EIC and transferred all of its holdings to the Crown. The court of directors met for the last time in September of that same year, and the Company's stock stopped paying dividends five years later. In its place the British government created a new administrative imperial entity known as the Raj (from the Hindi word for "government") to assert direct control over India. In London, the secretary of state for India, assisted by the India Office, appointed and supervised a viceroy who presided over a unified Indian bureaucracy. The India

Bill dispensed with the archaic Bengal, Bombay, and Madras presidencies and the Company's outdated civil administration. The new Indian
Civil Service (ICS) was theoretically a meritocracy open to educated
Indians, but the practice of holding the competitive entrance exams
in London ensured that only a handful of subject peoples entered its
senior ranks in the nineteenth century.

Like the EIC, the Raj remained an imperial state in its own right.
Its reconstituted armed forces were still separate from the regular
British army, and the viceroys still had considerable autonomy in setting its foreign policy. The reformers used Bahadur Shah's cooperation with the mutineers as an excuse to finally abolish the Mughal
Empire, and in his place Prime Minister Benjamin Disraeli made
Victoria queen-empress of India in 1876. As her first viceroy, Lord
Canning sought to win popular local support for the new imperial
regime by giving carefully chosen Indians seats on the viceregal and
provincial advisory councils. Assuming that the mutiny had demonstrated the ineffectiveness of western-educated Indians as allies and
intermediaries, Canning hoped to turn Indian nobles and aristocrats
into a primary prop of British rule. He ended the practice of annexing
the kingdoms of childless rulers and invented a grandiose array of
titles, coats of arms, and chivalric orders to reward princes who swore
allegiance to the Raj. Finally, he angered revenge-minded Britons and
earned himself the nickname of "Clemency Canning" by pardoning
former mutineers and rebels who were not directly implicated in the
killing of Europeans.

These reforms actually did very little to alter the realities of imperial governance and exploitation in India. The Raj was still concerned
primarily with generating and extracting wealth, and British officials
still believed that they could remake Indian society to increase their
returns by raising agricultural production. Formal taxation replaced
tribute collection, and investment instruments became important
new revenue sources as South Asia became more tightly integrated
into global capital markets. Ultimately, though, the wealth of India
still lay in the countryside, which forced the British to continue to
search for ways to make imperial extraction pay without provoking
further rebellions through their economic and social meddling.

The Raj also remained equally committed to defending the
boundaries of imperial subjecthood despite its loudly and piously
proclaimed commitment to opening government and commerce to

qualified Indians. Most British officials and their families lived within the segregated confines of opulent hill stations and fortified urban enclaves. Ever conscious that the mutiny had exposed their vulnerability as a privileged imperial elite, they became even more obsessed with protecting their personal safety under the guise of upholding law and order. A larger garrison of regular British forces provided a counterbalance to the reorganized Indian army, and the expanded railway network ensured that troops could deal quickly with potential threats. As a late nineteenth-century state, the Raj had the means to keep closer track of the Indian majority through a more modern police force, better censuses, and public health legislation that provided a legal cover for keeping Europeans segregated from the Indian majority. Angry Indians still occasionally attacked and murdered British officials, but these measures ensured that there would be no more uprisings on the scale of the 1857 mutiny.

As the threat of overt violent resistance receded, the western-educated Indian professionals and civil servants, whom the British continued to dismiss at best as an isolated elite and at worst as semi-European baboos, emerged as the most serious threat to the Raj. Frustrated by the smothering racism that still permeated imperial society, they refused to become permanent imperial subjects. In fact, their command of British law and culture was more dangerous to the Raj than any mutinous *sepoy* because they had means and opportunity to call attention to how the inherent exploitation and hypocrisy of imperial rule conflicted with the ideals of a western liberal democracy.

To this end, Indian lawyers and members of the civil service turned the Indian National Congress (INC), which a retired British bureaucrat founded in the 1880s as a supervised outlet for Indian political aspirations, into a powerful anti-imperial movement. Shifting from their initial goal of ending discrimination in the civil service, the INC leadership demanded political representation, judicial reform, and the abolition of the exploitive economic policies that they believed were draining India's wealth to Britain. These educated elites remained divided by region, caste, and religion, but they were far more successful in organizing popular resistance to the Raj than the British had ever imagined possible.

Belatedly recognizing the scope of the threat, imperial officials tried to appease them with a series of constitutional reforms that slowly expanded Indian participation in advisory councils that evolved gradually into provincial legislatures in the early twentieth century. But these stopgap measures were doomed because Mohandas Gandhi, a London-educated lawyer, and other INC leaders finally convinced the Indian majority to withdraw the tacit consent that had allowed foreigners to rule South Asia for almost two centuries. Recognizing that they were losing their grip on India following the First World War, desperate British officials subverted their own reformist agenda by resorting to coercive and illiberal extralegal measures to deal with dissent. When these tactics sparked even larger widespread popular opposition, Brigadier General Reginald Dyer took matters into his own hands by ordering his men to open fire on a peaceful protest in the Punjabi city of Amritsar. Pizarro would have approved, but the murder of almost four hundred unarmed demonstrators turned even more Indians against the Raj. In convincing enough Indians to think collectively, if not nationally, rather than locally or communally, Gandhi and his allies created sufficient social unity to render British India ungovernable through their noncooperation campaigns. Their progress toward independence in 1947 was halting and tragically bloody, but the Raj's relatively short life span in comparison to earlier empires demonstrated that the realities of empire had changed radically in the twentieth century.

Lasting from the victory at Plassey in 1757 to the violent partition of the Raj in 1947, Britain's South Asian empire appeared to be an imperial achievement on par with Umayyad Al-Andalus and the Spanish Andes in its coherency and durability. Yet there were actually three successive but very different British empires in India: the empire of the nabobs, the reformed Company empire, and the Raj. In retrospect, Britain's greatest imperial achievement in India was extending the shelf life of an archaic proxy empire from the early modern era into an age of nationalism and transnational global capitalist integration.

The original Company empire began as a commercial enterprise that had operated in South Asia for over a century before metastasizing into an empire. The nabobs built their Indian empire without the authorization of either the court of directors or the metropolitan British government. This set them apart from the conquistadors, whose New World empire building at least had the formal sanction of the Spanish Crown. Clive certainly matched Pizarro in his greed and ambition, but Mughal administrative and economic institutions proved sufficiently co-optable and adaptable to spare Company officials from having to adopt the conquistador commander's brutal tactics. Clive and his fellow Company servants did not have to concern themselves with finding ways to extract wealth from their subjects. The Mughal imperial institutions largely did it for them.

Therefore Plassey was not a nabobist Cajamarca. Instead it was a relatively minor battle that allowed Clive to supplant the *nawabs* as the imperial overlords of Bengal. This also explains why common Bengalis did not initially recognize that they had acquired a new and more ambitiously rapacious imperial master. It is fruitless to try to determine if there was more rural unrest under Mughal, *nawab*, or Company rule, but it is clear that *ryots* and craftsmen learned that their subjecthood had changed for the worse when the Company's rising tribute demands led to famine and destitution in the decades after Plassey.

In the short term, however, Clive's *jagir* was representative of the orientalist trappings that allowed the nabobs to pose as Indian rulers and conceal the full extent of their empire building from their superiors in London. Working through indigenous institutions of imperial governance, tribute, and commerce allowed them to form mutually beneficial alliances with key local Bengalis. These *banians, zamindars,* and *sepoys* did not betray a larger Indian nation in helping to build the Company empire; no such entity existed in eighteenth-century South Asia. The peoples of the British Isles were only just beginning to think of themselves as a nation during this period, but their stronger collective identity gave them an enormous advantage in India were identities were still primarily local, occupational, communal, or confessional. Moreover, the emergence of popular British patriotism allowed Clive and Hastings to escape censure for their excesses by wrapping themselves in the garb of national service.

The most successful nabobs became fabulously wealthy by transferring the real costs of empire to the metropole. Clive may have hoped that the Bengali *diwani* would generate millions of pounds of revenue each year, but it was little more than a cover for tribute collecting and stock speculation. The administrative and military costs of becoming an imperial power nearly bankrupted the Company, while Clive and his fellow nabobs made their fortunes. Bengali farmers and craftsmen of course bore the real cost of nabobism in the form of rising tribute obligations and famine, but British landed aristocrats and taxpayers also came to consider themselves its victims. From a metropolitan standpoint, the nabobs' greatest sins were forcing the treasury to rescue the Company from insolvency and disrupting the gentlemanly social order with their ill-gotten wealth.

The British authorities accordingly realized that empire was too lucrative and destabilizing to be left in the hands of private entrepreneurs. From one perspective, Parliament's move to assert more direct control over a territory that it had never originally intended to acquire was an inevitable sequence in the standard narrative of imperial history. Just as the Umayyad caliphs recalled Tariq ibn Ziyad and Musa ibn Nusayr from Iberia and the Spanish Crown sent Don Francisco de Toledo to mop up the Pizarrist mess in the Andes, the 1784 India Act put an end to nabobism by stripping the East India Company of most of its mercantile functions. Although its stock and court of directors made it still look like a commercial enterprise, the EIC essentially became a more closely regulated imperial state that allowed the metropolitan government to control India without incurring the heavy moral and economic cost of imperial governance and extraction.

The Romans, Umayyads, and Spaniards would have been well satisfied with such arrangements, but the proxy Company empire also introduced a new complication into the mechanism of imperial rule. Under pressure from the metropolitan reformist lobby, Company officials actually had to make at least a show of putting their self-serving humanitarian legitimizing ideologies of empire into practice. Although they may have been bigots by contemporary standards, British liberals, utilitarians, and evangelicals actually believed they could remake Indian society to the mutual benefit and profit of themselves and their subjects. Their public depiction of empire as moral and benevolent helped win support for the imperial enterprise in metropolitan Britain. The reformers therefore performed the useful service of obscuring the reality that the reconstituted Company still primarily benefited stockholders, civil servants, missionaries, planters, and private opium traders.

In South Asia, however, the continuing exploitive realities of empire exposed the hypocrisy of the reformist lobby's agenda. Its civilizing rhetoric implicitly depicted Indians as inherently primitive and condemned even aristocratic elites and Company allies to perpetual subjecthood. This inherent racism turned western-educated Indians into baboos and left common people at the mercy of the imperial special interests. Moreover, the charter revisions gave the reformers a lever to force the Company to intervene more directly in the daily lives of its subjects. The resulting social instability compounded local resentment over the Company's growing demands for tribute. As in Europe, social disruption and rural unrest were inevitable consequences of commercialization, industrialization, and integration into the global economy, but in Company India British rulers exacerbated the traumatic effects of these changes with their unchecked quest for privilege and profit.

It took several centuries for the Bengali *ryots* to rid themselves of these imperial parasites, but in Europe the surprisingly short lifespan of Napoleon's continental conquest state suggested that empires were losing their viability in the nationalist era. Although the French emperor portrayed himself as a modern Caesar, it was no longer possible to replicate the Roman achievements in Europe. The Roman Empire was the product of an era where identities were insular and narrow. Napoleon's defeat at Waterloo drove him from power, but simple peasants and townsmen were the most responsible for thwarting his imperial ambitions. Quite unexpectedly, the common peoples of the Italian peninsula and the rest of French-occupied Europe demonstrated that it was possible to stand up to conquistadors and nabobs.

Italy, 1799

5

NAPOLEONIC ITALY

Empire Aborted

History appeared poised to repeat itself in 1804 when the French first consul (soon to be emperor) Napoleon Bonaparte assembled a massive army of more than 150,000 men at the channel city of Boulogne, the same port from which Claudius most likely launched his conquest of the British Isles centuries earlier. The Grande Armée that threatened Britain with invasion roughly eighteen centuries later was a powerful instrument of French empire building, but it was actually a heterogeneous force recruited throughout Napoleonic Europe. Many of the soldiers were impressed conscripts, but others served their French conquerors voluntarily.

Ermolao Federigo, an Italian officer from Vicenza, was among the latter group of imperial auxiliaries. Although Napoleon had overrun his northern Italian homeland, Federigo was a willing retainer. In a letter home, the young Vicenzan assured his mother that service in the French military would teach his countrymen to be Italian. "I serve my *patria* when I learn to be a soldier, and even if I served the Turk it would be the same. Our Republic will certainly gain more reputation and glory from its few soldiers still too young to think of liberty. Let us think of being soldiers, and when we have a hundred thousand bayonets, then we can talk."[1] Federigo's *patria* was the Italian Republic, a recent invention that Napoleon had cobbled together from the various duchies, republics, and papal fiefdoms of northwestern Italy. The French emperor convinced young patriots like Federigo to fight and die for him by skillfully exploiting the nationalist sentiments that were breaking down local and communal identities in early nineteenth-century Europe.

While Phillip II's great sixteenth-century Habsburg Empire was on the decline, its hold on Italy remained largely intact. Some Italian ancien régime rulers were his vassals and others were independent, but most all tried to keep pace with the political and economic changes remaking western Europe by dabbling in state-directed absolutist reform. Nevertheless, the peninsula was largely a stagnant backwater. Only crumbling ruins testified to its grandeur as the heartland of the Roman Empire, and its influence as a center of arts and learning during the Renaissance had similarly declined. Mindful of their imperial and cultural heritage, Federigo and other ambitious young reformers took heart in Napoleon's destruction of the petty ancien régime states that stood in the way of reform. They were willing to overlook the brutal realities of the French Empire in return for Napoleon's promise that progressive imperial rule would restore Italy to its former greatness.

Napoleon willfully nurtured these ambitions as the titular president of the Italian Republic. Invoking self-determination as a new kind of legitimizing imperial ideology, he cast himself as the great patron of the Italian "nation" even after transforming the republic into a kingdom and crowning himself its king. His viceroy and stepson Eugène de Beauharnais reassured his subjects that their emperor had not betrayed them and promised that service in the French imperial forces was their best chance of becoming "a nation again, to make the power of Italy respected both now and in the future."[2]

Writing during his imprisonment on Elba, Napoleon insisted that one of his greatest accomplishments was to have raised "the Italian nation from its ruins" by creating a single "independent nation bounded by the Alps and the Adriatic, Ionian, and Mediterranean Seas." By his reasoning, it took an enlightened French empire to remove the roadblocks that the papacy, the Austrian Empire, and petty ancien régime princes placed in the way of Italian unification. Appealing to the judgment of history, Napoleon excused the excesses of his imperial regime by asserting: "There were now no Venetians, Piedmontese, or Tuscans: the inhabitants of the whole peninsula were no longer anything but Italians: all was ready to form the great Italian nation."[3]

At first glance, the French emperor seemed to have offered his subjects a new, more humane and inclusive brand of empire. His rule held out the offer of equality before the law, respect for private property, and national self-determination within the framework of a continental European empire that promised equality to his subjects. While Napoleon treated large swaths of rural France as conquered territory, his strategy of *ralliement* (rallying) represented a concerted effort to enlist propertied and influential Europeans in his imperial enterprise. Even more ambitiously, in adopting a policy of *amalgame* (amalgamation) he sought to create a new imperial elite that would assist France as loyally and usefully as romanized Britons and Gauls had served the Roman Empire.

In fact, there was actually very little that was new or revolutionary in Napoleon's amalgamist project. To varying degrees, the Umayyads, Spanish, and British nabobs had made similar compromises with Visigothic barons, Andean nobles, and Bengali aristocrats. The willingness of a significant cohort of elites to align their interests with foreign conquerors explains the longevity of ancient, medieval, and early modern empires. It is possible that Napoleon did not see a contradiction in *amalgame* and national self-determination, but in reality amalgamation was an impossibility in early nineteenth-century Europe. Napoleon conquered most of the continent by harnessing the emerging power of French nationalism, and the generals and administrators who followed him expected the new empire to bring material rewards for themselves and France.

The legitimizing ideologies of empire may have shifted at the dawn of the nationalist era, but the underlying nature of imperial rule had not. Extraction and exploitation were still the defining realities of imperial subjecthood, and no amount of inclusivist *amalgame* or benevolently nationalistic rhetoric could disguise this fact. Indeed, Napoleon may have portrayed himself as a humane empire builder, but he was actually part aspiring conquistador and part Caesar. He seized northern Italy in 1796 as a rising revolutionary general largely on his own initiative and used the resulting fame to claim first the consulship and then the imperial purple. Napoleon's reconquest of Italy in 1800 as first consul marked one of the rare occasions when a head of state led an imperial conquest and harked back to the Claudian invasion of Britain. His aspirations would have been familiar to most ancient Romans, for his first and primary goal was to empower himself by building a continental empire.

Napoleon courted Ermolao Federigo and other young would-be patriots as part of his amalgamist agenda, but he fully understood

that French nationalism was the key to his dynastic and imperial ambitions. At its core, his empire was an expression of French
greatness. Depicting himself as the personal embodiment of France,
he had as his primary goal to extract tribute, collect taxes, and conscript military manpower to advance his plans for continental dominance. This explains his candor in a 1805 order to his viceroy Eugène:
"Italy must not make calculations separate from the prosperity of
France...it must blend its interests with those of France....So take
as your motto: France before all."[4] Federigo would also have been disturbed to hear his patron describe Italians as "a people who are soft,
superstitious, deceitful and cowardly."[5]

Napoleon's Elba pronouncements about his benign imperial intentions were revisionist fiction. The non-French troops who assembled
in Boulogne for the stillborn invasion of Britain and fought for the
French throughout Europe were mostly unwilling conscripts. They
were subjects, not imperial partners. Napoleon nurtured the nationalist aspirations of the Italians, Germans, and Poles to enlist them in
his imperial enterprise; he had no intention of granting them social
or political autonomy, much less nation-states. Federigo represented
the small reformist and protonationalistic segment of Italian society
willing to embrace *amalgame*. Most Italians, however, viewed the
French Empire as alien, authoritarian, brutal, and invasively extractive. While *zamindars* stood between the full weight of nabobist rule
and Bengali *ryots*, Napoleon used the tools of the bureaucratic state
to create a far more efficient system of imperial administration that
reached down to the lowest, most basic levels of rural Italian society.
He did not need *zamindari*-type intermediaries to collect tribute, and
his demands for revenue and conscripts imposed a new, more oppressive form of subjecthood on conquered peoples throughout Europe.

Ironically, the very factors that made the early nineteenth-century
French Empire so powerful also led to its quick demise. Napoleon's
attempt to rule local communities directly sparked a powerful and popular anti-French backlash throughout the continent. This resistance
was not yet national, for most Europeans at this time still identified
themselves on the basis of local or communal loyalties. Nevertheless, the common experience of resisting the invasive French empire
helped build larger identities that were the raw material of European
nationalism. These expansive and coherent identities made it much
harder for would-be empire builders to recruit allies among subject

populations by exploiting their divisions. Federigo and his comrades eventually would realize that Napoleon had betrayed them, but at least the emperor's downfall appeared to signal the demise of the era of formal empire in Europe.

The quick rise and fall of the Napoleonic empire marked the end of a coherent mode of imperial conquest and rule that stretched back to the ancient world. Where the Roman, Umayyad, Spanish American, and British Indian empires lasted for centuries, the empire that began with the French Revolution and ended with Napoleon's defeat at Waterloo spanned only twenty-five years. Michael Broers attributes the French Empire's short life span to the violence that brought it into being. In his view, the brutality of the Napoleonic wars stunted its growth by giving conquered peoples a reason to hate the French. By this reasoning, forward-looking continental notables who would have valued Napoleon's commitment to good governance, stability, and the rule of law turned against him because they suffered at the hands of his soldiers. Broers is one of the most thoughtful and perceptive authorities on Napoleonic Europe, but in this case his perspective is too narrow.[6] Looking back over earlier imperial eras, it is clear that all empires were built by violent conquest and that conquered peoples invariably resented their subjecthood.

The Napoleonic empire was not abnormal; rather, it represented the end of a long tradition of empire that had lasted for several millennia. This imperial model lost its viability when common people came to see empires as foreign and thus illegitimate. Eighteenth-century absolutism and centralization made imperial rule far more burdensome by giving conquerors the means to extract wealth more directly from their subjects. Rural communities throughout Napoleonic Europe fell back on localism to defend themselves against this new, more invasive style of exploitation, but they gradually found common cause in resisting an oppressive imperial regime. It would take time for intellectuals and politicians to enlist or conscript the peoples of Europe in nation building, but the emergence of more coherent and broadly based collective identities steadily closed up the social divisions that empire builders needed to recruit the local allies that made long-term rule possible.

This enhanced social cohesion meant that conquistadors, nabobs, and other imperial entrepreneurs could no longer turn a quick military victory into an empire. Just as European Christians decided it was no longer acceptable to enslave each other in the early modern era, by the turn of the nineteenth century it became increasingly difficult to consign Europeans to the kind of subhuman subjecthood that was central to profitable imperial extraction. As Napoleon discovered, it now took a full-scale invasion and extended military occupation to create a continental European empire in the early national age. His empire was thus a transitional, absolutist conquest state that bridged the "old" early modern empire building and the last-gasp "new" imperialism of the modern nationalist era.

Napoleon certainly went to great lengths to depict himself as a benevolent emperor. Writing from his exile in St. Helena, he claimed that his main aim was to promote European unity and spread the ideals of the Enlightenment. Although he envisioned himself as the heir of Augustus and Charlemagne, he insisted that he had not gone to war to build a continental empire. Audaciously, he asserted: "All my victories and all my conquests were won in self-defense."[7] By this argument, he waged war to turn back the reactionary enemies of progress and had no intention of profiting unreasonably from his conquests.

Most imperial adventurers made similar claims, but the limited evidence from earlier eras made it difficult to refute them conclusively. Napoleon, however, produced one of the first bureaucratic empires. His more efficient systems of rule left a paper trail of letters, orders, and pronouncements that provided a much clearer picture of his imperial aspirations and practices. Consequently, it is easier to recognize his benevolent declarations for what they really were: propaganda to mobilize his subjects, win foreign allies, and embarrass his enemies. In reality, he spread rational secularism and legal equality to create a uniform administrative system and sweep away the aristocratic and feudal institutions that limited his ability to impose his will on conquered peoples.

Although Napoleon had more personal and state power than his imperial predecessors, he still shared their goals. As a nabobist general, he sought wealth and personal aggrandizement. As an emperor and head of state, he pursued these grandiose aspirations as the self-proclaimed personification of the French nation. He sought an empire to make his fortune, distract his French subjects with glorious foreign conquests, and acquire resources to underwrite his dynastic ambitions.

Moreover, the Napoleonic regime's legitimizing imperial ideologies were consistent with the excuses that the Romans, Umayyads, Spaniards, and British used to justify their empires. Indeed, Napoleon was entirely conscious of his imperial predecessors and often cast himself as their heirs. He adopted Roman symbols and titles and sponsored neoclassical interpretations in the fine arts, fashion, furnishings, and architecture. For all of his reformist and paternal rhetoric, Napoleon was more than willing to invoke the Roman privileges of conquest. Thus he bluntly answered his brother Jérôme, the ruler of the puppet state of Westphalia, who opposed seizing land to create new noble estates, with the dismissive rebuke: "These domains belong to my generals who conquered your kingdom."[8]

Furthermore, Napoleon never forgot that at its core his empire was fundamentally French. Although he was born on Corsica, he recognized the value of French cultural confidence as a potent imperial tool. Eighteenth-century Frenchmen saw themselves as the heirs of the Greeks and Romans and the center of the European Enlightenment. After the revolution of 1789, they grew even more certain of their superiority over the superstitious feudalistic societies of ancien régime Europe. Under Napoleon, French intellectuals reassured themselves that their culture combined the best of the classical tradition, Enlightenment science, revolutionary egalitarianism, and ancient French martial values.

Napoleonic empire builders thus used French culture as a yardstick to measure the societies they conquered. The notables, intellectuals, and city dwellers that came closest to the French ideal were worthy of enlistment in the French imperial project. Rural peoples were trapped in an earlier stage of development and therefore needed an extended lesson in "civilization" before they could qualify for *amalgame* and claim the privileges that came with French rule. In their eyes, the France of the revolution and Napoleon was fundamentally settled, cosmopolitan, and urban. French intellectuals in fact considered their own peasants to be just as barbarous and uncultured as their foreign rural subjects.

This is how Napoleon could depict himself as the liberator of subject nations even as he overran the continent. He pledged to help Europeans realize their national destinies by freeing them from the superstition of the Catholic Church and the narrow particularism of ancien régime feudalism. Promising to give Italians a national education, on the eve of his first invasion of Italy in 1796 he declared: "People of Italy, the French army is coming to break your chains. Meet it with confidence."[9] This was pure propaganda. Napoleon often pretended to support the national ambitions of his subjects, but toward the end of his reign he explicitly declared that his main concern was "the glory and power of France."[10]

Both the emperor and his representatives actually held Italians in contempt. French imperial proponents professed respect for the classical Romans, but they believed that their descendants were degenerate. Italian nobles and urban elites were lazy, soft, effeminate, and beholden to the Catholic Church. They wasted their time on billiards, opera, and love affairs. Rural peoples, particularly those of the Apennine highlands, were even worse. From the French perspective, they were irrational savages ruled by vendettas and superstition, and a French administrator went so far as to compare the villagers of Frosinone, a small hill town southeast of Rome, to Africans in their barbarity and "fierce nature."[11] By this account, common Italians were so uncivilized that they needed French imperial tutelage to regain their status as Europeans.

French empire builders thus envisioned themselves as secular missionaries charged with spreading the civilizing message of the Enlightenment to the backward corners of the continent. They would create a new enlightened European society by abolishing feudalism and introducing rational secularism, the rule of law, social equality, public education, and agricultural efficiency. Both Napoleon and the original French revolutionaries believed that their ideals were universal and transcended local cultural differences. Not surprisingly, they were equally confident that post-1789 France was the purest manifestation of this new enlightened, rational society.

The French told themselves that they had built an enlightened liberal empire to justify plunging Europe into a continental war, but this was nonsense. The primary function of Napoleon's reformist agenda was to create a powerful centralized imperial state to better extract wealth and military conscripts from subject societies. While he might have depicted himself as the enemy of feudal privilege, he was more than willing to work with the representatives of the ancien régime if they were sufficiently cooperative. In essence, the Napoleonic empire was a conquest state, and it is doubtful that many of its subjects considered the benefits of French civilization sufficient compensation for the men and wealth the emperor demanded in return.

Ultimately, Napoleon was just as ruthless as his imperial predecessors. He may have promised the Italians liberation, but in 1805 he betrayed his true intentions when he told Eugène de Beauharnais not to tolerate resistance in the Kingdom of Italy.

> There is evil in [Italians]. Do not let them forget that I am the master and can do whatever I wish. This needs to be drummed into all peoples, but especially the Italians, who only obey the voice of a master. They will respect you only if they fear you, and they will fear you only if they realize that you understand their false and deceitful character.[12]

Under Napoleonic rule, the Italians now had the same status as the ancient Britons, whom their Roman ancestors had conquered almost two millennia earlier. Napoleon's sprawling imperial state marked a turning point in the larger history of empire, but the dehumanizing realities of imperial subjecthood remained largely constant.

The nationalism that rendered imperial projects unworkable did not arise out of thin air at the close of Europe's early modern era. Undoubtedly, the kernels of ethnicity that formed the basis of western national identities were long-standing, if not ancient. But in the seventeenth and eighteenth centuries the linkage of identity with blood and ancestry, the translation of the Bible into vernacular languages, the expansion of secular printing, service in large nonprofessional armies, and the increased capacity of absolutist regimes to break down local particularism began to inspire at least some Europeans to see themselves as members of discrete, bounded, and ultimately superior "nations."

For the most part, these nation builders were princes, intellectuals, and cultural brokers who vied with each other to imagine and define the scope and membership of the larger national communities. Much like empire builders, they represented special interests who advanced their own personal agendas by framing them in broad idealistically collective terms. The stakes of the competition were formidable, for nationalism produced homogenous nation-states that empowered their leaders to claim specific territories and demand unprecedented levels of compliance and sacrifice from their citizens.

To make this work, would-be nation builders had to convince the wider population to accept and internalize their conception of the nation. This was a big step. In embracing national identities, local communities had to accept kinship with people they most likely would never meet. National rulers could also demand that they submit to military service, taxation, invasive laws, and the abolition of collective feudal rights and local privileges. This is why peasants and other common peoples resisted nation building with tax rebellions, food riots, and sullen indifference. Yet membership in a nation also had its compensations. Up until this point, citizenship simply meant insider status in comparison to even more marginal groups that had no protection from the full weight of imperial extraction. Now, citizenship in a nation-state brought the right of individuality, property ownership, assembly, expression, and eventually political participation. These national identities also provided a measure of stability and security during the social turmoil of the industrial revolution. Perhaps most important, nationalism imagined sovereignty invested in a national citizenry, and as "the people" of a nation, Europeans gradually acquired the capacity to place limits on state power.

Theoretically, the strength of a nation rested in its homogeneity. A people united by a shared sense of kinship might be defeated, but it was harder to turn them into imperial subjects because cooperation with a conquering power became much riskier. Of course, nationalism also had a dark side. Particularism became intolerable, and often it took compulsion to teach members of once distinct local communities to think nationally. In this sense, nation building could be even more oppressive than empire building. Imperial rulers were invariably authoritarian and often brutal, but they had to tolerate, if not respect, local identities because they played a central role in imperial administration and extraction. Nation-states, however, gave ethnic and religious minorities the choice of assimilation, marginalization, persecution, or emigration.

The French nationalism that underwrote Napoleon's imperial project reflected these liberating but coercive realities. Much like the Roman proconsuls who used military triumphs as a springboard to the imperial throne, Napoleon did not create his imperial state from scratch. Instead, he inherited the tools of empire from the Bourbon monarchs and their revolutionary successors. The architects of the French Revolution may have executed Louis XVI for treason in 1793, but they retained the centralizing instruments of his enlightened absolutism. Revolutionary changes made the royal guard into a national guard and the royal army into a national one. Yet although the members of the national assembly abolished feudal privilege, seized Church lands, and affirmed the natural rights of all men to liberty, property, and security, they shared the Bourbons' conviction that they could use state power to transform all levels of society. Their ambitious agenda included drafting a new calendar, inventing new children's names, and creating a "cult of reason" to break the power of the Catholic Church. While they fell far short of their egalitarian ambitions, they bequeathed Napoleon a strong centralized state.

In seeking a break with the past, the revolutionaries initially disavowed the centralized despotism of empire as a sin of the ancien régime. In 1790, the Constituent Assembly responsible for drafting a new constitution proudly declared: "The French nation renounces any intention of engaging in a war of conquest and will never employ its forces against the liberty of any people."[13] Nevertheless, the republican Girondins who controlled the assembly from 1791 to 1792 soon overcame their anti-imperial scruples once they acquired the means to build an empire. This began when they called upon the newly enfranchised French citizenry to defend the revolution from royalist conspiracies. Led by Jacques-Pierre Brissot, the Girondins forced the king to declare war on Austria and Prussia to rally popular support for the new regime. In convincing peasants and artisans to volunteer for the National Guard, Brissot harnessed the power of nationalism to the revolution.

The even more radical National Convention, which replaced the National Assembly in the summer of 1792, went a step further and declared France's intention to export the revolution by offering "fraternity and assistance to all peoples who seek to recover their liberty."[14] Suitably provoked, the Austrians and Prussians played their role by invading and, after some initial successes, losing to the better-led and better-motivated French national forces. This allowed the radical regime to occupy the left bank of the Rhine and Belgium (the Austrian Netherlands), thereby inciting the British, Dutch, Spanish, Portuguese, and northern Italian states to join the Austrians and Prussians in the anti-revolutionary First Coalition.

The threat of a hostile united Europe exacerbated simmering domestic disagreements over the shape and character of the new French nation that led the revolutionaries to turn on themselves. In 1793, the execution of the king, military reverses at the hands of the First Coalition, and economic trouble in Paris weakened the Girondins to the point where an extremist faction of Jacobins, known as the Montagnards, took control of the National Convention. Led by Maximilien Robespierre, their Committee of Public Safety suspended the constitution and coordinated the defense of France. For a little more than a year, this group of twelve deputies ruled as dictators and unleashed the infamous Reign of Terror against the real and imagined enemies of the revolution.

One of the committee's first actions was to introduce widespread conscription to fill out the flagging revolutionary armies. Surrounded by foreign enemies and facing a shortfall of three hundred thousand troops, the Convention ordered each French department (province) to produce a set quota of men. Theoretically, this *levée en masse* was a temporary requisition of manpower for the defense of the nation, but the conscripts' required service gradually stretched from months to years.

The defiant peasantry of Brittany and the Vendée refused to play their roles as revolutionary Frenchmen and allied with the Catholic clergy and royalist nobles in a localist counterrevolutionary revolt. The Committee of Public Safety responded with a brutal, near genocidal campaign against this "Christian army." The revolutionary forces destroyed crops, burned towns, and sometimes massacred resistant communities. Showing no sympathy for his fellow "citizens," General François-Joseph Westermann assured his superiors in Paris:

> The Vendée no longer exists. I've just buried it in the marshes and forests of Savenay. Following the orders I have received, I have crushed children beneath the hooves of our horses, and massacred women so that they don't spawn any more brigands. You can't reproach me with having taken any prisoners, the roads are littered with corpses.[15]

Westermann's ruthless treatment of the Vendée previewed the counterinsurgency measures that Napoleonic generals would use against rebels in Spain and the Kingdom of Naples. But these scorched-earth tactics weren't particularly effective in either western France or the wider empire. The fighting in the Vendée was so intractable that Napoleon refused a posting to the region on the assumption his military career would suffer in fighting a largely unwinnable war.

Abroad, the Convention's promise to bring liberty and fraternal assistance to the subject peoples of Europe was as hollow as its declarations of national solidarity with the common people of the Vendée. In July 1794, mass mobilization, high revolutionary morale, and better generalship enabled the French army to turn back an invasion by the First Coalition and push the boundaries of the revolution to the Rhine, Alps, and Pyrenees. These successes were not enough to defuse popular anger over the Committee of Public Safety's excesses, which included the arrest and execution of hundreds of thousands of enemies of the revolution. Two days after the great French victory at Fleurus, the more moderate members of the Convention ended the Reign of Terror by sending Robespierre and his most radical allies to the guillotine. By 1795, the result was a new constitution and a more moderate government under a five-man council known as the Directory. The Directory brought an end to the worst domestic abuses of the revolution, but its members had no intention of giving up the Convention's foreign conquests. In annexing borderlands deemed within France's "natural frontiers," the Directory implicitly acknowledged that the revolutionary regime had acquired an empire.

Ultimately, the promised returns of imperial rule proved as seductively irresistible to the French revolutionaries and republicans as they had been to their Bourbon predecessors. It took enormous financial resources to build a powerful centralized state, and the Directory insisted that the newly conquered territories had to reimburse France for the expense of their "liberation." Their continental French Empire consisted of annexed territories known as *départements réunis* (reunited departments) and puppet "sister republics." The former category included most of the Kingdom of Piedmont, the left bank of the Rhine, Geneva, and the lands comprising modern Belgium and Luxembourg. French administrators swept away the ancien régime's borders in these lands and subdivided their conquests into French departments. The Dutch United Provinces and what was left of the Swiss Confederation became the sister Batavian and Helvetic republics. Apart from Piedmont, which the French annexed, most of the Italian peninsula met a similar fate.

Napoleon carried out this imperial engineering as nothing more than a French general, but just as Julius Caesar used his victories in Gaul as a stepping-stone to power, Napoleon similarly made his reputation as the conqueror of northern Italy. Although he was the son of a noble Italian family that settled in Corsica when it was under Venetian control, he was very much a member of the French military caste.

Christened Napoleone Buonaparte, he became Napoleon Bonaparte after entering the École Militaire in Paris and earning a commission in the French military. Like many of his peers, the young officer, who spoke French with an Italian accent, found that the flight of senior royalists after the revolution created considerable opportunities for promotion in the nationalist army. It also helped that he became the protégé of Paul Barras, one of the five members of the Directory. In 1795, Napoleon reached the rank of general after distinguishing himself fighting royalist counterrevolutionaries, and one year later the Directory chose him to lead the invasion of Italy. The Directory designed the campaign as a feint to draw the First Coalition forces away from Germany, but Napoleon had other ideas. Demonstrating his superior generalship, he inflicted heavy casualties on the Austrians and drove them out of Italy entirely within the year. By October 1797, he was well on his way to Vienna when the Habsburgs dissolved the First Coalition by negotiating a peace treaty with France at Campo Formio.

As the supreme commander of French forces in Italy, Napoleon consequently found himself in control of most of the peninsula. Not unlike Clive and the Bengali nabobs, he was generally free to do as he pleased. Ignoring local appeals for an independent Italian republic, he grouped Bologna, Ferrara, Modena, and Reggio together to create the Cispadane Republic. In 1797, he folded this puppet state into the Cisalpine Republic along with the ex-Austrian Duchy of Milan and the Lombard Republic, in addition to transforming Genoa into the Ligurian Republic. Napoleon left Italy in 1798, but tensions with the Papal States and the Kingdom of Naples drew his successors southward, and their victories produced the Roman and Parthenopean republics.

These sister republics were little more than French client states. Napoleon assigned them restricted constitutions based on the Constitution of the Year III, which had brought the Directory to power in France. He had no intention of allowing them to challenge French interests and required his Italian allies to pay staggering amounts of tribute in the form of cash and requisitioned food and military supplies. Not surprisingly, this rapacious behavior soon provoked popular revolts against the French liberators.

The Italian experience of subjecthood under the empire of the Directory was fairly typical. The Dutch Batavian Republic had to pay one hundred million guilders to secure French diplomatic recognition, in addition to supporting a garrison of twenty-five thousand French troops. This was imperial extraction. Seeking to make this new empire pay, the Directory stripped conquered territories of useful machinery and destroyed what remained to ensure that it did not compete with French industry. As part of their plan to turn Paris into a new Rome, they similarly requisitioned great works of art and manuscripts from the museums, national archives, and stately homes of their sister republics. Predictably, the French revolutionary armies were even less restrained. Revolutionary generals may have cast France as the defender of western civilization, but they had more in common with the Ostrogothic plunderers of ancient Rome when they looted much of northern Italy. Chauvinistic rank-and-file French soldiers placed even less weight on the importance of solidarity with liberated peoples and followed the lead of their officers in living off the land.

Typically, the Directory's imperial accomplishments brought little security at home. Imperial tribute was not enough to offset the expense of nearly constant warfare, and the resulting economic instability undercut the regime's popular support. Additionally, the temporary truce in the Vendée collapsed when British meddling stirred up a new round of unrest. When the elections of 1797 returned a substantial number of conservatives to local assemblies and brought the royalist Marquis de Barthélemy to the Directory, the remaining directors called on Napoleon to save the republic. The general was happy to oblige. His men deported Barthélemy to South America, removed almost two hundred royalist councilors, and imposed martial law on much of the country. These authoritarian measures made the directors increasingly dependent on the military to stay in power. Their situation grew even more precarious as the demands of renewed warfare with Britain, Austria, and Russia (the Second Coalition) undermined what was left of their legitimacy. Unable to maintain the massive national army at full strength, the Directory suffered a series of military defeats in 1798 that once again left France open to invasion.

Napoleon took advantage of this situation when a cabal of senior officials, including the director Emmanuel-Joseph Sieyès, invited him to join a plot to save France by overthrowing the Directory. The conspirators planned to create a propertied oligarchy and viewed Napoleon as a pawn and popular figurehead. The general's reputation survived his 1798 failed invasion of Egypt, and he seemed the most malleable of the revolutionary generals. Instead, when the Coup of 18 Brumaire brought him to power as part of a three-consul triumvirate consisting of himself, Sieyès, and the ex-director Roger Ducos, he swiftly assumed real power. In 1799, a lopsided plebiscite confirmed the new Constitution of the Year VIII and legitimized his authority as first consul.

Napoleon was content with this role for almost five years as he gradually consolidated his power. Exploiting his fame as a war hero, the general outmaneuvered his fellow consuls to become consul for life. He ruled through a handpicked forty-member Council of State consisting of lawyers, judges, legislators, and administrators who wrote his laws and turned his orders into policy. Napoleon personally appointed the Senate, while special electoral colleges consisting of the richest taxpayers in each department chose members of national and local assemblies. This was largely for show, however, for these bodies existed only to consult rather than legislate.

Napoleon maintained the façade of revolutionary democracy by staging plebiscites to validate the constitutional changes that gradually gave him total control of France. Claiming to be above politics and factionalism, he invoked French nationalism to solidify his popular support and rallied the wealthy and professional classes with patronage and civil positions. After the revolutionary turmoil of the 1790s, French elites were now willing to back an absolutist leader who promised to respect their rank and property. Napoleon encouraged this rapprochement by granting amnesty to the royalist émigrés who accepted the loss of their estates and offered him an oath of loyalty.

This was the basis of *ralliement*. The revolutionaries and the men of the ancien régime would now work together for the glory of France under Napoleonic rule. The architects of the 1789 revolution could console themselves that Napoleon expanded and systematized many of their innovations, while French nobles and men of property were relieved to regain their status. Moreover, their sons were eligible for service in the Council of State's *auditoriat*, an elite body of select young men from prominent families who served as trusted couriers, bureaucrats, and imperial administrators in conquered territories and the sister republics. Napoleon similarly made peace with the Catholic Church. Under the Concordat of 1802, Pope Pius VII recognized Napoleon's consulate, renounced claims to former

Church property, and placed the French clergy under the authority of the secular government. In return, Napoleon acknowledged that Catholicism was the predominant religion of France.

Napoleon's success in using *ralliement* to lessen the divisions in French society gave him the support and resources to defeat the Second Coalition. In 1801, this alliance collapsed with the assassination of the Russian tsar Paul I and French victories over the Austrians. Napoleon owed his military successes to his skill in building on the innovations in recruiting, weapons, and tactics inherited from his revolutionary predecessors. His forces did not enjoy substantial advantages over their enemies in terms of military technology. They were, however, battle-hardened, professional, and superbly led by officers who owed Napoleon their personal loyalty. Most of the rank-and-file soldiery came into the army as conscripts, but nearly constant campaigning and a string of victories taught them to be loyal to each other, their supreme commander, and the larger French nation.

By 1802, no continental power could stand against this formidable force. Only Britain's Royal Navy and the English Channel blocked France's total control of western Europe. The British fought on after their Austrian and Russian allies deserted them, but eventually they also came to terms with Napoleon. The resulting accord signed at Amiens was more of a truce than a peace treaty; the British never renounced their opposition to a French empire in Europe. Nevertheless, they recognized the Napoleonic annexations and puppet republics in return for a break from their almost decade-long global struggle with the French.

The Peace of Amiens barely lasted a year, but Britain could do little to change the reality that the demise of the Second Coalition confirmed Napoleon as the master of continental Europe. Backed by his Grande Armée of roughly six hundred thousand men, he now had the stability and security to realize his dynastic ambitions. In December 1804, the Senate proclaimed him emperor. A sham plebiscite provided a veneer of legitimacy, with a vote of 3.5 million in favor of abolishing the last democratic vestiges of the revolution against only 2,579 dissenters.[16] France now was an empire in name as well as in practice.

In taking the final step of crowning himself emperor of the French, Napoleon formally linked the nation to his personal and family fortunes. He made no apologies for ending the revolutionaries' democratic experiment and portrayed himself as a new kind of liberal emperor. Where the Convention and Directory had been riven by factionalism and weakened by corruption, he claimed to blend the enlightened absolutism of the Bourbons with the nationalist social engineering of the revolution to rule for the good of France, its people, and ultimately all of Europe.

In practical terms, the French nation was the instrument of Napoleon's ambition and the stepping-stone to empire. He therefore sought to make France as strong as possible. Abandoning the Directory's distrust of central authority, he built one of the first modern state bureaucracies with a staff that almost tripled in size from 1,650 to roughly 4,000 civil servants over the course of his reign. These officials extended Napoleon's authority into the countryside. Prefects, whom Napoleon appointed personally, ran French departments with total authority, while subprefects oversaw *arrondissements* (districts). Like their master, the prefects were "little emperors" with absolute authority over almost all matters in their departments except for tax collection and policing. All told, 306 prefects served in France and the *départements réunis* between 1800 and 1814. The majority were under the age of forty and came from bourgeois French families, but over time some assimilated "new Frenchmen" from the annexed territories joined their ranks.

As would be expected, tax collection was one of the central functions of this expanded bureaucracy. Napoleon repudiated the Directory's unpaid debts, but he still inherited an empty treasury upon coming to power. Although tribute and loot from imperial conquests provided an important revenue stream, Napoleon recognized that he needed to tap the wealth of the French nation to fund his imperial ambitions. The Convention had already done much of the messy work by introducing direct taxation, and Napoleonic bureaucrats made the tax system more efficient by surveying the ownership and usage of all French land.

In terms of law, Napoleon co-opted and redirected the Directory's earlier efforts to create a uniform legal system. Focusing on personal and property rights, this new Civil Code, which became the Code Napoleon in 1807, abolished the last vestiges of feudal privilege and corporatism. The Church lost its role in keeping civil records, the guilds lost their influence, and all French men became equal before the law. Civil marriage and divorce became possible, but male householders retained absolute authority over their wives and daughters. While the new Criminal Code abolished arbitrary arrest and imprisonment, it allowed torture with judicial supervision. These illiberal contradictions are not surprising, for Napoleon's goals were more pragmatic than egalitarian. He sought to break down the communal and corporate barriers that had limited his monarchical predecessors' ability to rule directly. This is why he insisted on applying the Code Napoleon throughout the French Empire in all annexed territories and client states.

Napoleon was no revolutionary. In rallying French nobles, republicans, property owners, professionals, businessmen, bureaucrats, and military officers, he sought to engineer a class of elites that would draw their influence and status solely from ties to his regime. Claiming that state service was now the basis of aristocratic privilege, Napoleon created 31 dukes, 451 counts, and 1,474 chevaliers (knights) by 1808. But their backgrounds were hardly common. Most of the dukes were either Bonaparte family members or trusted generals and civil officials.[17] Unwilling to provoke further instability with another redivision of French estates, he rewarded this new imperial nobility with land grants (*majorats*) carved from conquered territory. By the end of his reign, there were approximately six thousand recipients of these bequests (*donataires*), mostly in eastern Europe, collecting thirty million francs' worth of rent from liberated French subjects.

Dismissing peasants and the urban lower orders, Napoleon courted the old nobility and the most able republican elites. Focusing on the next generation, he promoted *amalgame* by establishing prestigious secondary schools (*lycées*) to train their sons for state service. Although they taught conventional subjects such as mathematics, science, and modern languages, the *lycée* culture was ultimately martial. *Lycée* students wore uniforms, held military-style ranks, and marched and drilled regularly.

Napoleon's empire did not last long enough to give these experiments in social engineering a chance to run their course. *Ralliement* and *amalgame* might have eventually produced a loyal imperial citizenry, but in the near term his new imperial order was fundamentally coercive. For all of its commitment to legal reform and equality before the law, the Napoleonic regime was Europe's first modern police state. Building on the Directory's internal security apparatus, the Ministry of General Police under Joseph Fouché oversaw a network of uniformed policemen and clandestine informers. The eighteen-thousand-man paramilitary police force (*gendarmerie*), which the Convention created to enforce military conscription, gave the imperial regime an important counterbalance to the police. Ever mindful of the fate of the Bourbon monarchy, the Convention, and the Directory, Napoleon's men were constantly on the lookout for subversion. The Ministry of General Police monitored theaters for seditious plays and censored newspapers, journals, and illustrations. Postal inspectors opened the mail, and spies and unpaid informers listened in on barroom and café conversations and reported directly to the emperor. These measures were not born entirely of paranoia: the emperor survived several attacks on his life by royalist and republican plotters.

Political surveillance became particularly necessary after the resumption of war in 1805 cost the imperial regime much of its popular support. In the ensuing seven years, Napoleon pushed the borders of the French Empire to their greatest extent by dispatching the various alliances of Britain, Austria, Prussia, Russia, and Sweden that formed the Third, Fourth, and Fifth Coalitions. The Royal Navy's destruction of the French fleet at Trafalgar in 1805 ensured that Britain was safe from invasion, but the French victories over the Austrians, Prussians, and Russians made Napoleon master of the continent. In 1812, the Napoleonic empire covered three-quarters of a million square miles and ruled forty-four million subjects.[18]

The French people theoretically shared in this imperial glory, but the nearly continuous warfare placed enormous burdens on their resources and manpower. State spending rose from seven hundred million francs to one billion between 1806 and 1812, and 80 percent of these funds went directly to the military.[19] Similarly, although auxiliary troops from the wider empire rounded out the French forces, Napoleon needed mass conscription to force Frenchmen to take part in his imperial enterprise. The French people first experienced full military mobilization under the emergency *levée en masse* of 1793, and the Directory enacted permanent draft laws five years later. But as with the other state institutions inherited from the republican era, Napoleon expanded and centralized the military conscription system. From 1799 to 1813, his recruiters demanded roughly 2.8 million men, which amounted to approximately two-fifths of all eligible males or 7 percent of the population of preimperial France.[20]

Common Frenchmen may have reveled vicariously in France's new imperial glory, but only fifty-two thousand of them volunteered for Napoleon's armies before 1812. To meet the emperor's insatiable demand for soldiers, subprefects drew up comprehensive manpower lists for every locality. For a time, the wealthy could hire poorer men to take their place, but in the final years of the war the authorities conscripted rich and poor alike. In 1809, Napoleon needed a rushed levy of 174,000 men to repel an Austrian invasion during the War of the Fifth Coalition. As he grew more desperate, military recruiters turned French orphanages upside down in their dragnet for boys over the age of twelve. Many conscripts did not go willingly, and approximately 10 percent of all men called dodged the draft. In some areas the evasion rate was as high as 40 percent. In response, the *gendarmerie* tracked down resisters in mass manhunts, and the provincial authorities punished the parents of missing men with fines and billeted *gendarmes* in their homes. By 1811, the French authorities had swept up more than one hundred thousand fleeing conscripts.[21]

Thus, even more than taxation, conscription brought unprecedented levels of state intrusion into the daily lives of common people. Napoleonic officials imposed special taxes on localities that missed their quotas, and the brigades of *gendarmes* that hunted draft evaders were widely despised for their lack of respect for individual rights and privacy. It is not surprising that popular hostility toward conscription sparked another outbreak of resistance in the regions of western and southern France that had rejected revolutionary centralization in the 1790s. In the Vendée, columns of troops burned defiant villages, and special tribunes sentenced more than four hundred resisters to death.

These brutal tactics exposed the harsh realities and limits of Napoleonic rule. Faced with the distraction of a multifront war and the need to maintain the appearance of control, Napoleon quietly and pragmatically allowed communities in the Vendée to default on their tax and conscription obligations in the later years of his reign. He actually had greater authority in the settled areas of the inner empire than he did in some parts of France itself. The ability of people living in the Vendée and other relatively remote regions to resist his attempt to turn them into obedient French citizens demonstrated that localism was still a potent force. This rendered Napoleon's centralizing project incomplete.

Nevertheless, the people of the Vendée's nominal French citizenship spared them from the full tribute demands that Napoleon imposed on the common peoples of the wider empire. On paper, the Napoleonic regime was relatively unique in the larger history of empire because Napoleon and his officials pretended to make no distinction between the populations of old France and conquered territories, which meant that all of the peoples of the empire shared the same rights and obligations. This was in sharp contrast to Spanish and British imperial policy in Peru and Bengal, where the boundaries of subjecthood were pronounced and inherently discriminatory. In fact, however, only the most useful notable and urban middle classes were eligible for *ralliement* and imperial citizenship. Even the patriots and would-be nationalists such as Ermolao Federigo who accepted Napoleon's modernizing rhetoric eventually learned that he always kept French interests paramount.

From an administrative standpoint, the Napoleonic empire was remarkably homogenous. Although Napoleon manipulated political boundaries to create new departments and satellite states, he used essentially the same institutions and laws to govern the French metropole and his conquered territories. This was particularly true in the imperial inner core, comprising the settled and economically integrated regions of eastern France, western Germany, northern Italy, and the Low Countries. These territories contained the prosperous and tribute-rich urban centers and fertile river valleys most easily absorbed into the Napoleonic state system.

By contrast, the outer empire consisted of the mountainous and densely forested regions of metropolitan France, central Europe, and Italy, which stoutly resisted Napoleonic centralization. It took French soldiers, *gendarmes*, and policemen to force communities in these areas to acknowledge his authority, and the endemic banditry in the outer empire demonstrated the real limits of French imperial power. More significant, the resumption of warfare after 1805 led Napoleon to incorporate even more alien and inassimilable peoples in Spain, southern Italy, the Balkans, and eastern Europe into the empire. This included the unwise and ill-fated annexation of the former Austrian territories of Trieste, Croatia, and Dalmatia as the Illyrian Provinces. His hold on these regions was tenuous at best, and the expense of ruling them strained French resources during the final years of the Napoleonic empire.

In the inner empire, it usually took a period of transitional military rule to soften up the *départements réunis* and prepare them for integration into France. One of the first and most important steps was to organize a *gendarmerie* to extend French authority as deeply as possible into the countryside and the lower social orders. These forces used a heavy hand to break up the guilds, corporate feudal bodies, and local particularism that might hinder French attempts to tax and conscript. This is why Napoleon immediately imposed the Code Napoleon in every annexed territory. Aiming to deal directly with the subject population, his reforms established equality before the law but also ended collective peasant rights, abolished monastic charitable institutions, and appropriated local sources of revenue. Napoleonic officials similarly introduced the revolutionary practice of confiscating and reselling Church lands to raise revenue. Collectively, these policies were a radical shock to the society and culture of the *départements réunis*.

The weight of French imperial rule was slightly lighter in the territories that Napoleon allowed to retain a measure of autonomy as satellite republics and kingdoms. These were largely expedient artificial entities that reduced the strain of direct imperial administration in regions that were less suited, at least in the short term, for incorporation into France. During the years when Napoleon maintained the façade of the consulate he tended to call these puppet states republics, but after he assumed the imperial throne in 1805 most became kingdoms. Some territories had the unique experience of falling into all three categories. The Netherlands, for example, went from being the Batavian Republic to the Kingdom of Holland in 1806 and then was divided up and annexed as *départements réunis* four years later. In the German-speaking lands, Napoleon reconfigured the Holy Roman Empire to create the Confederation of the Rhine and the Kingdom of Westphalia. Further east, he undid the work of the Russians, Prussians, and Austrians by reconstituting Poland as the Duchy of Warsaw. In Iberia, Spain shifted from being a French ally to a puppet state after Napoleon deposed the inept Bourbon monarchy in 1808.

In terms of governance, a well-developed road network and message system allowed the emperor to keep the satellite states on a short leash. The French Ministry of Foreign Affairs handled their diplomatic relations, and Bonaparte family members became the kings of Naples, Holland, Westphalia, and eventually Spain. Napoleon kept the crown of the Kingdom of Italy for himself. Alternatively, cooperative foreign rulers retained a measure of their authority if they proved sufficiently useful. King Max Joseph of Bavaria kept his throne by enthusiastically adopting the Code Napoleon without French pressure, and Frederick Augustus of Saxony spared the French the costs of governing Poland by becoming the Duchy of Warsaw's nominal sovereign. Administratively, these satellite rulers still had to follow Napoleon's agenda. "Old Frenchmen" controlled their key ministries, and most adopted Napoleonic constitutions that abolished feudal privilege and instituted the primary elements of the French legal reforms.

In both the annexed *départements réunis* and the satellite kingdoms Napoleon sought to build a solid foundation for permanent imperial rule by fashioning a new social order through *ralliement* and *amalgame*. As in metropolitan France, he aimed to produce useful allies who derived their status and privilege from their active participation in the French imperial project. Napoleonic prefects may have aspired to rule the annexed *départements réunis* directly, but most lacked the linguistic and cultural expertise to communicate with their subjects. Recognizing that they needed local assistance to govern effectively, they courted ancien régime elites, urban notables, and professionals by offering political stability, respect for private property, and lucrative employment in the civil service, courts, and military. Napoleonic officials were also willing to work with cooperative local clergymen even though many revolutionary Frenchmen still believed that the Catholic Church promoted primitive superstition as a bastion of the ancien régime.

Napoleon actually had little use for the foreign Jacobins and republicans who had rallied to the French revolutionary cause in the 1790s. These radicals lacked sufficient influence with the general population and still entertained potentially subversive aspirations for national self-determination. When faced with reconciling their commitment to egalitarianism with their need for local allies the French watered down their reformist agenda and dismissed the radicals who embraced the ideals of the revolution in an effort to rally property owners to their cause.

The appeal of *ralliement* varied from territory to territory. In the Rhineland, the French regime won considerable support from urban notables, wealthy landowners, and former radicals by reducing banditry. Ignoring political ideology, French officials won over men of talent with jobs and social honors. It also helped that they gave wealthy elites an opportunity to buy confiscated Church property at reasonable prices. An even smaller handful of men, such as the onetime Genoese revolutionary Gian Carlo Serra, who enlisted in the Napoleonic imperial enterprise as a supporter of the Ligurian Republic in the 1790s, advanced through the civil service ranks. Serra even became the French resident in the Duchy of Warsaw in 1807. Napoleon also found it easy to win allies among populations that had suffered under the ancien régime. Poles served as loyal auxiliaries in most of his wars because they needed French protection from Prussia and Russia to realize their dream of an independent homeland. Jews, southern German Protestants, and Freemasons also gained a measure of security under the Napoleonic regime's emphasis on equality before the law.

More often, however, the inherent risks of *ralliement* outweighed its potential rewards. As in all empires, an alliance with an alien conquering power required imperial auxiliaries to cooperate in extracting wealth from their own communities. The men who rallied to the Napoleonic regime had to help the French enforce conscription, collect taxes, and uphold a series of administrative directives that interfered directly with the daily lives of common people. In doing so they earned popular disdain and risked violent retribution when the French empire began to waver. Moreover, relatively few men could match Serra's rapid rise in the imperial civil service because most French officials only trusted "old Frenchmen." This discrimination invariably alienated and disillusioned potential allies. Consequently, the preeminent notables in the conquered territories withdrew from civic life to avoid being drawn into the imperial administration on unfavorably subordinate terms.

Napoleon's problems recruiting and retaining local allies would have been quite familiar in earlier empires. The Romans, Umayyads, conquistadors, and nabobs all tried to implement their own versions of *ralliement*. Napoleon, however, broke new ground in the scope of his ambitiously systematized amalgamist agenda. While he sought to rally the most useful and prominent European social classes to his cause, in the long term his goal was to create a cohort of "new Frenchmen" to bridge the gap with his subjects. Theoretically, they would be loyal to the Napoleonic regime because they shared its goals and core values while retaining sufficient ties to their home cultures to be useful imperial intermediaries. The vast majority of conquered Europeans would remain subordinate subjects, but these assimilated elites would enjoy a measure of privilege and equality on par with that of romanized Britons under the later Roman Empire. Where it took centuries for romanization to run its course in Britain, Napoleon gambled that he could create a viable European continental empire in a single generation by reviving and updating Roman assimilationist policies.

The legacy of Bourbon absolutism and revolutionary centralization gave Napoleon the means and inspiration to attempt such an audacious feat of imperial social engineering. Banking on the malleability of youth, French administrators established special schools to draw the children of the aristocratic and notable classes into the new order. Always on the lookout out for promising recruits, they kept careful track of prominent families and maintained extensive files on their wealth, talents, loyalties, and reputations. No amount of gossip was too trivial, and police officials recorded the religion, dowries, physical appearance, and morals of unmarried young women of means. For those who passed muster, receptions, balls, salons, and tours of Paris highlighted the aesthetic rewards of imperial service, while the army and the *auditoriat* offered the prospect of status, rapid advancement, and, in the case of the military, glory. Napoleon even turned Freemasonry, which the Convention and Directory distrusted and condemned, into an amalgamist instrument. Bringing the various French rites under central state authority, Napoleon used Masonic lodges, particularly those tied to French army regiments, to co-opt the young Germans and Italians who joined the Napoleonic forces.

These amalgamist strategies achieved a small measure of success. Napoleon had roughly 150 foreign generals, and a little more than 10 percent of all prefects were "new Frenchmen."[22] *Amalgame* was most appealing to the small strata of urban and professional classes best equipped to take advantage of the stability and opportunities in the new continental empire. Young Italian, German, and Belgian notables could fit themselves into Napoleonic society because they shared the values of the French Enlightenment and revolution and had not yet committed themselves to an exclusive national identity. Napoleon claimed to be above the ancien régime's anti-Semitic prejudices, but he did not accord Jews equality before the law. Instead, French Jews had to serve a ten-year probationary term to demonstrate that they had given up their "superstitious" ways before qualifying as real Frenchmen.

Eastern Europeans were even harder to assimilate. Coming from more agrarian feudal societies, they were largely a mystery to French administrators. Napoleon therefore overreached himself in trying to impose *amalgame* on the Illyrian Provinces. When Serbs, Croats, Slovenes, and other Balkan communities refused to accept the Code Napoleon or attend French *lycées*, French officials concluded that they were too primitive and superstitious to ever become new Frenchmen.

Despite these French rationalizations, *ralliement* and *amalgame* failed because they offered no significant protection from the real burdens of imperial subjecthood. Austrian and Prussian elites and commoners alike had to pay tens of millions of francs into French coffers as penalties for their rulers' defiance of Napoleon's imperial agenda. In 1807, the *départements réunis* and satellite kingdoms surrendered a total of 359 million francs in tribute, which constituted half of France's annual national income. The weight of this unprecedented extractive regime took an equally heavy toll on both Napoleon's enemies and allies. The Kingdom of Holland had to take out a loan of forty million florins to meet its obligations to the emperor, and roughly two-thirds of the Kingdom of Naples' budget went to pay for the cost of its French garrison. Similarly, the Kingdom of Westphalia's yearly tribute obligations and mandatory military spending outstripped its annual revenues by more than six million francs.[23] The resulting fiscal insolvency ensured that the satellite kingdoms would never be even remotely autonomous.

The continental system, which embargoed British goods in the aftermath of the French navy's demise at Trafalgar, had an equally extractive dimension. Hoping to strangle Britain's emerging industrial economy, Napoleon turned the empire into a common but protected market for French industry and commerce. Under a blatant "France first" policy, discriminatory internal tariffs privileged French manufactures over those of rivals in the satellite kingdoms. As a result, Swiss, German, and Austrian producers lost access to key markets in northern Italy, Belgium, and the Rhineland that had become part of metropolitan France as annexed *départements réunis*. Even worse, the Royal Navy's retaliatory blockade closed off overseas markets, thereby swamping the continent with unsold excess goods.

This overproduction drove down prices and forced bankers to tighten credit and raise interest rates. Unemployment rose as small firms and large manufacturers alike went out of business. French merchants also openly violated the blockade when it suited them. They resold captured goods at a premium and even saved the British from a bad harvest in 1810 by selling them wheat.

While the continental system encouraged some import substitution to replace British and overseas products, it ultimately forced the rest of Europe to subsidize metropolitan France's standard of living. The development of more sophisticated financial instruments allowed Napoleon to dispense with some of the cruder extractive tactics of his imperial predecessors, but there was no mistaking the reality that his fiscal policies were simply an updated form of imperial plunder. Special agents drew up statistical assessments of the wealth of newly conquered territories, and prefects toured their departments annually to gather demographic and economic data for the purposes of conscription and tax collection.

Administrators, generals, speculators, and concessionaires also leveraged their privileged position to reap the personal benefits of empire. Just as military victories in India gave the nabobs the means to exploit Bengali rulers and *ryots* alike, the French scrambled to make their fortunes in the *départements réunis* and satellite kingdoms. They bought up the Catholic Church's nationalized lands at reduced prices and made off with its moveable treasures and works of art. Typically, the imperial administration also became a lucrative source of jobs, contracts, and patronage. Profit-seeking Frenchmen exposed the inherent corruption of empire by selling conscription exemptions, taking bribes to ignore smuggling, speculating in currency, and extorting gifts from local notables. This sort of graft was hardly unusual in early nineteenth-century Europe, but the power of empire gave venial Frenchmen the means to seek fortunes without fear of sanction or retribution from the local authorities.

Napoleon personally disapproved of this kind of corruption, but he also had no qualms about exploiting the opportunities of empire. Ignoring the protests of his German and Polish allies, he seized great swaths of Church and feudal land in the Kingdom of Westphalia and the Duchy of Warsaw to create estates for his new imperial nobility, who consisted primarily of Bonaparte family members and French generals. The common Poles and Germans who actually lived on these *donations* essentially acquired new feudal masters. These new French estates generated tens of millions of francs a year, most of which their absentee holders remitted to metropolitan France. Napoleon personally claimed a share of these spoils for his own use through a special fund known as the *domaine extraordinaire.* Although Polish and German peasants bore the heaviest burden of this exploitation, French revenue demands effectively hamstrung Napoleon's eastern puppet rulers. In addition to losing a significant portion of their annual budgets, the necessity of using authoritarian measures to generate the surplus required to meet French tribute demands cost them what little legitimacy they had with their subjects.

While this constituted a fairly conventional form of imperial extraction, the French also placed new burdens on their subjects by demanding military service as well as labor and tribute. Protonationalism justified mass conscription in metropolitan France, but Napoleon's insistence that the "modernizing" reforms of his empire placed a similar obligation on conquered populations rang hollow. Yet the Confederation of the Rhine, Switzerland, and the kingdoms of Italy and Westphalia actually supplied more conscripts than metropolitan France. To a degree this reflected the limited successes of *ralliement* and *amalgame* in convincing local notables to serve in and recruit for the French army. Napoleon's willingness to promote his officers on the basis of merit rather than birth helps to explain how more than one hundred Westphalians won the Legion d'Honneur.[24] However, the rulers of the satellite kingdoms also put their weight into conscription in the hope of gaining a greater degree of autonomy from their French overseers.

Roughly one million Italians, Germans, Belgians, Dutchmen, Poles, and other nationalities served Napoleon as conscripted soldiers. Estimates vary, but anywhere from one quarter to one half of the men in the Grande Armée that invaded Russia in 1812 were not French. French conscription policies thus constituted a new and highly oppressive form of imperial exploitation. The eighty thousand soldiers Napoleon took from the Rhineland amounted to 60 percent of all eligible men in 1813. Less than half of these troops returned home.[25]

These worsening conditions in the imperial forces eventually inspired the same kind of local resistance to conscription that broke out in the French Vendée. As in France, Napoleon's unending appetite for soldiers drove imperial officials and their allies to intervene ever more deeply into local affairs. The result was widespread draft evasion and anticonscription riots. Banditry also became more common as draft dodgers and deserters joined the outlaw gangs that had long resisted the ancien régime's attempts to extend their reach into the remote hinterlands. Resistance to conscription also often blended into local opposition to economic liberalization, land privatization, and the abolition of collective rights.

Napoleon was barely aware of these realities and treated this and every other form of dissent as unacceptable threats. The police imposed summary punishment without trial, and special criminal courts suspended regular legal codes to deal with captured rebels and bandits. The French success in improving law and order won over some notables, but these brutal tactics gave the great majority of Napoleon's rural subjects little opportunity to embrace *ralliement*. Seeing through the hypocrisy of Napoleonic propaganda, common peoples boycotted French sponsored festivals and ignored orders to celebrate the emperor's military victories. Others wore ribbons in the colors of deposed ancien régime rulers or refused to attend imperial Church services.

Napoleon's secular agenda and attempts to impose state control on the clergy were particularly divisive, and the Catholic Church emerged as one of his most entrenched and determined opponents after his accord with the Pope collapsed. The failure of the concordat was costly. The clergy were far more influential at the local level than their secular imperial counterparts and often directed both passive and active resistance to French rule. Some historically minded churchmen even compared the French Empire to the apocalyptical threat of the "heathen" Umayyad caliphate's invasion of Christian Europe. Rejecting Napoleon's secular legal code, lay Catholics held priestless masses and sheltered monks and nuns displaced by his closure of the monasteries.

Most popular resistance to Napoleonic rule was local and uncoordinated, but it had the capacity to grow into widespread rebellion in regions where geography and banditry limited French authority. Most of the German-speaking lands remained relatively stable, but large-scale revolts were common in the waning years of the empire in the Tyrolean Alps, southern Italy, the Illyrian Provinces, and Iberia. The most serious of these incidents took place in 1808 after

Napoleon invaded Spain. Although the Spanish Bourbons were technically French allies, they balked at enforcing the continental system. Napoleon therefore used a dynastic squabble between Charles IV and his son Ferdinand VII as an opportunity to depose them both and shift his brother Joseph from the puppet Kingdom of Naples to the Spanish throne. The consequences of this move reverberated all the way to the Andes, where the collapse of royal authority brought nearly four centuries of Spanish rule in Peru to an end.

In Spain, abuses by the hundred-thousand-man imperial invasion force and Napoleon's threat to the autonomy and privileges of local Iberian communities provoked a massive popular backlash. From the French perspective, it appeared that all of Spain had risen against them. Guerrilla bands dismembered or crucified captured imperial soldiers and murdered helpless French hospital patients. The rebel Spanish government at Cádiz and the local clergy sanctioned the execution of captured troops, and common villagers poisoned unsuspecting Frenchmen or pushed them down wells. The Napoleonic forces fought back by matching the guerrillas atrocity for atrocity, but they could neither subdue the Spanish countryside nor dislodge a British expeditionary force from Iberia. The situation grew so bad that many French units, which often consisted of Poles or conscripted Italians and Germans, lost the will to fight. As a result, the Peninsular War tied down some two hundred thousand imperial troops at a time when Napoleon desperately needed them in Russia.

Not surprisingly, many Spanish historians depict this widespread resistance to French empire building in nationalist terms. In reality, Spanish nationalism was not yet a coherent ideology, and the rebellion was not a popular mass uprising. In many cases, the guerrillas were little more than bandits who preyed on the rural population as much as they did on the French. More significant, Spanish peasants had little concept of a larger Spanish nation in this period, and few of them were willing to sacrifice themselves for the Bourbons. As in the rest of Napoleonic Europe, they fought the French because they opposed Napoleon's more extractive and intrusive form of subjecthood.

Most Italians felt the same way. At first glance, it seems remarkable that the heirs of the Roman Empire and the architects of the Renaissance would ever experience the harsh realities of imperial subjecthood. One of the great strengths of the ancient Roman Republic was the sense of unity that enabled local communities throughout the Italian peninsula to think of themselves as Roman and thus share the benefits of Roman citizenship. The collapse of the western empire in the seventh century and ensuing incursions by a steady parade of invaders including Germanic bands, Byzantines, Muslim Arabs, Normans, medieval Germans, and early modern Spaniards and Austrians fractured the peninsula politically. The great Renaissance city-states of northern Italy were formidable military powers and centers of learning and culture, but competition and mutual distrust kept them from turning this shared culture into larger political units.

These divisions left Italy vulnerable in the fifteenth and sixteenth centuries as the Italians became pawns in the wider struggles between the French, Spanish, and Austrians. Most of the main Italian states and regional powers became clients or vassals of various foreign rulers, with only Venice and Genoa retaining a measure of autonomy. Economic stagnation, widespread rural poverty, and the decline of the great Italian universities accelerated these trends. Europeans still respected Italians for their humanism, decorative arts, and opera, but the preeminence that Renaissance Italy had enjoyed throughout the continent was largely over.

The Spanish Habsburgs exploited this weakness in giving the Italians a strong lesson in imperial subjecthood. Building on his grandfather Ferdinand's claims to the kingdoms of Sicily and Naples, Charles V drove out the French and assumed control of most of the peninsula. Spanish rule was far from popular. Common Italians resented paying taxes to fund the Habsburg wars, and intellectuals looked down on the Spaniards as barbarians on par with the Turks.

The situation did not improve in the early eighteenth century when the Austrian Habsburgs became the dominant force on the peninsula after the War of the Spanish Succession. The change in masters meant little, and in 1725 a Piedmont diplomat lamented the Italians' continued imperial exploitation at the hands of the foreigners. "The provinces of Italy are the Indies of the Court of Vienna [Habsburgs]. For more than twenty-five years a good part of the silver of Italy has gone there."[26] Pursuing an agenda of absolutist reform, Empress Maria Theresa and her son Joseph II sought to improve revenue collection and extraction by asserting their sovereignty over feudal nobles and checking the power of the Church. Most of the remaining independent Italian ancien régime rulers followed suite.

In doing so they introduced many of the centralizing measures that Napoleon would continue and expand a century later.

The Austrian attempts to create more efficient forms of administration did not arrest Italy's economic decline. In spite of the cultural and commercial influence of the Renaissance city-states, Italian society remained predominantly rural and agrarian on the eve of the first Napoleonic conquest. Urban areas were the centers of absolutist reform and were the economic engine of the peninsula. They exercised only marginal influence on the mountainous hinterlands that ran down the spine of the peninsula through patronage and control of the judiciary. Most rural communities, particularly those in remote and rugged regions, remained largely autonomous. In these areas the clergy and important local families exercised the greatest authority.

In the fertile lowlands, the Church and great noble families dominated agricultural production through large estates worked primarily by sharecroppers. In the eighteenth century, urban elites sought security in rural holdings as the Italian manufacturing and commercial sectors contracted. Wealthy aristocrats and influential rural families enclosed common lands, squeezed greater returns from their tenants, and evicted peasant farmers. Stagnant wages, unemployment, and escalating food prices made life worse for the agrarian classes, and the result was a substantial increase in poverty, vagabondage, and outright banditry.

These sharp class and regional divisions prevented Italians from emulating the French. Overall, they shared a pride in their Roman heritage and Renaissance achievements, but they had no sense of how to create a unified nation-state. Their *patria* (fatherland) usually was their city or region of birth, and only a small handful of intellectuals aspired to create a *nazione* (nation). Men such as the playwright Vittorio Alfieri, the choreographer Gasparo Angiolini, and the philosopher Count Francesco Algarotti were immensely proud of Italy's vast cultural achievements and lamented that centuries of alien French, Spanish, and Austrian rule had left its people backward and divided.[27] In the late eighteenth century, the poet and novelist Ugo Foscolo had his character Jacopo Ortis lay out a plan for producing "Italians":

> There can be a country without inhabitants; but there can never be a
> people without a country.... Let's transform the masses, if not all at

least many of them, into well-to-do citizens who own land. But be careful! This must all be accomplished without bloodshed, without religious reforms that are sacrilegious, without factions, without pro-scriptions and exiles, without the aid and blood and plundering of foreign troops, without the division of lands with agrarian laws and the looting of a family's property.[28]

Yet neither Foscolo nor any of the other nation-minded thinkers had a specific blueprint for getting the common peoples of the pen-insula to recognize that they were Italians. For the *popolani* (lower classes), *campanilismo* (village patriotism) was far more potent than nebulous Italian nationalism. As was the case in most of continen-tal Europe, the identities of the vast majority of the peoples of Italy remained decidedly local.

This was the situation when the French revolutionary armies invaded Italy in 1796. At that time, the peninsula's ten major politi-cal units consisted of the Papal States, the kingdoms of Naples and Piedmont-Sardinia, the republics of Venice, Genoa, and Lucca, and the duchies of Modena, Parma, Milan, and Tuscany. Children or grandchildren of Empress Maria Theresa ruled Tuscany, Modena, Naples, Parma, and Milan, which, to varying degrees, placed them within the Austrian sphere of influence. Many of these rulers attempted to adopt the Habsburgs' centralizing absolutist agenda to break down entrenched feudal institutions, but only Piedmont, Milan, and Tuscany achieved any degree of success. Moreover, none of these largely foreign rulers had any intention of trying to unify the peninsula or granting their Italian subjects greater political rights.

Frustrated reform-minded Italians therefore saw an opportunity in the demise of the ancien régime in France. Viewing the revolutions in France and America as models for change, intellectuals, protona-tionalists ("patriots"), Freemasons, and university students followed the events in Paris closely. Each faction had its own distinct agenda, and in most cases all these groups had in common was a commitment to challenge the status quo in Italy. The most radical of them took the revolutionary regime in France as inspiration and founded Jacobin clubs. Even though these Italian Jacobins (Giacobini) and patriots were far less anticlerical and extreme than their French counterparts, they had relatively little popular support. Still, even the hint of subversion alarmed the foreign rulers of Italy. Most governments therefore tried to limit the revolutionary contagion by censoring newspapers and banning imports of subversive literature.

Despite these efforts, radical jargon still found its way into the language of local resistance as peasants shouted revolutionary slogans and threatened to "act like the French" during riots in Piedmont, Bologna, and Naples. Few had any real knowledge of Jacobinism, but they understood that it scared ancien régime rulers. Even more alarming to those in authority, the Giacobini drew some support from minor nobles, young middle-class professionals, junior army officers, and lower clergymen who were frustrated by the slow pace of reform. In time, the various Italian kings and dukes cracked down on the radicals and allied more closely with Austria when evidence emerged that the Convention was actively trying to instigate revolutions in Italy.

The Italian governments' aggressive tactics and retreat from enlightened reform led many Giacobini to look more directly to the French revolutionary regime for relief. In 1793, the Convention sent agents to Italy to organize them to assist a French invasion, but it eventually decided the Italian radicals were too divided and tradition-bound to be of much use. It fell to the Directory to launch the conquest of Italy two years later. Some of the directors backed the operation to gain bargaining chips in their peace negotiations with the Austrians, but others saw an opportunity to restructure the northern Italian states as model sister republics. None of them foresaw the consequences of choosing Napoleon to lead the expedition.

The Corsican general's rapid conquest of northern Italy far exceeded the Directory's and the Italian radicals' most ambitious expectations. From the Italian perspective, only a few patriots, such as the Tuscan nobleman Filippo Buonarroti, were farsighted enough to recognize the risks of allying with an imperial conqueror. Buonarroti tried to organize a pan-Italian revolt to preempt the French invasion, but the Italian authorities uncovered the plot and arrested him. Most of the Giacobini and patriots, however, were reassured that the French forces included exiled Italian republicans and were won over by Napoleon's rhetoric of revolutionary fraternalism and Italian nationalism. They therefore welcomed the French in the hope that they would bring reform and perhaps even unification.

The realities of the Directory's three years of rule in Italy, from 1796 through 1799 (the *triennio*), ultimately proved Buonarroti right. The French quickly demonstrated that they were empire builders, not liberators. Napoleon's first priorities in consolidating his victories over the Austrians and their local allies were stability and plunder. He worked with the Giacobini and patriots when it suited him, but he was equally willing to forge alliances with their more moderate and conservative countrymen. In fact, the Directory actually ordered Napoleon not to encourage the radicals because they expected to return northern Italy to the Austrians as part of a negotiated peace.

Consequently, the would-be nationalists in Piedmont who had cheered the French invasion forces were frustrated when Napoleon signed an armistice with their king. Equally troubling, the French-sponsored sister republics that replaced the ancien régime states proved to be little more than imperial puppets. The Giacobini and allied Italian moderates were initially well represented in the new governments, but they steadily lost influence as the French asserted more direct control. Moreover, Napoleon redrew and juggled their borders to suit his needs.

In northern Italy, the French turned Genoa into the Ligurian Republic and engineered the Cisalpine Republic by merging the Duchy of Milan, the Lombard Republic, the Cispadane Republic (consisting of Bologna, Ferrara, Modena, and Reggio), and parts of the Papal States. Napoleon appointed himself president, nominated the representatives to its assemblies, and had veto power over legislation. As president, he signed an unequal commercial treaty with France and forced the republic to pay for the twenty-five-thousand-man French military garrison on its soil.

The southern Italian puppet states were even more haphazard and tenuous. Napoleon left Italy to pursue grander ambitions in late 1797, but his deputies occupied what was left of the Papal States to suppress the highly conservative Pope Pius VI and radical democratic clubs in Rome. They proclaimed a Roman Republic in 1798, which in turn drew King Ferdinand of Naples into the conflict. Backed by Britain and seeking to restore the Pope, Ferdinand provoked a French counteroffensive that forced him to seek refugee on Sicily under the protection of the Royal Navy. The power vacuum allowed the professional classes in Naples to create the Parthenopean Republic.

Awakening to the realities of subjecthood, some Italian republicans called for the French to leave as early as 1797, but even then it was too late. Demonstrating that Napoleon's grand pronouncements about liberating Italy from the ancien régime were simple propaganda,

Frenchmen of every station quickly turned their attention to extraction. The Directory saddled the Italian sister republics with millions of francs in indemnities in addition to requisitioning an extensive inventory of military matériel. In Naples, the republican regime's marginal popular support evaporated when the French indemnity of two and a half million ducats and the Directory's insistence that it cover the cost of a French garrison forced the government to levy a range of invasive new taxes. The Directory also ordered Napoleon to seize great works of art and cultural treasures as compensation for the sacrifices of the French populace in Italy. This high-class plunder included paintings from Milanese churches, papal treasures, four bronze horses from the façade of the Basilica di San Marco in Venice, and thirteen volumes of Leonardo's manuscripts. At the opposite end of the spectrum, French troopers looted with impunity. Resistance simply invited violent retribution. Napoleon's men punished Pavia for defying French demands by sacking the city, shooting the members of the town council, and burning neighboring villages.

French imperial meddling was so unpopular that moderate reformers and Giacobini radicals paid a heavy price for cooperating with Napoleon when the *triennio* came to an abrupt and unexpected end. In 1799, the French suddenly lost their grip on Italy after Napoleon became bogged down in Egypt and the Austrian and Russian armies of the Second Coalition invaded from the north. The outbreaks of popular resistance that had cropped up sporadically during the triennio blossomed into full-scale rebellions. In what became known as the "Black Year," ancien régime rulers allied with the Catholic Church and peasant communities angered by French meddling attacked the Giacobini and aspiring nationalists throughout the peninsula. Popular distaste for the French and their radical clients was so strong that many commoners actually greeted the Austrian armies as liberators.

The Church was also a popular rallying point. Stories of church bells ringing by themselves and miraculous cures at religious shrines reflected a resurgence of popular faith in response to the radicals' anticlerical agenda. Putting aside their issues with the Pope, northern Italians shouted "Viva Maria" as they rose in revolt. In Lombardy, peasants rallied to a leader who claimed he had been called by Christ to punish the French. In the south, a "most Christian armada of the Holy Faith" of roughly one hundred thousand peasants and bandits under Cardinal Fabrizio Ruffo marched on Naples singing, "The French arrived, they taxed us; *liberté…égalité*, you rob me, I rob thee!"[29] Ruffo's main goal was to restore papal authority, but in raising the Armata della Santa Fede (Holy Faith army) he inflamed long-standing local tensions resulting from the ancien régime's centralizing agenda. This civil strife simmered just beneath the surface of what at face value appeared to be a counterrevolutionary popular rejection of the Parthenopean Republic and its French backers. The Sanfedists slaughtered thousands when they captured Naples, but this violence was as much due to widespread opposition to absolutist reform as it was to anti-French sentiment.

The Giacobini allied with the French conquerors in the hope that they could turn the Directory's imperial project to their own ends. The bloodshed of the Black Year demonstrated that they overreached dangerously in trying to harness the power of revolutionary absolutism. The Sanfedists executed the republicans in Naples, and northern mobs attacked radical reformers, Jews, and any other constituency that appeared to have prospered under French rule. Ever mindful of the threat of further revolution, the Austrians sent hundreds of Giacobini in the Cisalpine Republic to Balkan prisons.

Cardinal Ruffo and more sober aristocrats soon worried that this counterrevolutionary crusade might spin out of their control. It was not too far-fetched to imagine that the peasants and urban mobs might turn on the bastions of privilege and property once they finished with the Giacobini. Consequently, some Italian elites were receptive to Napoleon's offer of *ralliement* when the French retook control of Italy in 1800 after his victory over the Austrians at the Battle of Marengo. The ensuing Peace of Lunéville one year later recreated the Cisalpine and Ligurian republics that the Austrians and their ancien régime allies had so carefully dismantled.

This did not mean, however, that the Giacobini regained their influence. Much in the way that British empire builders dismissed western-educated Indians as useless after the violence of 1857, Napoleon gave up on the radicals because they proved poor imperial proxies during the Black Year. Instead he courted Italian moderates and pragmatic ancien régime notables. In turn, many disillusioned Giacobini and patriots joined the multitude of vaguely nationalist secret societies that sprang up throughout Italy at the turn of the nineteenth century. These disorganized and fractious cabals never constituted a serious threat, and the Giacobini either made their peace with the French or faded into obscurity.

With his hold on France secure and his victory over the Second Coalition complete, Napoleon had the means to reorder Italy to suite his grand imperial designs. In the ensuing years, he annexed Piedmont, Tuscany, Umbria, Parma, Rome, and the Ligurian Republic as fourteen *départements réunis*. The restored Cisalpine Republic became the Italian Republic (later the Kingdom of Italy) with the addition of the unannexed parts of the Papal States and territory in northern Italy taken from the Austrians. Napoleon did not get around to tinkering with the Kingdom of Naples until 1805, when he deposed the restored Bourbon regime. By the end of the decade, virtually every Italian experienced Napoleonic rule as a new Frenchman in the *départements réunis* or a subject of the puppet kingdoms of Italy and Naples.

In the first case, annexation should have spared Italians from the full weight of imperial extraction because they technically became French. Not since the days of romanization had an empire been so committed to assimilating subject communities, but as in Roman times, the realities of imperial subjecthood remained harsh and fundamentally oppressive. In Piedmont, French became the required language of education and business, while the Grand Armée absorbed its eight-thousand-man army. As in metropolitan France, prefects and subprefects administered each new department in accordance with Napoleon's centralizing program. Similarly, *gendarmerie* brigades imposed and enforced the Code Napoleon. The legitimizing ideology of the Napoleonic empire held that this expanded bureaucracy was open to assimilated men of talent, but in the Italian *départements réunis* the prefects, subprefects, gendarmes, judges, and policemen were overwhelmingly French.

Assimilated Piedmontese were the only new Frenchmen to play a significant role in the imperial bureaucracy. Although the French general who oversaw Piedmont's annexation initially warned that "generally [the people] heartily detest us," it was relatively easy to absorb the kingdom because the Piedmontese shared a similar culture with their French conquerers.[30] As a result, some ambitious young men embraced the opportunities of Napoleonic rule after an initial period of resistance. They were the only Italians to assume senior positions in the administration, police, and courts in noteworthy numbers. Yet French imperial officials never really accepted the Piedmontese as equals and held them to be slow, clannish, and incapable of grasping the complexities of the Code Napoleon.

In Rome, the French hoped to win over the notable and propertied classes after the city's annexation in 1809 through efficient rule and improved law and order. Cosmopolitan Romans, however, resented being treated as imperial subjects and disliked the Piedmontese who monopolized senior positions in the courts and administration. The Pope's call for mass nonviolent resistance to French rule after his exile also made it difficult to recruit suitable local men to staff the lower levels of the imperial administrative machinery.

French officials soon grew frustrated by their inability to exercise power at the local level. Not surprisingly, the Code Napoleon was simply too alien to impose on a rural population that had long practice in resisting centralized absolutist reform. However, the Napoleonic authorities blamed the Italians for their failure to recognize the benefits of French rule and civilization. If the assimilated Piedmontese were not worthy of full imperial citizenship in French eyes, then it was hardly surprising that they disdained the mass of Italian new Frenchmen as backward, if not blatantly barbarous.

In the rest of the peninsula, the theoretically autonomous status of the kingdoms of Italy and Naples offered no greater protection from the worst aspects of Napoleonic imperial rule than the paper citizenship the French imposed on the *départements réunis*. Napoleon himself resumed the presidency of the Italian Republic after both his brother Joseph and his Milanese ally Francesco Melzi turned it down on the grounds that the reconfigured government was too weak. In accepting the vice presidency, Melzi hoped to lay the groundwork for an elite-ruled unified Italian state, but he was never able to raise the Italian Republic above the status of a French puppet. Additionally, Napoleon banned all political parties and retained the power to appoint ministers and conduct foreign affairs. Most important, he had total control over the republic's Armée d'Italie, which was essentially part of the regular French army.

Napoleon delegated the responsibilities of day-to-day rule to Melzi, who oversaw an administration that followed France's prefectural bureaucratic template and religious policies. In 1803, he brushed aside his vice president's concerns about papal influence in negotiating a concordat that gave him the authority to redraw diocesan boundaries and appoint bishops in return for recognizing the primacy of the Church. The French emperor dispensed with Melzi entirely after crowning himself "king of all Italy" two years later and appointed his stepson Eugène de Beauharnais as viceroy. His imposition of the Code Napoleon and introduction of a new catechism acknowledging him as "the Lord's Anointed" demonstrated that there was relatively little difference between Italian subjecthood in the new kingdom and the *départements réunis*.

This was also the case in the Kingdom of Naples, where Napoleon handed over the throne first to his brother Joseph and then his brother-in-law Marshal Joachim Murat. In 1806, Joseph continued the Bourbon regime's absolutist reforms by imposing key elements of the Napoleonic administrative model, selling off Church lands, closing monasteries, and abolishing feudal institutions. On this score he attempted to be a relatively benevolent imperial ruler, for his main goal was to secure French rule by promoting political security and economic development. In attacking feudalism in the countryside he sought to create a taxable class of prosperous small to mid-sized farmers that would have an interest in underpinning his authority. This was an elusive goal. Feudal elites still had the means to buy up former Church estates and claim most of the common and municipal land in the kingdom. Many of the ex-tenants and peasant farmers who managed to purchase farms could not keep up with their mortgage and tax payments. The very poor lost the right to glean after harvests, hunt and fish on wasteland, and collect nuts and wood from forests. Consequently, Joseph's antifeudal reforms made life worse for the majority of common Italians and heightened rural tensions by spreading landlessness and poverty.

In 1808, Murat inherited the consequences of these policies when Joseph abdicated the crown of Naples to become Napoleon's puppet king of Spain. Unlike his predecessor, who was a relatively loyal viceroy, the marshal clashed frequently with Napoleon in his efforts to transform Naples into a truly sovereign kingdom. Murat sought to build the Army of Naples into an effective power base and flouted the continental system by trying to impose tariffs on French imports to raise revenue and protect local industry.

Napoleon had no patience for this unauthorized empire building. He forced Murat to drop his tariff barriers and implement the Code Napoleon. Caring only for the kingdom's capacity to produce troops and revenue, the emperor brushed aside Murat's protests that these policies took Naples to the brink of bankruptcy, mass unemployment, and dangerously high levels of social unrest. Indeed, the kingdom's debt to France was almost three times its annual revenue intake, and the simmering rebellion in the Calabria and Abruzzi hinterlands made it virtually impossible to collect taxes after 1809. Murat's troops went unpaid for months at a time, but Napoleon rebuked his viceroy when budget shortfalls forced Murat to reduce the kingdom's interest payments to France.

Given these realities, it might seem surprising that any Italian would willingly play a role in the Napoleonic imperial project. Yet the French efforts to rally useful Italians to their cause and amalgamate them into a new class of imperial intermediaries met with some success. For urban elites and aspiring bureaucrats the Napoleonic empire held out the promise of public order, patronage, and status. Property owners feared chaos more than the subjecthood that invariably fell most heavily on the lower classes. Mob attacks on moderate reformers and Giacobini during the anarchy of the Black Year made them much more inclined to put up with the indignities of French rule. They certainly had little reason to lament the demise of the foreign Bourbon and Habsburg ancien régime rulers.

With Italian nationalism still in its infancy, some elite Italians were willing to at least tacitly accept a regime that suppressed banditry, offered the chance of reasonably lucrative employment, and provided greater security for property via the Code Napoleon. The French antifeudal and anticlerical agenda also offered an opportunity to buy up Church estates and common land at bargain prices. Those who made themselves sufficiently useful could claim figurehead ministerial posts in the kingdoms of Italy and Naples and flattering ceremonial roles at Napoleon's Italian court. Businessmen appreciated Napoleon's destruction of tariff barriers within the peninsula, and French rule offered writers, artists, and scholars new opportunities for employment and patronage. Finally, the inherent corruption of empire allowed the second Cisalpine Republic's secretary of state, the mayor of Genoa, and other enterprising new Frenchmen to acquire personal fortunes.

Sometimes these inducements were enough to win over Napoleon's harshest Italian critics. At the height of his power, large crowds cheered his coronation as the king of Italy, and Foscolo's Venetians honored his defeat of the Austrians by building him a triumphal arch across the Grand Canal. The clergymen who balked at the new imperial catechism celebrating Napoleon's divine sanction sang Te Deums in celebration of his victories.

Napoleon enjoyed this adulation but understood that he needed more than the praise of a few respectable Italians to rule effectively. As in the wider empire, his long-term goal was to engineer a new class of intermediaries by incorporating the offspring of these notables into French imperial society. Operating under the assumption that their culture had made Italian men soft and unreliable, his amalgamist project focused on recruiting their sons into the military as a step toward turning them into new Frenchmen. In 1805, French officials in Parma tried to convert the College of Santa Caterina, one of the most prestigious boarding schools in Italy, into a military academy. They also organized university students in the Kingdom of Italy into battalions for military training and created an elite military unit (the *gardes d'honneur*) for aristocratic young men.

Ultimately, however, *amalgame* usually required force. The authorities in Piedmont threatened to confiscate the property of elite students who refused to attend the military academy at Saint-Cyr. In 1811, French officials subjected elites throughout the peninsula to a "golden levy" that pressed them to send their sons into the imperial military and civil services. In Umbria, the French prefect invited the heads of the twelve most prominent families of the department to a dinner party. The *gendarmes* that delivered the invitations sent a clear message that there would be serious consequences if they refused to cooperate. The French authorities in Rome jailed a renowned count for refusing to give up his son, and in the Kingdom of Italy they exiled the heads of four leading families to Paris to convince them to send their sons into the *gardes d'honneur*.

Amalgame also imposed French values and culture on an uncomfortable populace. Napoleonic officials in Rome introduced French currency and shifted clocks to Paris time. Ignoring Napoleon's various concordats with the Pope, they abolished the Inquisition and restrictions on the city's Jewish ghetto. Italian dialects remained the language of administration throughout most of the peninsula, but the French seeded it with new words reflecting their imperial needs. These included *funzionario* (civil servant), *controllo* (control), and *processo verbale* (court record).[31] As in all empires, these policies reflected Napoleon's arrogant assumption that military power could remake subject societies to suit his purposes. Moreover, he naively believed that assimilation and cooperation with the French imperial enterprise would not unduly compromise the amalgamated notables' influence over common Italians.

In reality, both *ralliement* and *amalgame* failed in Italy because there was no disguising the exploitation of imperial subjecthood. Some Italians may have forgiven Napoleon for his cynical and self-serving manipulation of Italian nationalism, but the majority of the population bitterly resented the extractive demands that made their lives measurably worse. French imperial economic policy treated Italy as a mercantilist colony. French officials tore down protective tariff barriers throughout the peninsula and dismantled the silk industries in Lombardy and Piedmont to clear the way for metropolitan French weavers. Their ultimate goal was to accelerate the ongoing decline of Italian industry that began during the ancien régime era and free up raw materials and foodstuffs for export to France.

Typically, the greatest burden of these exploitive policies fell on common Italians. Napoleon's refusal to let the kingdoms of Italy and Naples use tariffs to generate revenue meant that it took intrusive new taxes to meet tribute expectations. These included a poll tax and duties on salt, food, and milling grain. This unwelcome intervention came at a time when French demands for raw materials, wartime shortages, and the continental system made food scarce and drove up prices. Inflation, food exports to the wider empire, land shortages due to the sale of common land, and the closure of Church-run charitable organizations led to widespread poverty and the threat of famine. It is therefore hardly surprising that more and more Italians turned to crime and banditry to cope with the burden of Napoleonic rule.

Subject peoples had suffered under this kind of imperial exploitation since Roman times. Napoleon's empire, however, imposed a new kind of extraction in the form of his ravenous demand for masses of conscripted soldiers. To be sure, the Romans and their successors often turned their subjects into unwilling auxiliaries, but this coerced military service never approached the scale of conscription that Napoleon levied on the *départements réunis* and satellite kingdoms. He won over Ermolao Federigo and other patriots by manipulating their nationalist aspirations, but relatively few common Italians shared these sentiments. Thus, while cooperative Italian officers commanded Napoleon's Italian divisions, the vast majority of their rank-and-file soldiers were resentful conscripts. The French justified this wholesale impressment not on the grounds that Italians were imperial citizens but by claiming that French military service civilized barbarous mountain peasants and degenerate townsmen.

In the Kingdom of Italy, Melzi accepted this logic and supported the creation of the Armée d'Italie in the hope that it would pave the way for independence and unification. Rural elites often used conscription to get rid of their most troublesome tenants and sometimes even ill-disciplined sons. Notables in the *départements réunis* played a similar role in sweeping the most marginal and vulnerable members of society into the army. Altogether, these respectable Italians helped the French round up roughly two hundred thousand troops during the Napoleonic era, of whom only about 10 to 15 percent were volunteers. When Joseph Bonaparte and Murat tried to limit conscription in the Kingdom of Naples, Napoleon forced them to meet his manpower demands. Common people went to great lengths to avoid the dragnet. Italian troops earned less than metropolitan French soldiers, and they suffered enormous casualties during the brutal fighting in Spain and Russia. Estimates vary, but it appears that only thirteen thousand of the eighty-five thousand men from the Kingdom of Italy who fought in Russia returned home.[32]

Mass resistance to conscription in northern Italy began as early as 1802 when mobs turned on the Italian bureaucrats who conducted the draft. Similarly, angry Roman women attacked recruiting parties after the city's annexation. These incidents were a prelude to the most serious mass opposition to Napoleon's manpower demands. In 1809, armed bands in the Kingdom of Italy burned draft lists as part of a larger uprising against French rule. But challenging the empire directly was risky, and many Italians opted to resist conscription through more subtle means. Their tactics included faking medical disabilities, falsifying birth certificates, or marrying elderly women to claim a marriage exemption. Some went so far as to cut off their trigger fingers or pull the canine teeth needed to hold cartridges. Flight to neighboring territories was a less drastic recourse, and officials in the Kingdom of Italy estimated that more than twenty thousand eligible men dodged conscription in this manner. Those who did not escape the French roundup frequently took the first opportunity to desert. Approximately thirty thousand to forty thousand conscripted soldiers chose this option in the Italian kingdom between 1803 and 1812, and desertion rates climbed even higher in later years as news of the terrible losses in Russia and Spain reached Italy.[33]

The French authorities dealt with these overt and subtle forms of resistance aggressively. Not only did their armies need continual reinforcement after 1805, but as imperial rulers, they could not allow any expression of defiance to go unpunished. In 1808, the Kingdom of Italy created special labor camps to punish captured draft dodgers and fined their families. Villages with too many missing sons risked being burned to the ground by the *gendarmerie*. Prefects also exercised greater supervision over local draft councils, tightened medical exemptions, restricted movement through special internal passports, and even banned the marriage of young men to women over sixty.

Napoleonic officials considered desertion an even more serious offense. Escaping soldiers spread demoralizing news of French defeats and drained military resources by making off with their uniforms and weapons. Moreover, many joined the bandit gangs that grew in size and means in response to the inherent hardships of French rule. In 1809, the Kingdom of Italy assigned small military detachments to each of its departments to deal with armed ex-soldiers, and Italian military courts punished convicted deserters with sentences ranging from three years at hard labor to the death penalty. French officials considered these punishments too lax and often took matters into their own hands. In the sections of the Papal States added to the Kingdom of Italy they executed some resisters summarily, and Eugène personally condemned a few sons of Rome's leading families to death for deserting from the *gardes d'honneur*.

Although Napoleon counted the rule of law as one of the most substantial benefits of his empire, his men in Italy frequently resorted to extrajudicial measures to maintain control because local Italian courts and policemen would not take action against members of their own communities. In the more settled areas, the political or *haute* (high) police had the authority to dispense with the formal criminal courts in dealing with banditry and subversion, but in time they became embroiled in relatively petty controversies involving violations of public morality. This was a natural consequence of the amalgamist project, and French officials had to contend with local controversies involving adultery, wayward priests, and aristocratic intrigue. Italians rather than imperial officials brought many of these charges, and the French came to detest the spies and informers they needed to control urban and settled Italy. Imperial officials concluded that the Italians were too petty and depraved to qualify for full imperial citizenship.

These sentiments ran entirely contrary to their emperor's goal of rallying Italian notables, but in practice *ralliement* never stood a chance of success. Like all imperial conquerors, the French fell victim to bigotry in mistaking military power for cultural superiority. Concluding that luxury and superstition had made Italian men vain, cowardly, and effeminate, French officials decided that *amalgame* was unrealistic and ill-advised. Although they often depicted themselves as the heirs of classical Rome, they were particularly dismissive of contemporary Roman society. One senior administrator even refused to let his wife join him on his posting to Rome because he worried that the decadent Romans would corrupt an impressionable young woman.

This disdain for Italian culture did not prevent Frenchmen of all stations from using imperial privilege to take sexual advantage of Italian women. Prefects and prosecutors often kept local mistresses, and a French military veteran recalling his service in Germany could have just as easily been speaking about the Italians. "The hate which the Germans have for us should not be too surprising. They cannot pardon us for having for twenty years caressed their wives and daughters before their very faces."[34] This kind of sexual predation is an inherent part of the larger exploitive and dehumanizing realities of empire and must be considered alongside French demands for manpower and revenue in explaining the failure of *ralliement*.

Italian notables thus had good reasons for questioning the sincerity of Napoleon's invitation to enlist as junior partners and new Frenchmen in his imperial enterprise. Some of the emperor's most important Italian allies hedged their bets by treating with his enemies. Melzi was careful to maintain his contacts in Austria, and influential Neapolitans sent family members to both Paris and the exiled Bourbon court in Sicily. Most of these fence-sitters made up their minds to reject *ralliement* when the military tide turned against Napoleon and French rule became more precarious. Napoleon's arrest of the Pope struck a further blow to *ralliement*. Loyal Romans wore papal cockades as part of a passive resistance campaign that shut down the local administration and courts through a mass retreat from civic life.

While Italians were cool to Napoleon's call to rally, they were even more suspicious of his amalgamist project. The Piedmontese nobleman Massimo d'Azegilo was enraged when the French forced him to send his son to the military academy at Saint-Cyr because he felt it violated his paternal right to decide how his children should be educated. Similarly, the elite families of Parma withdrew their children from the College of Santa Caterina after Napoleonic officials tried to turn it into a military academy, and instead hired exiled Roman clergymen as tutors. Parents in Genoa and Tuscany shunned the new French-style schools. Only ex-Giacobini and the urban middle classes that found fruitful employment in imperial service gave the French full access to their children.

Ralliement and *amalgame* were never open to the common Italians who bore the real weight of French rule. Rural communities that had striven to thwart the centralizing reforms of ancien régime princes had no reason to accept the far more burdensome demands of a foreign imperial power. Admittedly, Napoleon's efforts to impose his will on the Italian countryside were an extension of his efforts to force the resistive populations of western and southern France to respect his authority. The difference, however, was that Napoleon considered the peoples of the Vendée and the Midi to be Frenchmen whether they liked it or not. He was far more ruthless with the peoples of the wider empire who dared to stand in the way of his extractive ambitions.

The necessity of intruding into rural communities to meet their emperor's treasure and manpower requirements forced Napoleonic officials to develop even more aggressive methods of disciplining their subjects. Special local guard formations and the National Guard in the Kingdom of Italy and the Civic Guard in Naples augmented French authority throughout the peninsula. French rule was relatively effective in Piedmont, but it grew weaker the further south one traveled. It waned considerably in the rural hinterlands where local institutions of authority remained largely immune to *ralliement*, much less *amalgame*. Although they disdained feudal institutions, necessity forced the French to depend on the rural clergy to execute imperial policy at the village level. They also needed vigilante groups to control banditry and maintain rural order. These irregular units, known popularly as *sbirri* (cops), were a holdover from the ancien régime era, and the imperial regime's efforts to control them through French officers were barely successful. More often than not, the *sbirri* bands were more inclined to prey on local communities instead of enforcing French rule.

As in much of early nineteenth-century Europe, rural opposition to the imposition of central authority, imperial or otherwise, often took the form of banditry. Peasants, herdsmen, sharecroppers, day laborers, draft dodgers, and military deserters, whose resistance the French criminalized as "brigandage," sought primarily to protect feudal-era rights and local privileges. Some of the lawless groups were indeed made up of criminals, but classifying resisting rural peoples as brigands, a particularly barbaric type of bandit, allowed Napoleonic officials to employ harsh extralegal measures against them. Military tribunals routinely handed down death sentences to brigands, and *gendarmerie* units punished resisters summarily without bothering to refer them to the courts at all. Imperial officials tried to improve security by banning the production and sale of daggers, but they could not prevent deserters from arming rural communities throughout the peninsula. Although property owners and feudal elites generally supported French efforts to promote rural order, few were willing to assist the imperial regime actively in confronting the outlaws.

Persistent and endemic banditry was a fertile medium for local discontent to grow into more serious mass challenges to the Napoleonic regime. As in the Black Year, these rebellions often took on an overtly Catholic veneer, but they were more concerned with thwarting French-led centralization than with defending the Church. The first significant uprising began near Genoa in 1805 and 1806. Led by a former militia captain and an innkeeper, local communities in Piacenza struck back against taxation, conscription, the closure of monasteries, and wartime requisitioning. Although it took French *gendarmes* and Italian reservists only a few weeks to restore order, the revolt unnerved the imperial authorities. Special military commissions in Parma and Piacenza sent captured rebels to the gallows or enslavement in Mediterranean galleys. The imperial authorities also turned the *sbirri* loose on defiant rural communities under the guise of imposing collective punishment. These draconian measures were out of proportion to the seriousness of the unrest, but Napoleonic officials rightly viewed any form of coordinated resistance as a threat to their hold on the rural majority. Lacking the manpower and resources to govern the countryside directly, they relied on intimidation and terror to extend their authority into upland Italy.

This imperial bluff largely collapsed in 1809. Encouraged by Austrian propaganda and inflamed by a new milling tax, the Kingdom of Italy's hinterlands again erupted in revolt. With the Armée d'Italie distracted by the war with Austria, the rebels killed policemen, drove off imperial officials, and burned tax and conscription records. The collapse of authority in the highlands gave bands of peasants numbering in the thousands the freedom to move on the urban areas that anchored Napoleonic rule in the region.

Further north, similar revolts broke out in the Tyrolean regions that Napoleon had added to the puppet Kingdom of Bavaria. Once again, peasant grievances centered on taxation, conscription, and the unwelcome expansion of state authority. They too attacked government offices, burned bureaucratic records, and chased off the imperial regime's local representatives. Swelled by the addition of military deserters, smugglers, and common criminals, the revolt lasted into 1810 and blocked commerce on the Po River. Austrian propaganda and subversion definitely played a role in instigating these revolts. Archduke John's attacks on Napoleonic exploitation, covert missions to the Tyrol, and short-term military victories gave the rebels hope that they might drive out the French. Some peasants even waved Austrian flags and shouted support for the Austrian emperor, but the vast majority of the rural people who took part in the 1809 uprisings were no more Habsburg partisans than they were Italian nationalists. Like the Catholic façade of the Black Year, the Austrians simply provided a useful rallying point for the defense of local autonomy.

Yet if localism drove the revolts, it was also the primary cause of their failure. The tendency of the rebels to resort to banditry cost them popular support, and their inability to unite left them fatally divided once Napoleon's troops turned back the Austrian invasion. It was then a relatively simple matter for *gendarmes*, civil guardsmen, and soldiers to hunt down the small, lightly armed groups. Thousands of peasants lost their lives, and special courts ordered the execution of more than one hundred captured "brigands." All the same, the scope of the revolt forced Napoleon's viceroy Eugène to repeal most of the new unpopular taxes.

Local resistance to Napoleonic centralization and extraction was even more pronounced and violent in the Kingdom of Naples, where French demands for tribute inflamed the already bitter opposition to absolutist reform. Beginning in 1806, rural poverty in the Calabria and Abruzzi regions, exacerbated by land privatization, increased taxation, and the closure of charitable religious institutions, led to an explosion of banditry. British forces in Sicily fanned these flames by funding bandit leaders such as the notorious Fra

Diavolo, or "Brother Devil," who had earned a reputation for brutality during the Black Year and continued to commit atrocities in the nominal service of the exiled Bourbon regime. Unlike the disorganized and lightly armed peasant rebels in the north, the guerrilla bands in Naples were a serious threat to the Napoleonic regime. They killed or wounded approximately twenty thousand imperial soldiers and made it impossible to collect taxes or conscripts in more than one-third of the kingdom.

As in Spain, the French met this overt defiance of imperial authority with equal ruthlessness and brutality. In 1806, Napoleon firmly told his brother Joseph: "Grant no pardons, execute at least six hundred rebels, for they have murdered a great many of my soldiers. Let the houses of at least thirty of the principal heads of the villages be burned and distribute their property among the troops. Disarm all the inhabitants and pillage five or six of the villages that have behaved the worst." Three years later, Murat issued similar instructions to his commanders when the rebellion showed no sign of breaking. "Remember, I want no more amnesty, and it is a war of extermination that I want waged against these miserable creatures."[35] Given these orders, the imperial forces castrated, flayed, impaled, crucified, and burned captured rebels. Unable to defeat the bandit bands directly, they tried to starve them into submission by making it a capital offense to feed them. In a particularly notorious incident, Murat's men slaughtered a group of women caught taking lunch to their men in the fields.

These sorts of atrocities were hardly a new innovation in imperial control. The Romans, Umayyads, and Spaniards used similar tactics against subject peoples who challenged their authority. But detailed accounts of their misdeeds are largely missing from the historical record. The vicious French counterinsurgency tactics in the Kingdom of Naples, coupled with the savagery that the British used to regain control over northeastern India after the mass uprising of 1857, brought the underlying brutality of imperial rule into sharper focus. Terror, intimidation, and barbarity had always been the unseen cornerstones of empire, but they were now more obvious at the dawn of the modern era. Moreover, they began to lose their effectiveness. The French imperial forces and the Neapolitan bandits essentially fought to a bloody stalemate in southern Italy. The guerrillas never overthrew the imperial regime, but Murat was equally unable to master the hinterlands.

It is tempting to attribute Napoleon's downfall in Italy to the strength of popular nationalism. But it would be anachronistic to suggest that defiant rural peoples refused to become imperial subjects because they were beginning to see themselves as Italians, Germans, or some other nationality. Most continued to identify with their local communities rather than a still-abstract notion of a larger nation, and if they resisted Napoleon, it was primarily because he continued and improved upon the ancien régime's centralizing reforms. The respectable and propertied classes in the cities and the settled countryside were more inclined to appreciate the improved security and opportunities that came with French rule. Indeed, nationalist sentiments were still weak enough at this time that many of these notables might well have followed the lead of earlier generations of elite Britons, Iberians, Andeans, and Bengalis in rallying to the new imperial order if French rule in Europe had lasted long enough.

In fact, Napoleon's European empire was remarkably short-lived in comparison to the venerable Roman, Umayyad, Spanish, and East India Company empires. It fell primarily because the main European powers would not share the continent with an expansionist power that aspired to become a new Rome. Napoleon therefore met his demise on the wider battlefields of Europe rather than in the hills of Italy or Spain. The British naval blockade goaded him into imposing the continental system on unwilling subjects and allies, which in turn made French rule increasingly unbearable. It soon became apparent to Europeans of all stations that there were no equal partners in the Napoleonic imperial enterprise. An alliance or treaty with the French brought a humiliating loss of sovereignty for princes, while overt subjecthood entailed the full weight of imperial exploitation for the wider population. Napoleon's empire was mighty but precarious, and its vulnerability gave Europeans the confidence to reject his call to *ralliement* and resist their subjecthood.

Enforcing the continental system drew France into the long-festering Peninsular War and the even more disastrous invasion of Russia. Napoleon's defeat at the hands of tsarist forces and the ravages of the Russian winter cost him the core of the Grande Armée, and only about 14 percent of the 650,000 soldiers who followed him into Russia survived the campaign in fighting condition. The incompatibility of empire and *ralliement* meant that he had to replace these losses with conscripts and tribute wrung from conquered territories.

The imperial budget ran a substantial deficit in the last years of the empire, and it took massive manpower sweeps to raise a new army to confront the combined forces of Britain, Russia, Austria, Spain, and the German powers that rolled back Napoleon's conquests in 1813.

The Confederation of the Rhine, the duchies of Berg and West-phalia, and the Italian puppet states began to collapse or defect after this Sixth Coalition won a decisive victory at the Battle of Nations in October 1813. Six months later, the French overthrew their emperor as his enemies bore down on Paris. The victorious powers sent Napoleon into exile on the Mediterranean island of Elba and reset the French borders to their 1792 frontiers. But the coalition's attempt to restore the Bourbon king Louis XVIII to the French throne provoked those who were not willing to surrender the glory of the revolution and empire. Many Frenchmen therefore rallied to Napoleon when he returned from Elba in March 1815. This popular support allowed him to regain control of France for the next one hundred days. It took a seventh and last coalition of European armies, which won the decisive victory at Waterloo, to bring down Napoleon and send him to his final exile and death on St. Helena in the south Atlantic.

The aftermath of Napoleon's demise is remarkable. It stood as one of the rare moments in the larger history of empire when it seemed possible to reverse the consequences of imperial conquest and rule. Having finally defeated the self-styled heir of ancient Rome, the victorious alliance of Britain, Austria, Prussia, and Russia set about dismantling his empire at the Congress of Vienna. This time they succeeded in forcing the French to accept the restoration of Louis XVIII. As punishment for returning to Napoleon during the One Hundred Days, the allies imposed an indemnity of seven hundred million francs and moved the French borders back to those of 1789. This meant France gave up what was left of the *départements réunis*. It also lost most of what was left of its original overseas empire, which succeeding French governments spent the following century rebuilding in Africa and Southeast Asia.

Despite these measures, the European powers could not dispense entirely with the primary innovations of the revolutionary and Napoleonic era. Absolutism was dead, and a constitution and Chamber of Deputies limited the power of the restored Bourbon monarchs. Ancien régime nobles regained some of their prestige, but much of their property was gone. They also had to accept Napoleon's new imperial aristocracy as relative equals. Surprisingly, there were no wholesale purges of Napoleonic officials, and even the widely hated minister of police, Joseph Fouché, escaped sanction. Institutionally, the Bourbons had to retain Napoleon's Bank of France, prefectural system, schools, and civil code to govern the new postimperial France.

It was equally difficult to turn back the clock in the rest of Europe. Napoleon's conquests swept away the decaying Holy Roman Empire, and in its place the Congress of Vienna created a German Confederation of thirty-nine German-speaking states ranging in size from Austria and Prussia to a handful of free cities. Although they wanted to make a clear break with the Napoleonic era, the restored rulers of these states retained many of the French emperor's more useful innovations. These included mass conscription, the *gendarmerie*, secular legal codes, and efficient local administrative systems. Conversely, the Catholic Church and most noblemen never regained their lost property. Further east, Napoleon's influence waned in the lands conquered after 1804, but the nationalistic gentry in Poland drew on his centralizing legacy in teaching, if not forcing, local communities to be Polish.

In Italy, there was no repeat of the violence of the Black Year when French authority collapsed because the invading Austrians and the respectable Italian classes shared a strong interest in preserving law and order. As a result, the elites who had rallied to the Napoleonic regime did not suffer the bloody fate of the Giacobini and patriots some fifteen years earlier. Italians, however, were at a loss as to what to do after the French retreat. Some advocated declaring an Italian kingdom to preempt the Austrians, but they could not agree on who would wear the crown. Most ordinary people were happy to see Napoleon go, but they were not ready to embrace unification or condemn Napoleon's allies and intermediaries as traitors to an imagined Italian nation. The French sponsorship and manipulation of Italian nationalism undercut its popular appeal by linking it to extraction, conscription, and intrusively centralized state authority. This helps to explain why Italians ignored Lord William Bentinck's nationalistic call to arms when he landed with a British force in Livorno in 1814: "Italians hesitate no longer; be Italians, and let Italy in arms be convinced that the great cause of the country is in your hands!"[36]

Murat similarly tried and failed to stay in power in Naples by recasting himself as a national leader. With armies of the Sixth Coalition closing in, he pledged to attack the Kingdom of Italy in return for recognition by Austria but reneged on his promise during the One Hundred Days. Expecting that Napoleon would keep the Austrians and British busy, he invoked Italian nationalism in a bid for popular support:

> Italians! The hour has come in which the great destiny of Italy must be fulfilled. Providence is summoning you at last to be an independent nation. From the Alps to the straits of Sicily one cry can be heard: 'The independence of Italy!'... Away with all foreign domination! You were once masters of the world, and you have paid for that perilous glory with twenty centuries of subjugation and slaughter. Let it be your glory now to break free from your masters.[37]

No one was fooled, and the Neapolitan Bourbons executed him after they returned to power.

Eugène de Beauharnais and the Kingdom of Italy fared only slightly better in the wake of the French collapse. Unlike Murat, the viceroy remained loyal to his stepfather, but the Austrians sent him into exile in Munich, where he married a daughter of the king of Bavaria. His finance minister Giuseppe Prina, whose role in enforcing the Napoleonic regime's tribute demands made him widely hated, did not get off as easily. Incited by vengeful nobles, an angry mob murdered him in 1814.

These internal divisions meant that Italians had little influence at the Congress of Vienna, where the delegates decided to return the Pope to Rome and the Bourbons to Naples. The various Habsburg princes got their duchies back in northern Italy, and an enlarged Kingdom of Piedmont and Sardinia acquired Genoa. Yet as in the rest of the former Napoleonic empire, these restored rulers kept its most useful centralizing tools in continuing the ongoing process of asserting state control over local communities. Similarly, the Church did not get its lands back and continued to lose influence in secular matters.

It would take another half century for the ruling dynasty in Piedmont to create the modern Italian state, and historians of Italy are divided over whether Napoleon advanced or retarded unification. At the very least, he opened politics to the middle classes, and his centralizing imperial program left Italian rulers with a greater capacity to impose their authority on the countryside. Broers is therefore probably correct in referring to the state-sponsored version of Italian nationalism that legitimized Italian unification as the "bastard child of Napoleonic cultural imperialism."[38] Indeed, the Italian experience of subjecthood under French imperial rule did not produce a unifying collective or popular sense of national identity. Napoleon's imperial project floundered in Italy because rural communities mobilized to resist him on the basis of local particularism rather than a larger nationalistic sense of Italian patriotism.

At first glance, the comparatively quick defeat and collapse of Napoleon's grand European empire seemed to suggest that the era of empire building was over. This was largely the case in western Europe, where local communities eventually and grudgingly made their peace with nationalism while defiantly rejecting the much more oppressive weight of imperial subjecthood. Rural Italians fought a rearguard action against Napoleonic centralization and direct state control, but in time they eventually became Italian "citizens." National consciousness thus spread, sometimes forcibly so, from intellectuals and romantic thinkers to the middle and lower classes. Citizenship was burdensome in many ways, but it also tempered the enhanced power of the western European nation-state to oppress them. Consequently, just as it became unacceptable in the early modern era for Europeans to be slaves, the slow emergence of nationalism in the nineteenth century meant that it gradually became equally unacceptable for them to be the subjects of a foreign imperial power. This was a halting process that slowly spread eastward, but it ultimately doomed the great multiethnic Habsburg and Ottoman empires. The Russian Empire survived into the twentieth century in the guise of the supposedly anti-imperial Soviet Union, but eventually its subjects also asserted their right to self-determination.

Thus nationalism corroded empires. Conventional imperial rule required local partners, and Spanish conquistadors and British nabobs built viable and long-lived empires in the early modern era by exploiting the divisions among Asians and Americans. As the nineteenth century progressed, the spread of nationalist sentiment in Europe made it difficult to rally local intermediaries as the strength of larger collective identities made it treasonous and dangerous to cooperate with a foreign regime. Similarly, liberal democracy and the collective rights of national citizenship made imperial extraction equally unfeasible and intolerable. Finally, the grand coalition that overthrew Napoleon demonstrated that the nations of Europe would not allow one of their number to upset the balance of power on the continent by building an empire by force of arms.

The nineteenth century therefore appeared to mark the end of empire. The once powerful early modern Spanish, Portuguese, and Dutch empires dwindled to a handful colonies scattered around the globe. Britain lost most of its original empire with the American Revolution, and the Indian revolt of 1857 marked the demise of the once powerful East India Company. At home, British liberals and free traders attacked empire as expensive, exploitive, and ultimately unnecessary at a time when Britain emerged from the Napoleonic wars as the world's dominant industrial and ocean-going power. In arguing that scattered outposts were an unnecessary drain on the metropolitan budget, they exposed how irrelevant and unproductive empire had become for nation-states.

Yet the age of formal empire was not yet over. In the final decades of the nineteenth century a new generation of imperial entrepreneurs and aspiring conquistadors tried to recapture the glory and wealth of the early modern empires. With Europe and the Americas wrapped in a protective carapace of emerging nationalism, they turned to Africa and Asia to exploit vulnerable communities who still identified themselves in local rather than collective terms. The British government underwrote the speculative conquest of what was to become Kenya because well-meaning Britons accepted the promise of the smugly confident "new imperialists" to create a liberal empire that would rule for the good of its subjects. This was a self-serving lie, but the new rulers of Africa found that the supposedly primitive population was not so different from the ordinary Italians who were so effective in thwarting Napoleon's ambitions. Like countless earlier generations of subjects who despised their imperial conquerors, the British army veteran Daniel Nguta disdained the British. The imperial enthusiasts who justified his subjugation on the grounds that he and his people were primitive and inferior soon realized that these supposedly simple "tribesmen" could bring down mighty empires.

Kenya

6

BRITISH KENYA

The Short Life of the New Imperialism

In 1905, some 373 years after Atawallpa met Pizarro on the plaza of Cajamarca, the Nandi *orkoiyot* Koitalel arap Samloei encountered another imperial entrepreneur in the highlands of Kenya. This heir of the conquistadors was a commissioned British military officer named Richard Meinertzhagen. In 1905, he was on secondment to the King's African Rifles (KAR), Britain's ragtag but grandly named East African colonial army. Unlike the Inka ruler, Koitalel was fully aware that this twentieth-century imperial soldier was a serious threat. Indeed, for the previous decade the Nandi had fought a war of attrition against the encroaching British Empire.

At first glance, it might seem odd that a supposedly "tribal" people such as the Nandi held a "modern" western power at bay for over ten years when the Inkas had succumbed to Pizarro and the conquistadors so quickly. Firmly entrenched in the cool, well-watered East African highlands, the Nandi had a conventional mixed agricultural and pastoral economy. Politically, they had no centralized institutions of authority and could be properly described as stateless. In the late nineteenth century, they divided their lands into six or seven counties (*emotinwek*) of two thousand to five thousand people under councils of elders (*kokwotinwek*) at which any married man could speak. In times of crisis special councils consisting of the most influential Nandi elders, military leaders, and ritual experts (*orkoiik*) made the key decisions.

The Nandi may have been stateless, but they were a significant military power in the highlands. In the decades before the British arrival, victories over neighboring communities allowed them to assimilate conquered populations and acquire new crops and technologies. Known originally as the Chemwal, they earned the name Mnandi from the coastal ivory traders whose caravans they raided repeatedly. This was the Swahili word for "cormorant," a bird with a reputation for rapaciousness in East Africa.

The rising Nandi fortunes were largely the work of an influential family of *orkoiik* that used their ability to divine the future to usurp the authority of the *kokwotinwek* councils. These ritual experts were actually refugees from a nearby Maasai community who took control of important agricultural and initiation rituals after finding refuge with a Nandi clan. The *orkoiyot* Kimnyole arap Turukat, who was Koitalel's father, organized the Nandi regiments into a powerful military force that drove off the Maasai and raided their remaining neighbors for cattle.

Later, the British claimed that these "witch doctors" were tyrannical autocrats, but the Nandi warriors beat Kimnyole to death in 1890 after he led them on a disastrous raid that resulted in the death of five hundred of their comrades. Nevertheless, Koitalel and his brother Kipchomber arap Koilegei retained significant influence in Nandi society and waged a fierce succession struggle to assume their father's place. Koitalel enjoyed the backing of an aggressive younger faction of Nandi warriors who wanted to continue the cattle raids, which gave him the means to drive his brother into exile. With his power secure, he directed the Nandi recovery from the epidemics, cattle blight, drought, locusts, and famine that disastrously weakened the East African highland communities at the turn of the twentieth century. The Nandi were therefore much better prepared than their neighbors to face the British imperial menace.

Richard Meinertzhagen personified that threat. When he met Koitalel under the equivalent of a flag of truce he did so as the military representative of the East Africa Protectorate (EAP), which became the Colony and Protectorate of Kenya in 1920. The EAP was actually the successor state to the anemic Imperial British East Africa Company (IBEAC), a chartered company that the metropolitan British government used to stake its initial claim to the region. The European chartered company was a powerful imperial tool in the early modern era, but it was an ineffectual anachronism in the late nineteenth century. Although the IBEAC reserved a slice of East Africa for Britain, its small and ill-equipped private army could not cope with the Nandi and other powerful local forces. Under both Kimny-ole and his son Koitalel the Nandi raided passing caravans and stole copper telegraph wire and raw materials from construction parties building a railway from the port of Mombasa to Uganda. The EAP, which replaced the company in 1895, mounted successive "pacifica-tion campaigns" against them, but the Nandi wisely avoided a direct confrontation with its Maxim guns and other western firearms.

Fed up with Nandi intransigence, the British demanded that Koitalel and his followers pay a fine of three hundred cattle or face the consequences. They knew full well that the Nandi would refuse, and Meinertzhagen was part of a massive punitive expedition con-sisting of eighty British officers, fifteen hundred African soldiers and policemen, thirty-five hundred armed and unarmed porters, one hundred Somali "levies," one thousand Maasai "auxiliaries," ten machine guns, and two armored trains. This represented the protec-torate's ultimate solution to the Nandi problem.[1] The Nandi Field Force's mission was to provoke the Nandi into standing and fighting by seizing their cattle. The Nandi elders' protests that they had little authority over Koitalel and his reckless younger followers were of no consequence.

The British framed their East African imperial project in moral and humanitarian terms. Denying that they were conquerors, they claimed that military force was the only way to compel the back-ward peoples of the highlands to respect civilized authority. By their count, the Nandi transgressions included the murder of Europeans, straightforward theft, and, most significant, demonstrating to other African communities that it was possible to defy imperial Britain. It mattered little that most of the Nandi's European victims were part of a marginal, often brutal rabble who sought to enrich themselves by leveraging their privileged status as "white men." They were clearly heirs of the Pizarrists, but the absence of lootable empires in the highlands forced them to seek their fortunes through cattle theft, petty fraud, and thinly disguised slave raiding. The Nandi recognized these men for what they were. Responding in kind, they murdered a British "trader" who had tortured two alleged cattle thieves to death. Even Meinertzhagen admitted that a grasping protectorate official provoked the Nandi by using punitive expeditions as an excuse to confiscate their cattle, which they kept primarily for themselves.

Yet Meinertzhagen was equally representative of the marginal men who sought wealth and status through empire in the highlands. While he disdained the company employees who were driven by simple greed, he and his fellow military officers sought fame and rapid promotion by winning glory on African battlefields. Likening the Nandi people to "a troublesome schoolboy" that had to be whipped, he had no reservations about using brutal and morally questionable tactics to achieve his goals. He admitted frankly in his memoirs: "I have no belief in the sanctity of human life or in the dignity of the human race. Human life has never been sacred; nor has man, except for a few occasional cases, been dignified."[2]

Meinertzhagen put this ruthless pragmatism into practice when he met Koitalel on October 19, 1905, to discuss a truce. The Nandi *orkoiyot* did not make Atawallpa's mistake in underestimating an invading foreigner, but he still made the fatal error of assuming that Meinertzhagen would behave honorably. Claiming that Koitalel was plotting an ambush, the British officer brazenly shot the *orkoiyot* to death when the two leaders met to shake hands. Meinertzhagen's men then opened fire and killed twenty-three more members of Koitalel's entourage. Accounts differ, but it appears that Koitalel was holding nothing more than a bundle of grass, which was the Nandi symbol for peace. In retelling the ambush story in his memoirs, Meinertzhagen professed to like the Nandi and claimed that he saved them from further destruction by removing a tyrant.[3]

Pizarro would have approved, but this tested the British liberal sympathies of the time. Although Meinertzhagen faced three separate army review boards to answer for his actions, there was no denying that the death of the *orkoiyot* broke the back of the Nandi resistance. The Nandi Field Force killed six hundred warriors and seized ten thousand of their cattle, which largely went into the herds of the rival Maasai. A follow-up punitive expedition killed fifty more people, seized more livestock, and burned almost 150 acres of crops. Faced with starvation, the Nandi capitulated. Under the terms of the peace settlement, they surrendered large sections of territory to the railway and European settlement.

Eventually, Meinertzhagen's superiors covered up the incident by recommending him for the Victoria Cross. He went on to distinguish himself in the First World War as the chief intelligence officer in Palestine and a friend of T. E. Lawrence, an aid at the Paris Peace

Conference, and the military advisor to the postwar Colonial Office. Upon retirement he achieved an additional measure of fame as an ornithologist with an enormous collection of stuffed birds ("study skins") and as a chronicler of Lawrence. It was only decades after his death that it came to light that he had stolen many of these specimens from other collections, plagiarized a book on Arabian birds, and written his supposedly contemporaneous diary entries about Lawrence in the 1950s.[4] Meinertzhagen's success and wealth never reached the levels of the conquistadors or nabobs, but he was reasonably typical of the "civilized" men who conquered Kenya for the British Empire.

The conquest of the highlands and Britain's rapid imperial expansion in the late nineteenth century were surprising given that Europeans appeared to have sworn off conventional imperial projects after the quick demise of Napoleon's continental empire. In Europe and to some extent North America, conquest and prolonged occupation now provoked violent resistance as westerners defiantly rejected imperial subjecthood as a violation of their natural rights as citizens of a nation. Many Britons accepted the loss of their North American colonies because they were confident in their global economic and strategic dominance in the postwar era. Many concluded that formal empire was an expensive tyrannical relic, particularly after the Indian Mutiny and the steady transition of the Canadian and Australian colonies to self-governing dominions by midcentury. Mindful of Adam Smith's attack on empire as a source of war, corruption, and financial drain, John Bright, Richard Cobden, and other free traders openly questioned the value of the remaining overseas territories.

These anti-imperial sentiments were at the root of Sir Charles Adderley's call to withdraw from West Africa in the 1860s. Arguing that disease made British naval bases and enclaves in the Gold Coast, Lagos, Freetown, and the Gambia "notoriously unfit for occupation by the Anglo-Saxon race," the member of Parliament charged that they were expensive luxuries that drew Britain into costly wars. Even more problematic, their inhabitants paid no taxes and thus contributed nothing to the one-million-pound annual maintenance costs of the naval bases. The proposal to withdraw from West Africa appeared radical, but only missionaries and palm oil merchants made the case for keeping a presence in West Africa. Adderley acknowledged the importance of tropical products, but in 1865 his Select Committee on Africa (Western Coast) concluded that while it was not yet possible to give up the coastal settlements, the British government should still "encourage in the natives the exercise of those qualities which may render it possible for us more and more to transfer to them the administration of all the Governments, with a view to our ultimate withdrawal from all, except, probably, Sierra Leone."[5]

These "natives" were mostly westernized Sierra Leonean Krios, who were descended from rescued slaves, black North American loyalists, and poor Britons of African descent. Adderley's committee wanted to make the West African enclaves more efficient by partnering with these Afro-Victorians to advance British interests. The Krios and other western-educated Africans warmly embraced this recommendation because they assumed that they would become the privileged imperial class in the West African territories. Their newspapers in Sierra Leone and the Gold Coast therefore openly advocated expansion into the interior, but they had no idea that in just a few short years they would be disenfranchised by the new imperialism's inherent racism.

In the 1860s, however, they had an important role in Adderley's vision of an informal empire. Arguing that Britain did not need permanent control to advance trade and investment, this pragmatic coalition of cost-cutters and free-traders assumed that the era of formal empire was over. They believed that this was true not only in sub-Saharan Africa and other remote places but also in Latin America, where British merchants and industrialists found profitable outlets for trade and investment without having to reimpose imperial rule on the former Spanish colonies. With most of continental Europe still struggling to recover from the Napoleonic wars, the British had no serious rivals at midcentury. In Africa, apart from the French conquest of Algeria and steady expansion up the Senegal River valley, British merchants largely had the continent to themselves until the 1870s.

This is not to say, however, that the British ever intended to give up their empire. In fact, the formal British Empire continued to grow by approximately one hundred square miles per year during this period, but most of the new acquisitions were strategically important naval bases or bits of territory claimed by the increasingly autonomous "white" settlement colonies in Australia, Canada, and South Africa. When the British public looked with pride on the pink-hued territories on the globe, they were gazing at these territories and not the tropical regions that became the hunting grounds of men such as Meinertzhagen.

British politicians lost faith in their network of informal influence and free trade only after European rivals, and to a lesser extent the United States and Japan, reentered the global arena as industrial and commercial powers. While British manufacturers still turned out simple products such as textiles and hardware, their continental rivals leapfrogged ahead in the production of steel, chemicals, and electrical goods. Consequently, Britain's share of global manufacturing output shrank from 33 percent to just 14 percent between 1870 and 1914. To make matters worse, the nation went from agricultural self-sufficiency to importing half its annual food needs as its farm output dropped steadily during the same period.[6]

These troubling developments provided the backdrop for the great depression of 1873, which was probably the single most important factor in sparking renewed interest in empire. Although crises of overproduction had beset the developing European industrial economies every seven to ten years in the preceding decades, the crash of 1873 was unprecedented in its scope and severity. Faced with dismal investment prospects, plummeting prices, and widespread unemployment, the industrial powers worried that their economies could grow no further. In Britain, panicked factory owners, financiers, and traders blamed the depression on the high tariff barriers of rival nations rather than admitting their inability to keep pace. Rejecting Adderley's warnings about the limited value of formal empire, they called for an expanded British imperial presence in tropical regions that were not yet open to western commerce and investment. Britain's continental rivals came to similar conclusions and rushed to reserve new African and Asian markets and sources of raw materials.

The subjugation of the East African highlands was part of this larger European conquest and partition of the African continent in the late nineteenth century. Historians lump this frenzy of empire building, along with the western powers' occupation of South Pacific islands, dismemberment of the Ottoman Empire, seizure of spheres of influence in China, and economic dominance of Latin America, under the heading of the "new imperialism." This global wave of imperial expansion was possible because the unifying power of nationalism and the industrial revolution gave westerners a relatively brief measure of military and commercial superiority over Africans and Asians.

Rather than being backward primitives, these new imperial victims were states and peoples whose sophistication, numbers, inhospitable climates, and/or geographical remoteness had spared them from early modern European empire building. In the late nineteenth century, ambitious European, American, and Japanese opportunists exploited these advantages to claim new empires and spheres of influence. For a brief window, permanent imperial rule once again appeared feasible and cost-effective in regions where the nation-state model had not yet taken hold.

Today, the new imperialism rivals Rome as the most popularly imagined model of empire, but the terms *new* and *imperialism* both require careful examination and explanation. The "old" imperialism referred to the American conquistador states and settlement colonies and the Asian chartered company empires of the early modern era. What was "new" about the conquest of the East African highlands was that it entailed the subjugation of the Nandi and other peoples who had escaped the first round of European imperial expansion but now lacked the means to deal with the growing power of the west. The discovery that quinine provided prophylactic protection from malaria allowed westerners to operate in tropical regions for extended periods, and repeating rifles, light field artillery, and the Maxim gun gave them the means to win inexpensive victories over much larger musket-equipped African armies. These advances made the new imperialism feasible by reducing the cost of conquest.

The new generation of late nineteenth-century imperial speculators first had to rehabilitate empire before they could exploit this imbalance. Imperial projects had a bad reputation in the mid-nineteenth-century western world after the devastation of the Napoleonic wars. Americans proudly imagined themselves as anti-imperial rebels, and in Europe Adderley and other liberals and free-traders dismissed empire as anachronistic and authoritarian. Indeed, the word *imperialism* first emerged as a pejorative synonym for *empire building* when British critics coined it to attack Napoleon III's Second French Empire. In 1858, an anonymous article in the *Westminster Review* charged that in proclaiming himself emperor Napoleon's nephew aspired to "permanent military despotism," and the author quite correctly noted that "the permanent continuance of Imperialism resolves itself plainly into the establishment of undisguised military rule and the triumph of brute force."[7] *Imperialism* never lost this negative meaning, particularly among twentieth-century critics of empire, but the imperial special-interest groups rehabilitated it in the 1880s by depicting empire as a profitable national enterprise.

Yet there were no more Bengals waiting to be conquered and exploited in the modern era. Partially commercialized African economies were poor outlets for western trade and investment, and J. A. Hobson, an imperial critic who covered the Anglo–South African War for the *Manchester Guardian*, was wrong in arguing that capitalist special interests sponsored the new wave of imperial expansion in Africa. In reality, British financiers put the bulk of their capital to work building railways and factories in the United States, Latin America, and Russia. The new imperialism stemmed primarily from fear and speculation, and only a small range of special-interest groups profited directly from the new empires. In addition to the merchants, missionaries, soldiers, and other men on the spot, these included the "gentlemanly capitalists" who controlled metropolitan banking, insurance, and shipping concerns.[8] Together, these latter-day nabobs exploited the temporary western advantage in technology, industry, and finance resulting from the uneven advance of globalization.

It is an open question as to how many people actually profited from the new imperialism. The overall value of the new empire to metropolitan Britain was certainly debatable. Britons at the turn of the twentieth century put 75 percent of their capital in nonimperial territories, and on average these investments brought approximately 1.58 percent higher returns than imperial ones.[9] For those willing to risk their money in the empire, India and the dominions remained the most lucrative outlets for trade and capital. The Raj was still unquestionably Britain's most valuable imperial possession. It offset Britain's trade imbalance with Europe, and the heavily subsidized Indian railways paid rich dividends to investors. The self-governing dominions were also important trading partners, but their value to Britain waned as they gained more control over their economies. By comparison, British Africa was nowhere near as valuable. The entire continent south of the Sahara took less than 5 percent of British exports in 1890, and when British capitalists did invest in the African empire they focused on the mines of southern Africa.[10] Lacking easily exploitable resources, sufficient infrastructure, and reliable labor supplies, the new protectorates were spectacularly poor investments, and the British government had to pay generous subsidies to draw capital to Africa.

Far from being a great engine of liberal free trade, this "new" British Empire was profoundly protectionist. Born of a deep sense of insecurity, it was Britain's desperate attempt to defend its global network of commerce and investment through non-economic means. Most British taxpayers probably would have preferred the cheaper option of informal empire, but the growing economic and military power of the United States, France, Germany, and to a lesser extent Russia and Japan scared the British government into indulging the imperial lobby's demands for more African and Asian territory. As a result, the British added almost five million square miles and ninety million more people to their formal empire in the last three decades of the nineteenth century. Although metropolitan Britain was a relatively small nation with a population of only forty-one and a half million, the new British Empire covered twelve million square miles (roughly one-quarter of the habitable world) and boasted more than four hundred million subjects at the turn of the twentieth century.[11]

As in the early modern era, bands of private explorers and chartered companies played the lead role in staking out claims to promising regions. In 1884, the European powers formalized this process at a conference in Berlin that the German chancellor Bismarck convened to ensure that squabbles over territory in Africa did not lead to war in Europe. In what amounted to the ground rules for the new imperialism, the delegates agreed that a nation wishing to claim a specific territory had to demonstrate that it occupied it "effectively." In practical terms, this meant direct administration and treaties in which the "natives" agreed to accept foreign protection. In many cases, the prominent local individuals who signed off on these protectorates did not realize that they were surrendering their sovereignty under European law. Instead, African leaders expected to be treated as equals and often hoped to use the foreigners against local rivals.

The British government was relatively restrained in this renewed rush for empire. In West Africa, it chartered Sir George Goldie's Royal Niger Company to claim Nigeria, but it only expanded territories surrounding the naval bases that Adderley wanted to give up. This is how the French came to claim most of West Africa. The central importance of India to the wider empire dictated the occupation of Egypt to safeguard the Suez Canal. Similarly, the Indian route around the Cape of Good Hope in southern Africa drew Britain into a war with the Transvaal and Orange Free State to ensure that these mineral-rich Afrikaner republics did not swallow up the strategically important Cape Colony. Britain had no significant military or economic interests in central and eastern Africa, so the metropolitan government left the region to state-sanctioned private speculators. Thus, Cecil Rhodes's British South Africa Company claimed and conquered northern and southern Rhodesia, and Sir William McKinnon's British East Africa Company did the same in Uganda and the East African highlands.

Imperial enthusiasts swelled with pride in seeing these territories colored British pink, but metropolitan reactions to the new imperialism were decidedly mixed. Many Britons assumed that imperialism meant building closer ties with the white settlement colonies and not the conquest of alien and inassimilable Africans and Asians. While Rhodes, Meinertzhagen, and other adventurers made fortunes and careers in the new territories, more often than not the British taxpayer paid for their empires. The Treasury was particularly suspicious of the new imperialism and criticized the expense of unnecessary imperial wars. The imperial special interests countered by appealing to the public's patriotic and humanitarian sentiments. Popular newspapers depicted the new empire as a heroic national enterprise, and music hall shows carried the message to the working classes. Rudyard Kipling, Rider Haggard, John Buchan, and other widely read authors spun romantic tales of adventure and national glory in the empire.

The resulting wave of popular enthusiasm generated by this celebration of empire meant that there was very little real political debate over the nature and merits of the new imperialism. Liberal and Tory politicians argued over its particulars, but both parties recognized the power of popular imperial sentiment. Benjamin Disraeli argued that the empire made Britain great, and Lord Randolph Churchill and Joseph Chamberlain courted working-class voters by promising that the new conquests provided markets and new lands for settlement. Alternatively, William Gladstone, H. H. Asquith, and other Liberals appealed to the publics' better nature by depicting the new empire as benevolent.

While this imperial expansion might appear inevitable in hindsight, it caught nonwestern peoples almost entirely by surprise. For nearly four centuries, coastal Africans interacted with Europeans as trading partners and allies in struggles with rival neighbors. Slave traders were certainly a threat, but on balance most African societies could deal with Europeans on relatively equal terms before the industrial era. Even more troubling, the new imperialism stripped them of their humanity.

Seeking to lend credence to their promise to civilize the "primitive races" of Africa, imperial speculators and their mission allies portrayed subject peoples as implicitly and often irredeemably backward. Most missionaries genuinely believed that the imperial wars of conquest were liberating, but the popular theories of social Darwinism and pseudoscientific racism, which depicted nonwesterners as biologically inferior, gave this seemingly benevolent imperial project an inherently sinister reality. While late nineteenth-century western intellectuals and politicians cited the unique characteristics of the British, French, and German "races" in making national distinctions, they placed all Europeans on a scale of cultural evolution far above the supposedly backward overseas peoples. Ethnographers and scientists confidently found evidence of this primitiveness by using comparative anatomy and craniology to prove that nonwestern peoples had smaller brains and diminished cognitive ability. E. S. Grogan, one of the most grasping new Kenyan imperialists, blithely declared that it was "patent to all who have observed the African native, that he is fundamentally inferior in mental development and ethical possibilities (call it a soul if you will) to the white man."[12]

Consequently, by the late nineteenth century it was no longer possible to be African and civilized within the British Empire. Africans became people without history, people who lived in timeless and unchanging backward tribal societies. This meant that westernized communities such as the Sierra Leonean Krios, who ran Britain's West African coastal enclaves, became "trousered natives" who, like the Indian baboos, aped a modern culture they did not understand. It did not matter that many were graduates of British universities, or that Samuel Adjai Crowther was an Anglican bishop and James Africanus Horton was a British army doctor. The new pseudoscientific racism created a liberal excuse for empire by turning all dark-complected peoples into primitives.

This was the grim scenario that played out in East Africa. Highland peoples, who traded with coastal Swahili city states through middlemen, became more directly integrated into global trade networks in the early nineteenth century when western middle-class demand for combs, piano keys, and billiard balls drove up the price of ivory. Additionally, the British abolitionists' success in outlawing the Atlantic slave trade had the unexpected consequence of pushing human trafficking into Central and East Africa. This was the result of a loophole that the British government inserted into the antislaving treaties to allow their Portuguese allies to buy and capture slaves south of the equator. Led by Afro-Arab adventurers and bankrolled by Indian investors, armed caravans hunted elephants and people in the highlands. Captured slaves carried the tusks to the coast, where these speculators doubled their profits by selling both commodities. Most of the ivory was destined for western markets, and the slaves went to Zanzibari plantations, the Middle East, and Brazil, where slavery remained legal until the 1880s.

These caravans integrated the highlands into the wider networks of trade and investment. Less advantageous, they spread firearms and contagious diseases. Merchant adventurers such as Tippu Tib carved out minor empires in the interior, and young highlanders who acquired guns to hunt elephants joined caravan deserters and runaway slaves in preying on local communities. This explains why Richard Burton, David Livingstone, and other explorers and missionaries encountered anarchy and violence when they mapped these regions at midcentury. Assuming that slave raiding, warfare, famine, and widespread misery were endemic, they had little clue that western demands for ivory and the misguided efforts of the humanitarian lobby were at the root of many of these problems.

This ignorance allowed the missionaries and fortune seekers who followed the explorers to portray Africans as primitive and in need of rescue and salvation. The metropolitan government initially paid little attention to these special interests. It saw no value in East Africa during the era of informal empire, and it took the threat of German expansion into the great lakes region to spur Prime Minister Lord Salisbury into action in the 1880s. Motivated by an unrealistic fear that a foreign presence on Lake Victoria/Nyanza and the headwaters of the Nile would threaten British control of Egypt and the Suez Canal, Salisbury's government chartered Sir William MacKinnon's IBEAC to stake a formal claim to the highlands. From the British government's standpoint, MacKinnon's enterprise was a cost effective way to establish "effective administration" of the northern end of the highlands under the terms of the Berlin Conference. Germany claimed what became modern Tanzania, and Britain acquired control over Zanzibar and, by extension, the Kenyan coastline by forcing the sultan to accept British "protection."

MacKinnon had vague but ambitious plans to develop the region and depicted his holdings as a "new Australia." But his company soon teetered on bankruptcy because the region lacked exploitable mineral resources and its local economies were not suited to easy extraction. Few East Africans in the interior produced commodities for the world market, which meant that MacKinnon could not emulate Clive's success in India by capturing preexisting trade and tax systems. To make matters worse, his charter required him to occupy the lake kingdom of Buganda at considerable expense. MacKinnon's only hope of survival was a government subsidy for a railway linking Mombasa to the highlands, but his enterprise was doomed once the Liberal prime minister William Gladstone refused to saddle the British taxpayers with such an expensive enterprise.

MacKinnon was a prototypical example of a failed imperial speculator. Although he benefited from western advances in commerce and technology, he had no means of extracting wealth from his new subjects. Many of his original employees were trained geologists, but their desperate search for economically viable mineral deposits was fruitless. Realizing that custom duties on the caravan trade were the region's only significant revenue source, MacKinnon essentially took over the old Afro-Arab trade network. His caravans employed many of the same coastal peoples who had initially chartered the highland trade, although they no longer engaged in slave raiding and elephant hunting.

Given these realities, it is hardly surprising that the IBEAC had difficulty attracting investors. Handicapped by a chronic capital shortage, MacKinnon lacked the means to govern and develop the highlands. He escaped total ruin when the more imperially minded prime minister Lord Rosebery claimed the Uganda and East Africa Protectorates in 1894 and 1895 on the assumption that the source of the Nile had sufficient strategic importance to warrant the expense of direct intervention. Having bought out MacKinnon and his investors, Rosebery concluded that the Treasury would have to take financial responsibility for replacing the caravan route from Mombasa to Uganda with a railway. In investing some nine million pounds of state funds in the project, he implicitly committed the British government to completing the IBEAC's conquest of East Africa. MacKinnon was off the hook, and most of his employees continued their careers in government service.

The Foreign Office had responsibility for the new protectorates until the Colonial Office took them over in 1906. This fit the overall pattern for the new British Empire. Administratively, the Crown was the source of executive authority in every British-controlled territory, but in practice there was no uniform or integrated system of governance. In London, a variety of government ministries instead shared responsibility for imperial oversight. The Foreign Office initially ran most of the African protectorates, but as in East Africa, it handed off most of these territories to the Colonial Office. The India Office oversaw the Raj and an extensive Indian Civil Service that was separate and distinct from the rest of the colonial service. In practical terms, however, the Treasury exercised the greatest influence of all the metropolitan ministries because the chancellors of the Exchequer stood in the way of speculators who sought to shift the costs of empire to the metropolitan government. The British East Africa Company was a notable exception to this rule.

Otherwise, the EAP followed the standard imperial template by dividing the newly conquered territory into provinces, districts, and African "locations." The Protestant missions adopted a similar strategy in apportioning the protectorate into spheres of influence to ensure that they did not compete with each other. In terms of governance, a commissioner, whose title later became governor, presided over a central secretariat, several specialized departments, and the larger field administration. These district officers supervised the chiefs who actually ruled the African majority under the doctrine of indirect rule.

In pretending to rule through local sovereigns, the British imported the Indian model of imperial rule to Africa. As in the Raj, British officials claimed to govern through African institutions of authority rather than ruling directly. This made the "tribe" the basis of imperial administration. Confused by the range of fluid and often overlapping ethnicities of preconquest Africa, British officials concluded that Africans lived in unchanging tribal societies. In the imperial imagination, a tribe was a lower form of political and social organization that, with proper paternal guidance, might one day evolve into a nation. Theoretically, these tribal identities were biologically ingrained, thereby making them fixed and corporate rather than individual. Working in the service of colonial governments, anthropologists mapped tribal languages, social institutions, and customary laws to fashion the tools of imperial administration for district officers. The African tribe was thus a useful fiction to update the venerable imperial strategy of co-opting local institutions of authority. This indirect rule lowered the cost of administration and allowed the new imperialists to portray themselves as philosopher-kings in the Platonic tradition.

However, British officials actually knew very little about the local institutions and customs they claimed to protect. Their igno-rance created opportunities for ambitious individuals to convince imperial officials and ethnographers to make them chiefs with the vested authority to define the tribal customs that became the basis of imperial administration. As John Iliffe famously noted: "Euro-peans believed Africans belonged to tribes; Africans built tribes to belong to," and the origins of the Mijikenda, Kalenjin, Luhya and other contemporary Kenyan "tribes" date from the imperial era.[13] The opportunities of imperially defined tribalism thus encouraged subject peoples to frame political and social debates in tribal terms. In doing so, they played into the hands of the new imperialists, for tribal status disqualified Africans from membership in the British nation-state. Metropolitan Britons were technically "subjects" of the British Crown, but in practice they were citizens with the full rights and protections of British law. Tribal Africans, conversely, were "protected persons," with no individual rights. Instead of citizenship, the British imperial system granted collective rights to tribes.

The complication was that while indirect rule worked relatively well in the Raj, where sultans and maharajas had substantial author-ity, these Indian rulers had few counterparts in sub-Saharan Africa, where, like the Nandi, most societies were stateless. This meant that there were multiple sites of authority in a given community and no single individual had the power to govern autonomously, collect taxes, or rule on "native law." In most territories, British officials compensated by turning cooperative individuals with some measure of influence into "chiefs." But this was not the equivalent of Napole-onic *ralliement*, for few of these men were true local notables. Simi-larly, imperial administrators solved the problem of statelessness by lumping related communities together into tribes under the nominal authority of these imperial proxies. While it did not have the power to force Africans to accept these tribal identities, the imperial regime created a powerful incentive for them to think tribally by refusing to acknowledge them as individuals. Tellingly, individualistic western-educated Africans such as the Sierra Leonean Krios had to be shunted aside because they were too individualistic and "modern."

It took some time for the Nandi and the rest of the highland communities to realize the consequences of these developments. Peoples living along the route to Lake Nyanza/Victoria, which IBEAC officials called the Buganda Road, saw both danger and opportunity in the expanding British presence. Initially, there were profits to be made by supplying the company with food, water, and labor. In the central highlands, a Kikuyu trader named Kinyanjui made himself useful by provisioning the caravans. Likewise, Mumia, a relatively minor Luhya clan leader on the northern shore of Lake Victoria/Nyanza, used his connections with the company to become a powerful chief. At the same time, MacKinnon's men also provoked highland communities when they resorted to foraging, which was essentially looting, to the expense of bartering supplies. That there were no rich treasures to plunder in the highlands did not mean that these latter-day conquistadors were any more virtuous than their predecessors.

Koitalel's followers and other young warriors who had no stake in commerce further hindered the company's ability to turn a profit. Preferring raiding to trading, they made the caravans' long trek from Mombasa to Buganda difficult and dangerous. Indian work gangs building the Uganda Railway were similarly at risk. The company initially dealt with this threat by fortifying its food stations, but the Foreign Office, which had little patience for local interference with a multimillion-pound construction project, adopted a more aggressive response. It reorganized the private company army into the KAR to bolster British authority in the new protectorates. This "native force" reduced the cost of empire by following the chartered company practice of recruiting ex-slaves and other poorly paid marginal peoples for service against more established communities.

Led by seconded regular army officers such as Richard Meinertzhagen, the KAR companies, backed by "native auxiliaries" and Indian troops on loan from the Raj, gradually forced the peoples of the highlands to accept imperial subjecthood. For the first decade of its existence the EAP's main business was conquest. From 1895 to 1905, the total cost of these pacification campaigns came to more than six thousand pounds, which was one-third of the protectorate's total expenditures.[14] The operations that led to Meinertzhagen's execution of Koitalel were fairly typical. Often devolving into mass cattle raids, these small but vicious wars usually ended when protectorate troops forced defiant communities to surrender by seizing their livestock and burning their huts and crops.

The resulting famines contributed to the devastatingly high mortality rates that afflicted the highlands at the end of the nineteenth century. Racked by hunger and epidemic disease, weakened East Africans struggled to cope with the British invasion. Once again, smallpox in particular played a central role in western empire building. Spread by the caravans along with cholera, pneumonia, and other deadly pathogens, it ravaged communities whose relative isolation in the highlands made them dangerously vulnerable to contagious Old World diseases. Rinderpest, a highly virulent cattle disease originating in South Asia, and bovine pleuropneumonia (lungsickness) made matters even worse by wiping out the herds that were both a food source and a measure of wealth. Estimates vary, but it appears that these human and biological disasters may have killed off as much as 30 to 50 percent of the population of the central and northern highlands.[15]

Although there were a few exceptions, the Nandi surrender in 1905 generally marked the end of open African resistance. With British rule secure, the pacification operations that brought glory to Meinertzhagen and other ambitious empire builders now became an expensive embarrassment and hindered the process of orderly extraction. As one of his fellow officers in the King's African Rifles candidly acknowledged, it was no longer "the object of the KAR to kill potential British subjects, especially as they are expected to become tax-payers and profitable customers."[16]

As with earlier empires, the imperial regime viewed the East Africans primarily as exploitable subjects rather than consumers. Anxious to recoup the nine million pounds that metropolitan taxpayers had invested in the Uganda Railway, protectorate authorities cast about for paying passengers and shippers. Giving far too much credibility to the denigrating ideologies of empire building, they failed to realize that many African farmers gladly would have produced crops for export if given sufficient access to global markets via the railway. Instead, the EAP's commissioner, Sir Charles Eliot, concluded that it would take a civilized people to develop the highlands. As the line neared completion in 1903, imperial officials considered and dismissed Indian peasants, Afrikaner homesteaders, and even Theodor Herzl's Zionists before committing themselves to enticing aristocratic Britons to settle in East Africa.

Building this elite settler society took some doing, for the pioneer empire builders in East Africa were anything but noble. As in the early stages of most imperial projects, the protectorate tended to attract marginal men and fortune hunters. They were a sorry collection of adventurers, hunters, con men, drunkards, and outright criminals who were hardly the best representatives of the civilized west. Slipping the bonds of metropolitan conceptions of morality, they had free rein to indulge their lust for wealth and power. Bartolomé de Las Casas, Edmund Burke, and other earlier metropolitan critics of empire would have recognized these corrupting imperial influences. Meinertzhagen at least was honest about how serving the East Africa Protectorate tested him.

> It is hard to resist the savagery of Africa when one falls under its spell. One soon reverts to one's ancestral character, both mind and temperament becoming brutalized. I have seen so much of it out here and I have myself felt the magnetic power of the African climate drawing me lower and lower to the level of a savage.[17]

In his eyes, most KAR officers were "regimental rejects" who failed this test by becoming obsessed with money, drink, pornography, mistresses, and small boys.[18] Precious few of the men who did the messy work of empire building were suited to be capitalist entrepreneurs or sober landed gentlemen, and migrants leaving Britain with agricultural experience had far better options in the United States and the dominions. Apart from about 280 itinerant Afrikaners from the Transvaal, there were only one hundred permanent settlers in the protectorate in 1903.

Eliot therefore recognized that it would take significant inducements to lure the right kind of men to East Africa. Seizing land from the Maasai, Kikuyu, Nandi, Kamba, and other highland communities, he offered settlers ninety-nine-year leases on parcels of 640 acres of prime agricultural land at the rock-bottom rate of less than one pence per acre. Companies could apply for even larger concessions ranging up to one hundred thousand acres, and a new ordinance in 1915 increased the tenure of the leases to 999 years. Even these generous inducements did not bring the expected rush of settlers, and land speculation proved far more profitable than farming. By the opening of the First World War, less than 10 percent of the alienated land was under cultivation, but farms that went for six pence per acre in 1903 were selling for one pound per acre in 1914. Moreover, powerful imperial interests and syndicates used political and family connections to buy up much of the available land. This gave five individuals and two syndicates the means to acquire 20 percent of the highlands, and in 1912 there were still only about one thousand permanent settlers in the protectorate.[19]

The imperial regime's legal authority for this blatant land theft was the Crown Lands Ordinance of 1902, which gave the Crown title to all "unoccupied" land in the protectorate. Linking land and identity, this legislation also set up a "native reserve" for each tribe. Theoretically, these reservations prevented unscrupulous European or South Asian speculators from duping ignorant tribesmen into selling lands that were their tribe's communal property. As one official paternalistically claimed, the Crown's ownership of African land was a legal fiction intended to "protect the natives from themselves." This was nonsense, and in reality the actual purpose of the reserve system was to open up the protectorate for expropriation by Europeans. The highlands thus became the "white highlands," which developed into a three-million-hectare settler "native" reserve off-limits to Africans. The peoples of the coast and the western Lake Nyanza/Victoria region did not lose land directly to western settlement, but they too became subject natives.

Imperial officials tried to legitimize these land seizures by depicting the highlands as underpopulated. Sir Harry Johnston described them as "admirably suited for a white man's country" because they were "utterly uninhabited for miles or at most its inhabitants are wandering hunters who have no settled home."[20] In fact, most highland communities were well on the way to demographic recovery from the devastation of the 1890s by the time Eliot began to promote European settlement. The Kikuyu in particular expanded rapidly during this period by sending landless young men to carve out new farms on the margins of their territory. British demands for food for caravan porters, railway laborers, and settlers accelerated this process by giving entrepreneurial Kikuyu farmers an incentive to increase their agricultural output. Ironically, these ambitious men would have

made ideal customers for the Uganda Railway. Company agents at
the time described the Kikuyu heartland as "one vast garden," and
even Johnston's comrade Frederick Lugard had to admit that their
"whole country may be said to be under tillage."[21]

The Maasai, by comparison, found another way to recover from
the disasters of the previous decade. Finding common cause with the
British invaders, they rebuilt their herds by enlisting as native auxiliaries in the pacification campaigns. While postindependence Kenyan
nationalists might have viewed this as treason, East Africans had no
reason to identify themselves collectively, much less nationally, until
the imperial era. From the Maasai standpoint, the IBEAC was a useful ally in their struggle with far more threatening rivals such as the
Nandi and Kikuyu. They had no reason to suspect that British settlers would eventually displace them by claiming three-quarters of
the Rift Valley.

This is why the totality of the imperial conquest shocked most
communities. In just a few decades, the British made a quick transition from useful trading partners and political allies to plundering but
manageable marauders and then to determined land-stealing empire
builders. The father of political activist Harry Thuku was stunned to
find that a government official suddenly claimed title to his farm, and
he had little recourse when the Europeans told him: "You have no
land. The land belongs to God. God has given it to the white man, and
they have it now."[22] Just as Iberians and Andeans turned to prophecy to explain the totality of their defeat, East Africans now recalled
the warnings of oracles and wise men who foretold the arrival of the
pale-skinned foreigners and their railway. The Nandi remembered
that Koitalel's father, Kimnyole, had prophesized that whites borne
by a giant shrieking, crawling, and smoking serpent would come to
kill his sons, take their cattle, and drive them from their homes. The
Kikuyu recorded that Mogo wa Kebiro issued similar warnings about
strangers colored like frogs and bearing magical fire-belching sticks.[23]
These tales were not the result of primitive superstition; they were
born of the highland communities' desperate need to make sense of
their enormous losses.

In time, their children recognized the conquest for the imperial power grab that it really was. Writing three decades later, Jomo
Kenyatta blamed the Kikuyu defeat on their willingness to befriend
the European strangers who appeared in the country as tired and

hungry vagrants and wanderers. Assuming that these people would be temporary sojourners, the Kikuyu elders signed their treaties and granted them permission to settle temporarily as clients. In Kenyatta's view, his people were defeated through treachery, not because they were somehow culturally inferior. "The Gikuyu lost their lands through their magnanimity, for the Gikuyu country was never wholly conquered by force of arms, but the people were put under the ruthless domination of European imperialism through the insidious trickery of hypocritical treaties."[24]

Protectorate officials and settlers dismissed or muzzled this opposition by portraying East Africans as primitive tribesmen lacking the capacity to make proper use of the rich highlands. But the EAP also struggled to attract the right kind of settler. Anxious to be rid of the politically embarrassing lumpen rabble that had undertaken the original conquest of the highlands, Eliot was determined to make the protectorate an aristocratic "white man's country."

The commissioner had an ally in Lord Cranworth, a member of the House of Lords with extensive interests in East Africa, who published a book promoting the EAP as the perfect place for English elites to create the feudal society of privilege and deference that they believed had withered away in democratic industrial Britain. With chapters on health, climate, agriculture, animal husbandry, hunting, horse racing, polo, and other sporting pursuits, the book claimed that the protectorate had everything a propertied Englishman could want.

> A perfect balmy climate? Take Nairobi and Kyambu. Something a little more bracing and with a touch of frost? Try Likipia or the Uasin Gishu plateau. Would you have a reminder of the West coast of Scotland with heavy rain, mist and lovely days interspersed? The Mau or the Nandi Escarpment will give it [to] you. A touch of the wind off the North Sea in East Anglia? The West Kenia plains can do that. While something really cold and bitter you must climb up into Kenia's glaciers.[25]

This sort of advertising drew men like Hugh Cholmondeley (Lord Delamere), who purchased one hundred thousand acres in the highlands for just five thousand pounds at the tender age of twenty-eight. Strict immigration controls required would-be immigrants to prove they had at least one thousand pounds in the bank, and the government deported to Bombay poorer undesirables who might diminish "white prestige" after first forcing them to work off the cost of their passage in the Mombasa jail.[26]

Although they had no formal position of authority in the EAP, Delamere and the settler aristocracy had considerable influence over sympathetic protectorate officials. In 1907, they won the right to elect representatives to the Legislative Council, and their Convention of Associations became a virtual lower parliamentary house. Opened by the governor (formerly the protectorate commissioner), the convention called officials to testify on government policy and debated bills under consideration in the formal legislative council.

Nevertheless, the settlers never felt physically or morally secure. Although they had their own militia, they relied on the European-led African soldiers of the KAR and "native" policemen for their protection. Those living on remote farms worried constantly about their safety, particularly when the press carried a report or rumor of an African assault on a European. The fact that these "outrages" were actually extremely rare was not reassuring. Ever mindful that they were a privileged minority, the settler community relied on the illusion of racial and cultural superiority to exercise authority. This is why Grogan insisted that European prestige "must be maintained at all costs, as it is the sole hold we have over the native."[27] Strict racial segregation concealed the settlers' inherent vulnerability, and they strove futilely to create all-white enclaves where Africans would only visit as domestic servants and temporary laborers.

The settlers staked their claim to the highlands by asserting that they alone had the means to develop the protectorate, but African produce accounted for 70 percent of the EAP's exports before the First World War. The settlers nevertheless justified their privileges by depicting Africans as irredeemably simple and slothful. The Kikuyu came in for particular abuse as the settlers' chief agricultural and political rivals, and Cranworth unashamedly described them as "a most miserable cowardly race."[28] This was empire at its most hypocritical, for Cranworth's estates would have been worthless without Kikuyu to work them.

As in earlier empires, the East Africa Protectorate's true wealth was in its people. The settlers reconciled their labor demands with the imperial lobby's humanitarian rhetoric by depicting toil as inherently civilizing. Frederick Lugard, Britain's foremost imperial ideologue, reassured the metropolitan public that it was possible to both uplift Africa's "native races" and exploit its resources. He asserted that the "white races" had a moral obligation to make the continent's wealth available to the wider world by directing their labor.[29] Invoking Lugard's declaration of this "dual mandate," the colonial secretary Leopold Amery confidently told the Houses of Commons: "Our first duty is to [our African subjects]; our object is not to exploit them, but to enable them materially, as well as in every other respect, to rise to a high plane of living and civilization."[30]

Rhetoric aside, the fortunes of settler farmers, concession holders, and speculators depended on a poorly paid, subservient African work force. Most westerners came to East Africa with the expectation that Africans would grow their food, build their houses, and tend to their most basic domestic needs. In the settlers' eyes, the EAP was obliged to supply this cheap if not free labor. The complication was that the moral veneer of the new imperialism prevented the EAP from simply forcing Africans to work. Eliot and his successors came under considerable criticism for taking their time in abolishing slavery on the Swahili coast. Unwilling to disrupt the relatively lucrative plantation economy, they tried to extend the immoral institution's life by pretending that it would gradually die out on its own accord. Realistically, slavery was no longer a viable tool of imperial extraction, and settlers and speculators had to find more civilized ways to harness African labor.

Initially, however, most East Africans had little incentive to work on imperial enterprises because their subsistence economies met most of their needs. Those that did accept paid employment usually did so just long enough to earn enough money to buy useful western material goods such as clothing, cutlery, or bicycles before returning home. Frustrated would-be employers therefore charged that Africans were inherently lazy. A settler newspaper published an unflinchingly racist poem that typified this view of African men as indolent, unmanly drunkards who lived off the labor of their wives.

> Jack Nigger you're as cute's can be
> Five beans to you make ten
> You drink and scrounge and sleep and laze
> And laze, scrounge and drink again!
> Your *bibis* [wives] do domestic jobs
> They sow and plough and reap
> And mend your pants and mind the kids
> While you lie fast asleep.

In fact they live for you alone
You gay and lazy dog
They make and fetch your *pombe* [beer] and
They feed you like a hog
And with it all but one thing can
Disturb your lordly rest
And that, Jack Nig, you likewise know
Is twenty of the best.[31]

The phrase "twenty of the best" referred to flogging.

Far from being embarrassed by the settlers' extensive use of corporal punishment, a member of the Kenyan Legislative Council unashamedly declared in open debate: "I always treat my natives the same as I treat children. I try to be kind to them, and to advise and direct them, but when kindness has no effect you have to do the same as they do in the public schools at home and throughout the empire—use the cane."[32] Exempted from western conceptions of morality and the rule of law by virtue of their race, the settlers sometimes beat their employees to death while teaching the value of "honest" work. The early years of British rule in Kenya were so corrupting that even Norman Leys, a vehement critic of the settlers, admitted that he too gave in to the seductive power of the racialized new imperialism. "You see I have lived in the fog myself. I have cuffed and kicked boys [Africans], sometimes because for the moment it seemed that [in no way] else could things be done, sometimes because my mind was tired beyond control, sometimes because I hated the people I kicked, though I never hated them as I hated myself."[33]

The protectorate government therefore cast about for more politically acceptable ways to produce African labor. The most obvious answer was to destroy local subsistence economies. On the whole, simple taxation proved the most effective strategy. The protectorate's relatively meager gross tax receipts were quiet small, but introducing the poll and hut tax, with mandatory payments in rupees and later shillings, required East Africans to find paying jobs. By 1910, they had to pay Rs 3 for each hut and Rs 3 for the individual poll tax each year. Defaulters lost their huts and crops and had to work one month for each rupee owed.[34] Europeans, in turn, did not pay a direct income tax until the late 1930s, leaving their "native" subjects to fund the settlers' schools, hospitals, and other amenities.

Africans could have raised their tax money by selling crops and livestock, but the native reserve system created land shortages that made it difficult to produce for the market. This meant that men and women had to sell their labor to avoid breaking the law. This subtle form of imperial coercion was both inexpensive and acceptable to the humanitarian lobby for all "civilized" people had to pay taxes. In the EAP, however, civilized people did not have an obligation to pay a fair wage. Desperate to keep the labor costs down, settlers and speculators used their influence to depress African pay scales. But even minimal wages were sufficient for most Africans to cover their taxes, which meant that most still avoided wage labor whenever they could. Moreover, the tendency of some of the EAP's poorly made coins to literally disintegrate when exposed to the elements hardly inspired confidence in the cash economy.

European employers therefore used every political resource at their disposal to press the EAP to institute a comprehensive program of forced labor. The settlers never got the government to recruit workers for them directly, but the imperial regime ordered district officers and chiefs to compel Africans to build roads, dams, and irrigation systems. These forced laborers even had to carry administrative officials on litters through the largely roadless rural areas. The EAP also turned a relatively blind eye to the abuses of unscrupulous private labor recruiters who used coercion and deception to get laborers to sign exploitive contracts. Those who ran away from abusive employers faced prosecution under a Master and Servants Ordinance. In 1912, reports of these excesses forced protectorate authorities to commission an investigation of "native labour" that acknowledged that chiefs and labor recruiters were forcing people to work by burning their huts, seizing their land, and fining them excessively.

The First World War only made matters worse. Dominating the protectorate war council, the settlers won new authority to round up laborers under martial law regulations by depicting African resistance to wage labor as traitorous. Even worse, the military authorities demanded huge numbers of men to support the largely futile three-year invasion of German East Africa (modern Tanzania). British, Indian, and South African troops initially took the lead in the operation, but mounting loses due to combat and disease led imperial generals to rely on local African troops. The East Africa, Uganda, and Nyasaland protectorates supplied more than thirty thousand African soldiers for the King's African Rifles during the campaign, but this paled in comparison to the hundreds of thousands of laborers the civil authorities conscripted to carry supplies. Recordkeeping from this era is poor, but it appears that at least fifty thousand of these "carriers" perished as a result of combat, disease, and gross mistreatment during the East African campaign.

The imperial authorities refused to even acknowledge African contributions to Britain's victory. Instead, the protectorate government seized half a million more acres of Nandi and Kikuyu land in 1919 to provide farms for demobilized British military officers. Designed to strengthen white settlement, the Soldier Settlement Scheme opened 685 new farms to qualified applicants of pure European origin with demonstrated assets worth at least one thousand pounds. A supplementary plan set aside additional land and one hundred thousand pounds for disabled veterans to grow flax. Precious few of the soldier settlers had any agricultural experience and most sold out to land speculators within a few short years. The participants in the flax scheme went bankrupt when global prices for the commodity crashed.

In 1920, the metropolitan government acknowledged the settlers' preeminent place in East Africa by transforming the EAP into the Kenya Colony and Protectorate. Most settlers expected this to set Kenya on the path to self-government and possibly even dominion status. They elected two representatives to the governor's Executive Council, which served as his cabinet. Their representatives in the Legislative Council had a majority on the Finance Committee and took a more direct role in drafting laws. A series of pro-settler governors worked closely with these "unofficial" elected legislators and often signed off on laws without sending them on to the Colonial Office for formal approval. A Chief Native Commissioner supposedly spoke for the African majority in the Executive Council, while a single appointed missionary represented "native" interests in the legislature.

Imperial apologists argued that tribal Africans were not sufficiently educated to speak for themselves. Not only was this absurd, it was also hypocritical. The imperial regime had no intention of giving its subjects the western-style education that was a prerequisite for the franchise. In 1924, the Kenyan government spent just 4 percent of its seventy-five-thousand pound education budget on African children.[35]

Apart from a few government schools, the Education Department left "native education" almost entirely in the hands of the missions, which were so powerful in East Africa that the evolutionary biologist Julian Huxley, who became an expert on imperial education, labeled them a "de facto Third Estate."

While the missions helped legitimize British imperial rule through their evangelical efforts, their schools served the equally important role of training the inexpensive African clerks, tradesmen, and skilled laborers that made indirect rule economically feasible. As the labor expert William Ormsby-Gore acknowledged: "The economic development of tropical Africa calls increasingly for Africans to man the railways, the motor lorries, to build, to carpenter, and to do a thousand things which are familiar to us and quite new and strange to the African."[36] At the same time, British administrators never forgot that Thomas Babington Macaulay's attempt to create a loyal western-educated class of Indians that was "English in taste, in opinions, in morals, and in intellect" helped produce the Indian National Congress. Anxious to avoid repeating that mistake in Africa, they sought to make Africans "better natives" by teaching them to respect manual labor and tribal chiefly authority instead of aspiring to be "black Europeans." As a babooist Tanganyikan official sneeringly observed: "Does anyone who sees the Europeanised African believe him to be genuine? Too often he seems only a caricature of a European and an insult to his own race."[37] The Colonial Office's Advisory Committee on Native Education in British Tropical Africa therefore embraced the southern American states' segregated industrial education model in the hope of training skilled laborers without also producing political agitators.

In Kenya, the Anglican and Presbyterian missions shared these views, but they were also reasonably committed to offering advanced schooling for at least some of their students. The Catholic Church and the heavily evangelical African Inland Mission, however, believed that their converts needed only a basic level of literacy to read the Bible. The resulting narrow educational pyramid denied African communities a political voice and ensured that they had to speak through chiefs and tribal representatives.

Comparatively speaking, the immigrant South Asian community was a much more serious threat to settler dominance in East Africa. Outnumbering Europeans by more than two to one in the interwar era, the approximately thirty-eight thousand Asians demanded equal political representation and permission to buy farms in the white highlands.[38] Although they had few legal rights, they had considerable economic influence in Kenya because long-standing and extensive commercial ties throughout the Indian Ocean allowed them to mobilize capital much more easily than the settlers could. They were the real driving force behind the growth of Nairobi, and a railway contractor named A. M. Jivanjee was one of the city's largest landowners in the 1920s.

The Asian challenge led the settlers to push for strict immigration limits and a formal declaration from the metropolitan government that Kenya was indeed a "white man's country." In doing so they overreached themselves, for the interwar Colonial Office was less sympathetic to their agenda. In 1923 the colonial secretary, Lord Devonshire, issued a white paper formally declaring that African interests in Kenya were "paramount" over those of both the British and Indian "immigrant races." The settlers were predictably outraged, and an extreme faction went so far as to hatch a ridiculous conspiracy for an armed uprising. They actually had little to worry about. Devonshire's declaration effectively blocked Asian expansion in Kenya, and a subsequent 1927 white paper affirmed the settlers' right to share in the "responsibilities of government" by declaring that Africans were best served by avoiding "clashes of interest" with the European community.

Assured that Kenya was a country for white men, the most ambitious imperial partisans dreamed of an East African Federation comprising Kenya, Uganda, and Tanganyika (the former German East Africa). Africans in the other two territories saw this as a bid by the Kenyan settlers for control of the entire East African highlands. "Natives" had no voice in high imperial policy, but the Ugandans and Tanganyikans were fortunate that the plan floundered with the depression.

Realistically, the imperial special interests were in no position to sustain an East African Federation. Large plantations on the coast brought the Kenyan government some revenue through export tariffs, but the neomercantilist nature of the new imperialism effectively ruled out industrial development in the colony. The Colonial Office blocked a bid by Asian entrepreneurs to build a textile mill, to ensure it did not compete with metropolitan weavers, and most manufacturing enterprises involved the production of soap, flour, fats, jam, tobacco, and beer for local consumption. The Magadi Soda Ash Company, which was Kenya's only viable export industry, needed a subsidized railway branch line simply to stay in business. In many years the metropolitan Treasury had to help balance the colony's budget, which demonstrated that the British government had made a particularly poor investment in choosing the settlers to drive Kenya's economic development. Most were inept farmers who spent most of their income on creature comforts instead of improving production. They depended on short-term loans to finance future plantings but had difficulty establishing good credit because speculation drove the value of their land beyond its actual capacity.

High production costs meant that the settlers needed protective tariffs, reduced railway rates, and extremely cheap labor to remain competitive. Securing abundant supplies of African labor was the most viable of the three strategies, for the Congo Basin Treaty limited the Kenyan government's ability to restrict trade. Furthermore, the Uganda government refused to pay higher freight costs on imports to subsidize Kenyan exports. The settlers therefore returned to the prewar strategy of trying to turn their political influence to extractive ends. In addition to demanding government assistance in labor recruiting, they also wanted higher African taxes, restrictive employment laws, and permission to forcibly discipline their workers.

While the Kenyan imperial authorities were sympathetic, coerced labor in any form was politically indefensible in interwar Britain. In 1919, settler leaders convinced Governor Sir Edward Northey to issue a series of circular orders directing district officers to "exercise every possible lawful influence" in pushing African men, women, and even children to "come out into the labour field." The first and most controversial circular warned that the government would have to resort to "special methods" if particular communities did not produce sufficient numbers of workers. Intense metropolitan criticism forced Northey to issue a follow-up order clarifying that he did not expect government officials to recruit labor directly for private employers. Instead he increased the African poll tax from ten shillings to sixteen and pointed out that while "no actual force can be employed to compel a man to go out to work, he can, however, be made to pay his tax." The unspoken assumption in this statement was that defaulters would work for the settlers. Finally, the governor took the particularly controversial step of making wage labor a greater priority than work on African peasant farms, which raised the risk of famine in many communities.[39] Northey, who, as a native-born South African, was particularly sympathetic to settler interests, was uncompromising in removing district officers who balked at implementing the circulars.

The Conservative imperial enthusiast Leopold Amery defended Northey's actions in Parliament by claiming that they would save East Africans from dying out like the Amerindians and Polynesians. This argument carried little weight with the humanitarian lobby. While this coalition of missionaries, antislavery activists, liberal civil servants, and socialists generally agreed with Northey that Africans should work, they absolutely rejected the concept of forced labor. Frank Weston, the Anglican bishop of Zanzibar, was one of the most uncompromising critics, and his scathing attack on the Kenyan labor policies entitled *The Serfs of Great Britain* helped push the Colonial Office to order Northey to issue a new circular spelling out greater protections for African laborers.

The Kenyan authorities had better luck defending the Registration of Natives Ordinance, which required all African men and boys over the age of fifteen to carry a special labor passport, known as a *kipande* (piece, slip) in Swahili, that recorded their fingerprints, tribal origins, biographical data, and employment record. Carried in a metal case worn around the neck, the *kipande* was one of the great innovations in the history of empire. For once, an imperial power had a viable way to keep track of rural people, and the *kipande* made it much harder for individuals to resist or evade oppressive policies by blending into a nameless subject majority. Men traveling outside their reserves had to supply it to any policeman or district officer on demand, and the chief registrar of natives kept a duplicate copy of each certificate, thereby making it possible to identify a man by his fingerprints.

Most significant, the system kept wages down because workers could not find a new job unless their previous employer signed off on their *kipande*. The most abusive settlers kept their laborers in virtual bondage by refusing to do so. Men who broke their contracts faced legal sanction, and the government made it easy for employers to prosecute them with a "Complaint of Desertion of Registered Native" form. The Kenyan authorities issued more than one million labor registration certificates by the end of the 1920s and charged roughly ten thousand men per year with *kipande* violations. Those who destroyed or tried to forge the certificates faced stiff fines and three months in jail.

Africans, understandably, detested the system. They found the fingerprinting demeaning and compared the metal *kipande* case and neck strap to a dog collar. Harry Thuku, a mission-educated telephone operator, fanned this widespread anger to organize the first mass African political resistance to imperial rule. Using popular discontent over wage cuts, high taxes, settler land seizures, and most particularly the *kipande* system as catalysts, he founded the East Africa Association (EAA) in 1921. The Association claimed to be nonpolitical, but it challenged the government's unqualified support for the settlers. Thuku audaciously held public meetings where women and girls recounted rapes on settler farms, and he called on people to turn in their *kipandes* en masse for delivery to the governor. The authorities found this sort of organized opposition intolerable. In 1922, the Kenyan police arrested Thuku for subversion and forcibly broke up a crowd that gathered to demand his release. In doing so they injured twenty-five and killed Mary Nyanjiru. By all accounts, she was of common origins, but her death and the mass protest forced the government to reduce the poll tax from sixteen shillings to twelve and address some of the worst labor abuses. However, the imperial regime refused to acknowledge that it had bowed to African pressure, and it tried to cover up the riot and Mary Nyanjiru's death by exiling Thuku and shutting down his association.

Banning the EAA appeared to smother the *kipande* protests, but the Kenyan authorities did not understand that simmering tensions in the countryside were the greatest threat to British rule. By the 1920s, many of the twenty-four separate native reserves, which covered more than forty-six thousand square miles, had become considerably overcrowded and eroded. With average population growth rates ranging from 1 to 2 percent per year, it was only a matter of time before they lost the capacity to support subsistence agriculture. Conditions were most severe in the three Kikuyu districts of Nyeri, Kiambu, and Fort Hall (Murang'a), where population densities of roughly 280 people per square mile forced up to three-quarters of the able-bodied men in some localities to leave home in search of work. The strain was almost as intense in the densely populated Luo and Luhya reserves in western Kenya, where between one-quarter and one-half of the adult men also became labor migrants.[40] Population pressure, land shortages, commercialized agriculture, and class formation were far more effective than the Northey circulars in forcing poorer Africans to work.

Many of these people, however, went to Nairobi, Mombasa, and corporate plantations instead of the white highlands. Unable to offer decent wages, the settlers had to court laborers by giving them permission to raise their own crops and cattle on the vast unused portions of their farms. Under Kenyan law, these were supposed to be contract workers, but by 1930 there were approximately 120,000 of these "squatters" permanently occupying 20 percent of the land in the highlands. Ironically, some were working land that had belonged to their families in the preconquest era. This squatter system was cheap but inefficient. Exploiting African peasant production was hardly a mark of progressive agricultural development, and the settler farm was more of a "feudal estate" than a capitalist enterprise.[41]

Seeking greater dignity and autonomy, some landless people understandably preferred "trespassing" in the native reserves of other tribes to squatting or working for Europeans. This illegal migration had the added benefit of providing an escape from chiefly supervision and taxation. In effect, it was a way to cease being a tribesman. For the Kikuyu, the nearby Maasai reserve was a tempting destination. Covering almost fifteen thousand square miles of prime agricultural land, it had a population density of just three people per square mile. The approximately forty thousand Maasai held title to such a vast swath of territory by virtue of a pair of treaties with the IBEAC that were a legacy of their participation in the conquest of the highlands.[42] These treaties barred the Kenyan government from redrawing their tribal boundaries to relieve population pressure in the most overcrowded regions on either side of the Rift Valley. District officers were legally bound to send interlopers back to their reserves, where they had little chance of competing with the chiefs and mission school graduates who had already appropriated the best land.

Although they were the privileged elite of the reserves, these chiefly and educated intermediaries also disliked being treated like imperial subjects and bitterly resented the settlers' dominance of the white highlands. In 1925, a more aggressive younger generation of Kikuyu took control of Thuku's East Africa Association and transformed it into the Kikuyu Central Association (KCA). Although the chiefs tended to distrust the mission-educated men of the KCA, almost every Kikuyu shared a deep antipathy toward the reserve system. For this reason, many of the imperial regime's most important allies quietly backed the association's decision to send Jomo Kenyatta to London in 1929 to petition the British Parliament for relief from oppressive land and labor policies.

The metropolitan authorities refused to even consider the KCA's appeal on the technicality that it did not come through the Kenyan government. Nevertheless, pressure from the humanitarian lobby forced the Colonial Office to create a special commission to investigate Kenya's ethnically based land policies. Although British officials had no sympathy for the KCA, the environmental degradation of the North American dust bowl and rapid African population growth raised the prospect that the agricultural foundation of the tribal economies might collapse, thereby rendering the entire system of indirect rule unsustainable. The Kenya Land Commission's main concern was to protect the settlers' claim to the highlands by repairing the native reserve system. Its report ruled that the reserves were sufficient for the needs of Kenya's tribes, but it recommended an ambitious conservation and development program to increase the carrying capacity of African land. Acknowledging the growing African land hunger, the commissioners called only for a small revision of the tribal boundaries as well as opening some marginal parts of the forest reserves for African settlement.

In defending the racial and ethnic division of land in the colony, the Land Commission gave the government sanction to begin expelling surplus squatters from the highlands. While they needed some Africans to work their land, by the 1930s the settlers were growing increasingly anxious about the size of squatter families on their farms. Coming to the realization that the generation of Kikuyu growing up in their midst was essentially colonizing the white highlands, the Kenyan authorities began a program of forced relocation that sent tens of thousands people back to the already overcrowded reserves on the premise that improved soil conservation would open more land for them.

This entirely unrealistic assumption demonstrated the imperial regime's commitment to favoring the interests of the European minority over those of its African subjects. The settlers' entrenched privileges subjected the African population of Kenya to an unprecedentedly burdensome form of imperial subjecthood. Ancient

Britons, medieval Iberians, early modern Andeans and Bengalis, and perhaps even Napoleon's Italian subjects would have recognized the basic template of the new imperialism's extractive policies. Imperial tribute took many forms throughout history, but its ultimate origin was always subject labor. This remained the case in British Kenya. What was really new about the Kenyan experience of empire was the biologically determined racism of the new imperial regime. Although earlier empires were equally, if not more, violent, they did not see their subjects as fundamentally and irredeemably inferior. Romanization was an avenue to imperial citizenship, Iberians converted to Islam, and at least some Andeans and Bengalis stood a reasonable chance of blending into the imperial ruling class during the early modern era. Indeed, even Napoleon held out the possibility of assimilation through *amalgame*. In the modern era, however, Kenyans were permanently inferior and at the mercy of the politically connected settler class.

Few of the young Britons staffing the lowest levels of the imperial administration in the interwar era were willing to stand up to the settlers, but at least they believed in the new imperialism's civilizing rhetoric. Nevertheless, they still spent most of their time traveling about their districts collecting taxes, recruiting labor, and supervising the chiefs. Their superiors in Nairobi expected them to do little more than maintain law and order while keeping revenue flowing. Just as Napoleon measured his prefects by their ability to extract tribute, the Kenyan district officer's reputation turned on tax collection. Terence Gavaghan was frank in his recollection of the unpleasant realities of wringing wealth from a poor and marginalized peasantry. "In itself the extraction of cash, often at the cost of sale of small stock, from people in bare subsistence, was unedifying and burdensome. It was also a tedious and grubby task."[43] Gavaghan's Roman, Umayyad, Spanish, and Napoleonic peers would have agreed with these sentiments. Yet in the Kenyan case tax collection generated embarrassingly small returns, and the real mission of Gavaghan and his colleagues was to drive Africans into the labor market.

Under the principles of indirect rule, the day-to-day responsibility for imperial administration fell to the chiefs rather than district officers. While it is tempting to view the Kenyan chiefs as the equivalents of the Andean *kurakas*, Bengali *zamindars*, and other earlier imperial intermediaries, the "native authorities" in British Kenya had far less power than their predecessors. Some had influence before the conquest, but the vast majority were imperial functionaries who drew their status from the Kenyan state. Many were ambitious men who had made themselves useful to the IBEAC. Others were former enemies, such as Koitalel's oldest son, Lelimo, who made their peace with the new regime. But in all cases, the key qualification for being a chief was outward obedience and the ability to enforce imperial policy. Although they claimed that "native custom" was the basis of indirect rule, British officials often simply invented new traditions to justify investing their allies with chiefly authority. Thus, the Luhya paramount chief Mumia acquired a cloak with a grandly embroidered fringe and a silver-topped baton as symbols of his office. These trappings fooled no one, and ultimately the chief's day-to-day power rested on the tribal police force and, by extension, the imperial regime.

Like most imperial rulers, however, the Kenyan authorities were actually poor patrons, and it was quite difficult to be a tribal chief. The British expected their proxies to assist in tax collection, maintain order, produce labor, and stifle political opposition. These were unpopular measures, and the inherent weakness of the imperial state meant that "native authorities" needed at least some measure of local support to govern effectively. But the chief who tried to be too popular by protecting his constituents faced replacement. As a British official admitted: "Either they had to work in our interests and risk unpopularity which in their un-natural position was fatal to them, or they had to side with their people against us and thus become the instruments of their subjects while they pretended to help us. Most of them tried to do both and failed all around."[44]

Those who managed this difficult balancing act reaped considerable dividends. By the interwar era, the chiefs earned annual salaries of up to eighteen hundred shillings at a time when an unskilled laborer was lucky to make two hundred shillings in a year.[45] Moreover, the chiefs' control of the native courts and tribal police created ample opportunities for graft and corruption. They could also manipulate young district officers, who rarely developed a conversational command of African languages. The chiefs further dominated the local native councils that managed tribal finances in the most politically active reserves. As virtual tyrants in their locations, with the privilege of defining custom and tradition, they could punish rivals and claim what was supposedly communal tribal land for themselves. Many Kikuyu chiefs used this land to grow cash crops and invested their earnings in businesses and education for their children.

The Kenyan government's insistence on treating Africans as primitive tribesmen legitimized and masked the chiefs' self-serving individualism. Assuming that African identities were exclusively collective, the imperial authorities would deal with Africans only as members of tribal communities. Common Africans understandably often found these designations limiting and oppressive, but the realities of the native reserve system meant that they had to accept their tribal status to gain access to land. The imperial authorities pretended that the reserves belonged collectively to the tribe and claimed that private land tenure was a western innovation with no precedent in native custom. In the 1920s, the Kenyan supreme court went so far as to rule officially that the Kikuyu in particular had no individual land rights. Arguing that privatization would create an exploitive landlord class, fragment the most productive land, and encourage social conflict, government officials repeatedly rejected petitions by wealthy Kikuyu for title deeds.

Profoundly suspicious of any practice or institution that might lead to "detribalization," the Kenyan government discouraged class formation and individualism. District officers and missionaries ridiculed Africans wearing western clothing, and the Education Department refused to let the mission schools teach in English on the grounds that, as one Colonial Office study put it, "tribal vernaculars" strengthened "the moral sanctions that rest on tribal membership."[46] In other words, peasant farmers did not need English, and European employers could use a simplified form of Swahili (popularly known as "ki-settler"), consisting largely of common objects and commands, to communicate with African workers. The Kenyan education authorities further mandated that government and mission schools teach an adapted curriculum that combined vocational training with tribal culture. They hoped that these measures would preserve the integrity of an imagined classless tribal society.

This imperial fiction was impractical and unsustainable given the social and economic realities of the new imperialism. The primary purpose of the native reserve system was to produce cheap African labor, not protect the viability of tribal society. The overcrowded Kikuyu reserves became particularly tense in the interwar era as family and clan members vied with each other to claim the most productive land. The stakes in these contests were high. Those who could control land and labor could produce lucrative cash crops for sale in nearby Nairobi or for export to the wider world via the railway. Although most of these entrepreneurs were Christians, their wealth enabled them to marry multiple wives. This meant that younger men, who could not afford to marry, faced the prospect of perpetual bachelorhood. Some worked for wealthy men, but the majority become labor migrants or squatters.

Those Africans who ventured outside their home reserves entered a world where Europeans enjoyed unquestioned preeminence and privilege. Asserting that there were no racial distinctions in Kenya law, the imperial regime claimed that the Europeans' preeminence in the colony stemmed from their superior civilization rather than their race. This fatuous assertion allowed the settlers to use their control of the local legislative process to create a formidable system of racial discrimination and segregation. Not only did this "colour bar" make it illegal for Africans to live permanently in the cities and the highlands, it also followed the American model of social segregation by banning them from European hospitals, hotels, bars, schools, and churches. The settlers even rejected the Carnegie Foundation's offer to build a free library in Nairobi because it would have been open to Africans, albeit through a separate door.

The settlers' nearly total dependence on cheap and plentiful subject labor made the colour bar supremely hypocritical. Real segregation would have bankrupted them and destroyed the greatest perquisites of empire. In addition to tending the settlers' crops and building their cities and towns, Africans also looked after the settlers' personal whims. By the end of the 1930s, there were more than eight thousand African domestic servants in Nairobi alone. Under Kenyan law these butlers, cooks, nurses, and nannies were the only natives eligible for permanent residence in European areas, and most settler' houses included extensive servant quarters. Western children led such an exceedingly privileged life that the imperial authorities actually became concerned that the boys would lapse into sloth and degeneracy.

The settlers worried even more about how life in imperial Africa would affect their wives and daughters. Imagining that western women were the embodiment of civilization and virtue, they believed that they needed constant protection, particularly from sexually rapacious native men. Most African household servants in Kenya were male, which meant they were a source of both domestic comfort and danger. Although they obsessed about this "black peril," the settlers would not give up the luxury of having Africans cook and clean for them. These gendered racial biases placed an enormous burden on western women to uphold the prestige of the settler class. Lord Cranworth cautioned that only the right kind of women who could learn when it was the "right time to have a servant beaten" should settle in Kenya, and any white woman caught in a voluntary "unlawful carnal connection with a native" faced up to five years in prison. Settler men were informally exempt from the ban on cross-cultural sex. Although the Colonial Office circulars banned conjugal relations with Africans, Terence Gavaghan's immediate superiors suggested that he take a mistress to help him polish his conversational Swahili. Too junior to attract the attention of a settler's daughter, he credited a series of African women with tutoring him in the "intricacies of sex."[47]

Gavaghan was free to indulge himself in the reserves, but Nairobi was supposed to be a safe and segregated bastion for European women. On paper, it was an exclusively white city, but this was never the case. In 1926 its population of roughly thirty thousand was approximately 60 percent African, 30 percent South Asian, and only 10 percent European. The vast majority of the African population lived in informal "villages" that the Nairobi municipal council refused to recognize as legitimate settlements. While these urban equivalents of rural "locations" in the reserves lacked even the most basic amenities, they offered refuge from taxation and the vagrancy laws that made it illegal for Africans to live permanently in the city. They were also good places to discuss politics, market produce from the reserves, and fence goods stolen from settler houses because they were largely outside the authority of the chiefs, district officers, and police. Crime was a problem in Nairobi from its earliest days, and in the 1920s African burglars had learned to break open safes, avoid leaving fingerprints, and escape in automobiles.

The municipal authorities therefore tried frantically to stamp out unauthorized African settlements and pulled down an average of thirty to forty illegal dwellings each week. But by the early 1920s, they had to accept the African "locations" of Pumwani and Kariokor (on the site of the old Carrier Corps depot) as permanent neighborhoods.

They could also do nothing about Kibera, a location that began as a settlement of discharged Sudanese veterans of the King's African Rifles. This did not, however, mean that they provided these African settlements with water, sewage, or other basic amenities.

The Nairobi municipal council justified this policy of malignant neglect on the grounds that Africans were temporary labor migrants who would eventually return to homes and families in the reserves. Apart from a small percentage of nurses and nannies, the logic of the colour bar also dictated that urban Africans were to be almost exclusively male. This freed employers from having to pay the higher wages needed to support a family in the city and allowed them to house their workers in simple barracks. The municipal authorities never could enforce these provisions, but their single-sex residence policies meant that the ratio of men to women in Nairobi was approximately eight to one by the end of the 1930s. The humanitarian lobby worried that this imbalance would lead to crime and vice, but more pragmatic government officials believed that a small number of prostitutes could tend to the migrants' needs.

The relatively few young African women who settled in Nairobi endured the indignities of urban imperial life because the cities provided an escape from the reserves, where the imperial regime rewarded the chiefs by backing their authority over tribeswomen. Some female migrants did work as prostitutes, but others provided rooms, home-brewed alcohol, and other basic domestic services. Although these arrangements made the government's gendered labor policies more bearable, the end result was a surge in rootless young people who swelled Nairobi's informal economy by the end of the interwar era. Worried that this "urban crowd" would follow political agitators like Harry Thuku, the municipal authorities finally admitted the necessity of allowing Africans to bring their families to the city.

The imperial regime's inability to keep the settled areas "white" exposed its inherent weakness. Illegal urban migration was just one of many strategies that Africans of all walks of life used to lessen the weight of the new imperialism. Lacking the means to resist openly, local communities took advantage of the Kenyan government's inability to govern them directly. A profusion of labor unrest and strikes in the late 1930s hinted at the potential of collective action, but in the interwar era vagrancy, trespassing, cattle rustling, prostitution, moonshining, and burglary were the most sensible and effective survival strategies for common people.

This was in contrast to the small handful of converts and mission school graduates whose mastery of western culture and English literacy qualified them for relatively lucrative careers as teachers, clerks, and interpreters. Free from the need to trespass in foreign reserves or live by their wits in the informal urban economy, they used the legitimizing ideologies of the new imperialism to attack the racist underpinnings of the Kenyan state. In founding their independent churches and schools, they sought to break the link between Christianity, western culture, and imperial authority by demonstrating that they too were a civilized people. The independent church movement first took hold among the Luo and Luhya communities before World War I and then spread to the Kikuyu reserves in the interwar period. Beginning with debates over the translation and interpretation of the Bible, independency rapidly became a moral and political force. Ultimately, the converts imagined a new African Christian society freed from the condescension of the missions and the political dominance of the settlers, but in the short term they wanted the freedom to conduct their own baptisms, marriages, and other religious rituals.

The Kikuyu independents in particular rejected Anglican and Presbyterian attacks on their culture and established a series of breakaway churches in the early 1920s. The confrontation came to a head in 1929 over the missionaries' insistence that their converts renounce female circumcision. Galvanized by Jomo Kenyatta's eloquent defense (if not reinterpretation) of Kikuyu tradition, large numbers of Kikuyu deserted the missions for these new churches. Many converts returned in time, but the independent churches remained viable. In the mid-1930s, church elders brought in an archbishop of the African Orthodox Church in South Africa named Daniel William Alexander to ordain their clergymen. The Kenyan police's Criminal Investigation Division kept the "coloured" Archbishop under surveillance, and the missions refused to recognize his baptisms and ordinations.

Despite these obstacles, Alexander's work legitimized the Kikuyu independent churches and, more important, their schools. In many ways, African demands for formal education lay at the root of the independence movement. At a time when schooling offered the best chance to escape the imperial regime's unyielding labor demands, African parents were immensely frustrated that the Kenyan government provided school spaces for only about thirty thousand of their children at the close of World War I.[48] This meant that just over 1 percent of the nearly three million Kenyan Africans had access to the "civilizing" western education that was a central ideological prop of the new imperialism. Even worse, there were only several hundred secondary school places for Africans.

This explains the school building boom in the Kikuyu reserves in the years before the Second World War. In 1936, the Education Department estimated that the independent institutions had enrollments of over five thousand students. Kenyan officials would have preferred to close them down, but they lacked the legal authority. While they probably could have an invented an excuse to do so, it would have been difficult to explain to the humanitarian lobby why teaching English, Christianity, and western values constituted an illegal act. At a time when modern communication gave the metropolitan government and general public the means to exercise unprecedented oversight over the wider empire, the imperial authorities had to appear to make good on their legitimizing rhetoric by giving their subjects at least some access to western culture and education.

The Kenyan government did not grasp the potential power of independence because its district officers still believed most Africans thought tribally and locally. The imperial authorities did not understand that discriminatory and oppressive land and labor policies and the inherent racism of the colour bar inspired Africans to imagine a larger, potentially violent, collective response to the imperial regime. In 1938, Jomo Kenyatta, the future president of Kenya, issued the prophetic warning that his fellow subjects were beginning to realize that it would take united action, if not force, to regain their freedom. Appropriating the imperial terminology of "the African," he cautioned that "he realises that he might fight unceasingly for his own complete emancipation; for without this he is doomed to remain the prey of rival imperialisms, which in every successive year will drive their fangs more deeply into his vitality and strength."[49]

Confident in their power, neither the metropolitan British government nor the Kenyan imperial regime paid much attention to Kenyatta's threat. Even as war with Germany loomed, most Britons still assumed that the empire would last for centuries. As Britain recovered from the depression, the African territories seemed particularly secure. Brushing aside the economic failures of the interwar era, the imperial lobby still promised to provide protected markets, new frontiers for settlement, and military manpower for the coming war. While some contemporary imperial sympathizers argue that the Colonial Office developed plans to train subject peoples for self-rule in the late 1930s, no one in official or unofficial imperial circles ever really imagined dismantling the empire at this point.

British officials optimistically believed that they could fix the imperial system to make it more acceptable to their subjects. On this score they were willing to grant non-Europeans a measure of self-government so long as they remained within the overall umbrella of the empire. In India, the first elections under the new Government of India Act gave the Indian National Congress control of India's provinces and most of its central administration in 1937. But loosening their hold on the Raj only made the British government more committed to retaining the rest of the empire. In 1938, the Colonial Office launched an ambitious new development initiative that promised to make good on the imperial lobby's grand promises about the mutual benefits of empire building. Its Colonial Development and Welfare Act of 1940 earmarked five million pounds per year for the development of "any colony or the welfare of its people." To a large degree, this was an answer to critics who equated the most oppressive and racist aspects of the new imperialism with Nazi fascism.

The realities of the Second World War postponed these development initiatives and forced Britain to instead make heavy demands on the empire. The wartime government implemented uncompromising extractive policies that wrung food, raw materials, manpower, and capital out of its remaining imperial territories around the world. Britain reasserted direct control over the Raj after the Indian National Congress withdrew from the government to protest its unilateral decision to draw India into the war with Germany. Putting aside the power-sharing compromises of the 1930s, British officials committed more than two million Indian men and 286.5 million pounds' worth of Indian goods to the imperial war effort and obligated the Raj to pay the operating costs of Indian Army units serving abroad. Common Indians paid the price for these contributions in the form of heavy manpower demands, higher taxes, and widespread food shortages.

By comparison, the war was a boon to the Kenyan settlers. Japanese conquests in the Far East eliminated much of their competition and the increased global demand for food and raw materials opened new markets and drove up prices. In 1941, Kenya and the other East African territories assumed primary responsibility for supplying British forces during the North African campaign. Never before had Kenya's exports been so profitable, but these factors alone did not account for the European community's sudden prosperity. African farmers were still much better equipped to produce for the global market, and the settlers remained hamstrung by inefficiency and high labor and transport costs. Wartime emergency measures made the Colonial Office much less likely to intervene to protect African interests, which gave the Kenyan government the opportunity to expand subsidies and price supports for European agriculture. Settler leaders also maneuvered Kenyan officials into buying their maize at nearly twice the African rate on the grounds that peasant farmers had lower production costs and should be discouraged from overplanting to protect the soil. In practice, speculators bought African maize for resale at the higher European rate and manipulated mandatory livestock auctions in the reserves to do the same thing with African cattle.

The imperial special interests also secured cheap African labor by convincing the government to classify their enterprises as "essential undertakings." While this designation was supposed to apply only to strategically important sectors of the economy, the Kenya authorities broadened its definition to include the production of tea, coffee, and virtually anything else that could grow in the white highlands. The essential undertakings legislation also allowed the settlers to requisition conscripted civilian laborers. Pressure from metropolitan Britain forced the Kenyan government to revise these rules in 1943 to exclude some of the most embarrassing abuses, but not before the settlers made windfall profits. Conversely, although some African farmers also benefited from rising wartime prices, in 1943 food exports and a labor shortage brought on by civil conscription and military recruiting caused widespread famine in many reserves.

Britain paid a political price for asking so much of its subjects during the war. Although Winston Churchill insisted that the 1941 Atlantic Charter, which affirmed that all peoples had the right of national self-determination, applied only to Nazi-occupied Europe, British imperial subjects thought otherwise. Others concluded that an Axis victory was their best hope for emancipation, and some West Indian movie audiences cheered newsreels reporting Allied defeats. Similar sentiments prevailed in Asia, where more than thirty thousand

Indian prisoners of war and deserters fought for the Japanese in Subhas Chandra Bose's Indian National Army. In 1942 and 1943, India itself experienced the worst outbreak of violent opposition since the 1857 mutiny when anti-imperial groups attacked post offices, train stations, and other government installations. The Raj responded to Gandhi's even more damaging nonviolent Quit India movement by jailing him and the rest of the Indian National Congress leadership. There were no comparable outbreaks of violence in Kenya, but the government took no chances and jailed the leaders of the Kikuyu Central Association on the trumped-up charge of conspiring with the Italians in Ethiopia.

These draconian measures bought the empire time, but the British government recognized that it would have to give its subjects a stronger reason to support the Allied war effort. In 1942, Sir Stafford Cripps, the leader of the House of Commons, offered the Indians full dominion status or some alternative form of complete autonomy within the British Commonwealth, which suggested an empire of consent rather than coercion. One year later, the secretary of state for the colonies made a broader pledge to guide all "colonial peoples along the road to self-government within the framework of the British Empire."[50] Imperial officials tried to qualify and retreat from these statements after the war, but there was no denying that peace would bring significant change to the empire.

This was apparent even in metropolitan Britain, where the Labour Party's victory in the 1945 elections testified to a general weariness with the war and the expense of empire. The British public wanted rapid demobilization, jobs, heat, and housing, and most people were unwilling to expend precious resources on retaining India or any other imperial territory by force. While retreat from India would have been unthinkable in the interwar era, these sentiments reflected the reality that Britain no longer profited from the Raj. Metropolitan manufacturers had already lost their share of Indian markets, and wartime spending and borrowing meant that Britain actually owed India more than one billion pounds in 1946. Acknowledging these realities, British officials hoped to guide India's path to independence and shape its postimperial government. Instead, violent sectarian civil strife resulting from irreconcilable differences between the Hindu and Muslim communities forced Britain to withdraw its troops rapidly in 1947 and accept the partition of the Raj into India and Pakistan.

Most people in Britain recognized the necessity of Indian independence by this point, but the demise of the Raj gave imperial partisans an opening to make the case for retaining the rest of the empire. As Cold War tensions mounted, the Labour foreign secretary Ernest Bevin spoke of turning the remaining African and Asian territories into a "third force" as a global counterbalance to the United States and Soviet Union. More important, the economic problems of the postwar era gave the Labour government a powerful incentive to try once again to make the empire pay its promised dividends. Nearly six years of total war left the nation with a debt approaching three billion pounds just as the United States ended its lend-lease program. In what angry British officials termed a "financial Dunkirk," the American government forced Britain to ratify the Bretton Woods accord and eliminate its imperial trade barriers as a condition for further aid. Clement Attlee came to power on a platform of reconstruction, economic development, and social reform, but his government lacked the dollars to retire its debts and pay for imports of food and building materials. As a result, the British public faced greater shortages and deprivation in 1946 and 1947 than it had during the war years.

Many Britons therefore hoped that the imperial interests' promises about the value of the African territories might hold true. Several members of Attlee's government had been strong critics of the imperial excesses of the interwar years, but they believed that they could create a more humane and mutually beneficial system of imperial development now that they were in power. They assumed they could transform subject societies through central planning, mechanization, and the 120 million pounds that an enhanced Colonial Development and Welfare Act allocated for investment in the empire. Colonial secretary Arthur Creech Jones, a onetime Fabian socialist, spoke optimistically about raising living standards in the colonies, but the real purpose of postwar colonial development was to earn dollars for Britain.

To this end the Labour government initiated an ambitious program of development in Africa that was channeled largely through the new Colonial Development Corporation and other semiofficial enterprises. Blaming stunted African economies on the failure of free market capitalism, the Labourites believed that rational economic planning and state-sponsored investment could unlock the economic potential of the remaining empire. One of their biggest and most infamous projects was the sprawling Tanganyika groundnut scheme, which spent thirty-six million pounds planting peanuts on tracts of land equal in size to the state of Connecticut. Similarly, a massive irrigation program in the Sudanese al-Jazirah province aimed to produce vast quantities of cotton. The overall goal of these initiatives was to provide raw materials that would reduce shortages in Britain and earn dollars in North American markets.

To this end, state marketing boards bought African produce at below-market prices on the promise that the banked surplus would guarantee stable returns in good times and bad. Rising global demand for commodities meant that there were no price downturns in the immediate postwar era, thereby allowing the territorial governments to keep the African deposits in London, where they were available for Britain's postwar recovery. The returns from African agriculture led the Colonial Office's development experts to meddle even more deeply in local communities. Failing to realize that African farmers were already willing and able to produce for the global market, their modernizing initiatives often alienated the very people they aimed to help.

The Labour development initiative also did very little to actually promote economic diversification or industrial development in Africa. In Kenya, the Colonial Development Corporation invested half a million pounds to turn a mix of improvised wartime industrial projects into East African Industries Ltd. (EAL), a semipublic conglomerate producing bricks, ceramics, tiles, chemicals, and cooking fats. These were money-losing ventures, and Asian investors and entrepreneurs had far more success in setting up small-scale industries that processed locally produced raw materials. None of these enterprises, however, altered Kenya's neomercantile relationship with Britain, and restrictive investment and licensing regulations ensured that commodity exports remained the central basis of the colony's economy.

From 1945 to 1951, Britain put forty million pounds into the empire, which was a fraction of the figure promised under the revised Colonial Development and Welfare Act. Nevertheless, the Labour government's various programs netted 140 million pounds for the metropolitan economy. This was in spite of debacles such as the Tanganyika groundnut scheme, which yielded only nine thousand tons of produce—meaning that a pound of its peanuts cost more than seventeen hundred pounds.[51] The resulting scandal almost brought down the Labour government.

Most Africans, however, gave more than they got, and the Labourites' promises of mutual development proved ephemeral. As in the prewar era, British interests always came first. Metropolitan buyers had first call on building materials for reconstruction, and the African territories had to reduce consumption to keep their dollar earnings within the empire. These policies led to shortages, inflation, and greater state interference in the daily lives of African workers and farmers. The result was a wave of rural unrest and urban strikes that swept through British Africa in the postwar years. Most were over low wages and commodity prices, but the imperial authorities gradually recognized that they had the potential to mushroom into organized political resistance to British rule.

The Labour government's imperial experts naively believed that they could defuse this discontent by granting Africans a measure of local autonomy and reforming the most flagrantly abusive legal and social institutions. Certain that "the natives" were not ready for full independence, they promised to put their subjects on a gradual path to self-government. Creech Jones sought to replace indirect rule with a democratic system of local administration to bind educated Africans more closely to the imperial regime. Theoretically, qualified men would move from elected local bodies to seats on territorial legislative councils, which in time might become national parliaments as the colonies and protectorates evolved into autonomous entities within the Commonwealth. In the meantime, the Colonial Office directed district officers to be scrupulously courteous in their day-to-day dealings with African constituents and began to retire old Africa hands who, in the words of a new Colonial Service handbook, tended to like "primitive people but could not get on well with the educated native."[52]

Not surprisingly, none of these developments sat well with the Kenyan government or settlers. The old Africa hands remained firmly entrenched in the colony, and the postwar governor Sir Philip Mitchell believed that Kenya should develop along Rhodesian lines into a self-governing dominion. He consequently continued his predecessors' policies of encouraging additional settlement in the white highlands. As a result, migration spiked in the postwar era as a new generation of settlers swelled the European population of the colony to thirty thousand on the premise that it would continue to be a white man's country.

Governor Mitchell shared this assumption. Seeking to lay the groundwork for a potential East African dominion, in 1946 he implemented a new legislative system that replaced his Executive Council with an "elected member system." This gave settler leaders control of key government departments, which evolved into formal ministries. Thus, Major Ferdinand Cavendish-Bentinck, the informal head of the postwar settler community, acquired the important portfolio for agriculture, animal husbandry and natural resources. By comparison, a former schoolteacher named Eliud Mathu became the sole appointed African representative in the lower Legislative Council until three more nominated African councilors joined him later in the decade.

On the surface, these measures appeared to make the Kenyan imperial regime more secure than ever. Population growth in the reserves ensured that employers had no difficulty recruiting African workers at comfortably low wages. Wartime profiteering gave the settler farmers the resources to invest in tractors and other forms of mechanization, which made them far less reliant on squatter labor. Able to dispense with the old imperial tools of labor extraction, they now sought to wall themselves off from all Africans but their domestic servants. Under settler pressure, sympathetic government officials resumed the mandatory relocations of the 1930s and forcibly returned roughly one hundred thousand squatters to the Kikuyu reserves between 1945 and 1952. These rural slums were no less crowded than they had been in the interwar era, but agricultural and social welfare experts hoped to develop them though soil conservation measures and modern agricultural technologies so that they could hold more people. This was entirely unrealistic, but it provided political cover for the Kenyan government's pro-settler policies.

The Labour government's mandate to end overt racism in the empire made this window dressing necessary. In 1948, the Colonial Office ordered the colonial governors to produce confidential memorandums justifying legislation in their territories that might be viewed as discriminatory. Mitchell's report was telling. While it boasted that Kenya had increased direct African representation on the Legislative Council, reformed the *kipande* system, and allowed lawful marriage between Africans and Europeans, it stoutly defended legal segregation in the colony on the basis of unequal "civilization." Arguing that the British government's earlier declarations in support of white settlement in Kenya amounted to a formal pledge to the "European race," the governor insisted that any attempt to end the racial exclusivity of the highlands would be "regarded by all European inhabitants of the Colony as a serious breach of faith." Additionally, Mitchell maintained that laws requiring Africans to live in designated urban locations were not discriminatory because that was where they wished to live. He also claimed that vagrancy laws designed to prevent illegal migration to the cities primarily targeted "prostitutes and undesirables" and generally spared respectable people. Finally, and most hypocritically, he justified urban segregation as necessary to protect the health of the "non-native community" on the grounds that most Africans did not yet know how to follow the "elementary rules of hygiene."[53]

R. Mugo Gatheru, an inspector in the Public Health Department, agreed that conditions in the urban native locations were unsanitary, but he correctly laid the blame for this on the municipal authorities, which refused to provide African neighborhoods with water and other basic services. Citing a single public lavatory in Nairobi that was used by more than a thousand people and was little more than an irrigated trench, he offered this stomach-churning description of the consequences:

> The water system was always defective and the faeces, therefore, could not be flushed away. Having no alternative, people would then continue "easing" themselves until the trench was full up. They would then be forced to use every inch of the floor until it became impossible to get inside—this became increasingly difficult to gauge since there were not enough lights within. The tins and floors were a sickening sight, and there were flies everywhere. One could see long threads or rings of tapeworms on the faeces dropped by people who were suffering from them, an inevitable disease amongst those forced to live in such circumstances.[54]

Mitchell justified segregation on the grounds that the more advanced European race made better productive use of Kenya's resources, but this public health disgrace and, by extension, the overall conditions in the slums and reserves were a more accurate record of the imperial regime's civilizing accomplishments.

These realities contributed directly to the increasing African unwillingness to tolerate imperial subjecthood in the postwar era. While their resistance tended to be local and relatively uncoordinated before the war, land shortages, rising prices, unemployment, intrusive government regulations, and settler harassment were powerful incentives to think and act collectively. This became most evident in the strike that shut down the port of Mombasa in 1947 and a more serious general strike in Nairobi three years later. New African labor unions and the Kenya African Union (KAU), which began as an advisory body for African members of the Legislative Council, organized much of this opposition under Jomo Kenyatta's leadership.

The imperial authorities kept the KAU and the unions under close surveillance, but the independent Kikuyu churches, schools, and other less formal bodies were a more serious threat. In appearing to be apolitical and respectable, they provided cover for common people to discuss how to oppose oppressive imperial policies. Police informers reported that many had become radicalized, but the new postwar environment required the Kenyan government to prove that the independent congregations and schools had actually broken a law. With its capacity to rule authoritatively on the wane, the imperial regime used a network of spies and intelligence agents to monitor this opposition and relied on paramilitary police units and the King's African Rifles to cow potential rebels.

These were stopgap measures, and the Kenyan government's internal security systems failed entirely in the early 1950s when landless and unemployed young Kikuyu men fought back violently against the exploitation and injustices of British imperial rule. The bluff and intimidation that were the coercive linchpins of the new imperialism simply could no longer deter the enormous Kikuyu underclass, who had grown so desperate that they lost their fear of the imperial regime and its monopoly on lethal force. It is not clear when the Kikuyu squatters and slum dwellers first turned to violence, but the first indications that something was amiss appeared in the late 1940s, when the settlers started to notice hamstrung and mutilated cattle. The Kenyan authorities were slow to see the import of these developments, and they did not grasp the scope of the danger until the early 1950s, when the rebels assassinated the Kikuyu senior chief Waruhiu and massacred a handful of European families on remote farms. These murders threw the settlers into a panic, but as was the case with the Tupac Amaru revolt in the eighteenth-century Andean highlands, the guerrillas' primary targets were the elite members of their own community who appeared to prosper from cooperating with the imperial regime.

Operating from the cover of Nairobi slums and forested regions in the highlands, the rebels fielded a decentralized force of five thousand to six thousand men. Fighting in small bands, their primary weapons were homemade guns or firearms bought or stolen from the settlers and the army. A much larger group of civilian sympathizers supplied this armed faction with food and refuge. These people bound themselves to each other with a series of powerful oaths that had great weight in Kikuyu culture. The Kenyan authorities propagandistically depicted their vows as tribal, barbaric, and satanic, but in reality they were an effective means of countering the imperial regime's strategy of dividing the Kikuyu community. By the end of the conflict, it appears that almost every Kikuyu had taken at least one of these oaths, if for no other reason than to avoid retribution by the guerrillas. Only the most committed mission converts, senior chiefs, and government allies took the risky step of breaking openly with the rebellion.

The British referred to the guerrillas and their sympathizers as "Mau Mau," but the Kikuyu fighters called themselves the Kenya Land Freedom Army. The term *mau mau* had no actual meaning in any Kenyan language, but it allowed the imperial regime to further portray its opponents as barbaric tribesmen who turned to violence because they could not cope with the pressures of "modernity." In hindsight, the Mau Mau upheaval was actually a civil war waged between the imperial regime's enemies and allies in local Kikuyu communities throughout central Kenya. In this sense it resembled the 1809 mass outbreak of popular peasant violence that targeted Napoleon's local proxies in the mountain of northern Italy.

Tellingly, the Kenyan authorities were not much better at controlling the countryside than their Napoleonic predecessors had been. Lacking the ability to rule directly, they tried to tip the scales in favor of their Kikuyu allies by recruiting a Home Guard under the command of the chiefs to fight the rebels. They claimed that these units consisted of "loyalists" who rejected the barbarism of Mau Mau, but most guardsmen enlisted under duress and many were at least tacit supporters of the rebellion. Caught between these opposing forces, many common Kikuyu tried to remain neutral and joined the Home Guard or took an oath only when they had to. Most understandably wanted to avoid fighting their neighbors and kinsmen and hoped to escape the imperial regime's violent response to the uprising.

This was a sensible strategy. Caught off guard by the scope of the revolt, the Kenyan authorities declared a state of emergency, banned the Kenya African Union, and falsely convicted Jomo Kenyatta for being the sinister force behind the insurgency. They also had no option but to turn to the metropolitan government for aid because they did not trust their own African soldiers and policemen even though most were not Kikuyu. The British military had few resources to spare at a time when its forces were tied down in Korea, Malaya, and West Germany, but the entrenched communist insurgency in Malaya demonstrated that it was risky to take an anti-imperial revolt lightly. Winston Churchill, whose Conservative Party returned to power in 1951, had this in mind when he sent an entire British army brigade to Kenya one year later.

Taking over military operations in the colony, the regular army pursued an effective counterinsurgency strategy that isolated the forest fighters from the general population by encircling the regions where they operated. These tactics, particularly using starvation as a weapon, harked back to the pacification campaigns of the late nineteenth century. All told, the army's search-and-destroy operations killed approximately twenty thousand Kikuyu, many of whom were not necessarily armed combatants, and brought the military dimension of the Emergency to an end by 1956.

The Kenya Land Freedom Army lost for a number of reasons. Although modern Kenyan nationalism depicted the revolt as an inclusive popular uprising, most of Kenya's other communities refrained from taking an active role because they viewed it as a Kikuyu movement. In this sense, the imperial regime's tribal policies paid a dividend. Equally significant, the Kenyan government took the draconian step of incarcerating almost the entire Kikuyu population in a network of prison camps and strategic villages on the assumption that all Kikuyu were guilty until proven innocent. This hearkened back to Viceroy Don Francisco de Toledo's plan to force the entire subject population of the Andeans into regimented *reducciones*. In keeping with their own collectivist rhetoric, the Kenyan imperial authorities essentially indicted and convicted the entire Kikuyu "tribe." Only documented loyalists escaped the sweep that emptied the white highlands and urban areas of Kikuyu, and by 1955 there were roughly seventy thousand people in detention camps scattered around Kenya, with about one million more in new fortified villages.

The new imperialism's civilizing veneer required the Kenyan authorities to promise to "rehabilitate" these captive Kikuyu through a program of social welfare, manual labor, and invented tribal counteroaths to break Mau Mau's hold on their superstitious minds. This seemingly humane enterprise masked the naked brutality of the government's anti–Mau Mau operations. Although the guerrillas killed only thirty-two Europeans during the Emergency (more died in road accidents during the same period), the imperial regime responded to the revolt with a retributive fury that rivaled its predecessor's violent response to the 1857 Indian Mutiny. Facing the prospect of the mass tribal uprising that had long haunted their deepest fears, the settlers fought ferociously to defend their imperial and racial privileges. They exercised considerable control over the counterinsurgency and rehabilitation programs through the elected member system that gave them a dominant voice in the Executive and Legislative Councils. Additionally, their young men filled the ranks of the Kenya Police Reserve, the all-white Kenya Regiment, the detention camp staffs, and much of the KAR's officer corps. This gave them the means to terrorize the Kikuyu population through murder, beatings, rape, physical mutilation, and torture.[55]

The Kenyan authorities covered up the vast majority of these incidents and excused those that came to light as a natural consequence of the public outrage over the slaughter of settler families. This was a fraud for the government itself was also deeply involved in the abuses. The Kenyan police frequently tortured confessions out of Kikuyu suspects, and state witnesses openly perjured themselves at trials that sent more than one thousand convicted Mau Mau members and supporters to the gallows.[56] Taken with Jomo Kenyatta's sham trial, these cases made a mockery of the British legal tradition that was supposedly one of the imperial regime's civilizing gifts to the subject peoples of the empire.

In time, reports of these abuses appeared in the metropolitan press, thereby shaming the British government and undermining public support for the imperial regime. Galvanized by the events in Kenya, an anti-imperial humanitarian lobby of liberally minded members of Parliament, socialists, and evangelicals came together to call for an end to settler colonialism throughout the empire. To a large degree their criticisms echoed the popular revulsion over the behavior of the nabobs in Bengal nearly three centuries earlier, but the realities of the post–World War II era made the Kenyan imperial abuses far more embarrassing and unsustainable. It was impossible to reconcile the reports of torture coming out of East Africa with Article Seventy-six of the United Nations Charter, which committed Britain to putting its imperial subjects on the path "toward self-government or independence." Britain's record on this score became even more awkward as more and more former imperial territories joined the General Assembly and British Commonwealth as member nations after gaining their independence.

The metropolitan public found little reason to excuse the damage that the Kenyan fiasco did to Britain's national reputation, particularly after it became obvious that the new imperialism's promised returns were ephemeral. India, one of the last vestiges of the first British Empire, had been unquestionably profitable, but now it was gone. While exports from the remaining imperial territories helped generate dollar earnings after the war, the key factors in Britain's recovery were a grant from the Marshall Plan and the devaluation of the pound. By the mid-1950s, the wider empire bought just 13 percent of Britain's exports and supplied only 10 percent of its imports. Most territories ran up their own dollar deficits, which meant that they no longer played a role in supporting the pound.[57] With the empire becoming more of an obvious burden, many Britons began to ask whether they would be better served by joining the European Common Market than by wasting economic, diplomatic, and military resources trying to hold together the last vestiges of the empire.

Recognizing these realities, the Conservative governments of the 1950s adopted a pragmatic strategy of granting individual territories self-rule, followed by independence, on the condition that the new rulers respected British investments and remained within the western sphere of influence. Essentially, they sought to turn the clock back a century to revive the institutions of informal empire. Senior Colonial Office officials and later generations of imperial apologists tried to portray this retreat as part of a planned strategy, but their revisionism was really just an attempt to put the best face on events that had spun out of control. Moreover, the fiction of planned decolonization was plausible only in the Caribbean and West Africa, where there were no significant British expatriate populations. African majority rule in the settler-dominated territories in eastern and southern

Africa was a nonstarter because the British government had theoretically pledged that they would remain white.

In Kenya, the expense and international embarrassment of Mau Mau led metropolitan British officials to make limited concessions to buy time and win over moderate African leaders. Over the vehement objections of the settlers, who refused to share power under any terms, they offered non-Europeans a political role through constitutional "multiracialism." Continuing the imperial policy of granting rights to communities rather than individuals, multiracialism denied Africans a full vote on the grounds that they were not sufficiently advanced to qualify for the franchise. Contending that civilization was the basis of political representation, the Colonial Office drew up constitutions that granted voting rights only to propertied or educated Africans and allocated legislative seats based on disproportionate ethnic quotas. This ensured that Europeans outnumbered African representatives by a ratio of two to one.

The vast majority of Africans understandably detested multiracialism, and in 1957 most African legislative council members boycotted the first elections held under the new constitution. Despite this opposition, the Kenyan authorities believed that they could water down this resistance. Sensing that popular opposition to multiracialism was breaking down tribal boundaries, they looked to divide the subject majority on the basis of class. To this end, they endeavored to create a small cadre of landed elites through a radical policy shift that gave their allies, particularly the Kikuyu chiefs and loyalists, the means to acquire private land titles in the reserves. Theoretically, these prosperous commercial farmers would have a vested interest in supporting continued British rule in Kenya. In finally backing African agricultural development, the imperial planners hoped that the resulting surplus would drive industrial development, thereby reducing unemployment and relieving the colony's chronic land shortage. Hard-core settlers opposed these reforms to the very end, but more pragmatic government officials realized the colour bar was politically unsustainable. Buoyed by an entirely unrealistic War Office plan to develop Kenya into a major military base in the late 1950s, they hoped to win enough African support to push back the day when they might have to enfranchise the subject majority.

The metropolitan authorities did not actually have an explicit plan to abandon the empire at this point, and it is possible that British rule in Africa might have lasted longer had it not been for the 1956 Suez crisis. The United States' opposition to the British, French, and Israeli plot to undo Gamal Abdel Nasser's nationalization of the canal by reoccupying the Canal Zone under the guise of a peacekeeping mission was a powerful demonstration that the new imperialism was unsustainable in the Cold War era. Fearing that the Soviets would exploit the nonwestern world's near universal hostility to the Franco-British invasion, the American government forced Britain to withdraw by threatening not to support its application for a loan from the International Monetary Fund.

This humiliation drove Prime Minister Anthony Eden from office and brought Harold Macmillan to power. At a time when the French and Belgians were making plans to leave Africa and a new United Nations resolution called for full independence for subject peoples, Macmillan resolved that Britain would not be the last imperial power on the continent. To this end he told the South African parliament in 1960: "The wind of change is blowing through this continent, and, whether we like it or not, this growth of national consciousness is a political fact."[58] This declaration of Britain's intention to retreat from Africa was also a tacit admission that multiracialism had failed to blunt African demands for full citizenship, if not total independence. The Afrikaners were entirely unmoved by Macmillan's warning about the power of African nationalism and calculated that violent repression would keep them in power. Startled imperial officials in the rest of British Africa, however, found that true national independence was no longer a vague promise but an immediate reality.

In Kenya, the settlers complained indignantly that Macmillan had betrayed them, but they were swiftly losing their remaining support in metropolitan Britain. It cost the British taxpayer roughly fifty-five million pounds to rescue them from the Mau Mau uprising, and reports that jailors at the Hola detention camp had beaten at least ten Kikuyu prisoners to death touched off a public scandal that threatened Macmillan's majority in Parliament. Although the Conservative Party had a history of defending the empire, the Tories were now unwilling to risk their party's larger political fortunes by defending a privileged imperial elite. As one of the new younger generation of Conservative politicians told the settler leader Michael Blundell: "What do I care about the fucking settlers, let them bloody well look after themselves."[59]

Thus the wind of change swept through Kenya along with the rest of British Africa. Accepting that independence would come within a matter of years instead of decades, the Kenyan authorities hoped to turn over power to a friendly African regime that would respect British investment and guarantee the settlers' lives and property. At first they tried to accomplish this by allying with the leaders of the Kenya African Democratic Union's (KADU) minority communities. Sharing fears of domination by the more numerous Kikuyu and Luo peoples that constituted the Kenya African National Union (KANU), KADU cooperated with the British government in drafting a federal constitution that divided the new nation into seven autonomous tribally based regions under a weak central government. This would have meant that the settlers would have become simply another minority tribe with a constitutional guarantee of autonomy in the postimperial era. However, KADU won only 20 percent of the vote in the 1961 elections that chose a provisional government to guide Kenya to independence.

Although the settlers reviled him as the satanic force behind Mau Mau, Jomo Kenyatta proved to be the imperial regime's most useful African ally during this transitional period. Far from being a radical or socialist, as his critics suggested, he actually had closer ties through marriage and sentiment to the landed Kikuyu elite. He was also unquestionably innocent of the government's fabricated charges that sent him into detention and internal exile for almost a decade, but this inequity had the silver lining of sparing him from having to take sides during the Mau Mau civil war and established his credentials as a national hero. In August 1961, the authorities gave into the inevitable and released him. Although he claimed to be above politics, he won a landslide victory in the 1963 independence elections as the KANU candidate.

One of Kenyatta's first priorities on taking power on December 12, 1963, was to abolish the federal system, but in almost every other regard he proved surprisingly cooperative in working with his former imperial rulers. Declaring that all Kenyans had fought for independence, he passed over the former forest fighters and Mau Mau detainees in favor of influential ex-chiefs and loyalists when forming his new government. He made it clear that there would be no radical redistribution of land or wealth, committing Kenya to a program of capitalist development and emphasizing economic continuity and respect for private property. Most important from the settlers' perspective, Kenyatta agreed to buy at above-market rates the land of any farmer who wanted to sell and to welcome those who wanted to stay. Although international donors provided the means for some common people to acquire a share of the former white highlands, most of the former settler farms went to the president's wealthy allies.

Many of the supporters who had hailed Kenyatta as a champion of the poor and landless during the imperial era were terribly disappointed by these policies. They assumed that *uhuru* (freedom) would bring land by breaking up the great highland farms and create jobs by forcing Europeans and Asians to leave Kenya. Yet the neomercantilist economy that the postimperial government inherited from the former regime largely tied Kenyatta's hands. Admittedly, his first priority was to secure his own power base by rewarding his closest allies, but the new president had few resources to make good on the promises of independence. After the transfer of power, the emptiness of the new imperialists' avowed commitment to civilize and modernize Kenya became painfully clear as Kenyatta's government strove to turn an artificial imperial conglomeration into a viable nation-state. The legacy of the colour bar and the dismally inadequate imperial education system meant that there were only a handful of Africans with the skills to guide Kenya through this transitional period. The new nation similarly inherited the imperial regime's narrow industrial base, inadequate infrastructure, and bleak urban slums. These were the new British Empire's true legacies.

The rapid and largely unexpected demise of the imperial regime in Kenya reflected the unstable and contradictory nature of the new imperialism. While the emergence of powerful national identities in the nineteenth century suggested there would be no more empires in Europe, western technological and capitalist advances appeared to give empire building a new lease on life in regions in Africa and Asia where identities remained dangerously local. Westerners took their short-term political, economic, and military advantages over these communities as evidence of their own cultural superiority, but the quick and relatively easy victories that built the new empires were simply the result of the uneven advance of globalization around the world. A broader historical view, coupled with the economic rise of the nonwestern world in recent years, reveals the fallacy of the racial and cultural chauvinism that legitimized the new imperialism.

What was actually novel about the new imperial projects was that largely democratic liberal nation-states were their sponsors. The voting western European public considered themselves civilized and moral and would not tolerate a return to the excesses of earlier imperial eras. Consequently, the new imperialists had to disguise their base ambitions by promising to create humane liberal empires that would reform and uplift subject societies in addition to bringing wealth and national glory to the imperial metropole. This intrinsic hypocrisy, which required empire builders to denigrate their Africans and Asians so they could save them, was also an innovative feature of the new imperialism. Early generations of empire builders were equally certain of their cultural superiority, but they never really pretended that their conquests were for the good of their subjects. No one in early modern Spain really took the rhetoric of the conquistadors' *requerimiento* seriously. Even more troubling, the rigidity of national thinking meant that there was little possibility of romanization or *amalgame* in the new imperialism.

The Kenyan imperial state was one of most oppressive manifestations of the new imperialism. It grafted its deceitful legitimizing ideologies onto a highly exploitive model of the kind of old-style settler colonialism that destroyed the Amerindian and Aboriginal civilizations of North America and Australia. Dressing the East Africa Protectorate's pacification campaigns in the garb of liberal humanitarianism was bad enough, but the settlers' argument that they were civilizing the peoples of the highlands by exploiting their labor was simply disgusting. As one dubious official in the Colonial Office acidly noted: "Does anyone really believe in the educative value of labour on a European farm?"[60] The reality of the settlers' self-avowed goal of making Kenya into a "white man's" country turned Africans into a permanent underclass. To be sure, ancient Britons, medieval Iberians, and early modern Andeans and Bengalis faced a similar fate, but at least their imperial rulers made no attempt to disguise their extractive agenda.

In the end, the African territories paid some of the worst returns in the history of empire. Although the native reserve system ultimately proved effective in forcing Africans to accept extremely low wages, inexpensive unskilled labor was not worth very much in the modern industrial era. At best, coerced African labor helped the settlers compensate for their lack of capital, high transportation costs, and basic agricultural incompetence, but it was not a basis for sustainable development or even old fashioned imperial extraction. These economic realities were fairly typical of most new imperial territories.

It is therefore hardly surprising that the new empires of the late nineteenth century proved so ephemeral. Lasting less than a century, they were almost as short-lived as the aborted Napoleonic empire. The new British Empire in Africa that Frederick Lugard assumed would last for centuries fell apart once Africans acquired the means to mount an effective resistance by developing larger collective, if not proto-national, identities based on the common experience of abuse and a mutual hatred of the imperial regime. In explaining the ultimate collapse of the Kenyan imperial state, Michael Blundell candidly admitted: "It boiled down to whether the British Government could or would shoot Africans to maintain the status quo for Europeans."[61] Earlier generations of empire builders would have unflinchingly obliged the settlers by killing people, but the Kenyan imperial regime had to at least make a show of living up to its humanitarian obligations.

Even more fundamentally, the metropolitan British government was bound by the new imperialism's legitimizing ideologies. Seeking to defuse African and Indian nationalism in the post–World War II era, the Labour government assured subject peoples that they were full and equal citizens of the empire. Its 1948 Nationality Act put this promise into law and opened the way for first tens and then hundreds of thousands of West Indians and South Asians to take the low-paying menial jobs that were vital to Britain's postwar reconstruction. Many stayed on to enjoy the higher standards of living in the imperial metropole. Never imagining that empire building would have such a profound impact on their own politics and culture, xenophobic Britons responded with race riots in the 1950s and a series of discriminatory immigration laws that gradually closed the door to non-European members of the Commonwealth a decade later.

There is no such thing as a liberal empire. The "new" British Empire in Africa fell quickly once Africans acquired the means to expose its inherent weaknesses. Like all empire builders, the architects of British Africa grossly underestimated their subjects. In Europe, however, another band of conquerors once again plunged the continent into tragedy and chaos by making the same mistake. Few historians see Adolf Hitler as product of the new imperial era, but his genocidal attempt to create a continental empire took the logic of the new imperialism to its bloody but inevitable conclusion.

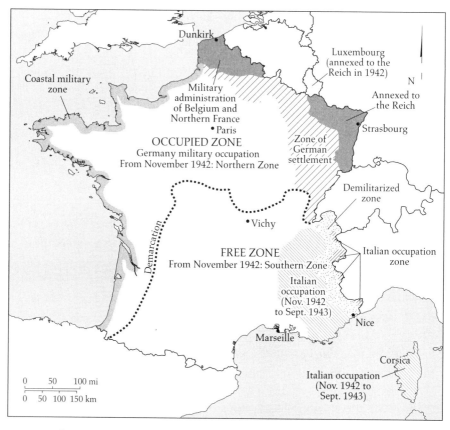

France during the Nazi Occupation

7

FRANCE UNDER THE NAZIS

Imperial Endpoint

In the summer of 1940, the French received a surprisingly unpleasant reminder of what it meant to become an imperial subject. After overrunning Poland and the Low Countries, Adolf Hitler's Nazi legions dealt them a crushing defeat that recalled the sudden and apocalyptic victories of earlier generations of empire builders. Although France was a global imperial power in its own right, it was vulnerable because a decade of economic decline and fratricidal infighting between left- and right-wing political factions left the nation unready for war. Moreover, many Frenchmen were determined to avoid being dragged into another continental conflict after the carnage of the First World War had demonstrated the devastating consequences of total war between "civilized" industrial nation-states.

Nevertheless, the French were aware of the Nazi threat and were hardly defenseless. With four and a half million men under arms and a modern air force and tank corps that rivaled the Germans', they had good reason to feel secure at the outbreak of the Second World War. The fall of France did not result from the pronounced military disparity that made the new imperialism in Africa and Asia feasible. The Nazis' advantage lay in their tactics and aggression, qualities that served earlier imperial conquerors well. While French strategists planned for the static trench warfare of an earlier era and concentrated on fortifying the border with Germany, the Nazi forces bypassed the Maginot Line entirely and invaded France through Luxembourg and Belgium. The French generals, who had assured themselves that German tanks could not operate in the Ardennes Forest, were caught flat-footed as Nazi armored columns backed by dive-bombers broke through their lines at Sedan and drove to the coast of the English Channel. In doing so they cut off a British Expeditionary Force and the bulk of the French army. After the British escaped from the beaches of Dunkirk, the Germans easily swept aside the remaining French divisions and advanced on Paris. Shocked French officials declared the French capital an open city, and the Germans rolled into Paris on June 13, 1940.

The effectiveness of the Nazi blitzkrieg (lightning war) threw the entire French populace into a panic. It was inconceivable that a modern imperial power would suffer such a rapid and overwhelming collapse, but the equally self-confident Iberian Visigoths and Inkan aristocrats would have identified with their profound shock. As in earlier eras, this astonishment gave way to fears of mass rape, looting, and destruction. As the Nazis advanced, some Frenchmen grew so despondent that they took their own lives. These suicides included an entire farm family in Burgundy, the mayor of Clichy, and Comte Thierry de Martel, a prominent brain surgeon who injected himself with strychnine. As the comfortable rhythms of modern life suddenly disintegrated, a newly subjugated people once again concluded that the world was coming to an end.

Terrified that they would suffer the fate of earlier generations of imperial subjects, between 8 million and 10 million Frenchmen fled south to escape the Nazi invasion. In a matter of days the population of Reims shrank from 250,000 to 5,000 people, while only 700,000 of 2.8 million Parisians remained behind to face the Germans. Spurred by rumors that internal enemies had betrayed France to the Nazis, bureaucrats burned state papers and museum directors packed up their collections. The capital's privileged and wealthy classes scrambled for cars, trains, and any other form of viable transportation. Thomas Kernan, the American editor of the French edition of *Vogue* magazine, was one of the few who remained behind. "I had a curious feeling of walking in a surrealist canvas by Salvador Dalí. In the streets of Paris, without autos, without noise, with only an occasional dwarfed figure on the vast esplanades, I could interpret for the first time the sense of isolation and alarm in my friend's weird painting."[1] With approximately one-sixth of its population on the clogged roads south, France was lucky to escape the devastating epidemics that accompanied the new imperial conquests in Africa.

This mass panic contributed to the sense of desperation that afflicted the remaining French forces. While some units stood bravely, in other cases infantrymen shot officers who insisted on carrying on the fight. Similarly, many mayors in the line of the German advance refused to let the French army establish defensive positions on the assumption that further resistance would lead only to the destruction of their towns. All told, the fighting killed approximately forty thousand French civilians, while the French army suffered about one hundred thousand casualties. This figure included approximately forty thousand to fifty thousand soldiers from France's North and West African colonies. Additionally, the Germans took almost two million prisoners of war. French men in general and the French soldiery in particular found this total collapse humiliating and ultimately emasculating. By comparison, the peoples of the East African highlands were actually far more successful in standing up to a conquering imperial power than the French. Where the Nandi fought a war of attrition against the new imperialists that lasted ten years, the French forces collapsed in a matter of weeks.

The German victory demonstrated how easy it was to take over a modern centralized state with a capitalist industrial economy. But at least the French were fortunate that the Nazis did not view them as racially inferior eastern European Slavs, much less subhuman Africans. Showing uncharacteristic restraint for a conquering imperial power, the German commander in chief promised that civilian lives and property would be safe so long as they followed orders. Simone de Beauvoir was pleasantly surprised to find this was the case in newly occupied Paris: "There were people boating and bathing [in the Seine], so that it had a strange holiday atmosphere. Moreover the season, people's nonchalance, and the low value of time—all that gives the days a gratuitous air, rather charming but rather disturbing."[2] De Beauvoir's only injury came from a chocolate bar thrown from a truck by a German soldier, and she observed that her friends never would have fled Paris had they known the invaders would have been so well behaved.

The Nazis' initially restrained behavior in France was the result of a specific policy termed Operation Seduction. Seeking to keep the population compliant while they completed the conquest of France, Germans gave up their seats to old women and young mothers on the Paris Métro and put up posters showing their men feeding emaciated children with the caption "Abandoned Populations—Put Your Trust in the German Soldier."[3] This hollow propaganda had echoes of the humanitarian rhetoric that the western powers used to legitimize the new imperialism, and Operation Seduction seduced few people. As a French student observed: "The *boche* is well disciplined; in Poland, he is ordered to murder and rape: he murders and rapes. In France, he must smile and excuse himself."[4] After more than three centuries of empire building, most Frenchmen understood that imperial conquest meant domination and extraction.

Faced with the prospect of a total Nazi victory, Prime Minister Paul Reynaud's government made choices that struck many contemporary observers as cowardly but were typical of how defeated peoples responded to an imperial conquest. While some of Reynaud's military advisors called for a last stand in Brittany under the cover of the British navy, the speed of the Nazi advance ruled this out. The prime minister also appealed to Franklin Roosevelt for military aid, but the American president provided only words of encouragement. Desperate to keep the French fighting, the British government offered to create a permanent political union with France that would have entailed common citizenship, economic integration, and full cooperation in postwar reconstruction. Right-wing politicians blocked the proposal by depicting it as a British plot to turn France into a dominion.

Instead, French leaders recalled Marshal Henri-Philippe Pétain, the eighty-four-year-old hero of World War I, to take control of the government and salvage what remained of France's pride and sovereignty. Pétain had made his reputation defending the Verdun fortress against relentless German attacks and was one of the forty "immortals" in the Académie Française. Now he concluded that France's cause was lost, and on June 17 he made a radio broadcast announcing his intention to seek a negotiated peace with Germany to preserve France's autonomy, fleet, and empire. In doing so, Pétain overruled a faction in the cabinet that called for a French government in exile, and he had the parliamentary deputies who escaped to Morocco arrested and brought home.

Casting himself as the savior of France, Pétain signed an armistice with the Nazis on June 22, 1940, in the same railway car in which Germany had accepted the Allied powers' terms for the end of the First World War. The agreement was not a formal peace treaty but a temporary truce under the international law of belligerent occupation that theoretically left French sovereignty intact. Both sides expected the British to come to terms with the Germans and bring the fighting in the west to a quick end. Ultimately, however, the Franco-German armistice lasted more than five years as the war dragged on.

While Pétain miscalculated tragically, the continuing conflict saved the French from bearing the full weight of imperial subjecthood. Hitler could not spare the resources to rule France directly while Germany remained at war with Britain and later the Soviet Union and the United States. At the very least, a hostile exiled French government and army in North Africa would have tied down his forces and put the French Empire in Allied hands. Scheming to turn Pétain into a client, the Nazis were relatively restrained in dictating the terms of the armistice, which in essence imposed a system of indirect imperial rule on France. The agreement froze the German advance and divided the country into an occupied northern zone and an autonomous southern zone that remained under Pétain's *état français* (French state). This arrangement left the strategic Atlantic coast and France's industrial and agricultural heartlands in German hands, but Pétain's regime, which took its informal name from the marshal's capital at Vichy, retained technical sovereignty over the entire country. In the occupied north, the French prefects and bureaucrats who in practice worked for the German military administration continued to answer to Pétain as the legitimate ruler of France.

Under the terms of the armistice, Vichy France nominally became a neutral power with the right to legislate and govern, but it bore little resemblance to the republican regime that it replaced. On July 10, 1940, the French parliament voted overwhelmingly to give Pétain absolute and authoritarian legislative and executive powers. But this was just the illusion of sovereignty. The armistice forced the French to pay the crippling costs of their own occupation, a figure that amounted to twenty million reichsmarks per day. The Vichy regime could not enact policies that conflicted with Germany's interests as the "occupying power," and the French army demobilized its major combat units and surrendered its heavy weapons. The two million prisoners of war in Germany also stayed in captivity as hostages to ensure that the French remained cooperative and compliant. In the end, Pétain's only major achievement was keeping the fleet and overseas empire under French control.

The Vichy authorities claimed that they came to terms with the Nazis to protect France from the destruction of total war and the full weight of imperial domination. Pétain clung to the illusion of sovereignty and promised the French public that "the government remains free, France will be administered by Frenchmen."[5] Pierre Laval, the Vichy minister of state, recalled the devastation of occupied France in World War I and asked rhetorically after the German defeat in 1945: "Would it have been in the greater interest of France to abandon it to disorder and to the cruel domination of the conqueror rather than to make the attempt...to hold off the conqueror by negotiation?"[6] The Atrebatian chieftain Togodumnus, the Visigothic nobleman Theodemir, the Inkan prince Manqu, and the Bengali *nawab* Mir Jafar all would have understood these sentiments. The Vichy regime also had much in common with the Italian notables who retained their status by rallying to Napoleon and with the Kikuyu elites who tried to make the most of their subjecthood by becoming colonial chiefs.

In signing the armistice agreement, Pétain and his allies assured themselves that they were working in partnership with the Germans rather than working for them as imperial subjects. They gambled that a quick Nazi victory would pave the way for a formal peace treaty, thereby ensuring France a prominent place in a new German Europe. As the right-wing ex-communist Jacques Doriot insisted: "France must pass from the camp of the conquered into the camp of the conquerors."[7] The Vichyites justified this desertion from the Allied cause by claiming that Britain conspired to destroy France by encouraging French forces to fight on while secretly negotiating a separate peace with Germany. On July 3, 1940, the British appeared to confirm these allegations when the Royal Navy attacked the Algerian ports of Oran and Mers-el-Kebir to keep the French fleet out of Nazi hands. The raid, which destroyed a battleship and killed more than thirteen hundred sailors, led Pétain to break off diplomatic relations with Britain.

History has judged the Vichy regime harshly, but in the summer of 1940 the French public largely supported Pétain's actions. Recalling the millions left dead and maimed from four years of carnage in the Great War, many people praised Pétain for sparing precious French blood. In casting about for scapegoats they blamed incompetent generals, cowardly Belgians, perfidious Britons, decadent and atheistic French socialists, two-faced domestic communists, and Jewish plotters for France's quick defeat. General Charles de Gaulle, the great hero of the resistance who fled to London after the armistice, initially had little success in rallying the French. Most people ignored his defiant call to reject Pétain and fight on:

> France has lost a battle! But France has not lost the war! Nothing is lost, because this war is a world war. In the free world, there are tremendous forces which have not yet been engaged. The day will come when these forces will crush the enemy. France, on that day, must be present at the victory. Then she will recover her liberty and her greatness.[8]

This passionate appeal fell on deaf ears, and most of the fifteen thousand French soldiers that the British evacuated from Dunkirk chose to return home to occupied France rather than join his Free French forces. Most Frenchmen wanted peace in 1940, which allowed Pétain to strip de Gaulle of his rank and ignore the British-sponsored Provisional French National Committee.

Just as Christian Iberians blamed the Umayyad invasion on Roderic's violation of Hercules's tower, and the peoples of the Andean and East African highlands used millenarian tales of pestilential butterflies and fire-belching iron snakes to explain how they fell victim to foreign invaders, many Frenchmen similarly equated the Nazi invasion with the end of the world. Religious pilgrimages increased in the first year of the occupation as many sought help from the Virgin Mary and Catholic saints. Aiming to turn this millenarian catastrophe into an opportunity for national redemption, the Vichyites pledged to create a revitalized France that would return to global preeminence.

Pétain and his followers should have known better. No imperial power ever allowed its subjects any measure of real autonomy. Hitler never ceased to view France as a mortal enemy and simply used Pétain and his allies as a means to an end. According to one of his confidants, the Nazi *Führer* (leader) had decided France's fate in 1939:

> I shall come to France as a liberator. We shall present ourselves to the French petite bourgeoisie as the champions of a fair social order and eternal peace.... I shall long since have established contacts with men who will form a new government, a government that suits me. We shall find plenty of men of that kind. We shall not even need to buy them. They will come to us of their own accord, driven by ambition, blindness, partisan discord and pride.[9]

Hitler always intended to impose the full weight of imperial subjecthood on the French by destroying them as a nation and co-opting and subverting their own institutions to wring as much wealth out of them as possible. Not surprisingly, Pétain's vision of a new France evaporated in the face of Nazi exploitation, and the marshal found himself and his government reduced to the status of imperial puppets.

In attempting to work with Hitler, the Vichyites introduced a new term into the vocabulary of empire: *collaboration*. In its most literal and benign sense, the word referred to some sort of mutually beneficial joint project or venture. But in the context of the Second World War it came to mean traitorous cooperation with the Nazis. Pétain spoke of "setting out along the road of collaboration" in seeking a working relationship with the Germans, a strategy that Togodumnus, Theodemir, Manqu, Mir Jafar, and Koitalel's son Lelimo all would have understood. Like his forerunners, the French marshal hoped to salvage a measure of dignity, autonomy, and prestige from the collapse of the old order and sought power and influence in the new imperial world.

Nevertheless, defeat did not obligate Pétain and his allies to collaborate. Like most people in occupied Europe, many Frenchmen adopted a strategy of *attentisme* (wait and see) instead of allying with the Nazis or the puppet Vichy regime. The Vichyites, however, viewed the Third Republic's defeat as an opportunity to remake France in their own image. Unlike the Italians who rallied to Napoleon or the Kenyan chiefs who made British indirect rule possible, they did not profit personally from collaboration. Pétain lived simply in a Vichy hotel room, and his state minister, Pierre Laval, was already rich. Hoping to exercise the same kind of civilizing influence on the Germans that the ancient Greeks had on the Romans, the Vichyites gambled that the Nazis would have to give them a real measure of autonomy to make their empire work. The French were imperial rulers themselves, and if they had bothered to understand the realities of imperial subjecthood, they would have realized that this assumption was tragically naive.

Conventional narratives of this dark period in European history rightly cast the German subjugation of France as brutal, totalitarian, and above all profoundly unjust. More fundamentally, European historians tend to depict the Nazi regime as exceptional and unique in its violence and barbarity. To be sure, the crimes of the Holocaust are without parallel in human history, but the Nazis clearly have their place in the long history of empire. The Martiniquais poet Aimé Césaire was certainly correct in arguing that Hitler "applied to Europe colonialist procedures which until then had been reserved exclusively for the Arabs of Algeria, the coolies of India, and the blacks of Africa."[10] While they were criminals of the highest order, the Nazis at least exposed the hypocrisy of the new imperialism by treating the French like Africans and Asians. Many Frenchmen would have been deeply offended by Césaire's charges, for they imagined themselves as civilized imperial rulers and not benighted natives. Yet just as decisive military victories turned earlier generations of defeated peoples into primitives and barbarians, their stunning military collapse in the summer of 1940 rendered twentieth-century Frenchmen inherently inferior in the eyes of the Nazis.

The French were not alone in their shock at becoming imperial subjects. After Napoleon's failed imperial project and the bloody stalemate of World War I, no one in western Europe believed that it was possible to create a formal continental empire in the era of the modern nation-state. France and Germany traded victories and defeats in the Franco-German War of 1870 and the First World War, but in neither case did the triumphant power consider occupying its vanquished foe on a permanent imperial basis. Instead, they imposed penalties and indemnities and swapped the disputed territories of Alsace-Lorraine back and forth. This restraint was not the result of European brotherhood. Rather, the continental powers assumed that it was not wise or possible to turn national peoples into imperial subjects.

Nationalism was a powerful counterweight to empire, but nations were not as coherent and immutable as the Europeans imagined. The idea that nation-states were composed of people who shared a common language, culture, and history was a useful fiction, but neither the Germans nor the French lived up to this ideal. Roughly one-third of the population of late nineteenth-century France did not actually speak French, and to the east, nineteenth-century Germans had even greater difficulty determining the scope and boundaries of the modern German nation. While French nationalism rested on the foundations of the centralized state system of Louis XVI and Napoleon, German-speakers were spread throughout central and eastern Europe. Most lived in the principalities, city-states, and religious fiefs that made up the German Confederation and the sprawling multiethnic Austro-Hungarian Empire, but there were also small enclaves of German-speakers in the Baltic states and tsarist Russia. For a long time, the creation of a single German nation seemed an impossibility.

Lacking formal state institutions to bridge these differences, aspiring nationalists and intellectuals debated whether the German nation-state should be based on the *klein Deutsch* (small German) model that would be restricted to northern Protestants or the *gross Deutsch* (large German) ideal that would theoretically include all German-speakers regardless of their religion or residence. On the all important question of what made a German, both camps generally agreed that the German *Volk* (people) shared a common bond based on blood and inheritance. This was in contrast to French and British nationalism, both of which were based primarily on citizenship in a particular state. Thus, while the French state could manufacture Frenchmen by forcing its minority Breton, Corsican, Flemish, Basque, and Alsatian populations to adopt French language and culture, German nation builders came to imagine a Germanness that was not tied to national boundaries.

It was no easy matter to build a coherent nation-state from this romantic but imprecise identity. Once moderate Germans failed to create a liberal constitutional monarchy out of the chaos of the revolutions of 1848, it fell to the Prussian prime minister Otto von Bismarck to bring about German unification on authoritarian terms. After defeating Austria in 1866, he forced the member states of the German Confederation to unite under the Prussian king (later emperor) Wilhelm I by goading Napoleon III of France into war four years later. The resulting German Empire, or Reich, hardly fit the model of a homogenous nation-state. Never forgetting that they had come late to the community of nations, the Reich's ruling elites were jealous of their national prestige and aggressive in defining the physical and cultural boundaries of the new state.

Imbued with a belligerent sense of nationalism, the Reich's leaders dreamed of a German-dominated *Mitteleuropa* (middle Europe) as a continental equivalent of the informal British Empire of the mid-nineteenth century. This sphere of commercial and political influence would provide the markets and raw materials that Germany needed to compete with the western industrial powers. Most Germans were not particularly interested in an overseas empire, and Bismarck took part in the new imperial scramble only to distract the French and acquire bargaining chips for future diplomatic negotiations.

While Hitler shared these dubious views of the new imperialism, the Nazi imperial project had much in common with its liberal democratic counterparts. What was truly distinctive about Hitler's empire was that he sought to create it in Europe rather than Africa or Asia. Although he disavowed overseas expansion in *Mein Kampf*, he had a clear imperial agenda that blended extractive rule in the industrial west with settler colonialism in the agricultural regions of the east. Kenya was a similar imperial/colonial hybrid, but the metropolitan British government and public never would have allowed the settlers to try to exterminate the African majority to claim the white highlands all for themselves.

The Nazis, on the other hand, never answered to a humanitarian lobby. Hitler disdained the liberal justification for empire, and in his view it was moral and right to defend the German people by any and all means. Citing the western destruction of Amerindians as a precedent, Hitler planned to carve out living space (*Lebensraum*) for German settlers in eastern Europe by enslaving and eventually exterminating "racially inferior" Slavs. Although he called the Ukraine Germany's "new Indian Empire," the Nazi leader emphatically disavowed the civilizing rhetoric that legitimized western styles of imperial rule. Declaring that "it is not our mission to lead the local inhabitants to a higher standard of life," Hitler proclaimed that the Reich's eastern subjects would not get any hospitals, schools, or even the simplest forms of social welfare. "No vaccinations for the Russians, and no soap to get the dirt off them. But let them have all the spirits and tobacco they want."[11] He defended these genocidal colonial plans as the justifiable prerogative of a master race faced with invasion by more fecund Slavic and Asiatic peoples, which made eastward military expansion just as moral and valid as the colonization of the Americas. While Hitler fantasized about reclaiming former Germanic lands in Flanders and Burgundy, he never envisioned replacing their populations with German settlers. Western Europeans may have been culturally inferior, but their shared racial heritage with Germany spared them from the worst abuses of Nazi rule in the east.

This Nazi blueprint for empire was both inherently brutal and foolishly unrealistic. Even so, conventional historical narratives are not correct in portraying Hitler's imperial project as exceptional or anomalous. The actual ambitions and methods of Nazi empire building were simply more extreme versions of the standard imperial template. In formulating their expansionist program, Hitler's men drew on both the continentalism of Germany's long-standing *Mitteleuropa* aspirations and lessons learned from limited overseas conquests during the new imperialism. The result was a powerful but unsustainable hybrid empire with a totalitarian metropole that combined genocidal settler colonialism with the extractive exploitation of subject communities.

In this sense, the Nazi empire was markedly different from the German Empire of Bismarck and Wilhelm I. The first unified German nation-state called itself a *Reich* (empire), but in Wilhelmian Germany this term referred as much to a national realm as it did a conventional empire. The Germans were not the clear-cut aggressors in the First World War, and apart from some boundary disputes, they did not have grand designs on their neighbors' territory in the west. They did have ambitious plans for the Ukraine, but had the Central Powers been victorious, Wilhelm's middle Europe most likely would have looked more like the informal British Empire than Napoleon's imperial continental state.

The Wilhelmian Reich's conduct in its African and Asian territories also did not explicitly presage the atrocities of the Nazi empire. While the early stages of German rule in Africa were marred by the same sorts of abuses that tarnished the reputations of Britain, France, and Belgium, in the years leading up to World War I, Bernhard Dernburg's Colonial Office won international respect for its plans to make imperial governance more rational, scientific, and humane. The settler colony of German Southwest Africa was the exception, but its brutal, if not genocidal, tactics in dealing with a revolt by the Herero people were quite similar to those employed by settlers in the neighboring British territories. Most of the German Reichstag was appalled by this incident and demanded that their representatives in Southwest Africa observe the rules of war set out in the Hague Conventions.

The victorious powers at the 1919 Paris Peace Conference therefore acted hypocritically when they passed judgment on the Wilhelmian Reich's record as an imperial power. In addition to forcing Germany to assume responsibility for starting the war, pay reparations, and surrender 13 percent of its European territory (including the contested

Alsace-Lorraine), they also convicted the Germans of being unfit to rule "primitive peoples." This was a poorly disguised excuse for the winners to take Germany's African and Asian territories as League of Nations mandates. Germany was thus the only participant in the new imperial scramble to answer for its record.

Even Germans who had little interest in overseas empires viewed the loss of their nonwestern territories under these circumstances as an affront to Germany's honor as a civilized nation. Heinrich Schnee, the last governor of German East Africa, made a telling point: "The colonial history of *no* nation is free from excesses, and indeed it would be easy to provide cases elsewhere exceeding in gravity anything to be found in the short history of German colonization."[12] In their defense, German apologists compiled a long list of imperial crimes committed by their accusers. These included forced labor in the French and Belgian Congo, Portuguese plantation slavery, British retaliation for the Indian Mutiny and the Amritsar massacre, the Rhodesians' demolition of caves sheltering Ndebele women and children, the deaths of more than twenty-six thousand Afrikaner women and children in Boer War concentration camps, and the Royal Air Force's bombardment of rebels in Southwest Africa, Iraq, and Afghanistan.

From the standpoint of the general German public, the loss of the overseas empire was one of the lesser indignities of the inequitable 1919 peace settlement. Like their counterparts in the other imperial metropoles, they paid little attention to imperial affairs because they derived few actual benefits from the new imperialism. Rampant postwar inflation, the war guilt clause, crushing reparations payments, restrictions on the German military, and the French occupation of the Ruhr industrial belt were far more onerous and pressing concerns. Nevertheless, Germany's imperial stigma contributed to the overall sense of anger and humiliation that undermined the Weimar Republic and helped bring the National Socialist German Workers' (Nazi) Party to power.

In the immediate interwar years, the Nazis were just one of many right-wing postwar factions that blamed Germany's defeat on Marxists, capitalists, and Jews. Incredibly and irrationally, these groups charged that Jews were the conspiratorial force behind both western imperialism and Russian Bolshevism. The German voting public paid the extremists relatively little attention once the country recovered a measure of stability in the 1920s. The Nazis became a national political force only when the Weimar regime's failure to manage the depression gave their conspiratorial theories credence with lower middle-class voters. Even this increased support brought Hitler's party only a third of the vote in the 1932 elections, leaving it the second-largest party in Germany. As the *Führer* of the Nazi Party, Hitler needed the backing of powerful industrialists and more mainstream conservatives to become the German Chancellor one year later.

The Nazis' capitalist sponsors and right-wing allies expected to use Hitler as a weapon against their enemies on the left. They never imagined that he would seize total control of the government through grassroots organizing, political terror, parliamentary maneuvering, and emergency decrees. Using an arson attack on the Reichstag in 1933 as an excuse to suspend the Weimar constitution, Hitler manipulated the legislators into giving him full executive and legislative powers. One year later, he assumed both the presidency and chancellorship on the death of President Paul von Hindenburg. This gave him the means to ban rival political parties and assert direct control over the Weimar Republic's constituent states.

Although Hitler only suspended the Weimar constitution rather than abolishing it, he used his dictatorial powers to establish the highly centralized Third Reich. This designation positioned the Nazis as the heirs of the first Holy Roman Empire and Bismarck's second Wilhelmian Reich, but they actually had no specific plan for a new empire. The Third Reich was in fact a highly inefficient and improvised state in which the organs of the party and the governmental bureaucracy overlapped and competed with each other.

As one of the key pillars of the new regime, the Nazi Party evolved into a hierarchical organization with Hitler and eighteen *Reichsleiters* (Reich leaders) presiding over a laddered bureaucracy reaching from powerful *Gauleiters* (regional leaders) down to *Zellenleiters* (neighborhood cell leaders). It also infiltrated and co-opted key elements of German society through the Hitler Youth, the National Socialist Women's Organization, the German Labor Front, and the Schutzstaffel (SS), a paramilitary unit that began as Hitler's personal guard and evolved into a massive state within a state by the end of the Second World War. Only the churches retained a measure of autonomy, but Hitler's 1933 concordat with the Catholic Church placed the German clergy under state protection in return for the Nazis' promise to let them manage their own affairs.

The Third Reich's second major prop was the old Weimar state structure, which Hitler still needed to handle the practical business of governance. On paper, the judiciary, central government ministries, and federal and state bureaucracies appeared relatively unchanged, but the Nazis infiltrated and undercut them at every level. The Reich ministries theoretically had the authority to draft legislation and decrees, but these needed the *Führer*'s personal approval to become law. The Ministry of Defense had responsibility for the German armed forces until 1938, when Hitler placed them under a more compliant Oberkommando der Wehrmacht (High Command of the Armed Forces) to better impose his will on the military. The Nazis also took over the state police forces and *gendarmerie* and placed them under the authority of the SS and the Reich Main Security Office. The Secret State Police (Gestapo), the party's Security Service Branch, special political courts, and a network of concentration camps dealt ruthlessly with Hitler's real and imagined enemies.

The Nazi regime's enormous scope made it seem omnipotent and highly disciplined, but it was more of an amorphous, ever-changing semicriminal syndicate in which party elites vied with each other constantly in pursuit of personal wealth and power. With nearly two million members in 1939, the Nazi Party tried to be both a popular movement of the masses and a vanguard party of the elite.[13] At first glance, it appeared unequipped to manage a modern state, much less an empire. This authoritarian chaos served Hitler well. As the head of both the party and the state, he had total control over the Reich's governing institutions. Every major policy decision required his personal approval, and the blurred lines of authority in the party and bureaucracy allowed him to intervene in any aspect of government that suited him.

Recalling that domestic turmoil brought down the Second Reich, the Nazis aspired to build what Götz Aly termed a "racist-totalitarian welfare state." This *Volkstaat* (people's state) put millions of Germans back to work, expanded education, supported families, and expanded health care. At the same time, the Third Reich undertook a massive rearmament campaign that increased defense spending as a percentage of the German gross national product from 1 to 25 percent between 1932 and 1939. To further complicate matters, Hitler devoted most of Germany's gold and foreign currency reserves to the military buildup, which led to shortages of food and other key industrial raw materials. The Nazis tried to address these problems through a state-directed development program to make the Reich self-sufficient, but in reality foreign conquest and plunder offered the only hope of bringing the national debt of 37.4 billion reichsmarks under control.[14]

German Jews were the first to bear the brunt of the Nazis' extractive agenda. Anti-Semitism was an inevitable outgrowth of hyper-racial nationalism and was relatively common throughout interwar Europe. Hitler courted popular support by tapping into the widely held right-wing suspicion that Jewish financiers had maneuvered Germany into the Great War and that Jewish conspirators had engineered its defeat. Karl Marx's Jewish ancestry also allowed the Nazis to depict communism as a Jewish plot. German Jews thus became an alien race that threatened the purity of the *Volk*. In 1935, this ugly lie led to the Nuremberg Laws, which defined German citizenship on the basis of blood and inheritance. Henceforth, Germans with demonstrable Jewish ancestry lost the franchise and suffered increasing social isolation in the name of racial self-defense. This largely propagandistic discrimination and abuse took on an explicitly economic dimension in 1938 when the Third Reich introduced an aryanization program to loot the German Jewish community systematically. All told, their assets covered 9 percent of the Third Reich's total budget outlays in 1939.[15]

This state-sponsored anti-Semitic extraction was only a stopgap measure. Jewish wealth was finite, and Hitler believed that the Reich had to expand to survive. The Nazis desperately needed the stolen wealth of Europe to pay for their massive military mobilization and comprehensive domestic social welfare programs. By 1939, Germany had a national debt of 37.4 billion reichsmarks, which led the national bank directors to warn Hitler that the economy was on the verge of collapse. Unwilling to test their popularity by raising taxes or sparking inflation, the Nazis needed enormous infusions of looted wealth to keep Germany solvent.[16]

On the eve of the Second World War, Germany had almost four million men under arms, a ridiculously large figure that undercut Hitler's claims that the Nazi rearmament program was for self-defense. In the short term, the Nazi leader's goal was to undo the humiliating 1919 peace settlement by reclaiming neighboring territories with measurable German populations. Recognizing that his military was not yet ready for war, he built this greater Germany by playing on the European powers' determination to avoid another continental conflagration at virtually any cost. Britain and France allowed Hitler to annex Austria, the Sudetenland, and all of Czechoslovakia between 1938 and 1939. German-speakers in these territories who could demonstrate their racial purity became full citizens of the Reich. Everyone else became the Nazis' first imperial subjects.

In contrast, Hitler made no move to reclaim Germany's overseas empire. While the Nazi Party platform of the 1920s called for the return of the Second Reich's lost African and Asian territories, this was largely a gambit to court the conservatives and industrialists who still believed that the remote holdings had some value. German imperial enthusiasts took the bait and aligned themselves with the Nazis even though some were uncomfortable with their extremist rhetoric. Hitler, however, raised the lost colonies only as part of his strategy of hoodwinking the British and French into believing that the Third Reich could be appeased with limited territorial concessions. He was actually telling the truth in *Mein Kampf* when he declared: "The German people will have no right to engage in a colonial policy until they shall have brought all their children together in the one State." In 1937, the Nazi economist Walther Funk ordered the Reich Colonial Federation to stop distracting the German public by romanticizing the African colonies, and during the war the *Führer* claimed: "If it were only a question of conquering a colony, I'd not continue the war a day longer."[17]

Although Hitler disavowed the new imperialism's goals and legitimizing ideologies, his grand strategy for the Second World War sought to emulate its tactics. Just as military superiority, ambition, and sheer ruthlessness gave the western powers quick and easy victories over Africans and Asians, the Nazis gambled that their blitzkrieg tactics would bring swift triumphs over continental enemies. Recognizing that Germany lacked the manpower and resources for a protracted war, they aimed to vanquish the western powers rapidly, with an eye to their grand expansionist plans in the east. Hitler's opportunistic 1939 nonaggression treaty with the Soviet Union, which made nonsense of his anticommunist rhetoric, was purely a pragmatic gambit to keep the Soviets out of the war until Germany finished its business in the west.

Nazi military strategists had planned to delay war until the mid-1940s to give them time to assimilate the Austrian and Czechoslovakian economies. Hitler brought on the war prematurely in September 1939 by ordering the invasion of Poland. He incorrectly calculated that the failure of Britain and France to protect the Czechs indicated that they would not honor their defense pact with the Poles. From then on, however, the first year of the war largely unfolded according to plan. After dispatching Poland in a matter of weeks, Nazi forces overran Denmark and Norway before winning their stunning victories in the Low Countries and France. Fascist Italy then opportunistically joined the war on the Axis side in the hope of claiming a share of the overseas French Empire. The Nazis needed the extra manpower, but Benito Mussolini did Hitler no favors in drawing the Germans into a broader Mediterranean war.

All the same, the Germans were the masters of most of continental Europe by the summer of 1941. Their first agenda was to reclaim the border regions of Poland, Belgium, and France that had once belonged to the Second Reich. These formally became part of Germany. As for the rest of their western conquests, the Nazis ruled Denmark and Norway through cooperative local officials, placed the Netherlands under a civilian German administration, and kept Belgium and occupied France under direct military control in preparation for an invasion of Britain that never materialized.

In the east, the Nazis surrendered eastern Poland to their Soviet "allies" and created the Poland General Government to administer what remained. Similarly, the non-German parts of Czechoslovakia became the Protectorate of Bohemia and Moravia. To the south, the Nazis helped Mussolini overrun Greece and conquer Yugoslavia in April 1941 when its young king refused to become a German lackey. Hungary, Romania, and Bulgaria became relatively willing Nazi puppets to escape the fate of the Czechs and reacquire bits of territory they had lost under the 1919 peace settlement. Hitler also won additional accomplices by playing upon the frustrated nationalist aspirations of the Ruthenians, Slovaks, Croats, Slovenes, and other minority communities who similarly felt betrayed by the delegates at Versailles. Conversely, the Finns joined the German camp to gain protection from Soviet aggression.

This preliminary empire building set the stage for Hitler's main imperial project: the defeat of the Soviet Union and the colonial settlement of its vast fertile heartland. Following in the footsteps of Napoleon 129 years earlier, he launched a massive invasion in

September 1941. The Nazi forces consisted of three million Germans and six hundred thousand of their Croat, Romanian, Hungarian, Slovakian, Italian, and Finnish auxiliaries. Anchored by more than three thousand armored vehicles, the Nazi blitzkrieg sought to seize the USSR's key industrial centers while encircling and destroying the five-million-man Red Army. Timed to last just four months, it was an audacious plan that almost succeeded. Within a matter of weeks, the Soviets lost two and a half million men and thousands of tanks and planes, but, as in 1812, the German advance ground to halt with the outbreak of winter. The Nazi legions suffered upward of eight hundred thousand casualties during the fall campaign and faced the first of many Soviet counterattacks in December 1941.[18] That same month Hitler acquired another formidable opponent by honoring his promise with the Japanese to declare war on the United States after Pearl Harbor.

Still, Nazi Europe seemed entirely secure at this point. German submarines kept Britain under siege and slowed the American deployment to Europe. In 1942, renewed German offensives pushed the Third Reich's boundaries to the Volga River. With a firm hold over western Europe and its armies advancing steadily in Russia and North Africa, the Nazi regime had the breathing space to begin the process of organizing its conquests into a formal empire.

In terms of administration, the workings of the German metropole remained largely unchanged from the prewar era, and the annexed territories restored to the fatherland became *Gaue*. Based on the old Reichstag electoral districts, these Nazi administrative units allowed party luminaries to exercise sweeping executive powers. The conquered peoples living in the new *Gaue* became eligible for citizenship if they were sufficiently "German" or faced expulsion and enslavement if they were not.

The necessity of keeping the Vichy French regime compliant dissuaded the Nazis from formally annexing Alsace-Lorraine, but both regions came under the authority of the adjoining German *Gaue*. Hitler ordered their *Gauleiters* to return the largely German-speaking Alsatian population to their Teutonic roots. The result was a program of forced Germanization that deported hundreds of thousands of Jews and French-speakers to France, imposed German as the language of administration and commerce, and imported uniformed teachers from the Reich to staff the schools. The Germans stripped buildings of French architectural features, pulled down statues of Joan of Arc, burned French books, and decreed that wedding rings be worn on the right hand, in the proper German fashion. Speaking French or even wearing berets brought fines and imprisonment, but those who embraced their new Germanness had the dubious privilege of becoming eligible for conscription into Hitler's army.

The Reich Ministry of the Interior was responsible for creating a uniform administrative system for the occupied territories that the Nazis did not annex. Not surprisingly, military viceroys and civilian governors answered directly to Hitler, who tended to make policy decisions based on personal whims. This meant that there never was a coherent system of Nazi imperial rule. The Third Reich actually governed Europe through a patchwork arrangement of satellite states, puppet regimes, military governments, and civil administrations.

In the occupied western territories Hitler was generally willing to make a show of following the Hague Conventions on conquest and occupation so long as their populations accepted their subject status passively. This policy produced the standard system of indirect rule that was common to most empires. Werner Best, the chief of the civil administration in France and Reich plenipotentiary in Denmark, described the German version of governance in western Europe as *wenig zu regieren* (govern little). This approach was born of the same realities that shaped earlier imperial administrative systems: the Nazis lacked the manpower and resources to rule directly. With only three thousand officials in all of occupied France, the German administration had no choice but to rely on French bureaucrats and policemen.[19] This meant they had to temper their demands on subject populations out of sheer necessity.

The Nazis treaded the most gently in Denmark and Norway because they considered Scandinavians fellow Aryans. Overruling the generals who lobbied for military rule, Hitler placed the Danes and Norwegians under the German Foreign Office. In Denmark, German troops had orders not to offend the Danes' national honor, and the government that surrendered in 1940 ran the country under German supervision until limited Danish resistance forced the Nazis to assert more direct control in 1943. In Norway, King Haakon escaped to Britain, but the Germans found willing allies in Vidkun Quisling and a small group of Norwegian fascists. Quisling's role in passing

Norwegian military secrets to the Nazis made him so unpopular that his name became synonymous with treason, but the Germans still managed to cobble together an effective government of Norwegian ministers under his nominal supervision.

In the Low Countries, the Nazi regime similarly ruled through senior bureaucrats after the Dutch and Belgian prime ministers established governments in exile in London. Queen Wilhelmina of the Netherlands also escaped, but King Leopold III let the Germans capture him. His unexpected decision to surrender the Belgian army during the Nazi invasion left the Allied forces vulnerable and cost him much of his legitimacy after the Belgian government in Britain repudiated his actions. The Austrian Nazi Party functionary Artur Seyss-Inquart was the *Reichskommissar* in the Netherlands, while Belgium's strategic value as a staging area for the air war against Britain kept it under direct military rule. The Germans had to carry out the day-to-day administration of both countries through high-ranking civil servants in key government ministries and insisted on direct control over only the police and security services.

While most western Europeans tried to keep the Nazis at arm's length, as in all imperial societies there were still individuals who made themselves useful to the conquering regime. Some were committed fascists who enthusiastically sought an influential role in the new Europe by forging an alliance with the Nazis, but Hitler distrusted them as potential competitors. They also lacked sufficient popular support to play an effective role in indirect rule. The most useful Nazi intermediaries were actually the civil servants who remained at their posts. Some simply hoped to spare their countrymen from the abuses of direct imperial rule, but others were apolitical functionaries who advanced their careers through service to the new regime. Jacobus Lambertus Lentz, the head of the Inspectorate for Population Registers, was one such opportunist who helped the Nazis implement a highly efficient identity card system in the Netherlands because the Dutch government had blocked his plans for a similar system on the grounds that it treated citizens like criminals.[20]

Eastern Europeans, by comparison, did not have the opportunity to collaborate in similar fashion. While the Nazis created puppet regimes in the Balkans, they followed a hybrid imperial/colonial strategy in the east that aimed to either exploit the labor of subject populations or destroy them entirely to create room for German settlers. These agendas were obviously contradictory, for it was impossible to wring wealth out of people that had been exterminated. As an army logistics expert in the Ukraine warned: "If we shoot the Jews, let the prisoners of war die, allow much of the big city population to starve to death, we cannot answer the question: who will then produce economic assets here?"[21] The Nazis' imperial incoherency was due primarily to the competition between civil administrators, labor ministry officials, central planners, social scientists, *Gauleiters*, and SS ideologues to advance their personal agendas in the occupied eastern territories. The result was a sort of reverse eastward barbarian invasion with the Nazis playing the role of the Goths and Huns who had preyed on the Roman Empire.

The Poles were the first to suffer the consequences of the German eastern imperial agenda. Just as the delegates to the Berlin Conference redrew the political map of Africa, the Nazis reordered what was left of Poland. To populate this new eastern frontier, Heinrich Himmler's Commissariat for the Strengthening of German Nationhood recruited two million ethnic Germans from throughout the region. After carving out German settlement colonies, they left the Poles a rump state called the General Government of the Occupied Polish Territories. Rejecting the Poles' right to nationhood, the Nazi imperial regime set out to destroy them as a people. It banished the Polish language from government, cut wages, instituted crushing taxes, plundered bank accounts, and banned all cultural activities. Even though they were burdened by Polish deportees from the annexed western regions, the General Government's population of eleven million still shrank at the rate of three thousand per day as the Poles perished from violence, disease, and starvation.[22]

Occupied Poland's governor-general and Reich minister, Hans Frank, alternatively depicted the Nazi rump state as part of the German fatherland and a model settlement colony. In fact, the Nazi imperial regime in Poland was an incoherent mess. Frank could not even decide whether he wanted to turn the Poles into helots or exterminate them. It also proved embarrassingly difficult to fix the boundary between citizen and subject in a population where intermarriage between Germans and Poles was not uncommon. To further complicate matters, the Nazis discovered illiterate "renegade Germans" who had betrayed their membership in the *Volk* by adopting elements of Polish culture. Frank's officials therefore had to issue special identity badges to distinguish who was really a German and who was not.

The German imperial agenda in the Soviet occupied territories was even more incoherent and bloody. Here too social scientists seeking to prove their racist *Lebensraum* theories vied with fortune-hunting party functionaries and strategically minded generals to set the agenda in the newly conquered lands. Imagining the possibilities of a German version of the North American frontier, Nazi ideologues came up with fantastically unrealistic but chillingly barbarous plans. They envisioned eliminating as many as thirty million Slavs through planned famines and mass prophylactic and sterilization programs. In their place they expected to settle millions of ethnic Germans in agrarian soldiers' colonies based on the ancient Roman model. Hitler spoke of linking these settlements to the Reich through enormous raised roads and building double-decker trains to take German veterans to Crimean vacation resorts.

This was pure fantasy, and the Nazis struggled to institute the most basic and rudimentary systems of imperial rule in the Soviet east. Officially, *Reichsleiter* Alfred Rosenberg's Reich Ministry for the Occupied Eastern Territories (OMi) had authority over all territory up to two hundred kilometers behind the front lines. Assuming that German troops would advance to the Urals by the end of 1941, the ministry planned to establish the Reich commissariats of Ostland, Ukraine, Moscovy, and the Caucasus in the conquered lands. In keeping with the standard geographical template of imperial administration, these commissariats would be divided into provincial and district units. Not content to wait for the expected flood of settlers from the Reich, the Ethnic German Liaison Office focused on organizing local communities of ethnic Germans into privileged settlement colonies.

In practice, the Nazis' shifting military fortunes meant that they were able to establish only the Ostland and Ukrainian commissariats. The OMi was also profoundly impotent when it came to actual imperial rule. The ministry's functionaries, whose yellow-brown uniforms earned them the derisive nickname of "gold pheasants," could not control the *Gauleiters* who used personal ties to Hitler to turn the commissariats into personal fiefs. Hermann Göring's Central Office of the Four-Year Plan, Fritz Sauckel's labor recruiting agency, and Albert Speer's armaments ministry also undercut Rosenberg's authority by following their own extractive agendas.

Reichsführer Heinrich Himmler, however, was the true power in the east. Although it was technically subordinate to the OMi, his SS exercised real authority in the Nazi commissariats through its control of the police and security forces. Himmler's troops operated independently in their campaign to murder Jews and Soviet commissars and turned the Ukraine and Ostland into unofficial SS police states. The *Reichsführer* also pursued his own pet projects, such as the *Hegewald* (forest reserve) that was to be the prototype for a string of fortified SS colonies for ethnic Germans designed to hold the conquered territories against Soviet counterattacks.

Although the Nazis never realized their genocidal ambition to wipe out the entire population of the east, they treated conquered Slavic peoples as an exploitable and expendable resource. This was a grim departure from the standard imperial model. Even the most brutal empire builders in earlier eras recognized the inherent value of sufficiently pacified subject communities. Furthermore, European settlers in Australia and the Americas did not explicitly seek to exterminate indigenous populations; they merely took advantage of the demographic collapse resulting from contagious Old World diseases and exploitive western imperial rule. By comparison, the Nazis conspired to murder the entire Jewish population of eastern Europe and condemned subject Christian communities to homicidal levels of forced labor and slow starvation.

These policies were both indefensibly barbaric and stupidly counterproductive. In the early months of the eastern campaign, the Ukrainians and other subject communities that had suffered under Soviet imperial rule were ready to welcome the advancing German armies as liberators. Instead, the Nazis executed Ukraine nationalist leaders and forced the entire community back into an unhappy alliance with Stalin through inhumanly brutal extractive policies. Captives of their own racist ideology, the Nazis abandoned the tried-and-true tactic of divide and rule. It was only in 1944 that Rosenberg found the backbone to complain publicly that the Germans had missed a golden opportunity to exploit the Ukrainians' deep hatred of the Soviets. This would prove shortsighted later in the war, but unalloyed ruthlessness made the Nazis' systems of imperial extraction exceptionally lucrative in the near term. Freed from the constraints of long-term planning and humanitarian sentiment, they set out to strip-mine their conquered territories.

In the west, Nazi empire builders manipulated the terms of the Hague Conventions, which allowed victorious powers to make defeated nations assume the costs of their occupation. The Netherlands' bill came to one hundred million guilders per month between 1940 and 1942, which increased the Dutch national budget by more than sixfold. Similarly, the Germans charged eighteen million francs to the Belgium government and seized its gold reserves.

The Nazis' greatest extractive innovation was turning modern financial mechanisms into instruments of imperial exploitation. They used the international clearing system, which European central banks used to balance imports and exports, to force conquered nations to fund the Reich's food and raw material imports. Normally, importers would pay for foreign goods by depositing the purchase price in clearing accounts in their own national bank. This bank would then transfer the sum to their trading partners' national bank, which would in turn credit the exporters' accounts in their own currency. The Nazis, however, never fulfilled their side of the bargain. This meant that state banks in the conquered territories had to reimburse their exporters by printing more money, which made them pay for the Third Reich's imports. This system was so efficient that Germany owed its "trading partners" twenty-nine billion reichsmarks by the summer of 1944.[23]

While high-ranking Nazis followed Napoleon's example in plundering Europe of its great works of art and moveable treasures, they found that currency manipulation was a much simpler alternative to the messy business of day-to-day looting. Instead of seizing food and materials from western Europeans, the conquering German forces "paid" for them with Reich Credit Bank certificates. These certificates, which were denominated in paper notes ranging from fifty pfennigs to fifty marks, looked like money, but they were not legal tender in Germany. The central banks of defeated nations had to redeem them, which forced them to cover the cost of German military requisitions. As with the clearing system, these banks had to make up the shortfall by issuing more money. This highly inflationary form of imperial extraction had the double virtue of appearing to be legal under the Hague Conventions because the Germans seemingly paid for their plunder. The Nazis usually withdrew the certificates at the end of a successful campaign to ensure that local economies did not collapse entirely, but they kept them in circulation in France until December 1943 to wring as much wealth as possible out of the Reich's rich historical enemy.

The Nazis also garnered popular support at home by giving common German soldiers and civilians a healthy share of the imperial spoils. They inflated the official exchange rate between the reichsmark and the currencies of defeated nations to increase German purchasing power. Families in Germany sent money and extensive shopping lists to their men in uniform. In return, they received packages of Greek tobacco, Norwegian herring, North African shoes, Russian bacon, and French velvet, silk, liqueurs, and coffee. Under what became known as the "schlep decree," Göring mandated that soldiers returning home on leave could bring back as much of this purchased booty as they could personally carry. The French bore the greatest weight of these policies by virtue of their shared border with Germany and because they had some of the most tempting goods. Even mayors and other civic officials in Germany took part in this form of modern looting by buying artificially inexpensive raw materials in France by the freight train load. All told, nonmilitary purchases of French goods came to 125 million marks by mid-1943.[24]

By comparison, most eastern economies were not sufficiently developed to sustain these more advanced extractive methods. The Nazis also had no inclination to be as gentle with their "subhuman" Slavic subjects as they were with "civilized" western nations. Dispensing with the niceties of bank certificates and clearing accounts, German forces stripped Poland and the occupied Soviet Union of food and other raw materials with the full knowledge that millions of people would starve. Western Europeans made similar forced contributions to the Reich's breadbasket, but their exports to Germany brought only severe malnutrition, not famine.

In addition to stealing their food, the Nazis also turned millions of eastern Europeans into slave laborers. This strategy reflected the reality that, as in the premodern empires, the Nazi empire's wealth was still in subject labor. Desperate for manpower to free German men for military service and spare German women from factory work, the Reich plenipotentiary for labor allocation, Fritz Sauckel, scoured occupied Europe for workers. While coerced Frenchmen, Belgians, Dutchmen, Danes, and Norwegians helped meet the Reich's labor needs, they were spared the worst of the Nazi forced labor policies. In the east, Sauckel's men grabbed people off the streets or seized them in churches and theaters. In Poland, every male between the ages of eighteen and sixty was liable for compulsory labor. As a result, there were approximately seven million foreign forced laborers in Germany by mid-1944.[25] Technically, these unfortunate people were not slaves because the Nazis paid them. But their employers imposed heavy payroll deductions for room and board on men and women who were living at virtual starvation levels in labor camps. The Nazi regime additionally transferred much of its labor costs to defeated governments by making them responsible for the back wages and family benefits of their citizens working in the Reich.

Even the Holocaust had an extractive element. Although the Nazis' hysterical anti-Semitism was highly irrational, their xenophobic policies paid economic returns. Initially, Hitler planned to move against the Jews only after a quick Nazi victory, but once the initial blitzkrieg in the east failed, he abandoned all restraint. As in the new imperial Africa, Nazi racial doctrines reduced Jews to the level of subhumans and left them dangerously vulnerable. The difference was that where western European empires simply sought profit, the Nazis plotted genocide. In preparation for their final solution to the "Jewish problem," Hitler's men set about segregating Jews from larger subject populations through special armbands, discriminatory laws, forced ghettoization, and eventually deportation to concentration and extermination camps.

These tactics made it easier for the Germans to seize the Jews' savings and material wealth. Inmates in the network of SS concentration camps produced fifty million marks per year through the production of crafts, construction and agricultural work, and industrial slave labor. The Nazis even shipped a million cubic meters of looted Jewish furniture to the Reich for resale at reduced rates to German families who had lost their homes to Allied bombing. Götz Aly estimated that the mandatory aryanization of Jewish assets and the outright theft of their personal property generated fifteen billion to twenty billion reichsmarks for the Reich and puppet governments in occupied nations.[26] This plundered Jewish wealth kept subject nations sufficiently solvent to meet their financial obligations to the Third Reich and bound collaborationist regimes more closely to the German cause by making them accomplices to genocide.

Upon reflection, the Nazi imperial balance sheet was impressive. Estimates vary, but it appears that the Third Reich extracted roughly 170 billion marks from its subjects, a figure that was approximately three times the total German domestic revenues for the same period.

Not only did this imperial windfall keep the Nazi armies in the field, it also kept the German people relatively comfortable for much of the war. In the Reich itself, German household income remained at approximately 78 percent of prewar levels for most of the conflict. The British and American rates, by comparison, were roughly half this figure.[27]

For common Germans, the returns of empire were even more significant in the occupied territories, where their status as a conquering power freed them from the conventional constraints of morality and civil society. Nazi doctrines of racial supremacy meant that an implicit perquisite of service in territorial administrations or military garrisons was the privilege of self-enrichment. In addition to extraterritorial protection from local laws and taxes, German men also acquired power over local women. As in earlier empires, their wealth and status made them desirable companions for those who sought to mitigate their subjecthood. These relationships ran the gamut from formal prostitution to marriage. Either way, a German military administrator's humiliation of his French counterpart in the days following France's capitulation exposed the lie behind Operation Seduction and made it clear that sexual domination was also a reality of occupation: "We are the victors! You have been beaten! The women, even the children of your country, are no longer yours! Our soldiers have the right to have fun, and if you do anything to slight the honor of the German army you will be arrested."[28] Typically, the subject women, particularly lower-class women, who suffered sexual abuse at the hands of German men rarely had any legal recourse.

Although desperate Jews in the Warsaw ghetto fought back against the Germans in 1943, the Nazi imperial regime's denigrating occupation policies and crushing extractive agenda produced surprisingly few incidents of open resistance in the first half of the war. This was due in part to the barbarity and utter ruthlessness of its internal security systems. Any village or community that had the courage to take up arms against the Nazis faced extermination. This was the fate of the Czechoslovakian town of Lidice, which the SS destroyed entirely in 1942 as retribution for the murder of *Obergruppenführer* Reinhard Heydrich, the deputy Reich protector of the puppet state of Bohemia and Moravia, by Czech partisans.

Freed from the constraints of conventional decency, the Nazis' use of brutality and terror as methods of imperial control were highly efficient. The SS and the Central Office for Reich Security, which coordinated and centralized the Reich's various paramilitary and secret police services, exercised direct control over domestic police forces in subject nations. Exempt from judicial oversight and local laws, these imperial enforcers had nearly total freedom of action and answered only to Himmler himself. While in the east SS men and security officers had the authority to punish subject populations summarily, in western Europe the Nazis pretended to respect the rule of law. But a special *Nacht und Nebel* (night and fog) decree empowered them to assassinate or abduct anyone who resisted openly. Those who disappeared and survived ended up in one of twenty-three major concentration camps, where overall survival rates were as low as 30 percent.

While this institutionalized brutality was formidable, violence and intimidation alone can never serve as the sole foundation of imperial rule. Even the Nazis needed local assistance to control their empire. As the German police chief in Amsterdam explained: "The main support of the German forces in the police sector and beyond was the Dutch police. Without it, not ten percent of the German occupation tasks would have been fulfilled.... Also it would have been practically impossible to seize even ten percent of Dutch Jewry without them."[29] While some of the functionaries who made themselves useful to the imperial regime were fanatics, more often than not the policemen who collaborated with the Nazi security services were motivated by duty and bureaucratic ambition. The Germans' success in co-opting defeated police forces further demonstrated how centralized nation-states were often more vulnerable to imperial conquest and domination than seemingly less advanced stateless societies.

Nevertheless, France should have been more resistant to Nazi imperial domination. Sustainable empires required sufficiently cooperative local allies, and in theory French patriotism was so strong that no Frenchman would betray his or her homeland by aiding an occupying power. This seemly dominant nationalism was actually an optimistic fiction that papered over significant economic, social, religious, and ethnic divisions. The Third Republic that emerged out of the chaos resulting from Bismarck's 1871 victory over the Second French Empire dedicated itself to turning peasants and ethnic minorities into Frenchmen, but it never put to rest the various feuds that had divided the French people since the revolution of 1789. Consequently,

Frenchmen continued to debate whether the dominant national order should be secular or Catholic, aristocratic or popular, centralized or regional, and urban or rural. Although France seemed strong and uniform under the Third Republic, the disaster of June 1940 brought all of these tensions to the surface, thereby creating an opening for Nazi empire builders.

The Third Republic was already under considerable internal strain well before the German victory. The prime ministership changed hands thirty-two times between 1924 and 1940 as various ideological and political factions vied for power. On the left, Radicals (who were essentially centrists), Socialists, and Communists fell out among themselves over questions of how much control the government should assert over the economy and the degree to which it should seek to make French society more egalitarian. Maurice Thorez's Communist Party was particularly strident in branding rival leftist parties "social fascists." The French right, which ranged from moderate conservatives to extreme reactionaries, was so divided in the interwar era that it largely conceded control of the government to the Socialists and Radicals. Frustrated, the rightists formed various paramilitary leagues and secret societies such as the Action Française (French Action), Croix-de-Feu (Cross of Fire), and Union Nationale des Combattants (National Combatants' Union) that advanced their agendas in the streets rather than at the polls.

In addition to these factional divisions, Frenchmen also continued to argue over the religious character of French society. Rural notables, clergymen, and lay Catholics never accepted their loss of influence under Napoleon and blamed the Third Republic's problems on immorality, decadence, and above all atheism. Conversely, republicans and secularists remained committed to traditions of the revolution, and many influential politicians and civil servants embraced Freemasonry as a counterweight to the Church. Deeply alarmed by the Masons' secrecy and unconventional religious beliefs, the French right believed their lodges were the sinister force behind many of the problems of the interwar era.

The lasting trauma of the Great War was the root cause of much of this political and social turmoil. The loss of 1.4 million soldiers and the wounding of 6.5 million more destroyed an entire generation. The result was an enormous gender imbalance and steadily falling birth rates. In the near term, immigration from eastern and southern Europe filled the population gap, and by 1931, 8 percent of the population was foreign-born. While these foreigners defused a labor shortage in the 1920s, they provoked a xenophobic backlash during the depression, when nearly one and a half million jobs disappeared and the flow of refugees from Nazi Germany increased. As the various political factions blamed each other for these problems, Frenchmen were largely unified in their determination to protect the blood of the nation by avoiding another continental war. They were much more deeply divided on how to manage the depression, resolve conflicts over immigration and women's rights, or cope with the twin threats of international fascism and Bolshevism.

These disputes nearly led to another revolution in 1934 when the right-wing leagues used a series of corruption scandals as an excuse to try to bring down the government through violent street protests. Calling for the elimination, if not murder, of foreigners, Jews, and leftist politicians, a mob numbering in the tens of thousands forced the police to open fire by charging the Chamber of Deputies. The result was fourteen rightists and one policeman dead and fourteen hundred injured, making it the worst outbreak of French political violence since the social strife that gave birth to the Third Republic in 1871.[30]

The riots brought down Edouard Daladier's Radical government and helped advance Pierre Laval to prominence as first the foreign minister and then the prime minister in a conservative unity government. But the street fighting also galvanized the left. Putting aside their differences temporarily in 1935, the Socialist, Radical, and Communist parties formed the Popular Front to deal with the right-wing leagues at home and the foreign fascist menace posed by the Nazi military buildup and the Italian invasion of Ethiopia. The Communists also found it easier to come to terms with their Socialist rivals after Stalin signed a five-year alliance with France.

Running on a platform promising bread, jobs, pensions, national unemployment insurance, women's rights, disarmament, and international peace, the Popular Front won a narrow parliamentary majority in the 1936 elections. Léon Blum became both the first Socialist prime minister and the first Jewish one, but with only 50 percent of the popular vote, his administration lacked the electoral muscle to make good on its promises. Although the Popular Front banned the rightist leagues, it was far less able to stand up to its own constituents.

Bowing to national workers' strikes, it forced employers to accept unionization, collective bargaining, a forty-hour workweek, paid holidays, and significant pay increases. While the French right detested these policies, it was too divided to mount a significant electoral threat to Blum. With the various leagues now outlawed, an extreme faction led by Eugène Deloncle formed the Comité Secret d'Action Révolutionnaire, more popularly known as the Cagoule (the hood), to use murder and political terror against what they saw as a communist menace. More sober conservatives, particularly bankers and industrialists, backed Jacques Doriot's Parti Populaire Français (French Popular Party), which was a fascist outgrowth of the banned Croix-de-Feu.

These rightist groups often took to the streets to advance their goals, but the Popular Front actually fell due to its own constituents' dissatisfaction with Blum's policies. In early 1937, Communists and Socialists broke with him over his refusal to ban the Parti Social Français, and price increases and the devaluation of the franc alienated both the working class and the middle class. Faced with intractable opposition on both the left and the right, Blum resigned in June 1937 when the French Senate refused him further emergency powers. He returned to office for a brief spell in 1938 and remained an extremely polarizing figure in French politics. The Communists and radicals castigated him for failing to rescue the republicans in the Spanish Civil War, while the extreme right detested him as a socialist Jew.

It is therefore hardly surprising that France was unprepared to deal with the Nazi threat. Consumed by internal squabbling, Frenchmen could agree only that they wanted to avoid war and that they despised the Third Republic. In 1937, the pacifist and World War I veteran Jean Giono declared: "What's the worst that can happen if Germany invades France?...Become Germans? For my part, I prefer being a living German to being a dead Frenchman." Alternatively, rightists swore: "Rather Hitler than Blum." Or as the Nazi sympathizer Marcel Deat asked during the tense months of early 1939: "Why die for Danzig?"[31] Instead of sympathizing with the Jewish refugees who flooded into the country as victims of Nazi aggression, many Frenchmen blamed them for provoking the Germans.

Ever mindful of the need to protect French blood, the various Third Republic governments of the 1930s favored appeasement over confrontation and defense over offense. Blum initiated a military modernization and rearmament program, but French strategists believed that they could best counter German advances in armor and airpower with a massive network of fortifications, known as the Maginot Line, on the Franco-German border. Budget shortfalls prevented them from extending it to the English Channel, which opened the way for the German blitzkrieg to skirt the French defenses by attacking through Luxembourg and Belgium.

When war broke out the Radical prime minister Edouard Daladier tried to repair France's deep political and social divisions by forming a coalition government with the conservatives. But Deat and many of the other right-wing extremists opposed honoring France's defense obligations to Poland, and the Communist Party shifted from promising to defend France to condemning "the imperialist and capitalist war" after Stalin signed the Nazi-Soviet Pact. The Communist Party leader Maurice Thorez deserted the French army and escaped to Moscow, and the French government responded to rumors of Soviet subversion by jailing six thousand French communists, including twenty-three members of the Chamber of Deputies. This infighting continued during the Phony War period between the Polish surrender and the Nazi assault on the Low Countries and eventually brought down Daladier's government in March 1940. It fell to the moderate Paul Reynaud, who had resisted his predecessor's appeasement policies, to surrender to Hitler four months later, but there was more than enough blame for France's greatest military disaster to go around.

The Nazis exploited these mutual recriminations effectively. The immediate pressures of war meant that the victorious German army did not have the time or the resources to rule France directly. In the short term, Hitler needed to keep the French obedient and complacent as he plundered their national wealth to fund his campaigns against Britain and the Soviet Union. As in all empires, the key was to induce a sufficient number of Frenchmen to play an active role in the new imperial regime.

In occupied France, the German military administration leaned heavily on French bureaucrats and policemen to run the country. Based at the Hotel Majestic in Paris, the Militärbefehlshaber in Frankreich (Military Command in France, MBF) consisted of a relatively small cadre of administrators and lawyers drawn from the army and Reich ministries. The civilian staff of the MBF totaled fifteen hundred in

1941, and roughly eighty thousand additional German businessmen, workers, and civil servants served in the occupation. The military garrison was one hundred thousand strong right after the armistice but declined to forty thousand second-rate troops in 1942. By comparison, the police forces for the Paris region numbered over thirty thousand, and the population of occupied France was twenty-three million.[32]

Lacking the manpower to rule the French directly, the Nazis attached the strategically important northern departments of Nord and Pas-de-Calais to the military regime in Belgium, but in the rest of occupied France, which consisted of forty-nine departments, they followed the existing French administrative template. This meant that provincial military governors and district commanders supervised prefects, subprefects, and mayors in the departments, *arrondissements*, and towns. French bureaucrats still answered to Pétain in Vichy, but as in colonial Kenya, German officers had full judicial authority and could appoint, fire, and transfer subordinate French bureaucrats.

Like all empires, this Nazi imperial regime parasitized the French economy. Demonstrating that an industrial nation-state was particularly vulnerable to imperial exploitation, they used the Reich Credit Bank certificates, currency manipulation (which overvalued the reichsmark by 50 percent), one-sided clearing advances, and grossly inflated occupation costs to wring roughly nine hundred billion francs out of France by the end of the occupation in 1944. This enormous sum, which amounted to nearly 60 percent of French governmental income, unquestionably made France the Third Reich's most valuable imperial acquisition.[33] As a result, the French suffered crippling inflation as the French banking authorities printed millions of francs' worth of unsupported currency to redeem the phony bank certificates and reimburse French suppliers for German "purchases." To add further insult to injury, the Germans used the proceeds of these one-sided transactions to buy shares in French companies. Almost comically, Nazi officials even carried the dress designs and records of the Chambre Syndicale de la Haute Couture back to the Reich as part of a ridiculous plan to have Berlin and Vienna replace Paris as the center of haute couture in Europe.[34]

While the French resented these exploitive policies, they dared not resist them openly. As the American journalist Thomas Kernan sympathetically observed: "The world's best army is sitting on [the Frenchman's] neck. If he owns a business and won't run it, it is taken away and given to a stranger. If he doesn't work, there is always the danger that he will be drafted for a labor camp and end up in a beet field in Silesia."[35] Nazi imperial rule in France rested on updated versions of the same inherent intimidation and brutality that were the foundations of earlier empires. Martial law and military courts allowed the Germans to ignore French law when it suited them. In the early days of the occupation, they ordered French mayors to round up local notables to live as hostages in requisitioned hotels until it became apparent that there would be no mass resistance. The SS, however, was not so lenient. With authority over all German police forces and eventually the French police as well, they were a power unto themselves. SS men and Gestapo officers in military uniforms dealt viciously with all forms of opposition and had no reservations about executing hostages.

As would be expected, Jews were particularly vulnerable. Numbering some three hundred thousand in 1939, the French Jewish population was evenly split between citizens and relatively recent migrants from central and eastern Europe. The latter group was most at risk because many Frenchmen blamed them for the war. Native-born Jews, however, were better protected because most were well assimilated into French society. The Nazis never succeeded in confining French Jews to ghettos, and the Générale des Israélites de France (French Jewish Council) they created to enforce German orders and collect a mass "atonement" fine of one billion francs was never as effective or compliant as the eastern *Judenrats* (Jewish councils) that helped round up victims for the concentration camps. Frustrated, the Nazis worked to isolate Jews by making the French citizenry accomplices in their exploitation and eventual extermination. They coerced French police officials to create a special section charged with carrying out a census of French Jews as a first step toward arrest and deportation. A 1940 MBF circular to military administrators explained: "The object is, in principle, to replace Jews by Frenchmen, so that in this way the French population can participate equally in the economic elimination of the Jews, and so avoid creating the impression that Germans alone wish to take the place of Jews."

While the French police dragged their heels in carrying out the census, the Nazis' aryanization program was far more effective in involving the French in their genocidal agenda. Rather than seizing Jewish assets directly, the imperial regime forced Jews to sell their businesses and assets to French owners. Driven by greed rather than ideology, Frenchmen scrambled to take advantage of this windfall. They turned on Jewish partners and flooded the authorities with requests to purchase specific companies or enterprises at cut-rate prices. Profits went into the French treasury, which in turn helped subsidize the larger Nazi extractive agenda. The French role also made the aryanization project appear permissible under the Hague Conventions. Although Hitler had no respect for the niceties of international law, the Nazis were careful to give their imperial agenda a legal veneer in France. Mindful of Allied propaganda depicting them as brutal despots, in the west they cloaked themselves in the same sorts of moral rationalizations that justified earlier imperial projects.

To this end, the Nazi imperial regime turned misinformation into an effective instrument of imperial control. The propagandists in the MBF and the German embassy in Paris flooded France with press releases, brochures, newsreels, and posters reminding the French of their subjecthood, warning of the consequences of rebellion, and highlighting Allied defeats. The French minorities were a primary target of this propaganda. Building on the standard imperial template of divide and rule, the Nazis sought to demoralize and split the French by playing up the ethnic divisions that the Third Republic worked so hard to eliminate. According to German propaganda, France was actually a French-dominated conglomeration of Occitans, Alsatians, Bretons, Corsicans, Flemings, Catalans, and Basques. The imperial regime promised Alsatian and Breton separatists, whose leaders had spent much of the interwar period in French jails, that it would sponsor their nationalist ambitions. The German military administration, however, would only let the Bretons form a watered-down national council, and Hitler dashed the hopes of the Alsatians by informally annexing Alsace-Lorraine.

More subtly, the Germans went to great lengths to demonstrate their cultural superiority and remind the French that their future lay in a Europe ruled by the Third Reich. Hitler styled himself as an heir of Napoleon and made an elaborate show of returning the remains of the French emperor's only son from Vienna for reburial on French soil. The German embassy also organized well-attended public exhibitions on the achievements of German agriculture, the secret conspiratorial workings of Freemasonry, the threat of Bolshevism, and the exploitive role of Jews in France. The Nazi ambassador to France, Otto Abetz, gave French authors large advances to produce German translations of their works (most were never published) and sent them on luxurious junkets to Germany along with prominent French actors, musicians, and architects. In return, he arranged for the Berlin Philharmonic Orchestra and Chamber Orchestra of Berlin to play the works of classical German composers in Paris.

The widespread and pervasive hopelessness arising from the military collapse of 1940 left many Frenchmen vulnerable to these sorts of soft methods of control in the early days of the occupation. French publishers voluntarily withdrew books that might provoke their imperial masters, and in western France a school inspector ordered Latin teachers not to assign Tacitus on the grounds that his depiction of Germanic peoples as barbarians might cause offense.[36] This sort of paranoia was symptomatic of imperial subjecthood. Deeply troubled by the scope and suddenness of the German victory, some people desperately sought stability and security.

Other Frenchmen viewed the conquest as an opportunity for social advance or to redress past wrongs, which made it relatively easy for the imperial regime to get them to report on each other. In some cases this took the seemingly benign form of helping Abetz gauge the effectiveness of the embassy's propaganda campaign. But in other instances Frenchmen denounced their neighbors to the French and German authorities as black marketeers, spies, communists, or Jews. French prefects and policemen usually discouraged such reports, but the Germans paid thousands of francs for useful information. Most denunciations took the form of unsigned letters and generally were born of personal animosity rather than ideological conviction. The ability to condemn a rival or enemy to arrest and deportation to a German concentration camp was a powerful weapon that Frenchmen used to break labor strikes, resolve neighborhood feuds, and even punish cheating spouses. Subject Italians did much the same thing in Napoleonic Italy.

This sense of traumatic dislocation was equally prevalent in the unoccupied portion of France, where the weight of German rule was much lighter. Although Pétain's *état français* had the illusion of sovereignty, it was still a Nazi imperial puppet state. In surrendering control of its diplomatic and military affairs in return for a measure of domestic and social autonomy, the Vichy regime resembled the Indian princely states and northern Nigerian emirates that the

British sponsored to defray the costs of empire. Pétain would have been deeply offended by such a comparison, and he certainly would have countered that his government still had nominal control of the French Empire, a lightly armed one-hundred-thousand-man army, and most of the French fleet. But in time, he discovered that he had no more sovereignty than his African or Indian counterparts.

Although the Vichyites were shocked deeply by the collapse of the Third Republic, they shed no tears over its passing. They instead assured themselves that the Nazi victory was an opportunity to build a new, stronger, and more moral France free from the influence of secularists, Protestants, Jews, and Freemasons. In guaranteeing the French people a quick return to national dignity, prosperity, and normalcy, Pétain was part of a long millenarian tradition, in which movements such as the Andean Taki Onqoy, the Sioux Ghost Dance, the Chinese Boxers, and the Kenya Land Freedom Army promised to create a new world free of imperial subjecthood. Yet where these nonwestern peoples employed religion and local custom to imagine a spiritually revitalized postimperial order, Pétain relied on politics, diplomacy, and ultimately collaboration.

The Nazis actively encouraged this kind of wishful thinking. Scheming to turn the French against Britain and reduce occupation expenses, Hitler let Pétain believe that France would have a place of influence in postwar Europe if it made itself sufficiently useful to the Third Reich. This was a total lie, but the Nazi imperial regime largely fulfilled its promise to leave the Vichyites to their own devices in the first two years of the occupation. The town of Vichy's population of three thousand more than quadrupled as all the major ministries except for the Ministry of Finance and the Banque de France relocated to the new center of French political power. Internationally, some forty foreign governments recognized the *état français* as a neutral sovereign state. Six, including the United States, even maintained embassies in Vichy.

Pétain drew his authority from a law passed by the Third Republic's National Assembly in July 1940 vesting him with all governmental powers as the president of the Council of Ministers. French civil and military officials swore an oath of loyalty to him as the chief of state, and the regime's propagandists built a fascist-style cult of loyalty around him as France's great savior. The marshal's photograph hung in every school classroom, traveling exhibitions highlighted his life and career, and towns throughout southern France renamed streets after him. Some artists even substituted his image for that of Marianne as the symbol of eternal France. Depicting himself as above politics, Pétain made the military his primary base of support. He amalgamated all prewar ex-servicemen's organizations into the Légion Française de Combattants (Legion of French Veterans), which infiltrated most every sector of Vichy society.

Pétain actually played a very small role in the day-to-day business of government, and there was a steady turnover in the Vichy ministries during the German occupation. Pierre Laval, who harbored a lasting grudge against the Third Republic over his downfall at the hands of the left in 1936, was the first Vichy minister of state. His influence stemmed from his behind-the-scenes role in negotiating the armistice and convincing the National Assembly to renounce exile and disband itself. As a primary architect of collaboration, Laval had close allies in the German military administration in Paris. This is probably why Pétain removed him in favor of Admiral François Darlan in early 1941. A profoundly anglophobic naval officer who never forgave the British attack on the French fleet at Mers-el-Kebir, Darlan was even more willing to collaborate with the Germans than his predecessor had been.

Laval and Darlan had considerable power because they were unhindered by the constraints of representative democracy. In theory, Pétain's first obligation was to draft a new constitution, but this was impossible while half of France was under German occupation. Instead, Pétain engaged in what Robert Paxton called "Bonapartist executive constitution-making."[37] In addition to appointing and dismissing ministers at will, he modified the Third Republic's administrative institutions to suit his needs. Bureaucrats in both the occupied and free zones who rallied to the new regime kept their jobs, but the Vichyites fired anyone whom they considered politically or socially suspect. They also ignored democratic election laws, appointing mayors and municipal councils directly. The Nazis were generally satisfied with these developments and pretended that Pétain's administrative reach extended to the entire country so long as he did not threaten their strategic interests and fulfilled France's financial obligations to the Reich.

For the most part, the Vichy regime rarely gave the Nazis any trouble, for it focused most of its attention inward. In justifying their collaboration, the Vichyites planned to restore the true France through what it called a National Revolution. Dispensing with the revolutionary virtues of *liberté, égalité, fraternité* (liberty, equality, fraternity), they made *travail, famille, patrie* (work, family, fatherland) their watchwords. Out of the ashes of the morally bankrupt Third Republic the National Revolution aimed to create a corporatist political and social order as an alternative to capitalism and communism. The Vichy social revolutionaries believed that they could substitute state-directed corporations of employers, workers, and peasants for the divisiveness of the free market and Marxist class struggle. They also forged an alliance with the church by banning Masonic lodges and repealing most of the Third Republic's anticlerical laws. In return, senior cardinals and archbishops issued a decree requiring Catholics to give their "absolute loyalty to the legitimate power in France."

Equally important, the National Revolution aimed to restore moral order by returning women and children to their proper places in society. Blaming France's defeat on falling birth rates and domestic chaos, Vichy ideologues stepped up their efforts to expel women from the workplace. They banned divorce and advertisements for contraceptives, increased penalties for abortions, and gave nursing mothers and women bearing more than four children medals and increased rations. To make these children proper Frenchmen the regime fired leftist teachers, restored religious instruction in the state curriculum, and subsidized private Catholic schools. Additionally, dour Vichy officials banned youths from cinemas on weekday afternoons and outlawed dancing and excessively strong alcoholic beverages. To make sure young men spent their time properly, they created the Compagnons de France (Companions of France) for boys fifteen to twenty and the Chantiers de la Jeunesse (Youth Workshops) for those of draft age who normally would have gone into the army. In the short term, the members of these groups would serve France through their labor. Eventually they would become the nucleus of a reconstituted national army.

While the Vichyites looked forward in imagining a new France, they also used the German victory as an opportunity for revenge. Obsessed with the need for national unity to ensure that anti-German resistance did not give the Nazis an excuse to interfere with the National Revolution, they went to great lengths to suppress dissent. This effectively made Vichy France a police state. The Vichyites took over and centralized municipal police forces into a new Police Nationale (National Police) and supplanted the *gendarmerie* with the paramilitary Groupes Mobiles de Reserve (Mobile Reserve Groups) that swore loyalty directly to Pétain. A state spy network tapped phones and read mail and telegrams to identify traitors and trouble-makers who faced prosecution in "special courts." In 1941, Pétain and Darlan allowed Joseph Darnand, a decorated veteran and former Cagoule member, to recruit a right-wing militia from the ranks of the more moderate French Legion of Veterans. Known as the Service d'Ordre Légionnaire (Legion Security Force, SOL), it specifically targeted the regime's enemies.

The roster of people and groups who fell into this category was quite extensive. It included communists, Freemasons, Jews, foreigners, followers of the exiled general Charles de Gaulle, and the leftist leaders of the Third Republic. The Vichy regime even prosecuted Blum, Dala-dier, Reynaud, and several other politicians and generals for leading France into a disastrous war, but the Germans ended the trials when they became nationalistic inquiries into the French defeat. Vichy offi-cials had a much freer hand in dealing with their other enemies and jailed them along with criminals and black marketeers in a network of forty-nine detention camps. To control the immigrant contamination, Pétain's government revoked the citizenship of half a million natural-ized Frenchmen to pave the way for their arrest and deportation.

Predictably, Vichy authoritarianism fell most heavily on Jews. Act-ing on their own initiative, Vichy officials enacted laws banning them from public office, the civil and colonial services, and the professions. Although they grudgingly accepted well-assimilated Jews as French-men, they created the General Commissariat for Jewish Questions in response to German pressure and set about segregating all Jews from greater French society. Only Jewish veterans, Legion of Honor holders, and distinguished artists were exempt. Some Vichyites hated Jews passionately, but their willingness to abet Hitler's anti-Semitic agenda was born as much from pragmatic self-interest as from ideol-ogy. In setting up their own version of the Nazi aryanization pro-grams, they hoped to defend French sovereignty and keep the wealth of French Jews out of German hands.

The Nazis approved, but they played no direct role in pushing the Vichy regime to adopt these anti-Semitic policies. More important, they had no interest in the National Revolution, and like all empire builders, their primary concern was obedience and extraction. From the German perspective, collaboration was a clever ruse to keep the French divided and complacent. Hitler reportedly had trouble even pronouncing the German version of the word, *Kollaboration*, and made no secret of his true intentions for France in discussions with his inner circle. According to Goebbels: "Talk of collaboration is only designed for the moment.... [Hitler] said, should the war turn out as he wished, then France must pay dearly, because it caused and inaugurated it."[38] In the short term, the *Führer* let the French believe that collaboration was an escape from full subjecthood. From the Nazi standpoint, the threat of direct military rule, German control of the Vichy border, and the millions of French POWs in Germany ensured that the *état français* did not become unmanageable.

Responding to the lure of restored sovereignty, the Vichyites were actually the driving force behind collaboration in the first two years of the occupation. After the British attack on Mers-el-Kebir, an enraged Pétain offered to give the Germans access to French bases in North Africa, while Laval suggested five hundred French pilots might help fight the Battle of Britain. In October 1940, Pétain and Laval went a step further by meeting directly with Hitler as he traveled through France to confer with General Francisco Franco in Spain. Seeking permission to rebuild the armed forces and reinforce the overseas empire, the Vichy leaders obligingly acknowledged that France was responsible for the war. They flinched, however, when Hitler demanded that France join the war as an Axis junior partner.

Laval's successor Darlan was more willing to accept the inherent risks of collaboration by accepting the German conditions. His primary objective was a formal peace treaty that would end Nazi occupation in exchange for France's acceptance of a supporting economic and strategic role in a unified Nazi Europe. Vichy economic planners proposed a network of highways and canals linking the French and German economies and offered to help develop the Reich's new eastern "colonies." In promising to use the French navy and empire to defend the continent as part of an "Atlantic shield," Darlan implicitly signaled a willingness to fight the Allies and acknowledge permanent Nazi rule in Europe. This bellicose stance was in part a response to the undeclared naval war in the Mediterranean resulting from attempts by French ships to run the Royal Navy's blockade of continental Europe. In May 1941, Darlan even made a radio broadcast accusing Britain of planning to seize the French Empire and reduce France to the status of a "second-class dominion, a continental Ireland."

The Vichy premier's offer to take a more active role in the fighting was tempting, and the Nazis strung him along. Ignoring his plea for a permanent peace treaty, they offered to reduce the occupation bill and relax control of Vichy's borders in exchange for tangible French military aid. The draft of these Paris Protocols gave the Afrika Korps access to French railways and military bases in North Africa, turned over fifteen hundred French trucks, and required the French fleet to escort German naval convoys in the Mediterranean. This was too much even for Pétain. Signing the Paris Protocols would have alienated the United States and exposed France's overseas territories to Allied attack. Overruling his minister of state, Pétain only allowed the Germans to use Syrian airfields to supply anti-British rebels in Iraq. Darlan trumpeted the Syrian arrangement as an example of successful collaboration, but Hitler's paltry concessions damaged the admiral's credibility. However, the Vichy regime was stuck with collaborationism, and in August 1942 Pétain congratulated Hitler publicly for "cleansing" French soil by repelling an Allied raid on the port of Dieppe. He then went on to offer to "open a French crenellation in the Atlantic Wall" if the Nazis allowed the French army back into the occupied zone.

While Hitler manipulated the Vichy leaders masterfully, earlier generations of conquerors would have recognized his bait-and-switch tactics as one of the most time-tested strategies of imperial rule. In accepting a subordinate role in the Nazi empire, the Vichyites tied their authority and status to the new imperial regime. Togodumnus, Theodemir, Prince Manqu, and Mir Jafar were in similar predicaments. While German officials were surprised at how closely the French obeyed the terms of the armistice agreement, Pétain and his allies cooperated with the Nazis primarily because they needed some sort of concession to demonstrate that collaboration worked.

The Nazis were able to control France with a relatively small cohort of troops and administrators by exploiting this Vichy quandary. The trauma of the French military collapse threw established conceptions of French patriotism into question and opened the way for Frenchmen to imagine alternative conceptions of France without appearing overtly treasonous. For these ambitious men the Germans became useful allies against rival nationalists.

The Nazis nurtured and profited from the resulting discord by alternately supporting and abandoning the various French factions who were still fighting the battles of the 1930s. Exploiting the partition of France, the Germans allowed some leftists and many right-wing extremists to operate relatively freely in Paris as a counterweight to Pétain. Prominent figures in the latter motley group included Marcel Deat, a former socialist turned Nazi sympathizer, Jacques Doriot, the ex-communist founder of the fascist Parti Populaire Français, and the Cagoulard leader Eugène Deloncle. All of these men founded new collaborationist versions of their organizations, but Doriot's Parti Populaire Français had the widest following and was Pétain's most serious rival. There was also Marcel Bucard, whose Mouvement Franciste (Francist Movement) made the easy transition from one of the most extreme interwar right-wing leagues to collaborationist party. Finally, Abetz introduced another divisive element into Paris politics by installing Laval in the French capital as a future bargaining chip after the premier fell from power in Vichy.

Although all of these groups professed an ultranationalistic love of France, they competed for the privilege of defining what form the French nation would take in the new Nazi Europe. The Germans indulged them by allowing them to recruit, organize, hold parades, and fly tricolor flags, but there were no elections to be won or political spoils to be divided. They often fought each other in the Paris streets and bars, and rumors flew that the "Gaullist agent" who tried to assassinate Laval and Deat at a public ceremony was really in the pay of Deloncle. Ultimately, however, the Paris collaborationists competed primarily by trying to outdo each other in proving their usefulness to the foreign imperial regime. Each aspired to supplant Pétain, but they all had to pay him public deference as one of France's greatest heroes. In practical terms, they understood that their fortunes were tied to the Nazis.

The collaborationists therefore put aside their differences in the summer of 1941 to form the Légion des Volontaires Français Contre le Bolchévisme (Legion of French Volunteers Against Bolshevism, LVF) for service in Hitler's war with the Soviet Union. The unit was well outside the mainstream French military establishment, and none of the recruits came from the largely toothless Vichy armistice army.

While its collaborationist sponsors generally despised each other, they agreed that they hated communists more. They also recognized that the LVF offered the only hope for French rearmament and envisioned that it would grow it into a full division. The unit drew recruits from the Vichy and unoccupied zones, but it was never larger than a battalion. Still, many Frenchmen initially embraced it as a symbol of French sovereignty. Pétain suspended the anti-Gaullist law banning Frenchmen from serving in military units outside France and told LVF members that they were participating in a great "anti-Bolshevik crusade" to save France and western civilization. The rector of the Catholic Institute in Paris, Cardinal Baudrillart, went even further in giving them his benediction.

> As a priest and a Frenchman, I venture to say that these Legionnaires rank among the best sons of France.... These soldiers are doing their part in helping to prepare the great French renaissance.... In its own way this Legion constitutes a new chivalry. These Legionnaires are the Crusaders of the twentieth century. May their arms be blessed.[39]

The LVF troops never lived up to this lofty praise and were little different from the countless native auxiliaries that served in imperial armies throughout history. Far from treating them as sovereign allies, the Nazis used them to patch their increasingly thin lines on the Soviet front. When the LVF fought in Russia it did so wearing German uniforms as the German 638th Infantry Regiment attached to the Seventh Bavarian Division. The unit was ill-disciplined, and when it took heavy casualties in the 1941 Soviet winter offensive German military authorities filled out its ranks with two hundred Algerian Arabs.

The collaborationist legionnaires were not the only Frenchmen to remain under arms after the armistice. Pétain and his Paris-based rivals faced a powerful adversary in Charles de Gaulle in their competition to define the character and scope of postwar France. Initially, the exiled general's Comité National Français (French National Committee), which was essentially a self-proclaimed government in exile, appeared of little consequence in the first years of the occupation. While he depicted himself as a patriot forced to defy his superiors when they seized power illegally, only a single parliamentary deputy and a few colonial army officers backed him. Most of the French soldiers that the Royal Navy rescued at Dunkirk chose to return to occupied France rather than join his Free French forces. Technically, to do so would have been desertion and treason given that the Vichy government declared that Frenchmen who left the country without permission automatically lost their citizenship. The British-sponsored Free French attack on Dakar in September 1940 further reinforced the impression that de Gaulle's followers were traitors.

This meant that the General had to look to the French Empire for allies against the Vichyites. This was problematical, for most imperial governors and army officers were conservatives who sympathized with Pétain, particularly after the British attack on Mers-el-Kebir. In the French West Africa Federation, every single territorial government rallied to the Vichy regime. Its governor-general, Pierre Boisson, enthusiastically put his own version of the National Revolution into practice by removing Jews, communists, and Freemasons from the civil service and made plans to attack the British West African territories. Renouncing the fundamental French legitimizing imperial ideology of assimilation, Boisson introduced racial segregation, purged military veterans and westernized *évolués* from the voting rolls, and placed all Africans under "native law" regardless of their education or level of westernization.

These discriminatory policies help to explain why Félix Éboué, the Guianan-born governor of Chad, offered de Gaulle a base of operations in French Equatorial Africa. Bravely acting without consideration for two sons in German POW camps, he used the support of Jacques-Philippe Leclerc, one of the few French army officers to join de Gaulle in exile, to convince his fellow equatorial governors to renounce Pétain and join the Free French cause. Brazzaville thus became Free France's first capital in exile, and it is worth noting that most of its soldiers at this time were conscripted Africans.

As committed French imperialists, both de Gaulle and Pétain exploited Africans because they agreed that France's greatness depended on its empire. The Vichyites were therefore outraged when their German occupiers behaved like an imperial elite in France. In doing so, they took their lead from Hitler, who considered the French a lesser Latin people occupying a middle ground between the German master race and the subhuman Slavs. In *Mein Kampf*, he declared that France's overseas empire had contaminated the French people and warned that France's reliance on African soldiers and obsession with "Negroid ideas" was a "threatening menace to the existence of the white race in Europe."[40] In his eyes the Third Republic's quick collapse in June 1940 confirmed this view.

While Hitler may have considered the French to be racially tainted, he still enjoyed the pleasures of Paris as he triumphantly toured the city after the French surrender. Putting into practice the common phrase *leben wie Gott in Frankreich* (living like God in France), Germans followed his example by taking advantage of the artificial currency imbalance to go on shopping sprees and enjoy Paris's finest hotels, restaurants, and nightclubs, where window signs now read *Hier spricht man Deutch* (German spoken here). They even advanced city clocks one hour forward to match "greater Reich time." A military tourist agency called Jeder einmal in Paris (Everyone in Paris Once) brought soldiers on leave to the city, where German-language newspapers and tourist books produced by commissioned French writers provided an introduction to the main attractions and French history and culture. Enlisted men enjoyed well-stocked canteens, reserved movie theaters, free rides on the Paris Métro, and their own medically supervised brothels. Senior officers socialized with French elites and dined on the best food and wine while being waited on by white-gloved servants. The top Paris fashion designers held special exhibitions for the wives and girlfriends of the Germans.

As was the norm in most empires, many of these women were from the subject population. At a time when the mass incarceration of young French men in German POW camps exacerbated the interwar gender imbalance, the young, robust, and relatively well-disciplined German soldier was appealing to many French women. The Germans' high wages and special privileges also offered women a chance to escape the more burdensome aspects of the occupation. Even a young Parisian woman with a brother in the Free French forces gave in to the temptation of dating a German officer: "He was all in white, like Lohengrin, in a white linen jacket, shining eagle emblem, knight commander of the Iron Cross, white cap and white gloves."[41] German men took full advantage of these sorts of sentiments. Additionally, German homosexuals also found willing partners and relatively little persecution in Paris.

Ironically, imperial subjecthood meant that the French themselves could no longer live up to the German vision of stereotypically decadent Frenchmen. The Nazis' brutally efficient extractive policies meant that there was virtually no coal for heat in the first winter of the occupation, and freezing Frenchmen got around on bicycles or in charcoal-fueled vehicles. Mandatory food exports and shortage-driven inflation meant that the average person subsisted on fifteen hundred calories per day. There was a tuberculosis epidemic and out-breaks of diseases caused by malnutrition. Children were particularly vulnerable. Infant mortality increased by 40 percent in the northern departments attached to the Belgian military government, and the average height of all French children dropped by seven centimeters for boys and eleven centimeters for girls between 1935 and 1944. Conditions were so bad that many French women, particularly those with missing husbands, were driven to prostitution to support them-selves and their children.[42]

The collapse of French political authority and the hardships of imperial occupation forced the French to look out for themselves. Parisian elites adapted particularly well and warmly feted leading Germans at cocktail parties, concerts, horse races, and other society events. Ambassador Abetz, who had an attractive French wife and a French movie star for a mistress, became a leading society figure by hosting glamorous parties at a confiscated rural estate. More common Frenchmen were of course not invited, but they too looked for ways to reach some sort of accord with the imperial power. The popularity of German-language study increased in French schools as language proficiency became an asset for those seeking German business con-tacts or a job in the military adminitration. The imperial authorities paid double wages for secretaries, and even housekeepers working for the Germans earned more than a policeman with eight years of service.

The nearly total Nazi dominance of the French economy meant that Germans became both primary employers and customers in the country. In the first case, roughly 350,000 Frenchmen worked for the MBF or military garrison in 1942, while an additional 184,000 vol-untarily took jobs in metropolitan Germany even before the Nazis demanded conscripted laborers. The Germans also accounted for between 70 and 90 percent of factory orders in some French industries during this period. This meant that the French willingly built ships, radios, airplanes, and other sorts of essential war matériel for their imperial masters. Marcel Michelin sold the Germans 80 percent of his company's tire production even though two of his sons were serving with the Free French.[43] Michelin supported de Gaulle enthusiastically, but industrialists who refused to do business with the imperial regime risked losing their factories and workers to confiscation and conscription. Less savory individuals helped the Nazis fence looted property and launder profits. Black marketeers supplied them with foodstuffs and luxury goods at prices well beyond the reach of the impoverished French consumer.

Many of these people would answer for their choices after the Nazi defeat, but their self-serving version of collaboration obscures the larger reality that most Frenchmen did their best to avoid taking sides during the first two years of the occupation. Although the Nazi victory seemed total and permanent, the changing fortunes of war led many to withdraw inward to wait for a clearer indication of what the new France would look like. In doing so, they stood aloof from the Nazi imperial regime, the Vichy state, de Gaulle's Free French government in exile, and the embryonic domestic resistance movements.

This did not mean that Frenchmen accepted their subjecthood passively. Recognizing that armed action would have been suicidal, many opted for the safer gambit of tweaking the occupiers. They pretended not to understand German and kept necessary social interaction to a minimum. More daring people sang "La Marseillaise," wore tricolor ribbons in their buttonholes, and observed Bastille Day and Armistice Day. Others made fun of the Nazis and their Vichy allies. German soldiers became "potato beetles" in popular slang, children in Nantes peppered Pétain's portrait with spitballs, and the illustrator and artist Tomi Ungerer recalled Alsatians turning the Nazi salute *"Heil Hitler"* into *"ein liter"* (one liter, presumably of beer). Angry German officials ordered that movie houses show films with the lights on because French audiences coughed and hissed at propaganda newsreels and cheered at the wrong moments. Graffiti turned *rauchen verboten* (smoking forbidden) signs on Paris Métro cars into *race verte verboten* ("the green race forbidden," a reference to German army uniforms). Scrawling the V-for-victory symbol popularized by British radio broadcasts on walls was more subversive, and in some areas anti-Vichy and anti-German graffiti became such a problem that the French police set up stakeouts to catch the perpetrators.

As in earlier empires, it was dangerous to be caught challenging imperial authority. Children and teenagers, who tended to blame their elders for failing to stand up to the Nazis, were often the most daring. In November 1940, a group of Parisian university students marched up the Champs-Élysées to lay a wreath of the Tomb of the Unknown Soldier to protest the arrest of one of their antifascist professors. This explicitly political protest crossed a line, and the Nazis arrested more than one hundred of the marchers. Similarly, when coal miners in northern France struck for better wages and rations, German troops forced them back to work at gunpoint. Generally speaking, the MBF was relatively patient in allowing the French their minor expressions of defiance, but it would not tolerate direct challenges to Nazi interests.

This was one of the primary reasons that there was little armed French resistance before 1942. Britain's Special Operations Executive, which promoted resistance and sabotage in occupied Europe, had very little success in stirring up the French during this period. Riddled by informers and divided by disagreements over the nature and leadership of postwar France, the first resistance groups initially focused on just making their presence known by publishing underground newspapers and putting up broadsides.

It was the French communists, who had refused to help defend France after the Nazi-Soviet pact, who became the most active resisters once Hitler invaded the Soviet Union. Beginning in August 1941, they sought to open a "home front" through sabotage, arson, and assassination. While their efforts were of little strategic consequence, communist assassination teams killed the *Feldkommandant* of Nantes and a few other German soldiers and military administrators in the fall of 1941. The Nantes case was the most serious, for the dispatch of a *Feldkommandant* was the equivalent of an African murdering a British provincial commissioner in Kenya. No imperial state could tolerate this kind of opposition because it exposed the inherent fragility of indirect rule. Like all imperial officials, the Germans could govern France only if the majority of Frenchmen believed active resistance was futile. This is why Hitler and the German high command took a direct role in formulating a response to the attacks. Vowing to execute one hundred French communists for each slain German soldier, the MBF ordered each district in occupied France to compile suitable lists of hostages. The military governor General Otto von Stülpnagel actually opposed these "Polish methods" on the grounds that the collective punishment tactics of the east would undermine collaboration and play into the hands of the British, but his superiors overruled him. The Nazis consequently murdered forty-eight French hostages in Nantes before von Stülpnagel arranged a pause to give the population a chance to cooperate.

The French response to these executions was telling. Rather than seeing the communist assassins as heroes, the city government in Nantes added seven hundred thousand francs to the German reward for the capture of the *Feldkommandant*'s killers and posted placards that eulogized the slain imperial official as a man of "intelligent understanding." An editorial in the local newspaper declared: "All good French people, all those who have a sense of honor, are outraged and have poured scorn on the criminals who acted under the cover of darkness, shot from behind, and ran away. *The assassins must be found*."[44] Most Frenchmen in 1941 blamed the communists for pushing the Germans to behave so brutally, particularly after further assassinations led to more retaliatory executions. Pétain tried his best to restrain the Nazis, but he blamed the communists for the crisis. While he disagreed with the marshal, de Gaulle also discouraged his followers from provoking the Nazis by attacking individual soldiers. Their rare point of accord reflected the implicit recognition that resisting a dominant empire was futile.

Although the Third Reich initially appeared impregnable, it was built on a relatively short-lived military imbalance that produced quick and easy victories at the beginning of the war. This came to an end in the winter of 1941 when the blitzkrieg in the Soviet Union bogged down at the gates of Moscow and the renewed German offensive the following year resulted in the bloody debacle at Stalingrad. Driven to desperation by the Nazis' genocidal version of settler colonialism, common Russians and Ukrainians put aside their divisions and formed guerrilla bands that made the Nazi predicament worse by wreaking havoc behind German lines. The partisans even murdered the *Gauleiter* of the Reich Commissariat of the Ukraine in his bed. The Nazi security forces responded with an unrestrained fury that made the execution of the Nantes hostages appear tame, but the necessity of fortifying their lines of communication diverted men and matériel from the front. The Red Army, by comparison, swelled to more than four hundred divisions by 1943 and handed the Germans another crushing defeat in a decisive tank battle near Kursk. By 1944, Soviet troops were advancing into Poland.

In the west, the Nazis faced similar reverses. Upholding their obligations under the Tripartite Pact, Hitler and Mussolini declared war on the United States after the attack on Pearl Harbor. The resulting American economic and military aid helped the British defeat the Afrika Korps decisively in Egypt at El Alamein. In November 1942, an Anglo-American invasion of French North Africa known as Operation Torch caught the Nazi armies in a vise that forced their surrender entirely in May 1943. Two months later, a seaborne assault on Italy opened up a new front and led Italians to overthrow Mussolini. The demise of his fascist ally in the fall of 1943 forced Hitler to occupy northern Italy to block the Allied advance. Additionally, attacks by British and American bombers brought the war home to the German people. All told, the Allies' relentless air assault killed six hundred thousand people, injured eight hundred thousand more, and destroyed two million homes.[45] No privileged metropolitan imperial population ever faced this level of immediate and crushing retribution at the hands of their intended victims.

Panicked by the Allied advances, the Nazis demanded even more wealth and manpower from their subjects. Conscripted civilian laborers from the occupied territories, prisoners of war, and concentration camp inmates became central in expanding war production and preserving living standards as German combat losses approached four million by 1944. As a result, foreign workers were so prevalent in the German heartland in the later years of the war that the Reich Office of Racial Purity worried that their presence and sexual availability would contaminate the *Volk*.[46]

Although they espoused a doctrine of racial purity, the vaunted Nazi legions eventually similarly relied heavily on non-German imperial auxiliaries. In addition to pressing Italian and Eastern European allies for more units to fill out their eastern lines, the Nazis enlisted subject peoples directly into the SS military arm under the guise of defending Christian Europe in a grand anticommunist crusade. At first Himmler insisted that only Danes, Norwegians, Dutchmen, and other nationalities with "Germanic blood" were eligible for the Waffen-SS, but as casualties mounted his recruiters became more practical in meeting their manpower needs. In addition to giving the French LVF SS status and raising a sixteen-thousand-man French SS grenadier regiment, the Nazis put aside their racist rhetoric by raising foreign legions of supposedly subhuman Bosnian Muslims and Ukrainians.

This racial pragmatism had no bearing on the Third Reich's assault on Jews and other "inferior" peoples. Nazi ideologues at first claimed that they intended to resettle the Jews imprisoned in ghettos and concentration camps somewhere in the vast eastern spaces of their empire, but the Red Army's westward advance led Hitler and his men to turn to genocide. Working largely in secret, they built death camps near the main concentration complexes where they systematically murdered millions of Jews, Slavs, Roma (Gypsies), and other racial enemies of the *Volk*.

Relatively few Frenchmen suffered this fate, but the Third Reich's failing fortunes had a substantial impact on the Nazi imperial regime in France. From the Vichy standpoint, Operation Torch was not a liberation but an invasion of sovereign French territory. An outraged Pétain declared: "We are being attacked, we shall defend ourselves."[47] Consequently, many French units in Morocco and Algeria fought back against the Allied invasion until common sense led Darlan, who by chance happened to be visiting his son in Algiers, to negotiate a cease-fire. Claiming Pétain's secret blessing, the Vichy premier formed a council of senior French officials and officers to govern the "liberated" colonies. It is difficult to know if Darlan truly intended to switch sides because a young monarchist officer assassinated him in late December 1942.

Surprisingly, the Americans and British allowed the Vichy administration to remain in power in North Africa because they suspected de Gaulle aspired to become a military dictator. They hoped to install General Henri Giraud as the leader of the Comité Français de Libération Nationale (French Committee of National Liberation), but de Gaulle got the better of both the Allies and the Vichyites by depicting himself successfully as the legitimate leader of the true France. His establishment of Algiers as the next French capital in exile after Brazzaville was the first step toward asserting his authority over the disorganized French resistance and liberating France on his terms.

In France, Hitler used Darlan's passive response to the Operation Torch landings as an excuse to occupy the entire Vichy zone and disband the remaining units of the token French army. He did not, however, extend the MBF's authority into southern France. Still lacking the manpower and resources to govern all of France directly, he needed to preserve the illusion that Pétain was still in charge. For his part, the marshal also remained willing to play his assigned role. Although Operation Torch shocked them, the Vichyites were prisoners of collaboration.

The Germans never really trusted Pétain, and after Darlan's murder they forced their client to reappoint his old rival Laval to the premiership with enhanced extralegal powers. Although the marshal remained the nominal head of state, Laval gained the authority to appoint ministers. He also took direct control of the ministries of Internal Affairs, Foreign Affairs, and Information, which gave him the means to expand the Vichy security apparatus. At his postwar trial Laval claimed that he did this to protect France, but in reality he had become a creature of the Nazis. On the second anniversary of the armistice agreement he made this clear by issuing the declaration that would later hang him: "I desire the victory of Germany, because, without it, Bolshevism would tomorrow establish itself everywhere. France cannot remain passive or indifferent before the immensity of the sacrifices Germany is willing to make in order to construct a Europe in which we must take our place."[48]

Using the fallacious excuse that collaboration tempered German demands for men and material, Laval stood by as the imperial regime's claims on the French economy increased from one-third to one-half of the country's total prewar revenues. He also bowed to Sauckel's demand for French labor by introducing a program called the *relève* (relief shift) that was supposed to send 150,000 voluntary skilled workers to Germany in exchange for the release of 50,000 French POWs.[49] When only a fraction of the promised workers materialized, Laval turned to conscription, for there was no way he could refuse the Nazi manpower demands and remain in power. In early 1943, the Vichy premier became Sauckel's recruiting agent by creating the Service du Travail Obligatoire (Mandatory Labor Service, STO). Required to supply almost half a million workers for the Nazi war effort, the STO combed France for available men. Facing censure for missed recruiting quotas, Vichy prefects even emptied jails to meet their targets. Ironically, the Nazi armaments minister Albert Speer did a better job of protecting French workers from conscription. Unlike Sauckel, Speer believed that Frenchmen best served the Reich's extractive needs by keeping France's economy functioning. However, Sauckel was not to be denied, and more than one in five Frenchmen ended up working in Germany as either civilian laborers or POWs during the war.[50]

Nearly universal revulsion over labor conscription played a central role in turning public opinion against the Vichy regime and inspiring more Frenchmen to resist the occupation actively. No longer able to sit on the fence with the Vichy labor dragnet hanging over their heads, many young men escaped to the mountainous regions of southern France. Although these bands of labor deserters, who came to be known as the *maquis* after the scrublands where they sheltered, initially had no direct tie to de Gaulle or the resistance, they challenged Vichy authority by raiding STO offices for money and supplies. In this sense they resembled the Italian bandits who bedeviled Napoleonic officials.

This shift in popular sentiment led resistance groups that had been fragmented and largely inconsequential in the early years of the occupation to become more active. They distributed propaganda, intimidated collaborators, cut phone lines, burned crops, planted bombs, and derailed trains. Most significant, some groups executed Vichyite officials and policemen after convicting them of treason in absentia at secret trials. The communists remained the boldest faction, but they were joined by a variety of new organizations drawn primarily from the moderate and left wings of the French political spectrum. Reviving the Popular Front squabbles of the 1930s, these various resistance bands barely trusted each other. It therefore took considerable effort for de Gaulle's representative Jean Moulin to organize them into the Conseil National de la Résistance (National Council of the Resistance). The National Council gave the appearance of unity, but it actually reflected the resistance leaders' decision to defer debates over the nature and character of the new France until the postwar era.

Despite this growing opposition, there were still many Frenchmen who remained committed to Pétain because they considered the resistance and *maquis* fighters criminals and terrorists. For those with conservative sympathies, a communist postwar France would have meant exchanging the German occupation for an even more hateful form of tyranny. The Vichy regime also had the support of bureaucrats and functionaries who preferred order and stability to the chaos of the resistance, and many officials gambled that the Allies could not mount an invasion on a sufficient scale to liberate France. Lastly, the resistance executions of convicted traitors demonstrated that those who rallied to Pétain would have a hard time switching sides.

This meant that the Nazis still had the necessary local allies to maintain imperial control over France even as their rule became progressively more brutal. Having lost faith in Pétain and the French police after the 1941 communist assassination campaign, Hitler gave the SS and Gestapo greater freedom to operate. This provoked General von Stülpnagel into resigning as head of the MFB in early 1942, and his replacement and cousin, Carl-Heinrich von Stülpnagel, had authority only over explicitly military matters. This gave Higher SS and Police Commander Carl-Albrecht Oberg a free hand to deal with the resistance. Dispensing with wholesale hostage executions, his men attacked the families of resistance members and spirited off to concentration camps suspects not immediately worthy of being shot. Oberg also raised a French arm of the Gestapo, comprised largely of criminals, that further terrorized the imperial regime's enemies through extortion, torture, and outright murder. When these more targeted tactics failed to suppress French opposition sufficiently, German soldiers and SS men fell back on the time-honored methods of imperial intimidation by wiping out communities they suspected of aiding resistance groups.

Even the slaughter of French civilians did not dissuade Vichy bureaucrats and policemen from cooperating with the Nazis. René Bousquet, Laval's youthful secretary general of police, convinced himself that he was helping the Germans arrest anarchists, terrorists, communists, and other mutual enemies of the two regimes. Seeking to salvage as much French sovereignty as possible by demonstrating to their imperial masters that the Vichy courts and security forces could maintain order, Laval and Bousquet directed French policemen to help the Nazis round up victims when Himmler demanded at least one hundred thousand French Jews for the concentration camps. Although some officers tipped off people marked for arrest, the Paris police seized more than twelve thousand Jews in July 1942. Most were foreign-born because Laval refused to turn over French citizens on the grounds of national sovereignty. All told, Vichy officials sent between forty thousand and sixty thousand Jews from France to their deaths in Nazi concentration camps.

The Vichyites had little to show for this complicity in genocide. Deeming Bousquet too timid, the Nazis took direct control of the French police and forced Laval to make Joseph Darnand police secretary general in December 1943. Darnand had proved his worth to both Laval and the Germans by transforming the paramilitary SOL into the Milice Française (French Militia). Composed largely of fanatics, opportunists, and blatant criminals, the Milice grew steadily from Laval's praetorian guard into a uniformed forty-thousand-man army that was Vichy's main weapon against the resistance. Darnand was also doubly trustworthy in German eyes because as an honorary colonel in the French SS volunteer grenadier regiment, he was the first high-ranking Vichy official to swear loyalty to Hitler.

Darnand's total embrace of the Nazi cause was symptomatic of the Vichy regime's political and moral bankruptcy in the final years of the war. As mounting Allied victories and the stench of Laval's collaborationist policies alienated French moderates, the leaders of the Paris-based extremist groups joined him in taking over what was left of the Vichy state. Pétain was still popular, but his authority waned even further when Laval returned the main French ministries to Paris and Darnand's men arrested any official they suspected of cooperating with the resistance.

This bitter civil war raging just below the surface of occupied France made switching sides extremely complicated and dangerous. When Pierre Pucheu, the Vichy minister of the interior from 1941 to 1942, fled to North Africa after the Operation Torch landings, de Gaulle's National Committee of Liberation tried and executed him for treason. Declaring their intention to rid France of "all men who played politics with the Vichy government, without any distinction between the *bons* (good) and *mauvais* (bad)," the committee created a Purge Commission to "mete out adequate punishment" to those who "by their acts, their writings, or their personal attitude, either encouraged enemy undertakings, or prejudiced the action of the United Nations and of Frenchmen who are resisting; or have interfered with constitutional institutions or basic public liberties."[51] Pucheu more than fit this description given his role in selecting communist hostages for execution.

Pucheu's failed gambit demonstrated how profoundly Nazi imperial rule had blurred French conceptions of political and social legitimacy. Far from resolving the divisions of the 1930s, the French surrender and armistice threw wide open the struggle to define the boundaries and character of the French nation. In 1944, this competition took the form of bloody battles between the Milice and the *maquis*, as well as audacious resistance attacks on the collaborationists. All told, thousands of Frenchmen died in this fratricidal violence during the course of the occupation. Popular French history recalls this as a great national struggle, but the resistance's appearance of unity as the Nazi regime weakened obscured sharp divisions between the communists, Gaullists, and even monarchists over who would take control of France after the liberation. Additionally, as in Napoleonic Italy, some of the people who styled themselves resistance members were little more than criminals and thugs who preyed on local communities under the cover of attacking collaborators.

These tensions became more apparent after the Allied landing in Normandy on June 6, 1944. In returning to France for the first time since 1940, de Gaulle's goal was to preempt the communists and head off British and American plans to create a transitional military government by making it appear that his forces liberated France. Betraying his own imperial biases, he "whitened" the Second French Armored Division, the sole Free French formation operating with the Allied forces, by replacing twenty thousand Arab and African soldiers with resistance members. This unit was not part of the initial D-Day invasion force, but de Gaulle convinced the Allied generals to send it into Paris ahead of the British, Canadian, and American troops who had done most of the fighting during the breakout from Normandy. Radio broadcasts and newsreels showed white Free French soldiers marching through the capital, but they never would have been able to defeat the Nazi garrison, which had swelled to one million men by 1944, with a single division. Indeed, the French were fortunate that the German commander ignored direct orders to destroy the city.

The Normandy landings and the subsequent fall of Paris on August 25, 1944, threw the Vichyites into shock. While they understood that the Third Reich was losing the war, they appear to have convinced themselves that the liberation would never actually come. The Paris extremists wanted the Germans to bring the LVF and French SS grenadier regiment back from the eastern front to fight the invasion, but Laval and Pétain simply asked French officials not to take sides and remain at their posts on the delusional grounds that: "we are not in the war." Laval plotted to preempt de Gaulle by recalling the National Assembly to lead a transitional government, while Pétain hoped to negotiate a truce between the Americans and Nazis in preparation for a Christian war with the Soviets. The French police, by comparison, deftly switched sides by staging a timely uprising on the eve of the liberation of Paris. As the last of the fence sitters finally chose sides,

Parisians derisively referred to army officers who suddenly turned up in long-mothballed uniforms as "naphthalenes."

While these small fish hoped to navigate the liberation's shifting tides, the Nazis had no intention of letting their Vichy clients come to terms with the Allies. They forced Pétain and Laval to join the German retreat back into the Reich and installed them in a castle at Sirmaringen, a small Danube River town near the Swiss border, as a French government in exile. Both leaders finally refused to play the role of puppet any longer, and Jacques Doriot, the leader of the fascist Parti Populaire Français, assumed the Vichy leadership. With France overrun, he ruled a pathetic exile community of collaborationist and *milicien* diehards that numbered over forty thousand men, women, and children. Conditions at Sirmaringen deteriorated markedly as the Allied armies pressed in on Germany, and alcoholism and malnutrition led to a growing sense of hopelessness among the refugees.

Nevertheless, the most committed and desperate collaborators still joined their Nazi masters in the suicidal defense of the Third Reich. The German forces facing the Soviet Union's January 1945 offensive were outnumbered five to one and largely stood alone as the Nazi satellite states in Eastern Europe surrendered or were overrun. Lacking the manpower and material to fight a multifront war, Hitler was caught in a vise as the allied armies closed in from Poland, Italy, and France. Fearing retribution for their genocidal *Lebensraum* policies in the east, Nazi leaders were most concerned with holding off the vengeance-driven Soviets. Consequently, they desperately filled out their eastern lines with old men, boys, and the most loyal subject auxiliaries from the Reich's lost territories.

This last group included thousands of Frenchmen. In the summer of 1944, the Nazis cobbled the LVF, the French SS, the French Gestapo, and the remnants of the Milice into the Charlemagne SS Division. Equipped with antiquated tanks and numbering only seven thousand men, the unit stood little chance against the Red Army and was destroyed defending Pomerania in February 1945. Two months later, a German SS general organized the most diehard French survivors of the Pomeranian debacle into the Charlemagne Battalion for a bloody last stand in the ruins of Berlin. There they joined the most extreme anti-Bolshevik and reactionary fanatics that Europe had to offer in defending the Reich's capital. As the Soviets took the city in savage block-by-block fighting, Hitler relied on these Norwegians,

Danes, Belgians, Spaniards, and Frenchmen to defend his bunker. They bought Hitler time to kill himself, and few survived to see the formal German surrender on May 8, 1945.

The Charlemagne Battalion's suicidal defense of Berlin seems nonsensical. At best the Nazis exploited the collaborationists; at worst they despised them. At least some of the French SS men had to have understood this. While their decision to stand with the Third Reich to the bitter end was born in part of their extremist right-wing ideology, it also reflected the desperation that came from having bet incorrectly that Nazi rule in France would stand. Although historical hindsight makes it easy to see that Hitler's imperial enterprise was doomed from the start, the seeming finality of the German victory in 1940 made the prospect of a permanent Nazi European empire seem plausible. Its collapse in 1945 put the collaborationists in the unusual position of having to answer for their decision to cooperate with a conquering imperial regime.

It is impossible to know what would have happened to the noble-man Theodemir if Roderic's heirs had reclaimed the Visigothic throne from the Umayyads. The fate of chiefs such as Mumia and Koitalel's son Lelimo if the British Empire did not hold the Kenya highlands is similarly unforeseeable. Indeed, there are very few documented cases of imperial clients or auxiliaries ever having to answer for throwing in with foreign empire builders. Some of the Vichyites gambled that they could reach some sort of accord with de Gaulle, but the willingness of the most extreme collaborationists to go down fighting for a lost cause testifies to the difficulty that conquered peoples faced in trying to come to terms with their subjecthood. Choosing the right sponsor paid enormous rewards, but prematurely choosing sides could be disastrous if the new order failed to stand.

De Gaulle and his allies faced the equally unprecedented question of how to undo an imperial conquest. Should they try to revive the Third Republic by turning the clock back to 1939, or should they emulate Pétain by using the liberation as an opportunity to create a new France? Both options were risky. The disaster of 1940 inflamed the bitter ideological and social tensions that had so deeply divided the nation in the interwar era. During the Nazi occupation thousands of Frenchmen died as a result of the unacknowledged civil war between the Vichyites and the communists and Gaullists. The Allied victory restored France to the French, but it also raised the difficult question of what to do with the people who had been somehow involved in sustaining the vanquished Nazi imperial regime. While the prospect of vengeance was tempting, criminalizing collaboration threatened to keep France weak and divided in the perilous postwar world.

Depicting the liberation as a restoration rather than a revolution, de Gaulle opted for unity by pretending that only a few extremist traitors had really collaborated and that most Frenchmen had backed the resistance. According to de Gaulle's idealized nationalistic narrative, the French majority waged a heroic struggle against the Nazis throughout the entire occupation and the Free French forces restored France's honor by spearheading the liberation without foreign help. Not only would this useful fiction reunite France, it also conveniently reinforced the general's claim to power by downplaying the role of the communists, *maquisards*, and Allied armies in driving out the Nazis.

With Allied forces still fighting in Germany, de Gaulle sought to restore order quickly to make this the official version of French history. Recognizing that allowing the civil war to continue would open the way for an American military government to play the role of peacekeeper, he appointed handpicked prefects with the authority to make or repeal laws, dismiss local officials, freeze bank accounts, and order summary executions. He gave independent-minded resistance fighters and *maquisards* the choice of disarming or joining the French army, but the communists were more difficult to rein in. With an armed following numbering in the tens of thousands, many French communist leaders wanted to use the liberation to launch a Marxist-Leninist revolution. However, Stalin held them back because he needed American lend-lease aid and did not want to provoke the western powers into allying with the Nazis. Lacking direction and foreign patronage, the communist partisans had little choice but to disarm.

Without question, the most ticklish question facing the new regime was what to do with the Vichyites. While collaboration seemed a valid choice during the first two years of the occupation, the brutal German crackdown after Operation Torch and the occupation of the Vichy zone had undermined its legitimacy substantially. In 1942, a three-man legal commission operating in secret in occupied Lyon ruled that any Frenchman cooperating with the Nazi regime was guilty of treason because a state of war still existed under the armistice. As Vichy and German authority collapsed in 1944, resistance leaders put this ruling into practice by court-martialing captured collaborators. They summarily executed French Gestapo officers, SS men, *miliciens*, and any other Frenchman in a German uniform, and their impromptu courts tried as many as nine thousand of the more passive supporters and enablers of the Nazi regime for treason.

The popular sentiment driving these improvised trials reflected a widespread shift in French public opinion favoring the resistance in the final year of the war. Predictably, people who had spent much of the Nazi era sitting on the fence turned conclusively against the discredited Vichy regime as it became clear that its Nazi sponsors would lose. Prosecution of the Vichy leaders would have to wait for the full restoration of French sovereignty after the war, but in the meantime resistance commanders and local communities throughout France took the law into their own hands. Long-festering grievances and animosities came to the fore as mobs turned on people whom they accused of prospering from the occupation. The social order that appeared to have collapsed with the Nazi victory was now reborn, or at least reimagined, thereby making the people who had accepted the new imperial regime accountable for their conduct under Nazi rule.

More often than not, French women were the primary targets of this vigilante justice. As in earlier empires, women were most able to cross the boundary between citizen and subject by forming conjugal relationships with male empire builders. To be sure, Nazi officials, German soldiers, and *miliciens* were often guilty of rape and other forms of sexual abuse, but other French women entered into these relationships willingly. In 1943, the MFB received more than eighty thousand claims for domestic benefits from the French mothers of children sired by its troops even though regulations barred German soldiers from marrying subject women.[52] While some of these women were probably in love, the ability of German men to provide material benefits and physical protection during the harsh occupation years was also a driving force behind these relationships.

In the eyes of many French men, however, any intimate association with the German occupiers was treasonous. Stung by the humiliation of the Nazi victory, they felt deeply threatened by the disloyalty of their women. The contempt that a French teenager recorded in her diary captured these emasculating consequences of becoming an imperial subject.

I have reached the point when I find the French no longer are men: I am renouncing my country. I no longer want to be French! When you see now how one and all have become collaborationist and are licking the boots of the Germans out of fear and cowardice, even in my own family![53]

The Inkan nobleman Don Felipe Huamán Poma de Ayala, who complained that Andean women became "big whores" in preferring Spaniards to Indians, would have recognized these sentiments. This made sex one of the riskiest forms of collaboration. Those who slept with Nazi or Vichy men might betray secrets about resistance or black market activities, while the wives of French POWs in Germany who committed adultery with German lovers betrayed the French nation as well as their husbands.

The Allied victory thus brought masculine redemption as well as national liberation. While French men might have been divided politically during the occupation, they bridged their differences by sharing in the punishment of disloyal French women. In one case, Free French interrogators slapped and humiliated such a woman into using a ruler to show the size of her German lover's penis. More commonly, however, vigilantes punished sexual collaborators by shaving their heads, but there was actually no French law that explicitly banned sex with foreign men. Neighbors, policemen, local courts, and rank-and-file resistance men essentially took the law into their own hands in shaving the approximately twenty thousand women who suffered this fate between 1943 and 1946. Recognized prostitutes often escaped similar sanction due to their professional status, but resistance men were inclined to view any female who had close contact with members of the former imperial regime as suspect and contaminated.

De Gaulle recognized that this sexual vigilantism complicated his efforts to reunite France. Concerned primarily with punishing high Vichy officials and purging all remaining traces of collaboration from French society, he used his authority as president of the Cours de Justice de la Liberation (Liberation Courts) to pardon women, youths under twenty-one, and those who worked with the Nazis under actual duress. All told, these courts, which ran from 1944 to 1951, investigated some 300,000 cases of collaboration. A little more than 124,000 went to trial and resulted in roughly 45,000 dismissals, 28,000 acquittals, and 23,000 guilty verdicts. In keeping with the general trend toward amnesty, the vast majority of convicted collaborators served relatively short prison terms, and the courts handed down only 2,173 life sentences and 6,763 death sentences. Ultimately, the French executed just 767 people for their role in the occupation, and most of these were Milice and French Gestapo members. Even French SS men tended to receive pardons if they never actually fought in France.[54]

Collaborationists who did not violate a specific law stood trial in *chambres civiques*, civil courts that had the authority to impose the *indignité nationale* (national indignity) on those whose actions had dishonored the nation. These transgressors included profiteers, minor officials, and women who had sexual relationships with the Germans. The civil courts examined approximately two hundred and fifty thousand cases and imposed the *indignité nationale* a little less than fifty thousand times. Those convicted lost the right to vote, medical coverage, state pensions, and other benefits of citizenship.[55] The 569 Third Republic senators and deputies who voted to give Pétain full executive and legislative powers correspondingly lost the right to stand for elected office, and prefects and senior magistrates had to prove they had cooperated with the resistance to keep their jobs. These punishments were not permanent, and many people regained their rights and positions after a relatively brief period.

Businessmen and bankers faced the Committee for the Confiscation of Illicit Profits, which sat in judgment on companies and individuals accused of enriching themselves through the black market or illicit commerce with the imperial regime. While convicted profiteers faced fines and the nationalization of their businesses, most major industrialists escaped censure by arguing that they had to do business with the Nazis to protect their factories and workers from confiscation and conscription. The French authorities spared these men the indignities visited on suspect French women because they were unwilling to jeopardize France's postwar reconstruction and economic recovery by delving too deeply into the high economics of collaboration.

Vengeance-minded Frenchmen criticized the Liberation Courts for being too slow and lenient, but de Gaulle's strategy was to hold the Vichy leadership responsible for all the crimes of the occupation. His aim was to spare the French people from having to account for their conduct during their brief experience of imperial subjecthood. De Gaulle's preference was to put the entire Vichy regime in the dock as a single institution, but the resistance's legal experts ruled that there had to be individual trials. Most of the Paris-based fascists and extremists died in the war, and the provisional French government swiftly tried and executed Darnand without creating much attention. Pétain and Laval, however, were another matter. Anxious to prove they were not traitors, they welcomed the opportunity to defend their actions in open court.

Pétain, who was the first to stand trial in July 1945, depicted himself as a nationalist martyr who sacrificed his personal reputation to protect fellow Frenchmen from the worst aspects of direct Nazi imperial rule. This argument carried little weight with the French tribunal that sentenced him to death for treason. De Gaulle, who could afford to be merciful with his thoroughly discredited but still widely respected rival, commuted the sentence to life imprisonment after humiliatingly stripping him of his rank as a marshal of France. The vanquished Vichy leader died broken and senile six years later in a military fortress on a remote island off France's western Atlantic coast. Hitler's telling dismissal of the Vichy regime under his leadership was Pétain's most fitting epitaph: "Because [the Vichyites] were anxious to sit on every chair at the same time, they have not succeeded in sitting firmly on any one of them."[56]

Laval, by comparison, mounted a far more passionate defense of collaboration. After initially avoiding capture in Spain and Austria, he faced trial for treason in October 1945. The specific charge accused him of betraying France by conspiring to create a fascist state, dissuading the French government from escaping into exile in June 1940, making French resources available to the Nazis, and cooperating in the persecution and murder of French Jews. The former Vichy premier laid out his defense in a prison diary that his daughter smuggled out for publication. It offered an unprecedented look into the rationalizations that led a respected politician to become an imperial client and auxiliary.

Far from seeing himself as a traitor, Laval echoed Pétain in arguing that his version of collaboration had protected the French from Göring's threat to treat them like Poles. He rebutted the various points of the Gaullist indictment by denying a role in negotiating the armistice and blaming the Third Republic parliament for taking the unprepared nation to war without a formal vote. Parsing words, the Vichy premier noted that the armistice agreement required him to meet with Hitler and to "conform faithfully to the regulations issued by the German military authorities and *to collaborate* with the latter in a correct manner."[57] Laval acknowledged the authoritarian excesses of the Vichy regime but blamed them on Pétain. By his account, the marshal was the architect of a traitorous version of collaboration who blocked his efforts to secure the release of French POWs, reduce the occupation costs, and return the government to Paris. Moreover, he claimed that the *relève* and STO had headed off a German demand for two million conscripted French laborers and secured the release of thousands of French POWs. As for the most damning charge, abetting the Holocaust, Laval maintained that his willingness to turn over foreign Jews had blocked the Nazis from rounding up French citizens, and he audaciously depicted himself as the primary defender of French Jewry during the occupation.

In framing his final defense, Laval echoed Pétain in claiming that he sacrificed his personal honor and reputation to save France by grappling directly with the Nazi imperial regime while de Gaulle betrayed the nation by fleeing to the safety of exile. Correctly pointing out that he had nothing to gain personally from collaboration because he already had all the wealth and power he wanted, Laval summed up his defense by arguing:

> I have a different concept of honour. I subordinate my personal honour to the honour of my country. My ideal of honour was to make every sacrifice in order to spare our country the final indignity of being ruled by a Gauleiter or by a band of adventurers, to avoid a declaration of war on the Anglo-Saxon powers and to obviate an alliance with the German Reich. I achieved my goal.... Tens of thousands of men and women, Frenchmen and Frenchwomen, owe me their lives. Hundreds of thousands more can thank me for their freedom.[58]

In making this argument Laval glossed over the reality that imperial regimes cannot govern without allies from subject communities. His invocation of Göring's threat to treat France like Poland was effective in pointing out that there were far more brutal forms of Nazi imperial rule, but it is unlikely that Hitler would have risked the consequences of implementing his exterminationist *Lebensraum* policies in "civilized" western European nation-states.

The French judges certainly were not convinced by Laval's excuses and convicted him of treason. Unlike Pétain, who was a great military hero of the First World War, Laval was so widely despised that de Gaulle felt no pressure to commute the sentence of death. Resigned to his fate, the Vichy premier wrote confidently in his diary that he would take cyanide to avoid the "stain of execution" and "die in my own way like the Romans," but the poison he had hidden in his fur coat only made him sick. He faced a firing squad on October 15, 1945.

The Third Republic met its final demise that same month when French men and, for the first time, French women voted overwhelmingly to convene a national assembly to write a new constitution for the Fourth French Republic. The assembly, which was dominated by resistance men belonging to centrist and leftist parties, chose de Gaulle to be the provisional president, but the general resigned two months later when it produced a draft constitution that favored legislative power over executive power. Although they celebrated de Gaulle as a hero of the resistance, many postwar politicians feared that he had Bonapartist ambitions.

While the Fourth Republic was almost as unstable as its predecessor, de Gaulle largely succeeded in writing his unifying version of the occupation and resistance into French history. For nearly three decades the French successfully forgot the difficult choices they made as Nazi imperial subjects. The occupation became an unpleasant but brief digression in the grand narrative of French history that cast France as a great civilizing imperial nation in its own right. The French learned little from their subjecthood, and they fought brutal wars to keep the Malagasy, Vietnamese, and Algerians from leaving their empire.

France settled instead into a premeditated collective forgetfulness after the main collaborationist trials. Local officials destroyed documents dealing with embarrassing incidents during the occupation, and the French government closed the national wartime archives until 1979 and sealed more sensitive records dealing with conduct of important individuals for a century. Pétain, Laval, and the Paris fascists alone bore the weight of the national sin of collaboration, and those who survived the trials and purges of the immediate postwar years gradually found their way back into mainstream French society. This national amnesia allowed fourteen senior Vichyites to sit in the parliament in the 1950s, two of whom became government ministers. The Vichy police chief René Bousquet escaped conviction for treason by claiming to have been a secret resistance supporter and suffered the *indignité nationale* for only five years before returning to political life. Maurice Papon, a senior bureaucrat who avoided having to answer for his role in rounding up Jews for Laval by embracing the resistance in 1944, also went on to have a distinguished career as a civil servant, industrialist, parliamentarian, and government minister. Finally, many French conservatives, who never felt the need to justify their support for Vichy, remembered Pétain as a legitimate ruler who heroically sacrificed all to protect France.

The demands by French Jews for a more thorough accounting of the Vichy deportation policies finally jarred the French out of their comfortable collective amnesia in the 1990s. Global revulsion over the Holocaust led President Jacques Chirac to acknowledge the role of the French administration in sending Jews to the concentration camps. Surviving officials such as Bousquet and Papon, who could no longer use professional obligation and duty to justify their role in organizing the deportations, now had to answer legally for their actions. Bousquet was the first scheduled to go to court, in 1993, but he was murdered by a mentally unstable publicity seeker before the proceedings could begin. Papon did stand trial, and in 1998 a French court found him guilty of complicity in crimes against humanity. Although he killed no one and was not a Nazi, the French newspaper *Le Monde* astutely editorialized: "He signed what he shouldn't have signed, carried out what he shouldn't have carried out, organized what above all he shouldn't have organized."[59]

There is absolutely no excusing the Holocaust and the enormous crimes of the Nazis, but generations upon generations of imperial subjects made similar choices in deciding to work with their conquerors. They too collected tribute and labor and maintained law and order for their imperial masters. The only difference was that they were accomplices to older and less virulent kinds of empires that only sought to exploit their subjects rather than exterminate them. Bousquet, Papon, and the other bureaucrats and policemen who served the Vichy regime, and by extension the Nazis, did not see themselves as monsters or traitors. Rather, they were relatively average people who tried to come to terms with the consequences of imperial subjecthood. The French collaborators deliberately looked away from their masters' depravity and never imagined that the quick and sudden demise of the seemingly impregnable Nazi empire would force them to answer for their conduct as imperial intermediaries.

Most historians of the Third Reich and the French occupation do not consider Hitler's European war to be part of the long history of conventional empire. Instead, there is a tendency to view the Nazis as exceptional in their criminality, racism, and barbarity. In one sense this is unquestionably true. No other regime in history made mass murder the central focus of state policy. Yet there is also no denying that Nazism was born of the same extremist nationalism and social Darwinism that drove the new imperialism in Africa and Asia. To be sure, as the self-imagined heir of Napoleon, Hitler's imperial ambitions were continental, not global. Moreover, he was openly disdainful of the new imperialism's legitimizing humanitarian ideologies, and he correctly recognized that most African and Asian colonies were not particularly valuable. Nevertheless, the Nazis were inspired by the same racism and naked self-interest that led the liberal western democracies to seize overseas empires in the late nineteenth century. The Nazis did not bother themselves with trying to uplift their subjects, but in practice neither did most of the new imperialists and settlers.

Hitler's innovation was to systematically combine settler colonialism in the east with the standard template of imperial conquest and extraction in the west. The British followed a similar dual policy in Kenya and southern Africa, just not to the scope or the extremes of the Nazis. Where Kenyan settlers sought to exploit Africans, Hitler planned to exterminate eastern Europeans to create *Lebensraum*. These two strategies are not as different as they might seem. Conventional empires justified the conquest, domination, and exploitation of subject peoples by depicting them as alien, barbaric, and primitive. Imperial subjects were not entitled to the rights of citizenship because they were not fully human. The Nazis made the same arguments about their subjects, but they did not feel bound by a humanitarian conception of empire. Both Hitler and the new imperialists in Africa and Asia shared a belief in a hierarchical scale of human social evolution where some races were inherently superior to others. They differed only in whether lower orders could move up the civilizational ladder. According to the Nazis' extreme social Darwinism, moral empire building advanced the interests of the racially superior German *Volk*, who were the embodiment of western achievement and culture. This thinking was repulsive, but ultimately so were the hypocritical legitimizing ideologies of the new imperialism.

Once an imperial regime stripped its subjects of their humanity, it was not too great a step to move from extractive exploitation to murder, mass slaughter, and even genocide. In the late nineteenth century, W. A. Jarvis, a former member of the British Parliament, explained the necessity of eliminating the rebellious Ndebele to open southern Rhodesia for British settlers in a letter to his mother: "There are about 5,500 niggers in this district (Gwelo) and our plan of campaign will [be to] wipe them out, then move on towards Bulawayo wiping out every nigger and every kraal (homestead) we can find."[60] The campaign against the Ndebele and the German assault on the Herero did not move as far down this road as the Nazis did, but these incidents were a powerful harbinger of what would happen when the ideological underpinnings of the new imperialism were taken to an extreme. The human failings, if not sheer evil, of the Nazi leadership should never be dismissed in trying to explain their genocidal outrages, but their intention to open an eastern frontier for German settlement was not too far out of the mainstream of imperial thought. Ultimately, their unwavering commitment to genocide was the result of empire building descended into madness.

The criminal insanity of the Holocaust allowed the Allied powers to deny this connection with the Nazi imperial agenda. Seeking to demonstrate that the Third Reich was an aberration and not the product of modern western culture, they put the surviving Nazi leaders on trial at Nuremberg for war crimes and crimes against peace and humanity. Article Six of the Charter of the International Military Tribunal indicted them for conspiring to wage an aggressive war in violation of international treaties, mass murder, slave labor, the plunder of public and private property, the wanton destruction of cities and towns, and inhumanly persecuting civilian populations on the basis of race and religion. This sent the Polish governor general Hans Frank to the gallows for his declared intention to treat the country "like a colony," and Artur Seyss-Inquart and Alfred Rosenberg met the same fate for their governorships of the Netherlands and occupied Soviet territory. The Reich plenipotentiary for labor allocation, Fritz Sauckel, also hung for his role in enslaving millions of Europeans. More significant, the Nuremberg trials forced the German people to take collective responsibility for the Nazis' crimes. For the first time, a metropolitan population answered directly for the actions of the empire builders who operated in their name.

Although it is impossible to feel any sympathy for the Nazi leadership, it bears noting that the original architects of the new imperialism were responsible for the deaths of millions of their African subjects. Certainly King Leopold and his proxies could have been held accountable for the brutal and ultimately exterminationist forced labor policies in the Belgian Congo. Jarvis had equally genocidal intentions in declaring his intention to wipe out every "nigger" and homestead in Gwelo district. The only reason these imperial entrepreneurs would have escaped prosecution at Nuremberg was that their victims had no national rights. The Allies charged the Nazis with violating international law by forcing sovereign rulers to abdicate, annexing territory, imposing their own law and courts, conscripting defeated peoples, and, most serious, demanding excessive revenue and tribute, but they never suggested that building an empire was a crime.

While Europeans may have denied any connection between the new imperialism and the Holocaust, many educated Africans and Asians were not fooled. Aimé Césaire in particular minced no words in linking the western imperial project with Hitler's crimes: "No one colonizes innocently…no one colonizes with impunity…a nation which colonizes, that civilization which justifies colonization—and therefore force—is already a sick civilization, a civilization that is morally diseased."[61] Césaire was equally harsh in declaring that the French were just such a civilization and therefore deserved to be conquered by the Nazis.

France's embarrassing defeat in 1940 further demonstrated that a "modern" European people had a great deal in common with supposedly backward African and Asian subjects. The nation's humiliating descent into imperial subjecthood goes a long way toward explaining why the French tried so hard to forget their four-year occupation by the Germans. By definition, only primitive people were imperial subjects, much less collaborators. Yet the French did behave remarkably like Africans and Asians in trying to come to terms with their occupation, and the Nazis' success in dividing the French demonstrates that any defeated people or nation can be turned into imperial subjects. France's social and political wars of the 1930s made the Germans' task easier, but it is easy to imagine King Edward VIII as Pétain and the English fascist Oswald Mosley in Laval's role if Hitler had conquered Great Britain.

While the era of formal empire seemed to end with the Nazi demise and the breakup of the western empires in Africa and Asia, imperial logic still appeals to those who continue to believe that power and coercion can be put to productive purposes. Although no great power admits to seeking an empire in the modern era, military might and smug ethnocentrism still lead to imperial projects. The disastrous American occupation of Iraq testifies to the tragic consequences of this failure to understand the true history of empire.

CONCLUSION

Imperial Epitaph

In 1917, General Stanley Maude, who conquered Iraq for the British Empire, reassured the people of Baghdad that his troops came not "as conquerors or enemies but as liberators" from oppressive Turkish rule. In 2003, President George Bush promised the Iraqis that the United States military would save them from a barbarous despot who threatened global civilization. In a speech a month before the invasion of Iraq, he solemnly declared, "Any future the Iraqi people choose for themselves will be better than the nightmare world that Saddam Hussein has chosen for them....If we must use force, the United States and our coalition stand ready to help the citizens of a liberated Iraq."[1] In other words, the United States would use military force to achieve humane ends.

The American soldiers who invaded Iraq were not neoconquistadors, and they did not consider themselves empire builders. Their leaders told them that they were there to rescue the population from a brutal dictator, and unlike Richard Meinertzhagen, who justified his execution of the Nandi *orkoiyot* Koitalel arap Samloei with a similar excuse, most respected the sanctity of human life. The vast majority were deeply disturbed by their role in the deaths of the ninety-two hundred civilians inadvertently killed by American and coalition forces during the first two years of the invasion and occupation.[2]

This heavy toll gave common Iraqis a decidedly different view of Operation Iraqi Freedom. Watching American soldiers patrol the streets of his capital, a resident of Baghdad lamented: "They're walking over my heart. I feel like they're crushing my heart." To him it mattered little that the Americans were Iraq's self-declared saviors. "They came to liberate us. Liberate us from what?…We have [our own] traditions, morals, and customs."[3] Echoing Daniel Wambua Nguta's dismissal of the humanitarian ethos of the British Empire, an Iraqi doctor declared that there was only one positive change resulting from the American occupation of his country: "The free talking. Only only only."[4]

In dismissing this common perspective and justifying their decision to invade a sovereign state without a formal declaration of war, President Bush and his advisors claimed the right to use force against unfriendly nations that possessed weapons of mass destruction and harbored terrorist groups. In articulating what became known as the Bush Doctrine, a September 2002 White House policy statement declared: "To forestall or prevent such hostile acts by our adversaries, the United States will, if necessary, act preemptively.… In an age where the enemies of civilization openly and actively seek the world's most destructive technologies, the United States cannot remain idle while dangers gather."[5]

Although American officials assured the world that they did not seek an empire, the Bush Doctrine was a classic excuse for one. Acknowledging the popular hatred of imperial institutions in the non-western world, the president emphatically declared: "We have no territorial ambitions, we don't seek an empire. Our nation is committed to freedom for ourselves and for others."[6] This was an unremarkable guarantee, for not even the most committed neoconservatives in the White House or Pentagon actually suggested that the United States should conquer and govern Iraq permanently. Overt empire building was incompatible with decades of established American foreign policy, and it would have incurred nearly universal condemnation from around the globe. Rather, the Bush Doctrine was a declaration of America's intention to use the tools of empire to fight the "war on terror" and deal with enemy regimes that might give terrorists weapons of mass destruction. It was an attempt to use force to achieve nonmilitary aims.

The architects of Operation Iraqi Freedom were primarily advocates of hard power. They drew moral support from Niall Ferguson and the other revisionist members of his self-described "neoimperialist gang." These scholars and public intellectuals argued passionately that it was both ethical and feasible for the United States to impose what Deepak Lal called an "international moral order" by using force against rogue regimes. Falling back on imperial romanticism and nostalgia for their historical precedents, they imagined the twentieth-century western empires as the benevolent guarantors of global stability and prosperity.[7] In doing so, they sought to destigmatize imperial methods.

In this sense, the Bush administration assumed that it was still possible to employ the informal imperial tactics that earlier American administrations had used to replace uncooperative regimes in Central America. Just as U.S. expeditionary forces installed compliant client governments in Nicaragua, Honduras, Guatemala, and the small Caribbean island nations after a relatively short and inexpensive interval of direct American rule, the president's advisors reasoned they could do the same in the twenty-first-century Middle East. Instead, the Bush administration followed in the footsteps of William Gladstone, whose dispatch of troops to secure the Suez Canal and bolster a cooperative Egyptian client regime in 1882 committed Britain to ruling Egypt as a protectorate for the next four decades. Bush officials may not have been aware of the ominous Egyptian precedent, but the imperial boosters in academia and the media should not have missed this classic case of an entangling occupation.

While it was true that the United States did not seek a formal empire in the Middle East, the Iraq invasion's methods and goals were implicitly imperial. This did not mean that the Americans sought taxes or labor from common Iraqis. Rather, Iraq's vast petroleum reserves figured prominently in the Bush administration's planning. Although the president's advisors made little mention of Iraqi oil in making the case for a preemptive war, they assumed that it would pay for the invasion and occupation once they rebuilt the nation's wells, pipelines, and refineries. Estimating that they could increase Iraqi exports to eight million to ten million barrels per day, Bush officials aimed to drive down global energy prices and dilute the influence of oil-exporting nations such as Saudi Arabia and Russia by flooding the world with oil. It also went without saying that American companies would push aside rival French, Russian, and Chinese companies to play the leading role in helping the "liberated" Iraqis produce and market their oil.[8]

As with the new imperialism, Bush officials masked the inherent self-interest of Operation Iraqi Freedom with humanitarian rhetoric.

The benefits of western civilization once again justified an aggressive military enterprise, and the neoimperialist gang asserted that these "gifts" could be imposed from above and largely at gunpoint. Calling for an "imperial operation" in Iraq in a *New York Times* editorial two months before the invasion, Michael Ignatieff argued that the United States had a moral obligation to spread free markets, human rights, and democracy.[9] The inevitability of civilian casualties was largely absent from this legitimizing rhetoric.

The hard power advocates and imperial apologists who made the case for Operation Iraqi Freedom gave little thought to common Iraqis who died in the crossfire of the invasion, and they dismissed the "collateral damage" of Operation Iraqi Freedom as a necessary sacrifice for a greater good. Ignatieff asserted that "regime change" was the only way to deal with a tyrant who invaded his neighbors, practiced ethnic cleansing, and starved his citizens to build palaces and weapons. "The disagreeable reality for those who believe in human rights is that there are some occasions—and Iraq may be one of them—when war is the only remedy for regimes that live by terror."[10] He cited declarations by Iraqi exiles that Iraqis would accept civilian casualties as the price of overthrowing Saddam, thereby leaving unspoken the question of why these American allies had the privilege of determining who would actually make such a sacrifice. Moreover, Ignatieff's indictment of the Iraqi regime for warmongering and human rights violations raises questions as to whether a western power such as the United States should have to answer for the decimation of New World peoples, slavery, the Mexican-American War, and the monopolization of global resources. Imperial balance sheets are inevitably subjective and selective in deciding what constitutes the greater good and what does not.

The critics of Operation Iraqi Freedom often overlooked these realities. To be sure, scholars of empire such as Nicholas Dirks did their part by linking the theorists, politicians, and military contractors that profited from the invasion of Iraqi with the conquistadors, nabobs, and other specialist groups behind earlier imperial projects. In chronicling the scandals of British East India Company rule, he found himself "writing the history not just of the eighteenth century, but of the present as well."[11] However, most opponents of President Bush's preemptive war made the mistake of equating empire and imperialism solely with the unjust use of hard power. In doing so, they failed to point out that it is simply no longer feasible to reorder another society through military force alone. Empires are indeed immoral, but it would have been more convincing to argue against the Iraq invasion by using historical precedents to show why it was doomed to fail. Instead, the Bush administration's leftist critics assumed that empire was still practical; they just differed from the neoconservatives and imperial apologists in branding it a sin.

Some well-meaning scholars and policy makers were also ensnared by the temptation to leverage military power for philanthropic purposes. Noah Feldman, a Harvard law professor who helped the American-appointed Iraqi Governing Council draft an interim constitution, assured himself that the invasion of Iraq was an act of "trusteeship" rather than empire building. Acknowledging that this notion of paternalistic stewardship had imperial origins, he nonetheless argued that it was moral to deprive a defeated people of their sovereignty temporarily if the "trustee" abandoned its assumption of moral superiority and governed as an "ordinary" democratically elected government.[12] In other words, the American occupiers knew what was best for the Iraqis. Left unsaid was the reality that common Iraqis never asked to be a ward of a victorious power, even if that power promised to rule humanely and altruistically. Like all forms of imperial rule, trusteeship ultimately springs from the barrel of a gun, not the consent of the conquered.

The central mistake running through much of the debate over the Iraqi occupation was the assumption that imperial methods were still effective and could be put to legitimate uses. The Bush administration's adventure in Iraq was actually doomed from the outset because its planners made the fundamental mistake of believing their own legitimizing rhetoric. Most common Iraqis were happy to be rid of Saddam Hussein, but this did not mean that they wanted to be ruled by well-intentioned foreigners. In the immediate aftermath of the invasion, a Sunni Imam sermonized: "Do you know of anyone who can accept this humiliation? Do you just let them occupy your land while you sit and do nothing?" A university student turned insurgent echoed this anger by asking: "How would you feel if French soldiers or Arab soldiers invaded your city and killed your friends, your family?"[13] President Bush's promises that the United States had no imperial ambitions in Iraq carried little weight, and most Iraqis believed he wanted their oil and to defend Israel, stage attacks on Iran and Syria, and create opportunities for American businessmen. True or not, the Iraqis' nearly universal rejection of subjecthood taught the Americans a painful lesson in the limits of empire.

Operation Iraqi Freedom was an attempt to use imperial methods in an age when formal empires are no longer practical, viable, or defensible. By the 1970s, there were no major powers left in the world that admitted to being empires. Imperial nomenclature occasionally crops up in Britain, but as Doris Lessing put it in turning down the invitation to become a dame of the British Empire: "Well, first of all there is no British empire, no one seems to notice this."[14] Certainly Basques, Northern Irish, Kurds, Tamils, East Timorese, Tibetans, and many other peoples seeking national homelands continue to endure a form of subjecthood. However, their struggles are with nations, not self-described empires.

Over the past half century, the emergence of former African and Asian imperial territories as independent nation-states holding a commanding presence in the United Nations General Assembly, coupled with the excesses of the Nazis, rendered empire illegitimate in the court of world opinion. Conservatives and western chauvinists never ceased to imagine the empires of the new imperial era as humane and civilizing, but former subject peoples held them in contempt. Consequently, imperialism became a synonym for aggression and exploitation that the United States and the Soviet Union both used in Cold War propaganda. Each cast itself as the champion of oppressed peoples while depicting its rival as an imperial power. But of course this did not prevent them from occasionally giving in to the temptation to use imperial methods in seeking to dominate strategic territories and secure resources.

Of the two Cold War powers, the Soviet Union certainly came closest to the conventional definition of an empire. It was heir to tsarist Russia, which had so many non-Russian subjects under the Romanovs that nationalists referred to it as "the prison of peoples." The Soviet Union never called itself an empire and condemned the western excesses of the new imperialism, but in reality Lenin's regime ruled millions of unwilling and disenfranchised subject peoples. This made the USSR a de facto empire. Ever the pragmatist, Joseph Stalin reacquired the last missing pieces of the Romanovs' empire by annexing eastern Poland and the Baltic states under the terms of the Nazi-Soviet Pact. In the 1950s, Nikita Khrushchev sponsored a colonial endeavor to settle hundreds of thousands of Russians and Ukrainians on untilled "virgin lands" in Central Asia.

As in the western empires, this oppression and extraction eventually provoked an anti-imperial backlash. The resistance began in the Ukraine in the 1960s, but over the next two decades it spread to most of the Soviet republics. Seeking relief from Russian settlers, limits on central demands for resources, and greater autonomy, subject elites, who were mostly products of the Soviet system, mobilized their communities along ethnic lines. In time, they demanded their own nation-states, particularly after the Soviet Union gave its eastern European satellites greater independence in the 1970s. Ideologies of Marxist-Leninist brotherhood were poor firebreaks against this spreading nationalism.

Matters came to a head in the late 1980s when the disastrous Afghan War, the Polish Solidarity movement, and Mikhail Gorbachev's glasnost reforms weakened the Soviet Union's hold on its imperial periphery. But as was the case in most empires, subject rebellions did not bring down the Soviet Union. Instead, the Russians themselves decided that it was no longer worthwhile to hold the Soviet empire together by force. Taking a page from the nationalists' book, Boris Yeltsin destroyed the USSR in 1991 by declaring that the Russian Soviet Federated Socialist Republic was a nation-state. He did this to strengthen Russia by jettisoning imperial territories that stood in the way of its development as a liberal democratic society. Having survived an attempted coup by Soviet hard-liners, Yeltsin concluded treaties with the other Soviet republics acknowledging them as sovereign independent nations. Thus, the last true empire in the world dissolved into fifteen independent successor states.

By comparison, if the USSR was an old-style empire in denial, the United States was a hegemonic global power that its friends and critics frequently mistook for an empire. To be sure, Americans often resorted to colonial and imperial methods in pursuing personal and national goals. The founding fathers framed the War of Independence as a just revolution against the tyrannical British Empire, but this did not prevent the new nation from acquiring enormous swaths of additional territory by either purchase or conquest. The 1846 Mexican-American War, for example, was a largely imperial enterprise that brought the United States most of its southwestern states.

More significant, America's westward expansion entailed the defeat and near total destruction of New World peoples. In this sense it was more colonial than imperial. In pursuing its "Manifest Destiny," the United States did not seek to turn Amerindians into tribute-paying subjects; it wanted their land. This did not mean that the settlers had a specific genocidal agenda in the west. Rather, most nineteenth-century Americans believed that the Amerindians were a lower order of humanity who were dying out because they could not survive in the modern world. Thomas Hart Benton put these sentiments into words on the Senate floor in 1846 when he said, "Civilization or extinction has been the fate of all people who have found themselves in the track of the advancing Whites."[15] Americans thus assured themselves that the United States' transformation into a continental nation was neither imperial nor immoral.

Modern debates over whether the United States was an empire or not overlook the fact that successive administrations in the nineteenth century followed an inherently nonimperial assimilationist policy in gradually recognizing surviving Native Americans as citizens, albeit inferior ones. Similarly, emancipation turned former slaves into Americans of African descent rather than imperial subjects. Alaskans and Hawaiians eventually won the same status, but these concessions were not particularly grand or magnanimous. Nevertheless, America's treatment of nonwestern peoples living within its borders was not, by strict definition, imperial. Although they suffered institutionalized racism and discrimination, by the twentieth century Native Americans, indigenous Hawaiians and Alaskans, and African Americans were citizens, not subjects. This reality stands in contrast to the national minorities in the Soviet Union who acquired their own separate nation-states when the Soviet empire collapsed.

The United States' assimilationist policies reinforced its egalitarian self-image, but the ingrained American antipathy toward empire did not prevent the nation from falling victim to the new imperial mania of the late nineteenth century. Although the United States did not take part in the scramble for Africa, President William McKinley's administration could not resist the temptation to take over most of Spain's remaining empire after its victory in the 1898 Spanish-American War. An unabashedly proimperial lobby failed to secure the annexation of Cuba, but McKinley obligingly claimed Guam, Puerto Rico, and the Philippines.

The United States proved a surprisingly ambivalent imperial master. Struggling to reconcile their democratic values with the realities

of ruling millions of unwilling and seemingly inassimilable subjects, Americans questioned the price of empire. The Supreme Court
ruled that the Bill of Rights applied to the former Spanish territories,
and the United States governed the Philippines through an elected
national assembly and senate that was largely free to legislate as it
saw fit, subject to the veto of an American governor general. In the
1930s, Franklin Roosevelt sought to shed an expensive imperial white
elephant by setting the Filipinos on the path to formal independence.
Acting over the objections of some Filipino elites who did not want to
lose access to American markets, he declared that the territory would
become independent after a ten-year transitional period of internal
self-government. The Second World War interrupted these plans, but
on July 4, 1946, Harry Truman held to Roosevelt's original timetable
and transferred power to the Filipinos.

After the Allied victory, the United States also refused to bankroll
the resuscitation of the British Empire, but Cold War pragmatism led
Truman to underwrite France's return to Indochina. For the most part,
the Truman and Eisenhower administrations tolerated the tottering
postwar European empires as long as they did not become a liability
in the struggle with the Soviet Union for influence in Africa and Asia.
It took the British, French, and Israeli invasion of the Suez Canal Zone
in 1956 for the United States to formally denounce imperialism. This
public break with the British and the French over empire allowed the
Americans to reconcile with the growing caucus of nonaligned nations
at the United Nations, most of whom were former imperial subjects.

Although they depicted the United States as an anti-imperial
power, American policy makers still naively believed that they could
use imperial methods without incurring the political and fiscal costs
of formal empire building. Their paramount goal was to create an
informal network of influence and free market capitalism to contain
communist subversion in the "Third World." Continuing to operate under the assumption that nonwestern peoples were inherently
backward, they aimed to keep African and Asian nations within the
western sphere of influence. Where the western European nations
had pursued this goal through empire, the United States would set
developing nations on the path to "modernity" through economic
aid, political patronage, and military assistance.

The practitioners of modernization theory thus fought the Cold
War not through formal empire building but by trying to make

the United States into a liberal global hegemon. Although Charles de Gaulle grumbled that western Europe had become an American economic protectorate, the Soviet threat and the centrality of the dollar in the postwar economy forced most nations to acknowledge America's global leadership. Certain in their moral superiority, postwar Americans were confident that the United States used its hard power benevolently to provide developing nations with the security to embrace the American brand of liberal capitalism. As in earlier imperial eras, they never imagined that other people might have their own definition of freedom or prefer an alternative path of development.

This conceit prevented American strategists from realizing that the short-term military interventionist strategy that was so effective in Latin America during the first half of the twentieth century was no longer feasible in the postimperial era. President John Kennedy certainly had no intention of establishing a formal empire in Vietnam when he tried to prop up the government of Ngo Dinh Diem. Failing to recognize that Diem had little legitimacy as an American client in what most Vietnamese viewed as a struggle for national liberation, Kennedy's advisors made the mistake of believing that they could use imperial methods compassionately and creatively. Their central aim was to encourage Diem to keep the nation within the western camp by winning the struggle for influence with the North Vietnamese communists through modernization, capitalism, and representative government.

The central flaw in this unrealistic strategy was that nearly a century of French and Japanese imperial rule had left the majority of Vietnamese unwilling to tolerate any form of foreign dominance, no matter how benign or indirect. The Vietnam War was a test of wills in which the United States broke first. Although they could not counter the United States' overwhelming military supremacy, the Vietnamese communists were ultimately victorious because they accepted enormous casualties as the price of sovereignty. As General Vo Nguyen Giap told Stanley Karnow in 1990: "Despite its military power, America misgauged the limits of its power. In war there are two factors—human beings and weapons. Ultimately, though, human beings are the decisive factor. Human beings! Human beings!"[16] All told, the Vietnam War cost the United States 120 billion dollars and fifty-eight thousand of its soldiers. Approximately four million Vietnamese soldiers and civilians died in the conflict, which amounted to 10 percent of their population.[17]

At first, it appeared that American strategists and public intellectuals learned the right lessons from the Vietnam disaster. The conflict appeared to demonstrate the limits of brute force conclusively, and succeeding administrations became far more cautious in trying to use hard power to achieve nonmilitary ends. Colin Powell, an infantry officer in Vietnam who became the chairman of the Joint Chiefs of Staff during the first Gulf War, argued convincingly that America should resort to military action only when its national security was clearly threatened, it committed overwhelming force, there was a clear exit strategy, and there was conclusive public support for the enterprise.

Hard power partisans disagreed, but they had little actual influence on American foreign and military policy until George W. Bush's victory in the 2000 election brought hawks such as Richard Cheney, Donald Rumsfeld, Paul Wolfowitz, Lewis Libby, Douglas Feith, and many other less well-known advocates of imperial methods into government. Nonetheless, it took the widespread fear and paranoia following the terrorist attacks of September 11, 2001, to give their doctrines credibility. Thus the Bush Doctrine replaced the Powell Doctrine.

Looking beyond the immediate "liberation" of Iraq, the president's advisors gave in to even grander imperial ambitions. In overthrowing Saddam Hussein, they sought to change the balance of power in the Middle East by creating a liberal, democratic, and prowestern Arab nation that would make peace with Israel, embrace free market capitalism, and offer the United States access to its oil and military bases. Giving free rein to these neoconservative fantasies, Max Boot, a journalist and fellow at the Council of Foreign Relations, declared confidently: "Once we have deposed Saddam, we can impose an American-led international regency in Baghdad, to go along with the one in Kabul. With American seriousness and credibility thus restored, we will enjoy fruitful cooperation from the region's many opportunists, who will show a newfound eagerness to be helpful in our larger task of rolling up the international terror network that threatens us."[18]

Although the Bush administration never intended to occupy Iraq permanently, the planners of Operation Iraqi Freedom expected to use imperial methods to create this post-Saddam utopia. Their academic and media allies cheered them on by providing skewed historical precedents from the defunct formal empires to prove that it was possible to use military force to restructure a conquered society. These imperial experts proved remarkably inept in understanding the true lessons of empire. Failing to recognize that conquerors need allies from the subject population to govern effectively, they made the fundamental mistake of believing their own rhetoric. The scholars and theorists who provided the moral and practical backing for the Iraq invasion similarly endorsed unequivocally President Bush's assertion that western values and culture constituted the "single surviving model of human progress" in the post–Cold War era. They thus joined Bush strategists in assuming that common Iraqis would welcome the opportunity to become more western under a period of benevolent foreign rule.

At first, Operation Iraqi Freedom resembled the lightning conquests that established so many earlier formal empires. As promised, the conventional Iraqi military collapsed as General Tommy Franks's invasion force raced northward. Saddam Hussein was a poor military strategist and his troops had little reason to stand and fight. But virtually by accident Saddam laid the groundwork for an effective anti-American insurgency by positioning plainclothes members of the Fedayeen Saddam (Saddam's Martyrs) and hidden arms caches in the cities and towns of southern Iraq. Their primary mission was not to fight the Americans but to keep an eye on the restive Shi'a population.

The Iraqi leader stiffened his irregular forces by enlisting thousands of foreign fighters to defend his country from western aggression. Some of these men belonged to terrorist groups that had trained in Iraq in the 1990s, but others were civilians motivated by pan-Arabism. As an Egyptian volunteer explained: "Look, Saddam is not an angel from Allah, we know that. But if they take Tikrit, then is Cairo next?"[19] Few of these foreigners were formal members of al-Qaeda, but captured passports with visas listing "jihad" as the purpose of visiting Iraq indicated that a significant number of Saddam's foreign forces were Islamicists. All told, American intelligence experts estimated, there were roughly forty thousand non-Iraqis resisting the invasion force in March 2003.[20]

Working in cooperation with the Fedayeen Saddam, these foreigners accomplished what the Iraqi army could not. Operating in small bands, they delayed the advance by ambushing American troops who expected anyone in civilian clothing to welcome them as liberators. In cities such as Samawah and Nasiriyah, the irregulars' hit-and-run tactics threatened Franks's supply lines, and for a time it appeared that Operation Iraqi Freedom might flounder in the face of protracted guerrilla resistance. The Americans' enormous advantage eventually won out, but the surviving fighters formed the nucleus of the insurgency.

Bush administration strategists paid the insurgents little attention as U.S. forces surrounded Baghdad in early April. Prodded by "thunder runs" that pierced the city's defenses and produced extensive civilian casualties, Saddam's Baathist regime collapsed. In the American media, the victory seemed relatively clean and tidy. President Bush flew to the aircraft carrier USS *Abraham Lincoln* to declare an end to major combat operations in a sovereign nation that was now an American protectorate. Under a banner declaring "Mission Accomplished," the president proclaimed: "The transition from dictatorship to democracy will take time, but it is worth every effort. Our coalition will stay until our work is done. Then we will leave, and we will leave behind a free Iraq."[21]

Bush's speech implicitly spelled out America's new global agenda. The president renounced formal empire, but he declared that the United States would use imperial methods to protect its interests by overthrowing unfriendly regimes and bestowing the American gift of "freedom" on liberated populations. The actual opinions and desires of conquered peoples did not matter. This imperial reasoning doomed the ensuing American occupation of Iraq.

Predictably, law and order broke down in Baghdad within a month of the president's "mission accomplished" speech. The Office of Rehabilitation and Humanitarian Assistance (ORHA, which critics dubbed the Office of Really Helpless Americans) had no forces directly at its disposal and was powerless to intervene. This was due in part to meddling by Vice President Dick Cheney and the Defense Department's Douglas Feith. Aiming to ensure a quick handoff of power to Ahmed Chalabi and their Iraqi exile clients, Cheney and Feith blocked Jay Garner from appointing a provisional Iraqi government with authority over the remnants of the Iraqi military. Defense Secretary Donald Rumsfeld seemed remarkably unconcerned as looters emptied the city's banks, museums, and government ministries. Cavalierly dismissing the gravity of the situation by declaring that "freedom's untidy," he only ordered his commanders to defend the Ministry of Oil. It never occurred to the Bush administration and its top generals that their failure to fill the power vacuum created by the Baathist collapse would create an opening for the very terrorists they were certain they had just defeated.

While there is no question that the officials responsible for running Iraq after Saddam's downfall were guilty of gross incompetence, many of the critics of the Iraq war made the fundamental mistake of assuming that the right combination of nation-building strategies and troop deployments would have produced the prowestern Iraqi regime that the Bush administration had promised. Comparatively speaking, the new imperialists who conquered much of Africa and Asia in the preceding century were far more undermanned and underfinanced than Garner and the ORHA. But they never had to deal with the level of resistance that the United States faced in Iraq because their subjects' identities were largely still local. This made it comparatively easy to recruit allies from the subject population by exploiting local rivalries. In the late nineteenth century, there were no powerful transnational sources of aid to help defeated peoples such as Koitalel arap Samloei's Nandi in Kenya resist the British Empire.

The Bush administration and its academic allies assumed that they could still use imperial tactics to govern Iraq, but divide-and-rule strategies were less feasible in an era when a foreign invasion inspired nationalist resistance and drew enemy combatants and weapons from abroad. Consequently, the Coalition Provisional Authority (CPA), which replaced Garner's ORHA in early May 2003, never actually controlled Iraq because its authority extended only as far as the United States military could shoot. Liberated from Saddamist controls, common Iraqis were free to do as they pleased outside the immediate gaze of the Americans. Unlike in earlier empires, there were no chiefs and native auxiliaries to force them to accept the authority of the foreign conquerors. President Bush may have been sincere in disavowing imperial ambitions in Iraq, but his advisors apparently never warned him that using military force to seize direct sovereignty over millions of unwilling foreign subjects would lead to imperial rule.

Bush officials therefore made no provision for the messy realities of imperial governance and control. The CPA, which acquired the popular moniker "Condescending and Patronizing Americans," was a formal imperial state because it sought to govern Iraq directly. But it was also unquestionably one of the most pathetically inept imperial regimes in recorded history. Critics often referred to Ambassador L. Paul Bremer, the CPA administrator, as an American viceroy, but the former diplomat with strong Republican Party ties had no real sense of what the job entailed. He was confident that he had learned how to deal with "tribes" during a previous posting to Malawi, and he equated Iraqi leaders with African "tribal chiefs." Bremer compared himself to the American generals who oversaw the reconstruction of Germany and Japan after World War II, but he had more in common with the paternalistic but naive missionaries who legitimized the new imperialism. Wearing a suit and tie to demonstrate his respect for Iraqis, he envisioned himself as a platonic guardian wielding benevolent authoritarianism to transform Iraq into a liberal western society. In the 2006 memoir of his year in Iraq, Bremer acknowledged that Saddam Hussein did not have weapons of mass destruction, but he used a typical balance sheet argument to justify the invasion on the grounds it had "prevented the tyrant from massacring more innocent people."[22]

Although there were exceptions, much of the rest of the CPA was equally imperially minded. Just as imperial Kenya drew ambitious careerists such as Meinertzhagen, Bremer's staff consisted primarily of eager recent college graduates whose only real qualifications were neoconservative zealotry and Republican political ties. President Bush recruited some personally. Others got their jobs through Republican congressmen, conservative think tanks, or party activists. Claiming an exemption from federal employment regulations on the grounds that they were hiring temporary political appointees, CPA recruiters asked potential candidates how they voted in the 2000 elections and their position on abortion. Although Bremer's aides included some older businessmen and retired civil servants, this young "brat pack" ran most of the CPA. A twenty-four-year-old oversaw the Baghdad stock market, and the six staffers who managed the thirteen-billion-dollar Iraqi budget were all under thirty.[23]

The CPA itself operated out of one of Saddam Hussein's palace complexes in a fortified redoubt known as the Green Zone. Almost entirely isolated from common Iraqis within this bunkered enclave, which cynics dubbed the "Emerald City," Bremer's staffers pretended they were still in America. In addition to bars, discos, GMC Suburban

SUVs, and FM 107.7 "Freedom Radio" (classic rock and propaganda), their reliable electricity and running water were the envy of Baghdad residents who found necessities in short supply after the looting.[24]

Initially, Bremer was reasonably confident that he could address such problems. Drawing his authority from a personal letter from George Bush, the CPA administrator had total control over all executive, legislative, judicial, and fiscal functions in Iraq. He was in this sense no more accountable to common Iraqis than Saddam Hussein. More significant, his decision to delay indefinitely the transfer of power clashed directly with Donald Rumsfeld's plans to create a puppet Iraqi regime. Assuming that American power gave him the means to remake Iraqi society, Bremer disbanded the army and "de-Baathified" Iraqi society by expelling former high- and middle-ranking party members from their jobs. American commanders objected strongly because they were counting on Iraqi units to help maintain law and order, but Bremer justified his purge by equating it with the de-Nazification of German society after the Second World War.

The neophyte American viceroy claimed that these moves were part of a master plan to build a "unified and stable, democratic Iraq." He aimed to accomplish this feat of imperial social engineering by creating a new army, restoring power generation, reopening schools and hospitals, introducing a new currency, imposing a market economy, and, most important, restarting oil production. Predictably, Bremer did not include representative democracy on his list of immediate objectives. Rejecting as reckless Garner's plan to appoint an interim Iraqi government, he envisioned a drawn-out and incremental period of American tutelage whereby Iraqis would write a constitution, conduct a census, pass election laws, and create political parties before having the privilege of choosing their own government.

Bremer's grand vision floundered on a number of complicating realities, not the least of which was the flood of special-interest groups that parasitized the occupation. These contractors, speculators, civil service careerists, and outright criminals resembled earlier generations of imperial opportunists and nabobs that preyed on subject societies. In the Iraqi case, however, their prime target was the incredibly inept occupying power. With Iraq's oil industry in a shambles, the real prize was the staggering sums that the Bush administration set aside for reconstruction. Roughly twenty billion dollars of these funds came from the Baathist regime's unfrozen bank accounts and

reserves from the United Nation's preinvasion "oil-for-food" program. The American government then had to add another eighteen
billion dollars of its own money in November 2003 when it became
clear that Wolfowitz's promises of a self-financing invasion and
occupation had fallen flat. Acknowledging World Bank and United
Nations estimates that it would take roughly fifty billion dollars to
rebuild Iraq, the Bush administration tried and failed to get its allies
to make up the shortfall. Between 2002 and 2008 it therefore spent
approximately fifty billion dollars of American taxpayers' money in
Iraq. This was the largest foreign aid package for a single nation in
U.S. history.[25]

Just as they had bungled the planning for Operation Iraqi Freedom,
Bush officials were remarkably inept in managing and protecting this
tempting windfall. They gave their friends and allies no-bid contracts
to provide everything from logistical support for the invasion force
to large-scale development and state-building projects in Iraq itself.
Predictably, most of the Iraqi reconstruction funding went to a small
group of politically influential corporations and companies. By far,
the largest bonanza went to Halliburton. Leveraging its connections
with Vice President Cheney, Halliburton's former CEO, the corporation won contracts to rebuild the Iraqi oil industry, construct power
and water treatment plants, and supply virtually all of the United
States military's logistical needs in Iraq. Free from direct oversight,
the company racked up billions of dollars in questionable billings,
including a $61 million overcharge for importing oil and single $247
cans of soft drinks for American troops.[26]

While Halliburton's bounty made it a symbol of Bush administration mismanagement, it was by no means the only special interest to profit from imperial-style privileges. An engineer working for
the Parsons Corporation made $150,000 per year ($90,000 of which
was tax free), a civilian American truck driver made $80,000, and a
"shooter" for a private security firm could earn an annual salary of
up to $200,000. This last opportunity arose from Rumsfeld's decision
to keep U.S. troop levels unworkably low. Missing what amounted to
an entire army division, American commanders needed private military contractors to provide basic security throughout the country.
Blackwater Worldwide had a $21 million contract to guard Bremer
and the CPA, while an improbably named firm called Custer Battles
earned $16 million plus costs to protect the Baghdad airport.[27]

The opportunities for corruption in this barely supervised flood of cash, millions of which arrived in shrink-wrapped bundles of hundred-dollar bills, were painfully obvious. The owners of Custer Battles used front companies in the Cayman Islands and Lebanon to inflate their costs and barely escaped prosecution for fraud when they left an incriminating spreadsheet on a CPA conference table showing they had billed more than $9 million for work costing $3.7 million. On a smaller scale, some of the less idealistic CPA officials were equally vulnerable to temptation. One manager oversaw a fund of $82 million and accepted $3 million worth of first-class plane tickets, real estate, vehicles, jewelry, and sexual services from prostitutes in return for reconstruction contracts.[28]

Although some of these looted funds came from Iraqi oil money, the Americans did not practice conventional imperial extraction in Iraq. They collected no tribute and never forced anyone to work for them. Still, most Iraqis suffered considerably upon becoming subjects of the United States. Bremer's ill-conceived mass demobilization of the army and de-Baathification policies threw more than half a million people out of work and produced a 40 percent spike in the national unemployment rate. Thousands of jobless veterans took to the streets of Baghdad in protest, and a former sergeant reduced to peddling tea spoke for many of them when he asked, quite legitimately: "Where are my rights and salary? Did U.S. democracy come and devour them?"[29] To make matters worse, Bremer and his advisors moved to cut food subsidies and close or sell off state-owned industries as part of their plan to liberalize the Iraqi economy.

Comparatively speaking, earlier generations of imperial subjects suffered far worse indignities than those endured by the Iraqis under American rule. Nevertheless, the experience of invasion and occupation was extraordinarily traumatic for a great many people, even if they hated Saddam Hussein. Ahmed Hashim, a counterinsurgency expert with the United States Central Command (CENTCOM), argued convincingly that the American conquest and elimination of the Iraqi army created a profound identity crisis for most of the country's Sunni Arabs. As Majid Hamid al-Bayati sermonized in a Baghdad mosque in the immediate aftermath of Bremer's directives: "They have destroyed our institutions, our people and our security. They have totally erased us."[30]

Faced with impoverishment and the loss of the privileges and status from the Baathist era, many Sunnis opted to fight the Americans. The first serious incident took place in April 2003 when U.S. troops killed or wounded eight people by shooting into a crowd of protesters in the town of Fallujah. Accounts differ as to which side fired first, but most Iraqis were certain it was the Americans. As attacks on the occupation forces mounted, President Bush rashly declared: "My answer is bring 'em on. We've got the force necessary to deal with the security situation."

In point of fact, the CPA did not have the manpower to control Iraq. The so-called Multi-National Division of Poles, Ukrainians, and Central Americans was actually only a brigade of three thousand soldiers. The New Iraqi Corps (NIC), which Bremer expected to replace the Baathist-dominated Iraqi army, was entirely unreliable, and very few of the nations that joined the Bush administration's "coalition of the willing" were willing to commit their troops to actual combat.

The consequences of the Bush administration's inability to assert authority over Iraq were enormous. Earlier empires understood that effective imperial rule depended on maintaining the illusion of invincibility to convince subjects that it was futile, if not suicidal, to resist. The Americans, however, were dangerously vulnerable. In an incident widely reported in the U.S. media, a Yemeni engineering student walked up to a Florida National Guardsman drinking a ginger ale at Baghdad University and shot him in the head. The Iraqi insurgents effectively called the Americans' bluff by murdering and intimidating anyone who became too closely associated with the occupying power. A former Baathist general active in the resistance made the explicit link between cooperation and the crime of collaboration. "Every Iraqi or foreigner who works with the Coalition is a target. Ministries, mercenaries, translators, businessmen, cooks or maids, it doesn't matter the degree of collaboration. To sign a contract with the occupiers is to sign your death certificate. Iraqi or not, these are traitors."[31]

This intimidation made it impossible for the CPA to recruit the local allies it needed to run the country. Insurgents shot down Aqila al-Hashemi, a female member of Bremer's showcase Iraqi Governing Council, on her own doorstep. They also assassinated one of Saddam Hussein's senior revenue officials when he began to work with the CPA, and they forced the governor of al-Anbar Province to retire by kidnapping his sons. In the Shi'a south, the young radical cleric

Muqtada al-Sadr's men murdered several high-ranking clerics who had signaled a willingness to work with the American occupiers.

Bush officials denied that the insurgents had any legitimacy or popular support by dismissing them as "regime dead-enders," Nazi-style Baathist thugs, or foreign Islamicists. Regarding the last claim, there was indeed a strong transnational element to the resistance. The CPA's inability to control Iraq's borders allowed those who detested the United States' global hegemony to surge into the country to kill Americans. Nonetheless, U.S. intelligence experts estimated that most of the fighters in the insurgency were native-born Iraqis. Senior Baathist leaders in hiding organized and funded much of their operations, but there was no denying that many guerrillas were common Iraqis who simply would not tolerate the occupation. As a laborer explained: "[U.S. soldiers] searched my house. They kicked my Koran. They speak to me so poorly in front of my children. It's not that I encourage my son to hate Americans. It's not that I make him want to join the resistance. Americans do that for me."[32] In April 2004, reports that guards and intelligence officers were systematically humiliating, if not torturing, detainees at Baghdad's Abu Ghraib prison deepened this widespread resolve to fight the occupation.

The Iraqis were no more organized in their opposition to the American occupation than the French were under Nazi rule in the previous century. The Jordanian Abu Musab al-Zarqawi's al-Qaeda in Iraq organization, which had no significant ties to the preinvasion Saddamist regime, was the most significant foreign element in the insurgency. In the Baghdad slums and the Shi'a south, Muqtada al-Sadr's sixty-thousand-man Mahdi Army also fought the American occupiers. Most insurgents, however, were Iraqi Sunnis, but they were divided over whether they were seeking the restoration of secular Baathist rule or an Islamic theocracy. Although they may have been split along sectarian, ethnic, and ideological lines, the various factions still generally agreed on the fundamental goal of expelling the Americans. Most significant, they never would have been able to operate effectively if the general public had not been willing to shelter them.

These largely common people successfully defied the United States, which friend and foe alike described as the world's sole superpower, for more than five years. Earlier generations of imperial subjects had the same goal, but they lacked the organization and means to resist.

In the twenty-first century, transnational flows of funding and support and the accessibility of advanced technology made it much easier to resist a foreign occupier. Former army officers provided essential training, but the insurgents also learned how to make improvised explosive devices (IEDs) and suicide bombs from the Internet. They used common household devices such as cell phones and garage door openers to set them off. These tools gave Iraqis the means to reject subjecthood.

Even more ruthlessly, the foreign fighters demonstrated the CPA's impotency and made Iraq ungovernable by inflaming sectarian divisions through suicide bombing attacks that indiscriminately killed people as they went about their daily lives. The Iraq insurgency thus wrecked the Bush administration's grand blueprint for Iraq. The guerrillas destroyed the CPA's infrastructure projects and forced contractors to shelter in fortified camps for safety. Most consequential, they sabotaged the Americans' primary extractive agenda by preventing the CPA from restarting oil production. Exasperated, Bremer noted that the coalition forces could not protect traffic to the Baghdad airport, and he compared their overstretched units to "an understrength fire crew racing from one blaze to another."

The Bush administration eventually had to acknowledge that direct American rule in Iraq was unworkable. It therefore cast about desperately for ways to withdraw from Iraq without giving the foreign Islamicists free rein or plunging the country into anarchy and full-scale civil war. President Bush's only viable option was "nation building," a long and expensive process that he had openly derided during the 2000 election campaign. From 2004 to 2006, the Americans guided their Iraqi clients through a series of incremental steps that included constitution writing, provisional and transitional administrations, and eventually elections for an Iraqi National Assembly and a nominally independent government under Prime Minister Nouri al-Maliki. While this was Bremer's original goal in 2003, the resulting regime looked nothing like his imaginary liberal Arab democracy.

Yet the emergence of a nominally sovereign Iraqi government did not end the American occupation, for al-Maliki needed U.S. aid to stay in power. As President Bush's second term of office drew to a close, more than five years after he launched Operation Iraqi Freedom, there were still approximately 130,000 American soldiers in Iraq. A new security arrangement with the al-Maliki regime set 2011 as the date for their final withdrawal, a process that his successor, Barack Obama, endorsed and accelerated.

Many of the hard power advocates who had argued so passionately for the invasion sought to regain a measure of credibility by attacking the Bush administration for failing to make proper use of America's vast military might. Latching on to the seeming effectiveness of a "surge" in American troops levels in 2007, they blamed Rumsfeld for grossly underestimating the number of men under arms that it would take to occupy and control Iraq. In fact, popular revulsion over the chronic violence stemming from the civil war and insurgency was the real reason that the unrest appeared to wane. Common Iraqis lost patience with foreign fighters and jihadis who were behind the bloodiest and most devastating bombings. Similarly, many Sunnis began to work with the occupation forces when they realized that they needed U.S. support as a counterweight to al-Maliki's Shi'a regime.

These sectarian divisions would have allowed earlier generations of imperial rulers to recruit local allies, but the United States simply could not find dependable Iraqi clients. As Ali Allawi, a western-educated Shi'a who briefly held several cabinet positions in the transition governments, explained: "There was no 'American party' in Iraq, no people who were open advocates of an alliance with America because it was not in the manifest interest of the country to have such an arrangement. America's only allies in Iraq were those who sought to manipulate the great power to their narrow advantage."[33] Bush officials never made a concerted effort to recruit more effective intermediaries because they were afraid of what might happen if they gave too much power to any particular faction. Indeed, it would have been difficult to explain to the American public how Operation Iraqi Freedom produced a Shi'a theocracy, a Sunni fundamentalist state, or a revived Baathist regime rather than the promised secular liberal democracy.

By any measure, the Bush administration's attempt to use unilateral military force to remake Iraq was, without question, an unmitigated failure. The disastrous consequences of this semi-imperial enterprise were so high in terms of casualties and resources that no subjective balance sheet could conceal them. The primary function of a formal empire has always been to extract tribute, but the CPA's inability to restart the Iraqi oil industry meant that wealth flowed from the United States to Iraq to sustain the occupation. As a result, the price of

Operation Iraqi Freedom, which Rumsfeld and his planners assumed would last only a few months and cost forty to fifty billion dollars, reached approximately three trillion dollars by 2008 and most likely played a role in the ensuing global financial crash. It also squandered American hard power, as every major army and marine unit served at least one, if not several, tours in Iraq during the Bush years. All told, the invasion and occupation cost the American military more than four thousand killed and thirty thousand wounded by 2008.[34]

The average Iraqi paid an even higher price for Operation Iraqi Freedom. Diehard Bush partisans and their neoimperial allies tried to excuse the deaths of thousands of civilians by claiming that the overthrow of Saddam Hussein and the liberation of Iraq was a greater good. CPA head Paul Bremer frequently equated the Baathists with the Nazis and cited humanitarian anecdotes such as the suffering of "little Khadija," a premature infant struggling to survive in a forty-year-old incubator, as an example of what the American occupation would fix. Bremer liked to blame the media for failing to report the "good news" in Iraq, but by any measure imaginable the American gift of "freedom" was devastatingly expensive. Estimates vary, but it may be that as many as half a million civilian casualties resulted from the invasion, insurgency, and civil war.[35] Furthermore, the violence resulting from the occupation forced roughly 1.6 million people to leave their homes to seek shelter in other parts of the country and drove an addition 1.8 million Iraqis into foreign exile.[36] It was therefore little wonder that an Iraqi journalist marked George W. Bush's farewell visit to Baghdad by throwing his shoes (a profound insult in the Arab world) at the American president while shouting, "This is a gift from the Iraqis; this is the farewell kiss, you dog. This is from the widows, the orphans, and those who were killed in Iraq."

It is also easy to understand why so many Iraqis either joined the insurgents and foreign fighters or refused to help the Americans root them out. A combined public opinion poll conducted by American and British media companies in March 2007 found that 78 percent of Iraqis surveyed opposed the occupation, and a staggering 51 percent believed that it was acceptable to use violence to drive the Americans out of Iraq. Additionally, almost two-thirds of the respondents believed that the United States, rather than the al-Maliki government, actually ran the country.[37] Most of these people did not take up arms against U.S. forces, but they made the occupation unworkable.

Neither the Bush administration nor its Pentagon strategists ever imagined that these common people had the capacity to thwart their grand plans. Many of the neoconservatives and imperial enthusiasts who had argued so strenuously for the Iraq invasion tried to salvage their reputations and explain this fundamental miscalculation by blaming the Bush administration for mismanaging the invasion. And the frustrated commanders, who found themselves trying to run the occupation on a shoestring, can be forgiven for calling ideologically driven administration strategists such as Paul Wolfowitz "dangerously idealistic and crack-smoking stupid."[38]

Yet the fundamental reality is that Operation Iraqi Freedom was never feasible, no matter how well or poorly it might have been planned. Imperial methods are simply no longer viable in the transnational era. The great imperial powers of history would have been able to isolate the Iraqi insurgents and counter their resistance with ruthless naked force. Some even would have slaughtered anyone who gave them support or shelter. The days of empire, however, are over.

Bush officials may have believed that their vast military power gave them the means to act unilaterally, but they failed because the world will no longer tolerate empire building, even if it is informal and temporary. The international community turned a deaf ear to the Bush administration's pleas to help shoulder the costs of the occupation, but ultimately common Iraqis defeated Operation Iraqi Freedom by refusing to cooperate with the conquering power. The American military's devastatingly powerful modern weapons and superbly trained soldiers were of no value whatsoever in governing an unwilling subject population.

The American occupation of Iraq is a powerful cautionary example for those who would misuse or selectively interpret history to further an ideological or self-aggrandizing agenda. From their comfortably safe positions of power and privilege in the White House, the Pentagon, the halls of Congress, think tanks, editorial boards, and academia, imperial enthusiasts advocated vital policy decisions that were based on a selective reading of history. In 2007, Niall Ferguson's acknowledgment of Iraq's descent into civil war began with the comment "Oh dear."[39]

While much of the work that drew on imperial precedents to legitimize the Bush administration's adventure in Iraq was inherently flawed and propagandistic, there are still lessons to be learned from a comparative historical study of actual imperial regimes. The first of these is that there never was a static, idealized Aristotelian model of empire. Imperial institutions evolved over time, and it is facile to cite the Roman Empire, a product of the ancient world, as a precedent in formulating contemporary foreign policy.

The late nineteenth-century British Empire was a more modern institution, but it was not the benevolent force for good that imperial partisans recall it to be. Empires are, by definition, a form of permanent authoritarian rule that consigns a defeated community to perpetual subjecthood, most often for the purposes of exploitation and extraction. Empire builders justified this inequitable relationship by portraying subject peoples as inherently primitive and backward, and their promises to reform and uplift them were just empty rhetoric. Imperial rulers were fundamentally guilty of disgusting hypocrisy in implying that they exploited their subjects for their own good.

Empires were never humane, and imperial subjecthood was always demeaning and intolerable. The current romanticization of the British and French empires of the last century as stable, omnipotent, and benevolent rests on anachronistic nostalgia, willful historical ignorance, and the intentional racist denigration and exoticization of nonwestern peoples. Throughout history, imperial special interests covered up these realities by disguising their avarice and self-interest in the garb of patriotism and humanitarianism. In doing so they obscured the true fiscal, military, and moral price of empire. Metropolitan populations shared these costs with foreign subjects, but they gullibly supported empire building because legitimizing imperial stereotypes confirmed their own inherent sense of cultural superiority.

Imperial subjects were not primitive, and conquerors became empire builders by exploiting short-term political and technological advantages resulting from the uneven advance of globalization. Imperial rulers often became subjects themselves after suffering a military defeat, while former subjects rarely passed up the opportunity to build empires when they acquired the means to do so. In other words, the global imbalances that facilitated empire building were largely self-correcting and were by no means a measure of cultural superiority or inferiority.

The empires covered in this book demonstrate that imperial conquerors were never as powerful as they imagined. Lacking the political will, manpower, and financial resources to govern an entire population directly, imperial states needed the assistance of allies from subject communities to assert their authority at the local level. In addition to drawing wealth and privilege from their participation in imperial governance, these intermediaries often manipulated their sponsors by exploiting their ignorance.

Although it may seem counterintuitive, the simple fact is that the longest-lived empires were those that proved most adept at recruiting reliable local allies and least efficient in extracting tribute. Roman historical texts and architectural ruins are grand, but the Romans themselves had little direct influence over their subjects. The Umayyad conquerors of Al-Andalus suffered from the same problem. In the premodern era, conquistadors and nabobs found it relatively easy to turn subject communities against each other when most identities were narrow and local, but they also had to share power with subject clients in order to collect taxes and rule effectively. This meant that while common people suffered individually under foreign rule, the strength of local privileges and particularism limited the overall extractive reach of premodern imperial states.

Imperial enthusiasts laud the great empires of the modern era for their scope and power, but they were ephemeral. The Napoleonic and Nazi empires conquered continental Europe but floundered on the strength of the Europeans' inherent anti-imperialism. Overseas, the nation-state's robust bureaucratic and coercive tools allowed the new imperialists to reach directly into local communities to extract tribute and labor. In doing so, however, they provoked enormous popular resistance and broke down the narrow and more parochial identities that had kept their subjects manageably compartmentalized. It therefore became much harder to enlist imperial proxies when cooperation became treasonous collaboration. In the twentieth century, imperial life spans shrank proportionately as the scope of identity expanded from the local to the national and then the global, and self-determination became a natural right. One can easily imagine Romans, Andalusis, conquistadors, and nabobs laughing at the "great" empires of the modern era that failed to last a single century.

Empire became even more impossible in the twenty-first century when accelerated globalization largely erased the west's technological, economic, and political advantages. Nationalism played a central role in destroying the world's last formal empires, but in the contemporary era, flows of ideas, capital, migrants, weapons, and willing practitioners of political violence mean that conquerors have lost the capacity to isolate and reduce a defeated population to subjecthood. The American and Soviet failures in Vietnam and Afghanistan were the first indication that common people could blunt hard power by drawing on aid from sympathetic rival powers. The collapse of the Soviet Union lulled the Bush administration into thinking that it could still use imperial methods because Saddam Hussein was isolated and had no influential foreign patrons. Yet the successful anti-American insurgency in Iraq demonstrates that larger transnational identities such as Arabism and Islamicism have given even weak and divided communities the means to defy a seemingly omnipotent conquering power.

In surrendering to the temptation to try to rule Iraq directly, Americans learned that imperial methods are inherently corrupting. They give free rein to hubris, greed, and other base human vices that are tempered within the confines of any civilized society. Sponsoring governments may try to keep this contamination safely walled off in the imperial hinterlands, but as Edmund Burke warned in the case of the Indian nabobs, there is always the danger that it will poison metropolitan society when the conquerors return home. In ruing the costs of empire, Pliny had good reason to complain that "through conquering we have been conquered." The theorists and historians who assured the world that the American imperial project in Iraq was feasible and moral ignored this reality.

As memories of the bloodshed and chaos of the occupation recede, the architects of Operation Iraqi Freedom inevitably will argue that it ultimately achieved its goals and served a greater good. In doing so, they will try to obscure their role in the deaths of tens of thousands of people, if not hundreds of thousands, by returning to the lie that imperial projects can achieve liberal and humanitarian ends. History has forgotten the earlier generations of subject peoples who suffered the results of similar hypocritical imperial promises, and there is no reason to assume that the experiences of ordinary Iraqis will have any greater resonance in America's popular imagination. Yet we ignore the lessons of this book at our peril. Common people now have the capacity to thwart imperial ambitions, and history shows us that imperial fortunes can turn quickly. Inkan nobles, Mughal emperors, and twentieth-century Frenchmen all learned that it was possible to go from ruler to ruled virtually overnight. Conquerors may self-servingly portray defeated peoples as exotic or backward, but we are all potential imperial subjects.

NOTES

Introduction

1. Quoted in Timothy Parsons, *The African Rank and File: Social Implications of Colonial Service in the King's African Rifles, 1902–1964* (Portsmouth: Heinemann, 1999), 106.

2. Bertram Francis Gordon Cranworth, *A Colony in the Making: Or Sport and Profit in British East Africa* (London: Macmillan, 1912), 166.

3. Sarah Joseph, "Table Talk: The Archbishop of Canterbury," *Emel*, December 2007.

4. Cranworth, *Colony in the Making*, 52, 55.

5. White House press release, "President Bush Delivers Graduation Speech at West Point," June 1, 2002.

6. Niall Ferguson, "The Empire Slinks Back," *New York Times*, April 27, 2003; Niall Ferguson, "An Empire in Denial: The Limits of U.S. Imperialism," *Harvard International Review*, Fall 2003, 69; Niall Ferguson, *Empire: How Britain Made the Modern World* (London: Penguin, 2003); Niall Ferguson, *Colossus: The Price of America's Empire* (New York: Penguin, 2004).

7. Deepak Lal, *In Praise of Empires: Globalization and Order* (New York: Palgrave MacMillan, 2004), xix, 4, 210–11.

8. Harold James, *The Roman Predicament: How the Rules of International Order Create the Politics of Empire* (Princeton: Princeton University Press, 2006), 88; Strobe Talbott, *The Great Experiment: The Story of Ancient Empires, Modern States, and the Quest for a Global Nation* (New York: Simon & Schuster, 2008), 3–4; Amy Chua, *Day of Empire: How Hyperpowers Rise to Global Dominance—And Why They Fall* (New York: Doubleday, 2007).

9. Benedict Anderson, *Imagined Communities: Reflections on the Origin and Spread of Nationalism,* rev. ed. (London: Verso, 1991), 6–7.

451

10. H. W. Brands, *Bound to Empire: The United States and the Philippines* (New York: Oxford University Press, 1992), x; James, *Roman Predicament*, 131.

11. Andrew Lintott, *Imperium Romanum: Politics and Administration* (London: Routledge, 1993), 22; Martin Goodman, *The Roman World, 44 B.C.–A.D. 180* (London: Routledge, 1997), 106; Craige Champion and Arthur Eckstein, "Introduction: The Study of Roman Imperialism," in *Roman Imperialism: Readings and Sources*, ed. Craige Champion (Oxford: Blackwell, 2004), 309.

12. Hannah Arendt, *The Origins of Totalitarianism*, 2nd ed. (New York: Meridian, 1960), 131; Richard Koebner and Helmut Dan Schmidt, *Imperialism: The Story and Significance of a Political Word, 1840–1960* (Cambridge: Cambridge University Press, 1964), xiii, 10, 324–25.

13. Ferguson, *Colossus*, 19.

14. Paul Passavant, "Introduction," in *Empire's New Clothes: Reading Hardt and Negri*, ed. Paul Passavant and Jodi Dean (New York: Routledge, 2004), 3.

15. Andrew Bacevich, *American Empire: The Realities and Consequences of U.S. Diplomacy* (Cambridge, MA: Harvard University Press, 2002); Michael Mann, *Incoherent Empire* (New York: Verso, 2003); Jim Garrison, *America as Empire: Global Leader or Rogue Power?* (San Francisco: Berret-Koehler, 2004); Chalmers Johnson, *The Sorrows of Empire: Militarism, Secrecy, and the End of the Republic* (New York: Metropolitan Books, 2004); Rashid Khalidi, *Resurrecting Empire: Western Footprints and America's Perilous Path in the Middle East* (Boston: Beacon, 2005).

16. L. H. Gann and Peter Duignan, *Burden of Empire* (Stanford: Stanford University Press, 1971), ix–x, 367.

17. Stanley Kurtz, "Democratic Imperialism: A Blueprint," *Policy Review Online*, April 2003; Ferguson, *Empire*, xx–xxii, 358–59, 362.

18. Nicholas Dirks, *The Scandal of Empire: India and the Creation of Imperial Britain* (Cambridge, MA: Harvard University Press, 2006), 322.

19. Quoted in Dane Kennedy, *Islands of White: Settler Society and Culture in Kenya and Southern Rhodesia, 1890–1939* (Durham, NC: Duke University Press, 1987), 130.

20. Aimé Césaire, *Discourse on Colonialism*, trans. Joan Pinkham (New York: Monthly Review Press, 1972), 21–22.

21. Daniel Headrick, *The Tools of Empire: Technology and European Imperialism in the Nineteenth Century* (New York: Oxford University Press, 1981), 199.

Chapter 1

1. Cassius Dio, *Dio's Roman History*, trans. Earnest Cary (Cambridge, MA: Harvard University Press, 1931), 7:421–23.

2. Sabine MacCormack, *On the Wings of Time: Rome, the Incas, Spain, and Peru* (Princeton: Princeton University Press, 2007), xviii; Richard Hingley, *Roman Officers and English Gentlemen* (London: Routledge, 2000), 4, 21.

3. Catharine Edwards, "Introduction: Shadows and Fragments," in *Roman Presences: Receptions of Rome in European Culture, 1789–1945*, ed. Catharine Edwards (Cambridge: Cambridge University Press, 1999), 3, 9.

4. Citations from Susan Mattern, "Rome and the Enemy: Imperial Strategy in the Principate," in *Roman Imperialism: Readings and Sources*, ed. Craige Champion (Oxford: Blackwell, 2004), 202–3.

5. Benjamin Isaac, *The Invention of Racism in Classical Antiquity* (Princeton: Princeton University Press, 2004), 190–92, 503; P. S. Wells, "The Barbarians Speak: How Conquered Peoples Shaped Roman Europe," in *Roman Imperialism*, 244–46.

6. Naphtali Lewis and Meyer Reinhold, eds., *Roman Civilization Source Book I: The Republic* (New York: Columbia University Press, 1966), 373–34.

7. Quoted in Isaac, *Invention of Racism*, 225.

8. Quoted in Mattern, "Rome and the Enemy," 203.

9. David Mattingly, *An Imperial Possession: Britain in the Roman Empire, 54 B.C.–A.D. 409* (London: Allen Lane, 2006), 6.

10. Livy, *The Dawn of the Roman Empire: Books 31–40*, trans. J. C. Yardley (Oxford: Oxford University Press, 2000), 188–89.

11. Quoted in Mattern, "Rome and the Enemy," 212.

12. Lewis and Reinhold, *Roman Civilization Source Book I: The Republic*, 313.

13. P. A. Brunt, "Reflections on British and Roman Imperialism," *Comparative Studies in Society and History* 7, 3 (1965): 271–72; Keith Hopkins, "Taxes and Trade in the Roman Empire, 200 B.C.–A.D. 400," *Journal of Roman Studies* 70 (1980): 105–8.

14. Quoted in Mattern, "Rome and the Enemy," 263.

15. Neil Faulkner, *The Decline and Fall of Roman Britain* (Charleston, SC: Tempus, 2000), 157; Martin Goodman, *The Roman World, 44 B.C.–A.D. 180* (London: Routledge, 1997), 214.

16. Martin Henig, *The Heirs of King Verica* (Charleston, SC: Tempus, 2002), 55.

17. Josephus, *The Jewish War*, ed. Gaalya Cornfeld et al. (Grand Rapids, MI: Zondervan, 1982), 444.

18. Keith Bradley, *Slavery and Society at Rome* (Cambridge: Cambridge University Press, 1994), 13–14, 32.

19. Cassius Dio, *Dio's Roman History*, 327–29; Faulkner, *Decline and Fall of Roman Britain*, 50–53.

20. Strabo, *The Geography of Strabo*, book 4: *Gaul*, trans. Horace Leonard Jones (Cambridge, MA: Harvard University Press, 1988), 255–57; Julius Caesar,

The Conquest of Gaul, trans. S. A. Handford (Baltimore, MD: Penguin, 1951), 135–36; Tacitus, *On Britain and Germany,* trans. H. Mattingly (Baltimore: Penguin, 1964), 61–62.

21. P. C. N. Stewart, "Inventing Britain: The Roman Creation of an Image," *Britannia* 26 (1995): 1–7; Katherine Clarke, "An Island Nation: Re-Reading Tacitus' 'Agricola,'" *Journal of Roman Studies* 91 (2001): 101–2.

22. Strabo, *Geography of Strabo,* book 4: *Gaul,* 255.

23. Caesar, *Conquest of Gaul,* 119–25.

24. Ibid., 135–39; Strabo, *Geography of Strabo,* book 4: *Gaul,* 257–59.

25. S. S. Frere, "Verulamium: Urban Development and the Local Region," in *Invasion and Response,* 273; Todd, *Roman Britain,* 29–30.

26. Suetonius, *The Lives of the Twelve Caesars,* trans. J. C. Rolfe (London: Heinemann, 1914), 2:287.

27. Tacitus, *On Britain and Germany,* 85–88.

28. Martin Millet, *The Romanization of Britain* (Cambridge: Cambridge University Press, 1990), 56.

29. Peter Salway, "Conclusion," in *The Roman Era: The British Isles, 55 B.C.–A.D. 410,* ed. Peter Salway (Oxford: Oxford University Press, 2002), 205; Henig, *Heirs of King Verica,* 42–44, 55.

30. Cassius Dio, *Dio's Roman History,* trans. Earnest Cary (Cambridge, MA: Harvard University Press, 1931), 8:83, 95.

31. Ibid., 85–87.

32. Tacitus, *The Annals of Imperial Rome,* trans. Michael Grant (New York: Penguin, 1986), 328.

33. Tacitus, *On Britain and Germany,* 72.

34. Anthony Barrett, "The Career of Tiberius Claudius Cogidubnus," *Britannia* 10 (1979): 242.

35. Lindsay Allason-Jones, *Women in Roman Britain* (London: British Museum, 1989), 59.

36. This may simply refer to an assessment of their military value as auxiliaries. Alan Bowman, *Life and Letters on the Roman Frontier: Vindolanda and Its People* (New York: Routledge, 1994), 29, 106.

37. John Wacher, *The Coming of Rome* (London: Routledge and Kegan Paul, 1979), 74.

R. Hingley, "Resistance and Domination: Social Change in Roman Britain," in *Dialogues in Roman Imperialism: Power, Discourse, and Discrepant Experience in the Roman Empire,* ed. D. J. Mattingly (Portsmouth, RI: Society for the Promotion of Roman Studies, 1997), 90.

38. Hopkins, "Taxes and Trade in the Roman Empire," 123.

39. Quoted in Millet, *Romanization of Britain,* 131.

40. Ammianus Marcellinus, *Ammianus Marcellinus,* trans. John Rolfe (Cambridge, MA: Harvard University Press, 1958), 2:3–5.

41. Zosimus, *Zosimus: Historia Nova*, trans. James Buchanon and Harold Davis (San Antonio, TX: Trinity University Press, 1967), 253.

Chapter 2

1. Charles Morris, *The Romance of Reality*, vol. 7: *Spain* (New York: R. H. Whitten, 1904), 17–20; Colin Smith, *Christians and Moors in Spain*, vol. 1: *711–1150* (Warminster: Aris and Phillips, 1988), 9, 19; Richard Fletcher, *Moorish Spain* (New York: Henry Holt, 1992), 15; Ibn Abd al-Hakam, "Narrative of the Conquest of al-Andalus," in *Medieval Iberia: Readings from Christian, Muslim, and Jewish Sources*, ed. Olivia Remie Constable (Philadelphia: University of Pennsylvania Press, 1997), 34.

2. *The Chronicle of 754*, in *Medieval Iberia*, 31.

3. Richard Bulliet, *Conversion to Islam in the Medieval Period: An Essay in Quantitative History* (Cambridge, MA: Harvard University Press, 1979), 33.

4. Khalid Yahya Blankinship, *The End of the Jihad State: The Reign of Hisham ibn Abd al-Malik and the Collapse of the Umayyads* (Albany: State University of New York Press, 1994), 42–44.

5. G. R. Hawting, *The First Dynasty of Islam: The Umayyad Caliphate, A.D. 661–750* (Carbondale: Southern Illinois University Press, 1987), 5; Patricia Crone, "Imperial Trauma: The Case of the Arabs," *Common Knowledge* 12, 1 (2006): 110–12.

6. Edward Gibbon, *History of the Decline and Fall of the Roman Empire*, ed. Hans-Friedrich Mueller (New York: Modern Library, 2003), 5:964.

7. Efraim Karsh, *Islamic Imperialism: A History* (New Haven: Yale University Press, 2006), 230–31.

8. In time the followers of Ali organized themselves into the Shi'a branch of Islam.

9. Hugh Kennedy, *The Prophet and the Age of the Caliphates*, 2nd ed. (London: Pearson, 2004), 68–69.

10. Hagith Sivan, "On Foederati, Hospitalitas, and the Settlement of the Goths in A.D. 41," *American Journal of Philology* 108 (1987): 767.

11. Jerrilynn Dodds, *Architecture and Ideology in Early Medieval Spain* (University Park: Pennsylvania State University Press, 1989), 8.

12. Hugh Kennedy, *Muslim Spain and Portugal: A Political History of al-Andalus* (London: Longman, 1996), 2.

13. "The Treaty of Tudmir," in *Medieval Iberia*, 37–38.

14. Migeul Cruz Hernandez, "The Social Structure of Al-Andalus during the Muslim Occupation and the Founding of the Umayyad Monarchy," in *The Formation of al-Andalus: Part I, History and Society*, ed. Manuela Marin (Aldershot: Ashgate, 1998), 77; Fletcher, *Moorish Spain*, 25.

15. Roger Collins, *Early Medieval Spain: Unity in Diversity, 400–1000* (New York: St. Martin's, 1983), 176.

16. Pedro Chalmeta, "An Approximate Picture of the Economy of al-Andalus," in *The Legacy of Muslim Spain*, ed. Salma Khadra Jayyusi (Leiden: E. J. Brill, 1992), 755.

17. Quoted in Ann Christys, *Christians in al-Andalus, 711–1000* (Richmond Surrey: Curzon Press, 2002), 15–16.

18. Fletcher, *Moorish Spain*, 37–38.

19. Thomas Glick and Oriol Pi-Sunyer, "Acculturation as an Explanatory Concept in Spanish History," *Comparative Studies in Society and History* 11 (1969): 144; Pierre Guichard, "The Social History of Muslim Spain from the Conquest to the End of the Almohad Regime, Early 8th–Early 13th Centuries," in Jayyusi, *Legacy of Muslim Spain*, 679.

20. Fletcher, *Moorish Spain*, 2, 8; Mahmoud Makki, "The Political History of al-Andalus," in Jayyusi, *Legacy of Muslim Spain*, 3.

21. David Wasserstein, "The Language Situation in al-Andalus," in *The Formation of al-Andalus: Part II, Language, Religion, Culture and the Sciences*, ed. Manuela Marin (Aldershot: Ashgate, 1998), 7; Christys, *Christians in al-Andalus*, 2, 29, 79.

22. Bernard Reilly, *The Contest of Christian and Muslim Spain, 1031–1157* (Oxford: Blackwell, 1950), 19.

23. Quoted in Christys, *Christians in al-Andalus*, 10.

24. Smith, *Christians and Moors in Spain*, 45.

25. Wasserstein, "Language Situation in al-Andalus," 12; Mikel De Epalza, "Mozarabs: An Emblematic Christian Minority in Islamic al-Andalus," in Jayyusi, *Legacy of Muslim Spain*, 161.

26. James Boone and Nancy Benco, "Islamic Settlement in North Africa and the Iberian Peninsula," *Annual Review of Anthropology* 28 (1999): 66.

27. Quoted in Noble David Cook, *Demographic Collapse: Indian Peru, 1520–1620* (Cambridge: Cambridge University Press, 1981), 254.

Chapter 3

1. Terence D'Altroy, *The Incas* (Malden, MA: Blackwell, 2002), 48; Kenneth Andrien, *Andean Worlds: Indigenous History, Culture, and Consciousness under Spanish Rule, 1532–1825* (Albuquerque: University of New Mexico Press, 2001), 3.

2. The exact origins of this term are unclear. It may come from a mythical tribe called the Viru or Biru or a Quechua word meaning "rich land." John Hemming, *The Conquest of the Incas* (New York: Macmillan, 1970), 24; *National Geographic* website.

3. Pedro Cieza de Leon, *The Discovery and Conquest of Peru*, ed. and trans. Parma Cook and Noble David Cook (Durham, NC: Duke University Press, 1998), 201–12; D'Altroy, *Incas*, 315; Hemming, *Conquest of the Incas*, 33–35, 39–44.

4. John Parry and Robert Keith, eds., *New Iberian World: A Documentary History of the Discovery and Settlement of Latin America to the Early 17th Century*, vol. 4: *The Andes* (New York: Times Books, 1984), 67.

5. Mark Burkholder and Lyman Johnson, *Colonial Latin America*, 3rd ed. (New York: Oxford University Press, 1998), 51–54; Henry Kamen, *Empire: How Spain Became a World Power, 1492–1763* (New York: HarperCollins, 2003), 106–11; Cieza de Leon, *Discovery and Conquest of Peru*, 243–44.

6. John Parry and Robert Keith, eds., *New Iberian World: A Documentary History of the Discovery and Settlement of Latin America to the Early 17th Century*, vol. 1: *The Conquerors and the Conquered* (New York: Times Books, 1984), 290.

7. Andrien, *Andean Worlds*, 114.

8. Steve Stern, *Peru's Indian Peoples and the Challenge of Spanish Conquest: Huamanga to 1640*, 2nd ed. (Madison: University of Wisconsin Press, 1993), 72–73.

9. Quoted in Sara Castro-Klaren, " 'May We Not Perish': The Incas and Spain," *Wilson Quarterly* 4 (1981): 171.

10. Quoted in Kamen, *Empire*, 83.

11. J. H. Elliot, *Imperial Spain, 1469–1716* (London: Penguin, 2002), 65; Rafael Varon Gabai and Auke Pieter Jacobs, "Peruvian Wealth and Spanish Investments: The Pizarro Family during the Sixteenth Century," *Hispanic American Historical Review* 67 (1987): 680.

12. Burkholder and Johnson, *Colonial Latin America*, 14–18.

13. Matthew Restall, *Seven Myths of the Spanish Conquest* (New York: Oxford University Press, 2003), 3, 45–47.

14. Alfred Crosby, *Germs, Seeds and Animals: Studies in Ecological History* (Armonk, NY: M. E. Sharpe, 1994), 22–23; Kamen, *Empire*, 85.

15. Karen Spalding, *Huarochiri: An Andean Society under Inca and Spanish Rule* (Stanford, CA: Stanford University Press, 1984), 47.

16. John Parry and Robert Keith, eds., *New Iberian World: A Documentary History of the Discovery and Settlement of Latin America to the Early 17th Century*, vol. 2: *The Caribbean* (New York: Times Books, 1984), 310.

17. Quoted in Castro-Klaren, " 'May We Not Perish,' " 173.

18. Klaren, *Peru*, 84.

19. Kamen, *Empire*, 188; Gabai and Jacobs, "Peruvian Wealth and Spanish Investments," 668.

20. Quoted in Kamen, *Empire*, 155.

21. D'Altroy, *Incas*, 280–83; Maria Rostworowski, *History of the Inca Realm*, trans. Harry Iceland (Cambridge: Cambridge University Press, 1999), 836.

22. Cieza de Leon, *Discovery and Conquest of Peru*, 188–91.

23. D'Altroy, *Incas*, 2.

24. Cieza de Leon, *Discovery and Conquest of Peru*, 256–57, 417.

25. Ibid., 213.

26. Quoted in Sabine Hyland, *The Jesuit and the Incas: The Extraordinary Life of Padre Blas Valera* (Ann Arbor: University of Michigan Press, 2003), 30.

27. Powers, *Women in the Crucible of Conquest*, 96, 162.

28. Parry and Keith, *New Iberian World*, 4:124.

29. Castro-Klaren, " 'May We Not Perish,' " 172.

30. Cieza de Leon, *Discovery and Conquest of Peru*, 408.

31. Ibid., 245.

32. Andrien, *Andean Worlds*, 78–79.

33. Cook, *Demographic Collapse*, 247.

34. Sabine MacCormack, *On the Wings of Time: Rome, the Incas, Spain, and Peru* (Princeton: Princeton University Press, 2007), xv–xviii.

35. James Lockhart, *Spanish Peru, 1532–1560: A Social History*, 2nd ed. (Madison: University of Wisconsin Press, 1994), 240.

36. Garcialaso de la Vega, *Royal Commentaries of the Incas: And General History of Peru, Part Two*, trans. Harold Livermore (Austin: University of Texas Press, 1966), 1475.

37. Father Pablo Joseph de Arriaga, *The Extirpation of Idolatry in Peru*, trans. L. Clark Keating (Lexington: University of Kentucky Press, 1968), 20.

38. Quoted in Kamen, *Empire*, 376.

39. Quoted in Peter Bakewell, *Miners of the Red Mountain: Indian Labor in Potosí, 1545–1650* (Albuquerque: University of New Mexico Press, 1984), 163.

40. Kamen, *Empire*, 286.

41. Spalding, *Huarochiri*, 165–67; Bakewell, *Miners of the Red Mountain*, 59; Andrien, *Andean Worlds*, 52; Gongora, *Studies in the Colonial History of Spanish America*, 148.

42. Bakewell, *Miners of the Red Mountain*, 153; Stern, *Peru's Indian Peoples and the Challenge of Spanish Conquest*, 85; Enrique Tandeter, *Coercion and Market: Silver Mining in Colonial Potosí, 1692–1826*, trans. Richard Warren (Albuquerque: University of New Mexico Press, 1993), 3–4.

43. Karen Vieira Powers, *Women in the Crucible of Conquest: The Gendered Genesis of Spanish American Society, 1500–1600* (Albuquerque: University of New Mexico Press, 2005), 148.

44. Quoted in Stern, *Peru's Indian Peoples and the Challenge of Spanish Conquest*, 171.

45. Quoted in Castro-Klaren, " 'May We Not Perish,' " 175.

46. Ward Stavig, *The World of Tupac Amaru: Conflict, Community, and Identity in Colonial Peru* (Lincoln: University of Nebraska Press, 1999), 28.

47. Cieza de Leon, *Discovery and Conquest of Peru*, 216.

48. Klaren, *Peru*, 75.

49. Scarlet O'Phelan Godoy, *Rebellions and Revolts in Eighteenth Century Peru and Upper Peru* (Köln: Böhlau Verlag, 1985), 47.

50. Restall, *Seven Myths of the Spanish Conquest*, 129.

51. David Garrett, "'His Majesty's Most Loyal Vassals': The Indian Nobility and Tupac Amaru," *Hispanic American Historical Review* 84, 4 (2004): 600; Leon Campbell, "Social Structure of the Tupac Amaru Army in Cuzco, 1780–81," *Hispanic American Historical Review* 61, 4 (1981): 691.

Chapter 4

1. The peoples of the British Isles did not begin to identify themselves as explicitly "British" until the late eighteenth century. Nevertheless, in the interests of simplicity this chapter will use the term to refer to the employees of the East India Company who had been living and working in India since the sixteenth century.

2. Radha Kumud Mookerj, *Indian Land-System: Ancient, Medieval, and Modern (With Special Reference to Bengal)* (Alipore, India: West Bengal Government Press, 1958), 36; Farhat Hasan, "Indigenous Cooperation and the Birth of a Colonial City: Calcutta, 1698–1750," *Modern Asian Studies* 26 (1992): 66–70.

3. Quoted in Abdul Majed Khan, "The Twilight of Mughal Bengal," in *The Eighteenth Century in Indian History: Evolution or Revolution*, ed. P. J. Marshall (Oxford: Oxford University Press, 2003), 362.

4. Anthony Wild, *The East India Company: Trade and Conquest from 1600* (New York: Lyons, 2000), 95–96.

5. Quoted in Nicholas Dirks, *The Scandal of Empire: India and the Creation of Imperial Britain* (Cambridge, MA: Harvard University Press, 2006), 174.

6. Quoted in Mookerj, *Indian Land-System*, 59.

7. Quoted in Atis Dasgupta, "Variations in Perceptions of the Insurgent Peasants of Bengal in the Late Eighteenth Century," *Social Scientist* 16 (1988): 31–32.

8. David Eltis, *The Rise of African Slavery in the Americas* (Cambridge: Cambridge University Press, 2000), 138–39; Bayly, *Imperial Meridian*, 76.

9. Bernard Cohn, "The Recruitment and Training of British Civil Servants in India, 1600–1800," in *An Anthropologist Among the Historians and Other Essays*, ed. Bernard Cohn (Oxford: Oxford University Press, 2003), 502.

10. T. O. Lloyd, *The British Empire, 1558–1995*, 2nd ed. (Oxford: Oxford University Press, 1996), 14, 91; Philip Lawson, *The East India Company: A History* (London: Longman, 1993), 44, 79.

11. John Richards, *The Mughal Empire* (Cambridge: Cambridge University Press, 1993), 1, 139.

12. Prakash, *European Commercial Enterprise in Pre-Colonial India*, 155–60; Dennis Flynn and Arturo Giraldez, "Cycles of Silver: Global Economic Unity through the Mid-Eighteenth Century," *Journal of World History* 13 (2002): 400; Richards, *Mughal Empire*, 198.

13. Khan, "Twilight of Mughal Bengal," 367.

14. Bruce Lenman and Philip Lawson, "Robert Clive, the 'Black Jagir,' and British Politics," *Historical Journal* 26 (1983): 812–14; Mookerji, *Indian Land-System*, 37–39.

15. Wild, *East India Company*, 95.

16. Rajat Kanta Ray, "Indian Society and the Establishment of British Supremacy, 1765–1818," in Marshall, *Eighteenth Century*, 508.

17. Shubhra Chakrabarti, "Collaboration and Resistance: Bengal Merchants and the English East India Company, 1757–1833," *Studies in History* 10 (1994): 107–8.

18. Quoted in Dirks, *Scandal of Empire*, 291–94.

19. Quoted in Huw Bowen, "Lord Clive and Speculation in East India Company Stock, 1766," *Historical Journal* 30 (1987): 907.

20. Marshall, *Bengal*, 89–90; Bowen, "Lord Clive and Speculation," 916–18.

21. Ray, *Change in Bengal Agrarian Society*, 111–19; Bowen, "Lord Clive and Speculation," 916–18.

22. Susan Bayly, *Caste, Society and Politics in India from the Eighteenth Century to the Modern Age* (Cambridge: Cambridge University Press, 1999), 106.

23. Quoted in G. J. Bryant, "Asymmetric Warfare: The British Experience in Eighteenth-Century India," *Journal of Military History* 68 (2004): 14.

24. Dirks, *Scandal of Empire*, 60–65, 71–74.

25. Quoted in Kathleen Wilson, *The Island Race: Englishness, Empire and Gender in the Eighteenth Century* (London: Routledge, 2003), 50.

26. Quoted in Wild, *East India Company*, 73.

27. Edmund Burke, *On Empire, Liberty, and Reform: Speeches and Letters*, ed. David Bromwich (New Haven: Yale University Press, 2000), 311.

28. Samuel Foote, *The Nabob: A Comedy, in Three Acts* (London, 1778); Marshall, *Problems of Empire*, 147–48.

29. Adam Smith, *An Inquiry into the Nature and Causes of the Wealth of Nations*, ed. Edwin Cannan (London: Methuen, 1904), retrieved October 20, 2007, www.econlib.org/library/Smith/smWN21.html.

30. Burke, *On Empire, Liberty, and Reform*, 297–98.

31. Dirks, *Scandal of Empire*, 191, 197.

32. Quoted in P. J. Marshall, *Problems of Empire: Britain and India, 1757–1813* (London: George Allen and Unwin, 1968), 118.

33. Quoted in Ray, "Indian Society," 519–20.

34. Quoted in Dirks, *Scandal of Empire*, 302; E. Daniel Potts, "Missionaries and the Beginnings of the Secular State in India," in *Essays in Indian History*, ed. D. Williams and E. D. Potts (New York: Asia Publishing House, 1973), 123.

35. Thomas Babington Macaulay, *Macaulay: Prose and Poetry*, ed. G. M. Young (Cambridge: Harvard University Press, 1967), 729.

36. Quoted in Sudipata Sen, "Colonial Aversions and Domestic Desires: Blood, Race, Sex, and the Decline of Intimacy in Early British India," *South Asia* 24 (2001): 25.

37. Quoted in Michael Fischer, "Indian Political Representations in Britain during the Transition to Colonialism," *Modern Asian Studies* 38 (2004): 672.

38. G. Subba Rao, *Indian Words in English: A Study in Indo-British Cultural and Linguistic Relations* (Oxford: Clarendon Press, 1969), 20–25, 44.

39. Irfan Habib, "The Coming of 1857," *Social Scientist* 26 (1998): 8.

40. Rudrangshu Mukherjee, "'Satan Let Loose upon Earth': The Kanpur Massacres in India in the Revolt of 1857," *Past and Present* 128 (1990): 104; Gautam Bhadra, "Four Rebels of Eighteen-Fifty-Seven," in *Selected Subaltern Studies*, ed. Ranajit Guha and G. C. Spivak (New York: Oxford University Press, 1988), 151–53.

41. Quoted in Raffi Gregorian, "Unfit for Service: British Law and Looting in India in the Mid-Nineteenth Century," *South Asia* 13 (1990): 77.

Chapter 5

1. Quoted in Stuart Woolf, *Napoleon's Integration of Europe* (London: Routledge, 1991), 229.

2. Quoted in M. G. Broers, "Noble Romans and Regenerated Citizens: The Morality of Conscription in Napoleonic Italy, 1800–1814," *War and Society* 8 (2001): 251.

3. Napoleon I, *Napoleon on Napoleon: An Autobiography of the Emperor*, ed. Somerset de Chair (London: Cassell, 1992), 39, 194.

4. Quoted in Stuart Woolf, *A History of Italy, 1700–1860: The Social Constraints of Political Change* (London: Methuen, 1979), 206.

5. This was after first conquering northern Italy in 1797. Quoted in Desmond Gregory, *Napoleon's Italy* (Teaneck, NJ: Fairleigh Dickinson University Press, 2001), 42.

6. Michael Broers, "The Empire behind the Lines," *History Today* 48 (1998): 24.

7. Quoted in Susan Connor, *The Age of Napoleon* (Westport, CT: Greenwood Press, 2004), 95.

8. Quoted in Woolf, *Napoleon's Integration of Europe*, 130.

9. Christopher Duggan, *The Force of Destiny: A History of Italy Since 1796* (London: Allen Lane, 2007), 3.

10. Geoffrey Ellis, "The Nature of Napoleonic Imperialism," in *Napoleon and Europe*, ed. Philip Dwyer (London: Pearson Education, 2001), 112.

11. Michael Broers, *The Napoleonic Empire in Italy, 1796–1814: Cultural Imperialism in a European Context* (New York: Palgrave Macmillan, 2005), 228–29.

12. Quoted in Duggan, *Force of Destiny*, 31.

13. Quoted in Woolf, *Napoleon's Integration of Europe*, 13.

14. Quoted in Geoffrey Best, *War and Society in Revolutionary Europe, 1770–1870* (Leicester: Leicester University Press, 1982), 82–83.

15. Quoted in Jonathan North, "General Hoche and Counterinsurgency," *Journal of Military History* 67 (2003): 530.

16. Owen Connelly, *The French Revolution and Napoleonic Era*, 2nd ed. (Fort Worth, TX: Holt, Rinehart and Winston, 1991), 209.

17. Connor, *Age of Napoleon*, 51–52; Ellis, *Napoleonic Empire*, 77–81.

18. These figures do not include the "independent" satellite states. Woolf, *Napoleon's Integration of Europe*, 30.

19. Ellis, *Napoleonic Empire*, 35–36.

20. Woolf, *Napoleon's Integration of Europe*, 158–59; Ellis, *Napoleonic Empire*, 60–63.

21. Best, *War and Society in Revolutionary Europe*, 116–17; Isser Woloch, "Napoleonic Conscription: State Power and Civil Society," *Past and Present* 111 (1986): 120–24.

22. Woolf, *Napoleon's Integration of Europe*, 171, 220–21; Edward Whitcomb, "Napoleon's Prefects," *American Historical Review* 79 (1974): 1099.

23. Charles Esdaile, "Popular Resistance to the Napoleonic Empire," in Dwyer, *Napoleon and Europe*, 138; Best, *War and Society in Revolutionary Europe*, 114; Woolf, *Napoleon's Integration of Europe*, 172–73.

24. Gunther Rothenberg, *The Art of Warfare in the Age of Napoleon* (Bloomington: Indiana University Press, 1978), 159–60.

25. Michael Rowe, "Between Empire and Home Town: Napoleonic Rule on the Rhine, 1799–1814," *Historical Journal* 42 (1999): 665–66.

26. Quoted in Woolf, *History of Italy*, 30.

27. Nicholas Doumanis, *Italy* (London: Oxford University Press, 2001), 44; Duggan, *Force of Destiny*, 4–5.

28. Douglas Radcliff-Umstead, *Ugo Foscolo's Ultime Lettere di Jacobo Ortis, A Translation* (Chapel Hill: University of North Carolina Press, 1970), 57.

29. Spencer Di Scala, *Italy from Revolution to Republic: 1700 to the Present*, 3rd ed. (Boulder, CO: Westview, 1995), 27.

30. Quoted in Gregory, *Napoleon's Italy*, 47–48.

31. Doumanis, *Italy*, 43.

32. Duggan, *Force of Destiny*, 52; Gregory, *Napoleon's Italy*, 137; Frederick Schneid, *Soldiers of Napoleon's Kingdom of Italy: Army, State, and Society, 1800–1815* (Boulder, CO: Westview, 1995), 61.

33. Alexander Grab, "State Power, Brigandage and Rural Resistance in Napoleonic Italy," *European History Quarterly* 25 (1995): 54; Gregory, *Napoleon's Italy*, 135–36.

34. Quoted in Charles Esdaile, "Popular Resistance to the Napoleonic Empire," in Dwyer, *Napoleon and Europe*, 140.

35. Quoted in Gregory, *Napoleon's Italy*, 172.

36. Quoted in ibid., 182.

37. Quoted in Duggan, *Force of Destiny*, 67.

38. Broers, *Napoleonic Empire in Italy*, 12.

Chapter 6

1. C. W. Hobley, *Kenya: From Chartered Company to Crown Colony*, 2nd ed. (London: Frank Cass, 1970), 109–17; Richard Meinertzhagen, *Kenya Diary 1902–1906* (New York: Hippocrene, 1984), 214, 224.

2. Meinertzhagen, *Kenya Diary*, 178.

3. Ibid., 223, 233; David Anderson, "Black Mischief: Crime, Protest and Resistance in Colonial Kenya," *Historical Journal* 36 (1993): 858.

4. John Seabrook, "Ruffled Feathers: Uncovering the Biggest Scandal in the Bird World," *New Yorker*, May 29, 2006.

5. Great Britain, House of Commons, *Report from the Select Committee on Africa (Western Coast)* (London, 1865), iii.

6. P. J. Cain and A. G. Hopkins, *British Imperialism: Innovation and Expansion, 1688–1914* (London: Longman, 1993), 112.

7. Anonymous, "France under Louis Napoleon," *Westminster Review* 344 (October 1858): 193; Richard Hingley, *Roman Officers and English Gentlemen* (London: Routledge, 2000), 20.

8. Lance Davis and Robert Huttenback, *Mammon and the Pursuit of Empire: The Political Economy of British Imperialism, 1860–1912* (Cambridge: Cambridge University Press, 1986), 71–75, 270; Cain and Hopkins, *British Imperialism*, 467.

9. Patrick K. O'Brien, "The Costs and Benefits of British Imperialism 1846–1914: Reply," *Past and Present* 125 (1989): 173, 176.

10. Cain and Hopkins, *British Imperialism*, 359.

11. Ronald Hyam, "The British Empire in the Edwardian Era," in *The Oxford History of the British Empire: The Twentieth Century* (New York: Oxford University Press, 1999), 5:48.

12. E. S. Grogan, *From the Cape to Cairo: The First Traverse of Africa from South to North* (Freeport: Books for Libraries, 1972), 356.

13. John Iliffe, *A Modern History of Tanganyika* (New York: Cambridge University Press, 1979), 324.

14. John Lonsdale and Bruce Berman, *Unhappy Valley: Conflict in Kenya and Africa* (London: James Curry, 1992), 18.

15. John Lonsdale, "The European Scramble and Conquest in African History," in *The Cambridge History of Africa*, ed. Roland Oliver (Cambridge: Cambridge University Press, 1985), 6:747–48.

16. William Lloyd-Jones, *K.A.R.; Being an Unofficial Account of the Origin and Activities of the Kings African Rifles* (London: Arrowsmith, 1926), 77.

17. Meinertzhagen, *Kenya Diary*, 218.

18. Ibid., 10–12, 148.

19. Bruce Berman, *Control and Crisis in Colonial Kenya: The Dialectic of Domination* (Nairobi: East African Publishers, 1990), 134; Simon S. S. Kenyanchui, "European Settler Agriculture," in *An Economic History of Kenya*, ed. W. R. Ochieng' and R. M. Maxon (Nairobi: East African Educational Publishers, 1992), 115.

20. Quoted in W. T. W. Morgan, "The 'White Highlands' of Kenya," *Geographical Journal* 129 (1963): 140.

21. Quoted in W. McGregor Ross, *Kenya from Within: A Short Political History* (London: George Allen and Unwin, 1927), 41.

22. Harry Thuku, *Harry Thuku: An Autobiography* (Nairobi: Oxford University Press, 1970), 2.

23. A. C. Hollis, *The Nandi: Their Language and Folk-Lore* (Westport, CT: Negro Universities Press, 1971), 50; Jomo Kenyatta, *Facing Mount Kenya: The Tribal Life of the Gikuyu* (New York: Vintage, 1965), 42–43.

24. Kenyatta, *Facing Mount Kenya*, 47.

25. Bertram Francis Gordon Cranworth, *A Colony in the Making: Or Sport and Profit in British East Africa* (London: Macmillan, 1912), 21.

26. Robert Foran, *The Kenya Police, 1887–1960* (London: Robert Hale, 1962), 21.

27. Grogan, *From the Cape to Cairo*, 378.

28. Cranworth, *Colony in the Making*, 48.

29. F. D. Lugard, *The Dual Mandate in British Tropical Africa* (London: Frank Cass, 1965); F. D. Lugard, "The Colour Problem," *Edinburgh Review* 233 (April 1921): 281.

30. Quoted in E. A. Brett, *Colonialism and Underdevelopment in East Africa: The Politics of Economic Change, 1919–1939* (New York: NOK, 1973), 73.

31. Quoted in Anthony Clayton and Donald Savage, *Government and Labour in Kenya, 1895–1963* (London: Frank Cass, 1974), 105.

32. Quoted in ibid., 172.

33. John Cell, ed., *By Kenya Possessed: The Correspondence of Norman Leys and J. H. Oldham, 1918–1926* (Chicago: University of Chicago Press, 1976), 140.

34. Hut Tax Ordinance, 1910, in G. H. Mungheam, ed., *Kenya: Select Historical Documents* (Nairobi: East African Publishing House, 1978).

35. Thomas Jesse Jones for the African Education Commission, *Education in East Africa (Phelps-Stokes Report)* (London: Edinburgh House, 1924), 118.

36. Quoted in Wyatt Rawson, ed., *Education for a Changing Commonwealth: Report of a British Commonwealth Education Conference, July 1931* (London: New Education Fellowship, 1931), 80.

37. Tanganyika Education Conference, *Conference between Government and Missions: Report of Proceedings 5–12 October 1925* (Dar es Salaam: Government Printer, 1925), 76.

38. William Malcom Hailey, *An African Survey: A Study of Problems Arising in Africa South of the Sahara* (London: Oxford University Press, 1938), 335.

39. Labour Circular No. 1, October 23, 1919, Labour Circular No. 2, February 17, 1920, in Mungheam, *Kenya: Select Historical Documents.*

40. Tiyambe Zeleza, "The Colonial Labour System in Kenya," in Ochieng' and Maxon, *Economic History of Kenya*, 180.

41. Ibid., 177.

42. Kenya Colony and Protectorate, *Report of the Kenya Land Commission* (Nairobi: Government Printer, 1933).

43. Terence Gavaghan, *Of Lions and Dung Beetles* (Ilfracombe: Arthur H. Stockwell, 1999), 36.

44. Quoted in Marshall Clough, *Fighting Two Sides: Kenyan Chiefs and Politicians, 1918–1940* (Niwot, CO: University Press of Colorado, 1990), 16.

45. Hailey, *African Survey*, 387–89.

46. Nuffield Foundation and Colonial Office, *African Education: A Study of Educational Policy and Practice in British Tropical Areas* (Oxford: Oxford University Press, 1953), 80.

47. Cranworth, *Colony in the Making*, 85; Gavaghan, *Of Lions and Dung Beetles*, 35–36, 66.

48. James R. Sheffield, *Education in Kenya: An Historical Study* (New York: Teachers College Press, 1973), 410.

49. Kenyatta, *Facing Mount Kenya*, 306.

50. Quoted in R. D. Pearce, "The Colonial Office and Planned Decolonisation in Africa," *African Affairs* 83 (1984): 80.

51. L. J. Butler, *Britain and Empire: Adjusting to a Post-Imperial World* (London: I. B. Tauris, 2002), 81–85; J. S. Hogendorn and K. M. Scott, "The East African Groundnut Scheme: Lessons of a Large Scale Agricultural Failure," *African Economic History* 10 (1981): 108.

52. Quoted in Anthony Kirk-Greene, *On Crown Service: A History of HM Colonial and Overseas Civil Services, 1837–1997* (London: I. B. Tauris, 1999), 9.

53. Report by Kenya Governor and Memoranda on What Legislation Is Discriminatory, February 28, 1949, Great Britain Public Records Office, CO 859 129/1.

54. R. Mugo Gatheru, *Child of Two Worlds* (London: Heinemann, 1966), 74.

55. Anthony Clayton, *Counterinsurgency in Kenya: A Study of Military Operations against the Mau Mau, 1952–1960* (Manhattan, KS: Sunflower University Press, 1984), 41.

56. David Anderson, *Histories of the Hanged: The Dirty War in Kenya and the End of Empire* (New York: W. W. Norton, 2005), 53–59.

57. John Hargreaves, *Decolonization in Africa*, 2nd ed. (London: Longmans, 1996), 171; Butler, *Britain and Empire*, 106–8.

58. Harold Macmillan, *Pointing the Way, 1959–1961* (London: Macmillan, 1972), 475.

59. Michael Blundell, *A Love Affair with the Sun: A Memoir of Seventy Years in Kenya* (Nairobi: East African Publishers, 1994), 97.

60. Quoted in Clayton and Savage, *Government and Labour in Kenya*, 189.

61. Michael Blundell, *So Rough a Wind* (London: Weidenfeld & Nicholson, 1964), 263.

Chapter 7

1. Thomas Kernan, *France on Berlin Time* (Philadelphia: J. B. Lippincott, 1941), 76.

2. Simone de Beauvoir, *Letters to Sartre*, trans. and ed. Quintin Hoare (New York: Arcade, 1991), 322.

3. Kernan, *France on Berlin Time*, 12–13.

4. Quoted in Richard Vinen, *The Unfree French: Life under the Occupation* (New Haven: Yale University Press, 2006), 23.

5. Philippe Burrin, *France under the Germans: Collaboration and Compromise*, trans. Janet Lloyd (New York: New Press, 1993), 14.

6. Pierre Laval, *The Unpublished Diary of Pierre Laval* (London: Falcon, 1948), 45.

7. David Pryce-Jones, *Paris in the Third Reich: A History of German Occupation, 1940–1944* (New York: Holt, Rinehart and Winston, 1981), 67.

8. Quoted in Karl Brandt, *Management of Agriculture and Food in the German-Occupied and Other Areas of Fortress Europe: A Study in Military Government* (Stanford, CA: Stanford University Press, 1953), 485.

9. Hermann Rauschning, *Hitler Told Me*, quoted in Burrin, *France under the Germans*, 47.

10. Aimé Césaire, *Discourse on Colonialism*, trans. Joan Pinkham (New York: Monthly Review Press, 1972), 14.

11. Adolf Hitler, *Hitler's Table Talk, 1941–1944*, trans. Norman Cameron and R. H. Stevens (London: Weidenfeld and Nicolson, 1953), 92, 319, 588–89.

12. Heinrich Schnee, *German Colonization Past and Future: The Truth about the German Colonies* (New York: Alfred Knopf, 1926), 105.

13. Michael Freeman, *Atlas of Nazi Germany* (New York: Macmillan, 1987), 58, 64; Klaus Fischer, *Nazi Germany: A New History* (New York: Continuum, 1995), 306–9.

14. Götz Aly, *Hitler's Beneficiaries: Plunder, Racial War, and the Nazi Welfare State*, trans. Jefferson Chase (New York: Metropolitan, 2005), 4, 39.

15. Ibid., 46–50.

16. Ibid., 39.

17. Adolf Hitler, *Mein Kampf*, trans. James Murphy (London: Hurst and Blackett, 1939); Hitler, *Hitler's Table Talk*, 74.

18. Wolfgang Benz, *A Concise History of the Third Reich*, trans. Thomas Dunlap (Berkeley: University of California Press, 2006), 188–89.

19. Michael Marrus and Robert Paxton, "The Nazis and the Jews in Occupied Western Europe, 1940–1944," *Journal of Modern History* 54 (1982): 690; Adam LeBor and Roger Boyes, *Seduced by Hitler: The Choices of a Nation and the Ethics of Survival* (Naperville, IL: Sourcebooks, 2000), 174–75.

20. Bob Moore, "Nazi Masters and Accommodating Dutch Bureaucrats: Working Towards the Führer in the Occupied Netherlands, 1940–45," in *Working towards the Führer*, ed. Anthony McElligott and Tim Kirk (Manchester: Manchester University Press, 2003), 194–98.

21. Quoted in Mark Mazower, *Hitler's Empire: How the Nazis Ruled Europe* (New York: Penguin, 2008), 164.

22. Michael Burleigh, *The Third Reich: A New History* (New York: Hill and Wang, 2000), 441–45.

23. Raphael Lemkin, *Axis Rule in Occupied Europe: Laws of Occupation, Analysis of Government, Proposals for Redress* (Washington: Carnegie Endowment for International Peace, 1944), 60–61; Aly, *Hitler's Beneficiaries*, 82–93.

24. Aly, *Hitler's Beneficiaries*, 94–97, 103–4, 111.

25. Lemkin, *Axis Rule in Occupied Europe*, 68–69; Fischer, *Nazi Germany*, 487.

26. Aly, *Hitler's Beneficiaries*, 123, 285.

27. Lemkin, *Axis Rule in Occupied Europe*, 87; Aly, *Hitler's Beneficiaries*, 72, 290–91.

28. Quoted in Robert Gildea, *Marianne in Chains: Daily Life in the Heart of France during the German Occupation* (New York: Henry Holt, 2002), 54.

29. Quoted in Moore, "Nazi Masters and Accommodating Dutch Bureaucrats," 194.

30. Rod Kedward, *La Vie en Bleu: France and the French Since 1900* (London: Allen Lane, 2005), 165–66.

31. Quotes from Eugen Weber, *The Hollow Years: France in the 1930s* (New York: W. W. Norton, 1994), 24; Kedward, *La Vie en Bleu*, 226.

32. Anthony Beevor and Artemis Cooper, *Paris after the Liberation, 1944–1949*, 2nd ed. (New York: Penguin, 2004), 12; Burrin, *France under the Germans*, 87–90.

33. Aly, *Hitler's Beneficiaries*, 147; Robert O. Paxton, *Vichy France: Old Guard and New Order, 1940–1944* (New York: Columbia University Press, 1982), 143–44.

34. Dominique Veiling, *Fashion under the Occupation*, trans. Miriam Kochan (Oxford: Berg, 2002), 85–86.

35. Kernan, *France on Berlin Time*, 19.

36. Gildea, *Marianne in Chains*, 3.

37. Paxton, *Vichy France*, 31.

38. Quoted in Burleigh, *Third Reich*, 422–23.

39. Quoted in Owen Anthony Davey, "The Origins of the Légion de Volontaires Français Contre le Bolchévisme," *Journal of Contemporary History* 6 (1971): 34.

40. Hitler, *Mein Kampf*.

41. Quoted in Pryce-Jones, *Paris in the Third Reich*, 160.

42. Lynne Taylor, "Collective Action in Northern France, 1940–1944," *French History* 11 (1997): 191–92; Denis Peschanski et al., *Collaboration and Resistance: Images of Life in Vichy France, 1940–1944*, trans. Lory Frankel (New York: Harry N. Abrams, 2000), 108; Burleigh, *Third Reich*, 417.

43. John Sweets, *Choices in Vichy France: The French under Nazi Occupation* (New York: Oxford University Press, 1986), 12–13, 196; Gildea, *Marianne in Chains*, 66; Burrin, *France under the Germans*, 283–85.

44. Quoted in Gildea, *Marianne in Chains*, 230–31.

45. Freeman, *Atlas of Nazi Germany*, 137.

46. Birthe Kundrus, "Forbidden Company: Romantic Relationships between Germans and Foreigners, 1939 to 1945," *Journal of the History of Sexuality* 11 (2002): 203–6.

47. Quoted in David Littlejohn, *Foreign Legions of the Third Reich*, vol. 1: *Norway, Denmark, France* (San Jose, CA: R. James Bender, 1987), 252–53.

48. Quoted in Burrin, *France under the Germans*, 480.

49. Ibid., 140, 283–85.

50. Sweets, *Choices in Vichy France*, 27, 102; Vinen, *The Unfree French*, 368.

51. France Forever, *Fighting France Year Book 1944*, 20–22.

52. Richard Cobb, *French and Germans, Germans and French: A Personal Interpretation of France under Two Occupations, 1914–1918, 1940–1944* (Hanover, NH: University Press of New England, 1983), 66–67.

53. Quoted in Pryce-Jones, *Paris in the Third Reich*, 157.

54. Yann Stephan, *A Broken Sword: Policing France during the German Occupation* (Chicago: Office of International Criminal Justice, 1992), 75–77.

55. Stephan, *Broken Sword*, 76–77.

56. Hitler, *Hitler's Table Talk*, 476.

57. Laval, *Unpublished Diary of Pierre Laval*, 76.

58. Ibid., 186.

59. Quoted in Nancy Wood, "Memory on Trial in Contemporary France: The Case of Maurice Papon," *History and Memory* 11 (1999): 42.

60. Quoted in T. O. Ranger, *Revolt in Southern Rhodesia, 1896–97: A Study in African Resistance* (Evanston, IL: Northwestern University Press, 1967), 131.

61. Césaire, *Discourse on Colonialism*, 17–18.

Conclusion

1. White House press release, "President Discusses the Future of Iraq," February 26, 2003.

2. These figures are based on cross-checked media accounts, official statistics, and morgue and hospital reports complied by the Iraq Body Count Project, a self-described "human security project" committed to enumerating violent civilian deaths resulting from the invasion and occupation of Iraq; www.iraqbodycount.org. For a graphic look at the perspective of American soldiers on Iraqi casualties, see Michael Gordon and Bernard Trainor, *Cobra II: The Inside Story of the Invasion and Occupation of Iraq* (New York: Pantheon, 2006), 382.

3. Quotes from Thomas Ricks, *Fiasco: The American Military Adventure in Iraq* (New York: Penguin, 2006), 177–78.

4. Quoted in George Packer, *The Assassin's Gate: America in Iraq* (New York: Farrar, Straus, and Giroux, 2005), 200.

5. The National Security Strategy of the United States of America, September 2002.

6. White House press release, "President Bush Salutes Veterans at White House Ceremony," November 11, 2002.

7. Niall Ferguson, "The Empire Slinks Back," *New York Times*, April 27, 2003; Niall Ferguson, "An Empire in Denial: The Limits of U.S. Imperialism," *Harvard International Review*, Fall 2003, 69; Deepak Lal, *In Praise of Empires: Globalization and Order* (New York: Palgrave MacMillan, 2004), 210–11.

8. Michael Renner, "Post-Saddam Iraq: Linchpin of a New Oil Order," in *The Iraq War Reader: History, Documents, and Opinions*, ed. Micah Sifry and Christopher Cerf (New York: Simon & Schuster, 2003), 582, 585.

9. Michael Ignatieff, "The American Empire: The Burden," *New York Times*, January 5, 2003.

10. Ibid.

11. Nicholas Dirks, *The Scandal of Empire: India and the Creation of Imperial Britain* (Cambridge, MA: Harvard University Press, 2006), xi.

12. Noah Feldman, *What We Owe Iraq: War and the Ethics of Nation Building* (Princeton: Princeton University Press, 2004), 3, 69, 71.

13. Quotes from Ahmed Hashim, *Insurgency and Counter-Insurgency in Iraq* (Ithaca, NY: Cornell University Press, 2006), 22, 29.

14. *Guardian*, October 13, 2007.

15. Quoted in Elias Lyman Magoon, ed., *Living Orators in America* (New York: Baker and Scribner), 2:334–35.

16. Quoted in Stanley Karnow, *Vietnam: A History* (New York: Penguin, 1997), 20–21.

17. Ibid., 11, 31.

18. Max Boot, "The Case for American Empire," *Weekly Standard*, October 15, 2001, 27.

19. Quoted in Hashim, *Insurgency and Counter-Insurgency in Iraq*, 13.

20. Gordon and Trainor, *Cobra II*, 366; Hashim, *Insurgency and Counter-Insurgency in Iraq*, 12.

21. White House press release, "President Bush Announces Major Combat Operations in Iraq Have Ended," May 1, 2003.

22. L. Paul Bremer, *My Year in Iraq: The Struggle to Build a Future of Hope* (New York: Simon & Schuster, 2006), 185.

23. Rajiv Chandrasekaran, *Imperial Life in the Emerald City: Inside Iraq's Green Zone* (New York: Borzoi, 2006), 12, 94; T. Christian Miller, *Blood Money: Wasted Billions, Lost Lives, and Corporate Greed in Iraq* (New York: Little, Brown, 2006), 39; Ferguson, "Empire Slinks Back."

24. Chandrasekaran, *Imperial Life in the Emerald City*, 14–16.

25. Stuart Bowen, "Hard Lessons: The Iraq Reconstruction Experience," unofficial draft, December 2008, http://www.sigir.mil/hardlessons/default.aspx; Miller, *Blood Money*, 3.

26. Miller, *Blood Money*, 72–74, 87–88, 117–18, 129.

27. Ibid., 133, 136, 157, 163–64.

28. Chandrasekaran, *Imperial Life in the Emerald City*, 139–41; Miller, *Blood Money*, 199–200.

29. Quoted in Hashim, *Insurgency and Counter-Insurgency in Iraq*, 96.

30. Quoted in ibid., 20.

31. Quoted in ibid., 195.

32. Quoted in ibid., 101.

33. Ali Allawi, *The Occupation of Iraq: Winning the War, Losing the Peace* (New Haven: Yale University Press, 2007), 459.

34. Linda Bilmes and Joseph Stiglitz, "The Iraq War Will Cost Us $3 Trillion, and Much More," *Washington Post*, March 9, 2008; Iraq Study Group, *The Iraq Study Group Report* (New York: Vintage Books, 2006), 3.

35. Hannah Fischer, "Iraqi Civilian Deaths Estimates," Congressional Research Service Report, August 27, 2008.

36. Iraq Study Group, *Iraq Study Group Report*, 4.

37. Patrick Cockburn, *The Occupation: War and Resistance in Iraq* (London: Verso, 2007), xvii, xix.

38. Quoted in Ricks, *Fiasco*, 17.

39. Niall Ferguson, "A War to Start All Wars," *Atlantic Monthly*, January/ February 2007.

INDEX